The Law Unbound!

I once fell in love with a voice over the radio that woke me up each morning with words of love for his people. I once loved a man because he could sing 101 songs in the fields as he worked as a farmworker.

I loved another because he had a laugh that embraced all those around him, though he had been tortured.

These men, I loved for their acts, I loved them as I have loved others, for the stories they gave me. They were not meant nor destined for romantic love. I shared with them "revolutionary love."

And then I began to love a man page by page, from a book he wrote about surviving death and disappearance. His revolutionary love called out to me....

       Patrisia Gonzales
       "Amor Revolucionario"
       Column of the Americas
       Universal Press Syndicate
       February 6, 2004

The Law Unbound!
A Richard Delgado Reader

Edited by
ADRIEN KATHERINE WING
and JEAN STEFANCIC

Paradigm Publishers
Boulder • London

Paradigm Publishers is committed to preserving ancient forests and natural resources. We elected to print *The Law Unbound!* on 50% post consumer recycled paper, processed chlorine free. As a result, for this printing, we have saved:

18 Trees (40' tall and 6-8" diameter)
7,600 Gallons of Wastewater
3,057 Kilowatt Hours of Electricity
838 Pounds of Solid Waste
1,646 Pounds of Greenhouse Gases

Paradigm Publishers made this paper choice because our printer, Thomson-Shore, Inc., is a member of Green Press Initiative, a nonprofit program dedicated to supporting authors, publishers, and suppliers in their efforts to reduce their use of fiber obtained from endangered forests.

For more information, visit www.greenpressinitiative.org

All rights reserved. No part of the publication may be transmitted or reproduced in any media or form, including electronic, mechanical, photocopy, recording, or informational storage and retrieval systems, without the express written consent of the publisher.

Copyright © 2007 Paradigm Publishers

Published in the United States by Paradigm Publishers, 3360 Mitchell Lane, Suite E, Boulder, CO 80301 USA.
Paradigm Publishers is the trade name of Birkenkamp & Company, LLC,
Dean Birkenkamp, President and Publisher.

Library of Congress Cataloging-in-Publication Data

The law unbound! : a Richard Delgado reader / edited by Adrien Katherine Wing and Jean Stefancic.
    p. cm.
  Includes bibliographical references and index.
  ISBN 978-1-59451-247-6 (hc)
  1. Race discrimination--Law and legislation—United States.   2. Discourse analysis, Narrative.   3. Critical legal studies—United States.   4. Hate speech—United States.
  I. Wing, Adrien Katherine.   I. Stefancic, Jean.
  KF4755.L39 2007
  340'.115—dc22

2007015066

Printed and bound in the United States of America on acid-free paper that meets the standards of the American National Standard for Permanence of Paper for Printed Library Materials. Designed and Typeset by Straight Creek Bookmakers.

11 10 09 08 07   1 2 3 4 5

Contents

Acknowledgments vii

Introduction ix

PART I. NARRATIVE AND LEGAL STORYTELLING 1

Storytelling for Oppositionists and Others: A Plea for Narrative, 3
Rodrigo's Chronicle, 20
Rodrigo's Third Chronicle: Care, Competition,
 and the Redemptive Tragedy of Race, 34
Rodrigo's Final Chronicle: Cultural Power, the Law Reviews,
 and the Attack on Narrative Jurisprudence, 52
Rodrigo's Eleventh Chronicle: Empathy and False Empathy, 69

PART II. CRITICAL THEORY 91

The Racial Double Helix: Watson, Crick, and
 Brown v. Board of Education, 93
Rodrigo's Fourth Chronicle: Neutrality and Stasis
 in Antidiscrimination Law, 101
Rodrigo's Eighth Chronicle: Black Crime, White Fears—
 On the Social Construction of Threat, 117
Rodrigo's Ninth Chronicle: Race, Legal Instrumentalism,
 and the Rule of Law, 137
Linking Arms: Interracial Coalition as an Avenue of Social Reform, 154

**PART III. LAW, LEGAL EDUCATION, AND THE LEGAL
 PROFESSION** 165

The Imperial Scholar: Reflections on a Review
 of Civil Rights Literature, 167
Rodrigo's Thirteenth Chronicle: Legal Formalism
 and Law's Discontents, 175
Official Elitism or Institutional Self-Interest?
 Ten Reasons Why Law Schools Should Abandon the LSAT, 197

PART IV. HATE SPEECH — 209
Words That Wound: A Tort Action for Racial Insults,
   Epithets, and Name-Calling, 211
The "More Speech" Solution: Can Free Expression
   Remedy Systemic Social Ills? 217
Campus Antiracism Rules: Constitutional Narratives in Collision, 225
Toward a Legal Realist View of the First Amendment, 234

PART V. LAW REFORM — 241
The Social Construction of *Brown v. Board of Education*:
   Law Reform and the Reconstructive Paradox, 243
Joseph Sax, the Public Trust Theory of Environmental Protection,
   and Some Dark Thoughts on the Possibility of Law Reform, 253
On Taking Back Our Civil Rights Promises:
   When Equality Doesn't Compute, 258
Rodrigo's Sixth Chronicle: Intersections, Essences,
   and the Dilemma of Social Reform, 262

PART VI. LATINOS AND OTHER NONBLACK MINORITIES — 283
Rodrigo's Fifteenth Chronicle: Racial Mixture, Latino-Critical
   Scholarship, and the Black-White Binary, 285
Derrick Bell's Toolkit: Fit to Dismantle That Famous House? 296

PART VII. POLITICS AND CRITIQUE — 307
Shadowboxing: An Essay on Power, 309
Rodrigo's Seventh Chronicle: Race, Democracy, and the State, 314
Rodrigo's Remonstrance: Love and Despair
   in an Age of Indifference, 327
Rodrigo's Roadmap: Is the Marketplace Theory for Eradicating
   Discrimination a Blind Alley? 338
Zero-Based Racial Politics: An Evaluation of Three Best-Case
   Arguments on Behalf of the Nonwhite Underclass, 356

PART VIII. AFFIRMATIVE ACTION — 363
1998 Hugo L. Black Lecture: Ten Arguments against
   Affirmative Action—How Valid? 365
Rodrigo's Tenth Chronicle: Merit and Affirmative Action, 375

Annotated Bibliography — 397

Index — 419

About the Author and Editors — 431

Acknowledgments

Portions of the excerpts in this book appeared in the following reviews and journals. Used by permission.

Alabama Law Review, for "Ten Arguments Against Affirmative Action: How Valid?" 50 Ala. L. Rev. 135 (1998)
California Law Review, for "Rodrigo's Third Chronicle: Care, Competition, and the Redemptive Tragedy of Race," 81 Cal. L. Rev. 387 (1993); and "Rodrigo's Eleventh Chronicle: Empathy and False Empathy," 84 Cal. L. Rev. 61 (1996)
Cornell Law Review, for "Linking Arms," 88 Cornell L. Rev. 855 (2003); "The 'More Speech' Solution: Can Free Expression Remedy Systemic Social Ills?" [Images of the Outsider], 77 Cornell L. Rev. 1258 (1992); and "Shadowboxing: An Essay on Power," 77 Cornell 813 (1992)
Georgetown Law Journal, for "Rodrigo's Remonstrance: Love and Despair in an Age of Indifference," 88 Geo. L.J. 263 (2000); "Zero-Based Racial Politics: An Evaluation of Three Best-Case Arguments on Behalf of the Nonwhite Underclass," 78 Geo. L.J. 1929 (1990); and "Rodrigo's Tenth Chronicle: Merit and Affirmative Action," 83 Geo. L.J. 1711 (1995)
Harvard Civil Rights–Civil Liberties Law Review, for "Words That Wound: A Tort Action for Insults, Epithets, and Name-Calling," 17 Harv. C.R.-C.L. L. Rev. 133 (1982)
Harvard Law Review, for "Toward a Legal Realist View of the First Amendment," 113 Harv. L. Rev. 778 (2000)
Howard Law Journal, for "The Racial Double Helix," 47 How. L.J. 473 (2004)
Michigan Law Review, for "Storytelling for Oppositionists and Others: A Plea for Narrative," 87 Mich. L. Rev. 2411 (1989); and "Rodrigo's Thirteenth Chronicle: Legal Formalism and Law's Discontents," 95 Mich. L. Rev. 1105 (1997)
New York University Law Review, for "Rodrigo's Sixth Chronicle: Intersections, Essences, and the Dilemma of Social Reform," 68 N.Y.U. L. Rev. 639 (1993); and "Derrick Bell's Toolkit—Fit to Dismantle That Famous House?" 75 N.Y.U. L. Rev. 283 (2000)
Northwestern University Law Review, for "Campus Antiracism Rules: Constitutional Narratives in Collision," 85 Nw. U. L. Rev. 343 (1991); and "Rodrigo's Roadmap: Is the Marketplace Theory for Eradicating Discrimination a Blind Alley?" 95 Nw. U. L. Rev. 215 (1998)

Southern California Law Review, for "Rodrigo's Final Chronicle: Cultural Power, the Law Reviews, and the Attack on Narrative Jurisprudence," 68 S. Cal. L. Rev. 545 (1995)

Stanford Law Review, for "Rodrigo's Fourth Chronicle: Neutrality and Stasis in Antidiscrimination Law," 45 Stan. L. Rev. 1133 (1993)

Texas Law Review, for "Rodrigo's Fifteenth Chronicle: Racial Mixture, Latino-Critical Scholarship, and the Black-White Binary," 75 Tex. L. Rev. 1181 (1997)

University of California at Davis Law Review, for "Official Elitism or Institutional Self-Interest? 10 Reasons Why Law Schools Should Abandon the LSAT," 34 U.C. Davis L. Rev. 593 (2001)

University of California at Los Angeles Law Review, for "Rodrigo's Seventh Chronicle: Race, Democracy, and the State," 41 UCLA L. Rev. 721 (1994)

University of Pennsylvania Law Review, for "Rodrigo's Ninth Chronicle: Race, Legal Instrumentalism, and the Rule of Law," 143 U. Pa. L. Rev. 379 (1994); and "The Imperial Scholar: Reflections on a Review of Civil Rights Literature," 132 U. Pa. L. Rev. 561 (1984)

Vanderbilt Law Review, for "Joseph Sax, the Public Trust Theory of Environmental Protection, and Some Dark Thoughts on the Possibility of Law Reform" [Our Better Natures], 44 Vand. L. Rev. 1209 (1991)

Virginia Law Review, for "Rodrigo's Eighth Chronicle: Black Crime, White Fears—On the Social Construction of Threat," 80 Va. L. Rev. 503 (1994)

William and Mary Law Review, for "The Social Construction of *Brown v. Board of Education,*" 36 Wm. & Mary L. Rev. 547 (1995)

Wisconsin Law Review, for "On Taking Back Our Civil Rights Promises," 1989 Wis. L. Rev. 579

Yale Law Journal, for "Rodrigo's Chronicle," 101 Yale L.J. 1357 (1992)

Adrien Wing acknowledges several sets of research assistants from the University of Iowa College of Law, in particular those who helped on the final version: Brendan Hug, Cynthia Lockett, Shaun Naidu, Ruben Pagán, Jonathan Stagg, and Andrea Suzuki. As always, thanks go to her steadfast partner, James Sommerville.

Jean Stefancic thanks research assistants Jamison Arimoto and Matthew Fergus for exceptional service. Jenna Cramer contributed expert technical assistance. LuAnn Driscoll, Phyllis Gentille, Karen Knochel, Darleen Mocello, and Barbara Salopek prepared the manuscript with intelligence and dispatch.

Dean Mary Crossley and the University of Pittsburgh Law School, as always, provided steadfast support. The Centrum Institute at Port Townsend, Washington, graciously supplied a space, solitude, and time for this work to come together.

Introduction

The tall black-haired man leaned back in his office chair at the University of Colorado Law School and looked out the window, a furrow crossing his indigenous-looking Latin brow. The Flatiron mountains framed the view outside, but inside, the professor's mind was racing.

He needed a new vehicle for his thoughts. All knowledge—or at any rate, social knowledge—is dialogic, he pondered, reflecting a give-and-take of opposing visions and points of view. This suggested to him that some form of storytelling might be what he was looking for. But in law? He had already made his reputation by writing "straight," orthodox, expository prose in articles such as "The Imperial Scholar" and "Words That Wound," the first article to name and analyze hate speech as a legally redressable harm.

But other topics that he wanted to write about—colonialism, the decline of the West, the role of love and compassion in social regulation—did not easily lend themselves to linear, heavily footnoted presentations such as those that appeared in the pages of the top law reviews.

I could invent a character who is multiracial; maybe I'll call him Rodrigo, he mused. Perhaps he will be a distant relative of one of Derrick Bell's characters. (I'll have to ask him first.) I'll make him multiracial. That way, my topics won't have to be limited to ones mainly affecting the African-American community. I'd like to go beyond the black-white binary. Jean urged me to do that a few years ago.

"That's it!" he exclaimed to himself. "I'll write a series of chronicles, like Bell's 'Geneva Chronicles,' and use my character as a foil to develop audacious new ideas. He'll be a young scholar, full of vinegar and spirit, a black man but with Latino roots, too. He'll be educated in a foreign country, perhaps Italy—maybe his father will be a U.S. serviceman who was stationed there—and the reader will meet him when he returns to the United States to look into a graduate law degree. He'll seek out an older figure, an experienced law professor of color, for advice. The older man can be the voice of caution and a counterpoint to the young fellow's bravura performances."

"This might work," he said, and turned to his typewriter. "Let me play with these ideas for a while. I do have that sabbatical coming up. If I manage to publish the first one in a good review, maybe I can turn this into a book."

The sound of his fingers clattering on the keyboard could be heard in the hallway off and on for the remainder of the afternoon. After a while, the custodian came in to empty his wastebasket. The professor hardly looked up.

And, as they say, the rest was history.

A prominent scholar once described Delgado's work in the following terms: "Delgado is a triple pioneer. He was the first to question free speech ideology; he and a few others invented Critical Race Theory; and he is both a theorist and an exemplar of the importance of storytelling in the workings of the law.... [*The Rodrigo Chronicles*] brings all of Delgado's strengths together in a stunning performance."

Hyperbole aside, Delgado's contributions to law do fall into those three main areas—free speech ideology, where he is a relentless critic of the status quo; critical race theory, where he is considered a founding figure; and legal storytelling, where the breadth and depth of his work are unique in legal scholarship. But he also has made major contributions in other areas, including Latino-critical scholarship (where he has been a major contributor and critic), law and medicine (for which he supplied a pathbreaking article on the psychology of religious cultism), tort theory (in an article on causation rules that influenced how courts approach mass torts such as Agent Orange exposure and radiation poisoning), and criminal law (for which he authored a much-cited article on the "rotten social background" defense). He also began writing about right-wing social movements and think tanks in the mid-1990s while much of the left was sleeping, and about the need to socialize the costs of health care before certain liberal theorists began doing so. And his book *The Coming Race War* may have helped spur the Clinton administration to establish a national yearlong dialogue on race.

The current volume collects the best of Delgado's work. We have identified his most foundational and easily accessible essays and grouped them under eight broad themes. We have edited them to eliminate overlapping material and most footnotes. The reader seeking an unabridged version should consult the acknowledgments, which identifies where they may be found.

Each part begins with a short introduction, written by the editors, setting out the main ideas that the reader will find in the material to follow and, in some cases, mentioning further selections that we could not fit into the confines of the book but that an interested reader might wish to consult. At the end of the volume, the reader will find an annotated bibliography of Delgado's main works and a comprehensive index that will enable him or her to identify where Delgado discusses particular themes or ideas.

The reader interested in Delgado's "Rodrigo Chronicles" will find several of them included in Part I, which is concerned with narrative jurisprudence and storytelling, as well as others throughout the rest of the book. These include a chronicle dealing with empathy and false empathy, which puts forward the astonishing notion that emotions can replicate hierarchy just as legal doctrine and conservative jurisprudence can. Another shows that white crime, not black, is the main source of danger today. And another locates the source of racism in the Enlightenment. Rodrigo appears in the book in various stages of his life and of his relationship with the Professor, not all chronological.

The reader intrigued by Delgado's work in reforming the law should consult Parts IV (Hate Speech), V (Law Reform), and VIII (Affirmative Action). These sections include classic articles on campus hate-speech rules, *Brown v. Board of Education,* and the predicament of women of color.

Delgado's contribution to critical race theory—and his own criticisms of the direction the movement has recently taken—appears in Part II (Critical Theory). Readers interested in his contribution to "Lat-crit" scholarship, a spinoff movement that grew out of critical race theory, should not miss Part VI (Latinos and Other Nonblack Minorities). Those intrigued by his critique of the United States political scene should consult Part VII (Politics and Critique). This latter section contains groundbreaking essays on power, democracy, and the law-and-economics movement, and one positing the sobering suggestion that minorities should consider making common cause with their traditional adversaries, the Republican Party.

Delgado is ecumenical. Some of the pieces in this book are about African Americans. Others are about Latinos. Some are about the environment and the world of nature. One details a charming love story between the seventy-year-old narrator and the mother of Rodrigo's love interest. A number of the characters in the Rodrigo dialogues are women. One is gay.

Excerpts in the storytelling mode give the reader a glimpse into what two intellectuals of color talk about. Others reveal a restless mind, one of the country's leading social critics, at work. This book is for everyone interested in understanding how law works, and how society succeeds and, more often, fails. It is for the reader who wonders why law seems so often unable to aid those it sets out to help and why social change is such hard work, requiring more than good intentions.

In introducing him to an audience at the University of Oregon, where Delgado gave the annual Wayne Morse Lecture in 1998, the dean of that law school described him as his colleagues knew him in his earliest years, as "an educational growth stock."

Delgado's early colleagues were right in their assessment of his potential. But he has also returned their favor by devoting some of his impressive body of scholarship to educational issues. Thus, the reader will find, in Part III (Law, Legal Education, and the Legal Profession), excerpts examining the very institution that he considers his home. Why are lawyers so unhappy? Are law schools bastions of elitism? Should white scholars withdraw from civil rights scholarship so that scholars of color can leave their mark?

A MAN'S LIFE

How did Delgado come to law and legal scholarship? The son of a Mexican (probably undocumented) immigrant from Aguascalientes and a Polish mother from the tenement district of Chicago, Delgado grew up poor. When he was young, his parents moved around frequently, as his father sought better or steadier jobs. He attended many schools and, because of his family's frequent moves, had few long-term friends. He became, as he says, "bookish," but few of his early teachers noticed his talent, because he would leave their classes before the year was out.

When Delgado was twelve, his father moved his family back to Mexico, where he renounced the American citizenship he had acquired through naturalization and became a Mexican citizen once again. For the next several years, Delgado attended the American High School, then returned to the United States for college at the University of Washington, where he majored in mathematics and philosophy. After a period of military service, he attended law school at the University of California at Berkeley, where he served on the law review and became convinced that he wanted to become a law professor. Lacking a mentor, he aimed low, applying to a neighboring school for a position as a teaching fellow. Fortune intervened, however, in the form of an invitation to interview for what turned out to be his first teaching position at Arizona State University College of Law.

Two years later, Delgado resigned to take a similar position at his alma mater, the University of Washington Law School, where he served for two years. He then received a phone call from UCLA, inviting him to teach for a year as a visiting professor. The visit went well, resulting in a tenure offer from this prominent law school, where he taught for eight years. He then transferred to the University of Wisconsin–Madison, as part of a bold social experiment known as the "Madison Plan," then returned to the West. As a chaired professor at the University of Colorado Law School in Boulder, where he taught for fourteen years, Delgado enjoyed a secure and congenial environment. Aided by a visionary dean and surrounded by energetic colleagues, Delgado's scholarship blossomed. He published article after article and began writing books, some with his second wife (and coeditor of this volume), Jean Stefancic. Presently a university distinguished professor at the University of Pittsburgh Law School, he continues mentoring young professors and junior scholars, particularly of color, throughout the nation. He also serves as series editor for three academic presses, in which capacity he is able to bring his passion for scholarship to the world of publishing.

"Why write?" he once asked. "Several reasons," he answered. "Because your colleagues are writing, because you have something to say, because you want to change the law, because it's enjoyable (at least sometimes), because you want professional advancement and recognition. Personally, I prefer the intrinsic reasons—writing as self-expression, writing because it is satisfying. But I also enjoy the result when something I have written has an impact—stirs people up, helps a court make the right decision. Everyone's motivation is, I think, mixed, and the mix varies from person to person and article to article."

A signature piece in this collection ends with the vision of a homeless man, "his few possessions stacked neatly on the bench beside him," looking up at the narrator inquiringly. The Professor thinks of Rodrigo, who has just left, perhaps not to be seen again. Delgado, though approaching seventy, is still full of life and almost surely will be heard from again. We invite you to leaf through this volume and immerse yourself in the world of this provocative legal scholar and writer.

Adrien Wing and Jean Stefancic
Iowa City, Iowa, and Pittsburgh, Pennsylvania

PART I
Narrative and Legal Storytelling

The selections that follow show Delgado developing one of his signature themes—legal storytelling.

In a much-cited article, "Storytelling for Oppositionists and Others," Delgado examines the struggle over how social reality is constructed through stories and counterstories. In this excerpt he shows ways oppositionist legal storytellers can unearth bias in standards of objectivity by telling five versions of a story about why a minority candidate failed to get a job offer.

"Rodrigo's Chronicle" introduces the fictional character Rodrigo Crenshaw. A mixed-race graduate of an Italian law school, Rodrigo seeks out "the Professor," with whom he has a long conversation about merit, law school hiring practices, and the decline of the West.

In "Rodrigo's Third Chronicle," Rodrigo presents a countervision of American society in which caregiving activities, such as nursing homes, are socialized, and the productive sector governed by free-market principles. He outlines a civil rights strategy based on love in which leaders in minority communities serve as bridge people between those most in need and the dominant white society.

Rodrigo defends narrative scholarship in "Rodrigo's Final Chronicle," taking into account reasons why the storytelling movement meets resistance; then suddenly and mysteriously he disappears.

After an escapade in which his kidnappers release him, Rodrigo reappears in the "Eleventh Chronicle," in which he and the Professor talk about the way empathy not only reproduces hierarchy but fails to aid law reform. Rodrigo explains how rules of evidence, pleading, and cross-examination limit civil rights plaintiffs' abilities to tell their stories in court trials, and concludes by calling for a due process of legal storytelling.

Rodrigo, the Professor, and other characters appear in dozens of Delgado's chronicles and four of his books, which are annotated in the bibliography at the end of this book. Responses to critiques of the legal storytelling movement appear there as well.

Storytelling for Oppositionists and Others
A Plea for Narrative

Everyone has been writing stories these days. And I don't just mean writing *about* stories or narrative theory, important as that is. I mean actual stories, as in "once-upon-a-time" type stories. Derrick Bell has been writing "Chronicles," and in the *Harvard Law Review* at that. Others have been writing dialogues, stories, and metastories. Many others have been daring to become more personal in their writing, to inject narrative, perspective, and feeling—how it was for me—into their otherwise scholarly, footnoted articles and, in the case of the truly brave, into their teaching.

Many, but by no means all, who have been telling legal stories are members of groups whose marginality defines the boundaries of the mainstream, whose voice and perspective—whose consciousness—has been suppressed, devalued, and abnormalized. The attraction of stories for outgroups should come as no surprise. For stories create their own bonds, represent cohesion, shared understandings, and meanings. The cohesiveness that stories bring is part of the strength of the outgroup. An outgroup creates its own stories, which circulate within the group as a kind of counter-reality.

The dominant group creates its own stories, as well. The stories or narratives the ingroup tells remind it of its identity in relation to outgroups and provide it with a form of shared reality in which its own superior position is seen as natural.

The stories of outgroups aim to subvert that reality. In civil rights, for example, many in the majority hold that any inequality between blacks and whites is due either to cultural lag or inadequate enforcement of currently existing beneficial laws—both of which are easily correctable. For many minority persons, the principal instrument of their subordination is neither of these. Rather, it is the prevailing *mindset* by means of which members of the dominant group justify the world as it is, that is, with whites on top and browns and blacks at the bottom.

Stories, parables, chronicles, and narratives are powerful means for destroying mindset—the bundle of presuppositions, received wisdoms, and shared understandings against a background of which legal and political discourse takes place. These matters rarely come into focus. Like eyeglasses we have worn a long time, they are nearly invisible; we use them to scan and interpret the world, only rarely examining them for themselves. Ideology—the received wisdom—makes current social arrangements seem fair and natural. Those in power sleep well at night—their conduct does not seem to them like oppression.

The cure is storytelling (or as I shall sometimes call it, counterstorytelling). As Derrick Bell, Bruno Bettelheim, and others show, stories can shatter complacency and challenge the status quo. Stories told by underdogs are frequently ironic or satiric; a root word for "humor" is humus—bringing low, down to earth. Along with the tradition of storytelling in black culture flourishes the Spanish tradition of the picaresque novel or story, which tells of humble folk piquing the pompous or powerful and bringing them down to more human levels.

Most who write about storytelling focus on its community-building functions: stories build consensus, a common culture of shared understandings, and deeper, more vital ethics. Counterstories, which challenge the received wisdom, do that as well. They can open new windows into reality, showing us possibilities for life other than the ones we live. They enrich imagination and teach that by combining elements from the story and current reality, we may construct a new world richer than either alone. Counterstories can quicken and engage conscience. Their graphic quality can stir imagination in ways in which more conventional discourse cannot.

But stories and counterstories can serve an equally important destructive function. They can show that what we believe is ridiculous, self-serving, or cruel. They can show us the way out of the trap of unjustified exclusion. They can help us understand when it is time to reallocate power. They are the other half—the destructive half—of the creative dialectic.

Stories and counterstories, to be effective, must be or appear to be noncoercive. They invite the reader to suspend judgment, listen for their point or message, and then decide what measure of truth they contain. They are insinuative, not frontal; they offer a respite from the linear, coercive quality of much legal writing.

STORYTELLING AND COUNTERSTORYTELLING

The same object, as everyone knows, can be described in many ways. A rectangular red object on my living room floor may be a nuisance if I stub my toe on it in the dark, a doorstop if I use it for that purpose, further evidence of my lackadaisical housekeeping to my visiting mother, a toy to my young daughter, or simply a brick left over from my patio restoration project. There is no single true, or all-encompassing description. The same holds true of events. Watching an individual perform strenuous repetitive movements, we might say that he or she is exercising, discharging nervous energy, seeing to his or her health under doctor's orders, or suffering a seizure or convulsion. Often, we will not be able to ascertain the single best description or interpretation of what we have seen. We participate in creating what we see in the very act of describing it.

Social and moral realities are just as indeterminate and subject to interpretation as single objects or events, if not more so. For example, what is the "correct" answer to the question, American Indians are—(A) a colonized people; (B) tragic victims of technological progress; (C) subjects of a suffocating, misdirected federal beneficence; (D) a minority stubbornly resistant to assimilation; or (E) ———; or (F) ———?

My premise is that much of social reality is constructed. We decide what is, and, almost simultaneously, what ought to be. Narrative habits, patterns of seeing, shape what we see and that to which we aspire. These patterns of perception become habitual, tempting us to believe that the way things are is inevitable, or the best that can be in an imperfect world. Alternative visions of reality are not explored, or, if they are, rejected as extreme or implausible.

In the area of racial reform the majority story would go something like this:

> Early in our history there was slavery, which was a terrible thing. Blacks were brought to this country from Africa in chains and made to work in the fields. Some were viciously mistreated, which was, of course, an unforgivable wrong; others were treated kindly. Slavery ended with the Civil War, although many blacks remained poor, uneducated, and outside the cultural mainstream. As the country's racial sensitivity to blacks' plight increased, the vestiges of slavery were gradually eliminated by federal statutes and case law. Today, blacks enjoy many civil rights and receive protection from discrimination in such areas as housing, public education, employment, and voting. The gap between blacks and whites is steadily closing, although it may take some time for it to close completely. At the same time, it is important not to go too far in providing special benefits for blacks. Doing so induces dependency and welfare mentality. It can also cause a backlash among innocent white victims of reverse discrimination. Most Americans are fair-minded individuals who harbor little racial prejudice. The few who do can be punished when they act on those beliefs.

Yet, coexisting with that rather comforting tale is another story of black subordination in America, a history "gory, brutal, filled with more murder, mutilation, rape, and brutality than most of us can imagine or easily comprehend." This other history continues into the present, implicating individuals still alive. It includes infant death rates among blacks nearly double those of whites, unemployment rates among black males nearly triple those of whites, and a gap between the races in income, wealth, and life expectancy that is the same as it was fifteen years ago, if not greater. It includes despair, crime, and drug addiction in black neighborhoods, and college and university enrollment figures for blacks that are dropping for the first time in decades. It dares to call our most prized legal doctrines and protections shams—devices enacted with great fanfare, only to be ignored, obstructed, or cut back as soon as the celebrations die down.

How can such divergent stories circulate? Why do they not combine? Is it simply that members of the dominant group see the same glass as half full, blacks as half empty? I believe more than this is at work; there is a war between stories. To see how the dialectic of competition and rejection works and the normative implications of adopting one story rather than another, consider the following series of accounts, each describing the same event.

A Standard Event and a Stock Story That Explains It
A black lawyer interviews for a teaching position at a major law school (school *X*), and is rejected. Any other race-tinged event could have served equally well. This particular event was chosen because it occurs on familiar ground—most readers of this essay are past or present members of a law school community who have heard about or participated in events like the one described.

The Stock Story

Setting. A professor and student are talking in the professor's office. Both are white. The professor, Blas Vernier, is tenured, in mid-career, and well regarded by his colleagues and students. The student, Judith Rogers, is a member of the student advisory appointments committee.

Rogers: Professor Vernier, what happened with the black candidate, John Henry? I heard the faculty voted him down yesterday. The students on my committee liked him a lot.

Vernier: It was a difficult decision, Judith. We discussed him for over two hours. I can't tell you the final vote, of course, but it wasn't particularly close. Even some of my colleagues who were initially for his appointment voted against him when the full record came out.

Rogers: But we have no minority professors at all, except for Professor Chen, who is untenured, and Professor Tompkins, who teaches Trial Practice on loan from the district attorney's office once a year.

Vernier: Don't forget Mary Foster, the Assistant Dean.

Rogers: But she doesn't teach, just handles admissions and the placement office.

Vernier: And does those things very well. But I understand your disappointment. Henry was a strong candidate, one of the stronger blacks we've interviewed recently. But ultimately he didn't measure up. We didn't think he wanted to teach for the right reasons. He was vague and diffuse about his research interests. All he could say was that he wanted to write about equality and civil rights, but so far as we could tell, he had nothing new to say about those areas. What's more, we had some problems with his teaching interests. He wanted to teach peripheral courses, in areas where we already have enough people. And we had the sense that he wouldn't be really rigorous in those areas, either.

Rogers: But we need courses in employment discrimination and civil rights. And he's had a long career with the NAACP Legal Defense Fund and really seemed to know his stuff.

Vernier: It's true we could stand to add a course or two of that nature, although as you know our main needs are in Commercial Law and Corporations.

But I think our need is not as acute as you say. Many of the topics you're interested in are covered in the second half of the Constitutional Law course taught by Professor White, who has a national reputation for his work in civil liberties and freedom of speech.

Rogers: But Henry could have taught those topics from a black perspective. And he would have been a wonderful role model for our minority students.

Vernier: Those things are true, and we gave them considerable weight. But when it came right down to it, we felt we couldn't take that risk. Henry wasn't on the law review at school, as you are, Judith, and has never written a line in a legal journal. Some of us doubted he ever would. And then, what would happen five years from now when he came up for tenure? It wouldn't be fair to him. He'd just have to pick up his career and start over if he didn't produce.

Rogers: With all due respect, Professor, that's paternalistic. I think Henry should have been given the chance. He might have surprised us.

Vernier: So I thought, too, until I heard my colleagues' discussion, which I'm afraid, given the demands of confidentiality, I can't share with you. Just let me say that we examined his case long and hard and, I am convinced, fairly. The decision, while painful, was correct.

Rogers: So another year is going to go by without a minority candidate or professor?

Vernier: These things take time. I was on the appointments committee last year, chaired it in fact. And I can tell you we would love nothing better than to find a qualified black. Every year, we call the Supreme Court to check on current clerks, telephone our colleagues at other leading law schools, and place ads in black newspapers and journals. But the pool is so small. And the few good ones have many opportunities. We can't pay nearly as much as private practice, you know.

[*Rogers, who would like to be a legal services attorney, but is attracted to the higher salaries of corporate practice, nods glumly.*]

Vernier: It may be that we'll have to wait another few years, until the current crop of black and minority law students graduates and gets some experience. We have some excellent prospects, including some members of your very class.

Rogers: [*Thinks: I've heard that one before, but says*] Well, thanks, Professor. I know the students will be disappointed. But maybe when the committee considers visiting professors later in the season it will be able to find a professor of color who meets its standards and fits our needs.

Vernier: We'll try our best. Although you should know that some of us believe that merely shuffling the few minorities in teaching from one school to another does little to expand the pool. And once they get here, it's hard to say no if they express a desire to stay on.

Rogers: [*Thinks: That's a lot like tenure. How ironic; there are certain of your colleagues we would love to get rid of, too. But says*] Well, thanks, Professor. I've got to get to class. I still wish the vote had come out otherwise. Our student committee is preparing a list of minority candidates that we would like to see considered. Maybe you'll find one or more of them worthy of teaching here.

Vernier: Judith, believe me, nothing would please me more.

* * *

In the above dialogue, Professor Vernier's account represents the stock story—the one the institution forms and tells about itself. This story picks and chooses from among the available facts to present a picture of what happened: an account that justifies the world as it is. It emphasizes the school's benevolent motivation ("look how hard we're trying") and good faith. It stresses stability and risk avoidance. It measures the black candidate through the prism of preexisting, agreed-upon criteria of conventional scholarship and teaching. Given those standards, it professes to be scrupulously meritocratic and fair; Henry would have been hired had he measured up. No one raises the possibility that the merit criteria used in judging Henry are themselves debatable, *chosen*—not inevitable. No one, least of all Vernier, calls attention to the way in which merit functions to conceal the contingent connection between institutional power and the things rated.

It gives little consideration to the possibility that Henry's presence on the faculty might have altered the institution's character, helped introduce a different prism and different criteria for selecting future candidates. The account is highly procedural—it emphasizes that Henry got a full, careful hearing—rather than substantive: a black was rejected. It emphasizes certain "facts" without examining their truth—namely, that the pool is very small, that good minority candidates have many choices, and that the appropriate view is long; haste makes waste.

The dominant fact about this first story, however, is its seeming neutrality. It scrupulously avoids issues of blame or responsibility. Race played no part in the candidate's rejection; indeed the school leaned over backwards to accommodate him. A white candidate with similar credentials would not have made it as far as Henry did. The story comforts and soothes. And Vernier's sincerity makes him an effective apologist for his system.

Vernier's story is also deeply coercive, although the coercion is disguised. Judith was aware of it but chose not to confront it directly; Vernier holds all the cards. He pressures her to go along with the institution's story by threatening her job prospects at the same time that he flatters her achievements. A victim herself, she is invited to take on and share the consciousness of her oppressor. She does not accept Vernier's story, but he does slip a few doubts through cracks in her armor. The professor's story shows how forceful and repeated storytelling can perpetuate a particular view of reality. Naturally, the stock story is not the only one that can be told. By emphasizing other events and giving them slightly different interpretations, a quite different picture can be made to emerge.

The Same Event Told by John Henry

Scene. John Henry has just received his rejection letter from the head of the appointments committee. The letter is quite cheerful. It tells Henry how much the faculty enjoyed meeting him and hearing his presentation on trends in civil rights litigation. It advises him that because of curricular concerns, the school's prime emphasis this year will be on filling slots in the Commercial Law and Corporations area. It concludes by encouraging Henry to remain in contact with the school and wishes him luck in his search for a teaching position. It nowhere tells him that he has been rejected.

A few days after receiving the letter, John Henry is having lunch with a junior colleague from the Fund. The colleague, who is also black, wants to teach some day and so quizzes Henry about his experiences in interviewing at school X.

Henry: It was, how shall I put it? Worse than I hoped but better than I feared. I'm not going to get an offer, although they of course never came right out and said so. And, from what I saw, I'm not sure I would want to teach there, even if I had gotten one. If school *X* is any sample of what blacks can expect in this supposedly colorblind, erudite world of legal education, I think I prefer Howard, where, incidentally, I'm interviewing next week. I got more than a whiff of these attitudes when I went to law school almost 15 years ago, but had dared to hope that things might have changed in the interim. They haven't.

Junior colleague: But how did they treat you? Did you give a colloquium?

Henry: You bet I gave a colloquium, and that's where it began. A good half of the faculty looked bored or puzzled and asked no questions. A quarter jumped down my throat after I had spoken maybe ten minutes, wanting to know whether I would advocate the same approach if the plaintiff were white and the defendant black. The old "neutral principles" idea, thirty years later. In the question-and-answer period, several younger professors tried to rescue me; one even changed the subject and asked about my philosophy of teaching. That brought everybody to the edge of their chairs. I got the impression many of them merely wanted assurance that I would write *some* articles, even if they were mediocre. But they were *all* extremely concerned that I be a good teacher. I think many of them were looking for a mascot, not a fellow scholar—someone who would counsel and keep the students in line, not someone who could challenge his or her colleagues at their own game.

During the small-group interviews, many of them didn't even show up. The ones that did asked me about curricular matters, what courses I would like to teach, how I enjoyed going to law school at Michigan and whether I took courses from their friend, so-and-so, who teaches there. The few who asked me anything about my colloquium ignored what I had said but asked me questions based on recent law review articles, written by their friends, most of which, of course, I had not read. They all seemed to deal with issues of equality and bore little relation to my work and litigation perspective.

Several asked what my grade point average was in law school—fifteen years ago, can you believe it!—and whether I was on the law review. They had my resume in front of them, so they knew the answer to that perfectly well. The first two who asked seemed dumbfounded when I said I had been invited to join the review and even more so when I said I had declined in order to work part-time in a prison law program. After a while I just answered the question by saying no.

Don't get me wrong. They're a good law school; I could see myself teaching there. But I think they're looking for someone they will never find—a black who won't challenge them in any way, who is just like them. I tried telling them about the cases I have argued and the litigation strategies I have pioneered. Most of them couldn't have cared less. Their eyes glazed over after three minutes or they changed the subject.

Junior colleague: John, let me ask you something flat out. You don't have to answer this if you don't want to. You know that I practiced corporate law in a large firm in Atlanta for three years before coming to the Fund. I could see myself teaching business subjects some day, in addition of course to civil rights. The school you interviewed at is advertising that they need professors of business law. Do I want to teach there?

Henry: [*Slowly*] That's a tough one. If I went there, my greatest fear is that I would be marginalized and ignored—either that or co-opted into the mainstream. I doubt they would see my work in civil rights as on a level with theirs in, say, property. You might have a different experience, though, teaching corporate and business law courses. Are you serious about applying?

Junior colleague: I think so.

Henry: Okay, my man. Let me call the Asian professor I met there. His name is Chen, I think. He seemed sympathetic, and I guess he would level with you. I'll ask him what he thinks the climate would be like for someone like you. Maybe in the process I'll learn something about how I was seen and get some pointers on how to conduct myself the next time I interview at a white, elite law school—if I have to. I think Howard is quite interested in me, and frankly I'm tempted to just accept an offer there if they make one. It would simplify life a great deal.

Junior colleague: I would appreciate that. You're a good buddy. Let me know what you find out.

* * *

Henry and his younger colleague's story is, obviously, quite different from the institution's. It shows, among other things, how different "neutrality" can feel from the perspective of an outsider. Henry's story emphasizes certain facts, sequences, tones of voice, and body language that the stock story leaves out. It infers different intentions, attitudes, and states of mind on the part of the faculty he met. Although not completely condemnatory, it is not nearly so generous to the school. It implies that the supposedly colorblind hiring process is really monochromatic: School *X* hires professors of any color, so long as they are white. In Henry's story, process questions submerge; the bottom line becomes more important. The story specifically challenges the school's meritocratic premises. It questions, somewhat satirically, the school's conception of a "good" teaching prospect and asks what came first, the current faculty (with its strengths and weaknesses) or the criteria. Did the "is" give birth to the "ought"? Henry's account, although less obviously slanted than Vernier's, contains exaggerations of its own. This is perhaps natural and understandable; Henry wanted his younger colleague to think well of him. His account is self-serving. For example, he implied that many of the faculty asked him about his law school grades, when in fact only two did. And, although Henry does struggle to free himself from the process trap to which Vernier succumbed, he does not succeed entirely. He charges that his "hearing" at the law school was substantively biased by racism and inappropriate criteria. But he also charges that the hearing was afflicted by ordinary defects: For example, many of his hearers did not bother to show up—it was a mock hearing. Henry still accepts the system's dominant values, wants to play, and win, by its rules. Perhaps this explains the calmness, the tone of resignation about Henry's story. Whether this is because he has internalized some of his victimizers' consciousness, has a good alternative coming up next week at Howard, or simply despairs of changing School X we do not know. But this situation soon changed drastically.

Following Henry's lunch with his younger colleague, Henry telephoned Chen and one other younger, bearded faculty member he met at the law school. The other professor, who is white, had visibly warmed up to Henry. He had asked him to call any time if Henry had questions. As a result of talking with these two at length, Henry learns facts that leave him seriously upset. No longer resigned, Henry consults with several colleagues at the Fund about a lawsuit. After receiving an offer from Howard, Henry retains private counsel. The following two stories are the result.

The Legal Complaint and Judge's Order

The Complaint. About a year after his unsuccessful interview, and ten months after speaking with Chen and the white professor, Henry files the following complaint in the superior court of College County of State X:

Henry v. Regents, et al. Comes now the plaintiff and alleges as follows.

[Following various jurisdictional and exhaustion-of-remedies allegations]:
8) That the defendant has intentionally engaged in an unlawful employment practice in that the defendant has discriminated against plaintiff by denying him an appointment as Professor of Law, because of his race and color; that defendant has denied plaintiff employment as Professor of Law because of his engagement in civil rights activities; that defendant has denied plaintiff employment as Professor of Law because as a black Professor teaching Civil Rights he would not "fit in"; and that the above mentioned acts of discrimination violate 42 U.S.C. section 1981 in that they were based on race, color, and civil rights activities and orientations.

9) That the plaintiff has lost wages by reason of the illegal employment practices of defendant and has earned less money in other employment than he would have earned had he received appointment as Professor of Law at defendant institution.

Whereupon plaintiff prays that this Court find that the defendant has intentionally and illegally denied plaintiff employment because of his race, color, and civil rights activities, and because as a black man he would not "fit in"; that the Court enjoin defendant from engaging in these and similar practices; that the defendant be ordered to pay plaintiff all lost wages because of said unlawful employment practices; that the defendant pay plaintiff's reasonable attorney's fees; and that defendant be ordered to pay all costs in this action.

Phyllis M. Leventhal
Attorney for Plaintiff
Address: 49 State Building
Capitol City, State X

The Judge's Order Dismissing the Action

After a short period of discovery, the judge dismissed Henry's suit with a brief opinion:

The defendant's motion for summary judgment is granted.

Even viewing the evidence in the light most favorable to Plaintiff, it is clear to this Court that he cannot prevail. Plaintiff has adduced no evidence, save his own assertion that he was not hired, that he has suffered unlawful employment discrimination. Given the historic shortage of qualified minorities in the applicant pool, it is not surprising that white faces should preponderate on a law faculty. This imbalance is not irrelevant but by itself does not constitute invidious discrimination. It is of no greater or less significance than the proportion of blacks to whites on the school's athletic teams.

Even assuming that he is qualified to teach at School X, Plaintiff has not made out a claim that his failure to be hired there is a product of discrimination. If he could adduce even one example of obvious discrimination—for example, if he had been told that his lack of authorship disqualified him, but he could prove that some white faculty members had neither published nor perished—this would be a far different case. But we find no such smoking gun. Plaintiff believes he was blackballed as a potential "troublemaker," someone who might use his position atop the ivory tower to cry out against the university, to bite the very hand that had uplifted him. But a propensity toward disloyalty is simply one of the competing considerations in the hiring process, the weight of which our scales of justice shall not attempt to assay. Nothing is intrinsically wrong, however, with requiring a college professor to be true to his school.

Nor do we find that differential standards were applied to Plaintiff's application. It may be that the law faculty devalued his potential contributions as a teacher and scholar of civil rights law. But a faculty is entitled to make judgments that one class or area of study is more urgently needed to round out the school's curriculum than another.

Moreover, this Court would be most hesitant to substitute its own standards for those of the professors who make up the faculty of X School of Law. The Law School is an eminent institution, one of the nation's finest. The decisions of such a body are necessarily judgmental and highly subjective. It is not an appropriate function for this Court to tell the faculty whom to hire. That is a matter for their professional judgment, and short of manifest unfairness or illegality, this Court cannot and will not interfere. The factors that make a good law professor are many, subtle, and eminently professional in character. They are best made by those who, had he been hired, would have been Plaintiff's peers. It would ill serve the Plaintiff to force him on an unwilling institution. We find no actionable wrong. This case is dismissed.

* * *

Both the complaint and the order dismissing it are stylized versions of Henry's story. Both use existing statutory and case law as a type of "screen" that makes certain facts relevant and others not. Henry's lawyer struggled to present her client's story in terms a court would accept. She failed. Unless reversed on appeal, the complaint's story will remain a renegade version of the world, officially devalued.

Putting the facts in the linguistic code required by the court sterilized them. The interview was abstracted from its context and squeezed into a prescribed mold that stripped it of the features that gave it meaning for Henry. It lost its power to outrage. In a sense, even if successful the complaint would have legitimated the current social order.

Stories do not pose these risks. Stories do not try to seize a part of the body of received wisdom and use it against itself, jiujitsu fashion, as litigation does. Stories attack and subvert the very "institutional logic" of the system. On the rare occasions when law-reform litigation is effective for blacks, the hard-won new "rights" are quietly stolen away by narrow interpretation, foot dragging, delay, and outright obstruction. Stories' success is not so easily circumvented; a telling point is registered instantaneously and the stock story it wounds will never be the same.

John Henry's complaint was doubly unsuccessful. It was dismissed, its failure validating the dominant story, its principal opponent so far. It also gave the judge an opportunity to tell his own story—dismissive, curt, verging on insult—and give it circulation and currency.

Al-Hammar X's Counterstory
None of the above stories attempts to unseat the prevailing institutional story. Henry's account comes closest; it highlights different facts and interprets those it does share with the standard account differently. His formal complaint also challenges the school's account, but it must fit itself under existing law, which it failed to do.

A few days after word of Henry's rejection reached the student body, Noel Al-Hammar X, leader of the Third World Coalition, delivered a speech at noon on the steps of the law school patio. The audience consisted of most of the black and brown students at the law school, several dozen white students, and a few faculty members. Chen was absent, having a class to prepare for. The Assistant Dean was present, uneasily taking notes in case the Dean asked her later what she heard.

Al-Hammar's speech was scathing, denunciatory, and at times downright rude. He spoke several words that the campus newspaper reporter wondered if his paper would print. He impugned the good faith of the faculty, accused them of institutional if not garden-variety racism, and pointed out in great detail the long history of the faculty as an all-white club. He said that the law school was bent on hiring only white males, "ladies" only if they were well-behaved clones of white males, and would never hire a black unless forced to do so by student pressure or the courts. He exhorted his fellow students not to rest until the law faculty took steps to address its own ethnocentricity and racism. He urged boycotting or disrupting classes, writing letters to the state legislature, withholding alumni contributions, setting up a "shadow" appointments committee, and several other measures that made the Assistant Dean wince.

Al-Hammar's talk received a great deal of attention, particularly from the faculty who were not there to hear it. Several versions of his story circulated among the faculty offices and corridors ("Did you hear what he said?"). Many of the stories-about-the-story were wildly exaggerated. Nevertheless, Al-Hammar's story is an authentic counterstory. It directly challenges—both in its words and tone—the corporate story the law school carefully worked out to explain Henry's non-appointment. It rejects many of the institution's premises, including we-try-so-hard and the-pool-is-so-small, and even mocks the school's meritocratic self-concept. "They say Henry is mediocre, has a pedestrian mind. Well, they ain't sat in none of my classes and listened to themselves. Mediocrity they got. They're experts on mediocrity." Al-Hammar denounced the faculty's excuse making, saying there were dozens of qualified black candidates, if not hundreds. "There isn't that big a pool of Chancellors, or quarterbacks," he said. "But when they need one, they find one, don't they?"

Al-Hammar also deviates stylistically, as a storyteller, from John Henry. He rebels against the "reasonable discourse" of law. He is angry, and anger is out of bounds in legal discourse, even as a response to discrimination. John Henry was unsuccessful in getting others to listen. So was Al-Hammar, but for a different reason. His counterstory overwhelmed the audience. More than just a narrative, it was a call to action, a call to join him in destroying the current story. But his audience was not ready to act. Too many of his listeners felt challenged or coerced; their defenses went up. The campus newspaper the next day published a garbled version, saying that he had urged the law faculty to relax its standards in order to provide minority students with role models. This prompted three letters to the editor asking how an unqualified black professor could be a good role model for anyone, black or white.

Moreover, the audience Al-Hammar intended to affect, namely the faculty, was even more unmoved by his counterstory. It attacked them too frontally. They were quick to dismiss him as an extremist, a demagogue, a hothead—someone to be taken seriously only for the damage he might do should he attract a body of followers. Consequently, for the next week the faculty spent much time in one-on-one conversations with "responsible" student leaders, including Judith Rogers.

By the end of the week, a consensus story had formed about Al-Hammar's story. That story-about-a-story held that Al-Hammar had gone too far, that the situation had more to it than Al-Hammar knew or was prepared to admit. Moreover, Al-Hammar was portrayed *not* as someone who had reached out, in pain, for sympathy and friendship. Rather, he was depicted as a "bad actor," someone with a "chip on his shoulder," someone with whom no responsible member of the law school community should trade stories. Nonetheless, a few progressive students and faculty members believed Al-Hammar had done the institution a favor by raising the issues and demanding that they be addressed. They were a distinct minority.

The Anonymous Leaflet Counterstory

About a month after Al-Hammar spoke, the law faculty formed a special committee for minority hiring. The committee contained practically every young liberal on the faculty, two of its three female professors, and the Assistant Dean. The Dean announced the committee's formation in a memorandum sent to the law school's ethnic student associations, the student government, and the alumni newsletter, which gave it front-page coverage. It was also posted on bulletin boards around the law school.

The memo spoke about the committee and its mission in serious, measured phrases—"social need," "national search," "renewed effort," "balancing the various considerations," "identifying members of a future pool from which we might draw." Shortly after the memo was distributed, an anonymous four-page leaflet appeared in the student lounge, on the same bulletin boards on which the Dean's memo appeared, and in various mailboxes of faculty members and law school organizations. Its author, whether student or faculty member, was never identified.

The leaflet was entitled, "Another Committee, Aren't We Wonderful?" It began with a caricature of the Dean's memo, mocking its measured language and high-flown tone. Then, beginning in the middle of the page, the memo told, in conversational terms, the following story:

And so, friends and neighbors (the leaflet continued), how is it that the good law schools go about looking for new faculty members? Here is how it works. The appointments committee starts out the year with a model new faculty member in mind. This mythic creature went to a leading law school, graduated first or second in his or her class, clerked for the Supreme Court, and wrote the leading note in the law review on some topic dealing with the federal courts. This individual is brilliant, personable, humane, and has just the right amount of practice experience with the right firm.

Schools begin with this paragon in mind and energetically beat the bushes, beginning in September, in search of him or her. At this stage, they believe themselves genuinely and sincerely colorblind. If they find such a mythic figure who is black or Hispanic or gay or lesbian, they will hire this person in a flash. They will of course do the same if the person is white.

By February, however, the school has not hired many mythic figures. Some that they interviewed turned them down. Now, it's late in the year and they have to get someone to teach Trusts and Estates. Although none is left on their list who is a Supreme Court clerk, etc., they can easily find several who are a notch or two below that—who went to good schools, but not Harvard, or who went to Harvard, yet were not first or second in their classes. Still, they know, with a degree verging on certainty, that this person is smart and can do the job. They know this from personal acquaintance with this individual, or they hear it from someone they know and trust. Joe says Bill is really smart, a good lawyer, and will be terrific in the classroom.

So they hire this person because, although he or she is not a mythic figure, functionally equivalent guarantees—namely first- or second-hand experience—assure them that this person will be a good teacher and scholar. And so it generally turns out—the new professor does just fine.

Persons hired in this fashion are almost always white, male, and straight. The reason: We rarely know blacks, Hispanics, women, and gays. Moreover, when we hire the white male, the known but less-than-mythic quantity, late in February, *it does not seem to us like we are making an exception.* Yet we are. We are employing a form of affirmative action—bending the stated rules so as to hire the person we want.

The upshot is that whites have two chances of being hired—by meeting the formal criteria we start out with in September—that is, by being mythic figures—and also by meeting the second, informal, modified criteria we apply later to friends and acquaintances when we are in a pinch. Minorities have just one chance of being hired—the first.

To be sure, once every decade or so a law school, imbued with crusading zeal, will bend the rules and hire a minority with credentials just short of Superman or Wonder Woman. And, when it does so, *it will feel like an exception.* The school will congratulate itself—it has lifted up one of the downtrodden. And, it will remind the new professor repeatedly how lucky he or she is to be here in this wonderful place. It will also make sure, through subtle or not-so-subtle means, that the students know so, too.

But (the leaflet continued), there is a coda.

If, later, the minority professor hired this way unexpectedly succeeds, this will produce consternation among his or her colleagues. For, things were not intended to go that way. When he or she came aboard, the minority professor lacked those standard indicia of merit—Supreme Court clerkship, high LSAT score, prep school background—that the majority-race professors had and believe essential to scholarly success.

Yet the minority professor is succeeding all the same—publishing in good law reviews, receiving invitations to serve on important commissions, winning popularity with students. This is infuriating. Many majority-race professors are persons of relatively slender achievements—you can look up their publishing record any time you have five minutes. Their principal achievements lie in the distant past, when aided by their parents' upper class background, they did well in high school and college, and got the requisite test scores on standardized tests which tested exactly the accumulated cultural capital they acquired so easily and naturally at home. Shortly after that, their careers started to stagnate. They publish an article every five years or so, often in a minor law review, after gallingly having it turned down by the very review they served on as editor twenty years ago.

So, their claim to fame lies in their early exploits, the badges they acquired up to about the age of twenty-five, at which point the edge they acquired from Mummy and Daddy began to lose effect. Now, along comes the hungry minority professor, imbued with a fierce desire to get ahead, a good intellect, and a willingness to work 70 hours a week if necessary to make up for lost time. The minority person lacks the merit badges awarded early in life, the white professor's main source of security. So, the minority's colleagues don't like it and use perfectly predictable ways to transfer the costs of their discomfort to the misbehaving minority.

So that, my friends, is why minority professors (i) have a hard time getting hired; and, (ii) have a hard time if they are hired.

When you and I are running the world, we won't replicate this unfair system, will we? Of course not—unless, of course, it changes us in the process.

* * *

This second counterstory attacks the faculty less frontally in some respects—for example it does not focus on the fate of any particular black candidate, such as Henry, but attacks a general mindset. It employs several devices including narrative and careful observation—the latter to build credibility (the reader says, "That's right"), the former to beguile the reader and get him or her to suspend judgment. (Everyone loves a story.) The last part of the story is painful; it strikes close to home. Yet the earlier parts paved the way by painting a plausible picture of events, so that the final part demands consideration. It generalizes and exaggerates—many majority-race professors are *not* persons of slender achievement. But such broad strokes are part of the narrator's art. The realistically drawn first part of the story, despite shading off into caricature at the end, forces readers to focus on the flaws in the good face the dean attempted to put on events. And, despite its somewhat accusatory thrust, the story, as was mentioned, debunks only a mindset, not a person. Unlike Al-Hammar X's story, it does not call the chair of the appointments committee, a much-loved senior professor, a racist. (But did Al-Hammar's story, confrontational as it was, pave the way for the generally positive reception accorded the anonymous account?)

The story invites the reader to distance herself or himself from the events described and to enter into the mental set of the teller, whose view is different from the reader's own. The oppositional nature of the story, the manner in which it challenges and rebuffs the stock story, thus causes him or her to oscillate between poles. It is insinuative: At times, the reader is seduced by the story and its logical coherence—it is a plausible counter-view of what happened; it has a degree of explanatory power.

Yet the story places the majority-race reader on the defensive. He or she alternately leaves the storyteller's perspective to return to his or her own, saying, "That's outrageous, I'm being accused of. . . ." The reader thus moves back and forth between two worlds, the storyteller's, which the reader occupies vicariously to the extent the story is well told and rings true, and his or her own, which he or she returns to and reevaluates in light of the story's message. Can my world still stand? What parts of it remain valid? What parts of the story seem true? How can I reconcile the two worlds, and will the resulting world be a better one than the one with which I began?

These are in large part normative questions, which lead to the final two issues I want to explore. Why *should* members of outgroups tell stories? And, why *should* others listen?

WHY OUTGROUPS SHOULD TELL STORIES AND WHY OTHERS SHOULD LISTEN

Subordinated groups have always told stories. Black slaves told, in song, letters, and verse, about their own pain and oppression. They described the terrible wrongs they had experienced at the hands of whites, and mocked (behind whites' backs) the veneer of gentility whites purchased at the cost of the slaves' suffering. Mexican-Americans in the Southwest composed *corridos* (ballads) and stories, passed on from generation to generation, of abuse at the hands of gringo justice, the Texas Rangers, and ruthless lawyers and developers who cheated them out of their lands. Native American literature, both oral and written, deals with all these themes as well. Feminist consciousness-raising consists, in part, of the sharing of stories, of tales from personal experience, on the basis of which the group constructs a shared reality about women's status vis-à-vis men.

This proliferation of counterstories is not an accident or coincidence. Oppressed groups have known instinctively that stories are an essential tool to their own survival and liberation. Members of outgroups can use stories in two basic ways: first, as means of psychic self-preservation; and, second, as means of lessening their own subordination. These two means correspond to the two perspectives from which a story can be viewed—that of the teller, and that of the listener. The storyteller gains psychically, the listener morally and epistemologically.

How Storytelling Benefits Members of Outgroups
The member of an outgroup gains, first, psychic self-preservation. A principal cause of the demoralization of marginalized groups is self-condemnation. They internalize the images that society thrusts on them—they believe that their lowly position is their own fault.

The therapy is to tell stories. By becoming acquainted with the facts of their own historic oppression—with the violence, murder, deceit, co-optation, and connivance that have caused their desperate estate—members of outgroups gain healing.

The story need not lead to a violent act; Frantz Fanon was wrong in writing that it is only through exacting blood from the oppressor that colonized people gain liberation. Rather, the story need only lead to a realization of how one came to be oppressed and subjugated. Then, one can stop perpetrating (mental) violence on oneself.

So, stories—stories about oppression, about victimization, about one's own brutalization—far from deepening the despair of the oppressed, lead to healing, liberation, mental health. They also promote group solidarity. Storytelling emboldens the hearer, who may have had the same thoughts and experiences the storyteller describes, but hesitated to give them voice. Having heard another express them, he or she realizes, I am not alone.

Yet, stories help oppressed groups in a second way—through their effect on the oppressor. Most oppression, as was mentioned earlier, does not seem like it to those perpetrating it. It is rationalized, causing few pangs of conscience. The dominant group justifies its privileged position by means of stories, stock explanations that construct reality in ways favorable to it. One such story was put forward earlier—the stock story of race relations in this country.

This story is drastically at odds with the way most people of color would describe their condition. Artfully designed parables, chronicles, allegories, and pungent tales like the one in the anonymous leaflet can jar the comfortable dominant complacency that is the principal anchor dragging down reform. They can destroy—but the destruction they produce must be voluntary, a type of willing death. Because this is a white-dominated society in which the majority race controls the reins of power, racial reform must include them. Their complacency—born of comforting stories—is a major stumbling block to racial progress. Counterstories can attack that complacency.

What is more, they can do so in ways that promise at least the possibility of success. Most civil rights strategies confront the obstacle of blacks' otherness. The dominant group, noticing that a particular effort is waged on behalf of blacks, increases its resistance. Stories at times can overcome that otherness, hold that instinctive resistance in abeyance. Stories are the oldest, most primordial meeting ground in human experience. Their allure will often provide the most effective means of overcoming otherness, of forming a new collectivity based on the shared story.

Why Members of the Ingroup Should Listen to Stories

Members of outgroups should tell stories. Why should members of ingroups listen to them?

Members of the majority race should listen to stories, of all sorts, in order to enrich their own reality. Reality is not fixed, not a given. Rather, we construct it through conversations, through our lives together. Racial and class-based isolation prevents the hearing of diverse stories and counterstories. It diminishes the conversation through which we create reality, construct our communal lives. Deliberately exposing oneself to counterstories can avoid that impoverishment, heighten "suspicion," and enable the listener and the teller to build a world richer than either could make alone. On another occasion, the listener will be the teller, sharing a secret, a piece of information, or an angle of vision that will enrich the former teller; and so on dialectically, in a rich tapestry of conversation, of stories. It is through this process that we can overcome ethnocentrism and the unthinking conviction that our way of seeing the world is the only one—that the way things are is inevitable, natural, just, and best—when it is, for some, full of pain, exclusion, and both petty and major tyranny.

Listening to stories makes the adjustment to future stories easier; one acquires the ability to see the world through others' eyes. It can lead the way to new environments. A willing listener is generally "welcomed with open arms." Listening to the stories of outgroups can avoid intellectual apartheid. Shared words can banish sameness, stiffness, and monochromaticity, reducing the terror of otherness when hearing new voices for the first time.

If we would deepen and humanize ourselves, we must seek out storytellers different from ourselves and afford them the audience they deserve. The benefit will be reciprocal.

Stories humanize us. They emphasize our differences in ways that can ultimately bring us closer together. They allow us to see how the world looks from behind someone else's spectacles. They challenge us to wipe off our own lenses and ask, "Could I have been overlooking something all along?"

Telling stories invests text with feeling, gives voice to those who were taught to hide their emotions. Hearing stories invites hearers to participate, challenging their assumptions, jarring their complacency, lifting their spirits, lowering their defenses.

Stories are useful tools for the underdog because they invite the listener to suspend judgment, listen for the story's point, and test it against his or her own version of reality. This process is essential in a pluralist society like ours and is a practical necessity for underdogs: All movements for change must gain the support, or at least the understanding, of the dominant group, which is white.

Traditional legal writing purports to be neutral and dispassionately analytical, but too often it is not. In part, this is so because legal writers rarely focus on their own mindsets, the received wisdoms that serve as their starting points, themselves no more than stories, that lie behind their quasi-scientific string of deductions. The supposedly objective point of view often mischaracterizes, minimizes, dismisses, or derides without fully understanding opposing viewpoints. Implying that legal questions have objective, correct answers also obscures the moral and political value judgments that lie at the heart of any legal inquiry.

Legal storytelling is an engine built to hurl rocks over walls of social complacency that obscure the view out from the citadel. But the rocks all have messages tied to them that the defenders cannot help but read. The messages say, let us knock down the walls, and use the blocks to pave a road we can all walk together.

Rodrigo's Chronicle

ENTER RODRIGO

"Excuse me, Professor, I'm Rodrigo Crenshaw. I believe we have an appointment."

Startled, I put down the book I was reading and glanced quickly first at my visitor, then at my desk calendar. The tall, rangy man standing in my doorway was of indeterminate age—somewhere between twenty and forty—and, for that matter, ethnicity. His tightly curled hair and olive complexion suggested that he might be African American. But he could also be Latino, perhaps Mexican, Puerto Rican, or any one of the many Central American nationalities that have been applying in larger numbers to my law school in recent years.

"Come in," I said. "I think I remember a message from you, but I seem not to have entered it into my appointment book. Please excuse all this confusion," I added, pointing to the pile of papers and boxes that had littered my office floor since my recent move. I wondered: Was he an undergraduate seeking admission? A faculty candidate of color like the many who seek my advice about entering academia? I searched my memory without success.

"Please sit down," I said. "What can I do for you?"

"I'm Geneva Crenshaw's brother. I want to talk to you about the LSAT, as well as the procedure for obtaining an appointment as a law professor at an American university."

As though sensing my surprise, my visitor explained: "Shortly after Geneva's accident, I moved to Italy with my father, Lorenzo, who was in the Army. After he retired, we remained in Italy, where he worked as a civilian at the same base where he had been serving. I finished high school at the base, then attended an Italian university, earning my law degree last June. I've applied for the LL.M. program at a number of U.S. law schools, including your own. I want to talk to you about the LSAT, which all the schools want me to take, and which, believe it or not, I've never taken. I'd also like to discuss my chances of landing a teaching position after I earn the degree."

I reflected a moment, then said: "Your situation is somewhat unusual. But I'll do my best. I didn't know Geneva had a brother."

"We're only half-siblings," he explained, "and separated by nearly twenty years. But I've kept in touch as best I could, and I'm grateful to you for bringing her message to the attention of your friends. She respects you and your work enormously."

"Your sister is a remarkable woman," I said. "I have learned at least as much from her as she from me."

SMALL TALK: RODRIGO WORRIES ABOUT THE LSAT

I continued, "You said you are going to be taking the LSAT. What are your concerns about that?"

"The usual," he replied, "including that I don't see why I should have to take it at all. I graduated fourth in my class at a law school even older than yours. I should think it would be obvious to anyone that I can read a case or make a legal argument. But I'm more than a little worried about the cultural bias people tell me the test embodies. I'm proficient in English, as you can tell. But I've been away from the United States for many years; I'm afraid some of the questions may assume information I lack simply because I've taken half my schooling outside the culture."

"I've made the same argument myself in the case of minorities in the United States," I said. "But it goes nowhere. They say the test is not biased because it predicts law school grades, which always seemed like a non sequitur to me. I didn't realize that we required the test for foreign law graduates." I paused, then added, "Maybe they think it provides a check against grades, which might vary from one system to another."

"Yet in each system," Rodrigo countered levelly, "those grades reflect, in most cases, broader and more pervasive forms of cultural power, including the backgrounds and advantages of those who earn them. They also correspond to the law firm jobs and prestigious government positions the students will hold after they graduate. Identifying the LSAT as a predictor of grades, or even of later job performance, tells us only that this narrow test will identify people who thrive in particular types of environments—the ones, of course, that rely on the test to do a certain type of screening."

Not bad, I thought—I hoped he would come to my law school. But instead I asked: "So, what are you going to do? If you skip the test, you can kiss your LL.M. goodbye."

"I know, I know," he said, "if I have to take the test, I will. I bought one of those practice books. I'm sure I'll do OK—although I can't help thinking the whole thing is a waste of time."

"I agree—on both scores," I added.

RODRIGO AND THE PROFESSOR DISCUSS THE LAW SCHOOL HIRING MARKET

"But the main reason I'm here is to ask you about the law school hiring market. I've heard it's extremely tight. But I'm also worried about something else. Geneva said it's becoming saturated with minority professors. I think she used the term 'tipping point' and mentioned an experience she had recently at a school where she was teaching. She produced several good candidates of color but couldn't get her colleagues to take them seriously because the school already had six minority professors and was thought to be in danger of losing its character as a white-dominated institution. Is this happening at other places?"

"Too few!" I replied. "Most of them profess to be searching desperately for candidates of color."

"Profess?" Rodrigo's eyebrows arched.

"Those that say they are looking the hardest complain the loudest that the pool is too small. And, of course, if they start with that assumption, that is what they are likely to find, whether it's true or not."

"How can that be?" Rodrigo asked. "There must be many lawyers of color like Geneva and me with excellent grades, practical experience, and so on. Why are the schools having such trouble finding us?"

"It works something like this," I said, reaching for a much-thumbed reprint. "Every law school appointments committee starts out in September looking for a candidate with stellar credentials—a super-graduate with top grades from one of the top law schools, a law review editorship, a Supreme Court clerkship, and just the right amount of experience at the right firm. This individual should be humane, compassionate, and wise. Ideally, she or he should have published a classic Note in the law review."

"I have some of those things, but not all," Rodrigo noted with a trace of anxiety. "Do the schools actually find and hire people like that?"

"No, not at all," I replied. "They're looking for mythic figures, of which there are very few. To be sure, if they do find one who is black or Hispanic, they'll hire him or her in a flash—as they would, of course, if the person were white. But the AALS's own figures show that the pool of those actually hired, black or white, is much less prepossessing than that. Only about a third served on the law review, and half that figure were elected to Order of the Coif. Only a small percentage published anything at all."

"So they obviously lower their standards at some point."

"Precisely. Although the committee members all begin the hiring season with these paragons in mind, by February they have managed to hire few, if any, of them. Several show up for interviews, only to turn down offers. So, now it's February and the dean is pressuring them to find someone to teach the UCC course and Trusts and Estates. Although by then few candidates are left who were Supreme Court clerks and at the top of their classes at Harvard or Yale, several are still available who are a notch below that—who graduated high, but not from a top school, or went to a top school but did not graduate at the head of their class. Still, the committee members know that these people are intellectually able and can do the job. They know this either from personal experience—someone on the committee practiced, clerked, or went to law school with one of them—or from someone they trust. Harry told Bill that Smith is really smart and will be a fine teacher. And so it works out—Smith is hired and goes on to have a fine career."

"I see what you're saying," Rodrigo said. "Those hired according to the relaxed, informal criteria schools use near the end of the season when they are under pressure are always white—right?"

"Exactly," I said. "With the result that majority-race candidates have two chances of being hired, while we have just one. They can be hired early in the year, just as we can, by being mythic figures—by satisfying the formal criteria, the superstar ones you hear about. But they can also be hired by word of mouth, under the relaxed criteria that come into play late in the game."

"A sort of affirmative action for whites," Rodrigo observed.

"You *are* Geneva's brother. You may be twenty years younger, but something of her rubbed off on you."

"We've always kept in touch. I must also confess, Professor, I've been reading your stuff and that of your colleagues in the critical race theory movement. It's fairly popular in Europe; many Italian law students read and discuss it."

"I'm glad to hear it. But I wish the news were better. The trouble is that the patterns I mentioned are self-perpetuating. When the all-white appointments committee hires the white professor late in the year, it doesn't trouble them at all—although it should."

"It wouldn't feel like an exception," Rodrigo interjected, "because business as usual never does. One of our own intellectuals said something similar during a period of hard times for him."

"To be sure," I quickly added, "once in a great while a law school will bend the rules and hire a professor of color who falls slightly short of the nominal criteria, who is just shy of Paul Freund or Thurgood Marshall in attainments and promise. And when they do so, the hiring *will* seem like an exception. They will congratulate themselves for bending down to lift up one of the downtrodden. The conservatives among them will complain that something unethical has been done—a great injustice to whites."

"From my studies, it appears that those in the majority always see merit as God-given, fixed, and eternal," Rodrigo responded.

"And of course they are the ones who have it, while affirmative action is necessary for us who lack it," I replied.

"Yet your account of the two avenues for whites paints a different picture. I'm sure you've had the experience, Professor, of trying to get your colleagues to hire one of us."

"Many times," I replied. "They're some of the most frustrating moments in my career. Every year the same thing happens. They say they are looking for candidates with qualifications *A, B,* and *C*. I produce a hungry, hard-driving candidate of color with credentials *A, B,* and *C,* and they say, 'Well, there's really also qualification *D,* which your candidate does not have. So, we cannot hire him after all.' Then I produce a candidate who possesses credentials *A, B, C,* and *D,* and they say, 'We also meant *E*.' Or, 'We meant something different by *B* from what you understood.'"

"So, the criteria multiply until it dawns on you they are really talking about themselves—the criteria will fit only candidates who are like them, i.e., white."

"Exactly," I said. "Although every now and then I try a different approach—namely pointing out that many of their most highly valued colleagues are also glaringly deficient in one or more of the criteria. Professor Jones hasn't published anything in twenty years. Professor Smith is such a lackadaisical teacher that none but the unwary take his classes, and so on."

"And what happens when you point this out?"

"They always have some excuse. Jones wrote the leading article on contingent remainders in 1949 and is obviously germinating an equally impressive one, which accounts for his silence. Fifteen years ago Smith, the notorious teacher, sat on a prestigious commission. And so on. It turns out that a whole set of *defenses* enables my colleagues to justify their current positions—but not ours."

"Merit sounds like white people's affirmative action!" Rodrigo exclaimed. "A way of keeping their own deficiencies neatly hidden while assuring that only people like them get in."

"I've often thought that myself," I said.

Rodrigo was silent for a time. Then: "I wonder how they'll see me? I'm black, and my family is middle class. But I went to one of the great universities of the world."

"My guess is that one of them will hire you. And as with the rest of us, when it does so it will make sure that you know—and that the students do, too—what a huge favor it has done by extending an offer to you."

Rodrigo was silent for a long time. Then he mused, "Ironic, but I suppose that's the price I have to pay for wanting to return to the States."

"Ironic?" I questioned. "How so? Tragic, unjust, and wrong are words that more readily come to mind, mine at least. What is the irony that you see?"

"The irony is that those who most need our help are those who most resist getting it."

IN WHICH RODRIGO BEGINS TO SEEM A LITTLE DEMENTED

"I'm not sure I follow you."

"Let's start with something familiar—academic publishing. A recent article pointed out that nearly three-fourths of articles on equality or civil rights published in the leading journals during the last five years were written by women or minorities. Ten years ago, the situation was reversed: minorities were beginning to publish, but their work was largely ignored. The same is true in other areas as well. Critical legal studies and other modernist and postmodern approaches to law are virtually the norm in the top reviews. Formalism has run its course."

"Perhaps," I said. "You don't see many articles in the classic vein today. In fact, I haven't seen one of those plodding, case-crunching, 150-page blockbusters with 600 footnotes in a top journal for a while."

"No one believes that way of writing is useful anymore. Some are writing chronicles. Others are writing about storytelling in the law, narrative theory, or 'voice' scholarship. The feminists are writing about changing the terms of legal discourse and putting women at the center. Even mainstream writers—the serious ones, at any rate—have moved beyond mere doctrinal analysis to realms such as political theory, legal history, and interdisciplinary analysis. One sees a whole new emphasis on legal culture, perspective, and on what some call positionality, as well as a renewed focus on the sociopolitical dimension of judging and legal reasoning."

"I'm not up on all these postmodern approaches, Rodrigo," I said quickly, "although I have read your friend who, as you say, got into trouble with the authorities. I find his work quite helpful. And I gather that the current ferment in American law is one of the reasons why you are thinking of returning here for your graduate degree?"

"In part. But I was mainly responding to your question about irony. However progressive certain mainstream scholars may be in their writing and analysis, the institutions they control still exclude and oppress minorities by manipulating the status quo and refusing to challenge their own informal expectations. The irony is that the old, dying order is resisting the new, rather than welcoming it with open arms."

Hmm. I thought of the words of a Bob Dylan song, but instead asked: "And just who, or what, do you think this new order is, Rodrigo?"

"Well, let me put it this way," Rodrigo explained. "You've heard, I assume, of double consciousness?"

"Of course. It's W.E.B. Du Bois' term. It refers to the propensity of excluded people to see the world in terms of two perspectives at the same time—that of the majority race, according to which they are demonized, despised, and reviled, and their own, in which they are normal. Lately, some—particularly feminists of color—have invented the term multiple consciousness to describe their experience."

"And you know that many members of minority groups speak two languages, grow up in two cultures?"

"Of course, especially our Latino brothers and sisters; for them, bilingualism is as much an article of faith as, say, Martin Luther King and his writings are for African Americans."

"And so," Rodrigo continued, "who has the advantage in mastering and applying critical social thought? Who tends to think of everything in two or more ways at the same time? Who is a postmodernist virtually as a condition of his or her being?"

"I suppose you are going to say us—people of color."

Rodrigo hesitated. "Remember that I have been sitting in Italian law libraries all these years, reading and learning about legal movements in the United States secondhand. I suppose it looks different to you here."

"It has scarcely been a bed of roses," I replied dryly. "The old order, as you put it, has not welcomed the new voices with any great warmth, although I must agree that the law reviews seem much more open to them than my faculty colleagues. And your notion that it is we—persons of color—who have the edge in mastering critical analysis would strike most of them as preposterous. If double consciousness turns out to be an advantage, they'll either deny it exists or insist that they can have it too. Aren't you just trying to invert the hierarchy, placing at the top a group that until now has occupied the bottom—and isn't this just as wrong as what the others have been doing to us?"

Rodrigo paused. "I see your point. But maybe this way of looking at things seems harsh only because it is so unfamiliar. In my circles everyone talks about the decline of Western thought, so finding evidence of it in law and legal scholarship doesn't seem so strange. I'm surprised it does to you. Are you familiar with the term *false consciousness*?"

"Yes, of course," I said (with some irritation—the impudent pup!). "It's a mechanism whereby oppressed people take on the consciousness of the oppressor group, adjusting to and becoming parties to their own oppression. And I suppose you think I'm laboring under some form of it?"

"Not you, Professor. Far from it. But when you rebuked me a moment ago, I wondered if you weren't in effect counseling *me* to internalize the views of the majority group about such things as hierarchy and the definition of a 'troublemaker.'"

"Perhaps," I admitted. "But my main concern is for you and your prospects. If you want to succeed in your LL.M. studies, not to mention land a professorship at a

U.S. law school, perhaps you had better 'cool it' for a while. Criticizing mainstream scholarship is one thing; everyone expects that from young firebrands like you. But this business about a more general decline of the West—that's out of our field, frowned on as flaky rhetoric, and nearly impossible to support with evidence. Even if you did have evidence to support your claims, no one would want to listen to you."

"Yes, I suppose so," admitted Rodrigo. "It's not the story you usually hear. If I had told you that I'm returning to the United States because it's the best country on earth, with rosy prospects, a high quality of life, and the fairest political system for minorities, your countrymen would accept that without question. No one would think of asking me for documentation, even though that is surely as much an empirical claim as its opposite."

"You're right," I said. "The dominant story always seems true, not in need of proof. I've written about that myself. And you and I discussed a case of it earlier when we talked about minority hiring. But tell me more about your thoughts on the West."

"Well, as I mentioned, my program of studies at Bologna centered on the history of Western culture. I'm mainly interested in the rise of Northern European thought and its contribution to our current predicament. During my early work, I had hoped to extend my analysis to law and legal thought."

"I think I know what you will say about legal thought and scholarship. Tell me more about the big picture—how you see Northern European thought."

"I've been studying its rise in the late Middle Ages and decline beginning a few decades ago. I'm interested in what causes cultures to evolve, then go into eclipse. American society, even more than its European counterparts, is in the early stages of dissolution and crisis. It's like a wave that is just starting to crest. As you know, waves travel unimpeded across thousands of miles of ocean. When they approach the shore, they rise up for a short time, then crest and lose their energy. Western culture, particularly in this country, is approaching that stage. Which explains, in part, why I am back."

I had already switched off my telephone. Now, hearing my secretary's footsteps, I stepped out into the hallway to tell her to cancel my appointments for the rest of the afternoon. I had a feeling I wanted to hear what this strange young thinker had to say undisturbed. When I returned, I saw Rodrigo eyeing my computer inquiringly.

Returning his gaze to me, Rodrigo went on: "I'm sure all the things I'm going to say have occurred to you. Northern Europeans have been on top for a relatively short period—a mere wink in the eye of history. And during that time they have accomplished little—except causing a significant number of deaths and the disruption of a number of more peaceful cultures, which they conquered, enslaved, exterminated, or relocated on their way to empire. Their principal advantages were linear thought, which lent itself to the development and production of weapons and other industrial technologies, and a kind of messianic self-image that allowed them to dominate other nations and groups. But now, as you can see"—Rodrigo gestured in the direction of the window and the murky air outside—"Saxon-Teuton culture has arrived at a terminus, demonstrating its own absurdity."

"I'm not sure I follow you. Linear thought, as you call it, has surely conferred many benefits. And is it really on its last legs? Aside from smoggy air, Western culture looks firmly in control to me."

"So does a wave, even when it's cresting—and you know what happens shortly thereafter. If you turn on your computer, Professor," Rodrigo said, pointing at my new terminal, "I'll show you a few things."

For the next ten minutes, Rodrigo led me on a tour of articles and books on the West's economic and political condition. His fingers fairly danced over the keys of my computer. Accessing data bases I didn't even know existed, he showed me treatises on the theory of cultural cyclicity, articles and editorials from *The Economist, Corriere della Sera,* the *Wall Street Journal,* and other leading newspapers, all on our declining economic position; material from *Statistical Abstract* and other sources on our increasing crime rate, rapidly dwindling fossil fuels, loss of markets, and switch from a production- to a service-based economy with high unemployment, an increasingly restless underclass, and increasing rates of drug addiction, suicide, and infant mortality. It was a sobering display of technical virtuosity. I had the feeling he had done this before and wondered how he had come by this proficiency while in Italy.

Rodrigo finally turned off the computer and looked at me inquiringly. "A bibliography alone will not persuade me," I said. "But let's suppose for the sake of argument that you have made a prima facie case, at least with respect to our economic problems and to issues concerning race and the underclass. Do you have a theory on how we got into this predicament?"

"I do," Rodrigo said with that combination of brashness and modesty that I find so charming in the young. "As I mentioned a moment ago, it has to do with linear thought—the hallmark of the West. When developed, it conferred a great initial advantage. Because of it, the culture was able to spawn, early on, classical physics, which, with the aid of a few borrowings here and there, like gunpowder from the Chinese, quickly enabled it to develop impressive armies. And, because it was basically a ruthless, restless culture, it quickly dominated others that lay in its path. It eradicated ones that resisted, enslaved others, and removed the Indians, all in the name of progress. It opened up and mined new territories—here and elsewhere—as soon as they became available and extracted all the available mineral wealth so rapidly that fossil fuels and other mineral goods are now running out, as you and your colleagues have pointed out."

"But you are indicting just one civilization. Haven't all groups acted similarly? Non-linear societies are accomplishing at least as much environmental destruction as Western societies are capable of. And what about Genghis Khan, Columbus, the cruelties of the Chinese dynasties? The Turkish genocide of the Armenians, the war machine that was ancient Rome?"

"True. But at least these other groups limited their own imperial impulses at some point."

"Hah! With a little help from their friends," I retorted.

"Anyway," continued Rodrigo, "these groups produced valuable art, music, or literature along the way. Northern Europeans have produced next to nothing—little sculpture, art, or music worth listening to, and only a modest amount of truly great literature. And the few accomplishments they can cite with pride can be traced to the Egyptians, an African culture."

"Rodrigo, you greatly underestimate the dominant culture. Some of them may be derivative and warlike, as you say. Others are not; they are creative and humane. And even the ones you impeach have a kind of dogged ingenuity for which you do not give them credit. They have the staying and adaptive powers to remain on top. For example, when linear physics reached a dead end, as you pointed out, they developed relativity physics. When formalism expired, at least some of them developed critical legal studies, reaching back and drawing on existing strands of thought such as psychoanalysis, phenomenology, Marxism, and philosophy of science."

"Good point," admitted Rodrigo a little grudgingly, "although I've already pointed out the contributions of Gramsci, a Mediterranean. Fanon and your critical race theory friends are black or brown. And Freud and Einstein are, of course, Jews. Consider, as well, Cervantes, Verdi, Michelangelo, Duke Ellington, the current crop of black writers—non-Saxons all."

"But Northern Europeans, at least in the case of the two Jewish giants," I interrupted.

"True, people move," he countered.

"Don't be flip," I responded. "Since when are the Spanish and Italians exempt from criticism for 'Western' foibles? What about the exploitive capacity of the colonizing conquistadors? Wasn't the rise of commercial city-states in Renaissance Italy a central foundation for subsequent European cultural imperialism? Most ideas of Eurocentric superiority date to the Renaissance and draw on its rationalist, humanist intellectual, and artistic traditions."

"We've had our lapses," Rodrigo conceded. "But theirs are far worse and more systematic." Rodrigo was again eyeing my computer.

Wondering what else he had in mind, I continued: "What about Rembrandt, Mozart, Shakespeare, Milton? And American popular culture—is it not the envy of the rest of the world? What's more, even if some of our Saxon brothers and sisters are doggedly linear, or, as you put it, exploitive of nature and warlike—surely you cannot believe that their behavior is biologically based—that something genetic prevents them from doing anything except invent and manufacture weapons?" Rodrigo's earnest and shrewd retelling of history had intrigued me, although, to be honest, I was alarmed. Was he an Italian Louis Farrakhan?

"The Saxons do all that, plus dig up the earth to extract minerals that are sent to factories that darken the skies, until everything runs out and we find ourselves in the situation where we are now." Then, after a pause: "Why do you so strongly resist a biological explanation, Professor? Their own scientists are happy to conjure up and apply them to us. But from one point of view, it is they whose exploits—or rather lack of them—need explaining."

"I'd love to hear your evidence."

"Let me begin this way. Do you remember that famous photo of the finish of the hundred-meter dash at the World Games this past summer? It showed six magnificent athletes straining to break the tape. The first two finished under the world record. All were black."

"I do remember."

"Black athletes dominated most of the events, the shorter ones at any rate. People of color are simply faster and quicker than our white brothers and sisters. Even the marathon has come to be dominated by people of color. And, to anticipate your question, yes I do believe the same holds true in the mental realm. In the ghetto they play 'the dozens'—a game that requires throwaway speed. The dominant group has nothing similar. And take your field, law. Saxons developed the hundred-page linear, densely footnoted, impeccably crafted article—saying, in most cases, very little. They also brought us the LSAT, which tests the same boring, linear capacities they developed over time and that now exclude the very voices they need for salvation. Yet you, Matsuda, Lawrence, Torres, Peller, and others toss off articles with ridiculous ease—critical thought comes easy for you, less so for them. I can't, of course, prove your friends are genetically inferior; it may be their mindset or culture. But they act like lemmings. They go on building factories until the natural resources run out, thermonuclear weapons when their absurdity is apparent and everyone knows they cannot be used, hundred-page law review articles that rehash cases when everyone knows that vein of thought has run dry—and they fail to even sense their own danger. You say they are adaptive. I doubt it."

"Rodrigo," I burst in. "You seriously misread the times. Your ideas on cultural superiority and inferiority will obviously generate resistance, as you yourself concede. Wait till you see how they respond to your hundred-yard dash example; you're sure to find *yourself* labeled as racist. Maybe we both are—half the time I agree with you. But even the other things you say about the West's predicament and its need for an infusion of new thought—things I strongly agree with—will fall on deaf ears. All the movement is the other way. This is a time of retrenchment. The country is listening to the conservatives, not to people like you and me."

"I know," said Rodrigo. "I've been reading about that retrenchment. We do get the *New York Times* in Italy, even if it comes a few days late."

"And so you must know about conservative writers like Allan Bloom, Thomas Sowell, Glenn Loury, Roger Kimball, Shelby Steele, E. D. Hirsch, and Dinesh D'Souza and the tremendous reception they have been receiving, both in popular circles and in the academy?"

"Yes. I read D'Souza on the flight over, in fact. Like the others, he has a number of insightful things to say. But he's seriously wrong—and hardly represents the wave of the future, as you fear."

"They certainly represent the present," I grumbled. "I can't remember a period—except perhaps the late 1950s—when I have seen such resistance to racial reform. The public seems tired of minorities, and the current Administration is no different. The backlash is apparent in the university setting as well: African-American studies departments are underfunded and the exclusionary Eurocentric curriculum is making a comeback."

"But it's ordinary, natural—and will pass," Rodrigo responded. "In troubled times, a people turns to the past, to its own more glorious period. That's why these neoconservative writers are popular—they preach that the culture need not change direction to survive, but only do the things it did before, harder and more energetically."

"What our psychologist friends call 'perseveration,'" I said.

"Exactly. In my studies, I found that most beleaguered people do this, plus search for a scapegoat—a group they can depict as the source of all their troubles."

"An old story," I agreed ruefully. "D'Souza, for example, places most of the blame for colleges' troubles at the doorstep of those demanding minorities who, along with a few deluded white sympathizers, have been broadening the curriculum, instituting Third World courses, hiring minority professors, and recruiting 'unqualified' students of color—all at the expense of academic rigor and standards. He says the barbarians—meaning us—are running the place and urges university administrators to hold the line against what he sees as bullying and a new form of racism."

"Have you ever thought it curious," Rodrigo mused, "how some whites can see themselves as victimized by us—a pristine example of the sort of postmodern move they profess to hate. I suppose if one has been in power a long time, any change seems threatening, offensive, unprincipled, and wrong. But reality eventually intervenes. Western culture's predicament runs very deep—every indicator shows it. And, there are straws in the wind, harbingers of hopeful change."

"Rodrigo, I'll say this for you—you've proposed a novel approach to affirmative action. Until now, we've struggled with finding a moral basis for sustaining what looked like breaches of the merit principle, like hiring a less qualified person over a more qualified one for racial reasons. But you're saying that white people should welcome nonwhites into their fold as rapidly as possible out of simple self-interest—that is, if they want their society to survive. This is something that they are not accustomed to hearing, to put it mildly. Do you have any support for *this* assertion?"

"Turn on your computer again, Professor. This won't take but a minute."

I obliged him, and was treated to a second lightning display of technological wizardry as Rodrigo showed me books on Asian business organization, Eastern mysticism, Japanese schooling, ancient Egyptian origins of modern astronomy and physics, and even on the debt our Founding Fathers owed the Iroquois for the political ideas that shaped our Constitution. He showed me articles on the Japanese computer and automobile industries, the seemingly more successful approach that African and Latino societies have taken to family organization and the treatment of their own aged and destitute, and even the roots of popular American music in black composers and groups.

"It's only a beginning," Rodrigo said, switching off my computer. "I want to make this my life's work. Do you think anyone will listen to me?"

"It's hard to say. I don't know if the times are right. Most Americans believe that their economic problems are just temporary and that they have the best, fairest political system in the world—conveniently forgetting a chapter or two of their own history. But never mind that. Let me ask you instead a personal question: If things are really as bad as you say, why are you, who have a choice, thinking of returning? Shouldn't you remain safely in Italy while your native culture self-destructs? When a wave crests, then hits the beach, it creates an immediate commotion. There's a lot of foam, a loud noise, a great expenditure of energy, and sometimes an undertow. I should think someone like you would be at some risk here—particularly if you go around speaking as candidly as you have to me today—notwithstanding our much-vaunted system of free expression."

RODRIGO EXPLAINS WHY HE HAS RETURNED

"I'm back for family reasons. Geneva and my other half-brothers and sisters are here. And since my father died, I have no other relatives in Italy. Your decreasing quality of life and high white-collar crime rate gave me pause. And I could be quite comfortable in Italy, now that I've got my military service out of the way. I suppose I thought, as well, that with a little more training I could do something to ease the pain of my native country as it goes through a difficult transition."

"You mean helping America adjust to its new multiracial character, plus its own shrinking share of world markets?" I asked.

"That and more," Rodrigo answered quietly. "The dominant group will need help. All of us will."

"What if they don't see it that way?" I pressed. "Has a dominant group ever given up power gracefully? Has it ever abandoned the modes of thought, military organization, and extractive industries that brought it to power without a struggle? And if so, how are we—I mean those who believe like you—going to conduct such a campaign? I'm afraid they have all the power. You may think truth and history are on your side. But what if they don't go along?"

"They will," Rodrigo replied with conviction, "as soon as they recognize their own dilemma. The early Visigoths destroyed themselves by warring. We can help the current dominant culture avoid a similar fate. We may even have some friends and allies in the majority group—ones who believe as we do. Maybe we can bill our offerings as 'hybrid vigor'—something they already endorse."

"And, once again—what if they refuse? Paradigms change slowly. What if your transformation requires a hundred years?"

"In that case, we can simply use sabotage and what you call terrorism to speed things up. The more advanced, the more technologically complex a society becomes, the more vulnerable it is to disruption. Imagine what a few strategic—and nonviolent—taps on telephone switching stations around the country could do—or a few computer viruses, for that matter. Disruption is economically efficient for the subordinated group. In Italy, the government tried for a time to exclude leftist organizations. A few kidnappings and commando raids, and they were ready for serious negotiation. Something like that could happen here—or do you think I'm wrong, Professor?"

"Rodrigo, I have many doubts about all the things you have said—and particularly this one. If you repeat even half of what you have told me today to your colleagues or students, you will find yourself out of academia on your ear—and probably disbarred to boot."

"I had no idea those were the rules of discourse. On the Continent we discuss these things openly—especially since recent events in Eastern Europe showed that rapid reform is, in fact, possible. Your society certainly perpetrated plenty of terrorism on blacks, Chicanos, and Indians. Nevertheless, if one cannot discuss these things in—how do you put it?—polite company, I'll keep them to myself and for my close friends. I don't want to be seen as having an attitude problem."

Our conversation soon concluded. I had to prepare for a faculty colloquium I was to give at my new school that afternoon, and Rodrigo quickly excused himself, saying he had to get ready for the LSAT—"that dinosaur relic of an outmoded system of thought"—the coming Saturday. But I couldn't shake his image. Here was a man who spoke what he saw. I feared for him.

EXIT RODRIGO

I heard from him a few more times in the weeks ahead. He left a message the following Monday saying he had found the LSAT easier than expected and hoped he had done well. About a week later, I received a polite letter saying how much he had enjoyed meeting me and asking whether, in view of our lengthy conversation, I felt I could write letters of recommendation on his behalf to certain LL.M. programs. I called him at Geneva's apartment where he was staying, and we spoke for nearly half an hour, during which I tried to get a better sense of his professional and personal goals. In particular, I wanted assurance that he would not too openly advocate or prematurely engage in disruptive acts of the sort he had mentioned so casually in my office. Hearing enough to satisfy myself, I wrote four letters of recommendation, each to a different LL.M. program, over the next week.

All my work was wasted. Three weeks later, I received a long letter, on flimsy airmail stationery, written from a city in southern Italy. It read:

Dear Professor:
   Thank you for all your efforts on my behalf. As you can see, I am back in Italy, courtesy of your immigration authorities. It seems I made the fundamental error of performing six months of part-time military training in the Italian Army shortly after my twentieth birthday. At the time it seemed a reasonable way of paying back the Italian nation for subsidizing my education at a fine university. Also, I don't know if I told you, but my late mother was an Italian citizen. How all this came to the attention of your authorities, I do not know. Is it possible your office or telephone is monitored? The immigration officer who conducted my hearing seemed to know a great deal about my political attitudes and interests.

At any rate, I have been informed that I am subject to denaturalization, whatever that means. I have to apply for a U.S. visa like any other foreigner, which could mean a delay of several years. So you will be deprived of further exchanges with me, in person at any rate, for the foreseeable future. I've found decent employment here, but had looked forward to returning to my homeland. I guess there is no reason to assume that a culture bent on demonstrating its own destructive absurdity will interrupt that demonstration for critical remonstrance. Well, as they say, Que será, será.

Arrivederci,
Rodrigo

* * *

As I walked across Washington Square park that evening I thought: Have we lost a prophet, or a madman? A racist or a savior? One with a message of hope, or of hatred and confusion? All these things at once?

A homeless man, his few possessions stacked neatly on the bench beside him, looked up at me despairingly as I walked past. Rodrigo's image of a wave cresting rose in my consciousness. I wondered if I would see him again.

[Eds. He did, five minutes later, when he opened his mail, but only by proxy. Rodrigo had left, in his faculty mailbox, a long document entitled "Rodrigo's Printout," containing statistics on Western poverty, unemployment, and homelessness, books and articles on Asian business organization, on Mexican and European approaches to the family and old age care, and the cyclicity and rise and fall of civilizations—essentially all of the points he covered in the Professor's office. See Richard Delgado, *Rodrigo's Chronicle,* 101 YALE L.J. 1357 (1992).]

Rodrigo's Third Chronicle
Care, Competition, and the Redemptive Tragedy of Race

[Eds. In the Second Chronicle, not reprinted here, Rodrigo returns from Italy via an ingenious method and enrolls in an LL.M. program at a prominent law school. After settling in, he and the Professor meet for a bracing conversation on law and economics.]

INTRODUCTION: RODRIGO ACCOUNTS FOR HIS RECENT ACTIVITIES

"Rodrigo, I was just thinking about you." This was not the usual hyperbole busy professors use to flatter their favorite students. Since returning from my talk at the Economics-of-Race conference, I had been meaning to call Rodrigo to thank him for helping me prepare for it. "How has the term been treating you?"

"Not bad. How was your conference?"

"Good. They're thinking of making a book out of the proceedings. If so, I'll get a chapter out of it. My talk went over well, thanks in part to our conversation."

"You give me too much credit," Rodrigo replied. "I was just a sounding board. But if you have a minute, I need your ear in connection with something I'm working on myself."

"Glad to oblige, though I hope you'll first tell me about your LL.M. program. I feel I had some role in getting you started. How are things going?" I asked, motioning him to have a seat on my office couch. "Like some coffee?"

"You know my weakness," Rodrigo replied. "I've been staying up late with two seminar papers, including the one I need to talk to you about."

IN WHICH RODRIGO EXPLAINS HOW HE WON A NATIONAL ESSAY COMPETITION, SOLVED THE RIDDLE OF THE AGES, YET GOT INTO TROUBLE WITH HIS SEMINAR PROFESSOR

As I busied myself making a pot of espresso on my office coffeemaker, Rodrigo launched into his tale:

"Things are going fine. Your Socratic method takes a little getting used to. But I'm enjoying myself, except for something curious that happened in my Social Legislation seminar. It's taught by a famous professor, someone you probably know. We had to write papers, so I wrote on a problem that I'd been thinking about for a while—namely, how to reconcile socialism and capitalism."

"No small challenge, Rodrigo!" I replied. I was struck by his audacity but, on second thought, not really surprised. The brash, talented Rodrigo never had been one to shy away from difficult challenges. "So, you addressed the riddle of the ages, one that has troubled some of the finest political minds of our times?"

"You know that I studied world cultures before returning here. Plus, Italian intellectuals have long been intensely interested in socialism and Marxism. Yet, all my professors here in the U.S. seem deeply committed to free market solutions for everything. It struck me as an area warranting examination. So I resolved to see what I could do."

"And that's what you wrote about for your course paper?"

"Yes, and I won a national essay competition for student writing. The judges loved it. I even received a small cash award, which I gave to my sister to pay her back for some of the moving-in expenses she helped me with."

"Congratulations!" I replied. "Your professor must be very proud." Gesturing toward the shelf, I said, "Cream and sugar?"

"Thanks," said Rodrigo, pouring and stirring with gusto. "As a matter of fact, that's what I'm here to see you about. Patience has never been my strong point, and when I learned of the essay competition, I submitted a draft even before showing it to my professor. The deadline was in early November, and I felt confident enough of my analysis that I sent it in."

"And then what happened?"

"I got a phone call announcing the award. But my professor, although happy that I won, wants me to rewrite the paper. He says it's not legal enough. Plus, to do real justice to the topic, he says it really ought to be a book. But since there's not time for that, he wants me to scale it down. He suggested that my next draft focus on race—on the 'problems of my people,' as he put it."

"Fascinating," I replied. "They are always complaining that we cluster together in cafeterias and so forth, and only want to teach and write about civil rights. Then, when we address something of broad social interest, they want to herd us back into our cubbyholes as quickly as possible. It happens often. But tell me what your paper is about—the one that won the prize, I mean."

"As I said, I set out to reconcile socialism and capitalism, the two principal systems of economic organization in the world. They've long been thought to be in conflict. So I thought that trying to reconcile them would be a good thing to do, especially for a Social Legislation paper."

"Some very good minds have addressed this very problem, Rodrigo," I replied wryly. "If you've pulled it off, you'd be a candidate for the Nobel Prize in law, if there were such a thing, not just first place in a student competition. Tell me how your analysis goes. Later, we can talk about what your professor wants in the way of a redraft. Incidentally, you shouldn't feel offended that he wants you to submit two drafts. It's a very common requirement in American law school courses."

"I know. He explained that during the first meeting. I just didn't expect the revision would take the direction he suggested—although, as you know, I'm fascinated by problems of race." Rodrigo peered at the jacket of a book lying open on my desk. "I'm reading the same one. It looks like it might be useful for my rewrite."

I refilled Rodrigo's cup and sat back expectantly. Rodrigo loved to talk about books and ideas. And I was especially curious to learn his thoughts about socialism and free market capitalism, having just returned from a conference on a related subject.

"How did you decide on your topic?" I asked.

"I was reading about nursing home scandals, including a recent case in which an elderly patient died for lack of care. Another LL.M. student, a friend of mine from Ghana named Ali, is writing about the problem of regulating such homes, so the issue was on my mind. It occurred to me that we have no such problem in Italy, nor in any other Mediterranean country I know about. And the same seems to be true of black and Chicano culture here. No matter how poor an elderly person, someone will take care of them."

"I've heard of exceptions," I interjected. "But as a generalization, you may be right. It is mainly our friends of the majority race who seem most concerned about being alone and uncared for in their old age."

"And this got me to thinking, not so much about white versus non-white differences, but the problem of care generally. It struck me that the caregiving sector of a society should almost always be socialized, while the productive sector should be relegated to the free market economy."

"A nice, elegant solution," I replied. "But of course the law-and-economists will argue that everything should be governed by the market, including nursing homes. Where, and why, do you draw the line?"

"Recall the very example I just mentioned," Rodrigo replied, finishing his coffee and looking up animatedly. "The nursing home had hired the minimum number of employees they could get away with under the law. And they were all high school graduates or less. When the elderly patient went into a semi-coma, they were too busy to notice, even though the other patients tried to call his predicament to their attention. Three days later, the family came to visit him, noticed his condition, and called an outside doctor. But it was too late. The grandfather died the next day."

"And the moral you draw from this is ... ?"

"Caregiving and the profit motive are incompatible. The temptation is to cut corners, which is contrary to what's needed. With caregiving, the focus has to be on the individual, not on the profit line. If what you need to dispense is love, compassion, nurturance, then you need to socialize the caregiving enterprise. That way, we all bear the cost of it, and can, if we decide, hire high-quality caregivers."

I sat up with interest. "And since our society is getting older, and none of us knows if he or she will need a caretaker sometime in the future, people can perhaps be made to go along." I am considerably older than Rodrigo and had given more than passing thought to what would happen to me when I entered old age.

"With the productive sector," Rodrigo continued, "it's fine to try to cut corners. A firm that succeeds in reducing the price of a good or service will drive its competitors out, which is good and to be expected. But people are not commodities, not cans of soup. So with child care, nursing care, primary education, programs for the mentally ill and other dependent populations, we should socialize every one. Some we already do. We should do the same with all the rest, even if it costs more in the short run."

"So, the trick is to draw the right line between the productive sector, which should be governed by aggressive, dog-eat-dog capitalism—the sort of thing our conservative friends love—and the caregiving sector, which should be socialized. Model-fitting, as they say."

"Right. And that's what my original paper was about. I even gave examples of industries and services that we currently socialize, like the Post Office, that it makes no sense to treat that way. They ought to be relegated to the private sector as soon as possible."

"You may not know this, Rodrigo, because you've been living in Italy. But we've actually been coming around to that view. Recently, we've allowed companies like U.P.S. and Federal Express to compete with the Post Office for the delivery of mail and packages. They've become very popular because they're faster and don't charge any more."

"I know. A friend of mine got an express package in Dublin from some friends in America. It got there in only two days; the mail usually takes a week or more. And when you think of it, it makes sense. There is no reason at all to have the Post Office be a socialized bureaucracy, other than that your Constitution makes some vague reference to one. The clerks are bored and slow. The Post Office can't attract intensely idealistic persons with nurturing skills, since there's little about a letter to love. Nor is there the zest and *élan* associated with competitive enterprise—trying to deliver a service or good cheaper and better than the next business. No wonder complaints about the service run rampant."

"Let's say we do what you suggest, Rodrigo. We commit all the caregiving activities—the ones we can't handle as individuals, at any rate—to the public sector, and socialize them. And we relegate the Post Office, manufacturing, and other productive activities to the competitive sector. Won't this just set up two nations within one, with the idealistic caregivers working at jobs everyone will regard as second class? We already have this to some extent. Won't your plan just exacerbate it?"

"No," Rodrigo replied quickly, "because we'll be free to pay the caregivers a living salary. As you mentioned, this shouldn't be hard to arrange, because with an aging society, everyone fears that they might need care some day. But additional arguments weigh in favor of my plan."

"I'd love to hear them."

"Well, first of all, everyone today is seeing first hand the economic and psychic consequences of lack of care"—Rodrigo gestured toward the book on my desk—"all the things Professor Hacker writes about—increased crime, juvenile delinquency, school dropouts—and more. The case for socializing caregiving today is plainer and more urgent than ever before. Personalized, loving attention to dependent individuals is today a cultural mandate—one that even makes economic sense."

"Then why not leave it to the private sector?"

"Because by its very nature, it falls upon those who can least afford it. We must socialize caregiving if it is to be effective."

"You may have a point, Rodrigo, but I'm still worried about the problem of second-class citizenship. With caregiving a function of the socialized sector and production left to the private side, won't all the caregivers end up being minorities and women, just like in the bad old days?"

"No, I don't think so," Rodrigo replied. "Many white folks have idealistic impulses, too, and would gladly work taking care of children, the aged, or the disabled if those jobs paid a decent salary. Some of them do now, even with what they get paid. And for the many caregivers who now suffer demoralization and burn-out, the better pay and greater prestige that would go with socialization may be the tonic they need to stay with their stressful, demanding jobs longer."

I was silent for a moment while Rodrigo poured himself a third cup of coffee. I marvelled at his youthful constitution. Three cups in the afternoon would have had me awake half the night. "You mentioned arguments in favor of your plan. What are the others?"

"One is synergy—interactions between the two sectors. The productive sector would develop technology for high-quality caregiving—for example, monitoring machines, wheelchairs, interactive learning devices for young schoolchildren. They could sell these to the caregiving sector, compensating for the somewhat higher tax bill the productive sector would have to absorb. At the same time the caregivers, free to give first-rate attention to their charges, should be able to send many of them into the private sector equipped with skills, a high self-image, and good job prospects. Currently, half a generation of inner-city children grows up unemployed or underemployed—if they don't turn into criminals or drug dealers. Concentrated care from an early age will redeem many of them, enable them to become Thomas Edisons, Colin Powells, or Jonas Salks. Our economy would flourish, instead of sinking to the point where it is now barely in the top five in the world. You recall our discussion before, Professor."

"I do. And your ideas have a certain idealistic appeal. But what about the problem of incentive? Wouldn't those in the caregiving sector become lazy and refuse to work hard? Why should they, if they can't be fired, if their business can't ever go under?"

"Mothers are not paid, nor are fathers. Do they take frequent coffee breaks, become lazy and bored?"

"No, of course not. But that's because they have blood ties to their charges. Nature equips them to care. Why should anyone love other people's children, or an elderly, incontinent retiree in a nursing home?"

Rodrigo was silent for a moment. "Some people do care about others, even in our dog-eat-dog system. My approach would enable these people to do what they are inclined to do naturally—help others. As things now stand, those who go to work for Legal Aid, the public defender, or do social work with the inner-city poor, become demoralized. Society does not value their work. They are underpaid in relation to what they do—which often exceeds in importance that which a Madison Avenue advertising specialist does in a lifetime of getting people hooked on cigarettes."

"But, Rodrigo, if changing bedpans in a nursing home were highly valued, wages would not be what they are. People have little taste for that kind of work. Much of it is so simple, anyone can do it. That's why it's not highly recompensed. Aren't you trying to distort the market, and isn't that always inefficient, as our friends in the law-and-economics movement put it, and, therefore, a bad idea?"

"Good point," Rodrigo conceded. "But tastes are created. They come from somewhere. The same is true of distastes. People shy away from helping professions because they're taught those professions are low status. Consider your own students, for example. Don't many of them come to law school full of idealism, ready to change the world, to represent the poor and the underdogs?"

"Yes, of course. You're like that now, for some reason."

Rodrigo shrugged off the compliment. "And what happens to them over time?"

"You know as well as I do. They change. Law school holds out corporate law, big-firm practice as the best, and criminal and poverty law as not nearly so prestigious or challenging. After a year or two, most of the ones who began certain that they wanted to vindicate justice and defend the outcasts start to think of law as a technical game. And the game is more enjoyable when played in a large firm with secretaries, paralegals, Xerox and fax machines—and, of course, a high salary."

"So, every year you see first hand, Professor, that tastes and distastes change?"

"Unfortunately so."

"Could not the pattern be reversed? What if law school painted poverty practice as the best, and big-firm practice as repetitious, sterile, mechanical, and lacking in any serious intellectual content?"

"A few of my colleagues will actually say that in unguarded moments," I said. "If they preached it to the students as consistently as they preach the opposite message, we might get a better balance among our graduates going into each of the different worlds of practice."

"My point exactly," Rodrigo said quietly.

"Rodrigo, I'm trying to think of all the objections your plan would face so that you'll be prepared. Here's one: let's suppose you are right that care is best given by someone whose temperament, training, and job description incline him or her to treat the cared-for person individually, without rush or haste."

"Just the opposite of the factory system, in other words," Rodrigo interjected.

"Yes. And let's concede also that none of us knows whether he or she will need that kind of care later in life. Why does it follow that we should therefore socialize the entire caregiving industry? That goes against our national grain. And you must admit it might lead to a certain amount of sandbagging by halfhearted caregivers attracted to the helping professions because of the increased salary and prestige that will go along with them. Would not a better solution be to encourage persons to purchase private insurance? If someone feels he or she is likely to need a nursing home, or if young newlyweds think they may have children who may need child care, why not let them protect against those contingencies by buying insurance?"

"Then, if the need arose, they could use the insurance proceeds to buy care—is that the idea, Professor?"

"Something like that. I'm just trying to anticipate what the other side might say."

"You can't buy love," said Rodrigo levelly.

I couldn't believe what I had just heard, and wondered if Rodrigo knew he was echoing a line from a well-known Beatles song. In a moment, I learned the answer.

"It's trite, but true. Marriages based on money fall apart. Primates separated from their mothers by a glass wall die or fail to grow, even if they are fed and warmed adequately. Patients even in well-run nursing homes die sooner than ones who stay at home. And look at the crime and delinquency rate among the children our society currently neglects. The conservatives are right—you can't solve a problem by throwing money at it. But if you address it with care and concern, often you can. Yet in our society, overbalanced toward production values, there is not enough care and love to go around."

"Perhaps volunteerism is the answer, as the Republicans say," I suggested.

"That only goes so far," Rodrigo replied. "Our communal, loving instincts have atrophied from disuse. We are too caught up in a linear, production-oriented mentality. Not to demean it—it was highly useful during the period of colonial and industrial expansion. But now that our needs are more diverse, we are equipped with all the wrong impulses."

"And I suppose you think other societies have struck a better balance."

"Actually, yes," said Rodrigo, looking slightly uncomfortable. "Although to be truthful, some of them have gone overboard in the other direction, have sacrificed efficiency and productivity for a rather smarmy form of social life based on connection and—what do you call it? Good vibes."

I wondered if Rodrigo might be referring to countries associated with his own ethnic background and heritage. But noticing his discomfort, I decided not to press him too closely.

"I commend you for your honesty. I agree that the two faculties often exhibit an inverse relationship. The more productive a society becomes, the more stunted they tend to be in love, affection, spontaneity. But if a culture goes all out for love, emotion, develops its affective side too much, it may pay a price in efficiency or productivity. What you're saying, then, is that we have to keep them in balance—right?"

"Not quite. The idea is to relegate activities that lie on the caregiving side to intelligent socialist treatment, and ones on the productive side to aggressive *laissez faire* capitalism. Within each sphere, it's fine to be as unbalanced as one wants. The capitalists in my ideal society could be aggressive and even devoid of human feelings—so long as they did not break the law or interfere with what the more nurturing caregivers were doing on the other side. And so similarly with the caregivers. Oh—and by the way, Professor. To answer your question about sandbagging: Any caregiver caught doing substandard or halfhearted work would simply be fired and sent over to the private sector."

"An apt punishment. And you think that a society run along those lines would be efficient?"

"Yes, for two reasons. First we would see a decided trickle-up effect. A vibrant and well-funded helping sector would turn out able workers and reduce the number of delinquents and welfare drags. And the productive sector, realizing it can sell commodities to the caregiving sector—because that sector is now well-financed—would invest heavily in 'human capital' thereby developing powerful new domestic markets it does not have now. And by the way, Professor, yes, I do think that Latino and black populations have done a better job at providing care, certainly for their dependent elderly, and probably for children and the mentally ill as well. Your Anglo friends, with all their production expertise, could well look to these sources for models."

"But I thought that you said earlier that all one would need to do is put out the call and thousands of talented schoolteachers, childcare workers, and the like would come surging forward."

"Some would. But they might need lessons in how to do it."

"Kind of a reverse Peace Corps."

"Something like that," Rodrigo said. "We talked a little about these things before."

"I remember. Give me a second while I throw this out. Want another cup?" Rodrigo shook his head no, and I carried the coffeemaker and pot to the sink outside, where I deposited the grounds and now thick coffee. As I walked back, I reminded myself to ask Rodrigo about the matter that had brought him to my office in the first place.

When I returned, Rodrigo was leafing through the book on my desk, Andrew Hacker's *Two Nations*. I remembered that he had been reading it, too, and so seized on this to ask him about the matter that had been on my mind: "Rodrigo, I sense we're nearly finished talking about your paper—the first version, I mean. Now I'd like to find out why you have to revise it for your professor. But first, tell me a little more about the prize. How much did you win? Did you get to make a trip to receive your award?"

"Two hundred fifty dollars, but no trip. They sent me the certificate; the check, and a nice award letter by mail. None of this did me much good with my instructor, however. When I told him about the prize, he hardly blinked. He was having appointments with each of his students, one every fifteen minutes. He had a sheet of notes on each draft. The main gist of mine was that this was an interesting idea, but a little unfocused. He urged me to concentrate on the problems of inner-city blacks. I'm supposed to write up what the ideal civil rights policy would be—'if any,' he said."

"And so, does he want you to build on your insight about socialism and capitalism?"

"I think that's pretty much up to me, but I'm thinking of doing it if I can. There's actually a second essay competition I can enter if I write fast. It's entitled, 'A Civil Rights Policy for the 90s and Beyond,' and is sponsored by a conservative organization. But they make clear that no ideological restrictions apply. Liberals and folks like me are free to submit," Rodrigo said smiling at his own joke. "Since it would be a more or less completely revised paper, I'm pretty sure I could submit it."

"You might check with them first," I suggested. "Best to avoid any hint of scandal. Conservatives can get righteous about the darndest things."

"Maybe I'll disclose in a footnote how this essay builds on the previous one."

"That should do it," I said. "But before getting into this one, tell me: were you disappointed when your professor asked you to restructure your article?"

"No, not really," Rodrigo replied cheerfully. "He's a good teacher, even if he didn't warm up to my paper. I think his mindset was that I was going to write about civil rights. It's understandable, given who I am. And it's possible I gave him that impression when we met for our initial conference early in the semester. I don't really mind. It's an opportunity to look at some things I've always wanted to read."

I marvelled once again at Rodrigo's good nature in the face of what some would have seen as his professor's insufferable paternalism.

As though reading my mind, Rodrigo interjected: "You could see his reaction as an instantiation of the very mechanism I wrote about in the first paper: corruption of taste, disdain for anything smacking of social service. Civil rights has an urgent, social-engineering ring to some members of society's elites. Maybe the professor unconsciously thought all my talk about love, caregiving, and compassion was 'soft,' and that a paper focusing on ghetto crime would be more like it."

"Who knows?" I said as noncommittally as possible, not wanting to be too harsh on a fellow faculty member. "Tell me your thoughts on revising the paper. Do I get a cut if you win another prize?"

"How about dinner?"

"You're on. Now let's hear what you are thinking of saying."

IN WHICH RODRIGO ATTEMPTS TO SOLVE THE PROBLEMS OF "HIS PEOPLE"

"I'm thinking of linking the new paper to the general theory I outlined in the first one."

"I hope you're not going to maintain that all ghetto kids need is a little love."

"Not at all," Rodrigo replied, a little sharply. "Although love does have something to do with it. You see, I think your country—I mean, our country—has its civil rights policy exactly reversed. In terms of the structure I laid out earlier, I mean. We shower love, affection, and indulgent treatment on minority group members who least need it—the middle-class, well-trained, and intellectually able."

"I can definitely think of a few cases," I replied. "I've written about that myself."

"So we adulate and grease the skids for talented professionals of color—those who would have succeeded without that anyway. And we tell the rest to lift themselves by their bootstraps, get a job, stop being welfare leeches, and so on. We turn a cold shoulder to those who need individualized care and concern, implying that they should take their chances—nil, if the truth were known—in the free market. And we hold close to our bosoms those who are most like us—who do not need the embrace. Blacks at the bottom of the heap get little personalized treatment, unless, of course, they commit crimes. We exclude them from our consciousness as much as possible, while those who are bright, well-educated, and able we fawn over and promote."

"Like you."

"That remains to be seen. I'm going on the teaching market this winter—if I ever get my paper done, that is."

"It sounds like you have it well in hand. But tell me, what's your solution to the problem you've just identified? Your professor, like most white people, will want to know not just what's wrong with our civil rights approach, but how to fix it. Do you want to bring back massive social programs like in the sixties?"

"It *will* take a major national effort," Rodrigo conceded. "But it will require both targeting the poor of color with individual care and concern *and* integrating them into the economy. The essence of being a colonized people is to be both beyond love and excluded from the main avenues of economic well-being."

"I've read that literature. But the American race problem is different somehow," I said. "And harder."

"It is indeed," Rodrigo agreed. "I'm thinking of calling it the problem of being Beyond Love."

"Beyond Love?"

"Yes. And if you'll give me a second to call my roommate, I'll tell you what I mean. May I borrow your phone? We were going to go out for dinner, but I need some more time with you. This is helping me get my thoughts in order. You're a good listener—I like the way you push me."

I gestured toward the telephone, then picked up Hacker's book from my desk. I had been reading it avidly as a welcome relief from the raft of books written by conservatives which I had read in preparation for the Economics-of-Race meeting.

"Don't leave," said Rodrigo. "This will just take a minute. It has something to do with the subject of that very book."

As promised, Rodrigo's phone call was brief. I was intrigued to learn that his roommate was named "Giannina."

"Beyond Love": In Which Rodrigo Explains What Stands in the Way of Our National Civil Rights Policy

"There," said Rodrigo, putting down the phone. "We're all set for later. How much of that book have you read?"

"I'm just finishing. It presents a pretty dismal picture. Before starting, I sneaked a look at the conclusion to see if the author makes a grand proposal, offers any sort of hope or 'quick fix' at the end. Nothing that I could see. So your work is definitely cut out for you."

"The main task, as I see it, is to deal with the problem of blacks being, as I call it, 'Beyond Love.' For the vast majority, our society is prepared to offer neither entrée into the economic system nor love and concern. They are excluded both from the economy and from networks of love."

"So the program of enhanced, synergistic, and reinvigorated spheres of love and economic development which you outlined earlier would leave them out—i.e., unbenefitted."

"I'm afraid so. It would take something more."

"I agree. I and others have written that our current system of white-over-black ascendancy is far from accidental. It benefits whites; indeed, one can see our entire current system of civil rights laws and policies as a sort of homeostat, assuring that the system contains exactly the right amount of racism. Not too much, for that would be destabilizing, nor too little, for that would cause whites to forfeit important psychic and pecuniary advantages. We have written about interest-convergence, and the way in which periodic ringing victories, like *Brown v. Board of Education,* end up benefitting whites more than blacks, legitimize a basically unfair system, and, when they become too inconvenient, are simply cut back by narrow judicial construction, administrative foot-dragging, or delay."

"I've read that work and agree with it," Rodrigo said quietly. "I hope to build on it. The trick is to offer a solution that recognizes and takes into account the interest-maintaining, homeostatic element of our current approaches to race."

"If you pull *that* off, I'll nominate you for a second Nobel Prize," I said—then immediately regretted it when Rodrigo shot me an appraising look.

"I'm sorry," I said. "I'm on your side. The search for a solution is urgent and important. I'm just a battle-scarred veteran of many defeats. Don't let my jadedness put you off. It's an occupational hazard. Please continue."

As I had hoped, Rodrigo brightened up. "I'm glad. The change in Administration may open a window of opportunity for new approaches, ones that may actually do some good." He paused for a moment, then continued:

"Have you noticed, Professor, how few animals kill members of their own species?"

"I have. Although you should know some sociobiologists are pointing out exceptions. Jane Goodall has shown that the great apes, for example, do sometimes war against and kill each other."

"I didn't mean to make a universal point. But the generalization contains a grain of truth, don't you think?"

"Yes, of course. And if you mean to apply it to human beings, I suppose it's a valid starting point. We rarely go to war against those whom we see as closely related by blood and tradition. It's easier to demonize and kill members of that other tribe or clan or nation."

"And might not something like that account for our racial predicament? Society has marginalized and excluded African Americans from the beginning, rendered them the Other in so many settings that even after the enactment of civil rights laws, most Americans cannot think of them as their equals. Hacker points this out as forcefully as anyone. Blacks, especially the black poor, have so few chances, so little interaction with majority society, that they might as well be exiles, outcasts, permanent black sheep who will never be permitted into the family. Majority society has, in effect, written them off. We might as well erect walls around their communities—as a few neighborhoods have tried to do."

"I remember some of Hacker's figures."

"The man wields numbers and statistics the way a classical composer wields notes and instruments. His voice is calm and temperate. But the picture he renders is devastating."

[Eds. Rodrigo gives a summary of some of Hacker's dismal statistics after which the two continue as follows.]

"Of course, our conservative and neoliberal friends will concede these statistics, but maintain that they are the fault of welfare dependency or a culture of poverty," I asserted.

"Hacker has an answer to that," Rodrigo retorted. "Blacks live in deteriorated neighborhoods, suffer debilitating diseases, live shorter lives, and commit crimes in far greater frequency than do whites. In a few cases, these may be the products of individual choice, laziness, or inertia. But when large numbers of people live this way, the suspicion arises that social forces are responsible. And Hacker says he knows what the forces are: white racism and neglect. Whites, who hold all the cards, simply are unwilling to permit blacks to achieve equality with them."

"What about blacks who achieve wealth and fame? Some do."

"Most are in sports and entertainment. As Hacker points out, the average young black gang member, if he watched TV at all, would be amazed at the number of cardigan-wearing black doctors and lawyers that appear there—all out of proportion to their numbers in real life."

"But don't most black criminals prey on black victims?" I asked.

"Of course. But it's black-on-white crime that society finds terrifying. Blacks have a three-times greater chance of dying from a policeman's bullet than do whites. The prisons are nearly one-half black. And murderers who kill whites are many times more likely to receive the death sentence than ones who kill blacks."

"His statistics certainly help you establish your case. As a group, African Americans live in a condition of near-apartheid. Yet few whites will accept any responsibility for our deplorable condition. We're as far removed from national consciousness as I can ever remember. It is even fashionable to blame blacks for their predicament, to view us as the aggressors, to see us as opportunistic whiners who do not want to work."

"I'm rapidly getting that sense," replied Rodrigo, "both from things I read and from the remarks of my fellow students in class. It's been a revelation. Where I came from, I was little more than a curiosity for my skin color. Here, it's practically a badge of identification—although I must confess that a few whites and a professor or two have taken a great interest in me and my ideas. As have you."

"But, of course, I'm a man of color."

"True. Although you move in a white world. I hope to be like you one day."

"First things first. You need to finish this paper. And what a dilemma you've painted. Black people are desperate, poor, demoralized, and confined to inferior schools and all-black neighborhoods. As soon as a neighborhood becomes more than about eight percent black, all the whites start to leave. What does your scheme for adjusting love and production have to say about that?"

Rodrigo leaned forward. "We need both a new myth and a form of coercion." I sensed that he had thought about this, but he seemed more tentative now than before. So I said encouragingly:

"I love to hear about myths. I write about narratives and stories myself, and believe this is a fruitful line of scholarship. I'd like to hear what you mean by coercion, too."

Rodrigo began: "I'm sure you know about Hobbes and his belief in a commonwealth created through mutual covenants?"

I nodded, so he went on: "It's a powerful image, not so much because it's true in any literal sense—no one makes explicit promises when they are born into the human community—but because of its mythic significance. People in the majority group know that if all, or most of them, obey the law, everyone will be better off. And so they pay their taxes even if they could cheat, they stop at red lights in the middle of the night when no one is watching, and so on. The Rule of Law prevails because everyone knows that if we all adhere to society's rules and regulations, we will all benefit. Otherwise, we could decline into savagery, and it would be every person for himself or herself."

"What about the 'free rider' or sociopath who discovers that he or she can gain an edge simply by disobeying the law?"

"A few do that," Rodrigo replied, "but the myth discourages them by designating them bad. They know that if they're caught, they will earn everyone's disapproval."

"If not be prosecuted criminally," I added.

"That's where coercion comes in—for those who are not adequately socialized in the myth, or who simply succumb to temptation."

"And I gather you're saying that the social compact and the force of law are inadequate to protect minority people—to enforce and guarantee the success of our civil rights laws and policies?"

"Precisely. Would you like me to spell it out a little more, Professor?"

"I'm still going strong," I replied—even though I was definitely feeling the late hour and fast pace. "And it is my line of work. I hope we're not going to make you late for your dinner appointment."

"Giannina said it's okay, but only on condition that I agree to introduce her to you someday. She admires your work enormously."

"Is she a law student like you?"

"I'll let her explain that when you meet her. Perhaps we'll have you over when the term finishes."

"I'd be delighted," I said. "But tell me more about myths and coercion."

Rodrigo glanced over at the Hacker book on my desk, then continued.

In Which Rodrigo Explains the New Civil Rights Myth and Form of Coercion

"The basic problem is that blacks fall outside the social compact. We are, as I call it, Beyond Love. The majority group has figured out that they don't need us, that it's more profitable to keep us as a ready supply of menial workers and a source of psychic consolation for blue collar, working class whites. Outside these uses, we are surplus, annoyances, of concern only insofar as we impinge on society through the occasional violent crime or have too many babies, thus increasing the tax burden.

They are prepared to write us off, eliminate us from their concern, to accept little from us so long as we demand little in return."

"Some of them are calling for concern, for attention to our needs."

"But they are voices in the wilderness. The average middle class white, according to Hacker, knows and cares for no blacks, has none living in his or her neighborhood, sends his or her children to schools where few if any of us attend—and is quite satisfied with that state of affairs."

"A bleak indictment," I mused. "But you said you had a solution of some sort."

"More like an approach, more like what one would do if one desired to change things. But of course I admit that any desire to better our dire estate may be missing from society today."

"That may change with the new Administration. Given this, what would you do?"

"I would disseminate a new myth. The current one does not work for us. With ordinary laws, white folks know that if everyone follows them, we will all be better off. But with civil rights, the situation is exactly the reverse."

"Racism benefits whites," I chimed in. "They know that as a class they are better off with us marginalized and excluded. So, they don't take their civil rights obligations that seriously."

"Except for a few tokens needed to legitimate the system. Most of us fall outside the clan. Like a species of wild animal, we are entitled to little consideration. It's not that we may be killed at random, but fellow-feeling simply does not extend to us. We are beyond love and concern. Norm-breaking behavior by a member of the majority which breaches the country's professed ideals about brotherhood, equality, and dignity for all confers a benefit on the law breaker and his group. That's why even blatant law breakers who refuse to rent to or hire qualified ones of us rarely receive any punishment."

"With ordinary laws, someone who acts in a law-abiding manner, stopping at a red light in the middle of the night, for example, gets to feel good, satisfied, and proud; he believes himself a good citizen. Are you saying that the same isn't true for people who adhere to the civil rights laws?"

"Yes. The good-citizen myth is much weaker, if it exists at all. Enforcement is infrequent and ineffectual. There are all the well-known excuses. The breach was unintentional. It was justified by a business necessity. There was another cause for the rejection. And so on."

"So we need both a better, or at least a different, myth, and a new way of enforcing it."

"It's easier to think of what the new form of coercion would be," said Rodrigo. "And I think it must come from us, not from them, at least initially. I think it would be some form of what your society calls terrorism or sabotage. We might call it self-help, liberation, or something of the sort. But there would need to be some form of redress for flagrant breaches of equal respect. And it would need to be as swift and effective as the penalties society applies to ordinary law breakers."

I shuddered. "Rodrigo, it's fine for you to discuss these matters with friends like me, in the safety of my office. But I must urge you in the strongest terms to keep your ideas to yourself." I looked at the door to see if I had closed it after emptying the coffee; with great relief I saw I had. "Italy may be different, but here the very word 'terrorism' raises hackles. I wouldn't be surprised if your advocacy of such tactics did not have something to do with your earlier troubles with the INS."

"Fine," said Rodrigo, seeming not at all abashed by my heated warning. "Although surely the most perceptive among your white friends know that continued neglect can only cause more violence, more frustration, more uprisings like those in Newark and Los Angeles. I'm merely pointing out that at some point, this anger might get channelled."

"A few of us have dared to broach that suggestion. But unlike you, we have tenure. Perhaps you had better backpedal or at least glide over the part about coercion, and go on to the part about myth. White people love myths. All of us do."

"What's needed is a reason—a plausible and inspiring reason—for expanding one's circle of sympathies to include groups who are now excluded. Group self-interest, like that which accompanies paying one's taxes or stopping at red lights, doesn't work because with respect to us, the majority's incentives point the other way. We need a reason for caring when caring is costly and does not benefit the caregiver in any obvious way. We need a reason for making a group, now situated outside the social compact, a member of it. Current antidiscrimination law applies coercion, ineffectively, to disadvantage the broader group, to deny it benefits, places in law school, jobs, goods it wants. So the myth must take this into account."

"A tall order," I commented dryly.

"True, since with our treatment of minorities—in this area alone—when we break the law we are better off. And the 'free rider,' the deviationist who defiantly breaks the law, who stands up against affirmative action, is cheered as a hero, one who dares to tell the truth, to call a spade a spade."

"So to speak." I winced, resolving sometime to let the innocent Rodrigo in on the meaning of the term. "So, unlike with ordinary laws, one can't appeal to the myth of the social compact."

"Only weakly, at best. Blacks lie outside society. They are the Other. We refer to them as 'them,' as 'those people.' Hacker says lying behind this aversion is the sense that African Americans are an inferior order of being. This is a white society; they live here at our sufferance. They mustn't get too close, begin living in our neighborhoods, go to school with our children, date our women. African Americans were brought here for their labor, and an attitude—racism—was coined to justify that practice. Slavery was abolished, but the attitude remained, because society still needed blacks for menial work. After three centuries of this, it's hardly surprising that the dominant group sees blacks as outside their circle of friends and families, outside their sphere of concern. There are, of course, national norms of brotherhood, equality and so on—as a prime example, the fine words of the Declaration of Independence. But these have little impact. The dreadful conditions of which Hacker speaks are not at all upsetting because they are *their* problem, not ours."

"And the system works," I added glumly. "Discrimination benefits the dominant group."

"That's why many white folk cannot be made to see discrimination the way they do the red light. Obeying the civil rights laws does not make them feel particularly good and virtuous. In acting generously toward a black, they do not see themselves as building a safer, more cohesive community. And the reason is that the black is not part of their community."

"So the virtue myth doesn't work. What is your alternative?"

"This is the final part of my paper, and it's a little hard to explain," Rodrigo said. He paused, as though collecting his thoughts.

"Take your time." I leaned back in my chair and drained the last bit of coffee from my cup.

"My plan has two parts. First, the implementation would be put in the hands of 'bridge people'—those older folks, often themselves marginal yet working or respectable, who still live in the neighborhoods and barrios and have a degree of contact with the lost kids of the gangs. They might be the postal clerk, retired serviceman, or porter—people like the 'Mayor of the Block' in the movie *Do the Right Thing*. We would give them MacArthurs and large grants and put them in charge of redeeming their own neighborhoods, especially the least lovable residents who live there—the black kids in the sweatsuits, tennis shoes, and gang insignia—the ones who terrify whites, the ones that whites cannot relate to."

"A body of emerging writing says that empathy only goes so far, that we cannot identify with or love anyone who is too different from us, cannot resonate to a 'story' too unlike the one we usually hear. So your idea of finding bridge people, people who split the gap between the stable, taxpaying white suburbanite and the alienated ghetto kid, makes sense. But where would the money come from? How would you get middle class society to give millions of dollars to bridge people for the benefit of welfare mothers and teenage hoodlums?"

"That's the other part," Rodrigo said. "We need to persuade them that burdening themselves to relieve anguish among African Americans benefits them."

"And how would you do that?"

"We would tell them they should pay because the recipients—people of color—have a secret. The secret is one that they will learn only later, once the programs are in place, and that once disclosed will bring them an incalculable benefit." Rodrigo was speaking softly yet emphatically. "The secret is one they cannot learn until blacks and other outsiders are brought fully inside, are made equal members of society. They will learn it when they have relaxed the barriers, when they have decided, as a group, that blacks and Mexicans and gays and lesbians are no longer Beyond Love."

"So, by saying 'I love you,' whites will receive this benefit, learn this secret?" I wanted to get Rodrigo to clarify his thoughts before he handed in his paper, with its extraordinary thesis, to a skeptical professor at his law school.

"Yes, something like that. And by it I mean learning to love those who are least like you, those who frighten and put you off. I mean the sixteen-year-old black youths in jogging suits and gang paraphernalia, walking in groups of four and looking mean. I mean loving the unlovable, the ones you now think of as the enemy, the Other, the ones least like you."

"Whites are pragmatic. They'll want to know what the secret is before they agree to love the unloved, pay to redress centuries of neglect and indifference, remedy the deferred maintenance that in a thousand ways we have allowed to build up within populations of color."

I was silent a moment. Then I blurted out: "Rodrigo, the current situation brings benefits to the majority group, as you yourself conceded. You can't seriously think they will give them up in return for a vague 'secret' that they *might* receive at some undesignated future time. I'm not sure *I* would go along, and I'm not even white!"

"You give yourself too little credit, Professor. You have already been doing something like that—loving those who are least deserving of love."

I calmed down, sensing Rodrigo's seriousness. I did not want to deter him from telling me more, from exploring the vein he was following.

"Their own culture supplies a host of narratives, reasons we could draw on to support the new myth. It would not be so unlike stories they already subscribe to, ones about receiving a benefit by giving. We could tap these narratives to show why the current policy that relegates African Americans to a life Beyond Love is iniquitous and unworthy."

"I hope you're right."

"The effort would be redemptive. As society integrates outsiders, achieves unity, so would the individuals engaged in that task. The social healing would accompany a psychic, individual one."

"Bearing another's burden does sometimes make one feel lighter—particularly if it enables the other to do surprising things. And I suppose you think our white friends will know the reward when they have done enough?"

"Yes," Rodrigo replied. "The benefit will come naturally, in its time. You see, I believe that all are innocent at birth. Children come into the world asking only for health and care. They begin life helpless. Some become corrupted by circumstances. None chooses the corrupting conditions that society or outside influences create." Rodrigo was speaking with great animation now. I wondered what recent experiences he might have had with small children, or whether the mysterious 'Giannina' somehow lay behind this near-spiritual tack of his. I had imagined him to be an atheist or agnostic; I resolved to ask him sometime.

He continued: "And some children then change from innocent beings to THEM, a tragedy both for them and us. We can perhaps redeem them—and ourselves—by working to reverse the process. In some ways, the greater sin is ours for having allowed ourselves to become slothful, uncaring, unloving, hedonistic to the point where we think the anguish of the inner cities is 'their problem.'"

"So, *we* are the ones in the jogging suits, after all," I said slowly. "We are the ones in need of redemption."

"A little too harsh, Professor. I prefer to think we all wear the same jogging suit, whether we have bought it in a store or stolen it during a riot, whether we are rich or poor, black or white."

Something made me glance suddenly at my watch. "Rodrigo, this reminds me—I have a date to go jogging with Professor Abercrombie in the Park in five minutes. Fascinating as all this is, I'm afraid I must break it off. Would you like to join us?"

"Thanks, Professor, but Giannina is waiting for me. I'd better take off. So, you think my paper has promise?"

"Yes," I said. "The theological part at the end is a little surprising, coming from you, but I like it. I'm sure your professor will, too."

"I hope so. And keep your fingers crossed that the Federalist Society doesn't reject it out of hand when I send it in."

I had heard strains from the law school chorale group, which was practicing downstairs for its Christmas program.

"Title your last section 'Amazing Grace,'" I suggested.

Rodrigo looked back intently at me as he left my office, his things under his arm. "I think I will," he said.

Rodrigo's Final Chronicle
Cultural Power, the Law Reviews, and the Attack on Narrative Jurisprudence

INTRODUCTION: RODRIGO AND I MEET AT THE AALS

I was sipping a cup of nondescript, institutional tea in hopes of soothing my jangled nerves in the low-budget, take-out restaurant in the basement of the huge, 1200-room hotel where the Association of American Law Schools (AALS) was holding its annual meeting. It was only the third day of the conference, and I felt wearier than usual. I wondered whether this was because of my advancing age, or because I was simply suffering from overload: too many colleagues, too many hyperkinetic five-minute conversations with persons I hadn't seen in years, too many panels, too many speeches.

I had escaped to the dimly lit dive in hopes of dodging the flocks of highly wired law professors, all dressed in neat suits and carrying green vinyl AALS briefcases, who frequented the more high-toned eating establishments upstairs. This year's meeting was being held in a resort city, and many of the conferees had brought their families. Along the restaurant wall, a group of young teenagers were playing at the video arcade. After the steady diet of high-paced talk with which I had been bombarded the last three days, their aimless chatter oddly reassured me.

I was halfway through my tea and had just noticed that my hands were no longer shaking when I heard a familiar voice from behind me.

"Professor!"

I looked up. "Rodrigo! What are you doing here?"

"I'd been hoping to run into you," my young friend and protégé replied. "But this place is crawling with law professors. No offense intended, but after awhile they all look the same. I'd practically given up when I came down here. And here you are."

"I like your beard," I said. "How long have you been in Orlando?"

"Four days. I came for the new professors' workshop, then stayed on. Giannina joined me yesterday. We're both on a panel tomorrow."

"I came down here to get away, but to tell the truth am delighted to see you. Sit down. I was going to leave a note on the message board if I didn't run into you soon. How are things going with your new position? And did you and Giannina ever figure out how to arrange things with your far-flung jobs and the commute?"

"It's not working out too badly. She's keeping her place in the Village and I got a flat in town not far from the airport. We take turns commuting. She says her total travel time to come see me is no greater than that of some of her friends who take the train to work every day."

"How's the teaching going?"

Rodrigo looked up to catch the waiter's attention. "Not bad. Do you mind if I join you? I could use a cup of coffee or a snack."

"Not at all. I have nothing on my calendar tonight except getting caught up on what has been happening with you."

"The classes are a lot of work. Fall semester I had two new preps, but this spring I just have my seminar. I finished my blue books last night in the hotel, and I'm looking forward to getting some writing done, starting next week in fact."

"You don't waste any time," I said admiringly. "What are you going to write about?"

"Either trusts and estates..."

I must have made a face, because Rodrigo quickly said, "I know. It's one of the courses they assigned me. The other area is civil rights. Actually, I was hoping to ask your advice on something. Whichever one I write first I'm thinking of writing in the narrative, or storytelling, mode."

"Storytelling?" Secretly, of course, I was delighted, because I had been writing in that mode myself and indeed am considered to have made a modest contribution to the genre. Yet no one was more aware of its risks than I.

"Rodrigo, as you must know, the whole movement is under attack. Some consider it mushy, unrigorous, even nonlegal. You should think carefully before writing in that vein. Unless you have exceptional colleagues, it might be best to hold off until you have tenure."

"I've heard of the attack on narrativity, in fact have just been reading about it. I'd love to talk things over with you, if you have the time, because I'm genuinely undecided."

The waiter appeared. "Are you gentlemen ready to order?"

RODRIGO AND I DISCUSS THE CRITIQUE OF NARRATIVITY AND TRY TO DECIDE WHAT A YOUNG PROFESSOR SHOULD DO

A few minutes later, we were finishing our sandwiches—pastrami on Rodrigo's part, a vegetarian special on mine—when Rodrigo looked up and began:

"As I see it, the attack on narrative scholarship takes two or three forms. Daniel Farber and Suzanna Sherry say that narrative writing, especially within critical race theory, rests on essentialist premises, which of course isn't true. None of us is under the illusion that *all* minority scholars speak in the voice of color, much less that we always employ narratives or stories."

"Of course not," I said. "Derrick Bell's famous *Serving Two Masters* article is a classic of the traditional cases-and-policies mode. And every now and then one of us tosses off the 300-footnote blockbuster full of case-crunching citations and cites to Fuller and Dworkin."

"The kind that are passing into history."

"Agreed. Yet other critical race scholars do write chronicles, parables, and narratives. We use them to explore ideology and mindset. Stories are a great device for probing the dominant narrative. We use them to examine presupposition, the body of received wisdoms that pass as truth but actually are contingent, power-serving, and drastically disadvantage our people."

"But these are exactly the types of writing that are under siege right now. In addition to the essentialist accusation, Farber and Sherry charge that stories—our kind, at any rate—are inauthentic, atypical, and untrue. Moreover, they are apt not to be tied adequately to legal analysis and doctrine. They wonder why articles of this sort appear in the law reviews and ask why law schools should award their authors tenure. There is no way to evaluate them, because they are *sui generis* and fall outside the scholarly paradigm."

"That's not all," I added. "Scholars like Mark Tushnet say we don't merely fall outside the scholarly paradigm. We are positively damaging it. The degradation of constitutional discourse, of which he not so delicately accuses us, includes flat-out lying and distortion carried out by some of the genre's best exponents. He also accuses us of playing politics with our stories, of choosing just one interpretation—say racism—in explaining an incident at a clothing store, for example, when other explanations are just as valid."

"Pretty harsh," Rodrigo replied. "But we do have our defenders. Tom Ross, Gary Peller, Jane Baron, and Kathy Abrams write of the legitimacy and power of narratives, and the way they help readers understand the social world."

"Don't forget a third group," I added. "There's a vast iceberg out there of skeptics who are basically friendly to narrative scholarship but want us to play by conventional rules. I'm thinking of people like Ed Rubin and Mary Coombs. They think it's fine if we write in stories and narratives, so long as we can be evaluated and graded in some way. They're worried that when young firebrands like you come up for tenure their colleagues won't have the slightest idea how to vote. They won't understand what you've written, or if they do, won't know how to evaluate it. With case analysis the norms are well understood. But who's to say if Derrick Bell's *The Space Traders* is better or worse than Patricia Williams' Benetton story, or Marie Ashe's *Zig-zag Stitching* piece?"

"That's not so hard," Rodrigo said. "Pungency, irony, insight, vividness. Illumination of a new perspective or angle of analysis. Narrative coherence. I don't see why it's so difficult to come up with criteria. The ones I just mentioned would be a start."

"I agree that eventually those ideas may take hold. But in the meantime, narrative writing is highly controversial. You know, of course, about Lani Guinier, and how Derrick Bell had to leave Harvard."

"But she didn't write narratives, and Derrick left on principle because his school refused to hire a black woman."

"But his narrative scholarship may have played a part. And she was a critical race theorist who challenged current notions of political and electoral fairness."

Two of the boys from the video parlor interrupted us politely to ask if we had any change. Rodrigo and I exchanged amused looks, dug deep into our pockets, produced what we had, and the youths nodded wordlessly and ran off.

"Nice kids. Where were we? Oh—maybe we need to distinguish different kinds of storytelling," Rodrigo continued. "I've noticed at least two types, with one being much more controversial than the other."

"And the two are ...?" I coaxed.

"Actually there are three. On our side, there is the so-called 'agony' tale, or first-person account, usually of some outrage the author suffered. And then there is the counterstory, the one that mocks, jars, displaces, or attacks some majoritarian tale or narrative, such as without intent no discrimination; or the free market will drive out discrimination; or some other such tenet of the majoritarian faith."

"And you mentioned that one of these is more controversial than the other?"

"Yes, by far."

"Which one?"

"Everyone loves the agony tale. They find them so poignant, so moving, so authentic, so true. They accept them immediately and call them poetic and soulful."

"I agree," I said. "The reaction often reminds me of the Harlem Renaissance, when white folks discovered black culture. Suddenly, black writers, jazz musicians, and painters found themselves in vogue, their work a counterbalance for the predictability and blandness of the broader culture. But you think counterstories are another story, so to speak?"

"Yes, they don't go over nearly as well. Consider, for example, the strong reaction Derrick Bell's *Space Traders* elicited. The point of the chronicle is that white self-interest drives the civil rights movement, accounting for the many zigs and zags of our racial history. It ends by showing that white America would sell out black rights today, just as it did 200 years ago, if the price were right."

"When one of us takes on one or more of these comforting myths of racial progress, of course there is trouble. But you mentioned a third kind of story."

Rodrigo was silent for a moment. "Oh, yes. There is the majoritarian story or tale. White folks tell stories, too. But they don't seem like stories at all, just the truth. So when one of them tells a story, such as the pool is so small or affirmative action ends up stigmatizing and disadvantaging able blacks, few consider it a story or ask whether it is authentic, typical, or true. No one asks whether it is adequately tied to legal doctrine, because it and others like it are the very bases by which we evaluate legal doctrine. White tales like these seem unimpeachable—when one of us tells a counterstory, it comes under attack, not the original story itself."

"Something like that once happened to me," I said. "Early in my career I wrote an article that in some respects was a classic agony tale, except I didn't tell stories, just quoted cases and social scientists. It was an early piece on hate speech. I pointed out that the tort system provided little remedy for racial insults and name-calling."

"I know that article. Even though it's not on the computerized databases, I ran across a citation to it and looked it up. I liked it."

"So did all of my friends, including, interestingly, a lot of white people. I would go to conferences like this one, and people I never even knew would come up to me and say how much they loved the article, how moved they were, and how terrible it was that the law didn't redress the harm of racist insults."

"And you say you find this surprising?" Rodrigo looked up with interest.

"Don't misunderstand me—I still think you should be very careful if you plan to write in the narrative mode. You can do it, just be cautious, and maybe wait till you have tenure. You see, I finally figured out why everyone loved that first article. It's because they could empathize with the black subjected to the vicious racial slur. They could say how terrible it is that our legal system doesn't provide redress. They sincerely felt that way. Indeed, I think it allowed them to say to themselves how much they loved the First Amendment. They loved it so much that they had to sacrifice these unfortunate Negroes and Mexicans, for which they were genuinely sorry and apologetic."

"So that was your agony story. Did you write any of the other kind?"

"Oh, yes. A few years later I wrote one on the campus hate-speech controversy. In this one, I didn't so much make a case for curbing hate speech as I did for the indeterminacy of the usual First Amendment analysis. I showed that the problem of campus hate speech can be approached in one of two ways. You can either see it, basically, as a liberty or an equality problem, with mirror-image consequences flowing from the two approaches, except of course going off in opposite directions. This one my liberal friends welcomed much less, although in a way it was a more sophisticated analysis. Then, recently, I published a piece showing that the marketplace of ideas is unable to redress systemic injustice—although it can correct minor social ills and errors—because the more deeply inscribed, systemic ones are simply invisible: we don't see them as such at the time. My ACLU buddies absolutely hated this one. They ignored my argument and all my historical evidence for what I called the 'empathic fallacy,' and kept saying they knew of cases where speech in their opinion worked."

"Which of course wasn't your point at all," Rodrigo added.

"No, it was that the First Amendment doesn't work, not speech itself."

Rodrigo was silent for a minute while we sipped our drinks. "So, Professor, you think I should hold off on writing this sort of stuff until I get tenure?"

"I know it's ironic. I myself was counseled to do something similar in my early days. And here I am telling you to do the same thing."

"I could write about something safe, like trusts and estates. But what if I do write a narrative and get it accepted at a top review?"

"You might think that ought to satisfy any tenure committee. But your colleagues might dismiss it as the product of yet another level of affirmative action, namely that of the law review editors who lean over backward to accept an article written by a minority professor. It's a case of the reverse reasoning you and I discussed before. They insist that we meet the merit criteria, but when we do they dismiss our accomplishment. Since professors of color virtually by definition lack merit, when we do demonstrate it in any of the classic ways, this disconcerts. There must be a reason for such a strange event. And they find the reason in the very factor, affirmative action, that raises a question about our competence in the first place. When faced with deciding between two propositions—that Rodrigo Crenshaw, the affirmative action candidate, had merit after all (indeed more than most of them, who have never once published in the *Harvard Law Review* in their entire careers) or that affirmative action accounted for Rodrigo's article getting accepted at the top law review—guess which one they will choose to believe?"

"We can't win. Our successes are laid to affirmative action of one sort, and our failures to another."

"A double bind," I said.

"I could write a 600-footnote case-cruncher," Rodrigo said, a little doubtfully.

"I'm sure you could," I said. "And some of your colleagues would love it. That's the kind of article they wrote to get tenure twenty-five years ago. They'd see themselves in you. They'd be all smiles."

"The trouble is that I'd never get an article of that kind in *Harvard*. They're passé. The good reviews realize that that vein of formalistic scholarship has run dry and is producing fewer and fewer breakthroughs."

"If it ever produced any," I added.

"All the good writing these days is either critical or interdisciplinary. Yet the old-timers on our faculties roll their eyes when they meet this kind. Especially when it's written by one of us."

"Well, let's put format aside. What are you thinking of writing *about*? You mentioned something about trusts and estates. Sounds a little dull, but I'm sure you'll find a way of making it interesting," I added.

"I'd like to show that the famous public-trust doctrine that Joseph Sax pioneered in environmental protection law a quarter of a century ago put a halt to the search for more far-reaching reform in that area. I would argue that the theory was both conservative and progressive at the same time—conservative, because it imported ideas from trust law that ultimately froze environmental law into an unproductive model, and progressive because it offered a way to control some of mankind's worst impulses. The other paper I'm thinking about writing is a civil rights piece."

"It seems to me you could write the first one in the standard cases-and-policies mode."

"I could. But I could also write it employing narratives, analyzing the rhetoric and logic of reform. I could show, for example, that the language and mental pictures of Sax's trust approach are essentially male, revealing an unconscious fear of what might happen if we did not place the valued property beyond our reach, in the hands of someone else. It's a little like what wealthy men do for their children—fearing that they otherwise might be tempted to spend the child's college funds on a sports car."

"Like Ulysses lashing himself to the mast. I like this other approach much better. It lets you do more, go to the core of the problem, namely the way we think about natural goods like parks, beaches, and animal species."

"I thought so, too," Rodrigo replied a little wryly, "but then I talked to a few of my colleagues. They all preferred the standard version. A couple of them showed thinly disguised scorn when I spoke of using a storytelling and narrative-analysis approach."

"A session at this very conference yesterday considered problems of law review publishing. The program note says the session was to be a gathering of legal scholars concerned about the battle for what they call authorial authority. Evidently many law professors think that law review editors are pushing them around, exercising too much control, too much judgment over articles."

"I heard about that," Rodrigo replied. "I couldn't go. But I heard that some participants voiced unhappiness over the way in which law reviews are publishing storytelling articles, feminism, and critical theory pieces all to the exclusion, as they see it, of 'real law.' Some argued that the only solution is a faculty takeover of the law reviews; at one school something similar already has happened."

I shuddered. "I hate to think what that would mean for innovative scholarship. Students are not perfect, and the law reviews do make mistakes every now and then. A bad article creeps in; a good one gets turned down. But on the whole students are much more open to new forms and authors than our faculty colleagues are. Some of the latter are open-minded, to be sure, but too many would use their position on the board of advisors to perpetuate sameness—to assure that law review writing today looks exactly like what they remember from their youth—boring, circular,

100-page blockbusters full of case analysis, shuffling and reshuffling doctrine, and going nowhere. Nothing could bring greater disrepute to legal academia. In the eyes of sister disciplines, we are seen as always being a little behind. A faculty takeover of the law reviews would make us the laughing-stock of the scholarly world."

"I agree," Rodrigo said, "and that's why this session on control of the law reviews worries me."

"But that's not solving your own problem. Are you going to write that trusts-and-estates article in the narrative mode or not? And what was that other topic you were talking about?"

"It's all tied up with figuring out the reason behind the resistance to narrative scholarship and storytelling. I'd love to explore this with you, if you have the time."

"Of course I do," I said. "It sounds like you have been giving this some thought—not surprising since your career may ride on it," I added.

"I'm torn," Rodrigo replied. "I want to write the best possible article, yet I want to survive to fight again another day. Maybe we can discuss it over dessert. Could you use another bite?"

"I could."

RODRIGO PUTS FORWARD HIS THEORY ON WHY APPEALS FOR REFORM SPARK SUCH STRONG RESISTANCE

We returned from the counter, where we had gone to select our desserts—a fluffy apple concoction for my rail-thin friend, an abstemious-looking sherbet for me—and Rodrigo began as follows:

"Professor, have you ever wondered about the connection between law, especially academic law, and social change?"

"Every day of my life. Sometimes I wonder if I'm not just greasing the wheels of industry, turning out young lawyers who will advance the aims of the capitalist state. I wonder whether all my teaching and writing about racial justice will do any good. The job structure out there is fixed; my students have to fit in. Possibly I'm making them even more discontent by preaching to them about a better world, when the realities of law practice—billable hours, corporate clients, and so on—mean that they are locked into a certain type of life and practice."

"Some of your students go into public interest practice. You may be more of an inspiration to them than you know."

"But even those who do, find that law is not the trusty instrument of reform we like to think it is."

"And the reasons for that have begun to be explored in recent scholarship, including your own, Professor. Law can do little to bring about fundamental social change because it operates piecemeal. Courts can only adjudicate the cases before them. Doctrines of stare decisis, standing, mootness, and ripeness assure that. Yet, fundamental reform requires that 'everything change at once.' If you only change one thing, leaving everything else in place, the remaining elements simply swallow up the new decree. Even such a mighty case as *Brown v. Board of Education* ended up changing relatively little in the fortunes of black schoolchildren, whose plight today is little better than it was fifty years ago. Pupil assignment rules changed only slightly, especially in the South, and white families compensated by simply moving away, with the result that more African American children attend predominantly black schools today than did in *Brown*'s day. Shortly after *Brown,* the number of black teachers and school administrators actually dropped, and today the graduation and drop-out rates of black, Latino, and Native American children are an embarrassment to any developed country."

Rodrigo was speaking intently now and leaning forward slightly. I nodded encouragingly. "And you believe all this is not due simply to a lack of will or changes in the political climate, but to a basic limitation in law reform?"

Rodrigo nodded emphatically. "Consider what I'm thinking of calling 'cultural weight.' Every legal decree operates against a background of assumptions, presuppositions, and agreed-upon meanings. In addition, it has to contend with a network of existing social practices and narratives. All of these exercise a kind of gravitational pull back in the direction of the familiar, the known. Thus, when *Brown* came down a thousand local officials and lower courts were faced with figuring out what it meant in particular situations. Separate is no longer equal—but what did that mean for teacher assignments, public swimming pools, school bus routes, college counseling in the schools, disciplinary due process, and a myriad of other practices?"

"I suppose you're going to say it meant very little. Is this because local officials were determined to resist *Brown*? Sounds like a conspiracy theory to me."

"No, I don't think that was the main way it happened, although *Brown* did indeed spark some ugly resistance, especially in the South. I think the mechanism was both more and less sinister than that."

"What do you mean?"

"It's the general weight of culture that stands in the way. No one person does, usually at any rate. Rather, it's a host of background forces against which legal decrees are played out that confines reform. There's actually been some recent writing about this."

"You mean the narratives, presuppositions, and existing practices with which landmark cases like *Brown* have to contend?"

"Yes. These sabotage a decree without any conscious effort on anyone's part. When the *Brown* decision came down, southern officials interpreted the decree in terms of their own experience, training, and common sense. To them it meant the only thing it could mean—desegregation that came not too quickly, went not too far, and that changed existing personnel, curricula, and school practices as little as possible. Indeed, southern officials at first interpreted the case as applying only to primary schools, and not to public swimming pools, meeting halls, and other facilities. A few even took the view that *Brown* only applied to the school districts immediately before the Court. It took years for the message to get out that *Brown* meant what it said. Even today, forty years later, more black children attend segregated schools than did in *Brown*'s day."

"And you think this is because of culture and not because of outright resistance?" I pressed.

"There was outright resistance, at least at first. But the way *Brown* went against the cultural grain proved even more decisive. In dozens of formal decisions—school disciplinary cases, teacher assignment schemes, and decisions to locate a new school or program in this part of town rather than that—as well as a myriad of informal ones, majority-race school officials interpreted their legal obligation in light of what they knew: Schools should remain as much as possible like they were before."

"Doctrinal developments didn't help, either," I added.

"No," Rodrigo replied. "Courts soon decided that segregation that results from housing patterns is unredressable. Metropolitan desegregation plans are unconstitutional. Education is not a fundamental interest, nor poverty a suspect class, so that state schemes that fund property-rich districts lavishly and property-poor ones in miserly fashion are perfectly legal."

"All this even though U.S. constitutional law remains perfectly color-blind and committed to the principle of integrated schooling. I gather you think the same applies to law reform decisions across the board."

"I do. Girardeau Spann wrote a splendid book on the subject. He argues that litigators should not place great faith in the Supreme Court as an instrument of social progress. It is conservative, as are the federal courts in general. And even when they do hand down a ringing victory for us, as they do every decade or so, the gain is quickly cut back by foot-dragging, obstruction, narrow construction, and delay."

"Sometimes the gravitational pull seems to reverse itself," I said. "During the sixties, courts and the general culture were on our side. It was a period of breakthroughs."

"But it did not last long. The arrow of change is as apt to be backward as forward at any given moment. A recent poll showed that black parents think that conditions today are as bad for black families as they have been since the time of slavery."

"I saw that study," I added. "It showed that homicide is the leading cause of death for black youths between ages fifteen and twenty-four. Nearly half of all black children lived under the poverty level in a recent year. Thirty-four percent of all black teenagers looking for work could not find it, a rate twice that of their white counterparts. Nearly half of all black babies were not fully immunized. Sixty-five percent of black adults think their children will be denied jobs because of racial prejudice."

"Grim statistics," Rodrigo said. "Unfortunately, this sort of thing is institutionalizing itself. Black despair is more the norm today than the exception."

"And there is little we law-types can do?" I asked. "In our role as lawyers, I mean?"

"Litigation does little good. Even when the courts do give us a rare breakthrough, it succumbs quietly to cultural weight. I used to think another route had promise for us, but now I'm not so sure."

I looked up, hoping Rodrigo would explain. But just then the waiter approached. "Would you gentlemen like something else?"

I looked at Rodrigo who uncharacteristically shook his head. "Just the bill."

As the waiter disappeared, the lights flickered briefly.

"What's that?" Rodrigo asked.

"I don't know," I said. "It happened once before. Maybe it's the kids and the video games." I indicated the teenagers tirelessly pressing buttons along the wall. "Or maybe all the professors upstairs plugged in their laptops at once."

"Maybe it's an omen," Rodrigo mused, falling silent.

"I'd love to hear your theory, though," I said. "I'm going strong, and this restaurant has plenty of empty tables. I doubt they'll rush us to leave. Do you have the time?"

"Sure," Rodrigo replied with renewed energy. "It's all related to my career decision, the one we talked about earlier. I consider you my mentor, so I'd love to run it past you. Are you sure you have the time?"

I nodded. Rodrigo was silent for a moment. Then, he began.

EXIT RODRIGO: MY YOUNG FRIEND EXPLAINS HOW ONTOGENY RECAPITULATES PHYLOGENY AND THEN GOES OFF TO AN UNCERTAIN FATE

"Until recently, I thought that the solution to law's lock-step was storytelling," Rodrigo began.

"Storytelling? You mean, what we talked about before?"

"Yes. You see, Professor, storytelling has the potential to change the social background against which legal decisions are interpreted. It can make inroads into the interlocking system of meanings, cultural understandings, and interpretations that determine the 'common sense' southern officials and other actors bring to legal and cultural decisions. It can make cases like *Brown* succeed, not fail."

"It can change the cultural weight you were talking about!" I exclaimed, sitting up in the booth cushion into which I had been progressively slumping as the evening wore on.

"Or so I used to think," Rodrigo replied. "Stories—well-told ones, at any rate—like Patricia Williams' and some of yours, Professor—can change the baseline. They can change consciousness, change the narrative stock by which we interpret new stories, like that of *Brown*. Separate is no longer equal. Clever, engaging stories can alter the way we see and interpret the world. Law fails because, as we said, 'everything must change at once.' But law cannot change everything at once. So the surprising new edict is always outnumbered. No wonder new rulings bring about little change."

"But persistent, engaged storytelling can change everything at once," I said, leaping a little ahead of myself. I had resolved to remain quiet in order to let Rodrigo develop his case, but my excitement had gotten the better of me. "But please go on."

Rodrigo inconspicuously picked up the bill—something I remarked with surprise and a little satisfaction, akin to seeing my own children grow up. I didn't object, even though I knew his salary as a beginning professor was probably half mine.

"Let me get this. You've always paid before," Rodrigo said, as though reading my mind. "Legal storytelling is potentially the most revolutionary form of scholarship on the current scene, which, in turn, accounts for the resistance we all see, including here at this very conference."

"How do you know it's not just old-fogyism?" I asked. "Mature scholars always resist new genres of writing pioneered by young upstarts like you. You talk strange lingoes and use terms they don't understand like 'hegemony' and 'multiple consciousness.' And you cite authors they've never read. Gearing up to understand these new forms of scholarship takes a lot of work. I struggle with it sometimes, as you know, and I'm a friend and fellow traveler."

"We're grateful for your help, and that of others in your generation," Rodrigo replied quietly. "You don't know what an inspiration you've been. You give us courage to go on."

"Not to mention your own native talent," I said. "But please continue. I'd love to know why stories are not the answer, either."

Rodrigo paused. "Do you remember the resistance to stories that we talked about earlier?"

"You mean the spate of recent law review articles and journalistic pieces attacking the new jurisprudence, ridiculing or trying to rein it in?"

"Have you wondered why it has sprung up?"

"I assume you think it's more than simple inertia and resistance to that which is new?"

"Yes. There's a double mechanism, which I'll explain in a minute. But underlying everything is the sense, the fear really, that stories if well told can become part of the narrative base and so change the way we understand the world. That's truly subversive. And since societies, like most organic things, do not want to change, at least rapidly, we resist."

"Conservative stories seem to have real effect," I interjected. "Over the last decade or so, stories like the welfare queen, the pathogenic black family, Willie Horton, and so on, have swept the land. Maybe the political right are simply better storytellers than we are."

"I don't think they're better, although they do seem to have a knack for catchphrases, like 'political correctness.' I think the real reason has to do with memory. Conservative stories recall a distant past, which we remember in a rosy glow, when everything seemed to be better. Progressives and reformers urge us to move in directions we've never been. Stories like that raise anxieties. Why abandon safe ground for an uncharted future?"

"But society sometimes listens to our stories, as it did in the sixties. And even today some of our writers do get a favorable reception. Patricia Williams' book, for example, got good reviews."

"Stories have to be inveigling, insinuative. Ones that are too frontal create resistance. They have to engage the logic, build on the narratives of the dominant tradition. Agony tales always go over better than the other kind."

"The more hard-edged ones?"

"Yes. You've seen something like that in your own experience writing about hate speech. That first article was a classic 'agony' tale. Liberals, and even some conservatives, loved it."

"The reaction was like that of some reviewers of Pat Williams' book, who praised it as so poignant, so moving, so poetic."

"But as happened to you when you wrote about the logic and structure of the hate-speech problem, you saw that you elicited a different reaction."

"I certainly did," I admitted a little ruefully. "I stopped being a cult hero. People started inviting me to lectures in order to *debate* my views. Often they would invite a speaker from the ACLU to present 'the other side.' And then when I started writing about campus speech codes, resistance increased and the decibel level rose even higher. One columnist attacked me and my co-author, calling us fascists, Orwellian censors, and purveyors of dangerous, un-American double-think, all in one article."

"Quite an indictment," Rodrigo said, looking at me intently. "I'm glad to see you haven't begun pulling your punches. Where did the column appear?"

"A national newspaper. At least they gave me a chance to reply, even if it was several months later. But you said you had a theory to explain all this, something to do with a double axis or mechanism?"

Rodrigo Explains Why Society Resists the New Storytellers and Sets Out His Double Mechanism by Which We Deploy That Resistance

"I do," Rodrigo began. "Recall two related phenomena, both having to do with stories and images." Rodrigo took a long sip of his coffee, which the waiter had obligingly refilled, even though we had paid our bill. "Not bad, for institutional coffee, I mean."

"I gather you mean ethnic images, whose history we discussed before. But what's the second phenomenon?" I asked.

"It's resistance to reform in general," Rodrigo replied. "If you consider both together, you see what they have in common and how it explains the predicament of today's other storytellers and counterstorytellers, who are trying to get their readers to take a more humane approach to problems of racial justice."

"I'm not quite sure I see their commonality. You and I recently discussed the way our culture's system of racial imagery depicts black people. Early on, there were the Sambo and the Mammy images."

"Which we said were necessary to reassure white society that African Americans were content with their lot during slavery and the early Emancipation years."

"Indeed. A different image would have been disturbing. It would have implied that the slaves wanted a normal life, had human needs, just like the rest of us. But then the image changed."

"During Reconstruction, novels, stories, and early films began depicting blacks as bestial, primitive, hypersexual, with designs on things they did not own or deserve, including white women. Now, what society needed was repression. The new images served this purpose perfectly."

"The images are not always negative. Remember the Harlem Renaissance."

"Yes, society was then turning to other cultures for renewal. They adopted black music and art as a refuge from their own excesses. They found its primitivism refreshing, just as today many Americans look to Southwest culture for relief from the cares of industrialized life. The images of us are never particularly flattering—beast, lackey, primitive, and so on. But they are intensely *functional* for the dominant group, changing as its needs change—now for cheap or slave labor, now for repression, now for entertainment, and so on."

"A few courageous souls in every era resist those images, or write a book or play depicting us as normal—like anyone else," I pointed out.

"But they are ignored. The weight of the general system of narratives and images is too great. Harriet Beecher Stowe's novel sold well only after decades of abolitionist agitation had begun to make the American public understand that slavery might be wrong. Nadine Gordimer won the Nobel Prize only as her country was on the verge of repudiating apartheid. Or consider the recent 'rediscovery' of a generation of black novelists and writers, including Zora Neale Hurston and Charles Chesnutt. Those authors were writing many years ago; they had publishers and small audiences. Society was simply not ready to change its images of blacks. These authors wrote about black characters who were normal—like everyone else—who had feelings, hopes, dreams, and so on. They lacked an audience because society did not want to accept that image of blacks back then."

"I'm generally familiar with that functional view of racial imagery," I replied. "But you mentioned another strand?"

"Yes," Rodrigo continued. "Recent work has begun to focus on the problem of social reform in general. A few scholars, like Spann, have analyzed law's role."

"Or lack of it," I added wryly.

"Indeed," Rodrigo went on. "Various writers are studying the natural history of social reform movements, working their way toward a general theory of reform and regression."

"And this mirrors the course of ethnic imagery which you just reviewed for me?"

"In some ways it does. At first social reform movements tend to evoke sympathy and solicitude. We consider ourselves a generous and welcoming people. So we link arms with the newcomers, march with them, sing 'We shall overcome.' Everyone identifies with the underdog. And so it is with most social movements—feminism, civil rights, environmentalism—at first. Then at some point the tide turns. We begin to see the group as dangerous, aggressive. They are asking for things they have not earned, do not deserve, demanding concessions we cannot easily give. Now they are no longer in favor. We no longer invite them to fashionable parties. They are whiners, demanding, impossible, never satisfied. Now they are imposing on our just prerogatives. They are in the wrong, we in the right."

"I've seen something like that happen with many social movements, including our own," I said. "In the sixties, they loved us. We could do no wrong. Now we are almost completely out of favor. These days, it's almost a sick joke. When I pick up a newspaper and see a column about racism, it's almost always about Farrakhan, or some outrage a white has suffered at the hands of women or minorities."

Rodrigo nodded, and so I reminded him of the connection I hoped he would make: "And you think all of this has something to do with the resistance to legal stories and storytelling?"

"I do," Rodrigo replied. "The latest round of reaction recapitulates both of these themes. At first, society welcomed the new storytellers. We thought they were cute and endearing, like children. 'Oh, look, they're telling stories,' we said. We deemed the new stories poignant, moving, touching. At this early stage, we considered most of the stories 'agony tales,' personal accounts or journals of the writers' lives. But then we noticed that they were doing more than merely writing about their feelings, doing more than telling us how it feels to be black. They were making points about us, about the ways in which we think and live. And some of their points were not particularly flattering. Some were downbeat and pessimistic, like Derrick Bell's. Now we started to temper our praise, to find fault with storytelling. Reservations appeared. Writers called for criteria to evaluate, to get a handle on this new legal genre. Writers of color then turned to counterstories, tales, and parables that mocked, jarred, or displaced some comfortable majoritarian tale, myth, or narrative. Major tenets of the majoritarian faith came into question. This brought sharp attacks. Farber and Sherry appeared. Austin and Van Alstyne began ridiculing the new narrativists openly. Austin said crits only cite each other."

"A kind of reversal of the imperial-scholar complaint," I observed wryly.

"And Van Alstyne likened us to commissars and thought-police, saying that when he read us he was reminded of the tanks clanking into Tiananmen Square."

"As though we were the ones with all the power," I exclaimed.

"To him, it must actually look that way," Rodrigo replied. "It's a kind of surplus-power phenomenon. Changes from the cultural baseline appear unprincipled, ruthless, and wrong. Oh, and to draw out the parallel I mentioned, it's all there. Early on, we were the Harlem Renaissance—earthy, primitive, simple, appealing. Then we were the simple Sambos and Mammies, cheerfully writing in the civil rights fields but producing little of the really important work. Then the tide changed. Now we are the threatening, bestial, nearly out-of-control blacks of the late 1800s or post–civil rights black exploitation films."

"And so they are right to resist us; they have practically a moral duty to do so, since we are the unprincipled ones, the ones on the offensive."

"True," Rodrigo replied with a slight sigh. "It's all done solemnly and for the best of reasons—academic rigor, due process, the integrity of the personnel and promotions process."

I could sense Rodrigo was about to finish, and so decided to push for clarification of something that had been nagging at me. "Rodrigo, you mentioned earlier the attack on the law reviews. Did you mean to imply that this assault has something to do with the currents we have been discussing?"

"I think it does," Rodrigo said. "The reviews have been publishing our material, that and the work of the crits and feminists. The old-time, formalistic stuff is passing into history. All the bright young articles editors know this, realize that formalist jurisprudence is playing itself out, has yielded all the insights it is ever going to offer. Postmodern, critical, feminist, and critical race analysis, for now at least, offer much more—genuinely new and exciting ways of understanding our social condition. Many conventional scholars don't like that. Rather than compete intellectually, which would entail retooling and reading and learning to think differently, it's much simpler just to take over the law reviews."

"So you think a faculty takeover really is imminent?" I asked in alarm.

"Not really a takeover, although this may happen in a few schools. What I think is much more likely is some sort of effort to increase faculty participation, certainly in the selection of articles, perhaps also in their editing once they're accepted. You saw evidence of that type of discontent in the ad hoc section meeting we mentioned before. It's the first time, isn't it, Professor, that these matters have been discussed at the AALS annual meeting?"

"I'm not sure," I replied. "I don't go to all of them. But it's the first time that I can remember, although there has been the occasional article or essay in the *Journal of Legal Education* decrying the role mere students have in editing and selecting our writing. We mentioned the one review that already was taken over. And I wonder if you saw the three articles in a leading review just this last year, calling for reexamination of the role of the law reviews."

"Cultural power always reasserts itself. You make gains, then when you least expect it, there's the backlash. And those who participate in the reaction don't see themselves as counterrevolutionaries at all. Rather, they're just trying to set things right. And so when the law reviews change structure, it will just seem like a little infusion of rigor, integrity. It will seem like a restoration, rather than a destructive movement aimed at aborting a host of promising social movements in the law."

Rodrigo was silent for a moment. Then he continued as follows: "And so you can see, Professor, how the personal, the political, and the academic, even, come together. I really want to get tenure, want to live with Giannina, and yet these forces seem inexorable. They combine. Do you have any doubt that what we see with the history of ethnic depiction, with social reform generally, and with storytelling and the law reviews, is about to play itself out closer to home?"

I wasn't sure what I was hearing. "Rodrigo, you mean that you have decided not to write in the storytelling mode?"

Rodrigo nodded his head glumly. "Stories are potent—as we observed. They can change the base, and through that, law, and through that, society."

"But you're saying," I interjected, "that the base changes us as well. Social gravity restores itself, inevitably, after a few moments of exhilarating flight in which you thought you were weightless and could fly."

"It's as though society had a small, but very powerful, unseen homeostat. We replicate ourselves even when we think we are trying most sincerely to transform ourselves. Social momentum is preserved. The more things change, the more they stay the same."

"And so you are forswearing stories, giving up narrative analysis?"

Rodrigo looked me straight in the eye and said nothing.

"But Rodrigo, you can't do that. You are a character in a narrative. You would no longer exist!"

"We are all characters in a narrative, Professor. We just fool ourselves into thinking that things are otherwise. Perhaps we want to escape responsibility for our own stories."

The lights flickered again. I hoped our dialogue was not about to be interrupted by a blackout. But the kids over by the wall had been quiet for some time.

"Maybe you'll change your mind," I said. "I've found that when the young wax pessimistic, they never stay that way for long. What other topic were you going to write about? You mentioned another one," I said, trying to redirect his thoughts to something less dire.

"Oh," Rodrigo said with a start. "The level playing field. Everyone wants to know whether it is or not. I was going to show exactly in what respects it is not level. I think it's an important topic. Conservatives say things are now leveled, and minorities ought to play by the same rules as everyone else. Liberals and many minorities insist it is not. But everyone is vague on exactly what the concept means, and in what respects minorities are made to play an unequal game. I would have taken two or three principal playing fields as illustration, including the famous First Amendment free market of ideas, the economic marketplace of trades, exchanges, and competition, and perhaps another one. Maybe the problem of law school admissions."

"We talked about something similar before," I said.

"Right," Rodrigo recalled. "The first time we met. Then, I would have employed history, cultural analysis, and close examination of the governing narratives in each area to show the main disadvantaging mechanisms that render the playing field uneven."

"Simple, brilliant, and deeply subversive," I said. I could hardly contain my enthusiasm. "What do you mean, 'you would have written'? This is a great project, Rodrigo. It's needed, it's exactly the time to do it—the critical moment, so to speak. And you're precisely the person to carry it off."

"I wish I were as sure as you are, Professor. I just worry about the possibility that—what do you call it—that one can analyze a thing to death?"

The lights flickered again, then went out decisively. I know they were out perhaps for thirty seconds, because I heard voices in the hallway outside exclaiming.

I sat there quietly reflecting on our conversation. Looking back, I cannot be sure I did not drift off to sleep for a moment, worn out by the fast pace of the three days of convention and the high-pitched, although stimulating, talk with Rodrigo.

When I opened my eyes, a bare booth greeted me. Rodrigo was nowhere to be found. I was certain he had been there—his empty coffee cup remained to remind me of our conversation. But no note, then or later, confirmed this. And future efforts to get in touch with him turned up blank.

After a few minutes, I got up and walked outside the hotel on the off chance he had gone there for a breath of air. No Rodrigo, indeed no one at all. I had the walkway to myself. I looked up at the night sky. A meteor flashed through the dark resort sky and was gone.

Had Rodrigo been, as he put it, just a character in a narrative? And, if so, did he actually succumb to the critique of narrativity? What did he mean by his last lines, of being analyzed to death? Like all storytelling, had he and his lessons been lost in a cloud of abstraction, in which learned commentators paid endless attention to the form, the quality, the procedure of storytelling, and gradually lost sight of the content of the stories themselves? Was Rodrigo right that cultural momentum is preserved, while he himself turned out to be perfectly fallible, perfectly mortal?

The night was chilly. I walked back into the hotel, noticing on an easel just inside the basement door a notice about the meeting on "Publishing." I was sorry I had not attended, and wondered if I had somehow betrayed my young friend and protégé by not going.

Once before he had returned from exile as brash and full of life as ever. But this departure somehow to me seemed more final, more dire. I wondered if I would ever see him again.

Rodrigo's Eleventh Chronicle
Empathy and False Empathy

INTRODUCTION: RODRIGO RETURNS AND ACCOUNTS FOR HIS RECENT ACTIVITIES

I was sitting in my darkened office one afternoon, thinking about life. To tell the truth, I was missing Rodrigo. Not long ago, I had consigned him to the Great Beyond. But now, I was flooded with regret and sadness. I missed his brashness, his insouciant originality. Odd, I had not thought of myself as sentimental. How could I have allowed him to succumb to the critique of narrativity in *Rodrigo's Final Chronicle*? I *had* gotten a great series of articles out of our meetings. He had pushed and challenged my thinking, helping dispel some of the loneliness I've felt in this sometimes desolate job. And now, he was gone.

I was just getting ready to turn on the light and resume reading the pile of seminar papers that had awaited me since my return from the AALS, when I heard a shuffling sound outside my door. A brown envelope materialized on my carpet, pushed through the crack by someone whose footsteps I now heard disappearing down the hall. "I'm here," I shouted.

"Oh, I didn't see your light," a familiar voice said.

I turned on the switch and opened the door. "Rodrigo!" I exclaimed. "I was just thinking about you. What are you doing here?"

"We last parted rather suddenly," Rodrigo explained, "so I brought you a note explaining what happened to me after that incident at the AALS. I didn't want it to be too much of a shock. I also brought you a book—a magazine, actually."

"Come on in. What on earth happened to you? I was afraid I would never see you again."

Rodrigo picked up the envelope from the floor, deposited it on the corner of my desk, and glanced around my office. "Do you have a minute?" He gestured toward the pile of neatly typed student papers in the center of my desk. "It looks like you're busy."

"Quite the contrary," I assured him. "These grades aren't due for another week. I'm eager to hear what happened to you. And, before you begin, can I offer you some coffee?"

My young friend nodded enthusiastically, and sat down in the one chair in my office not presently used as a bookshelf or table. As I busied myself measuring the water and grounds for my new office coffee maker (a sleek European model), Rodrigo began.

"Do you remember, Professor, where we were when the lights went out?"

"Yes, we had been talking, rather late at night, in that basement dive in the giant AALS hotel. We were discussing the critique of narrativity and legal storytelling, in particular that section meeting where several of our colleagues attacked the new forms of scholarship as nonlegal, unfair, even exclusionary. Others questioned the role of student-run law reviews. You had just said something about how we are all creatures of our own narratives, which immediately filled me with alarm. Then the lights went out."

"I figured it was the kids playing at the video arcade next to our booth, and that the lights would be back on again in a matter of minutes," Rodrigo said. "I saw you put your head down, assumed you were tired, and got up to stretch my legs. I thought of leaving you a note . . ."

"When I woke up, you were nowhere to be seen," I interjected. "Regular for you, right?" I asked, reaching for two coffee mugs.

Rodrigo nodded. "Thanks. Cream and sugar, please."

"I was afraid you had deconstructed yourself, allowed yourself to become a casualty of Farber, Sherry, Tushnet, and the critique of narrativity."

"Nothing so fancy, Professor, although I think you'll enjoy the story. In fact, what took place prompted me to come see you. Aside from reassuring you that I haven't expired, I've really wanted to discuss something, if you've got a minute."

"Of course! I'd love to know what happened and what you're thinking. Here we are."

I handed Rodrigo a steaming mug, he stirred in creamer and his trademark four teaspoons of sugar, and continued. "You won't believe this, Professor, but I was kidnapped."

"Kidnapped? Are you serious?"

"I am. Do you remember those kids who were playing at the video games along the wall?"

"Sure. They borrowed change from us once. I remember that they looked at you closely, but thought nothing of it at the time. So what happened?"

"It turns out they were not kids at all, but members of an Irish anti-royalist gang. This I only found out later. I had just stood up from the table when, quick as a flash, a cloth bag was over my head, my hands and feet were being tied, and I was carried outside and into a car. The whole thing took maybe thirty seconds."

"My God!" I exclaimed. "What happened then? And why were they after you?"

"This requires some memory on your part, Professor. Do you recall how I got back to the U.S. that first time?"

"I do," I said. "It was a neat little two-step maneuver. After you were deported back to Italy, you resettled in Ireland, using your law degree and taking advantage of the liberalized guest-worker provisions in the European Community. You got a job as a paralegal in Dublin, hung around coffeehouses for awhile, then returned to the United States by means of a private bill."

"With a little help from the Irish Immigration Society and a certain famous U.S. Senator of Irish descent who sponsors these bills routinely. I'm sure you remember what I did before returning, Professor."

I hesitated a moment, and Rodrigo continued. "I think I mentioned this to you before. I bought a title of nobility from a down-at-the-heels member of the British aristocracy. I really wanted to get back and start my LL.M. studies, and didn't want to take any chances. It turned out my investment was probably unnecessary—my American forebears and Italian law degree were probably enough—but that small act led to my adventure."

"You mean your kidnappers thought you really were the third duke of Crenshaw?" I asked, beginning to catch on.

"They did. It turned out the group was a collection of exiles just chafing for something to do. And when they heard from headquarters that someone on their list was apparently right here in the U.S., they decided to pick me up and give me a going-over."

"But of course their grievance was not with you, but with the real duke of Crenshaw, the one who sold you the title."

"Apparently he was a Royalist and something of a bad actor, from the liberationists' perspective, at least. The whole thing didn't become clear until they got me to their hideaway."

"Did you have to do some fast talking?"

"The team that commandeered me did. You should have seen their faces when they took the bag off my head and saw a black man instead of a light-skinned English aristocrat! Their leader was furious. They tried to explain that the restaurant had been dimly lit. They got out the photos. I actually do look slightly like the duke, except for our skin color. I met him briefly when I paid for the title; we're about the same height, weight, and age. So, their mistake was understandable."

"What happened when they got through blaming each other?"

"That's when *I* had to talk fast. One of them wanted to give me a hard time for having bought the title of nobility in the first place. 'A little would-be Englisher' he called me. I could see trouble coming, so I explained to them how I was a leftist and a race reformer. I told them I only became a duke because I wanted to get back to the States. I explained that not only is this my homeland, but that I had a mission here. They looked dubious at first, then finally gave in when I applied critical race theory to their own anti-royalist movement. We ended up going to a local brewpub and debating philosophy and soccer. After a while, they swore me to secrecy for seventy-two hours and drove me back to the hotel. When I got in I tried to look you up, but you had already checked out and headed back to the airport."

"Quite a story," I said. "Reminds me of Morris Zapp's adventure in *Small World*."

"The parallel did strike me," Rodrigo acknowledged. "Although at the time I wasn't sure it would turn out so well."

"Well, I'm very happy you're back and in one piece."

While Rodrigo took a swig of his coffee, I took the opportunity to remind him: "But you said you had something you wanted to talk to me about. Did it have to do with your kidnapping?"

Rodrigo leaned forward on my ancient office chair. "It did, in a way. And also with that magazine I brought you. The whole experience got me to thinking of the role empathy plays in our society. The activists who snatched me, even though they were at first taken aback, came around when they learned I was a fellow reformer. At first, I was afraid they'd just throw me off a bridge somewhere. But we ended up comparing notes and having a good time. It turned out we had a surprising amount in common."

"They empathized with your struggle, and you with theirs, in other words." I was silent for a moment. "So, the critique of narrativity caused you to disappear, but empathy brought you back. Awfully tidy, and, I must say, a little upbeat for a young crit like you," I said, pushing Rodrigo. "Or am I reading you correctly?"

"You and I did talk about the role of empathy once before, Professor. We agreed it is getting in shorter and shorter supply, particularly with respect to minorities of color. Yet I was able to connect quickly with my captors, once they got over their shock at finding a black man under the bag when they expected a blueblood English aristocrat."

"Maybe there's some level on which marginalized people of all sorts can understand each other," I suggested. "And so, do you think this is something our people can tap into in these troubled times, when society seems to be devoting less and less attention to our needs, the Republican right is in full cry, affirmative action is under attack, and welfare programs are being cut left and right?"

"No," Rodrigo said, shifting uncomfortably. "I believe the opposite is the case. I'd like to start with a thought experiment that occurred to me as my Irish friends were driving me back to the hotel."

"I'd love to hear."

Rodrigo drained his coffee mug, set it carefully on my desk, and began.

RODRIGO'S INQUISPRO EXAMPLE AND THE UNRELIABILITY OF EMPATHY AS A SOURCE OF SUCCOR FOR OUTSIDER GROUPS

"Professor, imagine that some scientific genius develops a computer called Inquispro, which discovers and evaluates the facts behind any lawsuit and issues an objective ruling. Inquispro can scan any segment of space and time and tell us what happened."

"So, we wouldn't have to rely on witnesses with fading memories, or speculative and inferential evidence," I said.

"Not only that," Rodrigo continued, "but Inquispro knows all the substantive law. We would program it so that it knows the elements of every cause of action or crime."

"So, for example, suppose Smith accuses Jones of negligence in failing to clear his sidewalks of snow. With Inquispro, we could simply ask the computer to apply the elements of a negligence cause of action to what happened when Smith slipped in front of Jones' house the day of the accident."

"Exactly," Rodrigo replied. "And so with the thousands of other causes of action on judges' dockets. Inquispro could methodically go through all of them, apply the relevant law to the facts, and solve them each in a fraction of a second."

"This would obviously be a great boon to our overworked judiciary," I said. "Indeed, it could eliminate our need for judges and jurors. And there wouldn't be much need for lawyers or law professors, either, although I suppose someone would have to program the computer with the relevant substantive law."

"Do you remember our recent conversation, Professor, in which we talked about white and black crime? We discussed the role of discretion and leniency in prosecuting the sorts of crimes committed by corporate executives, suburban youth, and governmental figures."

"Of course," I said. "Everyone knows what happens: the inner city black youth guilty of stealing hubcaps or selling a small amount of drugs is sent away for a long period, while the well-regarded white figure receives probation or a light sentence, even though the latter's crimes may be more serious, in both a monetary and a physical-safety sense. And so this is the type of thing your computer could not take into account: differential treatment based upon the race or class of the criminal?"

"That's right," Rodrigo replied. "And so, after a while, society would rebel. We would insist on programming sentencing discretion and plea-bargaining laxity into the computer. Otherwise automobile executives would receive long sentences when one of their poorly designed cars killed someone. Savings and loan executives would receive fifty-year sentences. And so on."

Seeking to play the devil's advocate, I interjected. "But doesn't a sentencing system in which the jury decides on the appropriate punishment, either in the sentence itself or through the choice of offense, provide exactly the discretionary empathy whose absence you deplore? Don't we need a jury, influenced by witnesses, lawyers, and the courtroom itself, to reflect our community's sense of reasonable conduct, morality, and approbation?"

"That's right," Rodrigo explained calmly, leaning back in what must be by now a very uncomfortable chair. "But empathy is apt to be quite selective. Society's rejection of Inquispro shows that we expect a judicial system that recognizes the individuality of white defendants, but not black ones. Take the federal sentencing guidelines for drug offenses. Judges in these cases, in which the defendants are overwhelmingly poor and of color, are statutorily prevented from considering leniency in sentencing. No such requirements exist, to my knowledge, for securities fraud, tax evasion, or environmental pollution."

The impact of what Rodrigo was saying sank in on me. "So, Rodrigo, you are saying that society would never tolerate Inquispro. A genuinely fair judiciary that provided equal justice for whites and blacks would be intolerable. We would insist on reprogramming Inquispro so that it was, basically, racist. So that it had a bias in favor of clean, neat, well-educated white defendants and against black ones, in favor of upper-class people of all colors and against poor ones."

"We would. Otherwise, society wouldn't accept it."

"And the moral you draw from this fiendish experiment, Rodrigo, is . . . ?"

"Our society doesn't really want empathy for outgroups or minorities, any more than it wants equal treatment for all people. Quite the contrary, we prefer preferential treatment for ourselves and our kind. We would never accept anything less than that, in fact."

"Which is what your Inquispro example shows," I replied glumly. I took the chance to offer Rodrigo another mug of coffee (had he ever declined, I wondered?).

Rodrigo glanced at my shiny black coffee machine, nodded enthusiastically and held out his cup. As he was stirring in his condiments, I asked, "And I gather you think this lack of empathy is somehow responsible for our current predicament?"

"I do. I've been thinking about it a great deal," Rodrigo explained, cupping both hands around the now-hot mug. "Although I hope you won't jump on me for the rough form of my ideas, Professor. I've developed not so much a theory as a way of seeing why things aren't better for our people. I'll be glad to tell you about it, if you have the time."

"I do, although I don't want to make you late for dinner. Is Giannina expecting you?"

"She's attending a writer's workshop uptown. My schedule's my own tonight, although I may want to borrow your phone later, if it's okay, and give her a call. We usually talk to each other around dinner time when one of us is away doing something."

"Of course," I replied, pointing at the phone. "Anytime you want. I'll punch in the code, and give you privacy."

"Thanks, Professor. Maybe a little later. And no, I won't be needing privacy. Giannina considers you almost one of the family."

"I'm honored. But tell me more about your theory of empathy. And incidentally, if you get hungry, let me know. I have snack food in the refrigerator . . ." I indicated my small office fridge, which I had recently purchased and of which I was proud. "Or we could go out for a bite."

"Thanks a lot," Rodrigo said, smiling. "Maybe a little later. Back to our subject. I start with two observations. One is that empathy is highly limited. Not only is it in short supply, but it also tends to become rarer over time. And the second is that we think we—and others—have much more empathy for the downtrodden than we, in fact, do. I even have a name for this. You've heard of Gramsci's concept of false consciousness?"

"Of course," I said, a little sharply. (These impudent young pups sometimes think us old-timers haven't read anything!) "Gramsci coined the term to mean the kind of identification with the aggressor that a subjugated people can easily develop. They internalize the perspectives, values, and points of view of the very people who conquer and oppress them, thus becoming unconscious agents in their own subordination."

"And so false consciousness is a danger for blacks, at least if we aren't careful. But have you ever wondered, Professor, if there is anything comparable for whites?"

"Comparable to false consciousness, you mean?" I wasn't sure what Rodrigo was driving at.

"I think there is, and it's empathy. Or rather, what I call false empathy, in which a white believes he or she is identifying with a person of color, but in fact is doing so only in a slight, superficial way."

"It *is* a kind of parallel," I said. "But I think I could use an example or two."

"Sure," Rodrigo replied. "Consider the early Settlement House movement. The upper-class ladies who worked there professed to be highly concerned over the plight of the immigrants who lived in the houses. But their sympathies did not extend to learning their languages or ways. Instead, they taught them personal hygiene, housekeeping, English—how to be American. Lawyers make this mistake, too, even public interest ones. Maybe especially public interest ones."

"I assume you are referring to Derrick Bell's famous article," I asked. "The one about serving two masters?"

"That one and others. Bell points out that lawyers working on behalf of black groups would often pursue one strategy, favored by the litigation team—say, desegregated schools—when what the client really wanted was better schools, ones with more resources. And sometimes even the best clinicians make similar mistakes."

Rodrigo continued. "My friend Kowalski and I were talking about this the other day. Even in those client-centered aspects of law like clinical scholarship, real empathy is lacking. Some of the young star scholars admit they sometimes make the mistake of thinking they know what the client wants, and imagine that they are able to tell the client's stories as he or she would want them told. Real empathy, putting the client first and getting fully inside the client's mind and experience, is rare."

"So, you are saying," I summarized, "that when a white empathizes with a black, it's always a white-black that he or she has in mind. The white surmises what he would be like if he were black, but with his same wants, needs, perspectives, and history. All grounded in white experience, of course."

"Right. False empathy, a sentimental, breast-beating kind, is common among white liberals, and is the mirror opposite of false consciousness, Gramsci's notion."

"Nice and neat," I said. "Like the periodic table." In truth, I was a bit stunned by the clear polarity Rodrigo had just outlined. His false empathy construct went some way, I thought, toward explaining how decades of liberal civil rights and legislative policy have left our people only marginally better off.

"False empathy is not just an elegant explanation," Rodrigo continued. "It has real consequences for civil rights strategy. With false consciousness, a person of color identifies with and adopts the consciousness of the oppressor, in this case a white. With false empathy, a white pretends to understand and sympathize with a black. Each is counterfeit. The first type, the upward climber, is readily recognized and unmasked. These are the Great Gatsbys, and they tend to be objects of ridicule by both whites and blacks. The second, false empathy, is likewise despised—but by blacks. We see through it, know by a kind of instinct that these folks won't be with us when trouble comes down. Derrick Bell got it right in his *Serving Two Masters* article. Gerald Lopez, in *Rebellious Lawyering*, did, too. But some of the top clinical theorists are getting it wrong, satisfying themselves and their clients with too little. A recent article shows how cognitive- and narrative-theory barriers render empathy difficult, a mechanism the authors call the 'empathic fallacy.'"

"You make it sound as though the problem lies mostly on the white folks' side. Don't our people sometimes commit the same mistakes?"

"They do, sometimes." Rodrigo conceded. "Although I think less frequently. Most whites lack double consciousness. As members of the majority culture, they have little practice viewing experience from two perspectives at once. We have to do so regularly."

"Someone who is in the grip of false empathy has a shallow identification with the other," I added. "He or she walks on the surface, uses the wrong metaphors and comparisons. It's a little bit like false piety, like those folks who go to church on Sunday but don't allow themselves to be seized by real religion."

"The most unsympathetic thing you can do is to think you have empathy with those of a radically different background. You can easily end up hurting them."

"You mean by doing the wrong thing, by not supplying what they need?" I asked.

"Even worse than that," Rodrigo replied. "Are you familiar with the story of La Malinche?"

I was silent for a moment, straining to remember. "You mean Hernan Cortés's translator?"

"Yes," Rodrigo replied. "I was talking with one of my Latina students the other day about her. La Malinche was a Native American woman who served as Cortés's translator. She ended up helping Cortés destroy her own people."

"I think our Mexican friends have a phrase for it."

"They do," Rodrigo replied. "*La traducción es traición.* Translation is treason. One who moves too easily back and forth between different communities can end up betraying the one with the least power, simply by making its secrets accessible to the other. Clinical theorists, some with the most impeccably liberal credentials, worry that they are doing something similar when they spill a client's stories out on the pages of a law review for all to read."

I stood up to switch my espresso machine to warm. "I'd love to come back to this later, Professor," Rodrigo remarked. "But can I interest you in a bite of dinner? I think I'm hungry, after all."

"You certainly can," I replied, looking at my watch. "And if we hurry, we can get to some good places before they fill up."

RODRIGO EXPLAINS HOW EMPATHY, LIKE KNOWLEDGE, REPRODUCES HIERARCHY AND WHY GENUINE SYMPATHY IS IN SHORT SUPPLY

We walked briskly down the sidewalk in front of my law school. "Is Vietnamese okay?" I asked. "This new place opened a couple of months ago. I haven't been there yet, but everyone tells me the food and service are good."

"Cool," Rodrigo replied casually. A few minutes later we were seated in a comfortable booth in the homey, dark restaurant. While waiting for the waiter to take our orders, I picked up our discussion where we had left off in my office. "Rodrigo, let me see if I understand you. Are you saying that empathy is bad, per se, or that it is good, but there is too little of the real article to go around?"

"In a way, both," Rodrigo replied, looking up at the waiter who had just brought our menus. After examining our options, we ordered appetizers and beverages (yet another cup of coffee for my irrepressible friend, herbal tea for me). "Empathy can harm if it's not genuine, as it often is not. Like knowledge, it has a power dimension. Empathy reproduces hierarchy. And the real kind, true empathy, is in extremely rare supply."

"Tell me about how the false, or superficial kind reproduces hierarchy," I asked. I had just been reading about the sociology of knowledge, and was intrigued by Rodrigo's notion that emotions might reinforce the status quo just as knowledge does.

"We mentioned the case of La Malinche a minute ago. A member of the oppressed group tells the oppressor what it wants to know. The more powerful group then uses the information to destroy the translator's group."

"The translator is a dupe, in other words," I said.

"It works the other way, as well," Rodrigo went on. "Some liberals write about horrible conditions in the community, believing that others will want to remedy them. Their readers may draw the opposite conclusion, however—that minorities are lazy, slothful, like to live that way, and so on. And there is a third way, in which the liberal does not actively harm the member of the weaker group, but merely does him no good. The Good Samaritan offers the wrong sort of rescue.

"Like the Settlement House ladies we were talking about before. They taught Italian immigrants how to cook and eat American food, although they already had perfectly satisfactory recipes and cuisines. The ladies urged immigrant mothers to use bottles and infant formula instead of breast feeding, which they considered un-American and not modern."

"It's what you were saying earlier," I interjected. "When we visualize helping another person, we end up helping ourselves in the form of that other person. A white helps a black who is, in effect white: a postulated recipient who will like and appreciate what the white would have wanted had the white been in exactly that situation. A church group helps the starving, but makes them pray first."

"I'm sure you've noticed, Professor, that people almost always give presents that they would like to receive themselves?"

I remembered with a pang a time or two when my late wife had scolded me for doing something similar. "It's something of a joke with married folks," I said. "The husband gives the wife a lug wrench. She gives him two tickets to the opera, and so on."

"So you see what I mean about the way empathy reproduces power relations," Rodrigo said. "And also how it can sometimes amount to outright betrayal."

We fell silent while the waiter set down our appetizers, some sort of skewered chicken for my rail-thin friend, a pungent hot-and-sour soup for me.

"You were also going to explain why it is in such short supply," I said, ladling myself a spoonful of the steaming delicacy. "The real kind, I mean. And I believe you were also going to explain why the other kind is not merely harmful, but can kill."

Rodrigo removed his chicken morsels from the skewer, neatly speared one with his fork, and began:

Rodrigo Explains Why Empathy Is in Short Supply

"Empathy ought to benefit the possessor," Rodrigo explained, "because it enables him or her to make beneficial trades. If one has the ability to perceive what the other person wants, one can offer him or her that and get what one wants in return. Our law and economics friends would say it promotes marketplace efficiency. Empathic people ought to get ahead. The capacity ought to confer an evolutionary advantage, enabling its possessors not merely to be good parents, friends, and lovers, but good traders, politicians, and marketers."

"But you believe things are not working out that way?" I asked.

"No. For some reason, the evolutionary momentum seems to have stopped, even reversed itself, with respect to people of color. I've been trying to figure out why this is so."

"No one can doubt that it is. Civil rights, affirmative action, Head Start, and dozens of other programs necessary to our people are under attack. The code words politicians and writers use when casting aspersions on us have become blatant and obvious. Black parents believe that things are now the worst they have been in more than a century, that their children will be denied jobs or educational opportunities because of discrimination, and that their sons are in constant danger from violence and drugs. And I gather you think this is not just an aberration or part of an ordinary political cycle."

"I wish it were," Rodrigo replied. "But the downturn in our fortunes is more serious than that. I think the increasing bureaucratization of modern life may account for part of the decrease in empathy and patience for the downtrodden. Modern social relations are apt to be distant and perfunctory. We may run across a few people of radically different classes or races from time to time, but we seldom interact closely with them. A new branch of social psychology called norm theory may supply part of the answer, as well."

I strained my memory. "Norm theory?" I asked.

"Yes. Norm theory holds that our reaction to another person in distress varies according to the normalcy or abnormalcy of his or her plight in our eyes. If you see an upper-class white family being evicted from their nice suburban home, you feel alarmed because you know that sort of situation is abnormal for them. You realize they must be experiencing real distress. But if you see starving Africans on TV, you feel less empathy because you know that is their ordinary situation. Famines are common in that part of the world, so your heart does not go out to them as it would to a neighbor who materialized on your doorstep not having eaten in eight days."

"I've read of experiments dealing with helping behavior that appear to bear that out," I said. "In one, a black man in the subway asks for change for a quarter and is refused; a white man does the same and everyone offers change. I had thought these experiments manifested simple racism, but maybe they illustrate your phenomenon as well. Everyone assumes the black person has a rough road in life, so hardly anyone will stop to help."

"Experiments with stranded motorists show much the same thing," Rodrigo added. "Norm theory explains why empathy decreases over time, even though it would seem to benefit the possessor. The poorer and more wretched blacks become, the less white people will empathize with them. They will dismiss our cries of pain, thinking to themselves that they are part of our normal condition."

"And the poorer and more wretched we become, the less we will have to offer in trade. Empathy with us will be useless. Who wants to trade with a slave who has nothing to offer? There is no reason for empathy with one who is permanently destitute."

"My point exactly," Rodrigo continued. "Empathy is least useful where we need it most. When inequality is deep and structural, empathy declines. It's a downward spiral. Empathy *would* work in a just world, one in which everyone's experience or access to resources was roughly the same. But we don't live in a world like that."

"Do you see any solution, any reason for hope?" I asked.

"The only one I see is to show that our people have something to offer whites. We were talking about this recently. If one can convince white folks in elite positions that blacks are necessary to them, have something to offer, our treatment will shift overnight, as it did in wartime. The prevailing narratives and myths will change magically to facilitate the trades and exchanges, services, and so on that the dominant group needs. None of this will take place on a conscious level."

"The trouble is that many of them seem ready to write us off. The Republicans now realize they don't need our votes. They can count on backlash voters, angry white males, while the Democrats seem not to want us, either. And, if I understand your argument, our few remaining liberal friends can't be counted on because their empathy is shallow. They think they know what we need, but don't. They visualize themselves in our places, and ask what they themselves would want."

"False empathy is worse than indifference, Professor. It encourages the possessor to believe he is beyond reproach. It's like a certain type of religiosity. If you believe you are saved, you can easily come to believe that you can do no wrong. Because you believe in God, you will believe you *are* God, or at least that you're in tight with Him. He's on your side; you understand each other. Once you reach this point, you can do no evil, as you *are* God—or at least His messenger."

"You will then think you are being extremely empathic, as the Spanish conquistadores did, because you are acting on behalf of God in the other person. Not what that other person is, but what he or she might be. The other person may not believe he or she has *that* God in him or her. But you will know better. Is that your general idea?" I asked.

"Yes," Rodrigo said. "In fact, I'm reminded that studies like the helping experiments we were talking about have shown that religious people did not help out any more than non-believers. For example, in one experiment, seminary students were no more likely than anyone else walking down the street to stop to help a man who was slumped over and groaning in a doorway. Ironically, some of the students were on their way to give a talk on the parable of the Good Samaritan."

"So ideology of all sorts decreases empathy," I summarized. "It allows one to exclude different or challenging ideas as outside the accepted paradigm. And the more politically fractured our nation becomes, the less important will seem its commitment to racial justice and help for the poor. Religiosity also decreases empathy, all things being equal, as does bureaucracy. And the conditions of modern life add a fourth element: as the gap in earnings and family wealth between blacks and whites grows wider, there is less to trade. And the poorer those others get, the more norm theory clicks in. Their poverty begins to seem natural and unsurprising, and thus one feels no need to remedy their misery."

"And don't forget the decreasing pie," Rodrigo added. "The slowing of job and income growth for the middle class, combined with the competition from foreign workers and markets, means that correspondingly less empathy is available to go around. The reason is that socioeconomic competition, as you know, increases racism as well as decreases empathy. Expanding markets give a reason for increased empathy: since one is in a position to make trades, understanding other people and their needs confers an advantage. One can trade with the newcomers. Bad times cause you to hunker down and conserve what you have. During human evolution, the main function of empathy was to facilitate bonding and solidarity, so that collectivities could form. But with racism, a relatively new phenomenon, the attitude promotes white bonding, white solidarity. This benefits elite whites, since it ensures that struggling white workers won't turn against them. And it consoles those workers. Even though their share of the pie gets smaller and smaller, they can say to themselves that they're at least better off than the blacks."

"In sum, six factors that augur little good for our people," I said. "A pretty gloomy scenario, coming from someone as young and upbeat as you. I hope you have a solution. Does it include law?"

"Oh, here's our waiter," Rodrigo interjected. "Can I tell you in a minute?" We both examined the menu in silence, while the waiter waited patiently.

"I'll have number twenty-seven," Rodrigo said.

"And I'll take thirteen. It doesn't have MSG, does it?" The waiter shook his head no and departed with our orders. "Doctor's orders," I added to Rodrigo, who shot back a sympathetic look. We continued our conversation as follows:

RODRIGO EXPLAINS WHY LAW IS NOT THE SOLUTION, AND WHY WE NEED A DUE PROCESS OF LEGAL STORYTELLING

"I do have a solution," Rodrigo replied, "but unfortunately it does not include law. At first, I thought it might. After all, one does not need empathy to file a lawsuit. A judge does not need it to rule on technical motions, or to see whether a complaint satisfies the elements of a statutory cause of action. Many of these acts are mechanical, requiring no large amount of judgment. In fact, some race-crits have advocated the formality of litigation as a positive advantage over nonformal dispute resolution, such as mediation, for cases presenting an imbalance of power between the plaintiff and the defendant, as most civil rights cases do. Unfortunately, I think litigation is not a very promising avenue of relief for society's poorest, most disadvantaged classes."

"We talked in a general way about some of these things before," I recalled.

"Your memory is good, Professor. We are not the only ones to question faith in law as an instrument of social reform. Many others do, both on the left and on the right. But some think things would be better if only we had more empathic judges, or ones with wider experience. Some think things would be better if lawyers just learned to tell better, more vivid, stories in their pleadings, for example."

"But you think this would not help at all?" I said, a little dubiously.

"Less than we might hope," Rodrigo replied. "Law is structurally biased against any display of empathy."

"Is that because of your Inquispro example?" I asked. "Namely, because we do not really want law to be uniform and nonracist, treating everyone alike. We *want* it to promote class advantage. If it didn't we'd change the system back."

"That's part of it," Rodrigo replied. "But even perfectly unbiased judges, ones like Inquispro who treat blacks and whites absolutely alike, would end up doing very little good. Incidentally, I think this is even more true for lawyers, but we'll come back to that later."

"Go ahead. I'm all ears," I said. "Why can't law redress the injuries of society's most needy and oppressed? What about the *Brown* decision and times like the sixties? Then, courts were in the forefront of the social revolution, handing down decrees protecting civil rights protesters, desegregating schools and lunch counters, requiring due process in school disciplinary cases, and so on."

"True," Rodrigo conceded. "Unfortunately, that was an aberration. Most of the time, courts are no more kindly disposed to us than they are to any other group, perhaps even less so."

"And I assume you have a theory for this?"

"I do—actually a group of explanations, corresponding to the different roles of judges, lawyers, and litigation as a whole."

Rodrigo Explains Why Civil Rights Litigants Cannot Command the Empathy They Should— Courts Recognize No Due Process of Storytelling

The Litigants Themselves. "Let's take the litigants first," Rodrigo began. "Let's say you are a plaintiff who has suffered a civil rights injury, maybe a black undergraduate or member of a family injured by hate speech. You file suit, but soon find out that it is very hard to tell your story in court. The legal system requires that you tell a different narrative from the one that happened. Law slices up your narrative into little bits, into unfamiliar pieces. The pleading rules require a 'short and plain statement' of your claim, with each allegation being 'simple, concise, and direct.' The law does contain master narratives corresponding fairly closely to commercial grievances, to what industrialists want to say about each other in antitrust cases for example. But it contains few narratives that seem written to remedy injuries to less entrenched interests. There is no pleading form for 'You treated me unfairly.' Thus, when a plaintiff starts to tell her story that her husband beat her for ten years, we interrupt and say, 'Don't tell us that story, tell us about imminent threats of death or violent injury. What was your husband about to do to you at the very moment when you killed him?' This focus on the imminence of the harm impairs the court's understanding of the totality of the harmful relationship. If it turns out the woman has nothing to tell of the official kind of story, we tell her to keep quiet. She had no story after all."

"So the law requires her to tell a stylized story that might or might not correspond to the injury she sustained."

"It can be even worse than that," Rodrigo continued. "Sometimes the law requires you to tell the other story—the perpetrator's—not your own. For example, in a civil rights complaint, you will end up having to tell and prove to the court that the other side acted intentionally."

"That's *Washington v. Davis*," I interjected. "The civil rights plaintiff has to prove that the defendant's conduct was intentionally discriminatory, not merely that it had a differential impact on persons like the plaintiff."

"Precisely," Rodrigo shot back. "And not only that, the plaintiff has to prove tight chains of causation between what the defendant did and his or her injury."

"And probably that the defendant had no legitimate business reason for denying the plaintiff a job or promotion," I added. "Half the plaintiff's case does seem to concern the defendant, not the plaintiff, who, after all, is the one who suffered the injury."

"Exactly. Consider the hate-speech case we mentioned a minute ago. The defendant, let's say, has burned a cross on the family's lawn. Or a group of fraternity kids shouts, 'Nigger, go back to Africa; you don't belong on this campus,' to an eighteen-year-old black undergraduate. If this case goes to court, the defendant immediately turns it into a First Amendment issue. The case will turn on whether he or she had a right to burn the cross or yell the epithet. You, who were merely walking home from the library late at night or trying to sleep in your room at home will find yourself on the defensive, depicted as someone who was trying to take away the precious free-speech rights of the skinhead or bigot."

"Indeed," I said. "We both know abridgments of the First Amendment are a dangerous precedent if more voices are to be heard in our society. Yet we know how hate speech tends to silence and decrease the exchange of ideas, and how not all categories of speech are equally deserving of protection." I paused momentarily, and glanced around the restaurant. "I see what you mean by the narratives all being against you. In fact, I was just re-reading Scalia's opinion in the St. Paul cross-burning case the other day. He hardly mentions the family at all. They were an abstraction, almost entirely missing from the opinion, which concerns speech categories, the dangers of censorship, and what Scalia calls 'viewpoint discrimination.'"

"A more perfect irony could not be imagined," Rodrigo continued. "The Jones family, who awoke to find a cross burning on their lawn, and the city that intervened on their behalf, considered guilty of discrimination!"

I paused for a moment while the waiter set down our food, a vegetarian stir fry for me and chicken in a lime-coconut curry for Rodrigo. "Looks fantastic," Rodrigo said, thanking our server.

"So," I summarized, "the plaintiff often does not get to tell her story at all. Even when she does, it's rarely the one the plaintiff naturally would tell. She cannot 'go back to the beginning.' She often finds that things she thought vital to the claim are irrelevant and cannot be told. The court interrupts, makes her tell her story in little slices, in response to direct examination. The other side gets to object every thirty seconds. Most of the 'material elements' concern the defendant and what she did. It's only when we get to the issue of damages that the plaintiff really gets to tell about herself and about what happened to her. The law makes one take what Alan Freeman calls the perpetrator perspective. Have I caught your meaning?"

"You have."

"It does sound worrisome," I said. "But surely, Rodrigo, courts must place some limits on storytelling. Otherwise, trials would be interminable. Without pleading rules anyone could go to court and enter any old generalized grievance against anyone else."

"True," Rodrigo replied. "But law makes our grievances particularly difficult to bring."

"Then maybe the solution is to litigate more, not less—to get the law to recognize new causes of action. Then it would become possible to tell new narratives, as happened with the tort of intentional infliction of emotional distress, for example. It took time for the legal system to recognize sexual harassment of women in the workplace. Before Catharine MacKinnon's path-breaking work, women could not tell those stories in court. Today they can. Maybe our people will eventually be able to tell their stories."

"I doubt it," Rodrigo replied gloomily. "The courts' and the country's mood is all in the other direction. American society is impatient with what they call activist judges. We believe the rights revolution has gone too far. Affirmative action is under attack. The dominant narratives of the sixties and seventies have shifted back toward a traditional and morally conservative posture. In the sixties, African Americans were long-suffering victims or righteous warriors. Then, the images changed to those of terrifying gangsters and black power advocates. In the last decade, we've had the Willie Hortons and Cadillac-owning lazy welfare cheat, the affirmative action hire who lacks traditional merit criteria and blocks the promotion of a supposedly more deserving white."

"So it is in the hate-speech debate," I said, returning to Rodrigo's previous example. "There, the narrative of harm receives short shrift, even though it's quite provable. Courts and commentators quickly substitute the wholly unproven narrative of censorship, as though every campus that enacts a mild hate-speech rule will immediately turn into an Orwellian nightmare with Big Brother looking over everyone's shoulder. This is quite speculative, and, in my opinion, extremely unlikely. Or take another narrative, the chilling effect that speakers are said to suffer if any speech-limiting code, like a hate-speech rule, is put into place. Set that alongside the terror, demoralization, and high dropout rates that are provably associated with campus hate speech, as dozens of studies show. Which one is more demonstrable?

One finds that all the prevailing narratives enable elite and not-so-elite whites to do what they are accustomed to doing, and then defend it in court. They have all these narratives going for them: Big Brother, the state as censor, the terrified speaker just waiting to be chilled, and the thin-skinned hypersensitive black just waiting to run to the authorities instead of shrugging it off."

I sat back. "I'm beginning to see why you have little faith in the legal system to solve our empathy crisis. Still, earnest, impassioned talking sometimes works. What about *Brown v. Board of Education*? And what about your own success in talking your way out of trouble with your captors. Did you not succeed in getting them to empathize with you?"

"We were about the same age and political orientation. They let me talk without interruption. Actually, I talked a blue streak for fifteen minutes, afraid for my life. Plus, I had something they wanted, namely that I would go away without making trouble or filing charges against them."

"They afforded you full due process of storytelling. In that respect, your situation was not parallel with the one that prevails in most courts."

"Not at all. But several other features reduce the possibility of empathy in court," Rodrigo continued. "Not only do we make it difficult for plaintiffs to tell their story. Consider how we treat witnesses."

Witnesses. "You're going to say rudely, I bet. I've just been reading about a famous criminal trial where many witnesses got raked over the coals and left the courtroom feeling impugned and maligned, even though they were just trying to do their job, namely, to tell what they saw."

"Exactly," Rodrigo replied. "Let's say the plaintiff tries to bring in some friends to help him tell his story. These are people who know something about the event that gave rise to the lawsuit, say, the act of discrimination. The witness soon learns that in our legal culture it is okay to treat witnesses with suspicion and contempt. The other side gets to badger them, imply they might be lying, insinuate all sorts of unsavory motives."

"Yet we insist that everyone treat the lawyers and judge with the greatest respect. Anyone who stood up in court and said that the prosecutor or judge might be lying or biased would be treated as having done something scandalous. Yet we do this sort of thing with plaintiffs' witnesses routinely."

"And with women who bring charges of rape," Rodrigo added.

"In the courtroom, certain types of emotional display will get you a contempt citation; others will not. Judges can shout, interrupt, and show exasperation or disbelief. But the plaintiff, her attorney, and the witnesses are expected to be models of decorum."

"Emotional rules are the underside of power and ideology," Rodrigo said. "It's okay for an empowered actor, say, your boss, to be angry at you. But you may not show anger at your boss. It's the same way in court. A power imbalance is always visible in courtroom interaction, conveyed in who speaks first, who interrupts, and who gets to paraphrase and sum up at the end."

"It's true," I said, taking the devil's advocate position, "that plaintiffs and witnesses find their roles limited in court by rules of evidence, relevancy, cross-examination, and so on. But that's the way things are in an adversary system. Without rules it would be a free-for-all and things would be even worse for what you call disempowered litigants. Aren't you forgetting that every plaintiff has a perfect counterbalance to all this power and cumbersome machinery that is deployed against him in court, namely the attorney, a gladiator trained to negotiate the maze of court rules, professionally and ethically bound to represent the client to the best of her ability? Doesn't the lawyer cancel all or most of that power imbalance out?"

The Lawyer. "I wish it were so," Rodrigo said with a sigh. "But a lawyer's training and culture disincline him or her to challenge the narrative structures we just mentioned. Lawyers who spoke up, or mimicked the emotional tone of the judge, would be sanctioned or disbarred. Lawyers cannot depart much from the stylized, desiccated stories spelled out in the rules of pleading. Gabel and Harris proposed different standards for lawyers representing political clients, but they were virtually the only ones who did. Recent clinical literature contains articles showing that even famous radical lawyers miss opportunities to tell their clients' stories. Instead, they settle for the dry, cautious tone set out in the pleading books and encouraged by the prevailing ethos, the bland decorousness of the courtroom."

"Even public interest lawyers litigating civil rights cases are prone to place the client's story second to their own," I added. "I'm reminded of the article you mentioned, in which Derrick Bell points out how civil rights attorneys end up litigating one thing when their clients really want another."

"It's not necessarily that the lawyer has a superficial understanding of the poor black client. Rather, it's that he believes he knows best. He believes he has to collaborate with the court by retelling the client's story so that it comes out in the sanitized, approved version. And since most lawyers are white, male, and middle-class, this can be a real problem. If the lawyer's experience, background, and history are radically different from those of the client, the lawyer can easily dismiss the client's objective and substitute his own. Lawyers may know the client's misery and understand fully the story he or she wants and needs to tell. But too often the lawyer puts the law story, the familiar one, the one he was trained to tell, first. The lawyer is trained to operate within the system."

I remembered something I had just read. "Rodrigo, you have some empirical evidence on your side. I was reading Paul Finkelman's review of a book by J. Clay Smith on the history of black lawyers in America. Finkelman commented on how few lawyers, black or white, were in the forefront of the civil rights movement. All the great leaders were nonlawyers: Martin Luther King, W.E.B. Du Bois, Frederick Douglass, Malcolm X, Jesse Jackson. They were historians, or teachers, or ministers; very few were lawyers. Do you think that's because a people in trouble know instinctively that a lawyer is not the one to tell its story as they need to have it heard? Or is it that lawyers shy away from leadership roles in social movements, preferring to remain in the background and conduct negotiations, file for injunctions, and do the nitty-gritty work that allows the real leaders to operate effectively and stay out of jail?"

"It may be both," Rodrigo replied. "Some lawyers do propose useful things. Thurgood Marshall and the other lawyers in the NAACP Legal Defense Fund certainly did, which Finkelman of course acknowledges. But the further removed a lawyer is by experience and background from the group represented, the less effective he or she seems to be. No white male middle-class lawyer advocated attention to racial slurs and hate speech until a minority lawyer did. Catharine MacKinnon, not a middle-class white male, proposed the elimination of sexual-history testimony in rape cases and developed a new cause of action for sexual harassment in the workplace. No white male—except that genius, Alan Freeman—proposed that civil rights law systematically disadvantages its very beneficiaries. The Supreme Court sees no serious problem with capital punishment that falls disproportionately on minorities. And so on."

"I'm sure you know you are ignoring a few notable exceptions, like Jack Greenberg," I said. "But as a generalization, you may be right. Why do you think that is?" I asked.

"I think something is fundamentally wrong with the legal narrative: one simply cannot tell stories of many kinds of injustice through the law. And if one's training is in the law, one has virtually de-trained oneself to represent society's outcasts. It takes a superhuman effort to be an empathic human being. To be both a lawyer and an empathic human is practically impossible. Our review of civil rights history shows that the legal narrative is less effective at promoting social change than that of practically any other profession, such as teaching, the ministry, or street-level activism, for that matter."

"You might be right. Lawyers are trained to observe courtroom rules until they become second nature. We are trained not to empathize but to be technocrats, concentrating on the small, not the big, picture. We focus on motions and pleadings, not stories, much less things like injustice, love, and compassion. The lawyer ends up telling his story, not the client's."

"We do allow victim-impact statements," Rodrigo mused. "That's one kind of new story we do like."

"We find it easy to empathize with the victims of crime," I said, "particularly if they are middle-class people like us."

"Even better, victims are not required to testify through a lawyer. They can speak for themselves. When we want someone to speak really effectively—that is, to help society condemn the criminal even more roundly—we let them speak uninterrupted. We could do the same for civil rights plaintiffs, but don't."

"But, Rodrigo," I interjected, "a new body of writing focuses on effective lawyering. Writers like Menkel-Meadow, López, Cunningham, Alfieri, and others are writing about client narratives, about the need to listen more carefully, to translate better, to get inside our clients' heads. They are warning about the dangers Derrick Bell raised of putting the law and the lawyer's objective first. Do you not think things are changing for the better?"

"I would like to think so," Rodrigo answered. "But a lawyer cannot easily escape the confines of background, culture, and professional discipline. Herb Eastman shows that even top lawyers, like the late William Kunstler, can tell dull, lifeless, stereotyped stories. And Anthony Alfieri, one of the best of the young clinicians, confesses that he often falls short in empowering his clients and letting their voices and personalities shine through. He writes about how he erased the pain and identity of one of his clients, a certain Mrs. Field. Progressive lawyers may go on and on about their consciences, because they want empathy not for their clients, but for themselves. They lose all their cases. Their clients sometimes lie to them. The judges are rude. Often their clients want X when the lawyers want Y—the grand declaration of principle—as we mentioned before. In the end, liberal empathy is often false, misdirected, or solipsistic."

The waiter, who had materialized at our table side while we were talking, asked us if we cared for dessert. I looked at Rodrigo who shrugged back, a little eagerly, I thought. What the heck, I thought, I'll go running tomorrow.

"Could we see your dessert tray?" I asked the waiter. He disappeared, taking our empty dinner plates with him. I picked up our conversation. "But you mentioned another way in which litigation prevents people from telling their stories."

The Court System. "Oh, yes," Rodrigo replied. "Law disaggregates and atomizes, treating as separate many grievances that have a group dimension. This leaves the litigant lonely and without allies. It encourages her to think about her own grievance, not those of the group."

"I can think of a few ways it does this," I chimed in. "Doctrines of standing and real party in interest limit who can sue or be sued. While joinder is possible to a degree, and class actions are possible in some situations...."

"Although we both know how the federal courts have been cutting back on that vehicle in recent years," Rodrigo interjected. "They insist on satisfaction of the minimum amount in controversy for every plaintiff, for example, and require notice to all class members who are identifiable through reasonable effort. These make group redress—out of which a group story may grow—difficult."

"True. But other features play a role, too. Courts are bound by precedent, which may contain bad stories. If the only narrative law recognizes is a bad one—one that requires that you demean yourself or tell your story in a strange and contorted way, or jump through very high hoops even to be heard at all—you will not choose to tell your story there very often. Judges' experiences and life perspectives are those of a certain class. Very few judges are African American, lesbian, disabled, or from a working-class background. Since their experience is limited, judges may be ill-equipped to understand your plea. Rules relating to ripeness, mootness, and standing mean that the court can only consider the case before it, not the broad story of dashed hopes and centuries-long mistreatment that afflicts an entire people and forms the historical and cultural background of your complaint. And the decree, even if favorable, will fix only your story, not that of others, especially after recent cutbacks in res judicata law and the class action vehicle. In short, courts are ill-equipped to hear and act on the stories many in our society most urgently need to tell."

"Another way of putting it," Rodrigo said, summing up, "is what I'm thinking of calling the reconstructive paradox. It's an aspect of what you said just now. It begins by observing that the greater the evil—say, black or female subjugation—the more entrenched it will be. The more entrenched any evil, the more massive the social effort required to dislodge it. An entrenched social evil will be invisible to many—maybe most—in the culture, simply because it is embedded, entrenched, and ordinary-seeming. The massive social effort will inevitably collide with other social values, settled expectations, the way things are, and so on. It will entail dislocations, new priorities, and spending shifts. These latter efforts, civil rights marches, for example, or revisions in college curricula, will be highly visible, by contrast, and will spark resistance and opposition. One is apt to be characterized as 'Big Brother,' a fascist, a reverse racist, and so on. Resistance then will feel principled to the resister, because the other side will appear to be sacrificing real liberty, real money for a nebulous and dubious social goal, like helping blacks."

"Reconstruction and reform, then," I said gloomily, "will always seem unprincipled, premature, wrong, and will spark resistance—until one hundred years later when consciousness changes, at which time we will look back and wonder how we possibly could have resisted that."

[Eds. Rodrigo concludes by offering two solutions to the false-empathy dilemma. In one, whites take on the role of "race traitor." In the other, they subvert the system from within.]

PART II
Critical Theory

In this section Delgado uses classical tools of critical race theory, such as structural determinism, interest convergence, differential racialization, the critique of neutral principles, social construction, and racial realism, to evaluate conventional social thought and law.

In the opening selection, "The Racial Double Helix," Delgado uses structural determinism and differential racialization to show how society replicates a hierarchy of social relations in a kind of triple helix consisting of three strands: race relations, economics and class, and culture.

"Rodrigo's Fourth Chronicle" examines the role that neutral principles and colorblindness play in antidiscrimination law. Rodrigo and the Professor discuss two types of equality: The first, equality of opportunity—advocated by conservatives—places everyone at the same starting line, even though a level playing field disadvantages racial minorities whose lives are very different from those of whites. The second, equality of results—the liberals' approach—examines why whites almost always end up at the finish line first.

"Rodrigo's Eighth Chronicle" uses statistics, interest convergence, and social construction to show that the cost and harm of black crime pale by comparison with those of white-collar crime, though society perceives the former to be the greater threat.

Rodrigo proposes a radical civil rights strategy called legal instrumentalism in the "Ninth Chronicle," declaring that minorities might as well adopt an instrumental view of law as an institution, summoning and following it when it serves their interests and ignoring or breaking it when it does not.

"Linking Arms" presents Delgado's skeptical assessment of the possibility of coalitions between racial groups in seeking change that will work for the betterment of all groups. After laying out an algebra of intergroup dynamics and past efforts, he cautions that the hope for successful coalitions may be a vain one.

The Racial Double Helix
Watson, Crick, and *Brown v. Board of Education*

INTRODUCTION: CULTURAL DNA

Legal interpretation takes place in a field of pain and death.

But even that graphic statement by Robert Cover—perhaps the most famous ever written in a law review article—may understate. It is not merely that judges' dockets are full of murders, rapes, assaults, and other forms of gore that they are left to clean up because no one else will. Courts are also the *agents* of pain and death. They deal in it, dish it out, and administer it, both directly and indirectly. When they impose capital punishment on a homeless, mentally retarded man who spent his last years in a shelter, was addicted to alcohol and drugs, and suffered abuse as a youth, they administer death. Their hands are not tied; courts in many other countries do not do that sort of thing, and even here it is generally possible to find a way around it.

But courts also administer another, more subtle, kind of death when they ruthlessly suppress a narrative which differs from the one law recognizes—for example, that of the same homeless man who explodes in a drunken rage, haunted by visions that no one else sees, and kills another unfortunate soul over some incomprehensible dispute. That defendant does not get to tell his story—unless his mental illness meets the current legal standard of insanity. And courts do this sort of thing every time, not just every now and then. They do it intrinsically, inherently, and by their very nature. That is what they are in the business of doing—killing narratives by a process of framing, winnowing, limiting, and shortening what one is allowed to say.

Unless you are very lucky, so that your story is absolutely standard—absolutely aligned with convention and social power—you cannot tell that story, as you might want to tell it, to a court. The rules of evidence force you to tell only a stylized version of it. No hearsay, no opinion, please. And you cannot tell it out of your own mouth, in your own way, and without interruption. No—you must have your lawyer pull it out of you, one fact at a time, in response to questions and subject to the other side's objections if you stray too far from the kind of story the court wants to hear. The other side then gets to cross-examine you to carve up your story even further. The story you end up telling is not your own, not the one you would recount if you were telling it to a friend. You do not feel that comfortable with it; it is not you, in a way. But now the other side asks you probing questions—do you really believe that story, the one that is not yours? Why did you hesitate just now over this or that detail? Why did your story deviate in some minor respect from the one you told the police when you were excited and scared six months ago? If you fail to answer those questions the right way, the jury will find against you. You may even be found guilty of perjury and sent to jail.

Take another case. An immigrant appears before an administrative judge to ask for sanctuary. She wants asylum because she knows how to read, and back home they think she is a witch or a subversive. Or she joined the wrong church or disobeyed her husband and he beat her. The judge will interrupt—"But did you fear imminent bodily harm or death?" The woman hesitates. "Not exactly." But her life was intolerable. She could not stand it. So she fled. Anyone would. But the judge does not want to hear that story. He would hear another story, one that is not hers, not the way she would put it. But it is the only one the judge can hear.

So, courts carve up your stories into little, unfamiliar pieces, and then quiz you to see if you really believe in each of them. They kill your narrative and transform it into something you do not recognize. They force you to choose and defend a past that is unfamiliar to you—one that is not yours. This is a great injury and a form of systemic injustice. It alters memory and reorganizes a person's past for them. Systematically falsifying someone's life story is the epistemological analog of a stroke—a sudden cessation of blood to a part of the brain that causes part of it to die, erases memory and self-concept, requiring arduous rehabilitation, or bringing death, or death in life.

Or think of amnesia and the plight of people who, because of an accident or blow to the head, have lost their memory. Amnesia fascinates us because it deprives the sufferers of their sense of who they are. Their narratives are gone. They cannot tell the story of their lives anymore. They can be told who they are, but they still have lost their own self-narrative. They can recount the facts of their lives, but only because they memorize, not remember, them, as though they were the facts of another person's life.

Stroke and amnesia are terrifying because they destroy memory, the common thread of narrative. In killing a person's narrative capacity, they kill her as a person, leaving just a mass of skin, nerves, and bones. Law does much the same, although unlike a stroke, it is purposive. It commits narrative violence with an agenda in mind—its own, not yours and mine.

How does society replicate itself? How is it that the hierarchy of race remains almost exactly the same from year to year, decade to decade, century to century, with whites on top and people of color on the bottom? And with an earnings gap year after year of seventy-one cents on the dollar, sometimes a little more, sometimes a little less? In other ways our society exhibits a great deal of change. Cities grow or wither. Markets rise or fall. Regions gain or lose population. Companies succeed or fail. Products catch on or do not. Styles and fads succeed one another. One corporation makes its shareholders rich, another loses all its money and has to fire its workers and raid their pension funds to pay for golden parachutes for the president and the board. But the gap between whites and non-white minorities remains remarkably the same year after year, and that holds true whether you look at wages, longevity, infant mortality, school completion, family wealth, or anything else.

Fifty years ago, *Brown v. Board of Education* declared that racial segregation in public schools violated the equal protection guarantee of the United States Constitution. But in that same year, the nation also saw the publication of a scientific paper that began with the words, "we wish to suggest a structure for the salt of deoxyribose nucleic acid (D.N.A.)." The authors went on to describe that structure as a "double helix," with two spiral chains coiled around a single axis, paired in such a way as to repair and communicate genetic information needed by all living cells. We refer, of course, to James Watson and Francis Crick's discovery of the basic building block of life, the genetic code that enables organisms to replicate themselves generation after generation.

Two astonishing, world-transforming events in the same twelve-month period. As we write [Eds. 2004], celebrations are ringing out across the land for both. The double helix won the Nobel Prize for Watson and Crick. The question we pose is: Why not a Nobel Prize for the legal scholar or social scientist who figures out how *racial relations* replicate themselves, endlessly and ineluctably, generation after generation—the scholar who figures out why, fifty years after *Brown*, more black children attend segregated schools than did then, or even, what made *Brown* necessary in the first place. Our Constitution and Declaration of Independence declare freedom and equal rights transcendent values. How *did* slavery, Jim Crow, and separate but equal accommodations take root in a nation dedicated to those lofty values?

One would think that this discovery would be just as important as learning how a cell on your nose knows to grow into a nose and not, say, an ear. After all, learning the basic mechanisms by which the people on the top and their children stay on the top would seem to be just as vital a piece of information as knowing how a nose turns into a nose. An old adage holds that the most valuable thing to man is man. What it means is that if forced to choose between a friend and an invention or tool, one should choose the friend every time. Social relations, networks, and knowledge determine what capital we are born with, where we go to school, what solidarity we can count on, what chances we have in life, and where we and our children are apt to wind up. As they say, it is all heredity and environment. Watson and Crick won a Nobel Prize for figuring out the secret of heredity. How about the other half—environment?

One legal scholar who has contributed greatly to this other kind of knowledge—the way racial reality perpetuates itself—is Derrick Bell, author of path-breaking articles on school desegregation, the price of racial remedies, interest-convergence, and the structure of legal thought. Why no award for Bell? He has contributed a body of social knowledge as vital as Watson and Crick's discoveries, indeed probably as vital as ninety-five percent of those inventors and academic entrepreneurs who constitute the marquee of intellectual side-shows that make up Big Science.

Yet, honors go to legal figures who *obscure* how power works, how law enables the haves always to come out ahead, and how our system, even, of race-remedies law, subjugates its supposed beneficiaries. Consider Herbert Wechsler, the author of a famous *Harvard Law Review* article that declared *Brown* unprincipled, and instead, advocated a colorblind, neutralist approach under which *Plessy v. Ferguson* would probably still be the law of the land. He received honors and plaudits for raising such a troubling question. You see, for a formalist like Wechsler, *Brown* traded the rights of blacks to associate with whites for the rights of whites *not* to associate with blacks, without adequate justification—never mind history, never mind the obvious symbolism of separate but equal Jim Crow laws.

For his pains, Wechsler won widespread recognition, and his article has been cited hundreds of times. Yet, if courts insisted on his sort of neutral principle—one that justified a racial remedy without mentioning or taking account of race—they would not find it, at least not easily. So, the law of equality would stall, and school boards could continue to assign little black and brown kids to separate schools. Formalist analysis allows you to do just this: freeze the law, hide narratives such as the history of slavery, conceal the operation of official power, and maybe even, indirectly, kill little black kids, all the while masking what you have done. Narrative violence, pure and simple.

* * *

HOW DOES CULTURE REPLICATE ITSELF?

The structure of racial reality is a triple helix, consisting of blacks, Latinos, and Asians, arrayed in an unending sequence—a little like the stripes on a barber's pole—with each transmitting information to the others in response to outside forces so that things seem to be happening, but the whole system remains in equilibrium. That structure, in turn, is part of a larger helix, with economic and cultural relations constituting the other strands. Economic relations replicate by means of the laws of surplus value, artificially stimulated consumer demands, colonialism, immigration policy, and a weak labor movement. Karl Marx, 100 years ago, knew as much about this strand as anybody, although we must say, conservative Republicans seem to have figured out a few additional mechanisms of their own in recent years. Culture replicates itself through ever-larger media conglomerates, aggressive marketing, and the manipulation of public tastes. Andrew Ross, Judith Butler, Chon Noriega, and Spike Lee deserve serious recognition for their work in decoding *these* structures. We have, in short, a triple helix within a triple helix of forces. The remainder of this excerpt concerns itself with the racial strand, but it is worth noting that each of the strands—race, class, and culture—communicates with and limits the others, so that no one strand can be fully understood in isolation from the rest. Like the stripes on a barber's pole.

The Structure of Racial Reality
Racial reality in the United States consists of three large minority groups and a few smaller ones, in rough equilibrium vis-à-vis whites. The mechanisms of that equilibrium are seven in number, the first four having to do with interest-convergence.

INTEREST-CONVERGENCE MECHANISMS

Mechanism One: Pitting Outgroups, Including Poor Whites, Against Each Other

If one examines the history of minority groups in the United States, one is struck by how one group is often gaining ground at the very time another is losing it. For example, between 1846 and 1848, the United States was fighting an imperialist war against Mexico, at the end of which it walked away with roughly one-half of that nation's territory. After the war ended with the Treaty of Guadalupe Hidalgo, federal officials looked the other way while crafty lawyers and crooked local administrators conspired with land-hungry Anglos in the Southwest to cheat the Mexicans who chose to remain in the U.S. of their ancestral lands. Yet only a few years after this happened, the North fought an equally bloody war against the South, ostensibly to free the slaves. Gallantry and honor on behalf of one group; infamy, for another.

During Reconstruction, the country disbanded slavery, enacted the Fourteenth Amendment, and wrote black suffrage into the law. But society's generosity turned out to be selective—in 1871, Congress passed the Indian Appropriations Act, providing that no Indian nation would be sovereign and capable of entering into further treaties with the United States. Only eight years later, California adopted a constitutional provision that made it a crime to employ Chinese workers, after which Congress, in 1882, enacted the Chinese Exclusion Act that the Supreme Court obligingly upheld in *Chae Chan Ping v. United States*. And, just a few years later, the Dawes Act destroyed joint land tenure for Indians, resulting in the loss of nearly two-thirds of Indian land. In 1913, California enacted the Alien Land Law under which aliens ineligible for naturalization could not lease land for more than three years, a measure that devastated Japanese farming. Yet, during World War I, Congress *eased* immigration quotas for Mexicans who were needed to work on large farms in California and the West.

The history of minority groups in the U.S. thus demonstrates that one group gains ground at the expense of another's losing its tenuous grip. Oftentimes this does not seem to be accidental; rather, whites have affirmatively pitted one minority group against another in the struggle for opportunities and rights. [Eds. Delgado and his coauthor give four examples.]

No group is immune from this elaborate dance, including poor whites. As Derrick Bell and others have pointed out, one of the most important features of our system of white-over-black exploitation is interest-convergence: White elites arrange that black gains come only when they will also advance white self-interest. A corollary explains why working-class whites cast their lot with elite whites, when one would think that they would advance their interests more effectively by joining with blacks and Latinos to challenge their common exploiters. This happens because elite whites convey to their working-class counterparts the idea that blacks covet their paltry prerogatives and that poor whites are better off maintaining a sharp separation between themselves and those at the true bottom of society.

So society arranges things so that minority groups exchange places on the triple helix spiral, always and endlessly, with one now up a little, and the others down, and the groups trading places every now and then as society's needs change. This is the first, and perhaps the most fundamental, way empowered groups keep racial relations replicating and in perfect equilibrium.

Mechanism Two: Legal Formalism

Law plays an important role in the maintenance of our system of racial hierarchy, with certain groups on top and other ones at the bottom of the well. Race law through most of our history has meant discrimination law—a congeries of restrictive covenants, school assignment rules, Jim Crow laws, racist immigration statutes, alien land laws, Chinese Exclusion Acts, and anti-miscegenation laws that kept black, brown, red, and yellow people down. Anti-discrimination law, which one might have thought an exception, does much the same thing, narrowing, regularizing, and limiting the pace of change, persuading us that all is well, and providing periodic opportunities for rejoicing—like 2004 [Eds. The 50th anniversary of *Brown*]—so that newspaper editors and a multitude of liberals can persuade themselves that American society, while not perfect, still is the fairest, most non-racist, most inclusive society on earth, when it still has a very long way to go.

One way law does this is through formalism, which is ascendant right now. By downplaying power, emotion, history, context, purpose, justice, and equity, in favor of text and precedent, formalism keeps a great deal of the messiness of life out of view. For a formalist, a landlord can evict a poor single mother by giving three days' notice and reciting a few boilerplate facts. An execution is just if it is formally correct and the trial afforded the suspect all his rights. A war is formally just if Congress declares it or if the President gets that body to pass a resolution. Never mind that it is pre-emptive, the cause fabricated, and the real objective to impose U.S. power on a weak but resource-rich nation.

You can be a devotee of law and economics—a modern variety of formalism—and persuade yourself that efficiency is the chief criterion of any sensible set of laws, and that justice, fairness, or the past does not matter. Economic narratives are legal, those others merely sentimental.

The formalist is, of course, color-blind in matters of race, so that laws that disadvantage whites are just as suspect as ones that handicap Latinos, blacks, and other minorities. He is also color- and gender-blind in thinking that reasonable man standards, which select the favored group's perspective as the normative baseline for legal doctrine, are fair for everyone. By concealing how power works, how history has contributed to pervasive inequalities of wealth and power, and how the practical effect of affirmative action is radically different from that of a Jim Crow law intended to marginalize black railroad passengers, the formalist assures that the pace of social and racial change is glacial. The formalist can even persuade many of the general public that blind justice is best and anything else judicial activism.

Mechanism Three: The Diversity Rationale for Affirmative Action
As formalism is to conservatives, the diversity rationale in constitutional law is to liberals—a mechanism that papers over a great deal of blood, pain, and death embodied in a 400-year history of racist oppression in favor of a cheerful, forward-looking approach to racial remedies.

Consider that one can justify affirmative action in two ways, one backward, the other forward looking. A remedial rationale requires institutions that have discriminated against minorities in the past to make them whole—to put them in the condition they would have enjoyed had the institution not discriminated against them. If an employer, for example, is shown to have discriminated against blacks, it must give them an edge in hiring until the deficiency is made up. The law will tolerate, or even require, that degree of race-consciousness.

But in the university setting, a different justification—the diversity rationale—comes into play. It permits institutions to consider race in faculty hiring and student admissions in order to achieve a diverse intellectual community.

Many universities have perpetuated discrimination as pervasive and clear-cut as any you are apt to find in the employment sphere, including all-white admissions policies and fraternities, segregated dorms, Jewish quotas, and alumni preferences for children, all of whom just happen to be white. Universities have also collaborated with agribusiness to drive small farmers and migrant workers out of business and away from lands big farmers coveted. Expert academic witnesses have testified to the degraded condition of minority communities and the inability of their children to learn, thus inscribing a deeper stereotype in the minds of legislators, social workers, and teachers.

Despite, or perhaps because of, all this, universities, abetted by liberal lawyers and administrators, unerringly select the diversity rationale when conservatives challenge race-conscious admissions and hiring. It is easy to see why—the remedial rationale would require them to disclose much about their past that they would just as soon leave buried. The lives of great figures whose names grace campus buildings and statues, for example, may reveal a dark side—they might have been slaveowners, merchants who profited from the slave trade, or leaders of raids against Indians, and so on. Diversity emerges as a much safer rationale. With it, one simply observes that society would be better off with a few more black or Latino engineers (which it would), and lets it go at that. The jaded white professor would get an edgy, ghetto-style answer to his standard Socratic question from time to time, and so on.

Not only is diversity a rather pallid, morally unimaginative way to approach campus integration, it suppresses stories about universities' own racism and discrimination that would be better aired and reckoned with. The diversity rationale, in great favor among liberals, kills off these stories, making them irrelevant, the province of a few hotheads who want to stir up trouble and are unwilling to let bygones be bygones.

Mechanism Four: Alternative Dispute Resolution
A related mechanism, much favored by a certain type of liberal, is Alternative Dispute Resolution (ADR). The liberal counterpart of formalism in legal process, ADR treats

conflict as pathology, adjusting disputants to their roles in life, and pretending that individual and class conflict are not inevitable and necessary parts of our system, which they are. Nonformal chambers like mediation, arbitration, and consumer complaint panels magnify power differentials and increase the likelihood of a judgment based on race or status. Courts kill stories—mediation kills dreams.

[Eds. The authors discuss three additional mechanisms based on differential racialization, then conclude as follows.]

CONCLUSION

This excerpt explains how social relations, especially in the area of race, remain the same, year after year, with only minor changes in position. *Brown* set out to dismantle one aspect of that hierarchy—separate but equal school attendance laws. What about the rest of it?

Brown was decided fifty years ago. But that same year saw another celebrated event, when James Watson and Francis Crick won a Nobel Prize for their discovery of the structure of DNA, the building block of life. But as important as the laws that govern heredity are, the ones that govern social relations and expectations are just as important to the average citizen, since they determine much about the treatment you receive, your opportunity for upward mobility, and where you wind up.

We described social reality as a triple helix, consisting of race, class, and culture, each governed by cross-cutting forces and laws. Beginning with the role of the legal system, we first addressed legal storytelling and story-killing. We showed how law writes "in a field of pain and death," and does so daily, regularly, and routinely, sometimes by killing actual human beings but at other times by suppressing their narratives or life stories—that is to say, everything that they deem most vital, most personal about themselves. And it does this selectively—some stories routinely emerge mangled or rejected while others get through quite nicely. Then, focusing on race, we showed how society, with the law in constant attendance, maintains the three large racial minority groups in equilibrium—a bit like a triple helix or a barber's pole with three colors—succeeding and chasing each other in various designated ways, sometimes actively pitted against each other, but always and endlessly transmitting information and exchanging locations in a complex matrix with whites always on top.

We showed how a narrow, formalistic conception of legal reasoning neatly conceals how this happens and limits inquiry to a few stereotyped issues, about which it makes a great fuss, excluding much more important ones, such as distributive justice, history, and who benefits and who loses from the various rules.

We explained how liberals participate in this process when they choose a favorite constitutional narrative—diversity—over reparations in the debate over affirmative action. We also took liberals to task for helping conceal this country's racial histories, as the diversity rationale does, as well as for promoting ADR. The liberal counterpart of formalism in legal process, ADR treats conflict as pathology, adjusting disputants to their roles and pretending that individual and class conflict is not an inevitable and necessary part of our system, which it is.

We then discussed a series of measures having to do with differential racialization, including racial binaries, pet groups, and civil rights triumphalism. These, then, are our candidates for the nucleotide bases in the structure of cultural DNA, the collection of forces that keep race relations more or less the same, with minor shifts in position, from decade to decade.

Rodrigo's Fourth Chronicle
Neutrality and Stasis in Antidiscrimination Law

INTRODUCTION: IN WHICH RODRIGO AND I COMMISERATE AND CATCH UP WITH DEVELOPMENTS IN EACH OTHER'S LIVES

I was in my office late one afternoon, puzzling over how to incorporate four recent books addressing the role of courts in protecting minority rights into the next edition of my casebook. I was getting nowhere when a familiar lanky figure appeared as though by magic in my doorway.

"Rodrigo!" I exclaimed. "I'm glad to see you. Please come in." I peered at him closely. The usually ebullient Rodrigo stood in my doorway, looking down. "Is something wrong?"

"Well, as a matter of fact, yes. Do you have a minute? I tried phoning first, but you were out."

"Of course," I assured him, gladly pushing the four books aside. A discussion with Rodrigo was always a welcome break from my work. "The last time we talked, things were going well for you. You had won that writing prize and were hot on the track of a second paper that sounded intriguing. Has school taken a turn for the worse?"

"Well, yes. And in a way, it has to do with the paper that I am working on."

"I'd like to hear about it. Can I offer you a cup of coffee? I have a new coffeemaker."

"Yes, thanks. Oh—Giannina and I have one of those." Rodrigo examined my new gadget with interest. "We have the smaller version."

As I busied myself measuring the grounds and setting the switches, my visitor inquired: "Does your law school have an annual 'libel show,' Professor?"

"Yes. I think most do. Here, they're called the Follies—a little singing, some bad dancing, and a lot of good-natured mockery of the professors. They're a good way for students to let off steam, although the faculty sometimes grumble over the irreverent way they are portrayed."

"We had something similar back in Italy, too. But the one they had at my school this year set a new low. Half the skits were antifemale or antiminority. One made fun of affirmative action; another, of gays and lesbians. A third, perhaps the most tasteless of all, lampooned a gay scholar who had died less than a year earlier of AIDS—even though his one-time lover and young son were in the audience."

"In bad taste, to say the least," I commented. "Did anyone do anything about it?"

"A number of students and several of the faculty complained and signed a petition demanding action. But the administration did nothing. Several faculty members sided with the students who produced the show. They said that, despite the odiousness of some of the ideas expressed, it was free speech."

"Reminds me of the position certain liberal organizations take on the campus hate-speech controversy. They deplore racism and racist remarks but throw up their hands and say there is little we can do because cracking down would violate the mighty First Amendment."

"I know. But that's only the beginning. When the administration refused to take action, my group of nearly fifty LL.M. students decided to produce a show of our own. It was a kind of counter-parody. We made fun of the original production, as well as of a number of law school institutions, practices, and sacred cows. Many of us are from foreign countries, so we chose targets that struck us as funny about the U.S. or legal education here."

"And what happened?"

"A huge crowd turned out—probably as big as for the original event, even though we didn't serve alcohol. The crowd loved it. We satirized the Socratic method, recruiting season, casebooks with unanswerable questions, ultraconservative student organizations, and professors who take seven months to grade bluebooks that we write in three hours."

"Sounds inoffensive enough. How did this get you in trouble?"

"One of our skits poked fun at the law school for currying favor with rich alumni. We called the skit 'Blood Money' and performed it to the music of a popular tune. When word got out, one well-known donor rescinded his pledge to give the law school $3 million for a new library. The administration was furious. Several of us got letters reprimanding us for conduct inimical to the institution. Others of us were told informally that we had better not count on the school's help in getting teaching jobs."

"No small threat," I acknowledged. "If your program is at all like ours, most of the LL.M.s are there because they want to become academics. What's the point of getting the degree if you can't teach later?"

Rodrigo shrugged and then continued, "I couldn't help but be struck by the different treatment of the two programs. The first one was raunchy, meanspirited, and really pretty amateurish. Ours was much more lighthearted and, if I may say so, literate. Giannina helped with the lyrics—as you may know, she's a published playwright."

"No, I didn't know." Actually, I had not yet met Giannina, Rodrigo's companion, and was curious to find out more about her.

"So, the words were really funny. Swiftian, even Voltairean, in their deftness. But it made no difference to the administration. We all received reprimands, and now I'm not sure I'll be able to get a job."

"Rodrigo, don't worry. You're a top graduate of a major law school and winner of a national prize for student writing. You'll do fine."

"I hope so," Rodrigo responded, a little uneasily. "But the whole business got me thinking about neutrality and colorblindness. As you may recall, my second paper—the one I'm writing for that other contest—"

"You mean the one sponsored by the conservative organization?" I interjected.

"Yes, that one. I've been struggling with a way to articulate just what's wrong with neutrality. It seems logical to think that a society that sets out scrupulously to treat blacks and whites alike in every setting—jobs, housing, education, credit, and the like—should have no discrimination. Yet it obviously doesn't work that way."

"Rodrigo, I know you're widely read. But possibly you don't know that a number of us in the critical race theory movement have been saying just that: Mainstream jurisprudence's neutrality is bogus, a mask, a cover. In feminist theory, Catharine MacKinnon has been saying the same thing—that the law's procedural regularity, its emphasis on 'legality,' serves to conceal and legitimate an antiwoman bias. So, your observation, while trenchant, is not particularly novel, although in light of your recent experience I can see why it preoccupies you. Would you like me to refer you to some things to read?" I reached for the four books on the corner of my desk and began mentally composing a short additional reading list that would get Rodrigo started. In a moment, I regretted my offer.

"I've read those," Rodrigo replied levelly. "And I've read you, and Bell, and MacKinnon, and Freeman, and many others on this subject. But I want to go further."

I could feel the blood rushing into the tiny capillaries in my face. I should have known better than to patronize Rodrigo. If not two steps ahead of me, he's almost always at my own level.

"What do you mean, 'go further'?" I asked quickly, in part to cover my own gaffe, but also because I very much wanted to hear his thoughts. Perhaps Rodrigo could help me discover a way to incorporate the four books I had been struggling with into my teaching materials.

"Many critical race theorists condemn neutrality and colorblindness as merely maintaining the racial advantage of whites. But, aside from presenting the 'playing field' or 'starting line' analogy, they offer little explanation of *why* this is so."

"The coffee's almost ready. I assume you have some thoughts about this?"

"I do."

"I'd love to hear them. Let me wash out these cups."

IN WHICH RODRIGO EXPLAINS HOW NEUTRAL PRINCIPLES OF CONSTITUTIONAL LAW DISADVANTAGE OUTSIDERS

When I returned, Rodrigo was leafing through one of the books on my desk.

"I must correct myself," he said. "I haven't read this one. It looks like it's still in manuscript form."

"It is," I confirmed. "The author, Professor Spann, was kind enough to supply me with an advance copy. It's an expansion of his *Michigan Law Review* article."

"*Pure Politics?*" Rodrigo asked. "I read that article. I thought it was brilliant. He urges black people to stop relying on the Supreme Court as an instrument of social progress, and to concentrate instead on 'pure politics'—mass force, marches, and protests, as well as elections and representative government. Is that what his new book is about?"

"That and more."

"And does he explain what it is about the Supreme Court's fascination with neutrality that causes it to hand down one hurtful decision after another?"

"Not in the version of the manuscript that I have."

"That's disappointing," Rodrigo lamented. "None of the good leftist scholars seem to have addressed that question. And the right-wingers," Rodrigo continued, gesturing toward two of the books on my desk, "agree that the courts haven't been able to effect sweeping social change. But, unlike the folks on the left, they're not upset about that; they think it's fine. In their view, a neutralist, quietist Supreme Court is simply performing its assigned role in our political system."

As I mulled over Rodrigo's observation, I noticed that my coffeemaker had stopped making noise. "Ready for a cup?" I asked, rising from my chair. Rodrigo nodded enthusiastically. I poured two mugfuls of steaming espresso and handed one to Rodrigo. Sitting back down, I urged Rodrigo, "So tell me what you think lies at the bottom of it. I mean, if a legal system sincerely sets out to treat a person of color and a white exactly the same in every situation that counts, this should in the long run produce something like rough equality, shouldn't it?"

"But it's impossible to assume away the short run," Rodrigo countered. "African Americans and whites live in vastly different circumstances, as we discussed last time. I think the reason for the paradox has to do with the unspoken background against which people make all of these ostensibly neutral decisions."

"In other words," I mused, "are you saying that the various decisionmakers—employers, apartment managers, admissions committees, and so on—strive to decide fairly, but carry around subconscious biases that make it impossible to be truly impartial?"

"That's part of it," Rodrigo replied. "But there's more. Legal and cultural decisions are made against a background of assumptions, interpretations, and implied exceptions, things everyone in our culture understands but which seldom, if ever, get expressed explicitly."

"And I suppose you are going to say that all those assumptions favor whites?"

"Of course. And they have at least as much efficacy as law on the books."

"Could you give me an example?" I persisted. "It still seems to me that if every relevant decisionmaker sets out to treat two individuals, A and B, identically even though one is white and the other black, then we have achieved formal equality. How," I asked with a wry smile, "can a system like this possibly disadvantage minorities?"

"Take a different kind of promise," Rodrigo said, eyeing my coffee machine. The young wunderkind set a fast pace; I was happy to see he needed fuel from time to time, too.

"Like another cup?"

"In a minute. Let's say that a father promises his son a trip to the ice cream parlor if the child cleans up his room. The child says, 'No matter what?' The father answers, 'Sure.' So the child cleans up his room, but the father never ends up taking him out for the ice cream."

"Hmm," I murmured, turning the hypothetical over in my mind. "I suppose the father had an excuse of some sort?" I recalled with no small measure of guilt times in my own life as a parent when I had done something similar.

"Right. The father says, 'You couldn't have thought that I meant that you had *three whole days* just to clean that little room.' Or, the day after the promise, the local ice cream parlor goes out of business, and the nearest shop is an hour away. Or, the father loses his job. Or, the car develops engine trouble or suffers some other mishap and has to go to the garage, and the only way to get the cone would be for the two to take a $10 cab ride. Or, the child develops a milk allergy. It turns out, then, that the father's promise assumed dozens of conditions, implied exceptions, and unstated excuses. Although the father never spelled these out, he insists the child must have known of them. The same sort of unstated conditions underlie our society's promises of racial equality."

"So, you are saying that just as all the terms of the argument favor the father, legal decisionmakers construe the interpretive structure in a manner that inevitably favors whites and disadvantages nonwhites in situations like the ones we've been talking about? And they do this, you're saying, not because they're biased, but rather because they're fully acculturated members of society?"

"Exactly!" Rodrigo replied with animation that I didn't think was entirely due to the high caffeine content of my mocha java beans, obtained from a new supplier. "Imagine an African American applies for a job on the faculty of an institution like yours. The only other candidate for the position is white. The hiring committee declares its intention to use only scrupulously race-neutral criteria."

"Yet, the white gets the position, right?"

"Yes. Even though the two candidates went to the same law school, got the same grades—you name it—a difference will emerge, and that difference is not part of the formal, written criteria. One turns out to have a more pleasant demeanor than the other. The white strikes the hiring committee as better at small talk. The white has more seniority, more solid job experience, better 'communication skills,' or a stronger recommendation from a better-known professor. It turns out that the new merit criteria just happen to favor the white applicant. None of these requirements was mentioned in the formal job description circulated or advertised by the employer."

"Yet everyone knows they're there. The formal, 'on the books' rule—the only one explicitly stated—looks magnificently fair: 'Treat blacks and whites exactly the same.' But the cultural backdrop skews the application of the rule, producing discriminatory results," I summarized. "I bet you think this explains why the LL.M. skit got you into trouble, while those students who put on the main event got off unpunished."

"Exactly," Rodrigo replied. "There turned out to be an implied exception to the rule that satires are acceptable. Free speech reigns unless you poke fun at certain things or cause a wealthy alum to put his checkbook away."

"I'm sure that alum will reconsider once the fuss dies down. Alums love having their names prominently displayed on buildings, classrooms, and lounges throughout the law school. It reminds them of the good old days."

"Even if the law school is changing—if the composition of the student body and faculty is radically different from the way he remembers?" pressed Rodrigo.

"You may have a point. But in all fairness, I think the *original* skitsters would have earned retribution, too, if their program caused a rich alum to revoke a donation." I stopped, realizing I was uncomfortably close to apologizing for the system. Was I losing my own critical edge? I had a birthday coming up, and this had been on my mind for a while.

Rodrigo shot me an appraising look so I backtracked slightly. "I do agree with you that the one case called up the 'boys will be boys' excuse, and not the other. The school's reaction does seem more than a little harsh."

"Maybe I'll have my friend Ali write a letter asking the donor to reconsider. Ali's a great conciliator. Maybe he can remind the wealthy philanthropist that the true test of a great law school lies in its ability to withstand vigorous criticism, and that the LL.M. skit simply confirmed his old school's greatness."

"I'm sure it wouldn't hurt your job chances if he did," I added.

Rodrigo was silent for a while. Then, returning to his critique of neutrality, he posed another hypothetical: "Maybe this is a way to explain it. Imagine that a lawn treatment chemical turns out to be virulently poisonous. The suburbs disappear. Overnight, white people become a minority who must now deal with blacks (and other racial minorities) from a position of weakness. A long tradition of black subculture holds that one may freely disparage and ridicule anyone who is a 'jerk.' The definition of 'jerk' is a person who is naive, slow at sports, bad at repartee, lacking in street smarts. A whole culture of songs, myths, stories, and the like derides people who fit this description. Let's suppose that unflattering concept just happens to be associated, fairly or unfairly, with people who have light skins. Is there any doubt that in the new regime, white people would come out second-best, even if they were just as talented, smart, deserving, and motivated as members of the new majority group?"

"A vivid example, if a little far-fetched," I replied. "I can see how whites would end up second-best even if blacks set out to treat them fairly, humanely, and even-handedly. The background assumptions would cause them to lose out in the race for jobs, slots in law school classes, and so on, even if all the rules were colorblind."

I flipped the switch on the coffee warmer to "On." "But let's return to the world at hand. Much of the action these days concerns retributive, not distributive justice. White society has already figured out, to its own satisfaction at least, how to go about distributing jobs and other benefits to blacks—namely, very stintingly. But the attention is now beginning to focus on the remedial aspects of civil rights strategy—on what society should do, in light of its past mistreatment of blacks. How does your cultural background argument work here, Rodrigo?"

"In much the same way," Rodrigo confidently replied, rising and walking over to my coffeemaker. "May I?"

"Of course. The sugar and creamer are over there."

Rodrigo poured himself a second cup, while I marveled at his youthful constitution. "If you want decaffeinated, I can brew some," I offered.

Rodrigo made a face and returned to his chair, where he began gulping his steaming-hot high-octane. "Implied exceptions arise there, too. Any remedy for past discrimination must not be too costly to whites. So-called 'innocent' whites may not be made to pay the penalty for past injustices. Decrees may not bind whites who are not members of a class before the court. Discrimination is not redressable unless an intent to discriminate can be proven. Harms are not compensable unless tight chains of causation are shown. Standing rules limit who may complain. And so on."

"So, essentially what you're saying is that the dominant culture has somehow managed to take the sting out of civil rights remedies?" I asked.

"Right," Rodrigo responded.

"You know, Rodrigo," I said, "I think you may be onto something. Many of us critical race theorists have written about the way in which the costs of racial remedies always seem to be placed on blacks—the faces at the bottom of the well. Your insight helps explain why."

Rodrigo drained his cup. "Neutral rules rarely detect many breaches of the principle of nondiscrimination," Rodrigo continued. "And, when they do, they remedy those violations in as innocuous a way as possible."

"How does partisan politics affect all of this? Do you think it makes much difference whether the conservatives or the liberals are in power?"

"Not much," Rodrigo answered. "Partisan distinctions may be important in other areas, such as economic policy or foreign relations, but they make little difference for minorities. Both liberals and conservatives embrace neutrality in antidiscrimination law, as though treating blacks and whites exactly the same will make discrimination go away. We fare no better under one regime than the other."

"I'm not sure I'd go that far, Rodrigo," I asserted. "Obviously, rules dictating equal treatment of minorities and whites can't redress longstanding discrimination. But you must admit, such rules are better than the old blatantly racist ones. Perhaps they are way stations to something better."

"Maybe," Rodrigo replied somewhat skeptically. "But they can also lead to complacency. Since minorities and whites are definitionally equal under the law, we can tell ourselves that *that* problem is solved. We can even blame the victim. For, if after four decades of scrupulously neutral legal rules, African Americans and other people of color are still poor, marginalized, and discontented—well, what can be done? Since we've put in place all these wonderful legal rules which mandate equal treatment, if they haven't been able to prosper, then the problem must lie with them. They must be shiftless, or immoral, or not very smart."

"I recognize this danger, in fact, have actually written along somewhat similar lines myself."

"I know," Rodrigo said. "And even those who don't blame us end up distracted. With formal legal equality, the focus shifts to the courts. Everyone asks whether *Brown* was a justified decision, whether it was principled or not. Everyone talks earnestly about the proper judicial role, about whether courts can or should be in the business of propelling legal change."

Rodrigo gestured toward Gerald Rosenberg's *The Hollow Hope*, one of the books on my desk. "A prime example! Instead of writing about blacks and their predicament, everyone writes about courts—on law and the appropriate judicial function. We start out writing about racial wrongs, about racial justice. But, we end up writing about ourselves. It's a neat shift."

"Traditional legal scholarship seems much more concerned with procedure, the way one should go about solving a problem—rather than actually solving it. It's probably a universal human tendency."

"Perhaps so," Rodrigo replied. "The problem is how African Americans, a group that was brought here in chains, can achieve retributive justice. Yet we end up talking about legal principles. We discuss whether some deviation from perfect formal equality is principled, whether a limited affirmative action program benefiting a handful of African Americans can be justified. How can we ever hope to achieve justice when these are what we're calling the burning issues of race?"

"Rodrigo, I must admit I find your analysis intriguing, particularly the way you tie your ideas back to neutrality as the source of the trouble. Is this what you are writing about for your seminar paper: the one you plan to submit to the second competition?"

"Yes. I'm thinking of focusing on the dichotomy between equality of opportunity and equality of results. I'm sure the conservative sponsors will appreciate that."

"Bravo," I responded, with a trace of amusement. "Conservatives love equal opportunity as much as they hate equal results. In their view, the first is principled, neutral, and fair, while the second is unprincipled, result-oriented, and wrong. You will definitely get their attention, particularly if you can manage to present a new angle. Have you thought about how you are going to link it up with your insight about neutrality as a sham guarantee?"

"That's the trick," Rodrigo answered, a bit pensively. "I've got a few ideas, though. Can I tell you about them over dinner?"

"Sounds good," I said. "I'm starved. My doctor told me not to go too long between meals."

IN WHICH RODRIGO AND I DISCUSS EQUALITY OF OPPORTUNITY VERSUS EQUALITY OF RESULTS

About an hour later, Rodrigo and I found ourselves comfortably ensconced in a plain but comfortable Mexican restaurant in the meat-packing district that my friend Jose Oliveros had introduced me to the last time he was in town. I was struck that Rodrigo, who had been raised in Italy and only been back in the States a short time, knew to order Dos Equis beer with his meal. After the waiter left with our orders, Rodrigo began:

"As I mentioned earlier, I'm thinking of using the two types of equality, equality of opportunity and equality of result, to illustrate the problems with neutrality."

"A good choice. Do you intend to argue that they merge, that they constitute a false dichotomy?" I worried that my young friend might have fallen prey to the influence of the deconstruction movement, whose main goal, so far as I could determine, is to show that polar opposites collapse into each other upon close inspection. I hoped Rodrigo was not going to take me on a tour of Continental theory. Fortunately, my fears proved groundless.

"No, although I suspect one could do that," Rodrigo replied.

Relieved, I prodded: "I've always been struck by the way conservatives favor equality of opportunity over the other kind. If they were genuinely committed to neutrality, you would think that equal results would be the logical way to measure the effectiveness of most programs. Have you a theory for why conservatives—and many liberals, too—have such an aversion to equality of results?"

"I do," Rodrigo declared, pausing for a moment as the waiter set down our drinks. I resolved merely to sip my own Dos Equis until dinner arrived. I could see the outlines of a new subsection of my book forming, and wanted to remain alert. I made a mental note to figure out some way of giving Rodrigo credit. Maybe an effusive footnote would suffice for now. Later, when he got his first teaching position, I'd take him on as co-author, I mused. He certainly had more energy than I did these days, and these revisions were becoming increasingly tedious.

As though reading my mind, Rodrigo offered: "You or I might want to do something with this notion sometime. To my knowledge, no one has really addressed it. It is truly amazing, when you think about it, how all the leftists and civil rights activists, like yourself, prefer equality of results, while those of moderate or conservative persuasion prefer equality of opportunity."

"You said you had a theory for this difference?"

"I think it has to do with one's perspective or baseline. If you start out from a certain position, a given practice will look neutral. From a different perspective, the same practice will look unfair. For example, look at the quota issue. It's no secret that conservatives dislike quotas. They strike them as unfair, because they assure that a certain number of minorities will get jobs. Imposition of a quota seems nonneutral, because whites are treated differently from nonwhites. Without the quotas, that number would, no doubt, be much smaller. But that, in large part, is because in the absence of quotas the job criteria operate to hire artificially low numbers of minority applicants. Genuinely equal treatment will strike whites as unfair. Apparently, only advantage—a tilted playing field with criteria that favor them—seems neutral and normal. So, with any arrangement we look to see who benefits, who is advantaged or disadvantaged, and pronounce regimes fair or unfair accordingly."

"I'm still not sure I understand why everyone resists equality of result. Is it merely because such an approach is likely to provide more jobs and benefits to minorities?"

"Yes, in part, but the mechanism is a little more complicated. Notice how equality of opportunity is a much more nonformal, multifactorial measure than equality of results, which is starkly simple. You merely compare the number of minorities and whites at a job site, for example. But with equality of opportunity, many things come into play. This multiplies the opportunity for cultural factors to operate."

"By cultural factors you mean the host of background assumptions, interpretations, and implied exceptions that we discussed earlier?"

"Yes. Neutrality allows all of these culturally inscribed routines and understandings to come into play. Read into the culture long ago, these understandings now seem objective, unchallengeable, and true. I mean things like the merit principle, the idea that informed consent should insulate a doctor from malpractice liability, or the impression that objective standards for consumer warnings are somehow more fair than subjective standards."

"Women have been pointing out something similar in connection with date rape, urging that consent be scrutinized from a more searching perspective than 'What would most men think in this situation?'"

"I think that's an aspect of the same general idea. After we inscribe our ideas of power, authority, and legitimacy into the culture, we then pretend to consult that culture, meekly and humbly, in search of justice—for rules that are fair and neutral. A nice trick if you can get away with it."

Rodrigo paused, since the waiter had arrived with our food. Realizing that our long conversation had made us hungry, in unspoken agreement we ate for a few moments in silence. Rodrigo attacked his *chile relleno* with gusto, while I examined my burrito for anything forbidden by my doctor—a list that seemed to get longer and longer each time I visited her.

After his appetite subsided, Rodrigo continued: "So the nonformal nature of equality of opportunity allows members of an empowered group to invoke the many culturally established routines, practices, and understandings that benefit them."

"Could you give me an example?"

"Sure. Take the law school that can only hire one professor. Two finalists are before them, a black and a white. The formal job description contains the standard criteria: potential for scholarship, teaching, and public service. The finalists seem equally qualified in each of those respects. Equality of results would dictate that the black applicant get the job because of the small number of African Americans on the faculty. That is, the approach would strive for proportional representation, or some similar measure. But as we discussed before, under equality of opportunity the white will probably get the position. Equality of opportunity only guarantees that both will receive consideration. And when they do, a myriad of factors, some conscious, some unconscious, will come into play: inflection, small talk, background, bearing, social class, and the many imponderables that go into evaluating collegiality. Prudent distrust of a decisionmaker who judges persons of a different race suggests that formal, structured rules and strictly confined discretion are the key to just such decisions. But that is the opposite of what we have."

"Or take cases of pay increase and promotion," I added. "Formal equality says pay and promote minorities the same as whites doing the same work. But, in practice, this rule turns out to have exceptions. The white candidate got a higher test score. So, following the rule of equal treatment would be unfair to the white. The next time, the two candidates have exactly the same test score. Again, the white gets the promotion—this time because he or she had more seniority, or a richer job background, or better references. And so it goes."

"In each case," Rodrigo interjected, "some unstated cultural understanding comes into play. The more empowered person whose predecessors were in a position to dictate the cultural terms for these transactions comes out ahead. If one were to devise a system that would, first, produce racially discrepant results, and, second, enable those who manage and benefit from the system to sleep well at night, it would look very much like the present one."

"A serious charge, Rodrigo," I cautioned. "Not every white person deserves that indictment. Some well-wishers and sympathizers want us to succeed. When you go out on the hiring market, you will see that. Perhaps even now, you have found a professor or two of majority race who has taken you under his wing, recognized your talent, gone out of his or her way on your behalf."

"Perhaps," Rodrigo conceded. "But even they fail to appreciate the full impact of racism. Most view our current civil rights laws and regulations as adequate. The only thing missing, they believe, is the will to enforce them consistently."

"Isn't there something to that?" I prodded. "What if we simply retooled the current rules to exclude the type of favoritism you mentioned? Then, would the system be fair?"

"I'm skeptical," responded Rodrigo. "Such retooling would entail the majority group's agreement to relinquish its advantages. They would have to agree to abide by quite complex rules. But, even if they did, rules alone cannot remedy racism."

"Why not?"

IN WHICH RODRIGO EXPLAINS RACISM'S RESISTANCE TO LEGAL REGULATION

"Because something about racism makes it peculiarly difficult to dismantle through any system of laws. Racism would exist even if the dominant group treated minorities and whites similarly in all settings. Even if society recognized and canceled out the myriad cultural interpretations and background factors that now give whites an edge and render equal treatment a hollow illusion, I think it would still remain."

"Rodrigo, I've been accused of undue pessimism about the prospects for racial reform. But it sounds like I soon will have an ally—namely, you! Please explain your theory about the persistence of racism."

* * *

"You and others have written about racism's historical character," Rodrigo began. "Everyone knows that blacks were brought here in slave ships. The practice of chattel slavery remained in effect for over two centuries, then was replaced by a system of Jim Crow laws and social practices that continues to this day. So, racism's roots are long and deep. Neutral rules cannot do justice to the thickly embedded historical nature of American prejudice. We act today on a set stage. But the rules ignore this. They tell the actor not to favor the white over the black. The only thing the rules take into account is what happens right now. If the actor—say a school board commissioner—can truthfully say, 'I acted as I did for no racial animus,' that is the end of the inquiry. This is obviously not sufficient."

"Why not?"

"Let me try to give you an example." Rodrigo squinted into the late afternoon dusk that enveloped the sidewalk. "Imagine a school board needs to establish an attendance boundary. All of the children who live on one side of the boundary will go to one school; the ones who live on the other side, to another."

"And you would predict that the board will choose a boundary that maintains segregated housing patterns, with the practical effect of maintaining segregated schools?"

"No. This school board truly wants to do the right thing. Recognizing that some boards have drawn attendance lines tracking ethnic neighborhoods, this board has no desire to follow suit. Besides, it knows that if it does, the ACLU might sue it. So, instead they choose an existing freeway as the dividing line, reasoning that such a boundary will make the children's walk safer and their walk shorter."

"What the board ignores," I continued, following the logic of Rodrigo's hypothetical, "is that many years ago the government probably placed the freeway in that location precisely because minority people lived there. In the past, governments frequently placed freeways, dump sites, power substations, and other such undesirable things in minority neighborhoods. If the board today selects the freeway as the boundary, it gives effect to a past discriminatory practice. It may do this entirely innocently. Indeed, it may have a laudable motive, one nobody could quarrel with, of making children's walk to school as safe as possible."

"Exactly."

"In other words," I recapped, "neutrality employs a 'freeze-frame' approach, looking only at present factors, when redressing racism requires a longer view."

Rodrigo smiled. "Without that longer view, one misses things, takes action that seems innocuous but that actually hurts minority people. A second feature works in a similar way. It's that white-over-black domination is a concerted system. Racism derives its efficacy from its insidiousness. Many whites don't realize this. They equate racism with isolated, shocking acts such as lynchings or burning crosses. Most white folks, even ones of good will, perceive much less racism in the world than we do. In part, that is because they see fewer acts of out-and-out racism than we do. But it is also because they analogize racism to other misfortunes that beset everyone, regardless of race, like having a flat tire or being cursed by another driver whom one has inadvertently cut off."

"I've noticed that tendency in the controversy over hate speech and university conduct codes," I said. "Many whites fail to realize how often the victim of one insult is the victim of another, similar one. They analogize it to being called a 'fool lady driver,' something that might happen to them every six months or year, and which rarely threatens an important feature of their identity. By contrast, persons of color get almost daily reminders of how different they are. Even my friend Professor Oliveros, a light-skinned Latino, reports something similar. He says probably half the people he meets ask him where he is from, what kind of name he has, or how he learned to speak English so well."

"It's that 'freeze-frame' approach again, Professor. Law focuses on micro-transactions, looking for something outrageous in a single remark. Not finding anything, it denies the underlying racism. And if you do confine your attention to the here and now in this way, there's not that much difference between 'Go back to Africa' and 'Stay in your lane, you fool.' Campus racism so unremitting that young minority undergraduates sometimes drop out ends up analogized to a football cheer: 'Boo, Cal.'"

"I know academics who have presented similar arguments," I commented.

"This concerted quality of racism makes it an ever-present force even for those of us with high professional status and wealth. It's as though criminal law were to lack any remedy for conspiracy, monopoly, and other offenses of collusion or aggregation, and, instead, dealt with the underlying evils on a case-by-case basis."

"Or like trying to identify and avoid poisons by examining their atomic structure when it's the behavior of the molecule that gives strychnine its deadly character," I added. "It just doesn't show up at that level."

* * *

After a short pause, I returned to our earlier topic: "Your professor urged you to try to solve the 'problems of your people,' as he put it. But, Rodrigo, you seem ready to conclude that those problems are insoluble. Neutral antidiscrimination law cannot redress racism; instead, it allows society to blame blacks for their predicament. And, racism's very nature makes it resistant to legalized solution. What a bleak vision for someone so young! For a battered old crusader like me, taking that stance is understandable. I think people give me sympathy for being so downbeat, want to rush in, comfort me, and say, 'No, it's not so.' But, for you, what's the point of struggle, what's the point of working so hard to become a professor and scholar of civil rights, if you have so little hope of things ever getting better?"

"I didn't say that things would never get better, Professor. I merely observed that the law would not make them better. Any neutrality-based legal rule will look depressingly ineffectual to a black or person of color who lives in this society. By the same token, any practice that the majority group perceives as favoring minorities to promote racial justice will appear unprincipled and wrong."

"Like affirmative action?"

"Yes. Society has been based on racial privilege since its inception. Formal equality today serves the same purpose as the formal inequality of earlier years. It's a little bit like putting a car into neutral once you reach a downhill stretch. It just picks up speed; you don't even need to press the accelerator any more. The difference between society and the car is that most people don't even notice it's going downhill. So, society has trouble seeing the racism in a freeway boundary. Civil rights law has devolved into a system of 'nots'—'Thou shalt not this,' and 'Thou shalt not that'—all centered around the relatively few cases society is prepared to denounce as unquestionable breaches of the principle of neutral treatment."

"Like hiring a white high school dropout over a black Ph.D. and Nobel Prize laureate."

"Right. Nothing in the law requires anyone to do more, to lend a helping hand, to try to help blacks find jobs, befriend them, speak to them, make eye contact with them, help them fix a flat when they are stranded on the highway, help them feel like full persons. The law just says, 'Don't set quotas. Don't discriminate.' How can a system like that change anything?"

"It seems the only positive duties are concerned with capitalism—paying taxes, registering for the draft, and so on," I observed sardonically.

The waiter arrived, briefly interrupting our conversation to take our order for desserts. I was glad for the break. Rodrigo ordered a strawberry torte and espresso. Mindful of my doctor's orders and the late hour, I asked for a lemon biscuit and decaffeinated coffee.

As the waiter disappeared, Rodrigo continued: "The negative character of antidiscrimination laws, along with their inability to deal with the concerted and culturally rooted quality of racism, means that neutral law can do very little. Moreover, neutrality precludes white folks from seeing how their own system advantages them, indeed enables their more aggressive elements to blame minorities for their plight."

The waiter served our coffee. "Given the boost they receive from the cultural background, conservatives and moderates adore neutral rules like those providing for equality of opportunity. Actually, nothing is intrinsically wrong with neutral rules." I looked up with surprise. "They could be written and applied from minorities' perspective, in which case they would do a great deal to redress racism. But the rules that minorities would enact, and which would strike them as fair, would appear one-sided and biased to whites. And whites will use their social power to label such rules unconstitutional, unprincipled, bad."

"So, do you mean to say that neutrality always fails to redress racism in practice? If it is applied against a background of minority cultural assumptions, it is not politically feasible; if it is applied in the current manner, against a background of white cultural premises, it fails to achieve retributive justice for minorities and may even make matters worse."

"Much worse," Rodrigo nodded. "Whites simultaneously get to blame the victim, feel relieved of any responsibility for the victim's plight, and congratulate themselves on their fair-mindedness. It's no surprise that under the present regime, the gap between whites and blacks in life expectancy, income, total wealth, educational attainment, infant mortality, and virtually every other indicator of social well-being has remained roughly the same. Of course, we have seen *some* improvement. After all, only a few generations ago blacks were formally enslaved. But the economic, social, and political gap between whites and blacks manages to remain almost identical decade after decade."

"This harsh reality pains and embarrasses white liberals, most of whom don't understand why it persists. But, I think it's fair to say that it no longer seems to bother the conservatives. They are pleased with the idea that the courts cannot and should not function as a mechanism for propelling social change. For them social reform is purely a legislative function. And from us, they expect bootstrapping efforts, economic development, getting a job, tending to our families, and so on."

"I've been reading some of those books, too," Rodrigo said. "But I think the conservatives overlook something when they maintain that the courts have no efficacy, and that they can and should do little in the area of civil rights."

The waiter brought our desserts. Hungry again from our earlier walk and animated discussion, I immediately attacked my lemon biscuit. Looking up, I challenged Rodrigo: "I'll bite. What are they overlooking?"

"Very funny," he replied. "What conservatives overlook is that our system of cautious, incremental, negatively phrased, neutral civil rights laws is in fact quite efficacious."

"It is?" I questioned incredulously, nearly spilling my decaffeinated cappuccino. "In what way?"

"The system works just fine. It is just that its successes serve a different goal. For example, Gerald Rosenberg's book is full of tables, charts, regression equations, and historical analyses, all demonstrating that Supreme Court decisions have not brought about changes, for women's or minorities' rights, that were not already under way. He shows that *Roe v. Wade* did not increase access to abortion, that *Brown v. Board of Education* did not enlarge the numbers of black schoolchildren attending desegregated schools. But Rosenberg mistakenly concludes that the civil rights laws have no effect."

"I suppose you are going to say that their effect is too subtle to measure, that it lies in a symbolic dimension that will take years to make itself felt?"

"No, not at all," Rodrigo replied. "Rather, civil rights laws efficiently and smoothly replicate social reality, particularly black-white power relations. They are a little like the thermostat in your home or office. They assure that there is just the right amount of racism. Too much would be destabilizing—the victims would rebel. Too little would forfeit important pecuniary and psychic advantages. So, the existing system of race-remedies law does, in fact, grant minorities an occasional victory, an occasional *Brown v. Board of Education*. Every now and then, a bigot who burns a cross or beats a black youth will be convicted. Particularly in areas where concessions are not too costly, like voting rights, or media licensing, the courts will grant us an occasional breakthrough."

"I believe that you and others in the critical race theory movement have a term for this?" I prompted.

"Contradiction-closing cases," Rodrigo replied. "I used to think that the term verged on tautology. But now I think there might be something to it. What else explains such decisions as *Metro Broadcasting, Inc. v. FCC* or *United States v. Fordice* in an era in which the Court methodically has been eviscerating civil rights protection for minorities and women by imposing new burdens of proof, narrowing standing to sue for class-based relief, and requiring tight claims of causation?"

"Under your theory, then," I reviewed, motioning the waiter to bring the check, "courts are doing their job. We just misconceive what that job is. Civil rights proponents still believe that the courts want to stamp out racial unfairness, that the optimal amount of racism in society is zero. But it's not. It's a properly low level, maintained by neutral rules that reach little conduct of significance, administered and interpreted by judges whose experiences ill equip them to understand the nature of the problem and who dispense victories as parsimoniously as possible. Is that your thesis?"

"Yes, and I think it operates at the level of cultural assumptions, which is, after all, its beauty. No conscious conspiracy operates. Liberal whites are often as blithely ignorant of the workings of the system, as needlessly indignant as the most rock-ribbed conservative extolling the virtues of our system of individual achievement, where every person rises or falls on her merits."

"Spann is indignant, too."

"Like others on the left, he began by believing—or at least hoping—that the system means what it says when it issues those golden promises of equality. That's why he's so indignant, expressing such a sense of betrayal. It's a little like the law of gravity. Rosenberg says civil rights law has failed because the position of women and minorities has not improved much as a result of constitutional adjudication. But that's like arguing that the law of gravity has failed because not everything has fallen. In fact, gravity holds everything neatly in balance, the sun, the moon, the stars, and the planets. In that respect it is quite successful, as is our civil rights system."

"So law works," I said, slowly grasping the enormity of what Rodrigo had just articulated. "But it operates to preserve racial advantage, to maintain the status quo."

"Like the law of gravity," Rodrigo repeated, draining the last drop of espresso from his cup.

CONCLUSION

We soon parted. After watching my hyperkinetic young friend stride along the sidewalk in the direction of his law school thirty blocks away, I began my slow walk back to my apartment and yet another session with my casebook. As I walked, I reflected on our conversation. If culture determines our interpretation of legal texts and rules, and racism is woven so deeply into our cultural fabric that we hardly notice it, then how can civil rights laws ever eradicate racism in our culture? What did Rodrigo mean when he said there might be cause for hope, but not through law? Perhaps he meant that cultural change might occur, possibly through some form of direct action. I cursed my fate as a casebook writer for having removed me, if only temporarily, from some of the drama being played out on the pages of the law reviews. I resolved to get together again with Rodrigo soon. I wanted to hear how his second essay fared in the competition he had mentioned. But even more importantly, I wanted to know whether he saw any way out of the cultural trap whose gloomy outlines he had so remorselessly sketched for my benefit.

~

Rodrigo's Eighth Chronicle
Black Crime, White Fears—On the Social Construction of Threat

INTRODUCTION: IN WHICH I LEARN ABOUT AN EVENT AT RODRIGO'S INSTITUTION

I was staring disconsolately at the flashing light on the vending machine in the student lounge, where I had gone in search of a much-needed late afternoon pick-me-up, when I heard a familiar voice from behind me:
"Professor, do you need some help?"
"Rodrigo!" I said. "It's good to see you." To tell the truth, I felt slightly uncomfortable at being surprised while trying to satisfy my physical needs on someone else's turf, but I was glad to see a person who might help me out of my predicament. Rodrigo, a brilliant LL.M. student of African-American heritage, was enrolled at the famous law school across town. He had sought me out for career advice a year earlier, during a return trip from Italy. Despite our age difference,

we had become good friends, discussing affirmative action, the U.S. racial scene, welfare politics, law and economics, and a number of other subjects over the course of the year. I always looked forward to our meetings; indeed, felt that I learned as much from them as did my young protégé. Raised in Italy, the son of an American serviceman and an Italian mother, Rodrigo saw the United States with fresh eyes. His pungent, highly original observations concerning the American racial and political scene had sparked many a responsive idea in my aging mind and provided grist for lecturing and writing assignments I would have found much more arduous without them.

"What's the problem, Professor? Out of change?"

I stumblingly tried to explain the predicament that just minutes ago had caused me to curse my fate. "As luck would have it, I have exactly fifty cents in change." I held out my palm with the quarter, two dimes, and a nickel. "But the Diet Pepsi I desperately need to keep going costs fifty-five cents. I also have this dollar bill. As you can see, the machine takes dollars, but it won't take mine. It keeps rolling right out. 'Use exact change,' it says. So I'm stuck. Would you have a nickel, by any chance?"

"I wish I did, Professor, but the subway took my last dime. But let me try something. Could I have all that money?"

"Sure," I said, handing it over. "What are you going to do?"

Rodrigo first inserted all my change. Nothing happened. Then, muttering something to himself, he inserted my dollar bill and pressed the button.

Jackpot! The machine disgorged both the Diet Pepsi I had been waiting for and a great clatter of change. Scooping it up, Rodrigo counted it out. "Ninety-five cents, just as I thought."

"How did you know to do that?" I asked appreciatively.

"It's simple, Professor. The machine doesn't have the right change. That's why it can't take your dollar. But if you put everything in, the machine then has enough money to make change for you. And since it's honest—has a simple computer that remembers how much you've put in—you get your change back. And your Diet Pepsi."

"Thanks!" I said. "At my age, I've learned I really need to take an occasional break, especially in the afternoon."

Rodrigo smiled. "Maybe it's a metaphor for all of life, Professor. Sometimes if you put in more than anyone expects, you get more in return."

"My, you are getting upbeat in your old age," I retorted, "especially for someone trained in Bologna and steeped in neo-Marxism and economic-determinist analyses of race. But what brings you around? It's good to see you—it's been a while."

"I was hoping you could give me a few minutes. I tried calling, but your line was busy. I need to run some ideas past you. They're about black crime."

"I'd be happy to talk with you about that. As you know, a burgeoning critical literature, including the piece by Regina Austin we talked about last time, addresses that subject. And, of course, there are the three Chronicles by Derrick Bell."

"I'm familiar with all those. What I'm really interested in pursuing is the cultural phenomenon itself. I'm intrigued by the way the whole issue tends to be framed."

"What got you started thinking about this?" I asked. "I hope the INS is not on your trail again."

"No, nothing so personal. I'm thinking of adding a section to my dissertation on society's treatment of black crime. Did you hear about the professor at my school who got mugged and sent to the hospital?"

"My God!" I said. "I did. It was just in the paper. There was a lot of talk about it here. Do you know him? How is he doing?"

"No, I don't know him, and he is much better. He had a lot of bruises and a cracked rib or two. But he's back from the hospital and it looks like he'll recover completely."

"I'm relieved. We were all shocked. Some of us talked about getting more safety features and lighting in the parking lot. I think the administration is going to do something."

"I'm glad, Professor. Not that I think you couldn't outrun most thieves. You look pretty fit for a man your age. I imagine you run every day."

"Most days," I replied modestly. "But I don't have the speed I once had. I went running with Professor Bollicker the other day, and immediately regretted it. He's much faster."

"You and I should go jogging one day, Professor. I've started up again. Giannina says it makes me less hyper, and it does help me sleep."

"Maybe sometime. Now, what are your thoughts on black crime? I gather the professor's mugger was black?"

"Well, as it happened, he was. And the professor, as you probably know, is white. He's also a much-loved figure—a veritable institution—around the law school. Everybody admires him and was furious when he got robbed and sent to the hospital."

"A natural reaction," I replied. "And so where does all this lead you? Are you surprised by the amount of crime you find in this country? I imagine it's greater than when you left. You were a teenager then. It was a safer era."

"I guess it's not the amount of crime that surprises me. I had read about that in Italy. Every major industrialized society has crime. Italy has some, too, although a little less than here—of the violent, interpersonal variety, at any rate. What surprises me is the way it's perceived. The reaction at my law school is a prime example."

I drew myself up in mock horror. "I can't think of a worse crime than mugging a professor," I said. "It's like desecrating a cathedral. Besides, I have so few brain cells left functioning, I fear it would take just one good knock and I'd be finished."

"I agree," Rodrigo said, then blushed. "Not about you, but about what happened to the other professor. It *was* a despicable act. Yet what surprised me was the way some people generalized the event. I heard snatches of conversation—things like, 'those people'; 'something has to be done'; 'they're out of control.' Even white folks I had come to think of as liberals were talking about the 'breakdown of the black family,' and so on. Some of us African-American students felt distinctly uncomfortable, as though people were looking at us, wondering why we didn't do something, wondering if we were going to mug *them*. There was even a graffito in the bathroom: 'Bernhard Goetz was right.'"

"Ugly," I commiserated. "But not exactly new. Every widely publicized black crime seems to bring out the same reaction. I'm sure all this strikes you as shocking, coming from a more peaceful, sunny clime. The U.S. has changed in the last ten or twenty years. You're seeing it with new eyes."

"Maybe so," Rodrigo replied. "And maybe you'll think my vision is a little skewed. That Diet Pepsi is getting warm, Professor." Rodrigo looked in the direction of the unopened can in my hand. "Can I take you somewhere for a drink, or were you in the middle of something? There's a health food bar Giannina and I discovered the other day. It's only a short walk from here. They have fresh fruit juices, salads, and organic soft drinks."

"Organic soft drinks?" I said. "I'll try anything once. Maybe my doctor will approve. She's been trying to get me to cut down on caffeine."

"They also have snacks. I could use one if you have the time."

I recalled my young friend's famous appetite. "Okay," I said. "This will be on me. You paid for the espresso last time."

ON THE SOCIAL CONSTRUCTION OF BLACK CRIME

A few minutes later, we were comfortably seated in the health food bar Rodrigo had recommended.

"I never go to places like this, although I should," I said, patting my stomach. "I gained a couple of pounds when I visited your homeland this summer. What are you having?"

The waiter arrived and stood by expectantly. "I'll have your Avocado Supreme," Rodrigo said. Then, to me: "It reminds me of something I used to have back at Bologna."

"I'll have the same," I said. After the waiter disappeared with our orders, Rodrigo continued:

"Have you noticed, Professor, how your society—I mean, our society—virtually equates crime and the black underclass, as though they were practically one and the same thing?"

"I have," I answered. "The conservatives want to crack down on it, build walls around their communities, more prisons, and get tougher on what they call 'career criminals.' The liberals, for their part, lament it and want to do something about what they see as the causes of black crime—poverty, lack of jobs, and so on."

"We talked a little about these things before," Rodrigo replied. "But my thinking has taken a slightly different turn since then. The reaction to the professor's mugging got me thinking. What's common to both the liberals, who want to attack the problem at its roots, and the conservatives, who want to solve it with harsher punishment, is that both construct black criminality as a *problem*."

"But it *is* a problem," I insisted. "Rodrigo, I hope you're not going to put me through another one of your postmodern tours-de-force and try to make something that everyone knows exists disappear. Black crime, especially among young black men—your age, I might add—is a serious problem. About one-quarter of young African-American males are caught up in the criminal justice system. The jails are about forty-five percent black. Homicide is the leading cause of death for young black men. Drugs and gangs run rampant in the inner city. I hope you're not going to deny the very real pain our community suffers as a result of the criminal activity of its own youth. Nothing could bring you quicker disrepute."

"Not at all," Rodrigo replied mildly. "I know the problems exist. In fact, they touched me just the other day. I was shopping in a men's clothing store, looking for a tie, when the house detective asked me to empty my pockets and book bag. He seemed disappointed when all he found was lecture notes and a leftover apple from my lunch."

"I'm relieved you concede that our young—some of them, at any rate—commit crimes. But you said that you found something about society's perception of those crimes interesting?"

"Yes." Rodrigo stopped for a moment while the waiter put down our plates and asked us if we'd like anything to drink.

"Just a refill," I said, pointing at my water glass.

"Do you have espresso?" Rodrigo asked. He ordered a double and then continued.

"I've been looking at some of the statistics, Professor, and I don't think black criminality is a more serious problem than many other forms of it. But it's interesting to see how everyone came to think so. I believe that, in conjunction with other sociocultural developments, four or five books and a couple of well-known reports played a major role in creating our modern conception of black crime. Before then, there was simply crime. Some of it was committed by white people, and some by blacks. Then, beginning in the mid-1960s with three national reports, the Moynihan study, the Blumstein article, and three or four books that I'm sure you're familiar with, the whole thing changed. Now, crime became identified with us—people like you and me, I mean. Before this time, crime was no more identified with us than, say, playing the trombone, having a cold, or any other human activity that crosses racial lines. Everyone knew that many of us were poor and sometimes took things. But so did people of other colorations—it was not seen as a peculiarly black problem."

"I'm not sure that's literally true, Rodrigo," I cautioned. "I have seen some studies of ethnic stereotyping and imagery that seem to indicate the opposite. In certain periods, blacks, Mexicans, and other minority groups of color were depicted as lascivious, immoral, bent on raping white women, and so on. It's a control device. The authors say the images change from period to period, according to whether society needs to justify control, repression, or yet some third position vis-à-vis the group. But the image has been negative in virtually every period, and criminality is often part of it."

"It's the violent, interpersonal type of crime that intrigues me," Rodrigo explained. "Because *that* part of our image has not always been there. In the thirties and forties, for example, everyone knew that young black kids sometimes stole hubcaps. But white kids did, as well. The extraordinarily negative depiction of our people as violent muggers and burglars who might break into your house at night and surprise you with a knife at your throat—that's relatively new."

"Hmmm," I said. "You're not saying it doesn't happen, are you?"

"Not at all. But some people wake up at night, and the burglar is white. Other crimes are committed predominantly by whites, and they're just as devastating as those our people, our kids, perpetrate. At one time in history everyone knew the Irish did one sort of thing, and blacks another. Then the hubcaps became more serious stuff. It became a problem. Then their problem. Then our problem. Which is where we are today. Everyone wants to crack down on their—I mean our—problem, Professor."

"Rodrigo, as you know, I'm not a great fan of your poststructuralist theories. I'm just an earnest plodder trying to work in my own way for racial justice. It seems to me that society could not, as you put it, construct an image of our people as criminal if there were not a grain of truth to it. Some of our young people do commit crimes—violent, interpersonal ones, like the one that laid your professor low. I'm not sure what utility lies in focusing on the social construction angle. If the media were lying, that would be one thing. But there *is* a problem. And isn't it up to us to do something about it? I hope you're not trying to whitewash a serious social problem."

"Not at all, Professor." Rodrigo was silent for a minute. "Can I give you an illustration from another area?"

"Of course."

"Consider a different example—the teenager. In some ways teenagers are the opposite of blacks. They are a relatively favored segment of our society. Everyone tolerates their foibles. They have a lot of free time. Marketers are always trying to sell them things. They have allowances, and so on."

"Well, that's the social image," I replied. "Although the reality is often quite different. Some teenagers are troubled, work twenty hours a week, take care of their younger brothers and sisters, and so on."

"I'm not denying any of that. I'm just asking you to question where the concept came from. Today, it's part of the culture. But it was not always there."

"It wasn't?"

"The flesh-and-blood humans were always there, of course. People between the ages of twelve and twenty or so, who stand about three-fourths to four-fifths of their final height and have been or are going through puberty—those have always been there. But that's not to say there have always been 'teenagers.'"

"You mean no special term for them?"

"Exactly. They were just human beings who happened to be between those two ages. They had no more special status than people between the ages of five and twenty-two, or thirty-seven and forty-eight."

"No special name for them," I said. "No category of their own."

"Nor any special clothes, magazines, marketing strategies, or musical groups. Before the category was created, teenagers were just medium-high people who went through the daily tasks of life. Some mowed lawns. Most went to school. And so on."

"I see what you're saying," I said. "A self-conscious interest group, whose main purpose is to consume things—such a category would be wonderful for the economy."

"I'm not so sure I'd be quite that deterministic, Professor. But the category does serve certain purposes. In that sense, it didn't just happen. By the same token, there were periods in history when blacks were not seen as particularly criminal. Hapless, perhaps. Carefree, musically talented, lazy, happy-go-lucky—you name it, the many sides our image takes on from time to time, none of them particularly flattering."

"But you think the criminal image whites imposed upon blacks came about as a response to some social need, perhaps for repression?"

"It would certainly serve that purpose," Rodrigo replied. "A group that is criminal, vicious, animal-like, with designs on white people's lives and pocketbooks—such a group would need to be controlled. At other periods the criminal image would not serve society's purposes, for example when blacks (or members of other racial groups) were needed for their labor or for service during wartime."

The waiter arrived to take our dessert orders. "Would you like something?" I asked. "Please go ahead. I'm thinking of trying their *gelato*."

"It *is* good here," Rodrigo replied. "Giannina and I had some last time. It's not quite like what we have back in Italy. But it's the next best thing."

In a moment, the waiter had taken our orders and disappeared. I looked at Rodrigo expectantly.

"The social construction of us as criminal did not come about by accident," he continued. "The 1960s and early 1970s was a time of great breakthroughs and success for blacks. Repression set in shortly afterward."

The waiter set down our desserts. "That looks good," I said. "What kind are you having?"

"Mandarino," he replied. "What's yours?"

"Lime. I'm counting calories. But back to your point. Other ethnic groups had crime, too: Irish rum-running, Italian numbers rackets. Mayor Daley's machine in Chicago. Tammany Hall. And others that come to mind, as well. What's the difference between the social construction of these other groups, and ours?"

"There are two or three differences," Rodrigo said. "First of all, the kind of crime we associated with these other groups was often relatively harmless. At any rate, we winked at it, tolerated it, smiled at it, almost. Second, to the extent to which members of these white ethnic groups actually engaged in it, the group benefited. Crime, for many, was a means of upward mobility, a means by which fortunes were amassed and family empires created. The next generation left crime when their parents sent them to college. They became senators and members of Congress, had country homes, opened or managed legitimate businesses."

"So crime was a path of upward mobility for other immigrant groups, but one that was denied for us?"

"Correct," Rodrigo replied. "For African Americans alone this avenue was closed. Society decided to repress, not tolerate, crime from our group."

I made a mental note to ask Rodrigo about something later, but instead asked, "Why do you think that was so? I assume you have a theory?"

"Nothing especially original," Rodrigo replied. "We're a large group numerically, so a great deal was at stake. Moreover, society has more to live down with respect to us. And, of course, there's the color question. For all these reasons, society decided fairly recently that it did not want us to get ahead in this way. The notion of the sinister, out-of-control black served this purpose admirably."

"Rodrigo, I hope you're not saying there was something like a conscious conspiracy. That strikes me as a little paranoid."

"No," Rodrigo replied. "Not any more than the creation of the teenager was a conscious conspiracy. No group of executives sat down and said, 'Let's see. What group can we create that will have a lot of money to spend and that we can persuade to buy clothes and magazines and makeup and music?' Yet, the category did come into being, and did operate to produce benefits to the merchandising sector. I think that good and bad categories just sort of come about naturally, with little effort or conscious design, when society needs them to appear."

"I wish I could be convinced," I said. "It sounds almost too pat."

"Let's walk back to your office, Professor. Do you still have your computer?"

"Yes," I nodded.

"And it's still hooked up to your databases?"

I nodded yes, and Rodrigo gestured for the waiter. "I've been doing some research on just this question."

I wasn't sure what he meant by "just this question," but I wanted to hear what he was looking into, so I said, "Sure, come on over. I have some new art work in my office. I think I told you last time that I was lucky enough to get a permanent job here, following that one-semester visit. So now we're neighbors. At least until you go off somewhere else."

"I'd like very much to see your stuff, Professor. I loved that poster you had of the state fair."

As we walked out of the little restaurant, Rodrigo looked at me and said, "I hope you'll be careful, Professor. Even the streets around here aren't one-hundred percent safe. We need to have you around for a while."

I mumbled something about being neither that old nor that hard to replace, and a few minutes later we were walking up the steps of the law building to my office.

RODRIGO'S PRINTOUT: THE STATISTICS AND POLITICS OF CRIME

"Say, you've rearranged things. The computer used to be over there."

The alert Rodrigo pointed out my recent redecorating efforts, of which I was proud. "Yes, I moved all the plaques over to that wall, the couch over there, and switched my desk and computer to face the window. What do you think?"

Rodrigo ignored my question. His eyes were on my computer. "Do you mind if I sit here, Professor? I should have brought my notes. But this should just take a minute."

"Go ahead," I said, moving to where I could see the screen. As they had done once before, Rodrigo's fingers flew over the keyboard. Accessing databases I did not even know existed, he brought up a wealth of information from articles, book abstracts, the U.S. Census, and FBI annual crime reports. I envied his technological wizardry and lamented that I had come to computers so late in life.

"See, Professor," Rodrigo said, pointing at the screen. "Here are the figures we talked about before. They show that the figure for white-collar crime exceeds the dollar losses from all the crimes associated with African Americans put together. If you just take...." Rodrigo punched a few more keys. "See—if you add all the losses from street robbery, including mugging and purse snatching, and add to them this other figure for...." Rodrigo interrupted himself briefly while my screen flashed, dissolved, then flashed again—"For all household burglaries, you get...."

I squinted, then said: "A lot of money. It looks like almost $8.3 billion per year."

"Now, we *could* throw in malicious mischief," Rodrigo muttered, punching some other keys. "Oh, yes, I remember where I got that. It's here. See, the total for graffiti is about $600 million."

"That's a lot of losses," I replied. My young friend went on:

"And, oh—here it is. Just as I thought. The figure for white-collar crime is not just higher than the one for street crime. It's ... let's see ... *much* higher. I was working on this before but didn't quite finish. I hope you've got a minute, Professor. I have a feeling this will surprise you." *Click, click, click.* I wondered, once again, how Rodrigo had become so proficient at electronic searching while studying world cultures, then law, in Italy. "What are you trying to do?" I asked.

"I'm trying for a total. Does your computer have a split screen? No, too bad. I was trying to make a running tally. Here, let me borrow some paper—can I use that pad? There. Just as I thought. If you divide out by the proportion of the country that is white and the proportion that is black, it looks like ... the figures for the sorts of crime white people do are greater than the figures for the sorts of crime they associate with us."

"You mean," I said, "that our people commit less crime than people of the majority race?"

"The per person losses are actually a lot lower. I'm assuming, of course, that most white-collar crime is perpetrated by white people—I mean the classic categories of that kind of crime—such as embezzlement, bribery, price-fixing, and insider trading. Actually, I'd better check." *Click, click, click.* "Here we are. The crime reports. Just as I thought, mostly white. And when you add in *corporate* misconduct—marketing unsafe autos and dangerous pharmaceuticals, Love Canal, the Dalkon Shield, the savings and loan scandal, the General Electric price-fixing conspiracy ..." *click, click, click ...* "the Lockheed fiasco, Three Mile Island, asbestosis, and Agent Orange—you find that almost all the top executives were white."

"That's really interesting," I said.

"This is more or less where I stopped last time. But let's look at this."

I watched quietly as Rodrigo once again performed feats on my computer, stopping only to scribble a new entry on the rapidly growing list of figures on the yellow pad next to him.

"See, Professor. If you add these other figures to the total of white-collar crime that we got earlier...." Rodrigo looked down at his list. "For corporate crime, including defense procurement fraud and bribery, consumer fraud, and, let's see, oh yes, the savings-and-loan scandals. You have a net figure of ... hmmm. It looks like many times the per capita figure for black crime. So, in one way of looking at it, the crime that elite white people do, especially white males, is much more serious than that committed by blacks of all ages and types."

"Amazing," I said. "I wonder why this never comes out."

"It's inherent in the social construction, Professor. No one focuses on white crime or sees it as a problem. In fact, the very category, 'White Crime,' sounds funny, like some sort of debater's trick."

"But there it is, right in the crime reports," I said.

"Yes, but it's hidden in a mass of statistics no one focuses on or makes a big production of. The other kinds, the ones laid out with precise charts in the FBI's annual compilations, attract all the attention and seem like 'the problem.'" Rodrigo gestured toward the electronic bookmark he had stuck in my computer, a feature I did not even know I had.

"Oops!" we both said in unison, as the phone rang loudly. I looked at my watch and remembered, with a start, the journalist I had promised to speak with around this time, half wishing I had not agreed to talk with her.

"Do you need privacy, Professor?"

It was the journalist. I covered the receiver. "No problem. This shouldn't take long."

Rodrigo pressed a few buttons, my printer started whirring, then he wandered out into the hallway. I was depressed to learn that the journalist, with whom I had spoken before and was friendly, wanted a comment on hate-speech directed at lawyers. I had done some writing on hate-speech against blacks, and the journalist wanted to know what I thought of a state bar association president's suggestion that vilifying an attorney be considered a hate crime. I said a few guarded things, tried to explain Harry Kalven's thesis—which the reporter refused to take down as too technical—and after a few minutes hung up. A moment later, Rodrigo walked back in.

"What do you think of my printout?" he asked, gathering up the long, flowing computer sheet my printer had obligingly produced in his absence. "Oh—and what did your journalist friend want to know?"

"I haven't looked at your printout yet, but I will—I'm fascinated by your evidence that white people commit as much crime as our youth. And, as for the journalist, never mind. Talking to the press is both one of the best and worst aspects of this job, as you'll find out soon enough. Some of them are really smart, understand everything, and take their time to get the story straight. Other times, they just want a quick quote—usually something specific they have in mind and try their best to coax out of you."

"Do you generally oblige them?"

"I do. I think it's important to be helpful and forthcoming to the press, despite the occasional disappointments. Maybe when you start teaching, I'll refer calls to you. I'll tell them if you don't know the answer, you can find out anything in less than thirty seconds. You're pretty good with a computer."

Rodrigo beamed. "I've been working on it. Part of my dissertation is going to be statistical. So I've been boning up. You looked like you were going to ask me something."

"I can't remember what it was."

"Did it have something to do with street crime?" Rodrigo asked. "I was pulling up the figures on muggings when you looked like you wanted to interject."

"Oh. That's right. If you are going to make the case that black crime is a social construction, an illusion, or at any rate no worse than white crime—"

"Less bad, actually," Rodrigo interjected quietly.

"Then you're going to need to deal with the objection that black crime is scarier. It's violent. When a savings and loan officer carries out a scam or causes an institution to fail, it costs the investors and depositors money. But losing five hundred or a thousand dollars is not the same as being mugged and sent to the hospital, even if the medical bill turns out to be the same. Embezzling and tax fraud are bad, to be sure. But they're just plain not as terrifying as waking up in the middle of the night and seeing a shadowy figure standing behind a curtain."

"I agree," Rodrigo said.

"So you want to know my thoughts about violent crime, and also my solution. No small challenge, Professor! These parts of my thesis are not fully fleshed out. But I do have some ideas on how to begin to address them. Can I interest you in a bite of real supper? I noticed on the bulletin board just a minute ago that the Latino Law Students are having a feed in the student lounge. And judging from the smells in the hallway, it's already started. Do you like Mexican food?"

"I love it," I replied a little ruefully. "But I should eat more of the variety that we had before. My doctor's been after me. It is late, though, and she did tell me to have lots of small meals as I go through the day...."

"Maybe a corn burrito, Professor?" Rodrigo asked solicitously. "They're not too high in calories or cholesterol."

"Tell you what. If you agree to help me hold the line at just one, I'll help you critique the remaining parts of your paper."

"It's a deal," Rodrigo said.

IN WHICH RODRIGO EXPLAINS HIS THEORY ABOUT VIOLENT CRIME

Twenty minutes later, as we rode up the elevator, balancing paper plates and munching on the remains of our burritos, Rodrigo continued: "I'm learning to love Mexican food. Italian is my favorite, of course. But for some reason, Mexican is more plentiful in the neighborhood where Giannina and I live. And the prices are a little lower."

"Easier on a student budget," I sympathized, placing my plate on the wooden chair next to my office door while I fished out the key. "Have a napkin," I said once we were inside, indicating a stash on the end of a bookshelf. "I have cold drinks in the mini-fridge. I showed it to you before, right?"

"I think you did. I'm not thirsty, but maybe I'll have one of your famous coffees, if you're up to making some."

"I was just thinking that myself. I got in a new supply of beans. You were going to address my objection about violence. Much black crime is violent, and, while the net losses from white-collar and black crime may be similar, there's no comparison in terms of *in terrorem* effect."

Rodrigo looked pensive. "You're right, and I would be the last person to try to excuse muggings or Central Park beatings. Did I tell you I've taken up jogging? Anyway, I think the answer lies in recognizing two things. The one has to do with the construction of reality idea we talked about earlier. The other has to do with the way these figures look in the new light this analysis reveals."

"I'd love to hear," I said, flicking the switch to "On" and adding the beans. "I assume you want the real kind, with caffeine?"

I knew the answer already. "I love coffee," Rodrigo said. "And it's not too late. Giannina wants me to cut down. She says coffee makes me too hyper. But if I have my last cup before about six p.m., I find I sleep well."

I poured him a cup, then measured out the decaffeinated beans from the other jar.

"Mmmm. This is good. You make some of the best coffee I've had since leaving Italy, Professor."

"So, a new construction of crime and a sharper look at the statistics will yield an answer to our problem?" I prodded.

"Have you ever wondered about all the white people's derelictions that are not crimes at all, but torts or administrative offenses, punishable if at all by fines, but rarely imprisonment? At the same time, the things that black and poor people do—shoplifting, stealing hubcaps, joy riding, selling or buying marijuana—can net you quite a few years behind bars," Rodrigo said.

"I have noticed. It seems to me that society has neatly arranged to have the types of things high-level executives do—even ones that are clearly unethical or antisocial—be handled nonpenally, the same way they handle the youthful indiscretions of clean-cut suburban youth. You rarely hear of a corporate executive going to jail—for long stretches, at any rate—even if the malfeasance is fairly serious, like marketing DES or Ford Pintos once they know they are lethally dangerous."

"No one thinks of these as violent crimes, but of course they are. We treat them as a case of boys-will-be-boys, as ordinary, red-blooded business zeal that got a little out of hand. The perpetrators rarely serve prison sentences. If they do, it makes the news—and then they're out again in a few months."

"I read of one that was quietly released just the other day. He had been sentenced to several years for bilking the public of millions of dollars. A few months later, he was walking the streets again."

"Much such misconduct isn't even treated as a crime. For example, I'm sure you've heard of doctors who perform Cesarean sections on women during childbirth, not out of medical necessity but for the doctor's convenience. Giannina was reading an article the other day on excessive medical procedures—including mammograms and hysterectomies for women and prostate operations for men. These cost millions of dollars a year, and result in a great deal of pain and, in some cases, deaths, yet are almost never included in the yearly totals for white-collar crime."

"I've read, too," I added, "of physicians who refer patients for laboratory tests to facilities in which the doctors have an interest. These result in more unnecessary tests, with all the inconvenience, expense, and in some cases pain that these entail."

"Add to that the many deaths each year caused by the marketing of infant formula in Third World countries."

"Yes. The mother frequently cannot read the preparation instructions, because they are printed in English. Sometimes the mother simply cannot read. Safe water for mixing the formula is almost never available. The result is an expensive but unsafe formula to replace the mother's perfectly safe and completely free breast milk. Even if the mother eventually realizes that the formula is causing her baby's illness, she has stopped lactating. Her baby will die."

"None of this is regarded as a crime," Rodrigo went on. "And then there is toxic dumping. We've already mentioned the sale and marketing of dangerous products. Toxic dumping adds another several thousand deaths a decade." Rodrigo gestured toward my computer. "Mind if I turn that on again?" I waved no, so he continued. "Let me see, where did I find that figure for dumping? Let's try fulltext and Love Canal. Oh, look, here's the atomic fallout test case, *Allen v. United States*. Add a few thousand more thyroid cancers. . . ." Rodrigo stopped to jot a few more figures down on the yellow pad, rapidly filling up with numbers. "And here's one on children's car seats. For some reason I didn't bring that one up before. And if you add . . ."

Rodrigo was silent for a moment while he added up a column of figures. "How many white people did we say there are in the country? Okay, divide out and we get . . . Oh, look. Once again, just about the same. Hmmm. Actually a little higher for the whites. And if you add undeclared wars . . ."

"Undeclared wars?" I asked.

"They're illegal, and they kill you just as dead. Every last one violates the War Powers Act, not to mention the Constitution, which provides that only Congress can declare a war. All the others are technically illegal. Virtually all wars like that also violate international law, including treaties to which the United States is a signatory, like the United Nations Charter. Tens of thousands of lives lost, millions if you go back to the two world wars. These are things that elite whites do. They kill and cripple. They are violent crimes, just like rape, homicide, and assault and battery, and but for our social construction of black crime, these white-collar crimes would have the same *in terrorem* effect as street crime currently does."

"And if you add them in?" I asked.

"I had the figure before, when Giannina and I were doing this back at our place. But I'd better not rely on memory. Let's see. Wars. Where did I get that. Oh, I know—let's try this. There we are. Over forty million deaths, if you go back just through the Second World War. If you include noncombatants and deaths on the other side ... Oh, here we are. All wars—over eighty-seven million since the beginning of the century."

Rodrigo scribbled again while I watched transfixed.

"If you add wars and military excursions, elite whites cause about three times the number, I mean ratio, of deaths and dismemberments, as blacks. Without wars, they're only slightly ahead." Rodrigo turned off my computer. "Well, Professor?"

"You can't be sure that no African American sat on the board of the corporation that marketed DES or dumped toxic wastes into Love Canal. And a recent Chief of Staff, as you know, was black—Colin Powell." I quickly realized how lame my challenge sounded, so retracted it. "On the whole, though, I have to admit, in the United States, at any rate, white folks have caused more death by violence than anyone else. And that's not even including slavery."

"That's at least another seven million to fourteen million deaths—more if you add the Indians," Rodrigo replied soberly. "And of course Amnesty International and other organizations have been after us for years to reduce our number of executions, which in their opinion is far too high. Higher than in any other nation except the old Soviet Union."

"Not to mention that we alone execute the mentally retarded and the underage," I said.

"Death row is disproportionately black, as the Georgia study showed. Juries convict black men who commit crimes against white victims at a rate more than four times greater than when the victim is black. The jails are nearly half black, and over 60 percent minority. All this is indefensible in the eyes of many international authorities."

"And of course it's not black people who are declaring these wars or operating these criminal justice systems that treat black offenders so harshly."

"In general, no. Studies of race-by-race sentencing show that black offenders are punished more harshly than whites for the same offense, right across the board."

"I hadn't realized that," I said. "But it stands to reason."

We were both silent for a minute. "I think neither of us gets much pleasure from these dreary statistics," Rodrigo said. "But I think it's important to get them out, because without them, our people become more and more demonized. Society deems us the source of its miseries, the insecurity of life in the cities, the reason why life today is not as safe, not as sweet as it used to be. These are unfortunate facts, and no one can blink at them."

"But laying them at our doorstep is not fair," I summarized. "The empirical analysis you just conducted showed we should be more fearful of the depredation caused by white-collar crime than by street crime. It's more serious, more common, *and* more hurtful."

"Crime and suffering in the ghetto are serious problems. No reasonable person could dismiss them. Conservatives and progressives alike should be working to ameliorate the pain, the poverty, the blighted lives that occur there. The dropout, infant mortality, and incarceration figures for the poor black community are tragic. But the challenge is to find an approach that recognizes that crime and delinquency are societywide problems, not ours exclusively."

"I gather you've been thinking about that challenge," I said.

"I have some ideas—an outline, nothing more. If you'd like to hear, I'd love the feedback. My draft's not due 'til the end of the summer. It doesn't need to be a long chapter, but I need to talk about solutions."

"I'm all ears."

IN WHICH RODRIGO PROPOSES HIS SOLUTION TO THE CRIME PROBLEM

Rodrigo reached for the pad of yellow paper. "I hope you don't mind if I take notes. I find that talking with you often stimulates me, Professor."

"No more than it does me," I said. "As I may have mentioned before, I'm participating in a Federalist Society debate next month, and someone is sure to bring up the crime-and-punishment question. This talk is helping me at least as much as you."

"You're a good friend, Professor. I like the way you push me. This part of my thesis I've told to no one except Giannina. So I really value your opinion."

"Please go on," I said.

"I think the key lies in getting a handle on white-collar crime, including the corporate variety. It would help, too, if we could cut down on military crimes—mainly all those undeclared wars. Defense procurement fraud is a big item, but it's all those young bodies, brains, and bones that bother me. If we could reduce white-collar, corporate, and military crime and adventurism, I think we could make the desert bloom."

"We'd all be safer, surely, but how would that help our people, particularly our youth who are caught up in gangs, crack, drugs, drop out of school, and get pregnant at depressingly early ages?"

"It wouldn't address these issues directly," Rodrigo replied. "Although reducing military adventurism would save some young black lives. Most of the gain would be indirect. If my calculations are right"—Rodrigo looked down at his scratch sheet—"the average American loses between five hundred and a thousand dollars a year to white-collar crimes. If you define the category broadly, to include corporate fraud and misconduct, the figure is even higher."

"That's a lot of money," I replied. "Are you sure of your figures?"

"They're about what I got before," Rodrigo said. "I can leave you this printout, and you can check for yourself."

"Thanks. I appreciated it when you did that before. It made my job easier. So, what do you think we could do to stem the tide of white-collar crime? And even if we did, why do you think society would want to spend any of the savings to relieve the pain and poverty of ghetto youth, rather than apply it for lower taxes, trips to Disneyland, a second car, or that long-delayed family vacation?"

"Let me try to deal with each of those separately," Rodrigo said.

I sat back expectantly.

In Which Rodrigo Explains How He Would Reduce White (-Collar) Crime

"To reduce the excess amount of crime white people commit, especially those in the executive suite, I think we have to go to the source of it."

"And that source is ... ?" I asked.

"The white family," Rodrigo replied. "That and the crime/tort loophole we discussed a minute ago. The two work together. White people's peculiar family structure inclines them to commit certain kinds of crimes, engage in certain kinds of antisocial behavior. And the soft treatment they afford each other when they're caught encourages them to act irresponsibly, never to develop a full sense of responsibility for their acts."

"I'd love to hear more about the kinds of family pathology you have in mind. I think I have a pretty good grasp on what you mean by soft treatment of offenders, by coddling of white-collar and corporate criminals. But it's the family dynamics that interest me right now." (I had both a professional and personal interest in the relation of families to crime. As Rodrigo had been speaking, I remembered with a slight pang an incident in our own past when my wife and I had received a call from the neighborhood police station. Our eldest son had been arrested on suspicion of shoplifting. He was only ten at the time, and was later cleared, but the experience had left a deep impression on all three of us.)

"Would you like a cup of coffee first?" I asked.

Rodrigo nodded vigorously, so I got up, motioning him to continue while I prepared the coffee machine for another batch.

Getting to the Root of the Problem: The White Family Structure

As I busied myself measuring out the ingredients, Rodrigo began:

"As we were saying, Professor, white-collar crime is a serious social problem. Committed mostly by white people, its net social costs exceed those of street crime by a large margin. Indeed, if my figures are correct, they exceed those committed by the black population on a per capita, not just a net basis. Many such crimes go unpunished, even though they cause injury, disfigurement, and death. Moreover, the amount of interpersonal violence associated with this type of misdeed is greater, on both bases, than that associated with black crime."

"Here's your coffee."

Rodrigo stirred in some creamer and his trademark four teaspoons of sugar and began slurping his drink. After a short interval, he continued:

"We need a major study of the white family. Social scientists could examine what features contribute to the large amount of deadly white-collar crime it constantly produces. Psychologists would study the contribution of child-rearing patterns, punishment, inculcation of attitudes toward authority, TV-watching, and so on. Sociologists would try to figure out whether mobility, changes in jobs and job security, and divorce have anything to do with it. Statisticians would look for correlations—all converging on the central problem of high levels of white-collar crime, particularly ones of stealth and theft."

"And I suppose you have a hypothesis regarding what they will find if they undertake such a study?"

"I do," Rodrigo replied. "I have a hunch that crimes of stealth and theft tend to be associated with small family size. In Italian culture, for example, families tend to be larger. More generations live under one roof, with grandparents and aunts living with the nuclear couple and their children. The children get plenty of adult attention. Plus, there's always someone there to watch them and very few latchkey children. For all those reasons, there is much less theft, even when you take into account that it is a much poorer country."

"Some American corporate criminals I have read about come from large families."

"I know. Small size is not the only factor. Many American families—upper class, white ones, I mean—are also intensely private. Every child has his or her own bedroom. Children are urged to cover up. There is little nudity, even when the child is very small. I have a suspicion that this encourages a spirit in which crimes of silence, of secrecy, can flourish. A third element is acquisitiveness. In the U.S., children quickly learn that material things—toys, the latest clothes, musical equipment, and so on—are a measure of their worth. For some, later in school, this takes the form of competition for the highest grades. Little wonder that children raised in such a warped atmosphere grow up committing one of the highest rates of white-collar crime in the world."

"Competitiveness isn't so bad. It enabled us to develop the wilderness, set up a commercial empire, invent new machines and medical cures."

"But not when it spreads over into the realm of crime," Rodrigo retorted, "as it too often does. For example, in my law school, one of the librarians told me that books disappear all the time. Imagine—stealing a book! In some societies this would be unthinkable. And one of my fellow students, who is in the J.D. program, told me that during exams and moot court, people scissor pages and whole articles out of bound volumes. The library has to Xerox or buy a replacement sheet or article, and glue it back into place. This looks funny—I've seen them—and must cost a fortune."

"I'm sure it does."

"And then this attitude spreads into the world of work," Rodrigo continued. "Corporations have learned that they can make more money by taking over each other, by issuing fraudulent or near-fraudulent junk bonds, and so on, much more easily than they can by working hard to sell better products or services. I ran into an old friend who is now working for the mergers and acquisitions department of a major law firm on the other side of the river. He says they have a saying: 'We make money the old fashioned way—we take it.'"

"Even when legal, there's obviously a limit to how long American business can go on simply buying and selling and taking over each other," I said.

"But hardly anyone thinks to ask that question. The prevailing ethic and family structure tell all who grow up in the culture that if you can get away with taking something—if no one sees you or the law doesn't flatly pronounce it criminal—it's okay to do it. Ethics, caring, consideration for others rarely come into play. It all goes back to the family structure."

"Of course, that's the same accusation they make against us—that our families are pathological, too many single mothers, gangs, irresponsibility, and so on."

"Some truth inheres in that," Rodrigo acknowledged. "But the black family is the strangest possible scapegoat for America's social ills today. The real causes of our economic downturn, of our festering cities, and soaring unemployment rate, are white-collar crime and corruption."

"You think it's that pervasive?"

"I do. But leaving that aside, the train of abuses I just documented for you on your computer is largely the source of our business downturn. Today the U.S. has only the world's fifth strongest economy. It used to be first by a large margin. And to return to your question, yes, I think the solution to blacks' problems is interconnected with the solution to whites' problems."

"You mean in the sense that any general benefit redounds to the improvement of all?"

"In more than that 'trickle-down' sense, Professor. I believe the connecting link is the great middle class and its sense of what we can and cannot do as a nation."

I probably looked puzzled, for Rodrigo stopped for a moment, drained his coffee cup, and continued:

"The white middle class has most of the votes. And currently, they will not vote for, or tolerate, costly programs that benefit the black poor. And the reason is not hard to understand: The members of that class are themselves hurting. Both parents in many families are already working, yet are barely able to make ends meet. Their own children are exhibiting social pathology because of inattention at home. And the economic indicators show that things are unlikely to get better soon."

"In an atmosphere like that, no one is likely to feel generous toward outgroups, toward people even poorer, more desperate than oneself."

"No, but if we could get a grip on white-collar crime, everyone would see an immediate improvement in their situation. Look at the figures we jotted down earlier—five hundred dollars per year per American citizen, not even counting the costs of wars and other military aggressions. If every family had that much more in their pocket, they might be more generous toward those who have even less. We could help young black men in trouble. We could have Head Start programs and pediatric care for every black youngster. We could turn things around, reduce the amount of pain and desolation in our inner cities—not overnight, but in relatively short order."

"We could even give some of the white people's land back to the Indians," I said.

Rodrigo shot me a sharp look. "I'm serious," I said. "It's not a minor issue."

"I'm glad," Rodrigo replied. "Because it's a serious issue with me, too. Our indigenous tribes exhibit poverty, drop-out, and suicide rates that are some of the worst in the world. It's time society took making amends seriously."

"And you think that by encouraging white folks to get a grip on their own criminality, rein in the malefactors and malefactors-to-be in their midst, all this would become possible?"

"Five hundred dollars per person is a lot of money. Right now, neither the money nor the spirit is there. The money has flowed into the pockets of the corporate elite, which is richer and more confident than ever before, while the middle class of all colors is hurting. If we clamped down on the tax cheats, procurement fraud artists, and so on, the average American taxpayer would have a lower bill, would see higher returns on his or her money, and would be less reluctant to vote for programs that benefit the poor and the black underclass."

"But what makes you think that the extra money will change people's political views? The average conservative middle class voter will attribute the windfall to his own hard work and ingenuity. He will continue to believe that he is comfortable because he deserves it and that the poor are in their position because they have gotten what they deserve. And the wealthier may not even notice the extra money; they may simply notice with disapproval that the law is really cracking down on them, but that the kid who stole their hubcaps has yet to be apprehended."

"I'm sure some will react that way," Rodrigo conceded.

"And even if the extra money is freed up and the taxpayers are willing to use it for the benefit of all society, rather than for their trip to Disneyland or Susie's tuition, I am not sure that they would agree to have that money spent on the underclasses. Many middle class people believe that too much is being spent already on 'those people.' And with the recent emphasis on the deficit and national debt, I'm not sure the middle class wants to raise taxes only to increase spending. They want deficit reduction."

Rodrigo shot me a quizzical look, then replied:

"Yes, and we thought that third-party candidates couldn't have much of an impact on national elections. But I don't guess I'm saying that the spirit to deal with the oppressive conditions of the inner city will necessarily come with the financial means of doing so. What I am saying is that, if we don't come up with the money by cutting waste or crime then the desire to help the plight of the poor will definitely not be there. With the extra money, the will may come."

"That is still a very optimistic view of things for a neomarxist."

"I realize that, Professor, but even if the middle class does not see the savings or attribute them to the crackdown on white collar crime, some of the savings will automatically accrue to the poorer classes. Particularly the savings from consumer fraud. Because the poor spend a higher percentage of their income on consumption than do the middle class or the wealthy, they will receive a higher proportion of their income in savings than will the wealthy."

"And with that higher income will come improvements in quality of life, and with that will come less of a need to steal and commit the various other street crimes that we talked about."

"Cracking down on white-collar crime can help two ways. Benefits will come from the savings automatically accruing to the poor as well as to the middle class. And the extra money may help the middle class get out of its own financial bind and enable it to think about others."

"But you would still have what you call the social construction problem, would you not?"

"I think this would ease as society began to see that our folks do not include the biggest and worst criminals by a long shot. They would see us for what we are: a population that contains many poor—and some desperate—people living lives of danger because of the legacy of slavery, racism, and separate-but-equal treatment. Americans can be generous toward groups they do not see as demonized—flood victims, for example."

"Or children lost in the bottom of a well," I added.

"You have put your finger on an important point, though, Professor, one I'll have to ponder. I've argued that social need generated the stigma-picture, the stereotype of the black criminal. The question is: If we could destroy that stereotype, would things reverse—would the repression and cold treatment wither away, or would it return in yet another form and supported by yet another rationalizing structure?"

"That's a tough question," I replied. "It has to do with one's basic attitude to human nature, the fundamental goodness or badness of mankind. Some days, I think our people will not overcome, that we will never be saved, that we will be doomed to enjoy at most periodic peaks of progress, followed by a sickening thud as we fall right back where we started from—that white self-interest calls the tune. When it serves the purpose of elite whites to permit us an occasional breakthrough, then we get a *Brown v. Board of Education* or Civil Rights Act of 1964. Right now it seems to be in the self-interest of powerful whites to depict us as criminals. I doubt we'll escape that stereotype until conditions change."

"Some white folks will listen," Rodrigo replied, a little hesitantly. "My thesis advisor is white, and he seems genuinely open."

"But it's the opinion makers who really count," I replied. "And for all his brilliance, your professor really is not an opinion maker in the way the humblest reporter, news broadcaster, or assistant city mayor is."

CONCLUSION

We both sat back in my rapidly darkening office. I knew Rodrigo and I would soon have to return to our respective shelters, I to my nearby apartment, he to his and Giannina's place across town. The coffeepot's red switch glowed faintly in the gathering gloom. I reflected on the powerful case Rodrigo had made, both with statistics and interest-convergence/social-construction-of-reality theory, for why our people are invested these days with such a devastatingly negative image. I wondered if there was any hope for its abatement. Only strong friends with access to and a command of the media, the mechanisms of public information and opinion, could help us, I thought. I reflected on the huge costs of that "other kind" of crime and wondered what chance, if any, our nation had of bringing it under control. Further, if we did, what assurance was there that the gains would be transferred, put to the benefit of poor families in the ghetto?

The phone rang again. I picked it up, and as I feared, Rodrigo stood up and indicated he had to go. "By the way, Professor," he mouthed, "your office looks very nice."

I nodded, listened to the phone for a moment, then smiled broadly. Covering the receiver I told Rodrigo, who was about to disappear out my door: "It's the reporter. She wants to know how to spell 'Harry Kalven'!"

Rodrigo's Ninth Chronicle
Race, Legal Instrumentalism, and the Rule of Law

I was sitting dejectedly in the airport waiting lounge, cursing myself for having taken a winter flight that changed planes in a northern city, when I heard a familiar voice from behind me.

"Professor, is it you?"

I turned. "Rodrigo, for goodness' sake! What are you doing here?" A foreign-educated LL.M. student at the famous university across town, Rodrigo had sought me out for career advice nearly a year ago on a return trip to the States. The son of an African-American serviceman and an Italian mother, the brilliant and audacious young scholar saw the United States with new eyes. We had become friends, discussing law and economics, civil rights, essentialism, black crime, and many other subjects over the course of a year.

"I'm just getting back from job interviews. I think I told you I'm on the teaching market. I did four interviews in seven days."

"You must be exhausted," I commiserated.

"Oh, it wasn't so bad," my irrepressible protégé replied, "although it went by in something of a blur. I'm afraid I'll get a telephone call from Professor Jones and not remember what school he's from."

"Tell him you enjoyed meeting his colleagues. He may mention a name and that'll ring a bell. The older I get the more trouble I have remembering students' names. But I don't have your excuse—I have them all term long."

"Your students like you, Professor. If you forget an occasional name it doesn't matter. They know you care about them, just as I know you care about me."

"Enough flattery," I said. "Tell me about your trip. My flight was canceled. I've got nearly three hours before the next one. I was just sitting here trying to build up courage to open my briefcase, but I'd much rather talk with you."

"I've got plenty of time. I'm arriving early, having caught a standby flight in the nick of time from Chicago. Giannina's not expecting me till this evening. Can I buy you a drink or cup of coffee?"

"Maybe in a minute. Sit down," I said, indicating the empty seat next to me. "Tell me about your trip."

"Well, as I mentioned, I interviewed at four law schools, all in the Midwest. Next week I'm hitting the Northeast—two in four days. But something interesting happened at the one I left just this morning. If you have a minute, I'd love to tell you about it."

"Please do. As I've told you more than once, I get at least as much out of our conversations as you do. What happened?"

"I was having one of those small group interviews. Four professors and I were meeting in the office of one of them. It was my last one before going to meet the students and the Dean. It really got me going—I've done nothing but think about it the whole flight. It's providential that I met you here. I would have called you in a day or two to talk."

"Was it something that came up during your job talk?"

"Only tangentially. I addressed the relation of laissez-faire economics and the plight of the black poor, an aspect of my thesis. One professor apparently got the idea that I'm interested in critical race theory, which of course I am, even though my talk didn't touch on that at all. So he had this question ready for me when we met later in the office."

"What was it? The usual one about affirmative action?"

"No, not at all. It was about racial realism, but with a pedagogical twist. You're familiar with the critique of Derrick Bell's work as too despairing?"

"I am. A number of authors have taken Bell to task for what they consider his undue pessimism, notably Alan Freeman, an otherwise friendly writer, in a review of Bell's first casebook. A few of us have even questioned whether preaching gloom and doom is wise, particularly if it ends up discouraging students from going into public interest work. How did you answer the question?"

"I pointed out that Bell might well be right, and if so, there's little to be gained by holding on to false hopes. But it turned out the professor was making a much more subtle 'as if' argument, questioning whether, even if we thought the condition of blacks and other minorities of color is unlikely to improve, enjoying only periodic peaks of progress followed by regression, we ought to act as though we believed the opposite. Otherwise we'd be paralyzed. There would be no reason to struggle."

"That *is* a more powerful version," I agreed. "It reminds me of recent writing about myths and the way society organizes itself around certain beliefs and credos. Even if not literally true, the myths help society run more smoothly."

"I conceded as much, but nevertheless stuck to my position. We had a spirited discussion."

"I wish I had been there. Tell me, how did you defend Bell's thesis?"

"I began by laying it out, beginning with the interest-convergence idea—that whites will support and tolerate gains for blacks only when these also benefit them—then traced it through Bell's analysis of *Brown v. Board of Education*, and finally into its modern form, *racial realism*."

Just then, the public address system announced the arrival of a flight from Dallas, and I realized we would soon have a planeload of passengers streaming past us. "This area is filling up, Rodrigo. I'd love to hear how you answered the professor's question, which incidentally strikes me as both intelligent and admirable. It lets you show how you would deal with a recurring pedagogical issue. And at the same time it allows you to strut your stuff on an important point of legal theory. That professor had obviously done his homework. Why don't we continue this conversation somewhere else? There's a little noodle shop just down the concourse. It smelled good when I passed by. Could you use a bite?"

"Always," Rodrigo replied. "They didn't feed us much on the flight home—just a tiny, dry sandwich."

I made a sympathetic face and stood up. As we walked in the direction of the restaurant, Rodrigo continued: "The myth question wasn't too hard, at least until I started thinking more about it later. I told the group in the office that minorities and members of the majority group need different myths because they are differently situated. With respect to race, what white people need is hope. They need to believe in black progress, because otherwise they would be consumed by guilt. Most of them have a higher standard of living than ours, longer life expectancy, lower rates of incarceration and infant death, and so on—all directly traceable to slavery and social neglect. Consequently, they fasten onto any indicator of progress for blacks or other minorities, even during times when our misery index is higher than ever. They read somewhere that more left-handed Hispanic plumber's apprentices work in Ohio than twenty years ago and seize upon that as proof that things are getting better."

"The conservatives aren't consumed by guilt," I pointed out. "They think that if our progress is stalled, it's our fault. We have dysfunctional families or allow ourselves to succumb to a culture of poverty."

"You have a point," Rodrigo acknowledged. "Yet they do hold to a myth of progress—namely, that the race problem has been solved. The playing field is now level, as a result of the 1960s-era reforms, so that today any black or Latino who is not progressing has only himself or herself to blame."

"So white folks subscribe to and place great stock in the myth of black progress. I agree with you on that. A recent poll showed that black parents believe things are now as bad for black children as at any time since slavery. The same study showed that homicide is the leading cause of death for black youths between fifteen and twenty-four years of age. Nearly half of all black children live under the poverty level, and

34 percent of all black teenagers looking for work could not find it, a rate twice that of white teenagers. Nearly half of all black babies are not adequately immunized, and fully 65 percent of black adults believe that their kids will be denied jobs because of racial prejudice. Nevertheless, most of our white friends cannot be made to see that things are getting worse, not better for us. But you mentioned a counterpart myth on our side of the equation."

"Oh, yes. Whites need the myth of civil rights progress to be able to function. We, by contrast, need a stone-cold sober assessment of our chances, even if they are not very good. For just as whites need guilt-avoidance, we need to avoid self-blame. For us, the paralyzing mental process is internalization of the terrible images society has disseminated about us through the ages—unintelligent, lazy, sexually lascivious, and so on. We also need to avoid connecting our low estate—our poverty, high crime rate, high degree of social pathology, and so on—with ourselves and our own efforts. We need to keep in mind that our current condition is the direct result of our subordination. It is, in short, not our fault. For us, this bleak realization is healing, is psychically necessary, just as the more sanguine, upbeat interpretation is what whites need."

The hostess at the restaurant, where we had been waiting briefly, beckoned us to come in. We followed her to a booth, sat down, and picked up the menus. Before we started scanning them in earnest, I asked Rodrigo, "And did that answer satisfy them?"

"It seemed to, for then. At least, we soon moved on to something else. But it didn't fully satisfy me. On the flight back I realized there's more to it than that. I'd love to run some ideas past you, if you've got the time."

I nodded enthusiastically. "Should we order first?"

IN WHICH RODRIGO RECONCILES MAINSTREAM CIVIL RIGHTS LAW AND THE MORE PESSIMISTIC RACIAL-REALIST VERSION

A few minutes later the waitress took our orders, first patiently explaining to my ebullient young friend how a certain Korean dish differed from one he had learned to like in his favorite restaurant in Chinatown. After she had gone, Rodrigo continued:

"Nice woman. Where were we? Oh, yes—the optimism-pessimism gap. What I realized on the flight home is that it's not enough simply to explain *why* our folks are on the whole less upbeat than whites. We need a theory of what folks like us should *do*. Should we sit around in despair? Try harder? The principal purveyor of what we called 'bleak chic,' namely Derrick Bell, says that the situation is grim, but one must struggle nonetheless. Even though one knows in advance that the gains will be very slight, one must make the effort anyway. Yet he doesn't explain why, exactly."

"It seems to be an article of faith, a kind of existential commitment, something that gives life meaning, enabling us to carry on in an otherwise bleak and desolate world," I suggested.

"That's the interpretation I drew too, but then I began thinking we can go even beyond that. The theory I propose is not so much a replacement as a modification of Bell's. Under it, subordinated people would acknowledge that in many eras and in many courts, success is really not possible. At these times, it is best to look elsewhere for relief."

"To what Gerry Spann calls 'pure politics,'" I ventured, "mass marches, picketing, lobbying, the legislative arena—forums other than courts?"

"Exactly. And when these avenues seem foreclosed, when society as a whole seems to close its face to us, we can turn to our own sources, our own communities."

"That's self-help, cultural nationalism, building our own communities, looking to black colleges," I said in excitement. I could see the outlines of a long-awaited theory of social change forming, something that had eluded some of our finest minds. I longed to hear more. "And so, Rodrigo, you think that what's needed is an overarching theory to tell us which approach to use at any given moment in history. The interest-convergence theory tells us there will be times when courts will be hostile or indifferent, but if I understand you correctly, that need not be a counsel of despair. Rather, it simply means that we should then look to other means for progress and succor."

"Exactly," Rodrigo replied. "We should look upon law as we would any other social institution, a tool that is useful for certain purposes and at certain times, but less so for other purposes or at different times. We need not succumb to the totalizing despair of some of our most eminent theorists, one that actually can prove enervating, despite my rather flip answer to the group this morning. Nor need we embrace the saccharine optimism of conventional civil rights theories grounded in liberalism and faith in progress. That's dangerous too, because it leads to disillusionment and burnout. We need a more sustaining approach, which my more pragmatic view provides. What do you think, Professor?" Rodrigo looked up cheerfully.

"I'd love to hear more details. But my first impression is that the idea has much promise. It echoes some of the teachings of a new legal movement, pragmatism. And it avoids the Scylla and Charybdis of over-optimism on the one hand, and despair on the other. Do you have a name for your brain child?"

Rodrigo looked up and smiled, whether because of my question or because of the arrival of the waitress with a trayful of steaming, savory-smelling bowls, I could not tell. "Legal instrumentalism," he said, moving aside his water glass and making way for the bowls and dishes full of tempting soups and crepe-type dishes.

RODRIGO EXPLAINS LEGAL INSTRUMENTALISM AS A CIVIL RIGHTS STRATEGY

"What are you having?" I asked.

"A noodle dish. I can't remember what it's called. It's a lot like something Giannina and I have at a Chinese restaurant near where we live. But it's different—it has more ginger. Want a bite?"

We traded morsels, and Rodrigo commented, "Mmmmm. Your stir fry is really good. So you think my theory has promise?"

"Emphatically so. I like its synthetic quality, the way it allows for differentiation of strategy depending on the times and circumstances. And I especially like the—well, how shall I call it?—the mental health overtones. It promises a much more liberating way of looking at civil rights challenges, one that avoids both false optimism and undue despair. But I'd love to know two things. First, how you thought of it. And second, how you would defend it against the charge of cynicism. You've already explained more or less how it would work—we'd choose whatever tool seemed most promising at a given period in history. And I'd also like to know how you would respond to the accusation, one you are certain to hear leveled against you, that it goes against the noble ideal of the rule of law. If not frankly 'antilegal,' your theory verges on a demystification of law and litigation, for it seems to say, follow the law when it will work for you, and avoid or break it when it won't. Your theory has precursors, not all of which enjoy good favor."

Legal Instrumentalism
Rodrigo paused to spear a last noodle stuck in the bottom of his bowl, then continued. "I know about Thrasymachus and that other dialogue, as well as some of their latter-day versions including 'By any means necessary.' But Socrates was not vindicating a system of laws that systematically oppressed a minority of its citizens, and so the tribunal that sentenced him to death was much more legitimate than ours, at least vis-à-vis him. Our Constitution excluded blacks, women, and those without property from the very beginning. It provided for the institution of slavery in no fewer than ten passages. And even when we abolished that institution a hundred years later, a system of Jim Crow laws kept our people in circumstances little better than those they had just escaped. It was not until yet another hundred years passed that separate but equal—legal apartheid—began to be repealed, and ten more years before we were permitted to marry whites. The United States was not the first nation to repeal slavery—not even among the first ten."

"But surely, Rodrigo," I interjected, "things have changed. And even if our system of civil rights laws is not perfect, does it not provide at least a degree of protection? What do we have that is any better? Anarchy?"

"Good points," Rodrigo replied mildly. "I don't want to exaggerate. Sometimes the courts are our staunchest allies. But sometimes they are not. During these times we should look to other avenues. Otherwise one is just beating one's head against a stone wall."

"What you called perseveration."

"Actually, your two questions turn out to be related. Legal instrumentalism occurred to me in reflecting on the idea of legitimacy and the way in which recent revolutionary leaders have viewed law. Few of the great ones held to any sort of romantic ideal. Gandhi, of course, considered the British system of laws and civil service entirely illegitimate and had little hesitation about ordering strikes and boycotts, even though they were technically illegal. Martin Luther King believed one had no obligation to obey unjust laws."

"Although King did believe that one should be prepared to suffer punishment as a consequence," I interjected.

"To be sure. And in more recent times, the Black Panthers took a position very much like the one I am suggesting. Their leaders understood that the forces of law would often be arrayed against them, but that sometimes one could employ litigation, injunctions, and other legal strategies to make genuine progress for the community. Cesar Chavez and the farmworkers seem to have had a similar attitude. Outsider groups exhibit a long history of seeing law in pragmatic terms, as sometimes legitimate and helpful, and at other times not."

"Your point, then, is that people of color should straightforwardly recognize that the law will often not protect them because it is designed to promote the interests of others, and that they should make the best of the situation."

"You and I were discussing normativity and the intensely civic-minded turn legal theory has taken recently. While on the plane, it occurred to me that one of the main uses of normative discourse is to keep people like you and me from criticizing the rule of law. If everyone, including outsiders, reveres the law, even when it is doing obvious and demonstrable harm, we will reason: 'Oh, well, it's a great institution, so we shouldn't criticize.' We'll agree to remain silent, fixating on the few times that legal institutions have really helped us...."

"Like the sixties," I said.

"Right," Rodrigo agreed. "And ignore that the rest of the time the law is either indifferent or a positive obstacle. In no other area of human endeavor, with the possible exception of religion, do we succumb to such totalistic, all-or-nothing thinking. Imagine, for example, a butcher who sold rotted meat defending his action by saying, 'But I followed the procedure.' Or a teacher, all of whose students failed standardized tests, insisting 'I taught them that.' In all these other areas we insist on results. Imagine the butcher defending his practice by saying that the institution of butchery does more good than harm. We'd call this the nonsense it is!"

"I see what you mean," I agreed. "Many have pointed out that procedure is something that bad men love and follow most assiduously. Kafka and other novelists wrote about that."

"So, minorities should invoke and follow the law when it benefits them and break or ignore it otherwise—when it gets in the way, is unresponsive, or is adverse to their interests. We should treat it like any other social institution, the highway department, for example. No one hesitates to call the highway department to task, to criticize it if it is always fixing the potholes on the other side of town and ignoring the ones in their neighborhood. No one speaks of the majesty of the rule of highway procedure or the grandeur of pothole fixing. If the department is doing its job, we leave it alone or give it a pat on the back. If it's not, we call it to account, or else work out some other way of getting the potholes fixed."

"Rodrigo, you are saying that social reformers should subsume law under their agenda, which is to achieve progress for minorities. Law-types approach things in just the opposite way, insisting on subsuming racial reform under law. Law people place law at the center, and then ask where racial justice should fit in. Should Martin Luther King be allowed to march in the face of an injunction? Should civil disobedience be allowed? Should a white charged with discrimination be able to escape by showing a business necessity, or a lack of intent or causation?"

"I agree. We should demand the opposite—that race reform be placed in the center, and then ask where law fits in."

"It seems to me," I said, "that it all depends on what is uppermost in your mind, on what your objective is. The law-lover will subscribe to mythic, heroic views about the rule of law and insist that we address everything else within that framework. We, by contrast, will take a more utilitarian view of law, as the Panthers did. We'll ask: 'What can law do for us at this time and place?'"

"And that's what I mean by 'legal instrumentalism.' We should demystify law, see it as the social institution it is: good for some things, less so for others. As we said before, theory-fitting is everything. It makes no sense to use Gramsci to help you prepare a budget, nor law and economics to try to make this a fairer world for excluded groups. We should avoid counsels of despair. But, by the same token, we should disavow failed liberal programs that achieve too little because they promise too much. Hence, legal instrumentalism: try everything until you find what works."

Rodrigo Defends Instrumentalism against the Charge That It Is Unprincipled

The waitress appeared at our table: "Would you gentlemen like some dessert?" Despite my doctor's orders to cut down, I looked up at Rodrigo inquiringly, as I very much wanted to prolong our session. His enthusiastic nod did much to allay my guilt. "You've been through a lot," I said. "Besides, I don't think they're serving supper on this make-up flight I'm taking in two hours." We both scrutinized the dessert menu, gave the waitress our orders (apple strudel for my high-energy young friend, an abstemious fruit cup for me), and returned to our conversation.

"Rodrigo, I like your theory. It's exactly what we need. As you pointed out, it comes with much honorable precedent. And, it squares with my sense of how law works to preserve the advantage of the powerful, yet enables us to go on nevertheless. But perhaps your theory is something that we should not speak of too openly. Perhaps we should keep it in-group. Perhaps it should remain on the level of myth, as you said, and not be put out for public consumption."

"Why would we do that?" Rodrigo looked concerned.

"I meant no criticism of your theory as a way to interpret and organize experience. But won't mainstream scholars accuse you of cynicism, of weakening the social fabric? And won't they have a point? You do seem to be saying that obeying the law is not important, at least for minorities."

"I believe deeply in the social fabric," Rodrigo replied, suddenly solemn. "But I don't equate that with the law any more than I think we should equate society with the highway department, or with the institution of conscription. Each of these is a means to an end. Anyone who argued that we should venerate the highway department or the military draft would be seen as a little strange. I'm suggesting that we think of the law in the same way, and that for minorities, at least, even stronger reasons counsel doing so. None of us was at the Constitutional Convention, only three of us have been elected to the Senate and none to the presidency or vice-presidency, and not a single black CEO leads a Fortune 500 company. Not to mention the way in which legal doctrine, the law on the books, as well as the law in action, are almost always arrayed against us."

I was silent as Rodrigo stole a look at the items on the tray of the waitress as she passed by our table. "Those look good. Too bad they're not for us," he continued. "Notice that large institutions never worship the rule of law, at least not the way everyone tells minorities they are supposed to. A corporation that calculates that it is cheaper to market a product with a design defect the corporation knows will cause X injuries or Y deaths will often do so if it figures it can get away with it or that the cost of compensating the victims is cheaper than that of retooling its assembly line."

"Or they reason that some members of the public won't sue. The victims may know they have been injured but not by whom. Or they may not want to make trouble. Or they may fear that filing a lawsuit will take too long and cost too much money. So a corporation that causes ten injuries may only be sued five times. The cost of retooling a defective product may be great enough that they simply internalize the deaths, broken bones, and cases of cancer as costs of doing business," I added.

"Corporations are not the only ones who behave this way. Nations do as well. If a large power needs to take action to promote its interest, it will often do so even if this violates international law or a treaty it has signed. In doing so, it realizes this will have a cost—that other nations will be resentful and not trust it so much in the future. It knows its action will weaken the tenuous compact among nations to obey the law, even when no superpower can enforce the rules. It knows these things, but factors them in as just another cost of doing business, like the lives and airplanes that will be lost in the invasion or coup."

"Great political theorists, old and new, have recognized this: Nations act in their own self-interest."

"I'm sure we're thinking of the same people," Rodrigo added. "It only makes sense to approach civil rights law nonideologically. We should be zero-based and as dispassionate as possible, choosing legality when doing so will benefit us, and straightforwardly pursuing other means when it does not. Ideology—including slavish devotion to law—always has costs. It prevents you from making alliances with the other side, from pursuing an avenue that might bring you benefit. Nietzsche thought that was its whole purpose. He may have had a point."

[Eds. Rodrigo and the Professor next discuss whether minorities should abandon their historic and near-reflexive embrace of the Democratic Party, after which the Professor asks whether idealism, not cold calculation, might not be best in the long run.]

Rodrigo's eyes twinkled for a moment as he glanced up from his strudel. "I know it's kind of a big order, all for dessert. [I snorted at the double entendre.] But maybe we could make a start. Actually, I've got [he looked at his watch] almost an hour. So, if you have the energy, why don't we start."

I nodded, Rodrigo took a deep breath, and began.

RODRIGO EXPLAINS WHY SELF-INTEREST, NOT IDEALISM, IS THE BEST COURSE FOR MINORITIES AND WHY ONE SHOULD RARELY PUT TOO MUCH FAITH IN INTEREST-CONVERGENCE WITH THE DOMINANT GROUP

Why Self-Interest Is the Safest Course for Disempowered People

"We can only look to our own self-interest, Professor, and rarely to the altruism of the majority group because our social construction, the images and pictures of us that the majority culture disseminates and consumes, limits the amount of altruism that comes our way. We discussed some of this before—the way in which the dominant society finds it convenient to depict us as lazy, criminal, lascivious, not very smart, and so on. Over time these pictures begin to seem like the truth, begin to seem real."

"Some whites escape those forces," I replied quietly. "Some of them are humane, generous, treat us as equals. You mentioned your thesis advisor, for one."

"True," Rodrigo conceded. "But I'm talking about politics, about large numbers. And when you look at that level—by which I mean the level of polls, attitudes, the ways the American people as a group look at race—you find something that I call 'guilt by definition.'"

"The term is new to me, but I think I know what you mean. We're a group whose very social construction inclines members of the majority race to fear us, to regard us as potential troublemakers, to cross the street when we approach them on the sidewalk at night, that sort of thing?"

"That is indeed part of it. We discussed this earlier when we talked about black and white crime. But I think that some of those earlier observations support legal instrumentalism as the only sane approach to civil rights—for blacks and people of color, at any rate."

"Let me guess how that argument might go," I said. "For you, the incessant characterization of blacks in demeaning terms means that the average member of society virtually equates any one of us with trouble. We come to be seen as absent fathers, welfare mothers, lazy office worker 'quota queens,' and so on. Once this sets in, we have little chance of appealing to the better natures of persons who hold this unconscious image of us. The image renders us 'Other.' It means people simply don't think of us as individuals to whom love, respect, generosity, and friendliness are due. We are 'beyond love,' as we discussed before. Studies of helping behavior show this conclusively. A black female confederate spills a bag of groceries and only blacks will help her. A blond, blue-eyed woman does and whites rush to her aid. And the same with stranded motorists and other people in distress. Is this the general mechanism you were thinking of?"

"Yes. And to anticipate your question, I do believe one can extrapolate from the personal to the political—what is true of individuals is also true of groups. So that any theory of race must take into account this lack of good will or fellow-feeling. Do you have a garden, Professor?"

The question took me by surprise. "Yes, I have a small one. Not that I have been tending to it as much as I should. My late wife and I used to have a much larger one.

What connection are you trying to make between gardening and civil rights?" I half winced, knowing of Rodrigo's penchant for colorful metaphors and extrapolations. It turned out that my fears were unfounded.

"If you've gardened, Professor, you know about the concept of weeds. A weed is any plant that a society deems undesirable, such as dandelions. Yet, in my home country, there are regions where dandelions grow wild, populate entire hillsides, and are regarded as rather beautiful."

"I remember," I said. "I was in your country not long ago. As you know, I spent last summer at a conference study center in northern Italy. While there, I drove through the Dolomite mountains in the late spring. The fields of bright yellow dandelions were, indeed, very beautiful."

"Racial features are like weeds and dandelions. No DNA divide separates common weeds, like thistles, dandelions, and clover on the one hand, from fine grasses and flowers on the other. The category is constructed and varies from society to society. The same is true of race. Our facial features, skin color, and hair do not set us apart in any important way from white people, who according to scientists share virtually all of their genetic makeup with us. We are the same species. It is only because society chooses to regard the small physical differences between blacks and whites as marking out different races that we even construct such categories instead of some other ones, such as heavily eyebrowed persons versus thin-eyebrowed persons or something similar."

"But we do, and the categories come loaded. We place value judgments on them—they are not neutral," I said, building on Rodrigo's observation. "We notice color not just as a curiosity, but in order to assign people to statuses. You and I are the weeds, they the flowers."

"Our very category implies that we are one-down, the sort of people whom majority society can afford disparate, and usually worse, treatment, all with impunity and while feeling perfectly ethical about it. Therefore, we need to tend our own gardens. My approach—legal instrumentalism—is simply radical individualism applied to the racial predicament. If our construction were different, this approach might not be necessary. But because of our history and culture, because of how we were brought here, the institutions of slavery, conquest, Bracero programs, racist immigration quotas, and so on that kept minority populations suppressed for years, it is. In a way, it's like the bootstrapping and self-help approaches that neoconservatives like Thomas Sowell and Glenn Loury have been urging, but for different reasons."

"The negative images may change, may even now be changing," I said, determined to play the devil's advocate as long as possible. "In every era, some mainstream writers or moviemakers take our side, depict us sympathetically. The image may in time give way in favor of a more nuanced, humane one."

"I know," Rodrigo conceded. "The trouble is that our defenders tend to have no audience. Their work is seen as political, as 'message' pieces. It is only later, after consciousness changes, that we see that they were right after all. Harriet Beecher Stowe's abolitionist novel sold well only after much anti-slavery activism had sensitized the American public to the evil of slavery. Nadine Gordimer won the Nobel

Prize only when her country was on the verge of repudiating apartheid. And have you heard of the role of 'attestors,' Professor?"

I strained, trying to remember where I had recently read about such a thing. "Does it have to do with authentication of the slave narratives?" I asked.

"It may arise there," Rodrigo said. "But I was reading about it in connection with the work of some early African-American poets."

"Oh yes, now I remember," I said. "Phillis Wheatley was one. Didn't the American publishing world refuse to believe that she, a onetime slave, actually wrote certain collections of poems?"

"Exactly. Several Bostonians, including the Governor of Massachusetts and John Hancock, had to step in. They knew Ms. Wheatley and testified that she had indeed written the poems in question. Most others in American letters did not believe an African-American woman was capable of such a thing. But the odd thing is that the attestors themselves were not poets at all, whereas Wheatley had gained recognition in Boston and in England for her poetry. It's like going to the local mayor for confirmation that Alexander the Great was really a major political figure."

"And you think the history of attestors shows something about our social quandary?"

"It does. Attestors wouldn't be necessary if we had an equal chance to be recognized on our own merits. And when society today hears from, say, Frank Michelman or Gary Peller that minority work is good, it comes as a surprise, like hearing a scientist say that a certain kind of common weed in your garden might be good."

"I believe you said earlier that the situation today is even worse than it's been, that we are more ensconced as weeds now than in recent years."

Rodrigo smiled at my use of his metaphor. "I did. Not only are we one-down, we are on the defensive when we merely want to rise, want to change our position. Affirmative action, under which a paltry few of us get hired, has come under attack as unprincipled and an affront to innocent whites. Our poverty is seen as a choice, as something we enjoy or wallow in, as evidence of the pathological nature of our culture and family structure. Our demands for justice are seen as requests for entitlements, for things we don't deserve."

"Consider the whole 'political correctness' movement," I suggested.

"A prime case. Our detractors apply the term to those who are merely asking for a slight modification in the canon of books taught at universities, or who ask for ethnic studies courses in universities that offer hundreds of other courses of study, or who ask for controls on vicious slurs like 'nigger,' 'kike,' 'spic,' and 'fag.' The term is designed to put us on the defensive, as though we were nags pursuing petty concerns."

"The label has certainly caught on," I conceded ruefully.

"Despite its disreputable history. I wonder why nobody has pointed this out. Political correctness is little more than a modern, sanitized, prettified version of an old term. It means one who sympathizes with the blacks, who takes their point of view."

"I'm sure we both know what word you mean," I said.

"Nigger lover," Rodrigo replied with distaste. "That's what it comes down to. Although it's naturally a sanitized version, that's what it means. Those who use it ought to be ashamed of themselves. Yet they are not, which proves my point about our current estate. Most of our defenders, most liberals, do not identify the term for what it is, but rather back away from the accusation. 'Oh, no,' they say. 'I'm not being politically correct, I just ... "

"Just like in the old days," I observed wryly.

Just then the waitress arrived to ask if we wanted anything else. Rodrigo moved to get out his credit card, but I said, "Please let me. The airline said they'd pay. I have this voucher because of the canceled flight. Would you like some coffee?"

"Do we have time?" Rodrigo asked.

"I do. And I'm looking forward to hearing about that last point you promised to address. Two coffees, please—one decaf, the other ... ?"

"Do you have espresso?" Rodrigo asked. The waitress nodded. "A double please."

Rodrigo Explains Why His Plan Is Better Than Interest-Convergence, Which Can Easily Lead Reformers to Take the Short View and Make Sacrifices That Turn Out to Be Unwise

"I forgot to say regular," Rodrigo said with a slightly worried look on his face. "I've noticed that more and more places are selling decaffeinated espresso, which I consider practically a contradiction in terms, like a nice weed."

I looked at my animated, rail-thin young friend and said, "Don't worry, I have a feeling she'll bring you the high-octane kind. If not, we can send it back. I did order decaf, but that's no reason she should assume you'd want the same."

Rodrigo was silent for a moment then looked up. "Oh yes. My last point has to do with a serious disadvantage of the interest-convergence approach. I don't want to be too critical. My approach aims to reconcile the best of interest-convergence and the excessive and unwarranted optimism of liberal civil rights theory. So, in a way, legal instrumentalism includes interest-convergence as a special case and doesn't really contradict it."

"Never mind," I said. "Criticizing their elders is what young people do. Everyone expects it. People like Bell and me have come in for much worse criticism than what you are likely to deliver. So, get on with it. Do you mean that interest-convergence sends you looking for the rare miracle—the one moment in a decade or century when white and black interests coincide—and leaves you without direction the rest of the time?"

"It does have that drawback," Rodrigo said. "But I am thinking of a more serious one that Bell, for all his brilliance, did not see." Rodrigo paused.

"I want to hear it. I never thought I would accuse you of being too respectful, and here you are holding back. Besides, I've got to catch a plane in," I glanced at my watch, "less than forty minutes. They could announce my flight any time now."

The waitress arrived with our coffees. "Decaf for you, Professor," she said. "And the real thing for you," she added, smiling. I wondered idly how she knew I was a professor.

"Mmmmm. This is good," Rodrigo said, slurping his espresso. "I'm glad you suggested this." Then, after allowing me to take a sip of my own brew, he continued as follows:

"You know how the few great ringing victories, like *Brown v. Board of Education*, have a way of slipping away, cut back by narrow interpretation, obstruction, or delay?"

"Of course. Bell and others have pointed out that more black school children attend predominantly black schools now than when the Supreme Court decided *Brown* fifty years ago. The South mounted real resistance. And in the North many white families simply moved away. Courts eventually held that segregation that results from housing patterns is irreparable. Education is not a fundamental interest, nor poverty a suspect class, so that property-rich school districts may offer first-rate educations while poor districts offer much less. Our youth suffer suspension, dropout, and assignment to special education tracks and classes at rates that ought to be a national embarrassment."

Rodrigo agreed. "We seem destined, as Bell puts it, for periodic peaks of progress followed by valleys of regression. Once every blue moon the stars line up, and the system grants us a seeming victory for reasons of its own...."

"Such as Cold War politics, as Mary Dudziak and Bell have noted," I interjected.

"And other reasons, too," Rodrigo continued. "And in a way that points out a deficiency with the interest-convergence theory for understanding racial politics. It can deceive you into thinking the convergence will last longer, and prove more stable than it will, when in fact the stars only line up for a moment, like in an eclipse. But a more serious problem," Rodrigo continued, "is that one can easily take the short-term view and get so caught up with capturing and exploiting the approaching convergence that one gives away a long-term asset of inestimable value."

"Do you mean that we can become so hungry for a victory, so anxious for some sign of progress that we leap to the bait regardless of whether we should?" I didn't quite get Rodrigo's drift and hoped he would explain.

"Consider an example from recent history," he said. "Think of the period just before *Brown v. Board of Education*. Everyone knows that we were then in the early stages of the Cold War. Russia had emerged as a world power. We were engaged in a worldwide struggle for the loyalties of the uncommitted Third World."

"Most of which was black, brown, or Asian," I added.

"Indeed, Bell's thesis holds that is the reason why the U.S. establishment intervened on behalf of civil rights. It would hardly do for us to be maintaining that our system was better than godless communism when the front pages of newspapers around the world carried stories and pictures of lynchings, cross burnings, whites-only drinking fountains, and murders like that of Emmett Till."

"So, according to Bell, the American establishment pushed for civil rights breakthroughs, not to advance black interests, but their own. Mary Dudziak recently confirmed Bell's hypothesis through an analysis of State Department and other government documents, which showed that the U.S. Attorney General finally decided to throw its weight behind the NAACP Legal Defense Fund only when the State Department sent it urgent messages requesting that it do so."

"And so we got *Brown*," I added.

"And singing and dancing in the streets followed by disappointment a few years later when we learned the decision was scarcely going to restructure American society or even benefit that many black school kids."

"And you think that instrumentalism avoids this mistake?" I asked.

"Excessive optimism is always a risk with a group that has been down so long. But instrumentalism at least gets us to ask the right questions: Will this strategy work? What will happen to this breakthrough a few months or years later? If we put X dollars into litigation this year, will the Supreme Court reward us, with what, and for how long? Interest-convergence just tells you that this may (or may not) be the time to strike. One should always look further down the line and ask what the practical effect of anything will be."

"That seems to me quite useful," I observed. "But does it amount to anything more than reminding ourselves that 'interest' ought to be seen longitudinally, as a long-term thing? Smart revolutionaries do that now."

Rodrigo winced. "Touché. But let me go on a bit. Perhaps instrumentalism—the theory that one ought to resort to law in the way one would resort to any tool, like the yellow pages, only when it promises concrete benefits—does indeed offer a more fruitful approach than either of the principal alternatives."

"Just a minute," I said, indicating that I had heard something. We were silent a moment while I absorbed a message coming through on the loudspeaker. "Oh, no," I groaned. "Another twenty minute delay. Well, at least my flight seems to be coming in, even if it's late. Take your time, then. My gate is only two or three down the concourse, and I'm already checked in."

"My point is cautionary only. The idea is that you must always be careful about chasing after interest-convergence with the dominant group, because in your eagerness you can easily give away the store, sacrifice something of too great value. The dominant group gives you what you wanted, but the value of what you've gained quickly erodes, so that you have little left in the long run, and in the meantime you have forfeited something even more precious."

"I assume you are thinking of more than the thousands of hours of gallant lawyering and tens of thousands of dollars in legal costs that went into bringing about the *Brown* victory?"

"Those as well as human costs of a different sort. They have to do with self-definition. If a community begins to think of itself in terms of its relation to a different community, it may start to lose its sense of itself, who it is. If we and our folks are constantly placing ourselves in the mind-set of powerful white folks, trying to see what they will want, how they will factor us in, trying to stage-manage interest-convergence, we can easily start to change not just what we want, but who we are. Human beings are coterminous with their social surroundings. Our identities largely derive from whom we identify with, whom we try to please, whom we empathize with imaginatively. In some respects, the black community is safeguarded from overidentification with the majority of society because of the way the majority regards us."

"As we discussed earlier," I commented.

"Right. But some of us do have a tendency to try to identify with them. They have all the power, can dispense rewards, control who is seen as beautiful, smart, acceptable, and so on."

"It's a trap all subordinated people can fall into," I said. "Psychologists call it identification with the aggressor. A milder term is assimilation."

"It can easily happen. But a more serious problem arises from another means by which groups define themselves and change their contours: expulsion. At any given time, a subordinated group has leaders, theorists who rail against the group's mistreatment and are able to articulate it. These may be writers, playwrights or Marxists—persons with an acute understanding of the group's condition and a fervent commitment to changing it."

"And you're saying that a minority group bent on pursuing the interest-convergence strategy may too easily jettison geniuses such as these?"

"There have been many examples. In our day, there could soon be more."

"Could you give me an example?" I asked.

"Two who come to mind are Paul Robeson and W.E.B. Du Bois. Both were major figures, extremely serious losses. Both died in bitterness and sorrow, effectively cut off from their communities—purged really. All this happened because black leaders decided, in the late 1940s and early 1950s, that they were too radical, with too many ties with the Soviet Union. Du Bois, in particular, was a giant figure, yet he was expelled from the NAACP, an organization he had helped found decades earlier, only to be later reinstated, but relegated to a minor role. Both men were casualties of the Cold War, pure and simple. Our community expelled them, traded them in hopes of presenting a purified, sanitized, non-Communist front. The strategy worked—it brought about *Brown v. Board of Education*. But in one way of looking at it, it was not worth the price. *Brown* quickly faded, while the penetrating critiques these two figures had to offer were muffled and lost. It was not until the advent of the Black Panthers and of Malcolm X decades later that anything approaching a radical critique of American institutions and racism sprang up again. We sold our birthright for a mess of pottage."

"And you think this is inherent in interest-convergence philosophy?"

"Not inherent, but an ever-present risk. If you place momentary interest and alignment with the major power players as your first priority, what is to stop you from sacrificing your leaders, your young, or anything else that stands in the way, for that matter?"

"I see what you are saying. Instrumentalism at least makes you stop and ask whether your action has long-term costs, to think whether the powerful group you are trying to get to act in certain ways may not at the same time be seeing *you* in instrumental terms. The approach's radical individualism reminds you that others may not have your interests at heart, a useful thing for a subordinated group to keep in mind. You are less inclined to tell a towering figure like W.E.B. Du Bois that you do not need him any more. By the way, you seem to have been reading up on this period in history. Was Du Bois's banishment merely a coup within the NAACP, or broader than that?"

"Much broader," Rodrigo replied soberly. "The entire black community was turning to the right, just as America was jumping aboard the anti-Communist bandwagon, McCarthy was holding hearings, and people were seeing Communists under every bed. Before that time, the African-American community had been quite receptive to radicalism. Marxists and labor unionists held places of honor. Paul Robeson even traveled to the Soviet Union. Then, the tide changed. African-American newspapers, ministers, and other leaders began speaking out against communism, began urging black people to rekindle their patriotism, join the army, and so on, in hopes of securing better treatment as a race. If successful, it was only marginally so. The fifties were not a good period for us, and the sixties, although a time of breakthroughs, established little in the way of a lasting foundation. Yet we lost the beginnings of radicalism, so that today we are flailing about looking for theories and leaders."

An urgent message disturbed my reverie: my flight was boarding right now. With a start, I realized I must have missed the boarding announcement in my fascination with Rodrigo's story.

"Is that your flight?" Rodrigo asked.

"Unfortunately, yes," I replied, scrambling to pick up my things. "Will you give the cashier this voucher? It should take care of everything. It's been stimulating as always, Rodrigo. I'll call you when I get back, okay?"

We shook hands quickly, wished each other well, and three minutes later I was fastening my safety belt in preparation for takeoff.

CONCLUSION

As the plane banked steeply and gained altitude I wondered why, after forty years of civil rights scholarship, it was left to Rodrigo, a mere graduate student and youth of twenty-five years or so, to hit upon such an obvious solution as legal instrumentalism. Did it have something to do with Dewey, whom Rodrigo recently had described as a much-neglected, and very brilliant, philosopher? I realized that Dewey had written that experience and problem situations were what called upon and enabled people to develop intelligence. In that sense, all the brilliant constitutional scholars I had read would be unlikely to have come up with Rodrigo's insight. Not experiencing racial injustice as acutely as a black such as Rodrigo, they might not think as probingly, clear-headedly, or as urgently as one who has suffered such bigotry. I wondered if this solved the problem of "racial voice" and justified resisting imperial scholarship, the domination of civil rights theory deplored by some minority-race writers. Did it validate the unique insights of scholars of color, or were we just as likely to succumb to the intellectual and moral sins of sloth, lazy thinking, cowardice, and co-optation as anyone else?

Once again, I realized what good fortune I had to be a teacher, exposed to minds such as Rodrigo's. I pulled down the tray table from the seat in front of me and prepared to work on the speech I was to deliver the next day, taking pleasure in the thought that Rodrigo was not unique—many students of color had the same talent, the same insight of my friend and protégé—that there were many Rodrigos, all of them growing up, waiting to take their places in the world.

Linking Arms
Interracial Coalition as an Avenue of Social Reform

The prospect of death, they say, focuses the mind remarkably. Might other great changes do the same? As America approaches the point when minorities outnumber whites (estimated to happen sometime in the middle of this century), writers and columnists have begun writing about what that shift portends. Thus, recent books have emerged on the browning of America, on panethnicity, on the need to preserve precious white genes and culture, and on whether America is still the greatest country in the world.

Articles and books have also addressed the prospect that minority groups will form alliances, possibly with disaffected working-class whites, so as to translate their impending majority into political and cultural influence. Without such coalitions, these authors seem to suggest, 2050—the year of the predicted demographic tipping point—might come and go without noticeable effect. Well past that point, Euro-Americans will continue to be the single richest and largest racial group in the country. If minorities do not unite to challenge the white establishment, they are destined to remain poor and politically marginalized.

Recent books illustrate this preoccupation with interracial coalition. One forcefully argues that minorities should unite, beginning with local issues, in pursuit of social justice. Another outlines a program for minorities to bury their grievances and work together toward much the same ends. Although the two books differ greatly in organization, style, and scope, they share the faith that America's hope lies with a heady coalition of the dispossessed. They also argue that outsider scholars and communities, because of the legacy of oppression, enjoy a deeper, sharper sense of social justice than the more complacent majority. Accordingly, if blacks, Latinos,

Asians, Native Americans, and down-and-out whites join forces, not only they but also the country as a whole will benefit.

Will this happen?

THE ALGEBRA OF INTERRACIAL COALITION

A few coalitions worked. Many others, however, endured only until the dominant group offered a token concession; others turned out to be based on a misunderstanding and were short-lived. Why? Consider a hypothetical society containing three groups. Race and color are not factors. Group *A* is the most numerous and powerful. It comprises fifty percent of the population and, thus, has been able to translate most of its wishes into law. It also controls well over fifty percent of the country's wealth. Groups *B* and *C* each comprise twenty-five percent of the population and command much less wealth and political clout than the *A*s.

Suppose that, at some point, groups *B* and *C* decide to form a coalition to oppose the *A*s, who run the country in ways that benefit them and leave the *B*s and *C*s on the outside looking in. Because the country is a democracy, a coalition of *B*s and *C*s would wield enough voting power to enact measures and elect favorable officials.

Faced with this prospect, the *A*s might rationally approach both of their smaller adversaries separately and offer each a chance to abandon the other group and join instead with the *A*s. They might point out that they are far richer and more numerous than either competitor, so that a coalition with them will last forever. As an inducement to jump ship, the *A*s offer the small group—say, the *C*s—immediate access to some of the wealth the more powerful *A*s have amassed over the years.

Group *A* will, of course, offer the same deal to group *B*. After all, the *B*s might be willing to join the *A*s more cheaply than their counterparts. In effect, the *A*s would force the weaker *B*s and *C*s to bid against each other for solidarity with the dominant *A*s. This bargaining would, presumably, drive down the price the *A*s would have to pay to protect their position.

Still, the *A*s would have to pay something to induce one of the two outsider groups to join them. Moreover, not only would the *A*s need to bribe one of the smaller groups to abandon principle, honor, and the Three Musketeers creed, they would also have to underwrite the price of assimilating the group into their more advanced civilization. This might include teaching them the governing language, offering them affirmative action in schools and jobs, and other such costly programs.

The *A*s, faced with a drop in their formerly high standard of living, would look to the outsider group that did not join with it for payment. Suppose *B* is the group that jumped ship and joined with the *A*s. The *C*s are now greatly outnumbered and without allies, because their former friends, the *B*s, are now basking in the company of the powerful *A*s.

The *A*s now exact revenge on the *C*s, extracting from them exactly what they had to pay the *B*s, so that the *A*s' standard of living returns to its former level. What the *B*s gain, the *C*s lose. *A*'s position remains the same, *B*'s is better, and *C*'s is much worse. The *C*s will wish they had not broached the idea of coalition with the *B*s in the first place.

In the early years of the critical race theory movement, Derrick Bell propounded his interest-convergence theory of racial reform, which holds that advances for blacks come only when they benefit powerful whites as well. The logic of coalition politics yields a corollary to Bell's dismal proposition: a minority group (like *B* in the above example) will join with another in search for justice against the majority (*A*) only when it is in the first group's interest to do so. Furthermore, such a group will abandon its ally in favor of the more powerful adversary as soon as the adversary offers concessions. The minority group may even have entered into coalition with another group precisely to gain the attention of powerful whites, always having intended to jump ship when offered better terms.

WE SHALL OVERCOME: WHEN THE BASIS OF A COALITION IS RACE

The analysis until this point has proceeded without consideration of race. When *A*, *B*, and *C* are racial groups, alliances are, if anything, more unstable than those based on other factors.

The Drawing Power of Whiteness

Whites in this country are not only the most numerous and powerful group—something that could easily change over time—they are also normative, their ideas, hopes, values, holidays, heroes, traditions, language, and narratives enshrined in the culture. American children's heroes, like Snow White, are Euro-American. Language imagery associates whiteness with purity, innocence, and virtue. Think of our most sacred ceremonies: white is for weddings, black for funerals. Even many minorities carry these associations and attitudes in their minds. Phrases like "sisterhood is powerful," "brown and black power," and "power to the people" possess an undeniable appeal. But whiteness's rewards, which include acceptance, validation, power, and influence, can plant a seed of doubt in the mind of any but the most dedicated insurgent of color.

Consider, for example, how many once-radical 1960s leaders, such as Corky Gonzalez, toned down their rhetoric and moderated their demands once the white establishment offered them a Ford Foundation or Office of Economic Opportunity (OEO) grant to assume the role of community organizer, with patronage jobs to hand out to their friends. Consider, as well, how militant black organizations, like the Congress of Racial Equality, changed their agendas to emphasize economic development when wealthy foundations came calling. Finally, recall how many law students (and faculty members) of color enter law school with the intention of pursuing public interest careers, but, after three years in a setting that holds up large-firm corporate practice as the pinnacle of professional success, succumb to the lure of money and prestige.

Solidarity Problems: Defectors and the Paradox of Leadership
Because of whiteness's attraction, a multiracial coalition is always susceptible to breakup if a subgroup changes its mind and decides to make common cause with whites. A similar dynamic could weaken a steadfast group if individual members defect or if the leaders turn out to be assimilated people who fail to appreciate the needs of their group's most impoverished members.

Essentialism and the Problem of Internal Solidarity
Everyone knows of cases like Richard Rodriguez or Linda Chavez, the Latino/a writers who deplore affirmative action, bilingual education, and radical Chicano politics; Clarence Thomas, the African-American Supreme Court justice who almost always votes with the conservative majority; and J.C. Watts, the black Republican member of Congress who generally sided with his right-wing colleagues in restricting welfare, opposing election reform, supporting federalism, and criticizing liberal black leaders like Jesse Jackson and Al Sharpton. In California, a surprising number of voters of color endorsed the anti-immigrant Proposition 187. Moreover, English-only measures, anathema to most Latinos and Asians, draw considerable support among African Americans, working-class whites, and a few conservative Latinos.

It is true that the loss of some such defectors will be offset by the occasional liberal white who joins. But one cannot assume that two groups, which between them total fifty percent of a country's population, will, by virtue of that fact alone, be able to work together. Not only may another group in the coalition leave entirely, members in the group's own ranks may do so as well. It is unrealistic to hope that every person of color will embrace radical politics and mass action as a means of social reform. Some prefer individualism and personal initiative. Assuming that a group of color that numbers, say, thirty million members, will deliver that many votes for the Democratic Party, affirmative action, and a host of familiar programs may be a serious miscalculation.

The Paradox of Representative Leadership
A related problem concerns the inevitable differences likely to arise between the leaders of an outsider coalition and its rank and file. Especially in a large coalition, the leaders are likely to be college educated, media-savvy individuals from urban backgrounds. Their constituents, however, may include blue-collar or agricultural workers, single mothers, and others with a host of immediate, day-to-day struggles and issues. If the leaders are not attuned to these issues, the coalition will eventually reach a crisis point.

Consider, for example, the campaign for black reparations, a large national effort led by elites, including a Harvard law professor. The elite leadership, which includes many lawyers, has done valuable work in researching the history of black exploitation, calculating damages, and devising legal theories for pursuing relief. Less impressive is their thinking regarding the form that relief should take. One recurring suggestion is that the African-American community should receive amends in the form of college scholarships and other forms of affirmative action.

Nothing is wrong with affirmative action; I have written in support of it myself. Yet, as the exclusive or primary remedy for slavery and racial oppression, it leaves much to be desired. It will certainly benefit many upwardly mobile African Americans wishing to pursue college or university studies. Yet, as everyone knows, just as many young black men are in jail as are in college. Why did the reparations committees not propose a bail fund for young blacks charged with or convicted of crimes? Such a remedy would be as beneficial as college scholarships for those who are probably already on the path to a successful life. Perhaps the reparations committee considered a bail fund and decided that it was too controversial to win public support. If so, they might have considered educational programs for prisoners, halfway houses for the recently released, and anti-gang counseling aimed at keeping unemployed, alienated youths out of prison in the first place. My point is that these are remedies that would not occur naturally to the movement's elite leadership because of reasons that are likely to plague any large coalition.

Coalitions May Replicate Hierarchy
A further complication concerns relationships within a coalition. Yen Le Espiritu has noted that one sort of coalition—panethnic groups—is prone to a dynamic in which a high-status, influential, and relatively assimilated group, such as the Chinese in a pan-Asian movement, expects to assume a position of power and authority. Meanwhile, less educated, poorer, or non-English-speaking members, such as Vietnamese or Cambodians, may be left behind. This practice not only adopts the master's tools and thus unwittingly strengthens his house, but it also weakens the coalition. During the civil rights era of the 1960s, recall how women were asked to march in the back of protest parades (or in front if the group expected violence), and to perform routine tasks like making coffee at meetings. Recall, as well, how Latinos and Asians have often bowed out of local coalitions with African Americans when they found that blacks expected their concerns to occupy center stage, and how African Americans reacted negatively when the other groups turned out to expect similar attention.

The Set Stage
Recent First Amendment theorists have written about the limitations of our system of free speech to deal with socially harmful messages, such as hate speech, coining the term "empathic fallacy" for the error of thinking that a new, better narrative will always prevail over an old, socially pernicious one. Coalition-making among outgroups confronts a similar obstacle. Coalition-making efforts never occur in the abstract. Instead, they take place on a set stage replete with histories, grievances, and loyalties to third parties, which may interfere with a coalition that, in the abstract, would appear to be in everyone's best interest. Let us examine some of these factors.

Party Politics
Our political system contains two major parties, with rapidly diminishing differences between them. Suppose that a powerful coalition of minorities is interested in promoting policy X. If X is the kind of policy that requires national action, only

two avenues will be open for effectuating it. The coalition must solicit support from either the Republicans or the Democrats. If the coalition can interest neither, the policy will arrive at a dead end.

Material Factors
Latinos are not just blacks with slightly lighter skins and a habit of speaking Spanish. Nor are blacks just whites who happen not to have any money right now. All groups of color exhibit different histories, cultures, identities, and needs. Blacks tend to be urban people, whereas Mexican Americans are much more rural. South Asian Indian immigrants often find work in the computer and information science sector, and so on.

Differences in the material situations of groups interested in coalition can easily lead to problems. Consider immigration policy. Relatively few blacks immigrate to the United States, while many Latinos do. Immigration, thus, is a major goal for Latinos. Likewise, one might expect blacks to be neutral or mildly positive toward immigration because it brings newcomers who are apt to vote Democratic, favor affirmative action, and support workplace safety, all measures of interest to blacks. Nevertheless, blacks as a group do not support immigration because new arrivals would, in many cases, compete with blacks for lower-echelon jobs. Thus, differences in the material circumstances of partners can cause a coalition to fail even on issues presenting no readily apparent disagreement.

Consider a second way historical differences can cause problems. Affirmative action is presently under siege, with conservative commentators and litigation centers calling for its repeal and even some of its liberal supporters beginning to waver. One would think that a powerful coalition of minority groups, which now make up nearly one-third of the country's population, could offer serious resistance to this movement. Neoconservatives, however, are now calling for a different strategy: cutting affirmative action back to its "traditional core"—blacks. Some blacks have responded enthusiastically, because eliminating affirmative action for American Indians, Latinos, and Asian Americans would cost them nothing. Perhaps a scaled-back affirmative action program, limited to blacks, could be even more generous than the current one, featuring more slots, scholarships, and special programs for blacks than the current version.

Any party to a coalition of color must realize the benefits of abandoning the coalition for one with whites. As mentioned, such a coalition will be larger, more powerful, and potentially more durable than one with another minority group. Even when a coalition aims to advance only a single issue that would benefit all of its members, the coalition can still founder if whites offer a concession to one faction at the expense of the rest.

The Law of Historical Grievance
As mentioned, very few minority groups pondering a coalition will come to the table on equal terms and with a clean slate. They will not be similarly situated in every relevant respect; one group may have grievances with another, which, in turn, may

have a grievance with the first. Groups lacking any grievances with each other would hardly need a coalition. Being similarly situated, they might as well work for common issues separately. Little is gained from coalition; working in concert may even diminish efficiency, because it takes time to elect leaders and become familiar with each other. Blacks might need to learn Spanish, while Latinos might need to adjust to black ways of speaking, relating, and doing business.

Assume, then, that we are considering a coalition between groups where solidarity cannot be taken for granted. In our world, this situation is common: the dominant group frequently casts minorities against one another in competition for scarce resources. For example, blacks may remember the time Latinos sacrificed black interests and sought their own well-being first, whereas Latinos will remember when blacks sided with white power or voted against a measure vital to the Latino community.

Over time, the memory of a grievance is unlikely to fade. The group nursing the grievance will magnify it, recount it over and over, and become more and more certain that it is important and in need of redress. The other group, by contrast, will rationalize it. If the aggrieved group demands reparations or amends as a condition of coalition, the second group may respond with indignation or incredulity.

Consider, for example, the current debate over black reparations. Blacks, many of whom nurse grievances over slavery and Jim Crow laws, seek very large reparations from white society, believing that these historical atrocities are responsible for many, if not all, of the respects in which blacks trail whites in achievement and standard of living. Whites, by contrast, are apt to respond either petulantly or sorrowfully: Slavery took place a long time ago. The victims and perpetrators are long since dead. If we make reparations for one group.... Perhaps it is time to move on.

The law of historical grievances suggests that most coalitions will never get off the ground. Any two potential partners will come together with at least one grievance that requires resolution. The aggrieved party will set a very high price on settlement, while the other party will consider the aggrieved to be unreasonable, petty, and vindictive. Even if the guilty party agrees that it should pay reparations to the aggrieved party, it may lack the resources to do so. A third, even more powerful, group may have bled it white, so that both the guilty party and its historic victims lack the resources to make redress.

Consider a few examples of coalitions gone awry.

White Women in Plantation Society

Just as plantation society treated black men as beasts, it placed white women on a pedestal. The two are causally related, although the connection rarely has been noted. Consider white women's role: trained in the domestic arts, from an early age white girls in plantation society were taught ladylike skills—piano playing, French, interior decorating, making small talk, and parrying the advances of the well-born young men who would one day seek their hand in marriage. Ponder what such a young woman could not do: corseted, dressed in finery, her hair elaborately coiffed, she could not play hard, dig in the dirt, or go for a swim in the river, especially if it were located near the slave camp. She could not go for a long tramp in the woods, learn to fix a plow, or ride a horse at breakneck speed through the country.

She could not do any of these things, because Southern ladies were expected to be the repositories of civilization and refinement. And they grew up saddled with these limitations precisely because black men led the opposite life—brutalized, dirty, sweating, beaten, and deprived of the opportunity to learn to read, paint, or write. Because slave life was brutal and mean, white women, living in the big house, were expected to personify the opposite values.

At the time, Southern women may have thought themselves fortunate. They were not required to work, develop their minds, or learn a career. It was not until years later that feminist writers began to realize how limiting this conception of woman's role was and began to press for opportunities for women in the professions, politics, education, and the arts.

The institution of slavery thus oppressed both black slaves and white women. Their oppression was inextricably linked, yet they were not candidates for coalition politics in the ordinary sense. Slaves and white women were not oppressed in the same way—through unfair SAT requirements, for example, or low wages from a meatpacking plant. Rather, their oppressions were complementary. Few women appreciated the link at the time. Although some railed at their own bondage and fewer still at the crasser form of bondage visited on the slaves, none seems to have seen her oppression as closely related to that of the slaves. Slavery and women's subjugation were separately unjust. Because the connections between the two forms of injustice were indirect and veiled, the idea of coalition did not arise. Justice and injustice may be indivisible, but if we rely, as most coalition theorists do, on a tangible inequity visited on two groups by the same actor and in like fashion, we shall miss opportunities to redress the linked underlying structures that do the most damage.

The Ending of the Civil Rights Era

As a second example of how difficult it can be to discern the alignment of two groups' interests, consider the fate of the civil rights movement of the 1960s. As Derrick Bell and Mary Dudziak have persuasively argued, *Brown v. Board of Education* and the softening of racial attitudes that it ushered in were attributable not so much to moral breakthroughs on the part of whites, but rather to changes in elite self-interest, which in turn were the result of Cold War competition.

But what has only recently come to light is that many of the same factors that brought about *Brown*, the 1964 Civil Rights Act, and other similar successes also account for the demise of the civil rights era a decade later. By that time, the movement had taken a significant turn. At first prayerful, decorous, and nonviolent, the tenor changed with the appearance of Black Power. Panthers armed themselves, began quoting Mao, Marx, and Lenin, and preached cultural nationalism and pride. Malcolm X wrote that whites were Satanic. The white establishment responded in two ways: with deadly force for the Panthers, and with grants and jobs in the federal OEO program for black leaders who were willing to toe the line. Economic empowerment replaced confrontation and war protests. As it had done earlier with figures like

Paul Robeson, Geraldine Baker, and W.E.B. Du Bois, the mainstream black press condemned militant radicals who criticized America, foreign wars, or capitalism. And, as had happened before, incipient black radicalism was placed on hold, not to return again until the mid-1980s.

Today, black fortunes are again languishing, with cutbacks in affirmative action, contractions in welfare, and increasing housing and school segregation. Yet, a generation of radical leaders that might have given voice to the community's discontent is gone. If communities of color in the 1970s had perceived their collective self-interest, they might not have been so quick to reject their own indigenous radicalism in return for the helping hand of Ford Foundation dollars and jobs in the federal antipoverty program.

The point of these examples is that although the imperative of justice may be relatively clear at any moment in history, that of self-interest may not be. Not only can coalitions be ungainly, ephemeral, and difficult to hold together, they may center around the wrong measures entirely. If, as I believe, this difficulty inheres in coalition politics, the arsenal of civil rights remedies must contain much more than strategies that rely on collective action.

RACIAL SOLIDARITY: THE HISTORICAL RECORD

As we have seen, interminority solidarity faces formidable obstacles, both theoretical and actual. Recent books give these obstacles short shrift; most authors are selective and upbeat about the prospects of cooperation among minorities as a means of strengthening democracy and promoting justice. Unfortunately, the historical record is mixed. Missed opportunities for coalition are as numerous as the successes.

Consider how, shortly after being released from slavery, blacks joined the Buffalo Soldiers and helped put down Native-American rebellions. The Native Americans, who might have expected solidarity with blacks, got trained killers instead. A few years later, middle-class Mexican Americans adopted the "other white" strategy as a way of combating discrimination in housing, public accommodations, and schools. Under this approach, Mexican community organizations argued that discrimination against Mexicans in the United States is illegal because Mexicans are white, and unlike with blacks, no state statutes permitted discrimination against whites. This strategy, of course, left blacks out in the cold.

In World War II, neither the NAACP nor any other major black organization filed an amicus brief in *Hirabayashi* or *Korematsu*, Supreme Court cases challenging the legality of Japanese internment. No ethnic group of color has demonstrated conspicuous solidarity with Muslims facing discrimination in the United States today. In California, Japanese parents objected to a San Francisco school board policy of assigning their children to schools for Chinese and Koreans because they considered them inferior. Many years later, the Chinese successfully sued the same board to set aside an admissions policy at elite Lowell High School that favored the admission of

African Americans and Latinos and placed a ceiling on the admission of every group, including whites and Asians.

Even *within* groups, we see breaches of coalition when the payoff is high enough. In plantation society, the owner would frequently assign lighter-skinned slaves to desirable household work or jobs supervising the darker-skinned field hands. The higher-status blacks were expected to spy on their brothers and sisters and report any rumor of rebellion or escape. During World War II, many Japanese fought gallantly in the U.S. Armed Forces at a time when their families were languishing in concentration camps. In our time, law schools are happy to assign charming associate and assistant deans of color the tasks of dealing with student complaints, while major corporations frequently employ Asian or light-skinned, European-looking Latinos to serve as personnel directors charged with laying off minority workers. Who could charge discrimination if the person who fired you were a fellow person of color?

* * *

What avenue, then, is open to minority groups eager to claim a fair share of society's bounty? Why not abandon coalition—a device beset by a host of difficulties—and instead labor straightforwardly for social and material justice? This approach might include, for example, Latinos organizing for bilingual education and expanded immigration policies, blacks agitating against police profiling, and Native Americans fighting for sovereignty and self-rule. It might include all these groups pressing, individually or collectively, for retention of affirmative action in higher education.

In the movie *The Untouchables*, Robert DeNiro's character (Al Capone) uses a baseball metaphor to explain his philosophy of teamwork. Most of the time, he says, he is happy to be on a good team. He depends on his teammates to do their jobs, especially when he plays the field. But when he is batting, he relies on no one but himself. In similar fashion, today's outsider groups need to ponder what tasks are best accomplished in concert with others, and which are better undertaken individually. For some projects, justice turns out to be a solitary, though heroic, quest, and the road to justice one that must be traveled alone, or with our deepest, most trusted companions.

PART III

Law, Legal Education, and the Legal Profession

The articles in this section are three of many in which Delgado examines certain features of the legal academy and law practice.

The admonition of the much-cited and controversial "Imperial Scholar" seems like common sense today: bring minority scholars who are well equipped by training and life experience into the discussion of legal problems and solutions related to antidiscrimination law. Yet, in 1984 the article caused a great stir, provoking much conversation. Many white scholars' feelings were hurt; they accused Delgado of biting the hand that fed him. He updated his study eight years later and found that not much had changed.

"Rodrigo's Thirteenth Chronicle" takes up the unhappiness of lawyers and the public's disenchantment with them. Rodrigo attributes these discontents to the inability of the legal academy and profession to break free of formalism, which emphasizes case law and doctrine and the view that law can be taught and practiced as a science.

In "Official Elitism or Institutional Self-Interest?" Delgado critiques the standardized testing industry, especially the Law School Admissions Test (LSAT), examining its history, its ineffectiveness at predicting success in law school, and the way it reinforces and promotes the interests of elites. He offers suggestions for ways to reduce the influence of these tests or to eliminate them entirely.

The Imperial Scholar
Reflections on a Review of Civil Rights Literature

CIVIL RIGHTS SCHOLARSHIP: IDENTIFYING A TRADITION

When I began teaching law, a number of well-meaning senior colleagues advised me to "play things straight" in my scholarship—to establish a reputation as a scholar in some mainstream legal area and not get too caught up in civil rights or other "ethnic" subjects. Being young, impressionable, and anxious to succeed, I took their advice to heart and, for the first few years of my career produced a steady stream of articles, book reviews, and the like, impeccably traditional in substance and form. The dangers my friends warned me about were averted; the benefits accrued. Tenure securely in hand, I turned my attention to civil rights law and scholarship.

Realizing I had a great deal of catching up to do, I asked my research assistant to compile a list of the twenty or so leading law review articles on civil rights. I gave him the criteria you would expect: frequent citation by courts and commentators, publication in a major law review, theoretical rather than practical focus, and so on. When he submitted the list, I noticed with surprise that each of the authors was white. Each was also male. I checked his work myself, with the same result. Further, a review of the footnotes of these articles disclosed a second curiosity—the works cited were also written by authors who were themselves white and male. I was puzzled. I knew that by then many black, Latino, and Native American law professors were teaching at American law schools. Many of them were writing in areas about which they cared deeply: antidiscrimination law, the equality principle, and affirmative action. Much of that scholarship, however, seemed to have been consigned to oblivion. Courts rarely cited it, and the legal scholars whose work *really* counted almost never did. The important work was published in eight or ten law reviews and was written by a small group of professors, who taught in the major law schools.

Most of this latter work, to be sure, is strongly supportive of minority rights. All the more curious that these authors, the giants in the field, only infrequently cite a minority scholar. My assistant and I prepared an informal sociogram, a pictorial representation of who-cites-whom in the civil rights literature. It is fascinating. Paul Brest cites Laurence Tribe. Laurence Tribe cites Paul Brest and Owen Fiss. Owen Fiss cites Bruce Ackerman, who cites Paul Brest and Frank Michelman, who cites Owen Fiss and Laurence Tribe and Kenneth Karst....

It does not matter where one enters this universe; one comes to the same result: an inner circle of about a dozen white male writers who comment on, take polite issue with, extol, criticize, and expand on each other's ideas. It is something like an elaborate minuet.

The failure to acknowledge minority scholarship extends even to nonlegal propositions and assertions of fact. W.E.B. Du Bois, deceased black historian, receives an occasional citation. Aside from him, few others rate a mention. Higginbotham's monumental *In the Matter of Color* might as well not exist. The same is true of the work of Kenneth Clark, black psychologist and past president of the American Psychological Association, and Alvin Poussaint, Harvard Medical School professor and authority on the psychological impact of race. One searches in vain for references to the powerful book by physicians Grier and Cobbs, *Black Rage,* or to Frantz Fanon's *The Wretched of the Earth,* or even to writings of or about Martin Luther King, Jr., Cesar Chavez, and Malcolm X. When the inner-circle writers need authority for a factual or social scientific proposition about race they generally cite reports of the United States Commission on Civil Rights [Eds. On which they or their friends sat] or else each other.

A single anecdote may help to illustrate what I mean. Recently a law professor who writes about civil rights showed me, for my edification, a draft of an article of his. It is, on the whole, an excellent article. It extols the value of a principle I will call "equal personhood." Equal personhood is the notion, implicit in several constitutional provisions and much case law, that each human being, regardless of race, creed, or color, is entitled to be treated with equal respect. To treat someone as an outsider, a nonmember of human society, violates this principle and devalues the self-worth of the person so excluded.

I have no quarrel with this premise, but, on reading the one hundred–plus footnotes of the article, I noticed that its author failed to cite black or minority scholars, an exclusion from the community of kindred souls as glaring as any condemned in the paper. I pointed this out to the author, citing as illustration a passage in which he asserted that unequal treatment can cause a person to suffer a withered self-concept. Having just written an article on a related subject, I was more or less steeped in withered self-concepts. I knew who the major authorities were in that area.

The professor's authority for the proposition about withered self-concepts was a prominent law professor, writing in the *Harvard Law Review.* I pointed out that although the professor may be a superb scholar and teacher, he probably has relatively little first-hand knowledge about withered self-concepts. I suggested that the professor add references to such works as Kenneth Clark's *Dark Ghetto* and Grier and Cobbs's *Black Rage,* and he agreed to do so. To justify his selection of an authority for the proposition about withered self-concept, the author explained that the Yale professor's statement was "so elegant."

Could inelegance of expression explain the absence of minority scholarship from the text and footnotes of leading law review articles about civil rights? Elegance is, without question, a virtue in writing, conversation, or anything else in life. If Euro-American authors write elegantly and minority scholars do not, then it would not be surprising if the former were read and cited more frequently. But minority legal scholars seem to have less trouble being recognized and taken seriously in areas of scholarship other than civil rights theory. If elegance is a problem for minority scholars, it seems mainly to be so in the core areas of civil rights: affirmative action, the equality principle, and the theoretical foundations of race relations law.

In 1971, Judge Skelly Wright wrote an article entitled *Professor Bickel, the Scholarly Tradition, and the Supreme Court,* in which he took a group of scholars to task for their bloodless carping at the Warren Court's decisions in the areas of racial justice and human rights. He accused the group of missing the central point in these decisions—their moral clarity and passion for justice—and labelled the group's excessive preoccupation with procedure and institutional role and its insistence that the Court justify every element of a decision under general principles of universal application, a "scholarly tradition."

I think I have discovered a second scholarly tradition. It consists of systematic occupation of, and exclusion of minority scholars from, the central areas of civil rights scholarship. The mainstream writers tend to acknowledge only each other's work. It is even possible that, consciously or not, they resist entry by minority scholars into the field, perhaps counseling them, as I was counseled, to establish their reputations in other areas of law. I believe that this "scholarly tradition" exists mainly in civil rights; nonwhite scholars in other fields of law seem to confront no such tradition.

DEFECTS IN IMPERIAL SCHOLARSHIP

To this point, I have been making an empirical claim. A person who disagreed with my thesis could attempt to show that some white inner-circle authors do cite nonwhite scholars appropriately, perhaps by introducing a sociogram of his or her own. My examination of the literature in the field, while admittedly not a scientific study, leads me to believe this is a vain task. A second response would assert that the exclusion of minority viewpoints from white scholarship about civil rights is, as they say, harmless error; it doesn't matter *who* advocates freedom and equality, as long as someone does.

This assertion would echo the holding of *Trafficante v. Metropolitan Life Insurance Co.,* which gave white tenants standing to challenge a building owner's discriminatory renting practices on the ground that these rendered the building a white ghetto and deprived the tenants of interracial contacts. Everyone, not just minorities, has an interest in achieving a racially just society, so why should not anyone be free to advocate it in print? Does a contrary policy not deny free speech and constitute a gratuitous rejection of a helping hand?

Put in simple terms, what difference does it make if the scholarship about the rights of group *A* is written by members of group *B*? Although Derrick Bell raised this question in a footnote, no one seems to have addressed it directly. A number of legal doctrines and case law may suggest answers by way of analogy. Relevant doctrines include standing, real party in interest, and *jus tertii,* doctrines which in general insist that *B* does not belong in court if he or she is attempting, without good reason, to assert the rights of, or redress the injuries to, *A*. We also have rules pertaining to joinder of parties, intervention, and representation in class suits, all of which serve to assure that the appropriate parties are before the court. On a more general level, our political and legal values contain an antipaternalistic principle that forbids *B* from asserting *A*'s interest if *A* is a competent human being of adult years, capable of independently deciding upon and asserting that interest.

Abstracting from these principles, it is possible to compile an *a priori* list of reasons why we might look with concern on a situation in which the scholarship about group *A* is written by members of group *B*. First, members of group *B* may be ineffective advocates of the rights and interests of persons in group *A*. They may lack information; more important, perhaps, they may lack passion, or that passion may be misdirected. *B*'s scholarship may tend to be sentimental, diffusing passion in useless directions, or wasting time on unproductive breast-beating. Second, while the *B*s might advocate effectively, they might advocate the wrong things. Their agenda may differ from that of the *A*s; they may pull their punches, especially where remedying *A*'s situation entails uncomfortable consequences for *B*. Despite the best of intentions, *B*s may have stereotypes embedded deep in their psyches that distort their thinking, causing them to balance interests in ways inimical to, *A*s. Finally, domination by members of group *B* may paralyze members of group *A*, causing the *A*s to forget how to flex their legal muscles for themselves.

A careful reading of the inner-circle articles suggests that many of the above mentioned problems and pitfalls are not simply hypothetical, but do in fact occur. A number of the authors were unaware of basic facts about the situation in which minority persons live or ways in which they see the world. From the viewpoint of a minority member, the assertions and arguments made by nonminority authors were sometimes so naive as to seem incomprehensible and hardly merit serious consideration. For example, some writers took seriously the *reductio ad absurdum* argument about an infinitude of minorities (if blacks and Hispanics, why not Belgians, Swedes, and Italians; what about an individual who is one-half black, or three-quarters Hispanic?), or worried about whether a white citizen forced to associate with blacks has his or her freedom of association violated as much as a black compelled to attend segregated schools. One author reasoned that *Carolene Products* "footnote four" analysis is no longer fully applicable to American blacks, because they have ceased to be an insular minority in need of heightened judicial protection. Another placed the burden on proponents of preferential admissions to show that no nonracial alternative exists, because today's minority may become tomorrow's majority and vice versa.

In addition to factual ignorance or naiveté, some of the writing suffered from a failure of empathy, an inability to share the values, desires, and perspectives of the population whose rights are under consideration. In his article, *Serving Two Masters: Integration Ideals and Client Interests in School Desegregation Litigation*, Derrick Bell pointed out that litigators in school desegregation cases have often seemed unaware of what their clients really wanted, or have pursued one remedy (e.g., integration) out of ideological commitment, even though the client wanted something different (e.g., better schools). A similar distancing of the scholar from the community he writes about was visible in the civil rights commentaries. The authors in the core group tended to be very concerned about *procedure*. Many of the articles were devoted, in various measures, to scholarly discussions of the standard of judicial review that should be applied in different types of civil rights suits. Others were concerned with the relationship between federal and state authority in antidiscrimination law, or with the respective competence of a particular decisionmaker to recognize and redress racial discrimination. One could easily conclude that the questions of who goes to court, what court, and with what standard of review, are the burning issues of American race-relations law. Perhaps the emphasis on procedure and judicial role is harmless, just a peculiar kink lawyers get in law school; but, as I will argue later in this essay, there is more to it than that.

Other peculiarities of perspective surfaced in connection with choosing a principle on which to base (or oppose) affirmative action. Measures to increase minority representation in education and the work force have been justified in three broad ways: reparations (or retribution); social utility; and distributive justice. The reparations argument emphasizes that white society has mistreated blacks, Native Americans, and Hispanics and now must make amends for that mistreatment. Utility-based arguments justify affirmative action on the ground that increased representation of minorities will be useful to society. The distributive justice rationale says that a certain amount of wealth is available and argues that everyone is entitled to a minimum share of it. Many of the minority scholars emphasize the reparations argument and stress the inherent cost to whites; the authors of the inner-circle articles generally make the case on the grounds of utility or distributive justice.

Emphasizing utility or distributive justice has a number of significant consequences. It enables the writer to concentrate on the present and the future and overlook the past. No need to dwell on unpleasant matters like lynch mobs, segregated bathrooms, Bracero programs, migrant farm labor camps, race-based immigration laws, or professional schools that, until recently, were lily white. The past becomes irrelevant; one just asks where things are now and where we ought to go from here, a straightforward social-engineering inquiry of the sort that law professors are familiar with and good at. But just as the adoption of either of the two present-oriented perspectives renders the investigation comfortably safe, it robs affirmative action programs of their moral force in favor of a sterile theory of fairness or utility. No doubt great social utility inheres in affirmative action, but to base it solely on that ground ignores the *right* of minority communities to be made whole, and the *obligation* of the majority to render them so. Moreover, what if the utility calculus changes in the future, so that the programs no longer appear "useful" to the majority? Can society then ignore those who still suffer the effects of past discrimination?

Distributive justice is a somewhat less objectionable ground for justifying affirmative action, but it too ignores history, makes for a rather weak, pallid case, and invites the neutral-principles response: if the idea is to start playing fair now, how can we justify discriminating against whites? A "we-they" analysis, espoused by several of the commentators, justifies a disadvantage that *we* (the majority) want to impose on ourselves to favor *them* (the minority). This type of thinking, however, leaves the choice of remedy and the time frame for it in the hands of the majority; it converts affirmative action into a benefit, not a right, neatly overlooking that a disadvantaged minority may have a moral claim to a particular remedy.

The inner-circle commentators rarely deal with issues of guilt and reparation. When they do, it is often to attach responsibility to a scapegoat, someone of another time or place, and almost certainly of another social class than that of the writer. These writers tend to focus on intentional and determinable *acts* of discrimination inflicted on the victim by some perpetrator and ignore the more pervasive and invidious forms of discriminatory *conditions* inherent in our society. This "perpetrator" perspective deflects attention from the victim-class, the blacks, Native Americans, Chicanos, and Puerto Ricans who lead blighted lives for reasons directly traceable to social and institutional injustice.

A corollary of this perspective is that remedies for racism should not encroach too much on middle- or upper-class prerogatives. If racial inequality is mainly the fault of the isolated redneck, outmoded ritual violence, or long abrogated governmental actions, then remedies that would encroach on simple "conditions" of life—middle-class housing patterns, for example, or the autonomy of local school boards—are unnecessary. Many persons of minority race see racism as including institutional components that extend far beyond lynch mobs, segregated schools, or epithets like "nigger" or "spick." Self-interest, mixed with inexperience, may make it difficult for the privileged white male writer to adopt this perspective or face up to its implications. Recall how remedies pursued at "all deliberate speed" or couched in terms of vague targets and goals entered the law when the legal system turned in earnest to problems of race. Could their appearance be the product of a utility-based perspective which ignores past injustices and simply seeks to engineer a solution with the most utility to society and the minimal amount of disruption? If the issue is not one of simple injustice requiring immediate correction, but merely an unfortunate and abstractly created problem, that leisurely treatment is not surprising.

Moreover, regardless of the scope and pace of racial remedies, their costs are generally imposed disproportionately on minorities and lower-class whites. Most university affirmative action programs, for example, pit minorities against each other and against low-income whites. The programs generate hostility among these groups, while exempting from such unpleasantness the high-achieving white product of a private prep school and Ivy League college, who can remain aloof from these battles. An obvious alternative—a broad based overhaul of the admissions process and a rethinking of the criteria that make a person a deserving law student and future lawyer—seldom receives serious consideration even though one could easily devise standards that would result in a proportionate number of minorities, whites, and women gaining admission. Minority commentators have suggested such an approach, but it has been often ignored and never instituted.

My conclusion to this point is that a second scholarly tradition consists of the exclusion of minority writing about key issues of race law, and that this exclusion causes bluntings, skewings, and omissions in the literature dealing with race, racism, and American law. What accounts for, what sustains this tradition? And, can it be defended or justified?

IMPERIAL SCHOLARSHIP: EXPLAINING THE TRADITION

Studied indifference to minority writing on issues of race would be justified if the writing were second-rate, inelegant, unscholarly, or unimaginative. But, as was mentioned earlier, minority writers have experienced little difficulty gaining recognition outside the core areas of civil rights. Poor quality of the writing therefore seems an unlikely explanation. Might it be that minority authors who write about racial issues are not objective, that passion and anger render them unfit to reason rigorously or express themselves clearly, while white authors are above self-interest and thus capable of thinking and writing objectively? But this too seems implausible, for it presupposes that white writers have no vested interest in the status quo. Moreover, common experience suggests that most persons perform better, not worse, at tasks they care deeply about. And, even if minority authors were offering one-sided views, their suggestions are at least data, material that deserves mention for what it discloses; one would not expect such telling data to be completely ignored. When discussing women's issues, white male elite writers seem to cite at least some white female writers, such as Herma Hill Kay, Lenore Weitzman, and Ruth Bader Ginsburg. These women write with passion and commitment, qualities that evidently do not render them unfit to be taken seriously. Lack of objectivity on the part of minority authors, then, seems an inadequate explanation for their treatment at the hands of leading white scholars.

In explaining the strange absence of minority scholarship from the text and footnotes of the central arenas of legal scholarship dealing with civil rights, I reject conscious malevolence or crass indifference. I think the explanation lies at the level of unconscious action and choice. It may be that the explanation lies in a need to remain in *control,* to make sure that legal change occurs, but not too fast. The desire to shape events is a powerful human motive that could easily account for much of the exclusionary scholarship I have noted. The moment one makes such a statement, however, one is reminded that it is these same liberal authors who often have been the strongest supporters of affirmative action in their own university communities, and who have often been prepared to take chances (as they see it) to advance the goal of an integrated society. Perhaps one can reconcile the two behaviors by observing that the liberal professor may be pleased to have minority students and colleagues serve as figureheads, ambassadors of good will, and future community leaders, but not necessarily happy with the thought of a minority colleague who might go galloping off in a new direction.

Once, early in my career, I co-authored a law review article about Mexican-Americans (as they were called then) as a legally cognizable class, one that can sue in its own name for injuries to its members. This was in the mid-1970s when the results of Chicano activism were just reaching the courts. At that time, a few decisions, notably *Lopez Tijerina v. Henry,* had held that Chicanos could not sue collectively because of problems with class definition. Some Chicanos speak Spanish, some do not; some have Spanish surnames, some do not; some trace their ancestors to Mexico, some do not. Chicanos were thus held too amorphous a group to be permitted to sue for class-based relief. My article explained several valid ways of getting around the class-definition problem and gave several reasons why this should happen. Shortly after the article appeared, I received a long letter from a white litigator at a public interest law firm that concerns itself with the legal problems of Mexican-Americans. The letter told me, in clear, terse language, of the disservice I had done the cause of Chicano legal rights. Its essence was that the writer's organization had been successfully *finessing* the class-definition problem, and my article had instead focused attention on it, making matters worse. I suffered terrible remorse until the Supreme Court decided in the following term that Mexican-Americans are a legally cognizable class for the purpose of civil rights suits.

Had the litigator, a former professor at a major law school, simply made a mistake in judgment? Or did more lie behind the letter and its insistence that I stay out of the picture and leave things to persons like him? I think many civil-rights activists and scholars derive a sense of personal satisfaction from being at the forefront of a powerful social movement. Command and influence are heady things; it takes an alert person to realize when to step back, to know when his or her efforts have begun to interfere with the intended beneficiaries' effective engagement in their own affairs. The inner-circle authors' strong identification with their own role may prevent them from understanding when it is time to begin to leave it behind.

Another closely related motive is fear. Most of the white scholars who make up the inner circle spent some of their formative years of teaching during the late 1960s and early 1970s. Lawyers, and especially law professors, are deeply committed to the rule of law; but during those years the rule of law seemed to mean relatively little. Events were out of control. Law seemed powerless to stop the popular tides that surged—the civil rights movement, inner city riots, draft resistance. The professors who now dominate legal scholarship and dictate legal styles saw what excesses of passion can do. Perhaps, scarcely knowing it, they came to emphasize scholarship that is controlled, incremental, and seemingly nonideological, and to resist that of a more tempestuous, change-oriented nature. The fear of losing control would explain a number of things—the emphasis on procedure and role, the downplaying of substance. It would explain inattention to the reparations argument and avoidance of issues of guilt and complicity. It would explain the treatment of racism and discrimination as vestigial aberrant behavior not connected by any common thread, much less illustrating an implied social compact. It would explain the lack of citation to minority writers, who have drawn attention to some of these thorny issues.

Whatever the reason for it, the phenomenon has not gone unnoticed. Derrick Bell once observed that the exclusion of minority participants from litigation and scholarship about black issues reminds him of traditional families of former years in which parents would tell their children, "Keep quiet. We are talking about you, not to you."

What should be done? As a beginning, minority students and teachers should raise insistently and often the unsatisfactory quality of the scholarship being produced by the inner circle—its biases, omissions, and errors. Its presuppositions and world-views should be exposed and challenged. That feedback will increase the likelihood that when a well-wishing white scholar writes about minority problems, he or she will give minority viewpoints and literature the full consideration due. That consideration may help the author avoid the types of substantive error catalogued earlier.

But while no one could object if sensitive white scholars contribute occasional articles and useful proposals, must these scholars make a career of it? The time has come for white liberal authors who write in the field of civil rights to redirect their efforts and to encourage their colleagues to do so as well. Many other important subjects could, and should, engage their formidable talents. As these scholars stand aside, nature will take its course; I am reasonably certain that the gap will quickly be filled by talented and innovative minority writers and commentators. The dominant scholars should affirmatively encourage their minority colleagues to move in this direction, as well as simply make the change possible.

Only such a transformation will end the incongruity of one group's maintenance of a failed ideology for another, an irony that Judge Wyzanski saw as clearly as anyone:

> To leave non-whites at the mercy of whites in the presentation of non-white claims which are admittedly adverse to the whites would be a mockery of democracy. Suppression, intentional or otherwise, of the presentation of non-white claims cannot be tolerated in our society.... In presenting non-white issues non-whites cannot, against their will, be relegated to white spokesmen, mimicking black men. The day of the minstrel show is over.

The day of the minstrel show is, indeed, over.

Rodrigo's Thirteenth Chronicle
Legal Formalism and Law's Discontents

INTRODUCTION: IN WHICH THE PROFESSOR RETURNS TO THE UNITED STATES AND GETS CAUGHT UP ON WHAT HIS TWO YOUNG FRIENDS HAVE BEEN DOING

"Professor! You're back!" Rodrigo leaped to his feet and shook my hand fervently. "I heard a rumor you might be coming. It's good to see you! Sit down. Did the authorities give you any trouble?"

"Not at all," I replied, choosing one of the few uncluttered spots on my young friend's couch. "I breezed right across. They didn't even make me open my suitcase. I gather you didn't get my letter."

"No, but Laz got a card and mentioned it to Giannina. So we were hoping against hope that we'd hear from you."

"You'll probably get my letter next month. The mail is glacially slow. It's one of the few things that takes a little getting used to about my new home. [Eds. Since their last conversation, the Professor took semi-retirement and is living in Mexico.] I'm glad you're both in town."

"It's been a while," Rodrigo said. "How's the grandchild?"

"She and her mother are fine. They named her Gianna, after your Giannina, I suspect."

"We hoped the lure of grandchildren would bring you back. How long can you stay?"

"My visa's good for six months. But I'm thinking of heading back the week after next. I'm helping my son-in-law lay tile for their new patio, so that my daughter and the baby can go outside when the weather's good." I looked at a pile of papers and reports on Rodrigo's desk with yellow slips of paper sticking out. "What are you working on?"

"Oh, that stuff," Rodrigo said, looking down. "Déjà vu. I'm on my school's curriculum committee. Laz is the chair. The dean asked us to decide what, if anything, the law school should do in response to these reports. Are you familiar with this one, Professor?" Rodrigo asked, holding up one of the volumes.

I half stood up and peered at the thick paperbound volume Rodrigo was holding up for my benefit. "That must be the MacCrate Report. It came out just as I was leaving. It caused quite a stir. As I recall, it argued that legal education should be more practical. A number of my friends applauded it. Others were taken aback because they thought it threatened transformative scholarship and teaching."

"And have you seen this other one?" Rodrigo asked.

I leaned forward again. "Oh, that's Judge Harry Edwards' article. Boy, has he changed. Did you know that we knew each other?"

"No, I didn't. But it stands to reason," Rodrigo replied. "You're of the same generation. So you know he leveled quite a blast at law review scholarship, charging that a high proportion of it has little to do with law and judging."

"I don't know what got into him. He was quite a scholar before he went on the bench. Maybe I'll write him sometime. But you mentioned a second piece?"

"Yes. The Paul Carrington article. It accuses CLS scholars—and, by implication, critical race theorists, feminists, and interdisciplinary writers—of nihilism and invites them to leave the academy."

"I remember it. He said their message was counteraspirational and went against the central ethos of the law. People who write that way, he said, have no business teaching law students. They should either move over to other departments or leave teaching entirely. And so your dean asked you to look at all three?"

"She did. We're supposed to report on their implications for legal education. Her memo came with a sheaf of news clippings about the public's discontent with law and lawyers."

"Some of that was building when I left the U.S. The major newsmagazines have been covering it, even in their international editions, which are the only ones we get down there. But it's not just the public. Lawyers seem disenchanted with law practice as well. Some are leaving. Others are thinking of doing so."

"She asked us to look into all that. Can I offer you a cup of coffee? Giannina will be here soon. Can you join us for dinner?"

"I'd love to," I said. "If it wouldn't be too much trouble."

"Not at all," Rodrigo replied. "Did I tell you that Giannina is in law school now?"

"I had no idea! How does she like it? Where is she going? I hope she hasn't given up her writing," I said.

"By no means. She says the first year is so weird she writes for relief. She's finished half a book of poems and most of a play that she refuses to let me see. I think it's about law school, and I'm probably a character in it."

"Uh-oh," I said. "Reminds me of the time my daughter wrote a crime mystery for a high school English class. It was so realistic the teacher called home. My late wife and I had to do a lot of talking to persuade the teacher we weren't running some sort of crime ring out of our home!"

Rodrigo laughed. "She's going to the school across town. She got high test scores and could have gone anywhere. But we've had it with living apart."

"I'm glad you decided to stay together. I remember how hard commuting was on the two of you that first year of teaching. But tell me your thoughts on those three critiques. I assume you have a theory."

"I do. Oh, the coffee's ready." Rodrigo busied himself for a moment at his office espresso machine, then handed me a steaming mug. "It's Italian blend. Your favorite, if I recall. And I have cream and sugar right here."

"Just like the old days," I said.

IN WHICH RODRIGO AND THE PROFESSOR REVIEW LAW'S LAMENTS

As I mixed the condiments into my coffee, Rodrigo began:

"You asked if I had a theory, Professor. I do. As you know, the two dominant currents in legal education today are, first, the MacCrate-Edwards critique of legal education and scholarship as not practical enough, and second, deep discontent with law and lawyers, both on the part of the public and of lawyers themselves. My thesis is that these two are related, although not in the way or even in the direction most people think. And the connecting link is legal formalism."

"Legal formalism?" I said. "You mean teaching and scholarship that emphasize cases and doctrine over policy, critique, and interdisciplinary approaches? The Langdellian idea that law is a science with only one right answer?"

Rodrigo nodded animatedly, whether in response to my answer or to his own double-size mug of coffee, which he was rapidly draining, I could not tell. In any event, I went on: "So are you saying we need more formalistic classroom teaching and more boring, doctrinal scholarship? I certainly hope that is not where you are going."

"Quite the contrary, Professor. Those things are precisely what are causing all the trouble."

"That's a relief," I replied. "But I hope you can spell out the connection, for you are definitely swimming against the tide. In fact, you are saying the opposite of what the ABA report and my old friend Harry Edwards are saying."

"I'll be happy to," Rodrigo replied. "But first consider what the public is saying about lawyers, and also what lawyers are saying about themselves and their profession."

"I'm all ears," I said. "I haven't practiced in quite a while, as you know. But I've always done a little consulting, mostly in school desegregation cases. So I'm vitally interested in what you have to say."

In Which Rodrigo and the Professor Analyze the Public's Disenchantment with Law and Lawyers

"Let's take the public's attitudes first," Rodrigo began. "If you'll just give me a minute." Rodrigo, who I knew from past experience was well versed in the new technology, pushed a few buttons on his computer keyboard. "Where did I find that poll file? Oh, here it is. Where were we?"

"Public attitudes toward lawyers."

"Right," Rodrigo said, looking down at his desk. "These clippings from the dean turned out to be only the tip of the iceberg. I bet you've seen this one, at least."

I peered at what he was holding up for my benefit. "Yes, it's the ABA president saying that the profession isn't as bad as it's made out to be."

"The public doesn't trust us. Many think we are ambulance chasers who feast off the misfortunes of others. More interested in money than justice, we prolong suits in order to drive up our fees. A Gallup Poll—let's see, oh, here it is—rated lawyers below druggists, clergypersons, doctors, dentists, and college teachers for honesty and ethical standards. We ended up near the bottom, not much above professional admen and used car salespersons. In a survey of confidence in institutions, law firms rated dead last, behind every branch of government, the military, major companies, Wall Street, the press, colleges and universities, the medical profession, and TV news. Fifty-six percent of the public believed lawyers recommend more legal work than necessary because it increases their fees. Seventy-three percent said there are too many lawyers and that the glut causes disputes to be taken to court when they shouldn't be."

"Sounds dire," I said. "But, of course, you can prove almost anything with statistics. The very way a polltaker frames a question largely shapes the answer. Maybe the public associates lawyers with trouble—with divorces, drunk driving tickets, and other hassles. Maybe it's a case of shooting the messenger."

"If so, they certainly think ill of the messenger," Rodrigo replied. "Another survey—this one by the ABA—showed that the public views lawyers as being of uneven character and quality; another, that lawyers are deficient in compassion, caring, ethics, and honesty, motivated by money, and prone to engage in undignified advertising. Lawyer-bashing jokes are legion."

I winced. "Even I've heard those from time to time. I'm a law professor, but a certain type of person makes it their business to let me know at parties what they think of lawyers, as though I were some sort of media-hungry, ambulance-chasing, personal injury shark."

"The same happens to me. I tell them I'm an Italian lawyer, which I am. That usually shuts them up, because they have no idea of whether or not their stock criticisms hold true elsewhere. Oh, look here. Here's one on parents. Professor, would you want your new grandchild to be a lawyer someday?"

"I'd be honored," I said.

"Most parents wouldn't. This poll," Rodrigo indicated his screen, "shows that when parents were asked which of eight professions they would encourage their son or daughter to go into, only five percent said law. Ten years ago, the figure was twelve. Among the top six lawyers people today said they admire most, two are fictional and two are dead."

"I love fictional lawyers," I quipped. "Some of my best friends..."

Rodrigo rolled his eyes. "The dead lawyers are Thurgood Marshall and Abraham Lincoln. The fictional ones are Perry Mason and Matlock. Oh, here's another poll of honesty and integrity. In this one we rank only slightly ahead of prostitutes and politicians."

"And used car salesmen, I think you mentioned."

"Them too, but barely. And finally," Rodrigo said, pressing more buttons on his computer and peering intently, "a recent *National Law Journal* poll found that three-fourths of Americans think that litigation is hindering the country's economy."

"A stunning indictment," I replied. "Especially when you hear it all at once. We obviously have some work to do." I pointed toward the other folder that lay on Rodrigo's desk. "But I think you mentioned another side to the story."

In Which Rodrigo and the Professor Discuss Lawyers' Discontents
"More like another count to the indictment," Rodrigo continued. "Not only is the public fed up with law and lawyers, our colleagues are as well."

"Everyone pines for the good old days," I interjected. Then I added: "Except for women and minorities of color. My law school class boasted only four women and three students of color in addition to me. Even outstanding graduates like Sandra

Day O'Connor and my friend Santos Keller had trouble getting jobs. Surely, you don't maintain that conditions for today's lawyers are worse?"

"I'll let you decide," Rodrigo said, opening a second folder. "Here's a study of lawyer satisfaction. An estimated 40,000 lawyers a year are leaving the profession—almost as many as enter the law schools. A Maryland survey showed that more than one-third were unsure they would continue practicing law. *Time* cited a major increase in working hours and greater stress as contributing to the erosion of the quality of life for attorneys. Firms today often require that lawyers perform 2,000 to 2,500 hours of billable work—"

"Which, as we both know, means many more hours than that on the job," I interjected.

"Of course. One can't bill for time spent eating, talking with colleagues, or going to the bathroom. That 2,500-hour figure, by the way, is almost one-third greater than it was a decade ago. Many attorneys routinely put in twelve-hour days."

"It's gotten to the point that books are now warning students about the hazards of law school," I added. "While browsing at a bookstore in the airport, I noticed one entitled *Full Disclosure: Do You Really Want to Be a Lawyer?* Another was entitled *Running from the Law: Why Good Lawyers Are Getting Out of the Legal Profession.* Both warned that law practice is becoming all-consuming, repetitious, and dull. Lawyers say that law is not as enjoyable as it once was. It leaves little time for reflection, contemplation, or creativity, much less family life. It's a business, not a learned profession. I went back for my fortieth-year law school class reunion. All my friends were saying the same thing. Some were retiring or going into other lines of work."

"A whole new industry counsels lawyers who are unhappy with their situation," Rodrigo interjected. "They see lawyers who are dejected and liken themselves to hamsters in a cage. Studies reveal that many lawyers are dissatisfied, depressed, or even suicidal. Some good students don't even try for law jobs."

"I bet you have something on that right there," I said, indicating a pile of neatly clipped computer printouts nestled in Rodrigo's file folder.

"Do I ever," Rodrigo replied. "One American Bar Association study showed"—Rodrigo looked down—"a 'deterioration in the lawyer workplace that will likely continue until law firms and other employers begin to address the management practices that are causing the problem.' The same study showed that more attorneys describe themselves as seriously discontented than did in 1984."

"I have the impression this is even more true of women," I added.

"It is," Rodrigo said. "And it's on the rise for partners and senior associates as well as for sole practitioners and very young attorneys. Lawyers say the work atmosphere is not warm or personal; that they have difficulty advancing; that the work is monotonous and pressured. An ABA survey found that more than half of second-year associates in big firms were deeply dissatisfied. Even the big paycheck cannot compensate for the long hours and tedious detail. According to one analyst, 'many of the smartest college students don't know exactly what they want to do, so they turn to one of modern society's last refuges for the generalist—law school.' Those who do well win summer clerkships, then first-year associateships making one hundred thousand dollars a year or more. But then they learn how solitary law practice is, with so many hours passed in the library. Little time is spent with clients or learning to be a wise counselor. One law graduate says: 'There's an incredible amount of dissatisfaction out there ... [Associates would] come in and shut the door and literally start crying. So many wanted to leave ... but felt they couldn't. There's a conspiracy of silence among people who doubt that the law is for them.'"

"Former students of mine have told me they love the law and their jobs," I added, "right up until the day they quit. One writes me regularly about life on her strawberry farm. One of my top students, she had been in line to become partner at a prestigious law firm in Washington, D.C."

"Here's another one," Rodrigo exclaimed. "Twenty-three percent of New Jersey lawyers were certain they would leave law practice before they retire. The same percentage of North Carolina lawyers said that if they had to do it all over again, they would not become lawyers. A 1990 ABA study showed that about half of lawyers in solo practice complain they do not have enough time for their families. Three-fourths said they felt fatigued or exhausted by the end of the workday. A report cosponsored by the A.B.A. Young Lawyers Division, entitled *At the Breaking Point,* found that lawyers in their early years perceive law practice as almost unbearably intense. Associates juggle several projects at the same time, working nine to twelve hours a day in the office and still taking work home."

"I understand that many prop themselves up with drugs or alcohol."

"They do," Rodrigo replied. "Divorce is common, as well. Some marriage counselors and psychiatrists have practices devoted exclusively to attorneys. One laid the blame on changes in the structure of law and law practice. Forty or fifty years ago, many who entered law were motivated by money. But others were attracted by the intellectual challenge and opportunity to help people and society. Back then, law practice allowed you actually to fulfill those aspirations. Today, it does not. Law and legal education take broad-based humanists and generalists and turn them into narrow, driven specialists. Naturally, they end up unhappy."

"Did you find anything on specialization? Law today is much more compartmentalized than it was when I was starting out."

"I did. A number of studies mentioned how unsatisfying it is for many young associates to work on only one piece of a project over and over again—say, document retrieval or analysis of damages. They complain that they never see clients or even attorneys working on other parts of the case."

"I've read of a felt decline in civility," I said. "Some articles complain of hate speech directed by lawyers or judges against other lawyers. Others report dirty tricks and cutthroat tactics that old-time practitioners never would have tolerated."

Rodrigo was silent for a moment. Then: "It just occurred to me that the two types of discontent may be related. If lawyers believe the public hates them, their job satisfaction obviously will be affected. Almost nine of every ten attorneys believe the image of the profession has been suffering. The O.J. Simpson trial didn't help. *New Jersey Lawyer* asked attorneys, 'Is the public becoming more antilawyer?' Eighty-six percent answered yes. Only 12.1% said the image of the lawyer is not deteriorating.

Women are even more dissatisfied with their professional lives than men are. Just a couple of months ago, a Justice of the U.S. Supreme Court lamented 'legal capitalism'—the excessive influence of the profit motive in the practice of law."

"Ironic!" I exclaimed. "The Court has been a bastion and protector of corporations and capitalism."

"Scholars such as Mary Ann Glendon report the same thing—that law is overcommercialized. Oh, here's another poll. Seventy percent of California lawyers would choose another line of work; three-quarters would not want their children to be lawyers. Sol Linowitz says that today's lawyers and law firms no longer think of law as a learned profession. They are 'hired guns' for whom winning is everything. Lawyers no longer think of themselves as officers of the court. As someone put it, 'the mechanics have increasingly supplanted the humanists.' No one reads for pleasure any more. Work leaves little quiet time or opportunity for creativity."

A knock at the door caused both of us to start. "Giannina!" Rodrigo exclaimed. "Come in."

I leaped to my feet. "I'm so glad to see you."

The slim, dark-haired young woman set down her backpack and gave me, then Rodrigo, quick hugs. "I'm starved. My study group went almost two hours late. Have you two been entertaining each other?" Giannina looked down at the mess of papers on Rodrigo's desk. "Law's troubles again?" Then, to me: "How was your flight?"

"Fine. I got in just three days ago. Saw my daughter and the baby. And now I want to get caught up on the two of you."

"No babies on our side, yet," Giannina said with a laugh. "But I'm in law school, as Rodrigo no doubt told you. How's your grandchild?"

"Both are fine. They named the little one after you. I'll have to introduce all of you sometime. But for now, can I take you two out to dinner? Talking makes me hungry. And your friend here seems able to eat any time." I looked over at Rodrigo, who nodded vigorously. "Maybe we can find a quiet place. Rodrigo has been regaling me with tales of despair. But he promised to tell me his theory of why the profession has been in such a tailspin. Have you heard it?"

Giannina said, "I don't think so. But Rodrigo is never at a loss for theories. He and Laz have been toiling away on this committee. Although I must say, the first-year experience is so peculiar that it practically begs for reform. I can't believe the Socratic method. Professors seem to believe that not telling you something is more educational than telling you. And the way lawyers write—it's deplorable."

Giannina, a published poet and playwright, wrinkled her nose in disgust. "I've just gotten through moot court," she said. "The idea seems to be that when writing a brief, the flatter and more boring the better. My writing instructor is actually not too bad. She knows how to put words on paper pretty decently and sometimes lets me get away with a metaphor or simile. But the structure of a brief—I can't believe it. It goes against all the rules of good writing. I thought of using a flashback technique in my reply brief. She told me to get rid of it, for no good reason other than it just isn't done."

I gave her a sympathetic look and added, "I know. Hang in there. Will a bit of dinner help?"

IN WHICH THE PROFESSOR AND GIANNINA HEAR RODRIGO'S THESIS ABOUT LAW'S DISCONTENTS AND ATTEMPT TO FIND AN EXPLANATION FOR WOMEN'S AND MINORITIES' DISENCHANTMENT WITH LAW AND LAW SCHOOL

A few minutes later we were seated in a small but comfortable Japanese restaurant that Giannina pronounced, "Fine. I like this place. They have good food, plus it's far enough from the law school that I won't be running into uptight fellow students." The waiter took our orders: vegetable tempura for Giannina, some sort of fish stew for my omnivorous friend Rodrigo, and teriyaki tofu ("It doesn't have MSG, I hope?") for me. The waiter filled our teacups and departed.

"Now, Rodrigo," I said. "Why do you think that doctrinalism in teaching and scholarship is responsible for law's woes? It's a little counterintuitive. In fact, all the authorities your dean asked you to look at diagnosed the problem in exactly the opposite way. I love policy analysis and critical thought, as you know. But it seems to me that turning out technically well-trained lawyers is a law school's central mission. If lawyers knew their craft and made fewer mistakes, maybe the public and judges would like us more."

"Oh, we all have to know our craft," Rodrigo agreed. "The question is what that craft is. Carrington, MacCrate, and Harry Edwards speak as though critical theory and interdisciplinary scholarship have very little place in legal theory or practice. In this, they are completely wrong—one hundred percent off. *Ignoring* all these realist-based approaches and obsessing over doctrine and rules are what's responsible for our woes."

"I don't mind doctrine," Giannina said quietly, "up to a point. But I've noticed that most of the professors, and even some of the young ones, cut off discussion when it wanders too far afield, when it begins to get into politics, or when a student wants to talk about feelings. Even though the classes are plenty challenging, a sameness is beginning to set in. How does this case square with that? Can this rule and that be reconciled? What difference would it have made in the court's result if the plaintiff were left-handed, or a child? All my fellow students are beginning to comment on this. So, I'm curious why you think a steady diet of this is bad for you."

"Me, too," I chimed in.

Rodrigo took a deep draught of his tea. "Laz and I were talking about this the other day. In fact, it's his idea that something is wrong with doctrinalism. But it's because he loves law and economics and thinks the curriculum pays too little attention to his favorite approach. All the public-law courses teach about the majesty of *Brown v. Board of Education, Marbury v. Madison,* and all the other big liberal cases, over and over, he said, with very little about judicial restraint and other notions dear to conservatives. We're buddies, even though he's the sponsor of the local Federalist Society, as I may have mentioned."

"And yet you're best friends," I said with wonderment. "For a conservative, he certainly seems ecumenical: he gets along fine with minorities like you, as well as persons of his own persuasion. He also feels passionately about social justice and poverty, if I recall."

"His family grew up poor. Anyway, we had a good long talk, after which I did some more thinking. I think formalism—the sort of thing Judge Edwards and Paul Carrington admire and the MacCrate Report champions—is responsible for law's laments in a number of ways, some of which have special force for minorities."

"We'd love to hear them," Giannina and I broke in simultaneously.

Rodrigo's First Connection: The Mechanical Quality of Doctrinalism and Scientific Jurisprudence as Responsible for Law's Discontents

"I realize this is paradoxical," Rodrigo began. "But I believe that legal formalism—the kind of teaching and scholarship that all three of our authorities hold up as the ideal—makes matters worse, not better."

"That *is* paradoxical," I agreed. "Everyone thinks the opposite. This had better be good."

"You can decide for yourselves," Rodrigo replied evenly. "It's like prescribing that someone go stand in the rain to get rid of a cold. Today's exaggerated focus on doctrine and case law contributes to law's low estate in at least five ways."

"Your analyses always seem to break down into four or five parts," Giannina interjected with a wry smile. "You're like one of my professors. Everything is either a three- or a four-part test."

"I suppose I do sound like a doctrinalist," Rodrigo replied with a smile. We all paused as the waiter set our plates down before us. "This looks good," Rodrigo said, examining his fish stew. "A five-course meal to go with a five-part analysis. My favorite evening."

"Mine, too," I said, patting my stomach a little ruefully. "And how do Mac-Crate, Harry Edwards, and Carrington prescribe exactly the wrong cure?"

"The first way those three giants—who, incidentally, are quite correct about the problem—err is by overlooking the mechanical quality of extreme doctrinalism."

"It certainly makes for a dull classroom," Giannina chimed in. "The professor never gets to the big issues, the ones we're all dying to discuss. But how does that produce the laments you two were discussing earlier?"

"It's not responsible for all of them," Rodrigo replied. "But mechanical jurisprudence goes hand-in-hand with emotional insensitivity and underdevelopment of law students and lawyers. It's the famous 'hired gun' mentality that the public accuses us of. Lawyers seem equally prepared to take either side of a case, with no personal attachment or conviction."

"I don't agree," I said. "In the criminal law, for example, our system holds that every defendant is entitled to a lawyer. If lawyers were to decide on which side justice lies and refuse to take the other, half the cases would have no lawyer."

"It's not a case of black and white," Rodrigo conceded. "Rather, a subtle quality of mind sets in. Lawyers come to strike clients as mere craftsmen, going through the paces, citing cases and precedent, highlighting the worst-case scenario, and so on, when the client's life or property may be at stake. Clinical theorists like Lucie White and Anthony Alfieri describe how the lawyer may be cold and technical, wanting to vindicate principle above all, when the client, who may be poor or black, may want something else. Good lawyering is more an art than a science. Under the apprenticeship system that prevailed until not so long ago, lawyers learned to use intuition and creativity to solve problems; in today's Socratic classroom they do not. Even Paul Carrington acknowledges that technocratic learning can 'dehumanize' and that law professors need to teach the 'effective use of intuition going beyond technical knowledge' and precedent."

"If you mean clinical classes," Giannina interjected, "I'm greatly looking forward to taking some of those next year. Unfortunately, our school is thinking of closing one of its three clinics. The immigration clinic just lost its funding due to federal cutbacks."

"Bad news," Rodrigo commiserated. "Because clinical classes *would* indeed help. But they must offer theory, too. Otherwise they can easily become mere cookie-cutter exercises in which an experienced practitioner drills a student in the practitioner's favorite way of handling a certain kind of case. This sort of teaching, as much as the Socratic classroom, can miseducate. Both teach instrumental reasoning: If you want to get from A to B, use C or D. Cite the right holding. Bring your case under a certain rule. The means by which an attorney pursues an end for his or her client should be independently justifiable. But the ends should be as well. As Sol Linowitz says, we are a profession that no longer can say no to the desires of a client. The action may be technically legal, but it may be an abominable thing to do to a consumer or competitor. It may also not be what Mrs. G., an indigent client, wants. The mechanical approach says, go ahead and do it anyway."

"I'm not sure I would go that far," I said. "It seems to me a lawyer needs to know technique just as much as he or she needs to have a firm grasp of values. If you have the right values but don't know how to advance the client's cause because you don't know the precedents or statutes, your advocacy is going to be a mess. Your critique needs more than that, Rodrigo, to convince me, at least."

"I *do* have more," Rodrigo replied. "Mechanical jurisprudence goes hand-in-hand with some unlovely traits, including hyperaggressiveness and obsession with production. A focus in law school on borderline cases—which, of course, are the only ones in the casebook—fosters a litigator's mentality. Lawyers love to fight, in part because the cases on which they cut their teeth are ones in which someone staged a full-scale battle with someone else. The curriculum neglects planning, counseling, and preventing the mess in the first place. We don't train law students to be wise counselors and conciliators, much less to understand and empathize with clients from radically different cultures. We train them to be killers. The focus on appellate cases is one reason why."

Rodrigo was quiet for a moment. I took a bit of my tofu, swallowed, then: "You mentioned obsession with production."

"Oh, right," Rodrigo said, offering Giannina, then me, a morsel of his own steaming dish. After depositing small portions neatly on our plates with his chopsticks, he continued. "If citing cases and filing papers were all there are in life, then the only thing that separates you from the next lawyer is doing more of it. With case law, you go round and round in little circles like a hamster on a treadmill."

"And witness the rise of the Rambo lawyer," I added. "The lawyer who places winning above all. Older lawyers say that there weren't that many of them just fifteen years ago. Maybe the return to case law and doctrine has something to do with it."

"I'm sure it does," Rodrigo agreed. "Doctrinalism is a discourse of power and mastery. Like positivist thought in early social science, it serves the rise of specialization and meshes well with the profitmaking motive already prevalent in capitalist society. The rise of the megafirm, the introduction of departments within firms, and the decline of the generalist all are aspects of the same thing. Doctrinalism is a cause of all this, but it is also a symptom of something broader."

Giannina nodded vigorously. "It's a discourse of mastery. The case method and Socratic teaching foster arrogance, not humility. They reward the confident, snap answer rather than the thoughtful, modest response. I see it in my classes every day. The competitive individualism these traditional methods foster carries over into daily life. All my classmates notice that they have become more argumentative. Three couples have split up in my first-year class alone, and the year isn't half finished. It stands to reason that the habits of mind acquired in the traditional classroom could carry over into practice and replicate overzealous, uncollegial advocacy and relations inside the bar."

"Older practitioners complain that civility is declining and that lawyers treat each other with less respect, both in and out of the courtroom," I went on. "The educational goal may be to develop effective advocates, but doctrinalism contains no stopping points, no built-in checks. It goes hand-in-hand with confrontation and rabid advocacy at the expense of interpersonal decency, communicative skills, empathy, and justice. Negotiation, counseling, and compromise are fast becoming lost arts. In my day, a few professors emphasized these things. Today, I get the impression hardly any do."

"Maybe that is why many women and minorities of color are unhappy with the legal classroom," Giannina said. "I was just reading Professor Guinier's study. It mirrors some of the complaints I've read about from young women in the bar. If so, things won't change until we resolve to teach and practice differently."

"Just as it would counsel that we shy away from the Carrington-Edwards prescription in our scholarship," Rodrigo added. "And this concludes my first point. Should we order dessert? I think I can go through my remaining critiques a little more quickly."

I looked at my watch. "My daughter and her husband turn in around ten. I've got a little time, if you two do."

Giannina nodded and summoned the waiter, who materialized quickly, dessert menus in hand. We ordered—mint ice cream for my lanky friend, mango sherbet for Giannina and me. After the waiter departed, Rodrigo resumed as follows:

Rodrigo's Second Connection: Extreme Doctrinalism Dehumanizes Clients and Legal Problems—The Anarchy-and-Elegance Critique

"The second connection is related to the first. Legal formalism breeds dissatisfaction because it mistakenly tries to make law a science. Law deals with people and the myriad fact situations in which they find themselves, rather than the orderly and relatively predictable phenomena of, say, chemistry or physics. The attempt to map scientific epistemology onto a humanistic subject naturally produces frustration. People are not like molecules, solar systems, or microbes; nor their behavior like that of liquid in a tube or an object on an inclined plane. Chris Goodrich wrote a fine book, *Anarchy and Elegance* [Giannina and I both nodded to show we were familiar with it] about law and law school. A journalist who spent a year at Yale Law School in a program for journalists and writers, he wrote about how law, with its elegant structures of rules and principles, struggles to come to terms with an unruly world. In the words of his title, the law represents elegance; daily life, anarchy. He marveled at how well the elegant lectures and treatises he absorbed did the trick. But I think if he had stuck around for another year or two—or, better yet, visited a busy city court—he would have tempered his praise. Formalism tries to make law a science, reducing human factors and fact patterns into pre-existing forms called precedent. It minimizes the role of judgment, experience, politics, love, compassion, discretion, and what our friend Duncan Kennedy calls 'intersubjective zap.' Critical legal studies tells us that these other things are all there is, which I don't agree with. But even the more modified scientism of legal process and Paul Carrington manifestly give less scope than CLS and Derrick Bell do to politics, history, compassion, instinct, and all the rest."

"That's certainly true," Giannina replied. "I've been studying Duncan Kennedy in my reading group."

"Didn't you meet him last year?" Rodrigo asked.

"No, I was out of town when he spoke. You told me he was amazing."

"He was. Judges, however, being busy bureaucrats with large case loads, do not welcome such a broad role. They prefer to think of themselves as technicians whose hands are tied when they send prisoners to jail, deny welfare rights to the poor, reduce recovery for consumers injured by dangerous products, and so on. Clients also feel something is wrong when they find their own lawyer taking the other side and spelling out the worst case scenario. They want a friend, and they get a laboratory technician. 'Mr. Jones, I'm sorry, but your test shows you have cancer. Please make an appointment next week with the oncologist.'"

"Your scientific example reminds me—we seem to be back to positivism again. You mentioned that earlier, if I recall."

"I guess I did," Rodrigo exclaimed, seemingly pleased at discovering how his critiques fit together. "Dissatisfaction with mechanistic law may be part of a more general movement away from rigid, pseudoscientific approaches toward 'softer,' more modest, interdisciplinary ones. This new emphasis came on the heels of widespread criticism, mainly from philosophers and critical social scientists, some in Europe, of positivist epistemologies. In the old, discredited approach, social scientists would try to see human behavior as subject to unvarying rules, independent of social context. These 'dominant discourses,' as they came to be called, ultimately failed because they marginalized subjectivity and ignored perspective and positionality. They simply could not deal adequately with the heterogeneity of social life and the situated, contingent nature of knowledge."

"Well put. But I assume you mean human knowledge, not physics and mathematics," I said, resolving to push Rodrigo as long as possible.

"Well, at least in that realm, and maybe in math and science too. I assume you are familiar with Kuhn and the sociology of science?"

"I am," I said.

"Even scientific knowledge is constructed and has an element of convention. A real world exists outside of us, of course. But how we choose to describe it is contingent and subject to differing interpretations at different times."

"Granted," Giannina broke in. "But I'm still not sure what all this has to do with the public's dissatisfaction with law and lawyers. Science clings tenaciously to past paradigms, embraces objectivism, and yet the public worships scientists. But they detest lawyers. Why?"

"Nice question," Rodrigo conceded. "One reason, as we said, has to do with the habits of mind it creates. Another is the client's sense that you simply are not on the same wavelength as he or she is, that you don't care about—or even understand—the human dimensions of his or her situation. You talk about funny things—'material elements' of a cause of action, and so on. You slice their problem up into little pieces, so that they end up hardly recognizing it. You translate their injury into something they may hardly recognize. Good lawyering requires judgment and knowledge of human beings and their motives. It requires the ability to see the world in shades of gray, acting fearlessly in situations of factual uncertainty and even moral ambiguity."

"I know what you're going to say," Giannina said with excitement in her voice. "Good lawyering requires great literature, psychology, social science, even religion. All these may be better models than science for what lawyers do—good ones, anyway." (I recalled that in her pre–law school life, Giannina had been a poet and playwright, publishing a number of volumes and even winning a prize or two.)

"So," Giannina went on, "you think that the illness in lawyers' souls comes from *denial*—the failure to deal straightforwardly with the way one sometimes manipulates and maneuvers to promote your clients' ends."

"Which, optimistically, include justice," Rodrigo added. "Formalism leaves you with no moral anchor. You go out into the world, confront its anarchy, and quickly become cynical. Doctors deal with sick people; lawyers, sometimes anyway, with bad ones. But formalism overlooks all this. It's as though doctors were trained only in science, not in how to take care of sick people."

"I had a doctor like that once," Giannina shuddered. "He was a terrific technician but had a horrible bedside manner. I quickly changed to another."

"Would you folks like some coffee?" asked the waiter, who had materialized at the side of our table. "We have cappuccino, decaf, and herbal teas."

"Decaf for me," I said.

"Make mine the real thing," said my high-energy young friend.

"I'll pass," said Giannina. Then after the waiter left: "Although you can't do that in a Socratic classroom."

"It's a different discourse," said Rodrigo with a wink. "In restaurants, no one pretends everyone else is the same. But some harried judges and lawyers do. The crits who are calling attention to law's contingency and political underpinnings may be speaking for the widespread feelings of impoverishment many feel throughout the legal community. This is especially so of the growing minority communities, who are most poorly served of all by cookie-cutter law. Far from teaching cynicism or neglect of craft, the new critical scholars may be in tune with the public and its needs. Carrington, MacCrate, and Harry Edwards put their fingers on what's wrong. But they err in their prescription, urging instead what will only make matters worse."

"Like that brilliant doctor I had once," Giannina said. "He prescribed a regimen that should have worked, ignoring that my body was different from that of the usual person. I changed doctors fast. Oh, here's your coffee. Actually, it looks good."

"Will you have some, Miss?" the waiter asked. "We do have decaf."

"Okay. I'll have a decaf latté, if you have it."

"We can make it," the waiter said and departed.

"He's like a good lawyer," all three of us said at once.

"He didn't stick to the menu," said Giannina.

Rodrigo's Third Connection: Formalism and Doctrinal Pedagogy Deflect Us from Things That Matter

As the waiter wrote down her order and walked away, Rodrigo looked up at his friend.

"Giannina, do you remember how you said that formalism is a type of massive denial?" (Giannina nodded.) "Well, my third critique builds on that. I think formalism, whether in legal scholarship, teaching, or practice, is bad for our souls and our ethics. It narrows political options. And it predisposes lawyers to develop the personal traits that the public find so annoying."

"Oh, dear," Giannina sighed. "I knew I should have stayed with writing. I made less than three thousand dollars most years, but if you're right, at least I was able to preserve my immortal soul."

Rodrigo raised his eyebrows. "I expect this to be the most controversial part of my thesis. Nobody likes hearing that their soul is in danger."

"Get on with it," I said. "The public already think we're unscrupulous sharks. If you can draw a connection between their low opinion and the way we think, write, and practice, come right out and say so. It can't hurt and might do some good."

"Let's take the least controversial part first," Rodrigo said, stirring his characteristic four teaspoons of sugar into his coffee. "Formalism is a deflection. It points you neatly away from the things that matter. This is bad for you and, in the long run, for your reputation."

"By deflection, I assume you mean from politics," Giannina ventured. "I've been reading *The Politics of Law* in my reading group. So if that's your point, it's not exactly new."

Rodrigo shot her a quick look. "I do think the crits are right, but I had something a little different in mind. Have you gotten to *Erie v. Tompkins* yet in Civil Procedure?"

"We're starting it next week. I've read it, though. I often skip around in the casebook if I find something interesting."

"Then you know *Erie* is about the distribution of judicial power between the federal and state judiciaries. It's essentially a choice-of-law case. What you may not know yet is that a huge mystique surrounds it. Many consider it one of the most important cases in American law, the cornerstone of our federalist system."

"My goodness," Giannina exclaimed. "At first glance it just looked like an interesting choice-of-law case about somebody who was walking along a railroad."

"In the eyes of many, it's much more than that," Rodrigo elaborated. "It tells us when a state versus a federal judge has the right to proclaim the common law. In diversity of citizenship cases, it says that federal courts must look to state substantive law rules, but may apply their own procedure. In federal-question cases, more or less the opposite prevails."

"Nice and neat," Giannina commented. "But why is the case considered so important? It just seems to say that an earlier decision, *Swift v. Tyson,* was wrong—that is, too narrow—in its application of the Federal Rules of Decision Act, requiring that federal judges, sitting in diversity, bow only to state law incorporated squarely in a statute."

"According to the usual view, it's the fulcrum that divides power between the two levels of government, state and federal."

"Well, I can see how it's at least a moderately important case," Giannina said. "I assume you think the opposite. Such a contrarian! Why do you think the case is unimportant or misguided?"

"It's not misguided," Rodrigo replied. "It may well be rightly decided. What I find curious, though, is the veneration a number of very bright people shower on it. There's practically a cult following, going back to Justice Frankfurter and the Harvard school of institutional analysis, which holds that the most important questions have to do with determining which person, authority, or branch of government is the most appropriate decisionmaker for a particular question."

"A kind of latter-day formalism!" Giannina exclaimed.

"Exactly," Rodrigo replied. "A way of avoiding difficult substantive questions. It *is* important to know whether a federal or a state judge has the right to declare the common law, for example on tort duties toward trespassers who walk along railroad tracks at night. But in another sense, *Erie* is a trivial case. I hope I'm not poisoning your mind."

"Thank you very much, Professor," Giannina said. "But what I'd really love to know is why you think it isn't such a big deal."

"Well, consider the profile of the typical federal trial-court judge," Rodrigo replied. "How old? Say, fifty-five. Which color? White. Male. Socially moderate to conservative. Lives in a nice suburban community. Went to a good, but probably not great, law school. Plays golf on Sundays. Has two or three kids."

"I suppose you're going to say we need to do better than that," Giannina replied.

"We *should*, although that's not my point."

"Oh?"

"Now consider the profile of the average *state* judge. Fifty-five years old. A moderate Republican. White. Male. Went to a good, but not great law school. Plays golf on Sundays. My point is that the two sets of judges look pretty much alike. Not exactly, of course. The federal judiciary is sometimes a little better, a little more select. But the similarities overwhelm the differences. *Erie,* however, creates a huge fuss over which white, male, moderate Republican, fifty-five year old judge gets to have his version of the common law applied to the case at hand. Now, I'm not saying it makes *no* difference who gets to do so, in railroad cases or in any other. But consider how few female, black, working class, or gay or lesbian judges preside over our courtrooms. Few with disabilities. Few younger than thirty-five. Few single mothers. Few with working-class roots."

"Now *that's* a question that really matters," I said.

"Yet the *Erie* line of cases neatly blinds us to it, focusing instead on whether Tweedle Dee or Tweedle Dum gets to declare the law. This is what I mean by a deflection. Doctrinalism, the worship of the conventionally framed question, blinds us to questions that really matter, ones of power and authority."

"Now that's a serious critique," I conceded. "To me, it's more forceful than your first one. But is it limited to a few big cases like *Erie*? If so, the cure for doctrinalism would be simply to remind ourselves that the case is not the be-all and end-all, that many important questions remain even after this one is addressed—such as the racial composition of the very judiciary that propounds the rule."

"I think the risk is general," Rodrigo replied. "Are you familiar, Professor, with Laurence Tribe's notion of structural due process?"

"You mean his suggestion about an interaction between procedural law and social change?"

"Exactly. He proposed that judges and other legal decisionmakers apply rules and procedures with an eye to the moral and political status of the case being adjudicated. Cases that present few novel or controversial issues ought to be adjudicated summarily, via streamlined procedures and under uniform, bright-line, across-the-board rules. Cases that present novel, controversial issues ought to be treated differently. These other cases ought to be aired fully, openly, and by means of procedures that allow full consideration of the entire range of issues they present. Examples of such cases, lying in the zone of moral flux, might include constitutional challenges to sodomy statutes or ones concerning women's procreative rights or the right to die."

"So you are saying that with cases like these, we gain by forcing ourselves to undertake serious, prolonged analyses?" Giannina asked.

"Tribe thinks so," Rodrigo replied. "We will arrive more rapidly at consensus. Then, adjudication may become more summary and routinized. We can use presumptions, summary judgment, tight evidentiary rules, and other devices to confine discussion to the most centrally relevant points, since we will know what they are, and eliminate the others."

"A sensible approach," I commented. "Saves time and effort. One is not constantly reinventing the wheel."

"And quite liberal," Giannina added. "It seems to me an outgrowth of institutional analysis, as you mentioned before. Curve-fitting. And I suppose you think it has a whiff of formalism about it?"

"It does," Rodrigo acknowledged. "Consider the contrast with critical legal studies. CLS points out that vast reaches of law are shot through with contradiction and indeterminacy. A judge deciding a case can invoke different principles and precedents and come to diametrically opposite conclusions. We use rules and rights to make it appear as though law is fair, neutral—a science with only one right answer. Legal discourse and all the elements of legal culture—legal education, the bar exam, the rituals, robes, and esoteric jargon—all serve to conceal a series of result-oriented replications of the status quo. Why do we put up with this? CLS's answer is that the myth of law's objectivity and rationality compels our loyalty."

"In short, law's veneer of fairness leads us to believe it actually serves our interests when it does not," Giannina interjected. "David Kairys says much the same thing."

"CLS's solution, though, is not revolution in the ordinary sense. Most CLS writers are idealists who believe our main chains are mental. Because of the mystifying ideology we acquire starting in law school, we cannot conceive of a better world, one based on love and cooperation. We learn that the rule of law in its majesty must reign even though it does injustice in Mrs. G's case. The crits' solution, then, is to think and teach, to move methodically from one area of the law to the next, showing the political, contingent, interest-serving nature of doctrine in each area. In this program of 'trashing,' CLS scholars draw on methodologies such as neo-Marxism, literary interpretation, and structural analysis."

"I think I see where you are going," I interjected, snapping erect. "You are saying that CLS challenges Tribe's liberal thesis, in fact stands it on its head. Liberal theory focuses on the difficult, or controverted, case—the *Brown v. Board of Education* or *Erie v. Tompkins*—to which it devotes lavish attention. CLS, by contrast, says that we must be most on guard regarding matters and issues that seem routine—ones that seem comfortable and familiar, that have been relegated to 'rules.' The familiarity and comfort these rules give us—their 'naturalness'—mean that they are most likely to form part of the ideology by which we submit to illegitimate domination."

"The tyranny of the ordinary," Rodrigo replied. "Judge Edwards' notion of practical scholarship suffers from the same fault. Practical scholarship greases the wheels. It helps judges accomplish more easily and smoothly what they are doing already. But the point of scholarship is to make judging harder, not easier."

We were all silent for a moment, absorbing what Rodrigo had said. Then, I said: "To summarize then, Rodrigo, you believe the doctrinalist counterrevolution is misdirected. Edwards and Carrington ignore that in times of change, like now, the familiar is where the greatest danger lies; reform may be the most practical thing. Outsider and critical scholarship, of both the theoretical and clinical variety, may be what our profession needs most. The call for a return to doctrine is a form of collective denial."

"Many of my most doctrinal classes," Giannina began, "seem to have had the least practical effect in the real world. For example, doctrinal approaches to criminal law have had little or no effect in reducing the crime rate or understanding the forces that lead to crime. They lead to cases like the Georgia death penalty case, *McClesky v. Kemp,* which pretend that race does not exist and that a form of sterile neutralism compels us to ignore what everybody knows."

"Speaking of denial," Rodrigo interjected tactfully, "it's getting late, and the Professor may be tired. Do we need to think about calling it quits soon?"

"I'm going strong," I insisted. "I'd love to hear your two final connections. If it gets too close to ten o'clock, I'll just call and ask them to leave a key under the mat. This is all very stimulating. Did I tell you I'm serving as a consultant to Mexico's national law school? They're thinking of reorganizing their curriculum more along American lines. I'd like to be able to report the good as well as the bad. So, please go ahead. If you have the energy, I have the time."

Rodrigo's Fourth Connection: Doctrinalism Dulls the Moral Senses and Injures Minorities and Women

"I'm glad you find this useful, Professor. You're a great sounding board. Giannina and I are both in your debt. We hope you have lots of grandchildren and make dozens of return trips to this country."

"You two can always come down to see *me,*" I pointed out. "Other than that one visit, you haven't been down at all. My art collection has grown considerably since then. I'd love to show you my new pieces."

"Just as we'd love to see them," said Giannina with alacrity. "You also promised to introduce me to your friends in that writers' colony. I'll definitely be down, even if Rodrigo won't," she concluded, smiling at Rodrigo so he would see she was only half serious. "What's your theory about formalism's ethical deficiencies?"

"Formalism and its pedagogical equivalent," Rodrigo began, "rely on appellate cases. They have to—that's where the law resides. These cases have relatively few facts and a great deal of doctrine and case shuffling. No party stands before the court—that happened below—nor do any witnesses, police officers, or expert scientific or medical testimony. No documents, either, unless someone entered them into the record. All of this arrives in the form of a sterile, highly summarized 'record of the case.' The actors are stick figures—the 'plaintiff,' the 'appellee,' and so on. The concrete details—the drama of the trial—are missing. One finds little to excite one, to engage the imagination, or to inflame one's sense of justice."

"I think we spoke about something similar once before. We agreed it is only concreteness, not abstraction, that triggers conscience, that engages one's sense of moral outrage. It's as though medical students never studied using actual sick patients and only reviewed hospital records of deaths, accidents, medical dosages, erroneous diagnoses, and so on."

"I think it was the fourth or fifth time we met," Rodrigo agreed. "The Langdellian case method and Socratic teaching breed reductionism. For idealistic students, this approach is soul sapping, leading easily to a fatalistic acceptance of bad law. With less idealistic students, it can breed crooks. Doctrinalism, much more so than its critique, may be responsible for a pessimistic sense in students and young lawyers that the legal system is hopelessly confining and unfair and will always be that way."

Giannina added: "Doctrinalism also disadvantages women and minorities if only because of the great emphasis it places on precedent. It justifies a current action or rule by virtue of an earlier one. Yet that earlier rule, laid down in an age when women and people of color were less significant factors, will likely disadvantage them. In this way, law's rules and narratives incorporate the ruling group's sense of things. Doctrinalism passes that invisible advantage down to succeeding generations. Practical scholarship does the same—it ratifies and consolidates class advantage."

"In the classroom," Rodrigo summarized, "doctrinalism rewards a conventional sort of quick-witted cleverness that relies on a few formulaic maneuvers and axioms. It rewards posturing and self-assurance. And in legal scholarship, it greases the wheels of industry. In real life, it perpetuates past inequalities."

"Formalism always narrows the range of considerations a legal rule will take into account," I said. "That's its nature. But it has to. Otherwise, law would not work. The decisionmaker potentially could take into account an infinitude of details. But I gather you are not complaining about that, but rather the way doctrine submerges the interest of the weaker party?"

"I am," Rodrigo replied. "Legal rules neatly exclude nonstandard cases and people, such as minorities. We use nonformal rules when we want to do *real* justice, to corporations for example. Consider long-arm jurisdiction and the multifaceted minimum-contacts test we employ there. Or recall the large number of defenses antidiscrimination law provides to defendants: business necessity, lack of intent, lack of causation, and so on."

[Eds. After a short digression about the impact of formalism on lawyers' souls, the three continue as follows.]

Rodrigo's Fifth Connection: Extreme Doctrinalism Promotes Schizophrenia, Dishonesty, and Other Unfortunate Traits of Mind

"Formalism is a case of legal obsessionism, as one writer calls it. One devotes hours to small distinctions between this case and that, looking for minute differences, when they count for very little and society and the legal system are in tatters. It also makes you lie—to profess beliefs, for example, in the majesty of the rule of law, in its internal consistency, and in the underlying coherence of contradictory platitudes. It makes you recite things you know are not true—that racism exists only when someone intends it; that everyone knows the law; that all are rational-interest calculators and cost avoiders; and that judges are capable of balancing incommensurable values. All this amounts to a vast schizophrenia, in which one knows things in ordinary life that one is forced to forget when functioning as a lawyer. This allows the ACLU, for example, to assert that vicious hate speech ought to go unregulated and to maintain simultaneously that it is in the best interest of minorities that this be so. It allows lawyers solemnly to proclaim that our system of criminal law is the best in the world, when over ninety percent of defendants plead guilty and get no trial whatsoever. Doctrinal fascination, as that same writer calls it," Rodrigo said, reading from a sheet he pulled out from his briefcase, "breeds a mentality prone to 'coercion, wheedling, needling, harassment, and other rude and crude practices of lawyers.'"

"Why do judges like Harry Edwards seem so enthralled with it, then?" Giannina asked. "Is it merely professional self-interest, the natural hope to find a law review article on point that will make it easier to write that opinion?"

"Maybe so, in part," Rodrigo agreed. "But it may also be like that of a schizophrenic who looks for others to share his or her delusion. The desire may also contain an element of narcissism. Judges are like construction workers. They want the physics department to write about *them,* and complain that the theoretical physicists in the ivory tower never print anything they can use. Some practitioners make the same complaint: What are you crits doing for me, an overworked, harried legal services lawyer with a huge caseload of poor clients? And, in a way, both are right: their own work *is* vitally important. They are on the front lines. If the rivets aren't put in right, the building will fall down. But the physicist may be researching an altogether new principle of building. Judges are in some respects like the riveters, uninterested in what is going on over in the physics department and wishing they would do something for *me.*"

"I'm not sure I'd go that far, Rodrigo," I interjected. "I've known many fine judges who are interested in justice and willing to innovate, if necessary, to find it. Maybe it's that legal scholarship speaks to many different audiences, something our friend Harry Edwards hasn't realized yet. Sometimes we aim our writing at the courts; at other times for each other, our communities, or the legislature. Sometimes we aim to change the legal paradigm, not make small refinements within it."

"Can I bring you folks something else?" our waiter asked. I looked at my companions and shook my head. "Not for me."

"Could you bring us the bill?" Rodrigo asked.

"Let me take care of it," I offered. "I *am* on vacation, and you two have helped bring me up to date. It's hard for an old guy in retirement to keep up, especially spending much of my time outside the United States without a comprehensive law library, except the tiny one at the embassy."

"No, it's on us," Rodrigo said quietly, but firmly. "You are always an honored guest."

Resolving to let things lie for now but to make a lightning move when the check arrived, I asked Rodrigo (partly in hopes of distracting him): "But Rodrigo, what use is it to know that doctrinalism in the law schools and as a judicial and scholarly philosophy promotes all these ills we spoke of before? Doctrinalism is law on the cheap. It's easy, lazy, and bureaucratic. It deflects you away from things that would make you have to think hard, to take responsibility. By the same token, the Langdellian classroom is legal education on the cheap. One professor holds sway over 100 students, dazzling them with imponderable questions and trick riddles. The system has a big stake in formalism. How can we change that without altering the material conditions of our work—that is to say, virtually everything else?"

"Ouch," said Rodrigo, whether because I swiftly and sneakily seized the check the waiter had deposited next to me—probably as the most senior-looking diner at the table—or because of the aptness of my question, I could not tell. "You seem to have got me, Professor. A neo-Marxist in most things, I may nevertheless have fallen prey to idealism, to thinking that if one simply names and recognizes an evil, it will go away by itself. It obviously won't. The profit motive causes law firms to take on a certain structure, including hiring dozens of young associates they have no intention of making partner and assigning them to write endless formalistic briefs, for which in turn they charge the client a great deal of money, necessitating that the lawyer on the other side write yet another massive case-cruncher, and so on forever. If the modes of production—the system of incentives—stays the same, tinkering with legal education and reasoning won't help. Law practice gets more and more arcane just as the student pool becomes more and more talented, with LSATs, grades, and numbers of applicants soaring. Competition becomes ever more fierce for seats in law schools. Students become more cutthroat and less collegial than before, then go out into the world where they become even more that way. And the law schools cater to the large-firm mentality that now defines law practice. The cost of legal education skyrockets; students leave with huge debts, which means they must practice in the large firms, which pay the best salaries. The young associates lead lives of overwork, stress, competition, and early burnout."

"Not a very appealing prospect," said Giannina wryly, "for someone just starting out. But identifying an evil is a starting point. And discovering its source the second step. If so, we've made progress. At least I've decided to throw away the *Gilbert's* [Eds. Mass-produced outlines of the law, like *Cliffs Notes* for torts, civil procedure, property, etc.] and focus on legal issues in the casebook that really matter."

"I'm betting your grades won't go down if you do," I said.

"I hope you're right," said Rodrigo. And with a laugh: "Our family income is riding on it. But, seriously, costly, nit-picking, formalistic lawyering is not the solution. It is not craft, despite what some authorities think. In fact, it's the very thing that's causing all the trouble."

"Especially for women and minorities," Giannina added.

I signed the credit card bill the waiter had brought. "Would the two of you like to see the baby?"

Giannina looked at Rodrigo. "We'd love to," she said. "How about this weekend? My moot court reply brief is due Friday, so I'll be feeling less pressured."

I told them I'd check with my daughter and son-in-law and jotted down the address for them on a napkin. "She's been hoping to meet you. She's thinking of going to graduate school when the baby gets a little older, and, would you believe, one of the options she's thinking about is law school. I'm sure she'll have a lot of questions."

We soon parted, Rodrigo and Giannina back to their apartment, me to my daughter's home across town. As I rather sleepily rode the taxi through the darkened streets, I reflected on what we had said. The public was certainly disenchanted with law. Lawyers were as well. But was legal formalism the cause, as Rodrigo had argued? Or was it a type of refuge sought by a beleaguered profession—*both* cause and effect? Would outsider jurisprudence and the new clinical theory, with their emphasis on narrative, creativity, and a sophisticated understanding of the client, provide a way out? Rodrigo had argued once before that only outsider thought could release a deadlocked West from decline and stasis. Could legal storytelling and the insights of writers like Derrick Bell, Mari Matsuda, Anthony Alfieri, Margaret Montoya, and, indeed, Rodrigo, lead the way to a humanized law and better relations with our various publics?

All this had a personal dimension as well, in light of my own daughter's plans. I looked forward to her meeting in a few days with Rodrigo and Giannina—what fortune to have them as role models!—and wondered, idly, about the wisdom of my own self-exile from my native country, where so many intriguing currents were playing themselves out—ideas being tested, new approaches to scholarship surging forward almost daily.

"That's the street," I told the cabbie. "Turn here please."

The key was under the mat, just where my daughter had told me it would be. I resolved to take a look at my visa and ask a few questions at the consulate when I got home.

Official Elitism or Institutional Self-Interest?

Ten Reasons Why Law Schools Should Abandon the LSAT

[Eds. Delgado delivered this excerpt as the Edward L. Barrett, Jr. Lecture on Constitutional Law at UC-Davis Law School.]

My subject is the billion dollar a year testing industry and especially the Law School Admissions Test (LSAT). That little beauty, familiar to many from a terror-filled Saturday in October, is one of a family of tests that include the SAT, which hundreds of thousands of high school students take every year, the Graduate Record Exam (GRE), which you take to get into graduate school, and many others. Every year, 143 million Americans take standardized tests to get into a school or program, another 50 to 200 million for business and industry, and several million more for the military. The number of standardized tests taken is on the order of 600 million annually, with total costs running in the billions of dollars, more when you add in prep courses.

As you might imagine, the College Board (Board) and Educational Testing Service (ETS), which lie at the center of the testing movement, are comfortably wealthy organizations. Despite its nonprofit status, the Board paid its president $350,000 and its nine vice presidents more than $100,000 in a recent year. Even those pay scales are not particularly surprising when you consider that the Board earned more than $250,000,000 that year, passing nearly two thirds of it on to ETS. All three tests, the SAT, GRE, and LSAT, share a similar history and lineage, but the LSAT is comparatively unstudied because it is taken by a much smaller number of applicants than the SAT or GRE. For that reason, I will sometimes draw on studies of these other two tests as well.

Standardized testing originated early in the twentieth century as a way to demonstrate the intellectual superiority of northern European whites. [Eds. Delgado next reviews the disreputable history of IQ and standardized testing. See Part VIII.]

Threatened with underemployment after World War I ended—the Army had given it a great deal of business—the testing industry transferred its attentions to the university and college market. The College Board began in 1900 with 35 colleges using its early examinations. The Board expanded rapidly by tapping post–World War I enthusiasm for testing and the American penchant for organizational planning, later Cold War fervor, and, a little later, remarkably, the civil rights movement.

A few years after the reign of Carl Campbell Brigham [Eds. An early president of the College Board and an unapologetic race-purifier], in 1947 the Board created the Educational Testing Service (ETS) to supervise the construction and administration of the SAT. Its early promoters, including James Conant, former president of Harvard, saw the test as an attractive alternative to admissions based on family connections. They also saw it as a means of organizing society efficiently along Platonic lines with every citizen assigned a place according to ability and aptitude.

By 1948, thousands of ex-GIs were applying to law schools. ETS responded by creating the Law School Admissions Test Council (now LSAC), which soon incorporated and chose its parent, ETS, as the agency to operate its testing program. From the beginning, ETS worked diligently to enhance its progeny's image: scheduling conferences at fine resorts, assigning staff to produce reports on LSAC letterhead, and creating titles, committees, and consultant positions for law professors to forestall the possibility that the Association of American Law Schools might develop its own competing test.

ETS later developed programs, including the Law School Data Assembly Service (LSDAS), which provided law school admissions offices with class rankings, profiles, formulas, index numbers, and predicted first year averages, all designed to make law school admissions simple and pseudo-scientific. Despite LSDAS' formidable ability to crank out numbers, the organization concealed the race gap in LSAT scores until comparatively recently. And, when troublesome information does come to light, the testing industry tends to respond by stepping up publicity. For example, when the U.S. Justice Department found no significant relationship between National Teacher Examination scores and teaching effectiveness, ETS responded not by rethinking its test, but by increasing promotion and newspaper ads.

Because of conservative challenges to affirmative action, standardized testing today is emerging as the chief barrier to the educational ambitions of minorities and the poor. The same conservatives who have been attacking affirmative action strenuously support standardized testing, equating test scores with the objective merit that affirmative action is said to ignore. A host of critics take issue with that equation.

In a moment, I outline the case against standardized testing. But before doing so, let me note that many of us are deeply invested in test scores, having done well on standardized tests and seen them open doors for us as we have gone through life. Yet, I would like to give you some reasons to start thinking about those scores in a different light. And, toward the end of my talk, I offer a series of alternatives to the LSAT and ways to assure that they receive attention.

ARGUMENTS AGAINST STANDARDIZED TESTING

The first argument against standardized testing is that despite its origins in intelligence testing and white supremacy, the tests are surprisingly poorly written. Keen eyes are constantly finding mistakes in them. For example, on one multi-state bar examination, administered by ETS, thirty to forty answers were found to be wrong. On the Test of English as a Foreign Language, ETS had to re-grade an entire nationwide sample when it discovered it was using the wrong answers. And, on one administration of the SAT, four out of forty-five verbal test answers turned out to be wrong, and many others as plausibly correct as the ones ETS keyed correct.

Particular test items aside, many ETS tests do not test all relevant skills. The LSAT, for example, only requires verbal and reasoning fluency, not the ability to command probability, scientific reasoning, humanistic thought, historical thought, or knowledge of human motivation and psychology—all skills important for lawyers. Multiple choice test taking under severe time constraints, as one critic put it, "is a specialized kind of game which rewards certain kinds of people and penalizes others for reasons apart from their ability to handle words [concepts] and numbers." Many psychologists today recognize that intelligences are multiple and that complex intellectual tasks, such as lawyering, require a wide range of abilities. These abilities include empathy, communication skills, common sense, reasoning by analogy, synthetic reasoning, and the ability to make order out of ambiguous, complex, and uncertain situations. Using a two hour paper and pencil test of word comprehension and logical games to judge fitness for law school is like picking basketball players based on a trial of foul shots. Tests like the LSAT and the SAT do measure something, but what they measure may not be particularly important. How many real writers—not to mention lawyers—use obscure words or farfetched analogies?

Thinking styles vary from person to person. You and I, when faced with the same problem, may take radically different routes to get to the right answer. Or, we may come up with two answers that are slightly different but each arguably correct. Standardized tests punish takers who deviate from the path the designer has in mind. This enforced orthodoxy punishes those who think outside the box. This punishment becomes particularly troublesome considering that standardized tests came into wide use in the 1950s and 1960s, when the civil rights era was just starting, and froze standards as they stood at a time when many minorities could not possibly meet them because of segregated schools and widespread poverty.

Recall that the testing industry shifts its promotional material with the times. The industry has not, however, demonstrated this same flexibility with the contents of its tests, which have remained remarkably the same for decades. This is true even though what society needs today is vastly different from what it needed fifty years ago, and even though today's 180 ABA accredited law schools differ greatly in their missions and characters. The earliest versions of the LSAT were a hodge podge of questions from other occupational tests, not specific to law. Yet, they predicted law school performance just as well, or badly, as today's versions do.

Even aside from conceptual incoherence, or perhaps because of it, the LSAT and other standardized tests simply are not very good at doing what they profess to do, namely predict first year grades. The LSAT, for example, correlates with those grades with a coefficient of about .4, meaning that it predicts only about sixteen percent of the variation. Other factors, which we *could* focus on but do not because the test is so simple and convenient, account for the other eighty-four percent. And, a study of minority law students showed a sharp drop off in correlation after the first year—.27 for the second year and .17, barely positive, for the third. That is another way of saying that by year three, test scores were predicting less than three percent of the variation in performance.

The LSAT is not the only ETS test that does not predict what it professes. As mentioned earlier, the Justice Department found no significant relationship between National Teacher Exam scores and teacher effectiveness. In another study, high scorers on the GRE took longer to graduate than modest scorers. At Yale, the correlation between GRE scores and academic success was negative for female graduate psychology students. On the SAT, men score forty-five points higher than women, who nevertheless earn higher college grades. And, in the range of test scores in which admissions officers function, the SAT increases schools' ability to predict graduation only one tenth of one percent over class rank alone, while greatly reducing minorities' chances of admission. At the University of California, for example, the number of Latinos would double if the system dropped the test.

Many students with low scores perform well after graduation. Studies of large-scale mistakes in test scoring show that low scorers do as well as those admitted without the mistake. Additionally, studies of Ivy League legacies show that sons and daughters of alumni admitted with test scores far lower than those of their classmates go on to do just as well. (This is not an argument for legacy admits, however.) And, recent large-scale studies of minority graduates by William Bowen and Derek Bok and by four professors at the University of Michigan law school show that minorities admitted under affirmative action, with SAT scores in many cases considerably lower than those of their classmates, nevertheless perform superbly after graduation, publishing books, winning prizes, and earning Ph.Ds at rates exceeding even those of their high testing peers.

Test scores are, however, highly correlated with economic status. In the old days, elite schools achieved status by admitting students with the best family backgrounds—which of course included the right race, ethnicity, and religion. Current rankings of institutions, generated primarily by test scores, are exactly the same as the earlier hierarchy that turned on social status. An SAT taker can expect an extra thirty points for every ten thousand dollars of parental income; a graph of test scores by family income is a straight line rising steeply. Test scores correlate with family income even more highly than they do with first year grades. Social class also correlates with scores, so that the children of a professional making $70,000 a year do better on the average than those of a blue collar family earning the very same income. Even zip codes predict ETS test scores with startling accuracy.

Why such a strong correlation? Professor Lani Guinier reports an informal study in which Jesse Jackson went to Glenbrook South, a suburban high school outside of Chicago that spends $11,000 per year per pupil, has twenty-four hour service from janitors earning $45,000 a year, carpets on the floor, a ninety-eight percent graduation rate, and assumes every student is able to learn. If any student has trouble, the school simply assigns him or her a tutor and computer, if necessary. Jackson then went to the Cook County jail, where he interviewed the predominantly black and Hispanic population of inmates. Instead of a ninety-eight percent graduation rate, he found a ninety percent rate of high school dropouts, on whom Cook County was spending $22,000 a year to keep behind bars. Ninety-nine percent of the inmates were functionally illiterate.

A further reason why SAT scores and family wealth may be correlated is that crash/prep courses, some of which cost $1,200 or more, are said to boost one's score by 150 points or more on the SAT and a comparable amount on the LSAT. Because our society has the highest level of childhood poverty in the developed world, with over forty percent of black and Latino kids growing up poor, it is easy to guess who gets to take Kaplan courses and attend elite prep schools that emphasize college attendance.

A culture of test savviness compounds these inequities. A recent study gave undergraduates one hundred reading comprehension questions taken from actual SATs. In some cases, the researchers provided the reading passages, the questions, and the five possible answers; in others, only the questions and answers. One group of sixty-one honors students, who were given only the questions and answers, but not the reading passages, scored 52.8; a second group of non-honors students, who also only received the questions and answers, scored 37.6. Because choosing answers at random would lead to scores of about twenty (and both groups scored much higher) performance on reading comprehension tests may measure overall cleverness as much as developed ability.

SAT and LSAT scores freeze the advantages one enjoys while living under one's parents' roof, or shortly thereafter, and the disadvantages that poor people and minorities suffer by reason of under-funded schools and lack of college prep courses. In legislating its way out of the worst depression this country has suffered, the government invested in whiteness through the Social Security Act, which excluded blacks from many of its provisions; the Wagner Act of 1935, which approved collective bargaining for all-white unions; and racially coded mortgage programs. These legislative acts allowed whites to earn more money and buy houses in better neighborhoods. Standardized testing, which came along shortly thereafter, consolidated those advantages.

Test scores may be highly positively correlated with income and social class, but they are even more negatively correlated with race. Except for minorities, most admissions decisions do not change with the addition of test scores. Conversely, when graduate and professional school admissions officers ignore standardized test scores, they admit a much higher proportion of minority applicants. At every grade point average, minority applicants to law schools receive admission offers in lower proportions than whites. For example, whites with 3.50 to 3.74 GPAs were admitted to law schools eighty-five percent of the time, compared to seventy-six percent of African Americans and eighty percent of Hispanics with the same GPAs. As GPA decreased, disparities increased. Whites with 2.25 to 2.49 GPAs were admitted nearly half the time, blacks only one quarter. Minorities make up slightly more than ten percent of the U.S. lawyer population, lagging behind accountants and only slightly ahead of physicians, college professors, dentists, and natural scientists. The LSAT today is a principal reason for that disparity.

Consider the group of mainly poor and African-American students at Northampton East High School in rural North Carolina who, building on their physics and chemistry lessons, constructed an electric car that won a national competition that included many of the country's elite high schools. Although Northampton students made the best car, they might easily have been aced out of Harvard, Stanford, or the University of California by their competitors who scored 1500 or 1600 on their SATs and who society deems more meritorious by conventional criteria. ETS blandly insists that before standardized testing, elitism reigned and colleges admitted few blue collar students and minorities, whose numbers went up after their tests came into wide use. This proposition has not been proven and, in any event, today things are plainly working in the opposite direction.

Why do many minorities score poorly on these tests? As mentioned earlier, inferior schools, poverty, and lack of access to test prep courses are part of the reason. But the tests themselves share part of the blame as well. Many test questions presuppose knowledge that is only common in middle- or upper-class white communities. The Multi-State Bar Exam (MBE) and LSAT questions emphasize business and property concepts, not civil rights, minority history, or literature. One study of the

SAT found items requiring knowledge of golf, tennis, pirouettes, property taxes, minuets, kettle drums, tympani, polo, and horseback riding, items that are scarcely common in minority communities. A study of the LSAT showed reading passages disparaging W.E.B. Du Bois, Cesar Chavez, and Harriet Tubman. Other LSAT questions presupposed legal knowledge. And, although the industry assumes that conditions are the same for all, admissions officers have no way of knowing which applicants have taken a prep course, or whose scores reflect what Claude Steele and Joshua Aronson call stereotype threat.

Testing requires communication, which in turn requires understanding of language and situations. Test makers do not write test questions as culturally and socio-economically stripped, neutral beings. Rather, test writers, like all humans, reflect the culture and surroundings in which they were raised. The situations and circumstances they incorporate into test questions, and, more importantly, the meanings and thought patterns they deem "right" will inevitably favor test takers who share those meanings and thought patterns.

Bias can enter in one final way, namely, in how we interpret and ascribe meaning to test scores. Blacks, for example, today have entrance test scores that compare with those of whites admitted to college in 1951, when admission was much less competitive than it is today. That generation of students did not do so badly, and were, in fact, running the world until quite recently. Why do we imagine that today's minority students would do any worse? Imagine that someone designs a test of cultural competence that contains items on preference for types of music, willingness to wait in line, and attitudes toward credit. Suppose scores on this test were used to predict crime and who is likely to be arrested, expelled from school, and fired from work. Further suppose that the correlation between test scores and one of these other events turns out to be .41, with minorities earning most of the low scores. Does that mean that the test is valid? Of course not—arrest and school discipline rates are in many cases themselves a function of social prejudice, profiling, and other forms of structural bias against people of color. The test would serve, in effect, as a proxy for racism by measuring little of importance about blacks and other minorities, but much about our social attitudes toward them.

Reliance on standardized test scores may even be illegal. If the LSAT, for example, discriminates against certain groups, is not job related, and predicts scarcely better than chance, then its use in law school admissions may contravene federal guidelines. The United States Department of Education has released a series of drafts of a guidebook for the use of standardized tests in admissions decisions. Among other things, it warns that because the tests have disparate impacts on minorities, over-reliance on them could trigger legal action. The Department expects institutions to evaluate all tests and criteria on which certain racial or ethnic groups perform better or worse than others to make sure that they are educationally necessary and that no other device would impose less of a disparate impact. In California, the LSAT may constitute a racial preference for whites in violation of Proposition 209.

Over-reliance on standardized tests is not only bad for institutions, it is bad for society at large. The tests reward rote performance, guessing, gamesmanship, and the ability to sort artificial alternatives quickly under timed conditions. Not surprisingly, standardized test scores do not predict creativity, artistic achievement, or other forms of accomplishment later in life. In fact, one may speculate that our society's obsession with test scores is responsible, in part, for the marked decline in achievement in the arts, humanities, science, politics, and law visible in the last half century. It discourages teachers from teaching real material; instead they teach to the tests. Recall how early test boosters, like James Conant, were bureaucrats and Cold War warriors who were uninterested in promoting creative or divergent thinking. Tests penalize dreamers, young people who live in a world of ideas or imagination. A recent analysis found that the SAT can cause problems for students who are unusually clever or creative. As a thought experiment, try to imagine anyone whom the United States has produced in the last fifty years, the era of mass testing, who is as good a scientist as Einstein or Salk, a politician like Woodrow Wilson or John F. Kennedy, an artist like Frank Lloyd Wright, or a musical composer the equal of Aaron Copland or Igor Stravinsky. If, like me, you have trouble with that exercise you have no less an authority than Jacques Barzun, who wrote an entire book on the subject, on your side. Recent research shows that groups perform best when they are diverse, not uniform, and the same is likely to be true for society at large. Finally, standardized tests may limit opportunities for future leaders. Perhaps the greatest American civil rights figure of our time, Martin Luther King, Jr., a man whose name adorns this building [Eds. Delgado spoke at Davis' law building, named Martin Luther King Hall], could not get into graduate school because he flunked the GRE, enrolling instead in a theological school. Even a study of 1,300 millionaires found "no correlation between [earlier] SAT scores, grade point averages, and [later] economic achievement."

Our obsession with testing may even be responsible for the decline in public esteem for the legal profession. Like many similar tests, the LSAT correlates negatively with community activism, social empathy, a desire to help others in trouble, and wanting to make a contribution to knowledge. When the public complains that lawyers seem callous, uninterested in justice, have poor communication skills, and do not return phone calls, might it be that we are screening for exactly that sort of person? Most senior partners, judges, and law professors entered law school at a time when they did not require the LSAT, or when scores were much lower than they are today. Many could not get into the schools from which they graduated if they were applying today. As a further thought experiment, cast your mind back over the last fifty years and try to think of legal scholars the equal of Prosser, Fuller, Corbin, Llewellyn, or Jerome Frank; judges to match Felix Frankfurter, Louis Brandeis, or Oliver Wendell Holmes. Could our obsession with tests have something to do with that scarcity?

ETS could easily adjust its tests to produce a more equitable distribution of scores across race and class lines, but will not do so without external pressure. Until recently, men earned more National Merit Scholarship Awards than women. In 1999, the Board, embarrassed by this, made minor changes in the Preliminary SAT (PSAT), including adding a multiple choice writing section, that equalized scores for men and women. In law, for example, a certain type of personality scores high on the LSAT, gets into law school, then into teaching, and, finally, on the admissions committees where, unsurprisingly, they look for persons like themselves (except thirty years younger). Law professors who set out to teach in a different way find themselves at the receiving end of negative reinforcement by students, a critical mass of whom is quick, glib, and expects the professor to cater to that form of discourse. Professional norms push in the same direction. Law schools publish their average LSAT scores. If they are high, the alumni smile and reach for their checkbooks. Corporate recruiters take notice and add the school to their road show.

A final reason to get rid of the LSAT and its sister tests is that the standardized testing industry really deserves it. If their tests were to fall into total disuse, in my opinion, it could not happen to a nicer bunch of people. Now under scrutiny, the testing industry has responded by hype and self-promotion, rather than self-examination or meeting their critics half way. ETS has long appointed professors and university administrators to committees, commissions, and consultantships and invited them to lavish retreats and conferences. Realizing that it is now under attack by many in the minority community, it has hastily increased representation of blacks and Latinos on committees and working groups. It takes out full page ads and hires minority front men to advocate the "responsible use" of their tests. It knows that prep courses improve scores, but continues to deny it. ETS winks at teachers who teach to K–12 competency tests and suburban students who gain an unfair advantage by submitting doctors' certificates that they need more time.

Mental testing is an effective means of social control. Breaking ETS' monopoly will require real effort. Employer A won't hire the first black applicant with a lower test score out of concern for what others in the same industry will think, and the same is true for schools. Even though the black or Latina may be the best worker, employer A may find it rational to hire the second best worker who is socially constructed as "the best" in the eyes of employers B and C.

A ROADMAP FOR ABOLITIONISTS

What might we do to reduce reliance on standardized tests such as the SAT and LSAT? If a school believes that a standardized test "amounts to the academic lynching of children of color," it could insist that testing agencies provide it with scores adjusted for race or economic background, adding points when students "beat their demographic odds." Better yet, it could insist on test scores that are fair across the board.

Better still, as one university president has proposed, schools could stop using the test entirely or make it optional, as over 280 colleges and universities have done with the SAT, including a few elite ones like Bowdoin, Bates, Dennison, and Mt. Holyoke. A number of these schools report that the size and quality of their applicant pool went up in the wake of the change. In several high school districts today top students are boycotting graduation tests, believing them unfair to the less able. Pressures of this sort could hasten reform.

Law schools could give applicants the option to determine how much weight to afford LSAT scores. One law school changed its admissions form to allow applicants to check one of two boxes. If they checked one box, the school would give their LSAT score the usual weight. If they checked the other, it would give their LSAT scores less weight and other factors, such as community service, overcoming adversity, recommendation letters, and unusual life experiences, more. They now have forty percent minority enrollment and have not lost the near-elite status they enjoyed before the change.

A reputable organization such as the Association of American Law Schools (AALS) or Society of American Law Teachers (SALT) could develop its own culture-free test. Current accreditation requirements only oblige law schools to include some written test in the admission process. Since past "accomplishments are the best predictor of future accomplishments," schools might give that factor decisive weight.

For example, the University of California, Davis could work with Sacramento State University and local community colleges to offer guaranteed admission to law school for students who perform at a high level in their undergraduate curriculum.

We might interview applicants or create a character index composed of traits we consider indicative of a good lawyer. Cornell's Department of Human Development created a targeted test which gave applicants particular assignments such as "critique this article."

Law schools could open up their second year ranks to transfers from lesser institutions, thereby rewarding demonstrated merit. They could give the LSAT five or ten percent weight instead of the current thirty to fifty percent. They could offer summer try-out programs for borderline candidates, guaranteeing admission in the fall to those who performed well.

Law schools could agree not to report their test scores to *U.S. News & World Report,* as forty-four colleges and universities have done with the SAT.

We could make allowances, not only for underprivilege and surmounting adversity, but also for *privilege* so that applicants who come from wealthy families and have had many opportunities to excel but produced only mediocre credentials, say a GPA of 3.1 and an SAT of 1200, would have their scores reduced.

Corporate America loves affirmative action even though conservative think tanks do not. As courts cut it back, businesses will find it more difficult than ever to recruit workers of color, particularly if standardized testing continues unchallenged. Activists at law schools could seek guarantees of large contributions from local corporations to their schools on condition that those schools abolish the LSAT and other standardized tests.

Activists at the University of California, Davis could communicate with the Martin Luther King Foundation and inform them of how a law school that bears his martyred name is employing a version of the very test that kept him out of graduate school to screen out minorities of color. It could ask them to demand that the school discontinue using his name until it changes its admission procedures.

Small but elite law schools, like Yale, could simply expand; a much larger first year class could hold many more minorities, especially if the school were willing to broaden admission requirements at the same time. They could ask other law schools to sign a pledge de-emphasizing the LSAT. Student and faculty activists could point out that a more diverse student body would make the school more attractive to women and minority professors, easing its recruitment woes. I can assure you that well-regarded minority law professors would flock to the first school to take such a step. Finally, a school that is prepared to end the reign of tests will make admissions fairer for all students, including talented whites who do not test well or who simply prefer a more diverse, fairer atmosphere in which to learn the law.

PART IV
Hate Speech

Over a twenty-year period, Delgado has forcefully shaped the debate over legal regulation of hate speech.

The section begins with a portion of his pathbreaking "Words That Wound," written in 1982. Calling on a host of psychological and sociological studies, Delgado demonstrates the harms of racist hate speech, especially to the young. He shows how current law provides no remedy and calls for a tort action to address racial insults.

In "The 'More Speech' Solution," part of a longer coauthored article titled "Images of the Outsider in American Law and Culture," Delgado tackles the dilemma that hate-speech regulation poses for proponents of free expression. He casts doubt that any rational dialogue can take place between a victim and a perpetrator of hate speech in the "marketplace of ideas" that First Amendment absolutists hold dear, and notes that to engage in such a conversation often makes matters worse for the victim.

"Campus Antiracism Rules" frames the issue of what to do about hate speech in two ways. One can see it as a First Amendment free speech issue that puts freedom of expression at the center of the analysis. Or, one can give more weight to equality concerns, as expressed in the Equal Protection Clause of the Fourteenth Amendment, thereby placing greater value on protecting the less empowered. Delgado offers a way out of this impasse through an approach that takes account of the pervasive nature of most racist harms in the victim's life and experience. Outside the legal academy, Delgado worked with others to help enact the first hate-speech code at the University of Wisconsin, a code that has been widely followed elsewhere.

Delgado continues his analysis of hate-speech regulation in "Toward a Legal Realist View of the First Amendment," an article that originally appeared in the *Harvard Law Review*. Using a recent book by Steven Shiffrin as a springboard, he offers some thoughts on how our increasingly diverse society may motivate policymakers to adopt a more nuanced "realist" approach to First Amendment issues such as hate speech. "Mechanical jurisprudence" will recede into the past, he writes, giving way to a framework that takes account of the actual functions (including harmful ones) that speech performs.

Words That Wound
A Tort Action for Racial Insults, Epithets, and Name-Calling

[Eds. Delgado begins by discussing two early hate-speech cases that went in opposite directions, then continues as follows.]

The contrasting results in these two cases and the unsettled condition in which they leave tort actions for racial speech suggest that reappraisal is in order.

PSYCHOLOGICAL, SOCIOLOGICAL, AND POLITICAL EFFECTS OF RACIAL INSULTS

American society remains deeply afflicted by racism. Long before slavery became the mainstay of the plantation society of the antebellum South, Anglo-Saxon attitudes of racial superiority left their stamp on the developing culture of colonial America. Today, over a century after the abolition of slavery, many citizens suffer from discriminatory attitudes and practices infecting our economic system, our cultural and political institutions, and the daily interactions of individuals. The idea that color is a badge of inferiority and a justification for the denial of opportunity and equal treatment is deeply ingrained.

The racial insult remains one of the most pervasive channels for imparting discriminatory attitudes. Such language injures the dignity and self-regard of the person to whom it is addressed, communicating the message that distinctions of race are distinctions of merit, dignity, status, and personhood. Not only does the listener learn and internalize the messages contained in racial insults, these messages color our society's institutions and are transmitted to succeeding generations.

The Harms of Racism
The psychological harms caused by racial stigmatization are often much more severe than those created by other stereotyping actions. Unlike many characteristics upon which stigmatization may be based, membership in a racial minority can be considered neither self-induced, like alcoholism or prostitution, nor alterable. Race-based stigmatization is, therefore, "one of the most fruitful causes of human misery. Poverty can be eliminated—but skin color cannot." The plight of members of racial minorities may be compared with that of persons with physical disfigurements; the point has been made that

> [a] rebuff due to one's color puts [the victim] in very much the situation of the very ugly person or one suffering from a loathsome disease. The suffering ... may

be aggravated by a consciousness of incurability and even blameworthiness, a self-reproaching which tends to leave the individual still more aware of his loneliness and unwantedness.

As psychologist Kenneth Clark put it: "Human beings... whose daily experience tells them that almost nowhere in society are they respected and granted the ordinary dignity and courtesy accorded to others will, as a matter of course, begin to doubt their own worth." Minorities may come to believe the frequent accusations that they are lazy, ignorant, dirty, and superstitious. "The accumulation of negative images... presents them with one massive and destructive choice: either to hate one's self, as culture so systematically demands, or to have no self at all, to be nothing."

The psychological responses to such stigmatization consist of feelings of humiliation, isolation, and self-hatred. Consequently, it is neither unusual nor abnormal for stigmatized individuals to feel ambivalent about their self-worth and identity. This ambivalence arises from the stigmatized individual's awareness that others perceive him or her as falling short of societal standards, standards which the individual has adopted. Stigmatized individuals thus often are hypersensitive and anticipate pain at the prospect of contact with "normals."

It is no surprise, then, that racial stigmatization injures its victims' relationships with others. Racial tags deny minority individuals the possibility of neutral behavior in cross-racial contacts, thereby impairing the victims' capacity to form close interracial relationships. Moreover, the psychological responses of self-hatred and self-doubt unquestionably affect even the victims' relationships with members of their own group.

The psychological effects of racism may also result in mental illness and psychosomatic disease. The affected person may react by seeking escape through alcohol, drugs, or other kinds of anti-social behavior. The rates of narcotic use and admission to public psychiatric hospitals are higher in minority communities than in society as a whole.

The achievement of high socioeconomic status does not diminish the psychological harms caused by prejudice. The effort to achieve success in business and managerial careers exacts a psychological toll even among exceptionally ambitious and upwardly mobile members of minority groups. Furthermore, those who succeed "do not enjoy the full benefits of their professional status within their organizations, because of inconsistent treatment by others resulting in continual psychological stress, strain, and frustration." As a result, the incidence of severe psychological impairment caused by the environmental stress of prejudice and discrimination is not lower among minority group members of high socioeconomic status.

One of the most troubling effects of racial stigmatization is that it may affect parenting practices among minority group members, thereby perpetuating a tradition of failure. A recent study of minority mothers found that many denied the real significance of color in their lives, yet were morbidly sensitive to matters of race. Some, as a defense against aggression, identified excessively with whites, accepting whiteness as superior. Most had negative expectations concerning life's chances. Such self-conscious, hypersensitive parents, preoccupied with the ambiguity of their own social position, are unlikely to raise confident, achievement-oriented, and emotionally stable children.

In addition to these long-term psychological harms of racial labeling, racial abuse may have physical consequences. Evidence shows that high blood pressure is associated with inhibited, constrained, or restricted anger, as well as genetic factors, and that insults produce elevation in blood pressure. American blacks have higher blood pressure levels and higher morbidity and mortality rates from hypertension, hypertensive disease, and stroke than do white counterparts. Further, a strong correlation between degree of darkness of skin for blacks and level of stress may be the product of the greater discrimination experienced by dark-skinned blacks.

In addition to such emotional and physical consequences, racial stigmatization may damage a victim's pecuniary interests. The psychological injuries severely handicap the victim's pursuit of a career. The person who is timid, withdrawn, bitter, hypertense, or psychotic will almost certainly fare poorly in employment settings. An experiment in which blacks and whites of similar aptitudes and capacities were put into a competitive situation found that the blacks exhibited defeatism, half-hearted competitiveness, and "high expectancies of failure." For many minority group members, the equalization of such quantifiable variables as salary and entry level is an insufficient antidote to defeatist attitudes because the psychological price of attempting to compete is unaffordable; they are "programmed for failure." Additionally, career options for the victims of racism are closed off by institutional racism—the subtle and unconscious racism in schools, hiring decisions, and the other practices which determine the distribution of social benefits and responsibilities.

Unlike most of the actions for which tort law provides redress to the victim, racial labeling and racial insults directly harm the perpetrator. Bigotry harms the individuals who harbor it by reinforcing rigid thinking, thereby dulling their moral and social senses and possibly leading to a "mildly ... paranoid" mentality. Little evidence suggests that racial slurs serve as a "safety valve" for anxiety which would otherwise be expressed in violence.

Racism and racial stigmatization harm not only the victim and the perpetrator of individual racist acts but also society as a whole. Racism is a breach of the ideal of egalitarianism, that "all men are created equal" and each person is an equal moral agent, an ideal that is a cornerstone of the American moral and legal system. A society in which some members regularly experience degradation because of their race hardly exemplifies this ideal. The failure of the legal system to redress the harms of racism, and of racial insults, conveys to all the lesson that egalitarianism is not a fundamental principle; the law, through inaction, implicitly teaches that respect for individuals is of little importance. Moreover, unredressed breaches of the egalitarian ideal may demoralize all those who prefer to live in a truly equal society, making them unwilling participants in the perpetuation of racism and racial inequality.

To the extent that racism contributes to a class system, society has a paramount interest in suppressing it. Racism injuries the career prospects, social mobility, and interracial contacts of minority group members. This, in turn, impedes assimilation into the economic, social, and political mainstream of society and ensures that the victims of racism are seen and see themselves as outsiders. Indeed, racism can be seen as a force used by the majority to preserve an economically advantageous position for themselves. But when individuals cannot or choose not to contribute their talents to a social system because they are demoralized or angry, or when they are actively prevented by racist institutions from fully contributing their talents, society as a whole loses.

Finally, and perhaps most disturbingly, racism and racial labeling have an even greater impact on children than on adults. The effects of racial labeling are discernible early in life; at a young age, minority children exhibit self-hatred because of their color, and majority children learn to associate dark skin with undesirability and ugliness. When presented with otherwise identical dolls, a black child preferred the light-skinned one as a friend; she said that the dark-skinned one looked dirty or "not nice." Another child hated her skin color so intensely that she "vigorously lathered her arms and face with soap in an effort to wash away the dirt." She told the experimenter, "This morning I scrubbed and scrubbed and it came almost white." When asked about making a little girl out of clay, a black child said that the group should use the white clay rather than the brown "because it will make a better girl." When asked to describe dolls which had the physical characteristics of black people, young children chose adjectives such as "rough, funny, stupid, silly, smelly, stinky, dirty." Three-fourths of a group of four-year-old black children favored white play companions; over half felt themselves inferior to whites. Some engaged in denial or falsification.

The Harms of Racial Insults

The most obvious direct harm of a racial insult is immediate mental or emotional distress. Without question, mere words, whether racial or otherwise, can cause mental, emotional, or even physical harm to their target, especially if delivered in front of others or by a person in a position of authority. Racial insults, relying as they do on the unalterable fact of the victim's race and on the history of slavery and race discrimination in this country, have an even greater potential for harm than other insults.

Although the emotional damage caused is variable and depends on many factors, only one of which is its outrageousness, a racial insult is always a dignitary affront, a direct violation of the victim's right to be treated respectfully. Our moral and legal systems recognize that individuals are entitled to treatment that does not denigrate their humanity through disrespect for their privacy or moral worth. This ideal occupies a high place in our traditions, finding expression in such principles as universal suffrage, the prohibition against cruel and unusual punishment, the protection of the Fourth Amendment against unreasonable searches, and the abolition of slavery. A racial insult is a serious transgression of this principle because it derogates by race, a characteristic central to one's self-image.

The wrong of this dignitary affront consists of the expression of a judgment that the victim of the racial slur is entitled to less than that to which all other citizens are entitled. Such dignitary affronts are certainly no less harmful than others recognized by the law. Clearly, a society whose public law recognizes harm in the stigma of separate but equal schooling and the potential offensiveness of the required display of a state motto on automobile license plates, and whose private law sees actionable conduct in an unwanted kiss or the forcible removal of a person's hat, should also recognize the dignitary harm inflicted by a racial insult.

The need for legal redress for victims grows when one considers that racial insults are intentional acts. The intentionality of racial insults is obvious: what other purpose could the insult serve? There can be little doubt that the dignitary affront of racial insults, except perhaps those that are overheard, is intentional and therefore most reprehensible. Most people today know that certain words are offensive and only calculated to wound. What other use remains for such words as "nigger," "wop," "spick," or "kike"?

In addition to the harms of immediate emotional distress and infringement of dignity, racial insults inflict psychological harm upon the victim. Racial slurs may cause long-term emotional pain because they draw upon and intensify the effects of the stigmatization, labeling, and disrespectful treatment that the victim has previously undergone. Social scientists who have studied the effects of racism have found that speech that communicates low regard for an individual because of race "tends to create in the victim those very traits of 'inferiority' that it ascribes to him." Moreover, "even in the absence of more objective forms of discrimination—poor schools, menial jobs, and substandard housing—traditional stereotypes about the low ability and apathy of Negroes and other minorities can operate as 'self-fulfilling prophecies.'" These stereotypes, portraying members of a minority group as stupid, lazy, dirty, or untrustworthy, are often communicated either explicitly or implicitly through racial insults.

Victims of racial invective have few means of coping with the harms caused by the insults. Physical attacks are of course forbidden. "More speech" frequently is useless because it may provoke only further abuse or because the insulter is in a position of authority over the victim. Complaints to civil rights organizations also are meaningless unless they lead to action to punish the offender. Adoption of a "they're well-meaning but ignorant" attitude is another impotent response in light of the insidious psychological harms of racial slurs. When victimized by racist language, victims must be able to threaten and institute legal action, thereby relieving the sense of helplessness that leads to psychological harm and communicating to the perpetrator and to society that such abuse will not be tolerated, either by its victims or by the courts.

Minority children possess even fewer means for coping with racial insults than do adults. "A child who finds himself rejected and attacked ... is not likely to develop dignity and poise.... On the contrary he develops defenses. Like a dwarf in a world of menacing giants, he cannot fight on equal terms." The child who is the victim of belittlement can react with only two unsuccessful strategies—hostility or passivity. Aggressive reactions can lead to consequences which reinforce the harm caused by the insults; children who behave aggressively in school are marked by their teachers as troublemakers, adding to the children's alienation and sense of rejection. Seemingly passive reactions have no better results; children who are passive toward their insulters turn the aggressive response on themselves; robbed of confidence and motivation, these children withdraw into moroseness, fantasy, and fear.

It is, of course, impossible to predict the degree of deterrence a cause of action in tort would create. However, as Professor van den Berghe has written, "for most people living in racist societies racial prejudice is merely a special kind of convenient rationalization for rewarding behavior." In other words, in racist societies "most members of the dominant group will exhibit both prejudice and discrimination," but only in conforming to social norms. Thus, "[W]hen social pressures and rewards for racism are absent, racial bigotry is more likely to be restricted to people for whom prejudice fulfills a psychological 'need.' In such a tolerant milieu prejudiced persons may even refrain from discriminating behavior to escape social disapproval." Increasing the cost of racial insults thus would certainly decrease their frequency. Laws will never prevent violations altogether, but they will deter "whoever is deterrable."

Because most citizens comply with legal rules, and this compliance in turn "reinforce[s] their own sentiments toward conformity," a tort action for racial insults would discourage such harmful activity through the teaching function of the law. The establishment of a legal norm "creates a public conscience and a standard for expected behavior that check overt signs of prejudice." Legislation aims first at controlling only the acts that express undesired attitudes. But "when expression changes, thoughts too in the long run are likely to fall into line." "Laws ... restrain the middle range of mortals who need them as a mentor in molding their habits." Thus, "If we create institutional arrangements in which exploitive behaviors are no longer reinforced, we will then succeed in changing attitudes that underlie these behaviors." Because racial attitudes of white Americans "typically follow rather than precede actual institutional or legal alteration," a tort for racial slurs is a promising vehicle for the eradication of racism.

[Eds. Delgado next considers how current law, including suits for assaults, battery, defamation, and intentional infliction of emotional distress, deters outrageous racial insults to some extent, but does not go far enough. He also considers a number of objections to a new, freestanding test, including that it would violate the First Amendment, and concludes as follows.]

ELEMENTS OF THE CAUSE OF ACTION

In order to prevail in an action for a racial insult, the plaintiff should be required to prove that

> Language that was addressed to him or her by the defendant was intended to demean through reference to race; that the plaintiff understood as intended to demean through reference to race; and that a reasonable person would recognize as a racial insult.

Thus, it would be expected that an epithet such as "You damn nigger" would almost always be found actionable, as it is highly insulting and highly racial. However, an insult such as "You incompetent fool," directed at a black person by a white, even in a context which made it highly insulting, would not be actionable because it lacks a racial component. "Boy," directed at a young black male, might be actionable, depending on the speaker's intent, the hearer's understanding, and whether a reasonable person would consider it a racial insult in the particular context. "Hey, nigger," spoken affectionately between black persons and used as a greeting, would not be actionable. An insult such as "You dumb honkey," directed at a white person, could be actionable, but only in the unusual situations where the plaintiff suffered harm from such an insult.

The plaintiff may be able to show aggravating circumstances, such as abuse of a position of power or authority or knowledge of the victim's susceptibility to racial insults, which may render punitive damages appropriate. The common law defenses of privilege and mistake may be applicable, and retraction of the insult may mitigate damages.

An independent tort for racial slurs would protect the interests of personality and equal citizenship that are part of our highest political traditions and moral values, thereby affirming the right of all citizens to lead their lives free from attacks on their dignity and psychological integrity. It is an avenue of redress that deserves explicit judicial recognition.

The "More Speech" Solution

Can Free Expression Remedy Systemic Social Ills?

Conventional First Amendment doctrine is beginning to show signs of strain. Outsider groups and women argue that free speech law inadequately protects them against certain types of harm. Meanwhile, scholars are questioning whether free expression can perform the lofty functions of community-building and consensus-formation that society assigns to it.

We believe that in both situations the source of the difficulty is the same: failure to take account of the ways language and expression work. The results of this failure are more glaring in some areas than others. Much as Newtonian physics enabled us to explain the phenomena of daily life but required modification to address ones lying on a larger scale, First Amendment theory will need revision to deal with issues lying at its farthest reaches.

Our thesis is that conventional First Amendment doctrine is most helpful in connection with small, clearly bounded disputes. Free speech and debate can help resolve controversies over whether a school disciplinary or local zoning policy is adequate, over whether a new sales tax is likely to increase or decrease net revenues, and over whether one candidate for political office is a better choice than another. Speech is less able to deal with systemic social ills, such as racism or sexism, that are widespread and deeply woven into the fabric of society. Free speech, in short, is least helpful where we need it most.

Consider racism and racial depiction. Several museums have featured displays of racial memorabilia from the past. One exhibit recently toured the United States; *Time* reviewed the opening of another. Filmmaker Marlon Riggs' award-winning one-hour documentary, *Ethnic Notions,* like the museum collections, depicts a shocking parade of Sambos, mammies, coons, uncles—bestial or happy-go-lucky, watermelon-eating—African Americans. They show advertising logos and household commodities in the shape of blacks with grotesquely exaggerated facial features. They include minstrel shows and film clips depicting blacks as so incompetent, shuffling, and dim-witted that it is hard to see how they survived to adulthood. They depict primitive, terrifying, larger-than-life black men in threatening garb and postures, often with apparent designs on white women.

Seeing these haunting images today, one is tempted to ask: "How could their authors—cartoonists, writers, filmmakers, and graphic designers—individuals, certainly, of higher than average education, create such appalling images? And why did no one protest?" The collections mentioned focus on African Americans, but the two of us examined the history of ethnic depiction for each of the four main minority subgroups of color—Mexicans, African Americans, Asians, and Native Americans—in the United States. In each case we found the same sad story: Each group is depicted, in virtually every epoch, in terms that can only be described as demeaning or worse. In addition, we found striking parallels among the stigma-pictures that society disseminated of the four groups. The stock characters may have different names and appear at different times, but they bear remarkable likenesses and seem to serve similar purposes for the majority culture.

What about the "How could they" question? In brief, we hold that those who composed and disseminated these images simply did not see them as grotesque. Their consciences were clear—their blithe creations did not trouble them. It is only decades later that these images strike us as indefensible and shocking. Our much-vaunted system of free expression, with its marketplace of ideas, cannot correct serious systemic ills such as racism or sexism simply because we do not see them as such at the time. No one can formulate an effective contemporaneous response to the vicious depiction; this happens only much later, after consciousness shifts and society adopts a different narrative. Our own era is no different. This is the dominant, overpowering lesson we draw from reviewing two centuries of ethnic depiction.

The belief that we can somehow control our consciousness despite limitations of time and positionality we call the *empathic* fallacy. In literature, the *pathetic* fallacy holds that nature is like us, that it is endowed with feelings, moods, and goals we can understand. It is raining. The poet, feeling sad, writes that the world weeps with him or her. Its correlate, which we term the *empathic* fallacy, consists of believing that we can enlarge our sympathies through linguistic means alone. By exposing ourselves to ennobling narratives and great literature, we like to think, we can broaden our experience, deepen our empathy, and achieve new levels of sensitivity and fellow-feeling. We can think, talk, read, and write our way out of bigotry and narrow-mindedness, out of our limitations of experience and perspective. As we illustrate, however, we can do this only to a very limited extent. Indeed our system of free speech not only fails to correct the repression and abuse subjugated groups must face, but often deepens their dilemma.

IMAGES OF THE OUTSIDER

A small but excellent literature chronicles the depiction in popular culture of each of the major minority subgroups of color—African Americans, Mexicans, Native Americans, and Asians. [Eds. The authors summarize the 300-year history of American racial history and draw parallels among the ways that society depicts the four groups. The reader learns of tricky Mexicans, lazy, shuffling blacks, devious Asians, and bloodthirsty Indians. They then continue as follows.]

HOW COULD THEY? LESSONS FROM HISTORY

As we see, the depiction of ethnic groups of color is littered with negative images, although the content of those images changes over time. In some periods, society needed to suppress a group, as with blacks during Reconstruction. Society then coined an image to suit that purpose—that of primitive, powerful larger than life blacks, terrifying and barely under control. At other times, for example during slavery, society needed reassurance that blacks were docile, cheerful, and content with their lot. Images of sullen, rebellious blacks dissatisfied with their condition would have made white society uneasy. Accordingly, images of simple, happy blacks, content to do the master's work, proliferated.

In every era, then, ethnic imagery comes bearing an enormous amount of social weight. Nevertheless, we ignore this *functional* feature of racial imagery. We ignore that it is a social *good,* a tool for adjusting social classes and expectations. We naively believe that racist language is an evil, a kind of mistake. We believe that we are in control, that we can be better, things need not be that way. We believe we can use speech jiujitsu fashion, on behalf of oppressed peoples. We believe that speech can serve as a tool of destabilization. It is virtually a prime tenet of liberal jurisprudence that by talk, dialogue, exhortation, and so on, we present each other with passionate, appealing messages that will counter the evil ones of racism and sexism and thereby advance society to greater levels of fairness and humanity.

Consider, for example, the current debate about campus speech codes. In response to a rising tide of racist incidents, many campuses have enacted rules that forbid certain types of face-to-face insult. These codes invariably draw fire from free-speech absolutists on the ground that they would interfere with free speech. Campuses, they argue, ought to be "bastions of free speech." Racism and prejudice are matters of "ignorance and fear," for which the appropriate remedy is more speech. Suppression merely drives racism underground, where it will fester and emerge in even more hateful forms. Speech is the best corrective for error; regulation risks the spectre of censorship and state control. Efforts to regulate pornography, Klan marches, and other types of race-baiting often meet similar responses.

But recent insights about language and the social construction of reality show that reliance on countervailing speech that will, in theory, wrestle with bad or vicious speech is misplaced, for two reasons: First, the account rests on simplistic and erroneous notions of narrativity and change; and second, it rests on a misunderstanding of the relation between the subject, or self, and new narratives.

The First Reason: Time Warp—Why We (Can) Only Condemn the Old Narrative

History shows that we simply do not see many forms of discrimination, bias, and prejudice as wrong at the time. The racism of other times and places does strike us as glaringly and appallingly wrong. But this happens only decades or centuries later; we acquiesce in today's version with little realization that a later generation will ask "How could they?" about *us*. We only condemn the racism of another place (South Africa) or time. But that of our own place and time strikes us, if at all, as unexceptionable, trivial, or well within literary license. Every form of creative work (we tell ourselves) relies on stock characters. What's so wrong with a novel that employs a black who ..., or a Mexican who ...? Besides, the argument goes, those groups *are* disproportionately employed as domestics, are responsible for a high proportion of our crime, are they not? And some actually talk this way; why, just last week, I overheard....

This time-warp aspect of racism makes speech an ineffective tool to counter it. Racism is woven into the warp and woof of the way we see and organize the world—it is one of the many preconceptions we bring to experience and use to make sense of it. Racism forms part of the dominant narrative, the group of received understandings and basic principles that form the baseline from which we reason. How could these be in question? Recent scholarship shows that the dominant narrative changes very slowly, resisting alteration. We interpret new stories in light of the old. Ones that deviate too markedly from our pre-existing stock are dismissed as extreme, coercive, political, and wrong. The only stories about race we are prepared to condemn, then, are the old ones giving voice to the racism of an earlier age, ones that society has already begun to reject. We can condemn Justice Brown for writing as he did in *Plessy v. Ferguson,* but not free-speech absolutists who blithely oppose remedies for campus racism, failing to notice the remarkable parallels between the two.

The Second Reason: Our Narratives, Our Selves
Racial change is slow, then, because the story of race is part of the dominant narrative. The narrative teaches that race matters, that people are different, with the differences lying always in a predictable direction. It holds that certain cultures, unfortunately, have less ambition than others, that the majority group is largely innocent of racial wrongdoing, that the current distribution of comfort and well-being is roughly what merit and fairness dictate. Within that general framework, only certain matters are open for discussion: How different? In what ways? With how many exceptions? And what measures are due to deal with this unfortunate situation and at what cost to whites? This is so because the narrative leaves only certain things intelligible; other suggestions and texts would seem outlandish.

A second insight from modern scholarship focuses not on the role of narratives in confining change to manageable proportions, but on the relationship between our selves and those narratives. The reigning First Amendment metaphor—the marketplace of ideas—implies a separation between subjects who do the choosing and the ideas or messages that vie for their attention. Subjects are "in here," the messages "out there." The pre-existing subjects choose the idea that seems most valid and true—somewhat in the manner of a diner deciding what to eat at a buffet.

But scholars are beginning to realize that this mechanistic view of an autonomous subject choosing among separate, external ideas is simplistic. In an important sense, we *are* our current stock of narratives, and they us. We subscribe to a stock of explanatory scripts, plots, narratives, and understandings that enable us to make sense of—to construct—our social world. Because we then live in that world, it begins to shape and determine *us,* who we are, what we see, how we select, reject, interpret and order subsequent reality.

These observations imply that our ability to escape the confines of our own preconceptions is quite limited. The contrary belief—that through speech and remonstrance alone we can endlessly reform ourselves and each other—we call the *empathic fallacy.* It and its companion, the pathetic fallacy, are both examples of *hubris,* the belief that we can be more than we are. The empathic fallacy holds that through speech and remonstrance we can surmount our limitations of time, place, and culture, can transcend our own situatedness. But the notion of ideas competing with each other, with truth and goodness emerging victorious from the competition, has proven seriously deficient when applied to evils, like racism, that are deeply inscribed in the culture. We have constructed the social world so that racism seems normal, part of the status quo, in need of little correction. It is not until much later that what we believed begins to seem incredibly, monstrously wrong. How could we have believed *that*?

True, every few decades an occasional genius will rise up and offer a work that recognizes and denounces the racism of the day. Unfortunately, they are ignored—they have no audience. Witness, for example, the recent "discovery" of long-forgotten black writers such as Charles Chesnutt, Zora Neale Hurston, or the slave narratives. Consider that Nadine Gordimer won the Nobel Prize after nearly 40 years of writing about the evils of apartheid; Harriet Beecher Stowe's book sold well only after years of abolitionist sentiment and agitation had sensitized her public to the possibility that slavery was wrong. One should, of course, speak out against social evils. But we should not accord speech greater efficacy than it has.

THE NATURE OF THE EVIL

How Much Racism Exists? The Difference Perspective Makes
As we have seen, much racism is not seen as such at the time of its commission. But whites often underestimate the extent of even the blatant variety. The reason is simple: Few acts of clear-cut racism take place within their view. Racism is often covert; the vignettes tend to play themselves out behind the scenes when no one else is watching. A merchant who harasses well-behaved black teenage shoppers will probably not do so if other whites are watching. A white apartment owner or employer will probably not deny a superbly qualified black applicant an apartment or job if a friend or observer is present.

As a result of its often covert nature, many persons of the majority race, even those of good will, consistently underestimate the extent of racism in society. Persons of color, those who are on the receiving end of it, generally report much more than do whites and naturally place greater priority on remedying it. This puzzles some whites, who wonder whether blacks are exaggerating or trying to guilt-trip them to gain an unfair advantage. The problem is perspective: Imagine that one's body were somehow magnetically charged. One would go through life astonished at how many metal filings there are in the world and how much we need a clean-up operation. Those not caught in this Kafkaesque dilemma would naturally fail to appreciate the situation's urgency.

The Subtle Nuances
Racism's victims become sensitized to its subtle nuances and code-words—the body language, averted gazes, exasperated looks, terms such as "you people," ":innocent whites," "highly qualified black," "articulate," and so on—that, whether intended or not, convey racially charged meanings. Like an Aleut accustomed to reading the sky for signs of snow or a small household pet skilled at recognizing a clumsy footfall, racism's perpetual victims are alert to the various guises racism and racial signalling take. Sympathizers of majority hue often must labor to acquire the knowledge that for minorities comes all too easily.

On Seeing What One Does Not Want to See
Some refuse to see racism in acts that trigger suspicion in the mind of any person of color. A well-qualified black applicant fails to get the job. Perhaps it was his tie,

his posture, his age, or the way he held himself that caused his rejection. Perhaps he seemed too diffident or too anxious to get the job. Perhaps he had traits, such as voice intonations, that might irritate customers. Choosing to believe in a race-free world reduces guilt and the need for corrective action. Racism is often a matter of interpretation. When one interpretation renders one uncomfortable and another does not, which will a person often draw?

Unlearning the Lessons of the Past
Finally, many members of the majority race simply forget how to see and condemn racism. Society generalizes the wrong lesson from the past, namely that racism has virtually disappeared. We notice, for example, that today's media contain fewer Sambos than in the past. We thus conclude that those writers from the past must have been acting against conscience, that is, had vicious wills and realized that what they were doing was wrong (as we realize it today), but went ahead and did it anyway. Yet, we think, "I do not act against conscience and neither do my friends."

In fact, those earlier writers were acting blithely, not against conscience, any more than we do today in maintaining our own versions of racism and racist imagery. The Willie Horton commercial struck many as falling within the bounds of fair play, perhaps only slightly exaggerated—at any rate the sort of thing that one must expect in the rough-and-tumble world of politics. Besides, do not blacks in fact commit a high percentage of violent crime; did I not read that . . . ?

HOW THE SYSTEM OF FREE EXPRESSION SOMETIMES MAKES MATTERS WORSE

Speech and free expression are not only poorly adapted to remedy racism, they often make matters worse. First, they encourage writers, filmmakers, and other creative people to feel amoral, nonresponsible in what they do. Because of the marketplace of ideas, the rationalization goes, another filmmaker is free to make an antiracist movie that will cancel out any minor stereotyping in the one I am making. My movie may have other redeeming qualities; besides, it is good entertainment and everyone in the industry uses stock characters like the black maid or the bumbling Asian tourist. How can one create film without stock characters?

Second, when insurgent groups attempt to use speech as an instrument of reform, courts almost invariably construe First Amendment doctrine against them. As Charles Lawrence pointed out, civil rights activists in the sixties made the greatest strides when they acted in defiance of the First Amendment as then understood. They marched, were arrested and convicted; sat in, were arrested and convicted; distributed leaflets, were arrested and convicted. Many years later, after much gallant lawyering, their conviction might be reversed on appeal if the original action had been sufficiently prayerful, mannerly, and not too interlaced with an action component. This history of the civil rights movement does not bear out the usual assumption that the First Amendment is of great value for racial reformers.

Current First Amendment law is similarly skewed. Examination of the many "exceptions" to First Amendment protection discloses that the large majority favor the interests of the powerful. If one says something disparaging of a wealthy and well-regarded individual, one discovers that one's words were not free after all; the wealthy individual has a type of property interest in his or her image, damage to which is compensable even though words were the sole instrument of the harm. Similarly, if one infringes the copyright or trademark of a well-known writer or industrialist, again it turns out that one's action is punishable. Further, if one disseminates an official secret valuable to a powerful branch of the military or defense contractor, that speech is punishable. If one speaks disrespectfully to a judge, police officer, teacher, military official, or other powerful authority figure, again one discovers that one's words were not free; and so with words used to defraud, form a conspiracy, breach the peace, or untruthful words given under oath during a civil or criminal proceeding.

Yet the suggestion that we create a new exception to protect vulnerable members of our society, such as isolated, young black undergraduates attending dominantly white campuses, is often met with consternation: the First Amendment must be a seamless web, we say; minorities, if they knew their own self-interest, should appreciate this even more than others. This one-sidedness of free-speech doctrine makes the First Amendment much more valuable to the majority than to the minority.

The system of free expression also performs a powerful after-the-fact apologetic function. Elite groups use the supposed existence of a marketplace of ideas to justify their own superior position. Imagine a society in which all As were rich and happy, all Bs were moderately comfortable, and all Cs were poor, stigmatized, and reviled. Imagine also that this society scrupulously believes in a free marketplace of ideas. Might not the As benefit greatly from such a system? On looking about them and observing the inequality in the distribution of wealth, longevity, happiness, and safety between themselves and the others, they might be inclined to feel guilt. Perhaps their own superior position is undeserved, or at least requires explanation. But the existence of an ostensibly free marketplace of ideas renders that effort unnecessary. Rationalization is easy: our ideas, our culture competed with their more easygoing ones and won. It was a fair fight. It is up to them to change, not us.

A free market of racial depiction resists change for two final reasons. First, the dominant pictures, images, narratives, plots, roles, and stories ascribed to, and constituting the public perception of minorities, are almost always dominantly negative. Through an unfortunate psychological mechanism, incessant bombardment by images of the sort described earlier inscribes those images on the souls and minds of minority persons. Persons of color can easily become demoralized, blame themselves, and not speak up vigorously. The expense of speech also precludes the stigmatized from participating effectively in the marketplace of ideas. They are often poor—indeed, one theory of racism holds that maintenance of economic inequality is its prime function—and hence unlikely to command the means to bring countervailing messages to the eyes and ears of others.

Second, even when minorities do speak they have little credibility. Who would listen to, who would credit, a speaker or writer one associates with watermelon-eating, buffoonery, menial work, intellectual inadequacy, laziness, lasciviousness, and demanding resources beyond his or her deserved share?

Our very imagery of the outsider shows that, contrary to the usual view, society does not really want them to speak out effectively in their own behalf, in fact cannot visualize them doing so. Ask yourself: How do outsiders speak in the dominant narratives? Poorly, inarticulately, with broken syntax, short sentences, grunts, and unsophisticated ideas. Try to recall a single popular narrative of an eloquent, self-assured black (for example) orator or speaker. In the real world, of course, they exist in profusion. But when we stumble upon them, we are surprised: "What a welcome 'exception'!"

Words, then, can wound. But the fine thing about the current situation is that one gets to enjoy a superior position and feel virtuous at the same time. By supporting the system of free expression no matter the cost, one is upholding principle. One can belong to impeccably liberal organizations and believe one is doing the right thing, even while taking actions injurious to the least privileged, most defenseless segments of our society. In time, one's actions will seem wrong and be condemned as such, but paradigms change slowly. The world one helps to create—a world in which denigrating depiction is good or at least acceptable, in which minorities are buffoons, clowns, maids, or Willie Hortons, and only rarely fully individuated human beings with sensitivities, talents, personalities, and frailties—will survive into the future. One gets to create culture at outsiders' expense. And, one gets to sleep well at night, too.

Racism is not a mistake, not a matter of episodic, irrational behavior carried out by vicious-willed individuals, not a throwback to a long-gone era. It is ritual assertion of supremacy, like animals sneering and posturing to maintain their places in the hierarchy of a colony. It is performed largely unconsciously, just as the animals' behavior is. Racism seems right, customary, and inoffensive to those engaged in it, while bringing psychic and pecuniary advantages. The notion that more speech, more talking, more preaching, and more lecturing can counter this system of oppression is appealing, lofty, romantic—and wrong.

Campus Antiracism Rules
Constitutional Narratives in Collision

Nearly two hundred university and college campuses have experienced racial unrest serious or graphic enough to be reported in the press. Most observers believe the increase in racial tension on the nation's campuses is real, and not just the product of better reporting or record keeping.

In response, a number of campuses have enacted student conduct rules prohibiting slurs and disparaging remarks directed against persons on account of their ethnicity, religion, or sexual orientation. The University of Wisconsin rule, for example, prohibits remarks that (i) are directed to an individual; (ii) demean based on membership in a racial, religious, or sexual group; (iii) are intended to demean; and (iv) interfere with the victim's ability to take part in education or instruction. These codes have drawn intense criticism.

FRAMING THE ISSUES

Persons tend to react to the problem of racial insults in one of two ways. On hearing that a university has enacted rules forbidding certain forms of speech, some will frame the issue as a First Amendment problem: the rules limit speech, and the Constitution forbids official regulation of speech without a very good reason. If one takes that starting point, several consequences follow. First, the burden shifts to the other side to show that the need to protect members of the campus community from insults and name-calling is compelling enough to overcome the presumption in favor of free speech. Further, no less onerous ways must be available of accomplishing that objective. Moreover, some will worry whether the enforcer of the regulation will become a censor, imposing narrow-minded restraints on campus discussion. Others will be concerned about slippery slopes and line-drawing problems: if a campus restricts this type of expression, might we not one day end up doing the same with classroom speech or political satire in the campus newspaper?

Others, however, will frame the problem as one of protection of equality. They will ask whether an educational institution does not have the power to protect core values emanating from the Thirteenth and Fourteenth Amendments, to enact reasonable regulations aimed at assuring equal personhood on campus. If one characterizes the issue *this* way, other consequences follow. Now, the defenders of racially scathing speech are required to show that the interest in its protection is compelling enough to overcome our ordinary preference for equal personhood. We will also want to be sure that this interest is advanced in the way least damaging to equality. Concerns again arise about the decisionmaker who will enforce the rules, but from the opposite direction: the enforcer must be attuned to the nuances of insult and racial supremacy at issue, for example by incorporating multi-ethnic representation into the hearing process. Finally, a different set of slopes will look slippery. If we do *not* intervene to protect equality here, what will the next outrage be?

The legal analysis, therefore, leads to opposite conclusions depending on the starting point. But an even deeper indeterminacy looms: both sides invoke different narratives to rally support. Protectors of the First Amendment see campus antiracism rules as parts of a much longer story: the centuries-old struggle of Western society to free itself from superstition and enforced ignorance. The tellers of this story invoke martyrs like Socrates, Galileo, and Peter Zenger, and heroes like Locke, Hobbes, Voltaire, and Hume who fought for the right of free expression. They conjure up struggles against official censorship, book burning, witch trials, and communist blacklists. Compared to that richly textured, deeply stirring account, the minority-protector's interest in freeing a few (supersensitive?) individuals from momentary discomfort looks thin. A textured, historical account is pitted against a particularized, slice-of-life, dignitary one.

Those on the minority-protection side invoke a different, and no less powerful, narrative. They see a nation's centuries-long struggle to free itself from racial and other forms of tyranny, including slavery, lynching, Jim Crow laws, and separate-but-equal schools. They conjure up different milestones—Lincoln's Emancipation Proclamation, *Brown v. Board of Education*; they look to different heroes—Martin Luther King, the early Abolitionists, Rosa Parks, and Cesar Chavez, civil rights protesters who put their lives on the line for racial justice. Arrayed against that richly textured historical account, the racist's interest in insulting a person of color face-to-face looks weak.

One often hears that the problem of campus antiracism rules is that of balancing free speech and equality. But more is at stake than that. Each side wants not merely to have the balance struck in its favor; each wants to impose its own understanding of what is at stake. Minority protectors see the injury of one who has been subject to a racial assault as not a mere isolated event, but as part of an interrelated series of acts that will follow the victim wherever she goes. First Amendment defenders see the wrong of silencing the racist as much more than a momentary inconvenience: protection of his right to speak is part of the never-ending vigilance necessary to preserve freedom of expression in a society too prone to balance it away.

Both stories are equally valid. Judges and university administrators have no easy, a priori way of choosing between them, of privileging one over the other. They could coin an exception to free speech, thus giving primacy to the equal protection values at stake. Or, they could carve an exception to equality, saying in effect that universities may protect minority populations except where this abridges speech. Nothing in constitutional or moral theory requires one answer rather than the other. Social science, case law, and the experience of other nations provide some illumination. But ultimately, judges and university administrators must *choose*. And in making this choice, we are in uncharted terrain: we lack a pole star.

[Eds. Delgado next reviews leading incidents of hate speech at top universities, discusses arguments pro and con regulation, and reviews the experience of other developed nations with hate-speech controls. He then continues as follows.]

The debate surrounding campus antiracism rules has not only proceeded in an empirical vacuum, ignoring the experience of other countries; it has also proceeded in a theoretical one, blind to the insights of social scientists who have studied race and racism. Critics of antiracism rules, for example, often assert: (i) that rules forbidding racist remarks will simply cause racism to go underground or surface in a more virulent form; (ii) that racist speech serves as a pressure valve, allowing prejudiced individuals to blow off steam harmlessly; (iii) that punishing racist speech is ineffective because it does not deal with the "root" causes of racism; and (iv) that the harm of a racial insult is slight. For their part, defenders of anti-hate rules maintain that racial speech causes serious harm to the psyche and educational prospects of its victims, with little if any documentation of these effects. Social science research sheds light on these and other assertions central to the debate about antiracism rules.

Nature and Origin of Prejudice

Social scientists have put forward a number of overlapping theories—psychodynamic, socioeconomic, and social-psychological—that explain how persons come to harbor prejudiced attitudes toward members of outgroups. No theory is dominant; indeed, more than one approach may be essential to understand the complex phenomenon of racism.

Psychodynamic theories find the source of racism in personality traits of particular individuals. For example, Adorno and his coauthors write that the most severe forms of racism are associated with a group of traits labelled the "authoritarian personality." Authoritarian personalities are rigid, conventional, and have difficulty accepting impulses they consider deviant—fear, weakness, sex, and aggression. Because they reject these impulses in themselves, they are prone to displace them onto others, particularly members of disempowered groups.

Other social scientists believe that understanding racism requires going beyond personal pathology to broader currents in society. Many hold that two principal sources of racism and prejudice toward outgroups are economic dislocation and competition. The anxiety produced by rapid social change requires a scapegoat assigned traits of inferiority in order to preserve the myth that America is fair and just. Scapegoating also channels aggression and strengthens group loyalty against outsiders who are at fault for societal ills.

Finally, the social-psychological approach holds that racial antipathies are not innate but learned, often as an aspect of group membership. Humans have a natural propensity to generalize. Ethnic categories serve this purpose admirably, as well as satisfy the basic human need for group identity. Loyalties to the in-group accompany dislike of outgroups. The dislike increases the distance between the individual and the outgroup, so that the attitude becomes self-reinforcing.

The combined effect of all these forces—personal dynamics, scapegoating, economic dislocations, and ingroup-outgroup categories—is powerful: studies indicate that a majority of Americans harbor some prejudice toward groups other than their own. Yet, not all act on these attitudes; at times, we hold our prejudice in check.

Controlling Racism

Unlike with racism's etiology, social scientists exhibit broad agreement on how to control its expression. Much prejudice is situational—individuals express it because the environment encourages or tolerates it. The attitude may be relatively constant, but most of us express it selectively—at times we hold it in check, at other times we feel freer to express it. The main deterrent of prejudice is the certainty that it will be remarked and punished. This "confrontation theory" holds that most individuals are ambivalent in matters of race. We realize that the national values—those enshrined in the "American Creed"—call for fair and respectful treatment of all. But the fair-mindedness of our public norms does not always match our private behavior. During moments of intimacy we feel much freer to tell or laugh at an ethnic joke, to make a racist or sexist remark.

Rules, formalities, and other environmental reminders put us on notice that the occasion requires the higher formal values of our culture. Rules forbidding certain types of racist acts cause us not to be inclined to carry them out. Moreover, threat of public notice and disapproval operates as a reinforcer—the potential racist refrains from acting out of fear of notice and sanction. The confrontation theory is probably today the majority view among social scientists on how to control racism. Most who subscribe to it hold that laws and rules play a vital role in controlling racism. According to Allport, they "create a public conscience and a standard for expected behavior that check *overt* signs of prejudice." Nor is the change merely cosmetic. In time, rules are internalized, and the impulse to engage in racist behavior weakens.

The current understanding of racial prejudice thus lends support to campus antiracism rules. The mere existence of rules will often cause members of the campus community to refrain from racist behavior, particularly when others may be watching. Even in private settings, some people will refrain from acting because the law has set an example. Those whose prejudice is associated with authoritarianism will do so because the rules represent society's legitimate voice.

Social science casts doubt on both the "hydraulic" theory of racism, according to which controlling racism in one arena will simply cause it to crop up somewhere else, and the theory that racist remarks are relatively harmless. A large body of literature shows that incessant racial categorization and treatment seriously impair the prospects and development of persons of minority race, deepen rigidity, and set the stage for even more serious transgressions on the part of persons so disposed.

CONSTITUTIONAL PARADIGMS

As mentioned earlier, campus antiracism rules can be analyzed from two directions. One perspective puts speech at the center, and demands that proponents of antiracism rules justify the abridgment of that liberty. Another puts equal dignity at the center, and regards the speech-act as a violation. In this view, the university has the power (perhaps the duty) to protect vulnerable populations from racial abuse, while the advocates of free speech would need to show why the interest in hurling invective should nevertheless prevail. Let us consider both views.

A First Amendment View
The First Amendment appears to stand as a formidable barrier to campus rules prohibiting group-disparaging speech. Designed to assure that debate on public issues is "uninhibited, robust, and wide open," the First Amendment protects speech which we hate as much as that which we hold dear. Yet, racial insults implicate powerful social interests in equality and equal personhood. When uttered on university campuses, racial insults bring into play additional concerns. Few would question that the university has strong, legitimate interests in (i) teaching students and teachers to treat each other respectfully; (ii) protecting minority-group students from harassment; and (iii) protecting diversity,

which could be impaired if students of color become demoralized and leave the university, or minority parents decide to send their children elsewhere.

The United States Supreme Court has only on one occasion weighed free speech against the equal-protection values endangered by race-hate speech. In *Beauharnais v. Illinois,* the defendant was convicted under a statute prohibiting dissemination of materials promoting racial or religious hatred. Justice Frankfurter, citing the "fighting words" doctrine of *Chaplinsky v. New Hampshire,* ruled that libelous statements aimed at groups, like those aimed at individuals, fall outside First Amendment protection. Later decisions, notably *New York Times v. Sullivan,* have increased protection for libelous speech, with the result that some commentators and courts question whether *Beauharnais* today would be decided differently. Yet, the decision has never been overruled, and in the meantime many courts have afforded redress in tort for racially or sexually insulting language [Eds. And one for cross-burning with the intent to intimidate], few finding any constitutional problem in doing so.

Moreover, over the past century the courts have carved out or tolerated dozens of "exceptions" to free speech, including: speech used to form a criminal conspiracy or an ordinary contract; speech that disseminates an official secret; speech that defames or libels someone; speech that is obscene; speech that creates a hostile workplace; speech that violates a trademark or plagiarizes another's words; speech that creates an immediately harmful impact or is tantamount to shouting fire in a crowded theatre; "patently offensive" speech directed at captive audiences or broadcast on the airwaves; speech that constitutes "fighting words"; speech that disrespects a judge, teacher, military officer, or other authority figure; speech used to defraud a consumer; words used to fix prices; words ("stick 'em up—hand over the money") used to communicate a criminal threat; and untruthful or irrelevant speech given under oath or during a trial.

Much speech, then, is unprotected. The issues are whether the social interest in reining in racially offensive speech is as great as that which gives rise to these "exceptional" categories, and whether racially offensive language has speech value. Because no recent Supreme Court decision directly addresses these issues, one might look to the underlying policies of our system of free expression to understand how the Supreme Court may rule if an appropriate case comes before it.

Our system of free expression serves a number of societal and individual goals: the personal fulfillment of the speaker; ascertainment of the truth; participation in democratic decisionmaking; and achievement of a balance between social stability and change. Applying these policies to the controversy surrounding campus antiracism rules yields no clear result. Uttering racial slurs may afford the racially troubled speaker some immediate relief, but hardly seems essential to self-fulfillment in any ideal sense. Moreover, such remarks serve little dialogic purpose; they do not seek to connect the speaker and addressee in a community of shared ideals. They divide, rather than unite.

Additionally, slurs contribute little to the discovery of truth. Classroom discussion of racial matters and even the speech of a bigot aimed at proving the superiority of the white race might move us closer to the truth. But one-on-one insults do not. They neither state nor attack a proposition; they are like a slap in the face. By the same token, racial insults do little to help reach broad social consensuses. Indeed, by demoralizing their victim they may actually reduce speech, dialogue, and participation in political life. "More speech" is rarely a solution. Epithets often strike suddenly, immobilizing their victim and rendering her speechless. Often they arrive in cowardly, anonymous fashion—for example, in the form of a defaced poster or leaflet slipped under a student's door, or hurled by a group against a single victim, rendering response foolhardy. Nor do they help strike a healthy balance between stability and social change.

Yet racial epithets *are* speech, and as such we ought to protect them unless a very good reason counsels against it. A recent book by Kent Greenawalt suggests a framework for assessing laws against insults. Drawing on First Amendment principles and case law, Greenawalt writes that the setting, the speaker's intention, the forum's interest, and the relationship between the speaker and the victim must be considered. Moreover, abusive words (like kike, nigger, wop, and faggot) are punishable if spoken with intent, cause a harm subject to formulation in clear legal language, and form a message essentially devoid of ideas. Greenawalt offers as an example of words that could be criminally punishable, "You Spick whore" uttered by four men to a woman of color at a bus stop, intended to humiliate her.

Under Greenawalt's test, narrowly drawn university guidelines penalizing racial slurs might withstand scrutiny. The university forum has a strong interest in establishing a nonracist atmosphere. Moreover, most university rules are aimed at face-to-face remarks that are intentionally abusive. Most exclude classroom speech, speeches to a crowd, and satire published in a campus newspaper. Under Greenawalt's nonabsolutist approach, such rules might well be held constitutional.

An Equal Protection View
The First Amendment perspective yields no clear-cut result. Society has a strong interest in seeing that expression is as unfettered as possible, yet the kind of expression under consideration has little social worth and can cause serious harm. Unfortunately, looking at the problem of racist speech from the perspective of the equality-protecting amendments yields no clearer result.

Equality and equal respect are highly valued principles in our system of jurisprudence. Three constitutional amendments and a myriad of federal and state statutes aim to protect the rights of racial, religious, and sexual minorities to be free from discrimination in housing, education, jobs, and many other areas of life. Moreover, universities have considerable power to enact regulations protecting minority interests. Yet the equality principle is not without limits. State agencies may not redress breaches by means that too broadly encroach on the rights of whites, or on other constitutional principles. Rigorous rules of intent, causation, standing, and limiting relief circumscribe what may be done. New causes of action are not lightly recognized; for example, the legal system has resisted efforts by feminists to have pornography deemed a civil rights offense against women.

Moreover, courts have ruled that a university's power to effectuate campus policies, presumably including equality, is also limited. Cases stemming from efforts to regulate the wearing of armbands, what students may publish in the school newspaper, or their freedom to gather in open areas for worship or speech have shown that individual liberty will sometimes supersede an institution's interest in achieving its educational objectives—students do not abandon all their constitutional rights at the schoolhouse door. According to the author of a leading treatise on higher education law, rules bridling racist speech will be found constitutional if enacted in response to a local history of racial disruption; if narrowly tailored to punish only face-to-face insults and avoid encroaching on classroom and other protected speech; if consistently and even-handedly applied; and if due process protections such as the right to representation and a fair hearing are present. The author's guidelines seem plausible, but have yet to be tested. In several jurisdictions, the ACLU has announced that it is monitoring developments and may file suit.

RECONCILING THE FIRST AND FOURTEENTH AMENDMENTS: STIGMA-PICTURES AND THE SOCIAL CONSTRUCTION OF REALITY

As we have seen, neither the constitutional narrative of the First, nor of the Thirteenth and Fourteenth, Amendments clearly prevails in connection with campus antiracism rules. Judges must choose. The dilemma is embedded in the nature of our system of law and politics: we want and fear both equality and liberty. Ultimately, the problem of campus antiracism rules may yield to a post-modern insight: the speech by which society "constructs" a stigma picture of minorities may be regulated consistently with the First Amendment. Indeed, regulation may be necessary for full effectuation of the values of equal personhood we hold equally dear.

The first step is recognizing that racism is, in almost all its aspects, a class harm—the essence of which is subordination of one people by another. The mechanism of this subordination is a complex, interlocking series of acts, some physical, some symbolic. Although the physical acts (like lynchings and cross burnings) are often the most striking, the symbolic acts are the most insidious. By communicating and constructing a shared cultural image of the victim group as inferior, we enable ourselves to feel comfortable about the disparity in power and resources between ourselves and the stigmatized group. Most civil rights law, unfortunately, contributes to this stigmatization: the group is so vulnerable that it requires social help.

The ubiquity and incessancy of harmful racial depiction are thus the source of its virulence. Like water dripping on sandstone, it is a pervasive harm which only the most hardy can resist. Yet the prevailing First Amendment paradigm predisposes us to treat racist speech as an individual harm, as though we only had to evaluate the effect of a single drop of water. This approach—corresponding to liberal, individualistic theories of self and society—systematically misperceives the experience of racism for both victim and perpetrator. This mistake is natural, and corresponds to one aspect of our natures—our individualistic selves. In this capacity, we want and need liberty. But we also exist in a social capacity; we need others to fulfill ourselves as beings. In this group aspect, we require inclusion, equality, and equal respect. Constitutional narratives of equal protection and prohibition of slavery—narratives that encourage us to form and embrace collectivity and equal citizenship—reflect this second aspect of our existence.

When the tacit consent of a group begins to coordinate the exercise of individual rights so as seriously to jeopardize participation by a smaller group, the "rights" nature of the first group's actions acquires a different dimension. The exercise of an individual right now poses a group harm and must be weighed against this qualitatively more serious threat.

Racist speech is not readily repaired—it separates the victim from the storytellers who alone have credibility. Not only does racist speech, by placing all the credibility with the dominant group, strengthen the dominant story, it also works to disempower minority groups by crippling the effectiveness of *their* speech in rebuttal. This situation makes free speech a powerful asset to the dominant group, but a much less helpful one to subordinate groups—a result at odds, certainly, with marketplace theories of the First Amendment. Unless society is able to deal with this incongruity, the Thirteenth and Fourteenth Amendments and our complex system of civil rights statutes will be of little avail. At best, they will be able to obtain redress for episodic, blatant acts of individual prejudice and bigotry, but will do little to address the source of the problem: the speech that creates the stigma-picture that makes the acts hurtful in the first place, and that renders almost any other form of aid—social or legal—useless.

Could judges and legislators effectuate my suggestion that speech which constructs a stigma-picture of a subordinate group stands on a different footing from sporadic speech aimed at persons who are not disempowered? It might be argued that *all* speech constructs the world to some extent, and that every speech act could prove offensive to someone. Traditionalists find modern art troublesome, Republicans detest left-wing speech, and some men hate speech that constructs a sex-neutral world. Yet race—like gender and a few other characteristics—is different; our entire history and culture bespeak this difference. Thus, judges easily could differentiate speech which subordinates blacks, for example, from that which disparages factory owners. Will they choose to do so? Perhaps not; low-grade racism benefits the status quo. Moreover, our system's winners have a stake in liberal, marketplace interpretations of law and politics—the seeming neutrality and meritocratic nature of such interpretations reassure them that their social position is deserved.

Still, resurgent racism on our nation's campuses is rapidly becoming a national embarrassment. Almost daily, we read headlines featuring some of the ugliest forms of ethnic conflict and the spectre of virtually all-white universities. The need to avoid these consequences may have the beneficial effect of causing courts to reflect on, and tailor, constitutional doctrine. As Harry Kalven pointed out twenty five years ago, it would not be the first time that insights born of the cauldron of racial justice yielded reforms that ultimately redounded to the benefit of all society.

Toward a Legal Realist View of the First Amendment

Nearly three-quarters of a century ago, legal realism swept aside what Roscoe Pound called "mechanical jurisprudence," paving the way for a host of movements—law and society, critical legal studies (CLS), feminist legal theory, and critical race theory, to name a few—that broadened our concept of law, generally for the better. The one area that has resisted the legal realist revolution is First Amendment law, in which mechanistic rules (for example, no content-based regulation), special doctrines (for example, the dozens of "exceptions" to the realm of free speech), and thought-ending clichés ("the cure for bad speech is more speech") continue to hold sway. Recall, for example, Justice Scalia's opinion in *R.A.V. v. City of St. Paul*, which displays the formalism of a 1950s hornbook in its inattention to St. Paul's racial history, the rise of skinheads, the African-American family's reaction to the cross burning, the impact of hate messages in general, or anything else one might have thought relevant to the disposition of the case.

Under the influence of radical feminism and critical race theory, this last remnant of 1890s mechanical jurisprudence is beginning to give way to a view of speech that is flexible, policy-sensitive, and mindful of communication theory, politics, and setting. Steven Shiffrin's *Dissent, Injustice, and the Meanings of America* is a welcome addition to this emerging "First Amendment legal realism" vein of scholarship.

[Eds. Delgado next praises the Shiffrin book, while pointing out a few flaws. He then continues as follows.]

If dissent cannot serve as the only analytical tool for analyzing a complex free-speech question, what would a more expansive realist treatment look like? As was mentioned, it should, at a minimum, consider context, social science, and the politics of the area in question. Consider how some of these matters might play out in the controversy over hate-speech regulation.

HATE SPEECH AS A CONCERTED HARM

One realist observation concerns what some call the "social construction of reality" thesis. Hate speech never occurs in isolation; it picks as its target individuals who have been exposed to racist hate speech before and are likely to experience its sting again in the future. Like salt rubbed into a wound, hate speech digs at its victims' sensibilities, reminding them that they are different and that the source of that difference causes others to regard them as beneath the speaker in standing and human worth. Like water dripping on stone, hate speech harms by virtue of its incessancy—victims hear it again and again throughout their entire lives. The messages conveyed in hate speech sink in, so that over time the victims of those damaging messages begin to doubt their self-worth. This aspect of hate speech is what proponents of regulation have in mind when they write that hate speech contributes to a social order that falls far short of our national ideals.

But these messages also alter the environment for individuals of the majority race, including those who aspire to be nonracist and would never utter hate speech themselves. They hear others doing so and see images of minorities in demeaning or limited roles on television, in the movies, and in newspapers. Who would blame them if, after time, they began secretly to wonder whether the prevailing stereotypes of persons of color did not contain a small grain of truth? And, an insidious form of reinforcement known as "stereotype threat" validates those suspicions, as test-takers from groups subject to demeaning stereotypes perform poorly precisely because they fear that their performance will confirm the stereotype. Claude Steele and a co-investigator coined this term when they found that black test-takers, told that a fairly difficult paper-and-pencil test would measure their cognitive ability, performed poorly compared to a control group whose members were told that the test was aimed only at helping researchers to understand problem-solving behavior. Media and other messages broadcasting the inferiority of minorities may be a prime means of perpetuating stereotype threat.

These broader consequences of hate speech can easily escape scholars. Seeing the harm of hate speech as affecting dignity only, they end up weighing short-term, individual consequences—wounded feelings—against the broad, systemic benefits that we derive as a society from our system of free expression. Even a good writer (Steve Shiffrin) succumbs to this temptation at times, yet how fair is it to frame the problem in these terms? Suppose that a supporter of hate-speech regulation urged that the legal system weigh the *speaker's* "momentary discomfort" in reining in his or her thoughts against the massive gains that society reaps from enforcing antidiscrimination norms. A realist approach would regard *both* individual and social costs and benefits as duly weighing in the balance. It would deal with both the effects of hate speech on the life of a single individual as well as its impact across large groups.

HATE SPEECH AND INTERCLASS COMPETITION: THE WHO-BENEFITS QUESTION

A second realist insight concerns hate speech's role in promoting the interests of elite groups. Not only does such speech render its victims one-down, it often operates further to advantage its speakers and their class. Hate speech achieves these ends in a number of ways. First, it keeps the playing field uneven—recall the earlier discussion of stereotype threat, for example. If a system of pernicious images renders a minority of test-takers and job applicants nervous, fumbling, ill-at-ease—and less competent than they would otherwise be—then those who compete with them for test scores, jobs, and places in law school classes will gain an advantage; part of the competition will have been eliminated.

Hate speech also reinforces the class system in other, more straightforward ways. Some university administrators may hesitate to crack down on campus hate speech because of subtle self-interest. Although university officials are generally sympathetic to the plight of minorities, they may know, on some level, that tolerating a small degree of harassment and invective on campus confers benefits. I do not mean crude, graphic, glaring forms of racial acting-out like fraternity parties with racially offensive themes or slave auctions that bring press coverage and infamy to the campus, but the daily forms of near-invisible comments, double entendres, and slights directed against students of color and women. Consider, also, the unpunished defacement of interest groups' bulletin boards or graffiti written on campus buildings—events that rarely attract press attention but that students of color, Jews, and women notice and remember. Tolerating this level of "micro-aggression" keeps students of color on edge and defensive, prevents them from feeling too secure on campus, and discourages them from making demands—such as for curricular change, more financial aid, or professors of color—that might prove quite costly for the institution. Minority students of real spirit—apt to be a thorn in the side of administrators—may well leave or transfer to another institution.

Thus, although most campus officials themselves would never utter a racial slur and would disapprove strongly if a member of their social circle did so, they might treat lightly the occasional racist student, visitor, or lecturer who utters one, recognizing, perhaps unconsciously, that his transgression brings stability to the institution. Campus hate speech may, then, operate like a homeostat, assuring that the system contains just the right amount of racism. Not too much, for that would bring adverse consequences and instigate rebellion; nor too little, for that would forfeit important advantages that enable the campus to perform its work of reproducing social hierarchy.

The system of freedom of expression benefits the powerful in yet another way. A marketplace mechanism like so many others, freedom of expression allows those in control to believe that their positions are deserved. For if *our* superior ideas and forms of social organization competed with those of others and won fair and square, then the proponents of the weaker ideas have no legitimate complaint. If the losers find themselves poor, reviled, and excluded, their remedy is to bring themselves up to our standard. Free speech, then, serves an important after-the-fact, apologetic function. But, of course, the fight was not fair. Speech is expensive; not all can afford the cost of a microphone, computer, or television airtime; not all enjoy equal credibility in the eyes of the public. Yet our myth of a free marketplace of ideas enables us to ignore these inequalities, deepening the predicament of those whom it marginalizes.

HATE SPEECH AND DISTRIBUTED CREDIBILITY

This observation about selective access and credibility dovetails with yet another realist observation, namely, hate speech's falsification of a leading premise of our competitive, merit-driven system—the level playing field, which assumes that in a fair society, all will compete on equal terms for jobs, positions in a law school class, and other scarce commodities. Standardized tests, like the Scholastic Aptitude Test (SAT) or Law School Admissions Test (LSAT), are supposed to be administered under conditions that are the same for all. If a condition of the test required that blaring music bombard half the test-takers (for example, women and minorities) but not the other half, we would immediately pronounce the competition unfair and the playing field uneven. Stereotype anxiety, a mechanism documented by Steele and Aronson, afflicts minorities alone and is a product of hate speech, belittlement, and other forms of negative social characterization.

Hate messages also make the task of the minority speaker harder, because of the toll that they take on the credibility of speakers of color. Women know that often, in the course of a conversation among several people, a woman will make a suggestion and the conversation will continue as though little had happened. Later, a man will raise the same idea, which everyone will praise and then describe as "Bill's idea." The *very same message* from a woman will register differently from one delivered by a man. Minorities often have the same experience. How can this be? Because the message is the same irrespective of the speaker, the reason for the different reception cannot lie in the words themselves. Unless all women and minorities are inherently unworthy of belief—something no one is likely to maintain—the only possible origin of this differential credibility lies in the system of stories and messages that we choose to tell about, and to, minorities and women—in short, hate speech.

The speech of *A*, then, deprives *B* of effective speech, the one value that a First Amendment absolutist cannot deny. Note that this deprivation stems not from a merely contingent connection such as that between money and speech—the Supreme Court has held that this does not rise to constitutional dimensions. Instead, credibility stands as a logical precondition for successful communication—no one credits a lunatic or pathological liar; even if he or she speaks the truth on occasion, most auditors would seek independent verification.

Credibility, of course, occupies a vital place in our system of law. Dozens of evidentiary doctrines determine when a witness's lack of credibility may bar him or her from speaking. Rules dealing with conflict of interest, child witnesses, and those who have earlier testified inconsistently aim to weed out testimony that lacks credibility. Cross-examination endeavors to assure the same end. In earlier eras we refused to hear the testimony of Chinese or black witnesses against parties who were white—we deemed them unworthy to perform that function.

On a larger scale, the political marketplace of ideas rests on an assumption similar to that of the adversary system; it too assumes that evidence and testimony presented by opposing sides will allow the truth to emerge. If our system of freedom of expression exists, in part, to permit a vigorous give-and-take of ideas and contributions on important social subjects, then one must view with concern any mechanism that systematically denies a blameless group its due efficacy and credibility. At one time we straightforwardly excluded women and nonwhite minorities from voting or giving courtroom testimony. Today, we accomplish a milder version of the same exclusion through media-delivered and individual messages that slander and demean. Like lies in court, hate speech subverts a principal premise of democracy.

"BUT FREE SPEECH MADE AMERICA GREAT"

Some liberals and free speech absolutists deplore hate speech but argue against its regulation on the ground that freedom of expression has been minorities' best friend. If they knew their own best interest, the argument goes, they would not be clamoring for its restriction. A realist view of history shows, however, that our system of free speech law has not always served as a staunch ally of minority interests. In the sixties, black protesters sat in and were arrested and convicted; marched and were arrested and convicted; picketed and were arrested and convicted. True, years later and at the cost of thousands of dollars of legal fees and many hours of heroic lawyering, some of their convictions were reversed on appeal. But not always; courts often concluded that their speech was too muscular—too intermixed with action—or too disruptive of property rights to risk reversal. *Speech* may have been a vital tool for organizing and for quickening America's conscience; *free speech law* (at least as then interpreted) was not.

Just as that body of law did not play a central role in advancing minorities' struggle for civil rights, it also has not invariably furthered other social goals. Many believe uncritically that free speech and the First Amendment have made America great. But consider: the U.S. today unquestionably leads the rest of the world in two principal areas—economic production and military might. Arguably, both flourished not because of freedom of expression but because of exceptions to it, such as patents, copyrights, trade secrets, and official (military) secrets. A truly free press and citizenry, able to speak, learn, and circulate ideas freely in these areas, would have interfered with the development of the prodigious industrial and military base that we now enjoy.

At the same time, hate speech and hard-core pornography, which until recently have enjoyed virtually free rein, contribute greatly to inequality and social pathology. In contrast to industrial and military production, which the American legal system favors by restrictions on speech, social relations among classes and groups receive less protection. If dominant groups may carelessly revile and disparage weaker ones, then it can hardly be a surprise that America ranks low among western industrialized nations in equality of wealth and income, and that the figures for infant mortality, life expectancy, and broken families in black and brown communities remain abysmal. It seems highly likely that tolerating virulent hate speech and vicious public depiction plays a part in allowing these forms of social misery to develop and persist. Free speech, then, did not make America great. It would be truer to say that the exceptions to it did, at the same time that the lack of regulation of hate speech contributed to social conditions that are becoming a source of national embarrassment. Legal-realist analysis would question the celebratory manner in which some equate free speech with a vehicle of progress, modernity, and social justice, and would aim instead for a more balanced approach that concedes that unregulated speech may sometimes exact a high cost.

THE BALANCE TODAY MAY BE TIPPING: HATE SPEECH IS NO LONGER A SOCIAL GOOD

Although hate speech may have abetted the preservation of a system of social stratification that brought at least some benefits to the ruling class—at a considerable cost to the minority class—the equation may be changing. Our society today is much more diverse than before. It is also more populous, and channels of communication place us in closer contact with each other than ever before, multiplying opportunities for friction. For all these reasons, society may need to begin imposing some limits on virulently antisocial discourse. Most other areas of law have witnessed healthy (perhaps inevitable) evolution stemming from these and other social changes—for example, recall how the law of personal jurisdiction has moved from mechanistic reliance on physical presence to a more multifaceted minimum contacts approach, under which a state may assert jurisdiction over defendants who have had certain contacts with it or its citizens. To meet the current challenges of global competition, society needs the contributions and enthusiastic participation of all its members. Now that the era of rapid, unrestrained development has passed, controls on hate speech, like the sexual harassment limits developed over the past few years, may begin to seem logical and necessary to all segments of society, irrespective of class or race distinctions. This is not to say that devising sensible rules will be easy. Even now, hate speech comes in a variety of forms, not all of which lend themselves to regulation. Moreover, the very idea of what hate speech is may change over time (just as the idea of what constitutes defamation or plagiarism has) and vary from group to group. Realism teaches that no static, across-the-board approach will work for something as complex as language.

FROM REALISM TO MORALITY AND POLITICS

Restraints may become politically and morally imperative as well. In former times, neorepublican and social-contractarian notions of government assumed that all citizens were capable of deliberating about the good. These theories assumed a relatively homogeneous society. In today's more diverse society, no single, simple definition of the common good is attainable. Permanent truces and agreements to tolerate divergent opinions could well be the best that society can hope to achieve.

One precondition to such a tolerant society could be an agreement not to denigrate other groups needlessly.

Dealing with hate speech may then turn out to be a pre-political normative reckoning necessary before deliberation among equals—the keystone of democracy—may occur. Without such a reckoning, genuine dialogue based on equal participation and respect will be scarce. The costs of a regime that tolerates hate speech will inevitably fall heavily on minorities. To put it in Kantian terms, one cannot will a universal rule tolerating hate speech, any more than one can consider that such practice treats people as ends in themselves. History informs the content of hate speech and the context in which a person experiences racial slurs. Thus, words such as "honky," "cracker," and "redneck" are insulting for white individuals, but nonetheless lack the socially and politically laden and corrosively dispiriting quality of words such as "nigger," "wop," "spic," "chink," or "kike." These terms carry a historical message that often multiplies their impact, whereas the derogatory forms for non-minorities, who do not have a history of persecution that used these terms as symbols, often experience slurs on an individual and isolated level.

The legal creation of the "suspect class" also demonstrates the importance of pre-political normative reckoning. Courts apply a higher standard of judicial review to laws that disadvantage insular and discrete minorities disadvantaged in the political process. This standard, which owes its origin to a famous footnote in *United States v. Carolene Products Co.,* buttresses what previous writers have posited: that equality (or equal respect) and free speech presuppose and depend upon each other. That is, without some basic level of social respect, free speech will merely compound social inequality, yet without a degree of freedom to speak, minorities will be unable to advocate for social advancement. Both free speech and the protection of equality, then, are linked—we must advance both at the same time, or we will have little of either.

The legal recognition and protection of social groups, such as racial minorities, remind us that some segments of society are disenfranchised, politically isolated, and socially marginalized. Speech that targets them—indeed, "constructs" them—must therefore stand on different footing from speech that targets, for example, wealthy industrialists who are well-represented in the political process and bear no comparably damaging historic stigma or stereotype. On this point, Shiffrin's insight about the role of dissent in curbing the excesses of the powerful is true and helpful. It enables us to see that we need not tolerate all speech, especially not that which victimizes those who are already marginalized, and, as mentioned earlier, functions as the opposite of dissent.

PART V
Law Reform

Before critical race theory had a name, Delgado wrote about law reform from a critical perspective. Anticipating a number of controversies by several years, he set forth his opinions on such subjects as parental preference and selective abortion, medical malpractice, and the failure of alternate dispute resolution to address the problems of minorities and women. His articles on the "rotten social background" defense, brainwashing, and mass torts have been excerpted in a number of casebooks and readers. His broad-ranging interests found expression in articles about law and medicine, science as a First Amendment activity, cults, and social psychology.

In "The Social Construction of *Brown v. Board of Education*," Delgado attributes the inability of that famous case to effect a hoped-for social revolution to a "reconstructive paradox," by which a reform movement will stall unless everything can change at once. Law reform, alone, proceeds incrementally; too much or too rapid change sparks societal resistance.

Environmental reform, based on the public trust model put forward by Joseph Sax, comes under analysis in the second selection. In it Delgado shows how a moderate reform, which arrives too early in a movement's life cycle, satisfies and pacifies the needs of the majority, making more progressive change harder, if not impossible, to achieve.

Delgado next examines, in "On Taking Back Our Civil Rights Promises," whether computer-assisted analysis of data enables lawyers to be more successful in bringing lawsuits on behalf of disadvantaged groups than before such data were available. He concludes that during this period, doctrinal retrenchment has taken place and that new sophisticated data that prove inequality seem not to have made much difference at all in achieving social justice.

Rodrigo reappears in the "Sixth Chronicle" to discuss issues of essentialism, intersectionality, and social reform with his mentor, the Professor. Their wide-ranging conversation centers on the pitfalls awaiting a small group that attaches itself to a larger group in search of reforms or changes. Goals and agendas can easily change course or disappear into the larger group's agenda when, for example, black feminists form coalitions with their white counterparts. Rodrigo advocates a pragmatic theory of social change that values justice, even disruptive justice, over an artificial condition of stability and peace.

The Social Construction of *Brown v. Board of Education*
Law Reform and the Reconstructive Paradox

Two broad views of *Brown v. Board of Education* compete in the public mind. The conventional view holds that *Brown* is one of the two or three most important cases in American legal history. According to this interpretation, *Brown* supplied the impetus for the modern civil rights movement, demonstrated that courts, at least at times, can assert moral leadership, and emphasized that African Americans are entitled to live in the United States on equal terms with whites.

The other view, that of the revisionists, holds that *Brown v. Board of Education* accomplished relatively little, either in the short or long run. Revisionists argue that *Brown* is the product of a momentary convergence between white and black interests that began to fade soon thereafter. Some of them even argue that landmark cases like *Brown* may impair the cause of black rights by inducing a mood of unwarranted euphoria among supporters while stiffening resistance on the part of diehards and white supremacists. Revisionists and conventionalists are apt to differ not only in their understanding of *Brown,* but in their interpretation of how social change occurs. In general, revisionists hold that social reform is difficult to achieve, especially through law, and that gains have a way of slipping back. The more sanguine conventionalists argue that if *Brown* has not brought about racial justice by itself, we can at least move closer to this goal through further effort. *Brown* has certainly helped; and if it has fallen short, what we need is a Brown III or a Brown IV.

Although these and other differences separate the revisionists and the conventionalists, in one respect they both approach *Brown* in the same manner. Each examines the situation that prevailed before and after *Brown* and asks: Did the landmark decision make a difference? Were the forces that led to the 1960s-era reforms already in motion before that famous case came down? Did *Brown* benefit white elites more than it benefited blacks? If it benefited blacks, did it help mostly middle-class members of this group, leaving the underclass as badly off as before? Both schools of thought, in short, examine *Brown* longitudinally and temporally, looking for evidence of causation or its lack. The argument has what we might call a vertical character: One lines up the situation that prevailed before *Brown,* and that after, and looks for signs that *Brown* brought about a difference.

This excerpt argues that an ignored, and equally vital, axis is horizontal. To understand *Brown*'s role, and that of law reform cases generally, one must attend to contemporaneous events in society at the time *Brown* was decided. Focusing on this other dimension enables us to understand why *Brown v. Board of Education* struck many as a breakthrough case, even though it failed to accomplish much outside the

HOW *BROWN* FAILED TO GENERALIZE

Many critics have pointed out that *Brown* accomplished relatively little in the way of school desegregation, except in the Deep South, and that black children are as likely today as they were forty years ago to attend predominantly black schools. To this, one could add doctrinal retrenchment in closely related areas. Although subsequent courts have left *Brown* standing, in the sense that they did not expressly overrule it, they have done much to cut back its effect. School districts may not enact metropolitan desegregation plans, at least in the absence of a showing of prior discrimination. Education is not a fundamental interest, nor poverty a suspect class. States are under no obligation to fund property-rich and property-poor districts equally. Segregation that results from white flight is essentially irremediable. Black male academies are unconstitutional, minority scholarships under fire, and affirmative action that takes the form of reserving slots in state-funded professional schools is illegal.

Why did *Brown* end up having so little effect, even in the area of school reform? Elsewhere, we have posited that social reform through law is relatively limited because law's scope is so narrow. Because every social practice is part of an interlocking system of other practices, meanings, and interpretations, changing just one element (for example, school assignment rules) leaves the rest unchanged. Thus, when the Supreme Court decided *Brown,* its ruling was soon robbed of much effect when, in a myriad of decisions, school officials, lower courts, sheriffs, and others interpreted *Brown* against the familiar background. "Of course, the Supreme Court didn't mean *that,*" they would reason in close cases. It is as though legal decisions take place against a gravitational field, with the pull being toward the familiar, toward stasis. Because *Brown* set out to change just one element, leaving the force-field itself intact, its effect quickly eroded. For social reform to happen, "everything must change at once," but in the law, doctrines such as stare decisis, standing, mootness, ripeness, and political question mean that the law cannot change everything at once. It can only decide the case before it.

Disbelieving or obstructionist officials are not the only forces that rob landmark decisions of much of their effect. If that were true, all that would be necessary would be vigilance and dogged enforcement. Rather, such decisions fail to establish themselves in the wider legal culture, so that even those who are generally sympathetic to reform fail to see their applications in closely related areas.

Consider, for example, the debate over campus hate-speech rules. Beginning about a decade ago, college and university administrators began noticing an upsurge in the number of racist insults, graffiti, and namecalling on their campuses. At some institutions, the number of students of color began to drop as parents decided to send their sons and daughters elsewhere. Many campuses responded by enacting anti-hate-speech rules that punished certain forms of racial or sexual taunting or namecalling. The rules sparked immediate resistance.

Brown at least had some effect. Today, a school official who might be tempted to assign all the black children to one school and the white ones to another, would likely think, "I had better not do that, at least unless I disguise what I am doing." Today's opponents of hate-speech rules, however, show little such hesitation; they proceed as though *Brown* had not taken place at all. Hate-speech rules are in many respects like student-assignment rules. Yet, opponents make the same arguments against them, the same rhetorical moves, that we witnessed with the classic resistance to school desegregation.

Under *Plessy v. Ferguson,* schemes that allocated benefits along racial lines were upheld, so long as the benefit blacks received was roughly comparable to that received by whites. In *Plessy,* blacks were forced to ride in one railroad car, whites in another. The Supreme Court upheld the railroad's rule: separate but equal. Whites and blacks were equally disadvantaged: neither could ride in the other's car. A similar situation prevailed in the schools of Topeka, Kansas, at the time *Brown* was decided. Indeed, shortly after the decision was announced, a famous constitutional scholar wondered if the decision was principled: Why should the rights of blacks to associate with whites trump those of whites *not* to associate with blacks? One right balanced another, one claim against its perfect reciprocal.

In the debate about hate speech, we find an identical structure. The white insists on a right to say whatever is on his mind. The black demands protection when what is on the white's mind is a direct face-to-face racial insult. One claims a right to do X, the other the right not to have X done to him. One right emanates from one part of the Constitution—the First Amendment—the other, from a different part—the Fourteenth Amendment. As with separate but equal, today's debate over hate speech features commentators insisting that the black's injury is all in his head. This feature parallels early cases in which the Supreme Court told Negroes that the indignity of being herded into separate railroad cars is offensive only if they put that construction on it. Today's opponents of hate-speech rules dismiss the black's injury as merely dignitary, and not a real harm. One well-regarded constitutional scholar recently rejected the "silencing" argument by pointing out that it requires mental mediation—the victim decides to remain silent. As with *Brown,* the opposition to hate-speech rules portrays itself as highly principled. It is not in favor of hate speech (heaven forbid). Rather, other, higher principles are at stake here.

WHY *BROWN* FAILED TO GENERALIZE

Brown effected little change in doctrine, consciousness, or the realities of life for black schoolchildren. Yet, society has constructed the decision as a breakthrough of momentous proportions. We believe the two observations are related. *Brown*'s sharp departure from the past caused it to stand out, to seem a breathtaking advance. This departure also assured that it would fail to "take"—would succumb to a kind of social gravity. Consider now in greater detail what that gravity is and a "reconstructive paradox" that affects all reform movements, especially those that rely heavily on law and litigation.

The Forces That Swallow Social Reform Decisions Like Brown

What we have described as a kind of social gravity that affects all novel social claims, especially legal ones, has at least three components: a system of meanings and interpretations against which the new rule must operate; a set of narratives or "stock stories" with which the new ruling must seek accommodation; and a set of social practices with which the new command must contend. Each of these components reduces the new decision's effect. Each is an aspect of what we called the horizontal dimension of a case, that which was taking place in society at the time the case comes down.

Meanings and Social Interpretations

Any text, including a legal one, is interpreted against a background of meanings, presumptions, and preexisting understandings. If a parent tells a child, "Clean up your room," the terms "clean" and "room" have relatively well agreed-upon meanings: The child knows he or she is not expected to launder the drapes or vacuum the attic space above the room. If an adolescent tells the parent, "I'll be back by midnight," both understand that "midnight" means tonight, not next week, and that "back" means inside the house. The same is true of legal commands. Thus, when *Brown* ordered school districts to desegregate "with all deliberate speed," southern officials interpreted the decree in terms of their common sense. In hundreds of close cases, they construed *Brown* to mean the only thing it could mean, consistent with their experience: integration that went not too far, not too fast, and that left the school system as intact as possible.

Operators of public beaches, restaurants, colleges, and other facilities interpreted *Brown* as affecting only schools. Some school officials even took the position that it bound only the districts before the court. To recalcitrant officials, *Brown* looked like an exception, an improbable edict that should naturally be interpreted in that light. The only way to harmonize it with common sense was to construe it narrowly: "Of course, the Supreme Court did not mean that blacks and whites are strictly equal," they told themselves. "They surely didn't mean that we would have to do *this*" (assign black principals to white schools; provide college counseling to all; adopt due process protections in school discipline cases affecting black children facing expulsion; and so on). Because the public interpreted *Brown* against the background of a myriad of such understandings, traditions, and expectations, and because, unlike a parent, the Supreme Court was not instantly available to clarify what it meant, the case had relatively little impact. It did change one thing, pupil assignment rules, but the rest of society remained much the same. The gain in this one area was quickly swallowed up by interpretive effects emanating from all the others.

Social Practices

A second component of the gravitational field is a vast set of preexisting social practices, most of which the Supreme Court is powerless to change. These include friendship patterns, the way a teacher looks at or responds to a black child, and that child's own self-concept and expectations with respect to treatment from whites. They include the ways in which librarians, bus drivers, shop owners, and landlords deal with the young black schoolchild and his or her family, and who is chosen for student body president, the debate team, and the cheerleading squad. If all of these practices remain the same while only school assignment rules change, a black child's life will not be greatly improved after *Brown* (and may be considerably worse).

Of course, a forced change in one social practice theoretically could prompt reconsideration of all the others. Because white schoolchildren now are required to attend school in a building that will house some blacks, the other social practices we have mentioned might begin to change. But everything we know about cognitive dissonance and resistance to the unfamiliar suggests the opposite. New practices that are discordant with old ones spark resistance and are adopted, if at all, slowly and grudgingly. New reasons are found to justify now disputed social practices.

The Role of Narratives

A final component of the social milieu that affects the reception of a legal decision or rule is the backdrop of narratives or stories against which the new element will be forced to operate. Narratives are the simple, script-like interpretive structures—"he hit first," "I didn't know it was yours," "majority rules," or "I've been here longer"—that we use in ordering our understanding of the world.

In the school desegregation setting, court decrees confront a whole host of narratives and social perceptions that generate resistance: "Neighborhood schools are best"; "who are these outsiders trying to tell us what to do?"; "our Negroes were happy until ... "; "black people just want to push into where they are not wanted"; "they want things they don't deserve and haven't earned"; "integration might be okay, but the schools should remain predominantly white, and the curriculum, teachers, and so on, roughly as they are now"; etc.

As with meanings and social practices, these and other narratives could theoretically change. A person who holds a stock of hundreds of such narratives regarding minority people, neighborhood schools, and "the way things are" could radically revise his or her worldview when confronted by the image of a surprisingly nice, intelligent, reasonable black individual at a school or work place. But narratives change very slowly, in part because we interpret new experiences and new narratives in terms of the old ones—the ones we hold. These old narratives, indeed, form the basis for understanding new experiences, including that of our first close black associate. It is far easier to pronounce the black an "exception" than to revise one's entire stock of beliefs.

Eventually, of course, stories and practices change. But this happens much more slowly than we like to think. And when it does, courts and decrees play little role in bringing about the change. Courts are usually distant institutions. Unlike flesh-and-blood persons, they cannot follow up an exchange by saying, for example: "No, he is not an exception; most of them are like that if you take the trouble to get to know them." Courts are not in a position to engage society in the kind of continuing dialogue that could in theory change meanings and practices. They can only change one practice at a time. Everything else—the entire system of practices, traditions, and meanings—remains the same, exerting its gravitational tug toward the familiar. In giving obedience to the new decree—something the courts *are* in a position to enforce—hundreds of lower-level bureaucrats, state officials, and lower court judges will interpret the ringing words according to their common sense understandings about persons, relations, and what is just and deserved.

The Reconstructive Paradox

The combined effect of the forces just mentioned means that any reform measure other than the smallest and most incremental will meet predictable resistance, reinterpretation, and obstruction in ways that the legal system is ill equipped to manage and counter. One perspective from which to view these horizontal forces is in terms of what we call the "reconstructive paradox." After defining the paradox, we illustrate its operation by demonstrating that the current approach to race and race remedies shows the influence of the nineteenth-century cases, especially *Plessy v. Ferguson,* more than that of their more famous twentieth-century rival, *Brown v. Board of Education.*

Defining the Reconstructive Paradox

1. The greater a social evil (for example black subordination), the more it is apt to be entrenched in our national life.
2. The more entrenched the evil, the more massive the social effort that will be necessary to eradicate it.
3. The harm of an entrenched evil will be invisible to many because it is embedded and ordinary.
4. The massive social effort mentioned in number two will inevitably collide with other social values and things we hold dear (for example, settled expectations, religion, the family, privacy, the southern way of life, etc.). It will entail dislocations, shifts in spending priorities, new taxes, and changes in the way we speak and relate to each other.
5. These efforts, by contrast, will be highly visible and will spark resistance and accusations that the backers are engaging in totalitarian tactics, siding with big government, disadvantaging innocent whites, operating in derogation of the merit principle, elevating group over individual rights, reviving old grudges, whipping up division where none existed before, and so on.
6. Resisting these latter complaints will feel right and proper, for the other side will appear to be callously sacrificing real liberty, real security, and real resources for a nebulous goal.

Therefore, reconstruction will always strike many as unprincipled, unwarranted, and wrong. Little surprise, then, that few take up its cause, persist long in the face of the resistance, or even frame their programs and objectives broadly enough so that if they are adopted, they have a chance of remaining in place and achieving some real effects.

Back to Plessy and Dred Scott: *Present-Day Rhetoric and Evidence of the Reconstructive Paradox Operating in Our Time*

Reform through *law alone,* as we mentioned, is apt to have little effect, because legal decrees succumb silently to interpretation and other forms of cultural weight. Even when, as happened with the civil rights revolution of the 1960s, legal reform aligns with broader social forces to produce undeniable and much-needed gains, resistance is apt to set in at some point. Consider how today we no longer talk in terms of separateness as an inherent injury, of black schoolchildren as victims, or of racism as a harm whose injury "is unlikely ever to be undone." Instead, we speak of the need for formal neutrality, of the dangers affirmative action poses for innocent whites, and of the need for black Americans to look to their own resources. Moderates and conservatives alike have rolled back affirmative action and challenged university and college theme houses, special curricula, and ethnic studies departments, which they see as violations of the principle of fair and equal treatment. Courts are quick to strike down set-aside programs and affirmative action plans as "quota systems" likely to discriminate against "innocent whites." The narrative of *Plessy v. Ferguson* more aptly characterizes our attitudes with respect to race than do the stirring words of *Brown.*

In *Plessy,* United States Supreme Court Justice Brown could not see anything wrong with a system that required blacks to sit in separate railroad cars, overlooking the unmistakable damage inflicted on blacks' sense of dignity by such a discriminatory system. Indeed, he wrote:

> We consider the underlying fallacy of the plaintiff's argument to consist in the assumption that the enforced separation of the two races stamps the colored race with a badge of inferiority. If this be so, it is not by reason of anything found in the act, but solely because the colored race chooses to put that construction upon it.

In a recent case, *City of Memphis v. Greene,* Justice Stevens declared that a municipal decision to separate a white neighborhood from a black one by allowing the construction of a wall between them to regulate traffic flow was fair and not motivated by an intention to discriminate against blacks, but rather by an "interest in protecting the safety and tranquillity of a residential neighborhood." Echoing the earlier opinion of Justice Brown in *Plessy,* Stevens wrote:

> Because urban neighborhoods are so frequently characterized by a common ethnic or racial heritage, a regulation's adverse impact on a particular neighborhood will often have a disparate effect on an identifiable ethnic or racial group. To regard

an inevitable consequence of that kind as a form of stigma so severe as to violate the Thirteenth Amendment would trivialize the great purpose of that charter of freedom.

In both cases, separated by nearly a century, during which much progress in race relations was said to have been made, blacks confronted rhetorical trickery that tests both their ability to participate in society-wide self-deception and their inclination to prevail in spite of it.

Other modern-era cases show the same tendency to disregard blacks' long-standing predicament or whites' contribution to it. Because *Brown* only addressed the effects of segregated education on black schoolchildren, remaining silent on the issue of white responsibility, it was perhaps inevitable that the question of fault would become the next hurdle to blacks struggling to achieve social gains. *Washington v. Davis* is perhaps the most well-known example, but a number of others have followed suit. In *Arlington Heights v. Metropolitan Housing Development Corp.,* the Court held that zoning regulations that had excluded blacks were constitutionally valid because they were not enacted with that purpose in mind. *San Antonio Independent School District v. Rodriguez* upheld a school finance scheme that caused a great disparity in funding tax-rich and tax-poor schools despite its serious impact on poor and minority children. And, as mentioned earlier, *Greene* deemed a traffic control measure that took the form of a wall between white and black neighbors in Memphis as just that, a traffic control measure, despite the way in which it physically and symbolically separated the races.

Each of these cases foreshadows a retreat from the ringing words of *Brown*; each is reminiscent of the crabbed neutrality and unrealistic refusal to see discrimination that characterized *Plessy*. Not only has our time implicitly resurrected *Plessy* in its approach to racial justice, but a second notorious nineteenth century case's star is rising: the *Civil Rights Cases*. There, the Supreme Court wrote that blacks who were demanding equal access to various types of public accommodation were seriously overstepping and in effect demanding to be afforded special treatment. The Court wrote:

> When a man has emerged from slavery, and by the aid of beneficent legislation has shaken off the inseparable concomitants of that state, there must be some stage in the progress of his elevation when he takes the rank of a mere citizen, and ceases to be the special favorite of the laws, and when his rights as a citizen, or a man, are to be protected in the ordinary modes by which other men's rights are protected.

Cases in our time show much the same attitude. Blacks' demands for justice are themselves unjust, because they are a form of asking for special treatment and because they encroach on white privilege and settled expectations. [Eds. Delgado discusses a number of such cases.]

The most startling parallel is found in *City of Richmond v. J.A. Croson Co.,* where the Court struck down a minority set-aside program in the construction industry that the Richmond city council had adopted. The majority opinion found the council's action a potential case of "simple racial politics." A concurring opinion went even further, warning that society should be watchful against those who might attempt to "even the score" at the expense of whites.

Societal rhetoric follows suit. A host of commentators today rail against multicultural programs on university campuses; minority-only scholarships are under fire; welfare programs are under sustained attack as disguised give-aways to undeserving, unambitious, and oversexed blacks; and the use of code-words, like "political correctness," indicates that many in our society believe that blacks have gone too far. They are now receiving special, not just equal treatment. It is time to put a stop to it.

We believe, then, that dispassionate examination of today's dominant narratives shows that the themes of *Plessy* and the *Civil Rights Cases* are in ascension. We put forward an even more somber prediction: Without concerted action or a sharp change in national circumstances, one final step will be taken. Just as the clock of time seems to be rolling backward, a final narrative may soon regain prominence: that of *Dred Scott v. Sandford.*

In *Dred Scott,* the Supreme Court, in a case concerning a runaway slave, held that African Americans have "no rights which the white person is bound to respect." The claim of an African American to citizenship was absurd, both historically and legally: Blacks simply were not citizens because they never were and the framers of the Constitution, "great men," never regarded them that way. *Dred Scott* constitutes, certainly, the nadir of American law's treatment of African Americans, a blot on the record of the American legal conscience. Yet, its narrative retains vitality today. We see growing evidence of it in Supreme Court opinions and in popular culture.

Justice Taney's opinion depicted blacks as subhumans. Is this shocking portrayal of other beings so far from today's range of possibilities? Is the story of the primitive bestial black or Mexican completely missing in today's narratives, both in popular culture and in judicial opinions? No. Indeed, this account of groups of color is undergoing a resurgence.

Consider, for example, the revival of race-IQ theories, some seconded by well-regarded scientists and writers such as Charles Murray, Richard Herrnstein, Arthur Jensen and William Shockley. Consider the number of books, such as Ben Wattenberg's *The Birth Dearth,* and reports that have urged renewed attention to the question of selective breeding: Our "best" citizens have too few children; minorities and the poor, too many, so that the gene pool in the United States is declining. Consider the resurgence of nativism and movements to close the nation's borders particularly to brown-skinned immigrants. Consider also the English-Only movement. Much of this attitude is fueled by the conviction that "those people" are not fit to reside here, that their language, customs, and morals are inferior, and that they are and always will be second-class citizens. All of these cultural strands converge around the idea that this is a white country and that nonwhite persons, genes, ideas, languages, and culture are inferior to European ones, a principal theme in *Dred Scott.*

In *McCleskey v. Kemp,* the Supreme Court considered a challenge to Georgia's infliction of the death penalty, which fell disproportionately heavily on blacks, particularly ones whose victims were white. The Court rejected McClesky's claim, at the same time reprimanding him and his lawyers for even having brought it. Such claims, based on statistical disparities, might be raised in virtually any setting, the Court reasoned, resulting in repetitive demands "based upon any arbitrary variable." Cases brought by poor women—*Wyman v. James* (the welfare-search case), *Maher v. Roe,* and other abortion-funding cases—show the same thinly veiled exasperation on the part of the Court. These decisions stop barely short of telling poor women that they do not know their places and what is expected of them—to be as quiet, prudent, nondemanding, and nonsexual as possible. The demand for privacy in the face of a welfare inspection, or for an abortion from a state-funded clinic, appears outrageous. The women are chastised for the effrontery of wanting to live life on their own terms.

* * *

Brown, like all law reform cases, confronted built-in resistances that deprived it of the efficacy its supporters hoped for it. Social reform proceeds, if at all, in small increments; the pendulum swing is as apt to be backward at any given time as forward. *Brown*'s relatively slight effect is part of a broader form of social response—the reconstructive paradox—which holds that the greater the evil, the greater the need for reform; the greater the reform effort, the more unprincipled and unjust the effort will seem, and the greater the resistance it will generate. Even more than other avenues for reform, law is handicapped by its inability to engage in dialogue with the group whose values and practices need changing. Except in criminal law, where it can put violators in jail, law has little ability to provide the constant reinforcement necessary to change attitudes or behavior. Indeed, law is always outnumbered; doctrines such as standing ensure that any wide-ranging legal edict appears incomprehensible and wrong, evoking the reaction: Surely the court didn't mean *that.*

If we are right, reformers should hesitate to place much faith in the legal system as their primary instrument. Law is relatively powerless to effect social revolutions as both theory and history, including the case of *Brown,* demonstrate. Everything must change at once, so that a far greater focus than the merely legal is necessary before reform begins to be possible. Because the reconstructive paradox has greatest force with respect to courts, reformers ought to reserve judicial activism for the later stages of a revolution, using courts for the final mopping up steps to secure a social advance that society has already begun to accept.

Litigation is expensive and frustrating if conducted at the wrong time. We urge that reformers reconsider the appropriate time to use it. If employed too early, as it arguably may have been with *Brown,* it leads to false celebration, then disillusionment by persons who, like African Americans, have waited too long to see their just demands met—then betrayed.

~

Joseph Sax, the Public Trust Theory of Environmental Protection, and Some Dark Thoughts on the Possibility of Law Reform

When Professor Joseph Sax wrote his famous *Public Trust* article in 1970, the environmental movement was in a state of agitation and flux. Commentators were writing about *Ways Not to Think About Plastic Trees,* and whether we should bestow legal rights on natural objects. The Green Movement had taken hold in Europe, and in the United States scholars, activists, and ordinary citizens were calling for greater attention to decreasing quality of life, increasing pollution, and overdevelopment of the nation's farm and wilderness lands.

The time was exactly right for Sax's article. Sax proposed a simple, easily understood, and intuitively appealing approach to environmental protection. Because the nation's natural resources and parklands are limited commodities which, if too rapidly consumed, will not be available to ourselves and later generations, Sax argued, we should regard ourselves as trustees who hold these precious goods for the benefit of all. The nation's rivers, beaches, and other natural resources are not ours alone to spend; we must deplete them judiciously, setting aside as much as prudence dictates for our own use and that of future generations.

Sax's idea caught on quickly, influencing the National Environmental Policy Act and every environmental law casebook, hornbook, and law review article. Courts have cited it heavily.

This excerpt argues that Sax's public trust doctrine is a seriously flawed solution to our environmental crisis. Its answer—to regard the nation's environmental resources as goods held in trust—forestalled more searching reconsideration of our environmental predicament and postponed, perhaps indefinitely, the moment when society would come to terms with environmental problems in a serious and far-reaching way.

One can generalize the lesson of Sax's trust approach as follows: Most serious reform movements fail because society prefers incremental rather than wide-ranging change. In a version of the maxim that "bad money drives out good," we invariably find ourselves drawn to doomed, moderate approaches, like Sax's, when society needs more sweeping, ambitious ones. We resist precisely the medicine that could save us. We turn to strong solutions only when it is either too late, or when our thinking has advanced so far that the solutions seem commonplace and tame.

SAX'S ARTICLE: THE PUBLIC TRUST DOCTRINE IN ENVIRONMENTAL LAW

In his 1970 article and later work, Sax sets out his theory of environmental protection: that natural resources ought to be regarded as goods held in common. Because these goods are to be enjoyed by all, the government must assume a trust-like duty not to waste or expend them for the benefit of just a few. Further, the state must take into account future users—later generations who will be harmed if society depletes or damages the environment in irreversible ways.

Sax derives his doctrine from Roman law and traces it to early Supreme Court decisions in which the Court used trust language to protect shores, rivers, and other water-related resources. Although Sax initially applied the trust doctrine to water conservation, later commentators have urged its extension to dry beaches, wildlife, and parks, a suggestion that some states have adopted. The status of the public trust theory today seems secure; it has influenced legislation, case law, and, indeed, our basic thinking about the environment. The National Environmental Policy Act (NEPA) reflects trust notions, as do the federal Clean Water Act, Endangered Species Act, and environmental statutes in many states. The public trust theory has received criticism from a few conservative scholars as an impediment to economic development and by a few on the environmental fringe as unduly homocentric. Yet it seems to have withstood all such criticism and is today the leading approach to protection of the environment and natural resources. Even in areas where direct influence is difficult to trace, the doctrine marked out a realm of the "ideal," so that commentators often evaluated judicial and legislative actions in terms of it.

WHAT'S WRONG WITH THE TRUST SYSTEM OF ENVIRONMENTAL PROTECTION

Sax's public trust theory won widespread approval and was adopted into law. In the process, it inhibited the development of other approaches that would have enabled us—and might still—to cope better with our environmental problems. It can easily discourage innovative environmental thought. A trust is, by its nature, conservative—its purpose is to protect a corpus and put it to some use. The idea is to protect what one has, to reduce the risk of improvidence or improper expenditure. Trusts aim to serve an already defined purpose, not to prompt consideration of what that purpose should be. One establishes a trust for a child's college education, for example, once one has decided the child should attend college, not to prompt the child to reflect about his or her future, or about whether he or she should attend college, much less about whether college education, as currently constituted, is good or ideal.

In this view, the trust theory arrived on the scene too early in our debate about the environment, before we had explored adequately humanity's relationship with the environment. In short, the fit between it and the stage of social dialogue was poor. Yet something about it attracted us and made us adopt it—made us seize it before we knew precisely what we were protecting and to what extent. The trust theory froze thinking on our relationship to nature in the form in which it stood in the early 1970s. Serious reflection on environmental questions continued, of course, but in marginalized forms and confined to the pages of fringe journals and books. It was no longer center stage as it was during the period just prior to the advent of Sax's theory.

The public trust theory is also poorly suited to advance natural values. The approach places protection of the environment in the hands of a trustee, generally some agent of the sovereign, who receives a set of instructions and is told to protect the environment accordingly. Unfortunately, the trustee in whose hands the environment is placed is not in the classical position of trustee. Typically a government agency, it will be in no better position to understand how the environment is to be protected than we are.

Frequently, the impulse for setting up a trust is lack of confidence; we fear that we may act irresponsibly with respect to the valued good (say, a sum of money), so we place it in the hands of another whom we instruct to act in accord with our better natures—in the way we would act if we were trustworthy. Consider educational trusts, for example. In our society, men often are conditioned to measure their success by material gains, while women are conditioned to value responsibility to others, particularly their children. Men often set up trusts for their children's college education because they fear that otherwise they might spend the money on a sports car or European vacation. Women—and men who have developed a more immediate connection with their children—are less likely to resort to a trust; spending the children's college money on a consumer item simply is not a serious temptation. To the extent that this is true, one might say that Sax's reliance on a trust model is a particularly male approach to guarding against overconsumption of limited resources.

One of the reasons why we establish trusts, then, is that we sense in ourselves a dark impulse to act in ways that go against our better natures. This is particularly true with respect to environmental values. All of us, especially men, know that we have impulses to hunt, mine, dam, or cut things down—to treat nature, in short, in ways that contravene our collective ideals, which are not to hunt, mine, dam, and so on, to excess. Both men and women, in addition, often desire an easier, more resource- and energy-intensive life. Sax and other serious environmentalists know this—that if we are left to balance environmental values against short-term pleasure or economic gain, we are likely to favor the latter. But this goes against our ideal natures, hence we relinquish control over the valued object, like Ulysses who lashed himself to the mast to avoid succumbing to the sirens' song.

Nothing is wrong with the trust model. It can be a useful device in many situations. But in wilderness preservation, the trust approach may founder because the trustee will share the very same values we hold. Thus, the trustee will construe our wishes against a background of the same cultural assumptions, values, and meanings that we hold, and that render us poor defenders of the thing in question.

This is much more troublesome in connection with the environment than with areas where bright-line treatment is possible ("Issue Junior four hundred dollars a month as long as he remains a full-time student in an accredited college with a GPA above 2.5"). Environmental protection entails trade-offs and judgment calls. If the trustees—for example, government agencies—are prone to make the same mistakes we would, little gain is likely to accrue from transferring defense of the environment to them.

This is, of course, what has happened. Government trustees at both the federal and state level have done little to stop deterioration of air and water quality, to protect endangered environments from the growing problem of toxic wastes, and to protect endangered species. Certainly, they have generated little in the way of creative, wide-ranging thought about environmental questions; their role has been bureaucratic, routinized, and contained. Yet the public and scholarly community have reacted as though environmental issues are solved, or at least in capable hands. Self-scrutiny has ceased, with the result that several promising approaches to humanity's relationship with the natural world have not been developed.

Sax's public trust theory won rapid and widespread acceptance during a time of considerable agitation when new theories and approaches to environmental protection were under discussion. The trust approach stilled much of that fervor. [Eds. Delgado next considers Aldo Leopold's system of earth-centered ethics, Native American thought, and ecofeminism.]

Each of these approaches to environmental protection was put on the back burner when Sax's public trust theory appeared on the scene. In the meantime, our environmental problems have worsened. Halfway measures have proven ineffectual, and within the near future we surely again will have to reconsider our relationship to the natural world. We missed an opportunity in the 1970s, one whose loss we have only recently begun to appreciate. Was this inevitable—and what does this missed opportunity mean for our prospects for achieving social and legal reform in general?

THE CAREER OF SAX'S PUBLIC TRUST THEORY: WHAT IT ILLUSTRATES FOR LEGAL REFORM

One can generalize from society's experience with Sax's public trust theory of environmental protection as follows. Recall how during the middle years of the century, American society began to realize that unlimited exploitation of our natural resources could not continue much longer. We began to doubt the old ethic that prevailed during our period of rapid expansion, permitting practically any form of development or use of public lands that did not positively injure another person and that a majority of the citizenry would tolerate. After several decades of increasing ferment—which included a proliferation of creative essays and books addressing such basic environmental questions as: Why protect the natural environment? What status shall we afford natural objects and our wilderness heritage?—matters were ripe for a revolution in consciousness. Americans reached a collective decision that something had to be done. Business and a few others resisted change; members of "deep ecology," admirers of Aldo Leopold, and ecofeminists advocated far-reaching changes.

Hoping to capitalize on the manifest failures of the old mine-it-dam-it-cut-it-down approach, members of the latter groups wrote books, spoke at rallies, and organized political campaigns around the issue of environmental protection. Their programs were not particularly normative; they did not need to be. Rather, they rested on shrewd observation and imaginative (and for some, unflattering) reconceptions of how our relationship to nature could be.

Normativity was turned against them, however. As is generally the case when a paradigm change is in the wind, society welcomed normative analysis to: (1) praise and embrace the just-begun reforms; and (2) condemn the more ambitious reform programs as extreme and dangerous. There almost always arises, at exactly this point in historic transformations, a savior—an individual who captures the legitimate need for reform, as well as society's need to assure that matters do not change too far or too fast, an individual who sincerely condemns the old order, thereby assuring that the revolution has a ratchet effect—won't slip back—yet offers the assurance that the new paradigm is not too different from the old. We condemn and abandon the old order only when we are certain that the new one is not more discomforting than necessary.

In the environmental revolution, that savior was Joseph Sax, whose trust theory, *Mountains Without Handrails,* and other landmark works established his credentials as a serious reformer. At the same time, his public trust article dealt the coup de grace to environmentalists who were pushing for a radical transformation. His theory, then, was in some ways forward-looking, an imaginative, pragmatic—even gallant—effort to save the environment from further deterioration. Yet the theory won wide support largely because it did not promise far-reaching environmental protection. It offered exactly what society needs during the middle and late stages of a revolution—a way of confining change to a manageable level.

Sax's public trust doctrine was attractive because it offered protection from our base instincts. It enabled us to tell ourselves that we no longer needed to worry about the dark sides of our natures. It enabled us to tell ourselves and each other that we had finally done something about the environment. Yet by placing control over natural resources and wilderness areas in government agencies run by people like us, we could feel sure that familiar, comfortable values would shape and restrain environmental decisionmaking. The ecofeminists and others advocating sweeping change were shut out. The problem was taken care of in a way that would not change anything too fundamentally—which was all to the good.

On Taking Back Our Civil Rights Promises
When Equality Doesn't Compute

Only some twenty years old, the information revolution has already subtly altered the landscape of legal disputing. Although most of the changes to date have been facilitative—enabling us to do better the things we did before, such as researching cases, preparing documents, analyzing evidence, and billing clients—in one area the impact is likely to be powerfully substantive as well. This area is civil rights, where the advent of computers and sophisticated methods of statistical proof portends sobering changes in the way we think about equality and racial justice. My reasons for believing so consist of two observations plus a prediction. The first observation is that computer-assisted analysis of data has enabled us to prove inequality more powerfully than ever before. Inequality between blacks and whites, men and women, young and old can be made to stand out like figures carved in a mountainside, so boldly and clearly that no one can deny its existence. The potential for demonstrating this existed, of course, in the pencil and paper age. But computers enable us to show patterns of difference quickly, economically, and with any confidence level we see fit to require. The proof-of-facts side of a civil rights lawyer's life has thus taken a marked turn for the better.

My second observation concerns the law's response to this development. And that response has been, simply, doctrinal retrenchment. Rather than accept at face value the evidence tendered by attorneys for African Americans, Latinos, women, and others, our system has been telling them, "You have misconceived our promises of equality. Equality does not mean what you thought, and under the new, narrower version we hereby announce, you cannot prevail." This doctrinal retrenchment has exactly paralleled the advances in factual proof, so that the net result is zero: redress for most forms of race- and sex-based discrimination remains just as difficult as before.

My final step consists of a prediction—that the process described above is on a collision course with itself. The taking back of civil rights promises is producing a gap between our story of origins and that contained in current civil rights law. When this gap reaches a certain point a crisis will occur, and one of two things will happen.

Either our system will adjust the current story in the direction of the original version, or we will abandon our story of origins and drop the fiction that we are a nation committed to equal justice. The forces propelling us toward this confrontation are already in operation.

PROOF OF INEQUALITY: WHAT COMPUTERS AND STATISTICAL ANALYSIS CAN DO

Computers can carry out swiftly and accurately sophisticated statistical analyses of large amounts of data. They can hold certain variables constant and look for the effect of others (such as race or sex). They can analyze the contribution of dozens of variables at once. They can test hypotheses, analyze variance, and determine when and with what degree of confidence we can assert that a pattern is unlikely to be the result of chance.

Lawyers have used computer-generated data in suits brought by women alleging unequal pay, compared to men, in particular job categories, and even greater inequality for work of comparable worth. Black litigants have used statistical data to show that patterns of hiring, promotion, and firing for blacks are worse than for whites and that these patterns cannot be explained by chance. Lawyers have used computerized data to show racial disparities in sentencing patterns and in the rates at which probation and parole are granted and the death penalty imposed.

Investigators and advocates for blacks have shown that blacks' income is lower than whites', a difference that cannot be accounted for by years of seniority or education. They have shown black-white gaps with respect to longevity, infant mortality, income, wealth, rates of criminal conviction, suicide and other forms of self-endangerment, mental illness, and drug addiction. They have shown that the disparities between whites and blacks on most of these measures are growing, not closing, that the degree of residential segregation is increasing in America's neighborhoods, and that racial attitudes are hardening, not softening.

Attorneys have used statistical analysis to examine the decisions of particular courts or even individual judges in search of an unbiased forum—or, sometimes, one biased in their favor. None of these tasks was impossible in the pre-computer age; computers simply made them faster and easier.

LAW'S RESPONSE TO THE INEQUALITY EXPLOSION: RETRENCHMENT AND THE REPHRASING OF PROMISES

Aided by computerized analysis, attorneys have been vigorously pressing actions on behalf of disadvantaged groups. Initially some of these claims were successful, but recently successes have become rarer. Instead, what we have seen is doctrinal retrenchment; as the factual predicate for inequality claims advanced, legal doctrine retreated. The circle of redressable racism shrank as courts required proof of intent to discriminate and demanded tight chains of causation. Changes arrived in standing to sue, limitations on state action, and the type of relief allowed. Disparate impact was sharply curtailed, and in *McCleskey v. Kemp,* the Supreme Court devalued statistical proof—which all but the most skeptical would have found convincing—that blacks are executed in Georgia more frequently than whites. Thus, our response to blacks' "You promised" has been, in effect, "No, we didn't." Scarcely unprecedented—in everyday life we often do the same thing when reminded of promises we now find inconvenient. Yet, the consequences of repudiating our civil rights promises are greater than with ordinary ones, endangering the uneasy social contract among citizens in our society.

THE FOUNDING STORY AND CURRENT ANTIDISCRIMINATION LAW: CLOSING THE GAP BETWEEN "THAT WAS THEN" AND "THIS IS NOW"

Antidiscrimination law today increasingly exhibits an ectoplasmic quality—thin and more than a little pale. Its promises ring hollow. But the hollowness is not that of the parent who, having promised his child something, tells him or her that the promised item will not be forthcoming—straightforward breach. Rather, it is that of the parent who insists that the promised thing was another, less desirable, item entirely. A parent who does this too often, however, courts trouble; sooner or later the child will demand an explanation. The growing enfeeblement of civil rights law will spur a similar demand. In the ensuing accounting, our starting point will be the original promises—those constitutive ideals, principles, and narratives that form our founding story. That story, our story of origins, holds that our nation was founded on mutuality and equal personhood. All men are created equal and endowed with fundamental human rights. What is more, those truths are not just contingently, but self-evidently so; they are in the nature of things and supply the glue we rely on to form a more perfect union.

This founding story accompanies narratives emanating from dominant codes of ethics and the Judeo-Christian tradition. In this tradition, all persons are equal in the sight of God. We must act toward others as we would have them act toward us, respecting their humanity just as we respect our own. We must love other persons as ourselves.

This founding story is taught in our schools, preached in our churches, and enshrined in song and literature. It is part of our self-concept as a generous and inclusive people. Yet, alongside that story is set a much more somber one, a story of nonwhite people caught in poverty, neglect, and despair. In this other story, inequality is everywhere, and is everywhere unredressed. Law's story today tells blacks, "You may recover, but only if you satisfy us that your grievance meets our definition of racism, which is of course much narrower than yours. Moreover, you must satisfy requirements A through E and rebut several defenses that we have decided to let the other side use against you. You must wait several years for relief, and your measure of damages should you be successful will be less than you might have envisioned. Do you want to proceed?" Law's story and our story of origins cannot co-exist much longer; the differences between them are becoming too great. Soon we will have to decide between two ways of closing the gap. We can adjust current reality in the direction of the original promises. Or, we can decide in favor of present reality and forfeit our ideals. The former course would entail putting new vitality back into civil rights law. We could ease the requirements of intent and of near-straight line causation. We could define redressable discrimination more broadly and take firmer steps to remedy inequality even when it does not result from intentional discrimination. We could re-examine the many qualifications, exceptions, and defenses we have engrafted in antidiscrimination law. By such measures we could indicate to outgroups that we are serious about including them in our community. This course is costly; it will entail relinquishing privileges and prerogatives that many of us now enjoy. We may well decide not to pay this price. The alternative, however, is also costly. Its price is the admission that our founding story, with its myths about brotherhood, equality, and redress of grievances, is just that: a collection of myths. We will then confront the somber realization that, as a people, we are not serious about equality, that we embrace inequality and status so long as they benefit us, and that in these respects we are no different from the many nations that willingly accept permanent, ineradicable divisions of race, sex, and caste.

* * *

Computers and statistical analysis enable us to prove inequality and unequal treatment more compellingly than ever before. But as our ability to prove the facts necessary to sustain a discrimination case has advanced, legal doctrine has retreated, with the result that civil rights claims are exactly as difficult to win as before. As modern methods of proof shone a bright light on the inequality in our world, we dimmed the lights in doctrine, not wanting to see what was there.

But this has only postponed the moment of reckoning. The inequality we banished by verbal trickery from our field of vision now shows up in our spectacles. Doctrine's enfeeblement is now visible to all; its promises no longer come close to matching those contained in our story of origins. Potential claimants are beginning to realize that our once-proud system of civil rights statutes and case law is not for their benefit, that it has little to do with equal justice. We are thus entering the first stage of a civil rights crisis precipitated by this growing realization. Only two paths lead out. We can adjust the promises contained in civil rights law back in the direction of the original ones. Or, we can abandon our story of origins and face the realization that we are no longer committed to the vision of equality and racial justice it contains. Our decision will say much about what kind of people we are and will become. To say that much will ride on it is an understatement.

Rodrigo's Sixth Chronicle
Intersections, Essences, and the Dilemma of Social Reform

INTRODUCTION: IN WHICH RODRIGO TELLS ME ABOUT AN URGENT PROBLEM

I was returning to my office from the faculty library one flight below, annoyed that the book I hoped to find was off the shelf and not checked out, when I spied a familiar figure waiting outside my door.

"Rodrigo!" I said. "It's good to see you. Please come in."

I had not seen my young protégé in a while. A graduate of a fine law school in Italy, Rodrigo had returned to the United States recently to begin LL.M. studies at a well-known school across town in preparation for a career as a law professor. An African American by birth and ancestry, the talented Rodrigo had sought me out over the course of a year to discuss Critical Race Theory and many other ideas. For my part, I had gratefully used him as a foil and a sounding board for my own thoughts.

"Have a seat. You look a little agitated. Is everything OK?" Rodrigo had been pacing my office while I was putting my books down and activating my voice mail. I hoped it was intellectual excitement and his usual high-pitched energy that accounted for his restless demeanor.

"Professor, I'm afraid I'm in some trouble. Do you have a few minutes? There's something I need to talk over with someone older and wiser."

"I'm definitely older," I said. "The other part I'm not sure about. What's happening?"

"A big feud is going on in the Women's Law Caucus at my school. The women of color and the white members are going at it hammer and tongs. And like a dummy, I got caught right in the middle."

"You? How?" I asked.

"I'm not a member. I don't think any man is. But Giannina is an honorary member, as I think I mentioned once. The Caucus has tried to keep its struggle quiet, but I learned about it from Giannina. And I'm afraid I really—how do you put it?—put my foot in the mouth."

"In your mouth," I corrected. Although Rodrigo had been born in the States and spent his early childhood here, he occasionally failed to use an idiom correctly, a difficulty I had observed with other foreigners. "Tell me more," I continued. "How did it happen? Is it serious?"

"It's extremely serious," said Rodrigo, leaping to his feet and resuming his pacing. "They were having a meeting down in the basement, where I went after class to pick up Giannina. We were going to catch the subway home, and I thought her meeting would be over by then. I stood at the door a minute, when a woman I knew motioned me in. That was my mistake."

"Are the meetings closed to men?"

"I don't think so. But I was the only man there at the time. They were talking about essentialism—as I've learned to call it—and the organization's agenda. A woman of color was complaining that the group paid too little attention to the concerns of women like her. Some of the white women were getting upset. I made the mistake of raising my hand."

"What did you say?"

"I only tried to help analyze some of the issues. I drew a couple of distinctions, or tried to anyway. Both sides got mad at me. One called me an imperial scholar, an interloper, a typical male, and a pest. I got out of there fast. And now, no one will talk to me. Even Giannina made me move out of the bedroom. I've been sleeping on the couch for the last three nights. I feel like a leper."

A quarrel between lovers! I had not had to deal with one of those since my sons were young. "I'm sure you and she will patch it up," I offered. "You'd better—the two of you owe me dinner, remember?"

Rodrigo was not cheered by my joke nor my effort to console him. "I may never have Giannina's companionship again," he said, looking down.

"These things generally get better with time," I said. "It's part of life. But if talking would help, I'm game. I've been reading these things," I gestured toward some of the books and law review articles I had just carried up from the library, "on essentialism and feminist legal theory. They're for an annotated bibliography I'm preparing."

Rodrigo peered over at the pile on the corner of my desk. "I read that one last night. And I'm reading the two articles now. If you have the time, I'd love to talk. Since no one else will talk to me, I've got lots of time on my hands."

"Me too," I said. "Would you like a cup of coffee before we start?"

"I'd love one. I've been too distraught to eat."

I busied myself grinding the beans and setting the dials on my office espresso maker. "So, tell me what you know about essentialism. You like cream and sugar, right?"

Rodrigo nodded. After I left the machine to its own devices and returned to my chair, he began.

IN WHICH RODRIGO AND I REVIEW THE ESSENTIALISM DEBATE AND TRY TO UNDERSTAND WHAT HAPPENED AT THE WOMEN'S LAW CAUCUS

"The debate about essentialism has both a political and a theoretical component," Rodrigo began. "That book [Rodrigo nodded in the direction of *Yearning: Race, Gender and Cultural Politics,* by bell hooks, lying open on my desk] and those articles pay more attention to the political dimension. But there's also a linguistic-theory component."

"You mean the early philosophical discussion about whether words have essences?" I asked, pausing a moment to offer Rodrigo a cup of steaming espresso. I pointed out the tray of ingredients and said, "Help yourself if it needs more cream and sugar."

"Exactly," Rodrigo replied, slurping his coffee. "The early antiessentialists attacked the belief that words have core, or central, meanings. If I'm not mistaken, Wittgenstein was the first in our time to do so. In a way, it's a particularly powerful and persuasive version of the antinominalist argument."

As always, Rodrigo surprised me with his erudition. I wondered how an Italian-trained scholar, particularly one so young, had managed to learn about Wittgenstein, whose popularity I thought lay mainly in the English-speaking world. "How did you learn about Wittgenstein?" I asked.

"He's popular in Italy," Rodrigo explained. "I belonged to a study group that read him. The part of his teaching that laid the basis for anti-essentialism was his attack on the idea of core meanings. As you know, he wrote that the meaning of a term is its *use*."

"I haven't read him in a while," I added hastily. "But you mentioned that the controversy's political side seems to be moving into the fore right now. And I gather it's this aspect that you banged into at school."

"In its political guise," Rodrigo continued, "members of outgroups argue about the appropriate unit of analysis—about whether the black community, for example, is one or many, whether gays and lesbians have anything in common with straight activists, and so on. At the Women's Law Caucus, they were debating one aspect of this—namely, whether there is one, essential sisterhood, as opposed to many. The women of color were arguing that to think of the women's movement as singular and unitary disempowers them. They said that this view disenfranchises anyone—say lesbian mothers, disabled women, or working-class women—whose experience and status differ from what they term 'the norm.'"

"And the others, of course, were saying the opposite?"

"Not exactly," Rodrigo replied. "They were saying that vis-à-vis men, all women stood on a similar footing. All are oppressed by a common enemy, namely patriarchy, and ought to stand together to confront this evil."

"I've read something similar in the literature," I said.

"I'm not surprised. In a way, the debate the Caucus was having recapitulates an exchange between Angela Harris, a talented black writer, and Martha Fineman, a leading white feminist scholar."

"Those articles are on my list of things to read. In fact," I paused, ruffling through the papers on my littered desk, "they're right here. I skimmed this one and set this other one aside for more careful reading later. I have to annotate both for my editors."

"Then you have at least a general idea of how the political version goes," Rodrigo said. "It has to do with agendas and the sorts of compromises people have to make in any organization to keep the group working together. In the Caucus's version, the sisters were complaining that the organization did not pay enough attention to the needs of women of color. They were urging that the group write an amicus brief on behalf of Haitian women and take a stand for the largely all-black custodial workers at the university. While not unsympathetic, the Caucus leadership thought these projects should not have the highest priority."

"I see what you mean by recapitulation of the academic debate. Fineman and Harris argue over some of the same things. Not the specific examples, of course, but the general issues. Harris writes about the troubled relationship between black and white women, although she notes that many of the same issues reappear in exchanges between straight and gay women, working- and professional-class minorities, black women and black men, and so on. She and others write of the way in which these relationships often end up disempowering the less influential group. They point out that white feminist theorists, while powerful and brilliant in many ways, nevertheless base many of their insights on gender essentialism—the idea that women have a single, unitary nature, without taking into account differences of race or class. This approach obscures the identities and submerges the perspectives of women who differ from the norm. Not only does legal theory built on essentialist foundations marginalize and render certain groups invisible, it falls prey to the trap of over-abstraction, something the same writers deplore in other settings. It also promotes hierarchy and silencing, evils that women should, and do, seek to subvert."

"Much the same goes on within the black community," I pointed out. "This community is diverse, many communities in one. Black neoconservatives, for example, complain that folks like you and me leave little room for diversity by disparaging them as sellouts and belittling their views as unrepresentative. They accuse us of writing as though the community of color only has one voice—ours—and of arrogating to ourselves the power to make generalizations and declare ourselves the possessors of socio-political truth."

"I know that critique," Rodrigo replied. "We talked about it once before. It seems to me that they might well have a point, although it does sound a little strange to hear the complaint of being overwhelmed, smothered, spoken for by others coming from the mouth of someone at Yale or Harvard."

"Like you at the Law Caucus, I found myself on the end of some stinging criticism. I have Randall Kennedy and Steve Carter, particularly, in mind. They write powerfully, and of course many in the mainstream loved their message—so much so that they neglected to read any of the replies. But let's get back to what happened to you at the Women's Law meeting."

"Oh, yes. The discussion in many ways mirrored the debate in the legal literature and in that book." Rodrigo again pointed at the bell hooks book. "As you know, Harris's principal opponent in the anti-essentialism debate has been Martha Fineman, who takes black feminists to task for what she considers their overpreoccupation with difference. Their focus on their own unique experience contributes to a 'disunity' within the broader feminist movement that she finds troubling because it weakens the group's voice, the sum total of power it wields. Emphasizing minor differences between young and old, gay and straight, and black and white women is divisive, verging on self-indulgence. It contributes to the false idea that the individual is the unit of social change, not the group. It results in tokenism and plays into the hands of male power."

"And the discussion in the room was proceeding along these lines?" I asked.

"Yes," Rodrigo replied. "Although I had the sense that things had been brewing for some time. As soon as some of the leaders expressed coolness toward the black women's proposal for a day-care center, the level of acrimony increased sharply. A number of women of color said, 'This is just like what you said last time.' Some of the white women accused them of narrow parochialism. And so it went."

"The white feminists accusing the sisters of disloyalty, the sisters telling the others that they seem uncaring and dangerously empowered?"

Rodrigo nodded assent, so I continued, "And what got *you* into trouble?"

"Well, I started to draw an analogy between the controversy they were having and the one raging about Great Books and the canon. I had hardly gotten the words out of my mouth when both sides were up in arms. They accused me of butting in, of being condescending, and of trying to preach to them. I got out of there in a hurry. But ever since, I've felt a distinct chill. Before, we all had good relationships. Now, even Giannina won't speak to me."

Rodrigo's distracted look impressed on me the seriousness of his predicament, at least in his eyes. So, I resisted the temptation to joke, and instead went on as follows:

"Rodrigo, you might not know this because you've been out of the country for—what?—the last ten years?" Rodrigo nodded yes. "These issues are really heated right now. And they're not confined to feminist organizations. Many of the same arguments are raging within communities of color. Latinos and blacks are feuding. And, of course, everyone knows about Korean merchants and inner-city blacks. Black women are telling us men about our insufferable behavior. We're always finishing sentences for them, expecting them to make coffee at meetings. Some of them with long memories recall how we made them march in the second row during the civil rights movement. We make the same arguments right back at them: 'Don't criticize, you'll weaken the movement, the greater evil is racism, we need unity and common cause,' and so on. They're starting to get tired of that form of essentializing, and to point out our own chauvinism, our own patriarchal mannerisms and faults."

"Those are some of the things I got called at the meeting. It looks like I have company."

"We all need to think these things through. Can I offer you a second cup of coffee?"

"I'd love some."

IN WHICH RODRIGO AND THE PROFESSOR DISCUSS THE PERILS OF MAKING COMMON CAUSE

I started my espresso maker on a fresh pot. As it settled into its humming cycle, I looked up at Rodrigo. He began:

"What got me in trouble, as I mentioned, Professor, was the suggestion that the whole controversy mirrored the one about Great Books and the scholarly canon."

"How did that get you in trouble? I mean, I'm not sure I even see the connection."

"The white feminists were the angriest. I already told you some of the things they said. But even some of the sisters hissed. I got the sense that I should leave. But before my hasty exit, I explained that essentialism struck me as the usual response of a beleaguered group, one that needs solidarity in a struggle against a more powerful one. It has a close relation to perseveration—something you and I talked about before—in which a culture in decline insists on doing over and over again, with more and more energy, the very things that once brought it greatness but that now are bringing it doom. So you see how the Great Books analogy got me in hot water with the Law Caucus."

"I think I am beginning to understand," I said. "You are saying that essentialist thinking of any sort, white or black, male or female, is an effort to tame variety, to impose an artificial sameness on a situation that has bewildering diversity built into it."

"I think it's an insistence on a single narrative. You've been writing about narratives, Professor. I think this is something similar—an effort to impose a single 'story line' in order to make life simpler than it really is."

"I see a sort of progression," I said. "In linguistic theory, Wittgenstein and others showed that words don't have central, unitary meanings. Later, the focus shifted to culture, where outsider groups began to insist that their books, texts, experiences, language, and special-interest courses were as valid as those in the mainstream's canon. There is no one valid set of stories, in other words. Those battles have largely been won, as well. Now the controversy has moved into the arena of politics and power. Groups are attempting to coerce or persuade subgroups not to splinter off. And a main weapon in this battle is the narrative of a common enemy."

"After leaving the meeting, I thought of a good name for it," Rodrigo added: "Relational essentialism. It's the idea that black women, for example, must join white women, but not because both groups have the very same experience, perspective, needs, and agendas. They don't. Rather, it's because they stand on the same footing with respect to patriarchy. In this respect, they are essentially the same, that is, oppressed and in need of relief."

"Black men like you and me are guilty of the same thing when we tell the sisters to be quiet, to stop complaining, lest they weaken the community."

"I don't exempt us," Rodrigo said quietly. "We're all guilty of the same thing on occasion. It's a universal trait. We want to simplify the world by getting deviant, feisty, noncompliant others to come along. We want them to see the world and our struggle in exactly the same way that we do. In essentialism's political guise, we need others—sometimes urgently—to join in our fight against an oppressive force of some sort. What essentialism's three guises share is the search for narrative coherence. My audience at the meeting hated this idea."

"It's easy to see why," I said after a short pause. "Everyone likes to essentialize others—or themselves—on occasion. Is it possible that when you shared with me your concerns about being banished to the living room a little earlier, you and I were engaging in at least a mild variety of the same kind of essentialism? I'm sure you know the critique of 'male bonding' is based to a large degree on the sexual objectification of women. Some would say that your concern over the intimate consequences of your quarrel with Giannina reduces her to her sexual capacity as a woman."

"I know," Rodrigo replied. "I try not to do it. It just slipped out, like my remark at the Caucus meeting."

"We must all struggle against it—the desire to simplify others, I mean. It makes the essentialized person or group angry, of course. Plus, we miss a chance to learn something. You're right to suggest that it's a universal tendency," I said. "But it's nevertheless a power move."

"Which in turn is a response to a sense of one's own predicament, one's own disempowerment," Rodrigo said.

"Vis-à-vis someone else, I think you said. And I agree, it's often relational. A essentializes B, who essentializes C out of fear over D, and so on down the line."

Rodrigo nodded in agreement, so I continued: "It's easiest to see in personal life. The trick is to connect it to political and legal theory."

"I ran across a brilliant example the other day of why essentialism has real, sometimes debilitating consequences for individuals. Would you like to hear it, Professor?"

"I'd love to," I said. "Can I offer you a bagel to go with that second cup of coffee?" I motioned toward my compact office refrigerator, which I had just restocked. When Rodrigo nodded enthusiastically, I unwrapped my bag of bagels and spread them out on my desk. "Which kind would you like?"

"What are those?"

"Onion. Those others are sesame seed."

"I'll take one of those," Rodrigo said, pointing. "Where were we?"

"You were explaining your theory that essentialist thinking is not harmless."

"Oh, yes. The other author, Kimberle Crenshaw, is the one who offers the example. Let me know if you've heard it. She points out that black women often experience discrimination at the job site on account of their black womanhood. Often the employer is not particularly racist—that is, treats black men fairly decently—nor sexist—that is, treats white women decently. But the employer thinks black women are lazy, stupid, and sexually licentious. So the employer treats them poorly with regard to promotions and job assignments."

"Such a woman could clearly sue for employment discrimination," I said, "and recover damages."

"But how? I mean, under what theory? Crenshaw points out that a black woman plaintiff, until very recently, had only two options. She could sue for racial discrimination, in which case she would be able to use statutes and case law developed with blacks generally in mind. Or, she could sue for sex-based discrimination, invoking laws framed with women in mind. There was no legal category for black women who experienced discrimination on account of their black womanhood. So, they could either place themselves in a class of women dominated, numerically and in other ways, by white women, and use remedies framed with them in mind. Or, they could sue for racial discrimination, in which case they ended up lumped in a category containing black men. In either case, they wound up in a group—white women or black men—with more power, prestige, influence, and standing than they."

"I believe the author and others have a name for this."

"Intersectionality," Rodrigo replied quickly. "It's related to essentialism. As we have seen, the law of remedies assumes one essential black and one essential woman. The black is male, the woman white. The black woman has to choose, and neither choice is comfortable. Neither category is hers. Neither group has her agenda and needs in mind. And the law follows suit."

"But isn't it a wash?" I asked, offering Rodrigo some nicely aged brie I had overlooked in my refrigerator. "I got this on sale, but it's pretty good. Try some."

Rodrigo slathered his bagel with the cheese, and then continued: "I gather you mean that the person situated at the intersection of two categories, like the black woman, gets to have two sets of allies."

"Exactly," I replied. "In some settings, and in some eras, racism will be the major problem for her. When this is the case, she can call on black men as allies. In other situations, sexism will be the major concern. Then, she can call on the white women, who face the same problem. Black women may end up getting protection that has a poor 'fit' to their circumstances. But at least they can call on double the number of friends."

"So I thought, too. But then a cool remark that Giannina made as we rode home that night got me thinking that maybe it isn't so."

"What do you mean?"

"At first, I thought as you did. In fact, the algebra of it is kind of neat. Anyone who lies at the intersection of two categories gets half-hearted protection from each of the two groups. And so, you might think that person is at least as well off as the others. This would, of course, blunt the criticism that persons marginal to a particular group are injured when the group essentializes its own experience. It would blunt it because the reply would be, simply, that the intersectional person can call on double the number of allies, can find two (or more) groups, not just one, whose narratives will overlap, at least in part, with their own."

"But now you are thinking this is not so? I think I agree with you, but I can't quite put my finger on why," I said. Secretly, I was hoping Rodrigo would let his famous imagination loose. I had to write several annotations on these issues of intersectionality over the next few days, and was hoping our discussion would enable me to produce a better product.

"I hope you'll bear with me, Professor. This part of my theory is still pretty—how do they call it?—provisional. Please don't be too hard on me."

"Of course I won't. Intersectionality and anti-essentialism are emerging as important issues. If you can do anything to advance the debate, we'll all benefit. And besides, I've got a very concrete reason for wanting to hear what you have to say. So, please go ahead."

"Three reasons suggest that an outsider cannot play along, as it were, with the relatively more empowered group that wants to essentialize it. They're all related. And they all converge on a single moral, or maxim that Giannina said she has come to live by: namely, that if you are a relatively disempowered person, say a black man or woman or a lesbian single mother, it is always a big mistake to take the perspective of the larger, more empowered group, even for strategic reasons."

"I'd like to hear how you are going to document that, and I assume it has something to do with your three reasons."

"Right," the irrepressible Rodrigo responded with alacrity.

Rodrigo's First Reason Why the Social Reformer Is Caught in a Dilemma in Which the Solution Is Not Always Opting for the Largest Possible Coalition: On Marching in the Right Direction

"The first reason, Professor, is strategic. This is the one that Giannina alluded to that night. It's that it's better to march in the right direction rather than the wrong one. Suppose you're a black woman and you decide to go along with the feminist agenda, even if all the leaders are white, and all the goals seem more calculated to serve their interest than yours. You reason, 'what the heck, at least some of the things they hold important I hold important too'—for example, protecting the right to an abortion. Moreover, the group has access to power, money, and channels of communication. So, even though the group is lukewarm about programs that you feel are important, like Head Start, you at least get to march with them on an important issue."

"It's always nice to have company," I said.

"Unfortunately, it turns out that it's generally better to march along more slowly in your own direction. It assures that at the least you get closer to your destination. If you march with the larger group in a direction that is a little off from where you want to go—say, ten degrees skewed—you will have high morale. You will experience great solidarity. Sing great protest songs. You will link hands and present an impressive-looking phalanx. Your picture will be in the papers."

"But in time you'll notice that you are diverging, getting further and further away from your goal, right?"

"Yes. But the price of strategic essentialism is not only that you get away from your agenda and your heart-of-hearts goals. You'll develop what Antonio Gramsci calls false consciousness. You'll forget who you are and what your original goals and commitments were. Goals and personal identities and loyalties are socially constructed. If we work and struggle with people—no matter how well-intentioned—whose perspectives, culture, and agenda are different from ours, we will eventually change. Goals are not atomistic. I can't say, I'll go along with the Republicans because I agree with their ideas on tax reform, but I'll be a Democrat with respect to this other policy, and so on. Spending time with Republicans means you will inevitably take on their mindset. A black man active in a white-dominated civil rights organization will eventually take on the traits and concerns he finds there. A black woman working in a male-dominated group will risk losing her identity as a black feminist. Some social scientists call this 'alienation.'"

"I'm not sure I quite understand all this high-crit talk, Rodrigo. I do, however, think that your metaphor of marching determinedly off in the wrong direction, with lots of company and all the bands playing, is a vivid and useful one. But you mentioned other reasons for caution."

Rodrigo's Second Reason Why the Social Reformer Is Caught in a Dilemma: On the Need to Avoid Triumphalism
"The second reason has to do with something you and other writers in the critical race theory school have expressed—namely, skepticism of gains that seem to have been won through appeals to social altruism."

"I assume you mean our writing on the phenomenon of interest convergence and its pitfalls."

"Precisely. You and others have written of the way in which civil rights gains for blacks and others always seem to coincide with white self-interest. In eras in which white self-interest and black justice are not aligned, nothing happens. When, as happened around the time of *Brown v. Board of Education,* elite white groups need to allow a breakthrough for minorities, one miraculously appears. Altruism, a sense of compassion, and racial justice count for little, if anything."

"I know that hypothesis, and agree with it," I said. "But how does it connect with your thesis about essentialism and your idea that the weaker party gains little from affiliating with the stronger, even where both are struggling against a common oppressor?"

"I should have explained myself better," Rodrigo said. "What I meant is that temporary alliances always have a way of falling back, just as civil rights gains stemming from momentary interest-convergences between blacks and whites always erode."

"When the interest-convergence ceases, you mean?"

"Yes. Take *Brown v. Board of Education.* As everyone knows, the ringing words of the Court's opinion were quickly robbed of much effect by administrative foot-dragging, obstruction, and delay. The case ended up changing very little. School districts are as segregated today as they were in the days of *Brown.* And, of course, much the same has happened with women's issues. The right to abortion secured by *Roe v. Wade* was eventually cut back by narrow interpretation, refusal to provide funding, and the fervor of the religious right. Despite a small increase in the number of abortions since *Roe v. Wade,* women who obtain them often have to run a gauntlet of opposition and hassling. Giannina described an experience a friend of hers had. It was harrowing."

"And so the conclusion you draw is ... ?"

"Gains are ephemeral if one wins them by forming coalitions with individuals who really do not have your interest at heart. It's not just that the larger, more diverse group will forget you and your special needs. It's worse than that. You'll forget who you are. And even if you don't, you may still end up demonized, blamed for sabotaging the revolution when it inevitably and ineluctably fails."

"Sounds dire," I said. "I hope you'll explain how this happens."

Rodrigo's Third Reason: On Normativity and the Inevitable Egocentrism of Rights-Talk

"As I mentioned, Professor, the three reasons converge. The third one has to do with the way normativity—prescriptive discourse—finds use. Imagine that a group, say women, is successful in winning a concession from society at large, for example the right to an abortion. Who will reap the gains of the new right, and who will leave disappointed? Rights are precious things; they realign how we think about each other. Getting a new right recognized is a lot of work. In accomplishing this, one likely has made a lot of enemies and called in a lot of favors. The victory has not been cost-free. Who now will pay those costs? With abortion, recall how quickly the right came to be narrowed. Courts ruled that states need not fund abortions and that governments may prohibit them entirely in state-supported facilities. Poor women often cannot afford abortions and therefore, in effect, lack access. A few women in the majority group protested, but many went along since the restrictions did not affect them. But it's not merely that the right was cut back in predictable fashion, as *Brown v. Board of Education* was for blacks. Worse, as soon as the political climate changed, black women's sexuality came under fire. The new rights-and-responsibilities movement, championed by some well-known feminists, now designates black women's sexuality as irresponsible, and the employment of abortion as a means of birth control as an abuse of a right."

"Much the same happened in the wake of various civil rights breakthroughs," I pointed out.

"I think it's a general phenomenon," Rodrigo agreed. "Rights, once won, tend to be cut back. And even when part of them remains, the price of the newly won right is placed on the most marginal of its beneficiaries. For example, affirmative action benefited largely the middle-class, upward-striving black person, like me—ones who likely would have succeeded anyway. Desperately poor blacks benefited little. And the remedy, affirmative action, was so visible and controversial that it drew fire, assuring that all blacks paid the penalty of its benefits to the few—penalties in the form of stigma, hostility by the majority, and the overriding belief by whites that all blacks are so undeserving or so stupid that they require affirmative action to have a chance."

"So your third reason has to do with the way the gains one seems to win through coalescing with a more powerful group backfire, causing one to end up disappointed and demonized?"

"Normative discourse is always self-centered," Rodrigo replied. "The critique of normativity shows that in a number of ways. For example, society may tolerate or even celebrate new rights for women or minorities. But then it will invariably declare that your and my exercise of those rights is not what they had in mind at all. When a low-income black woman has an abortion, that will seem like lasciviousness and hypersexuality, an irresponsible exercise of the right. When the judicial system recognizes a right to nondiscriminatory treatment in employment, everyone celebrates. But when a black man with credentials short of Albert Einstein's gets a job, that will seem troublesome and unprincipled."

"So, the conclusion you draw from all this is . . . ?"

"That one should never adopt the perspective of the more powerful group, even strategically. Adopting another's perspective is always a mistake. One starts out thinking one can go along with the more numerous, better organized, and more influential group—say, white women in the case of sisters of color—and reap some benefits. You think that you can jump nimbly aside before the inevitable setbacks, disappointments, and double crosses set in. But you can't. You will march strongly and determinedly in the wrong direction, alienating yourself in the process. You'll end up having the newly deployed rights cut back in your case, perhaps suffer criticism as irresponsible when you try to exercise them. Moreover, any small suggestion for deviation in the agenda, any polite request that the larger group consider your own concerns, will bring quick denunciation. You are being divisive. You are weakening the movement."

"Rodrigo, you have me half convinced," I replied. "I've long thought that the interest-convergence hypothesis was right. You've just elegantly extended that hypothesis to the essentialism debate and embedded it in a linguistic and cultural context. But if you are ever going to restore your credibility in the eyes of the sisters of color at your law school—not to mention the rest—you can't stop at that. They will want to know where you go from there. If essentialism and making common cause with a too-large group is always a mistake, what do you do to replace it? You need more than a theory to explain what's wrong; you also need to explain what we ought to do. Otherwise you run the risk of being seen as a troublemaker, one who goes around stirring up animosity among potential allies and friends."

Rodrigo winced a little. "I think that may have already happened to me. But this part of my theory I'm much less certain about than the critique part. Do you have the time to listen? You're a great critic, Professor. And I have a most immediate need to refine my thoughts. Giannina and I may be finished if I don't."

I smiled at Rodrigo's earnestness, remembering my own youth.

"Can I offer you some fruit?" I asked. "We've been going at it for quite a while. I find I need something every now and then to keep my energy up. And my doctor, as you know, wants me to eat many small meals as I go through the day."

Rodrigo nodded gratefully. I took down a small tray of nuts and dried apricots I kept stowed in a cabinet next to my refrigerator. Rodrigo continued.

IN WHICH RODRIGO SKETCHES THE CONTOURS OF A THEORY OF ANTI-ESSENTIALISM AND THE RELATION OF SMALL GROUPS TO SOCIAL CHANGE

"Interest-convergence never lasts long, as I said, Professor. And it's a bad idea to try to stage-manage it by aligning yourself with the next-less-disempowered group, the one just up the scale from you, for all the reasons I mentioned."

"But if we drop out of larger groups, people will accuse us of being narrow nationalists, of being poor team players, of being obsessed with our own parochial interests. And won't they have a point—at least in their way of looking at it?" I asked.

"I see two challenges," Rodrigo replied. "The first is to remain oppositional, not to give in to the welcome embraces of the group that is not like you. This is fairly difficult. All the pressure is in the other direction. We are taught, even indoctrinated, to be team players. One who pursues his or her own way is depicted as disloyal, disruptive, and a 'single-issue' person. In our society, those are not nice words. But one can persevere. The second challenge is to understand why pursuing a nationalist, counter-essentialist course is a good idea, to explain how it brings benefits to everyone, not just to one's own kin-group."

"This I'd love to hear," I said, reaching for a walnut from the tray in front of us. "Have some."

"These are delicious. Where did you get them?" asked Rodrigo.

"At a place just down the street from where I live," I replied. "It's a Korean-run grocery store. They have great produce, and I go there in part to make a point. Have as many as you like. I've got more."

"The big supermarket where Giannina and I shop doesn't have nearly as good ones. We may switch. Where was I?"

"You were starting to explain why anti-essentialism is good for all, even the larger group, and not a case of disloyalty or excessive self-preoccupation."

"Oh, yes. My theory has to do with double consciousness. You're familiar with the term of course, Professor."

"Of course. The black scholar, W.E.B. Du Bois, wrote of it. It holds that persons of color see the world in two ways at the same time. The black person, for example, sees himself as normal and abnormal at the same time—as others see him, and also as he sees himself. It's a familiar feeling we all know."

"And in recent times, black and other feminists of color have expanded that notion to include the idea of multiple consciousness. A black female lesbian, for example, sees the world from at least those three different perspectives of race, gender, and sexuality. Her experience is not the same as that of the average black woman, or that of a black gay male. It's a complex interaction among those three points of view, and perhaps others as well."

"And you were saying, Rodrigo, that this confers an advantage? To the person bearing multiple consciousness, or to others?"

"To both. A person with multiple consciousness learns to see everything through two or more lenses at once. This gives you a better grasp of reality. It's kind of like looking through a pair of binoculars. Binocular vision is always better than the kind you get by looking at something through just one lens. So, it gives the possessor an advantage."

"I've heard it said that slaves observed their masters better than their masters observed them. Is your theory related to that idea?"

"In a way it is. The slave perceived the master more accurately than the master perceived him; he had to to survive. Reading the master's folkways and moods was an essential skill the slave developed to avoid harsh treatment. But he also observed the master more clearly because he had double consciousness—he saw the master both as a master and as a human being. The master, on the other hand, regarded the slave one-dimensionally as a slave or worker only, not as a human being. There were a few exceptions, of course."

"It's coming back to me. The first time we met, you argued that multiple consciousness enables the outsider to see defects in the prevailing order long before one immersed in that system could. You said that, in scholarship, this conferred an advantage, particularly with respect to grasping and deploying postmodern theory. But, if I hear you correctly, you are urging that outsiders ought to hang on to their peculiar form of social insight, maintain it pristine and separate, in order to benefit the larger group as well. But isn't it just this larger group that they plan to leave if they followed your advice?"

"I know it sounds paradoxical, Professor. But bear with me for a minute. Merging with the larger group causes you to forfeit a kind of sightedness. So it's bad for you. But it's also bad for the larger group because dissenters who agree to remain in the larger movements eventually become coopted and alienated from their own position, with the result that the larger group loses an important source of criticism, a kind of early warning from which they could learn something. Systemic evils, like racism and sexism, are never visible within the culture, because those evils are woven into the paradigm—into the system of meanings by which we construct and understand reality. Speech is paradigm-dependent. And, if racism—or any other evil—is embedded in that paradigm, one can't speak out against it without being heard as incoherent. That's why racism and sexism are harder to correct than scientific error."

"I'm not sure I see that. How about an example?"

Rodrigo was silent a long moment. Then, he looked up thoughtfully:

"Professor, does your school have an affirmative action program?"

"Of course. I think virtually every one does. Yours must, as well."

"It does. But I learned something interesting when I was working on a report for the curriculum committee. As you recall, we've been working with some of the faculty in revising the first- and second-year curriculum. This came up sort of tangentially, but now I think it's really important. At one point, my friend Ali, who is also on the committee, and I asked the law school for figures about employment, salary, job offers, etc. We were exploring quite a different hypothesis...."

"What they call serendipity," I interrupted.

"Exactly. And what we learned turned out, as you will see, to have a great bearing on the matter we are currently discussing: namely, the invisibility of the status quo. We learned that the minority students, most of whom were admitted to the school under an affirmative action program, tended to graduate at a rate almost identical to that of law students in general. Not only that, they tended to get jobs at roughly the same rate. Last year, in fact, they did better than the whites. They also earned a slightly higher average starting salary. More of them got judicial clerkships—I mean on a percentage basis, of course."

"That's fascinating. I remember hearing one or two figures like those at my school. What do you make of that?" I asked.

"Ali and I were intrigued, as you can imagine. So, we looked around further. It turned out that years after graduating, the same holds true. The minorities end up appointed to judgeships and commissions at a rate greater than their proportion in the alumni body. All the students, of course, are smart, and many of them go on to quite distinguished careers. But the minorities tend to do a little better. We checked at some other law schools and found the same story: The minorities did a little better than the whites, or at least not worse. Not in every case, of course, and not on every single measure, but in general."

"And the conclusion you draw from this is ... ?"

"I thought that there has to be some form of cultural preference encoded and deeply buried in the way we admit and grade students, something, perhaps in the way we use letters of recommendation, evaluate extracurricular activities, or perhaps the LSATs, that gives an edge to the whites and disadvantages the minorities. The output figures imply strongly that the minorities are just as able, or more so. But they get admitted in quite small numbers. My law school has only a handful of students of color."

"Mine, too."

"Yet the ones who do get in excel."

"From which you conclude that some form of favoritism is going on?"

"Some encoded cultural preference for the slightly less qualified whites. I don't want to overstate this, Professor. As I mentioned, all the graduates do well. But judging from output statistics, the minorities are superior to or undifferentiable from the rest."

"Perhaps they have an unfair advantage," I quipped, "namely, a sense of mission." I immediately regretted my tongue-in-cheek remark when Rodrigo shot me a rueful look.

"I'm joking. You've pointed out a serious problem. I don't mean to make light of it. I've often reflected on how brilliantly many of my minority students acquit themselves in class and later. But I think you were mentioning this en route to a point about perception, right?"

"Exactly. I found when I ran some of these figures past some of my white friends, they did *not* draw the inference I did. Rather, they looked puzzled, or disbelieving. They wanted to know where I got my statistics, and when I said the placement office, they looked flabbergasted. Several said that the minority-success figures I had unearthed must themselves be the product of affirmative action in wider society."

"In other words," I said, "they begin with the premise that minorities are inferior, indeed must be—otherwise why would there be affirmative action? Then, when it turns out that the minorities, despite all the obstacles they face, nevertheless do well, it must be because judges, employers, appointments committees, and so on are giving them favored treatment. You draw one conclusion, they another."

"And that's the whole point of a canonical mindset. It means that if you have two possible inferences from a set of data, one in which minorities are the equal of whites, or even have a slight edge, and one in which they don't, you immediately think of the second."

"I agree that preconception—what you call canonical thinking—functions that way. Paradigms always preserve themselves. But I'm unclear what connection all this has to your argument in favor of an anti-essentialist cultural nationalism that would renounce coalition politics."

"Let's see if I can bring myself back on track." Rodrigo was silent for a moment, his fingers lightly touching his forehead. I was glad to see that my quick-witted young friend, who often seemed able to dance miles ahead of me, occasionally needed to regroup. He continued at length:

"The connection is this. The larger group always has a canon—a set of principles, articles of faith, ways of seeing the world. These may exclude you—at least not include you as fully as you might like. If you go along with them, occasions will inevitably arise like the one I just mentioned between blacks and whites, except that you will be on the receiving end of poor or uncomprehending treatment from a group with whom you thought you had a lot in common.

"Since their narrative is designed for a different purpose—namely, theirs—your requests will seem unprincipled distractions, evidence of disloyalty or overpreoccupation with self. They may seem like reverse essentialism—a perverse insistence on the importance of such a petty and divisive thing as race.

"And so you are generally—maybe always—better off with your own," Rodrigo concluded.

"Yet you said, I think, that accepting this would benefit not just the insurrectionist group but the larger one from which it secedes, as it were. How can it benefit white women in the feminist movement, for example, if the black women go their own way? Is it the binocular vision idea you mentioned before?"

"The main benefits inure to the secessionist group. But the larger group benefits, as well. They get careful outside criticism. They get a certain degree of protection from complacency by reason of the need to vie for the support of outsider allies. They get constant reminders that their perspective is not the only one. I got one just the other day," Rodrigo concluded, a little ruefully.

"But Rodrigo, aren't you overlooking that the next-larger group, the one that suffers the defection, *needs* the smaller group? It needs it to consolidate cultural change, to install new conventions. It needs allies, as well, to institute ordinary, concrete reforms, like new civil rights laws. What might look to you like loyalty to self looks to others like a case of weakening a revolution that desperately needs you—needs your numbers, needs your genius, needs the credibility you bring by virtue of your very diversity. Revolutionary groups of all sorts need solidarity. When a reform movement starts to fragment, isn't it in trouble? Rodrigo, you ignore the *costs* of fragmentation. I don't see how anti-essentialism can possibly benefit the group whose solidarity is weakened. I think one revolution dies to give birth to another. Isn't that the best you can say?"

Rodrigo smiled as he listened to my earnest objection.

"Professor, I was about to say that I had a response and that it had to do with the role of hunger. Then I noticed that it is past dinnertime."

"We could get a bite to eat at the little Persian deli next door," I offered. "They just opened up last month. I've been there twice. They're pretty good, although I think they close at seven."

"It's a few minutes of. What do you say we get some take-out? I'll treat this time."

"Please let me," I said. "Your life is in enough turmoil right now, and I assume you have interviews coming up?"

"Starting next week."

"You'll have extra expenses. Let me pay. If you make up with Giannina, perhaps the two of you can have me over when you're back from the circuit."

"Okay, if you'll promise to come. Giannina has been wanting to meet you."

"It will be my pleasure."

IN WHICH RODRIGO POSITS A THEORY OF SOCIAL CHANGE AND EXPLAINS THE ROLE OF OPPOSITIONAL GROUPS IN BRINGING IT ABOUT

Ten minutes later, we were riding up the elevator to my office, balancing cups of hot tea and plates of dolmas, kebabs, and pita bread. "I'm glad you plan to elaborate on your theory of social change, Rodrigo. In one of our earlier discussions, you kind of left that hanging. As you know, I am a skeptic on that score. A number of friends and I have been developing a theory of what we call the 'empathic fallacy' to explain why reform is so halting and slow. The last time we talked you said something to the effect that social reform through law was unlikely. But you left open the possibility that it might come another way."

We arrived at my door. As I struggled to get out the key without spilling my food, Rodrigo said, "My theory—it's only vague and sketchy at this point—consists of two parts. The first explains why we never get lasting reform through legal means—litigation and legislation. The second part consists of showing how reform does come about, when it comes."

"Which is rare enough."

"I agree," Rodrigo said. "Need some help with that key?"

"No, I've got it." Moments later we were seated comfortably back in my office.

"This is like having a picnic," Rodrigo said as he dived into his meal. "I'm glad we got there before they closed."

Rodrigo Lays Out a Natural History of Social Ideas

"I think that virtually all revolutionary ideas start with an outsider of some sort," Rodrigo began. "We mentioned the reasons before. Few who operate within the system see its defects. They speak, read, and hear within a discourse that is self-satisfying. The primary function of our system of free speech is to effect stasis, not change. New ideas are ridiculed as absurd and extreme, and discounted as political. It's not until much later, when consciousness changes, that we look back and wonder why we resisted so strongly."

"Revolutionaries always lead rocky lives. You'll see that too, Rodrigo, although I don't know if you classify yourself as one or not. All the pressure is in the direction of conforming, of doing what others do, in teaching, in scholarship, in fact in all areas of life."

Rodrigo shrugged off my counsel. "So, new ideas and movements come along relatively rarely. And when they do, they are beleaguered. For a long time, they garner little support. Then, for some reason, they acquire a critical mass. Society begins to pay attention. Now, the situation is in flux. The group now needs all the allies they can muster. They begin to make inroads and need to make more. They see that they are beginning to approach the point where they might be able to effect change."

"Including the power to define who is 'divisive,'" I added.

"That, too—especially that," Rodrigo said animatedly, seeing how my observation fit into the theory he was developing. He looked up gratefully, then continued:

"At this point, they need all the help they can get. If they are you, they need Gary Peller and Alan Freeman. If they are feminists, they need Cass Sunstein. Earlier, they needed the religious right in their campaign against pornography. And so on. With a little growth in numbers, they may perhaps reach the point at which power begins to translate into knowledge. And knowledge, of course, is the beginning of social reform. When everyone knows you are right, knows you have a point, you are well on your way to victory."

"And for this the group needs numbers."

"Right. With them, they can change the interpretive community. They can remake the model of the essential woman, say, along lines that are genuinely more humane."

Rodrigo and I Discuss the Role of Reformers and Malcontent Groups

"So, Rodrigo," I continued, "you are saying that new knowledge of any important, radical sort begins with a small group. This group is dissatisfied, but believes it has a point. It agitates, acquires new members, begins to get society to take it seriously. And it's at this point that the essentialism/anti-essentialism debate usually sets in?"

"Before, it wouldn't arise. And later, when the large group is nearing its goals, it doesn't need the disaffected faction. So it's at this mid-point in a social revolution—for example, the feminist movement—that we have debates like the one I got caught in the middle of."

"But you were saying earlier that the disaffected cell ought to sit out the revolution, as it were, and not just for its own good but for that of the wider society as well?"

"It should. And often such groups do, consciously or unconsciously. I'm just saying that when they do, it's usually not a bad thing."

"And this is because of your theory of knowledge, I gather, in which canonical thinking always gets to a point where it no longer works and needs a fundamental challenge?"

"And this, in turn, can only come from a disaffected group. Every new idea, if it has merit, eventually turns into a canon. And every canonical idea at some point needs to be dislodged, challenged, and supplanted by a new one."

"So maverick, malcontent groups are the growing edge of social thought."

"Not every one. Some are regressive—want to roll back reform."

"I can think of several that fit that bill," I said shuddering. "But you said earlier that the outsider enjoys a kind of binocular vision that enables him or her to see defects in the bubbles in which we all live—to see the curvature, the limitations, the downward drift that eventually spells trouble. But just now you used another metaphor. What was it?"

Rodrigo thought for a moment. "Oh, I remember. It was just before we went out for food. The metaphor was the role of hunger."

"I'd love for you to explain."

"It's like this." Rodrigo pushed aside his plate. "Change comes from a small, dissatisfied group for whom canonical knowledge and the standard social arrangements don't work. Such a group needs allies. Thus, white women in the feminist movement reach out to women of color; black men in the civil rights movement try to include black women, and so on. Eventually, the larger group makes inroads, changes the paradigm, begins to be accepted, gets laws passed, and so on."

"Can I take that plate?" I asked. Rodrigo passed it over, and I put it in the nonrecyclable bin outside my office along with the other remnants of our snack. "This is what you argued before, so I assume you're getting to your theory about hunger."

"Correct. But you see, as soon as all this happens, the once-radical group begins to lose its edge. It enters a phase of consolidation, in which it is more concerned with defending and instituting reforms made possible by the new consensus, the new paradigm of Knowledge/Power, than with pushing the envelope towards more radical change. The group is beginning to lose binocular vision, the special form of insight most outgroups have, about social inequities and imbalances."

"And so the reform movement founders," I said.

"I'm not sure I'd say founders," Rodrigo interjected. "Rather, it enters into a different phase."

"But at any rate, it peters out," I said. "It loses vigor."

"And another group rises up to take its place. Often this is a disaffected subset of the larger group, the one that won reforms, that got the Supreme Court or Congress to recognize the legitimacy of its claims. It turns out that the reforms did not do much for it. The revolution came and went, but things stayed pretty much the same for it. So, it renews its effort."

"And that's what you meant by hunger?"

"Yes. Those who are hungry are most desperate for change. Human intelligence and progress spring from adversity, from a sense that the world is not supplying what the organism needs and requires. A famous American philosopher developed a theory of education based on this idea."

"I assume you mean John Dewey?"

"Him and others. He was a sometime member of the school of American pragmatists. But his approach differed in significant respects from that of the other pragmatists like William James and Charles Peirce. One was this. We can borrow from his theory to explain the natural history of revolutionary movements, applying what he saw for individuals to larger groups."

"Where you think it holds as well?" I asked. "It's always dangerous extrapolating from the individual to the group."

"I think the observation does hold for groups, as well," Rodrigo replied. "The basic idea is that victors become complacent. They lose their critical edge, because they don't need it. The social structure now works for them. If by intelligence, one means critical intelligence, we become dumber all the time. It's a kind of reverse evolution. Eventually society gets out of kilter enough that a dissident group rises up, its critical skills honed, its perception equal to that of the slave. It challenges the master by condemning the status quo as unjust, just as Giannina challenged me. Sometimes the injustices it complains of are ones that genuinely need mending, and not just for the discontented group. Rather, they signal a broader need to reform things in ways that will benefit everybody."

I leaned forward; the full force of what Rodrigo was saying had hit me. "So, Rodrigo, you are saying that the history of revolution is, by its nature, iterative. The unit of social intelligence is small; reform and retrenchment come in waves. This fits in with what you were saying earlier about the decline of the West and the need for infusion of outsider thought. And, it dovetails with other currents under way in environmental thought, economic thought—and, as you mentioned, in American political philosophy. Maybe you'll start a resurgence of attention to John Dewey, who I always thought was a neglected, but very brilliant, philosopher."

"Do you see any defects in my theory, anything I should consider?"

After a pause, I said, "Well, there's the World Trade Center issue."

"I'm not sure what you mean."

"Isn't the intelligence of radically disenfranchised groups and subgroups just as likely to turn criminal and take destructive forms, like blowing up the World Trade Center, as it is to take the constructive critical turn you posit?"

"This may happen occasionally," Rodrigo conceded.

"But it's no small objection, Rodrigo," I pressed. "Many believe that the need today is not for further fragmentation, further nationalism, further multiplication of small groups along lines of ethnicity, politics, or religion. Rather, the need is for the opposite—for peace, for cooperation, for everyone to acquire a large, ecumenical understanding of the world and our place in it. We can't solve problems piecemeal. Everything is connected. What's needed is a holistic vision, not the parochial concern, say, of Arab nationalists. We need to see problems in a national, if not global, perspective."

"But we won't get that unless the world is fair." Rodrigo was speaking slowly and emphatically now. He leaned forward in his seat. "You see, Professor, the ecumenical view requires that everyone see the regime as just. If not, they will unite with others disaffected like themselves and struggle their hardest to bring their grievances to the attention of the next-larger group. That group inevitably will preach to them about division, partisanship, and disloyalty, and will tell them that their cooperation is necessary to forward the larger group's agenda, whatever that is. But if the Palestinians thought their situation was fair, they would not be disturbing the peace in the Middle East. If black women thought they were being dealt with fairly in the women's movement—or at the hands of the black brothers, for that matter—they would not be agitating for increased attention to their needs."

"So justice comes before peace?"

"Logically, yes, and also in the natural history of ideas," Rodrigo replied. "Of course, if one is a member of a more empowered group, as you and I are vis-à-vis black women, one's need will be for peace, for unity, for consolidation, for other virtues of a stable and just age. But the smaller group will think just the opposite—that the age is not just and has no business being stable."

Just then I heard the phone ringing in my secretary's office down the hall and realized we were about to be interrupted by call-forwarding if the caller persevered beyond four rings. While waiting for the call to flip over, I mused to Rodrigo:

"Rodrigo, I think I agree with you about your general analysis. Moreover, I want to write your epitaph. It will say ..."

Just then my office phone started to ring, so I quickly finished my thought:

"'Justice first, then peace'—a motto that others have employed in different versions to highlight the incompatibility between an oppressive regime that contains structures of unfairness, and social stability. Such a regime is inherently unstable because of the ever-present possibility of revolt."

Rodrigo smiled in appreciation. I picked up the phone. What I then told him made him smile even more:

"It's Giannina," I said. "She wants to know if the three of us would like to go to a movie."

PART VI
Latinos and Other Nonblack Minorities

An examination of early critical race theory scholarship will show that most of those writings addressed broad principles of antidiscrimination law, examining primarily problems of African Americans. Delgado's prolific scholarship contributed immensely to this genre. Yet, in one of his first articles in 1975, he and his coauthor focused solely on Mexican Americans. They proposed that for purposes of legal recognition, Latinos should qualify as a cognizable class because they shared a common culture and language and, because of it, were subject to discrimination as well. Other early articles addressed the legal education of Chicano students and a law school admissions study by the Mexican American Legal Defense Fund. Over the following decades, as the legal academy became more diverse, scores of other writers began to examine problems of African Americans. This body of scholarship, loosely defined as critical race theory, began to receive recognition in the larger academy in large part due to Delgado's admonition to white scholars in his "Imperial Scholar" article (see Part III) to let minority scholars have a voice in scholarship about their respective communities.

Meanwhile, Delgado, like his character Rodrigo, refocused his attention from the particular issues affecting African Americans to those of Latinos and other groups. In the two selections that follow, he examines the black-white binary paradigm of race. According to this dominant way of thinking about remedies for racial discrimination, African Americans are the primary group for whom antidiscrimination law was crafted. Other groups appear only as variants of blacks or are absent altogether because the Equal Protection Clause of the Fourteenth Amendment and the Civil War amendments do not apply to them.

In "Rodrigo's Fifteenth Chronicle," Rodrigo and the Professor discuss the way the black-white binary functions as a subordinating mechanism for Latinos because it offers no racial remedies for the particular facets of Latino histories as colonized or immigrant groups that put them beyond the protection of antidiscrimination law.

In "Derrick Bell's Toolkit," Delgado questions whether Bell's analysis of racial remedies is broad enough to address issues of other minority groups, and even of blacks. Delgado develops his in-depth analysis of the role of revisionist history, the checkerboard of racial progress, differential racialization, how coalitions fail or occasionally succeed, and how the reformer must consider the situations of all the groups at the same time.

RODRIGO'S FIFTEENTH CHRONICLE
Racial Mixture, Latino-Critical Scholarship, and the Black-White Binary

"Rodrigo, here I am," I announced, raising my voice over the din of the airport loudspeaker and voices of fellow passengers waiting at curbside. "How kind of you to pick me up."

"No problem. Giannina's back home, reviewing for a midterm. Here, let me take that bag."

"Nice car," I said. "Did you have it last time?"

"No, it's new. We tried doing without one, but our schedules are so different now that we needed it in order to have any time at all together. So, we got this little beauty."

"It's Italian, right?" I asked.

"Right. Mom and Dad had one when I was growing up, although it was a larger model. Have you ever driven one?"

"I don't think so," I said. "At my age, my tastes run to something a little more sedate."

"You can drive it to your meeting tomorrow if you want. I'm staying home for the day. You could drop Giannina off at her law school on the way."

"We'll see," I said as Rodrigo slowed for the short-term parking booth. He showed his ticket to the attendant, who waved him on—"Free, less than thirty minutes"—and then I asked, "I gather you've been doing some traveling, too."

"I have," Rodrigo replied. "I just got back from a two-day conference hosted by the Latino law students of a major school. It drew an impressive cast, with speakers like Rodolfo Acuña and Carlos Muñoz, as well as the usual complement of law professors. I've been meaning to ask you about something, if you're not too tired."

"Not at all," I replied. "My flight was nonstop and, despite my best intentions to get some work done, I spent the last half of it sleeping. I'm wide awake—ask away."

"As I mentioned, Professor, the event was richly interdisciplinary. But the panel that sparked the most excitement, among the law types at any rate, focused on the role of racial mixture in America's future."

"As a multiracial person yourself, I can see how you must have found that one intriguing. Were you one of the speakers?"

"No," Rodrigo replied. "I was on a different panel. But on this one, practically every one of the speakers was a member of the group called Latino-Critical scholars, or Lat-Crits, that has sprung up over the last few years."

"I've been reading about them," I said. "They seem to be a spinoff from critical race theory, which in turn traces its origins to earlier progressive movements, including critical legal studies. What were some of the issues the panel discussed?"

"Mainly interracial marriage and adoption. But afterwards some of us were talking about the role of Latinos in American politics. We wondered why our relatively large group has had so little impact on national civil rights policy, especially in areas like immigration reform, bilingual education, poverty, and English-only laws. On all these fronts, we've been relatively ineffectual, compared to blacks. Some thought it had to do with inter-marriage, assimilation, or lack of cohesion, since Latinos are made up of so many different national-origin groups. But after reading a certain book on the flight home, I think it's something different."

"You mean that one?" I said, pointing to a volume lying on the back seat of the little car, a neat bookmark sticking out. "I saw it when I got in."

Rodrigo craned around. "Yes, that one. I brought it along to show you. Entitled *All Rise: Reynaldo Garza, the First Mexican American Federal Judge* and written by a Washington, D.C.-area writer, it details the life and career of Reynaldo Garza. It's a good read."

IN WHICH RODRIGO AND I DISCUSS *ALL RISE* AND WHAT IT TEACHES ABOUT THE STRUCTURE OF CIVIL RIGHTS THOUGHT

"I think I saw a notice for it the other day," I said. "And of course I'm familiar with some of the judge's opinions; in fact have taught a few in my courses over the years. What does the book say about him? Nothing too harsh, I hope. It's tough being a first of any kind. Sometimes biographers and critics expect more of you than you can possibly deliver."

"It's favorable," Rodrigo replied. "As well as intelligently written. Like all good biography, it helps you understand the person and his or her times—how the circumstances in which he or she lived affected the possibilities for that person's life and thought."

"What's the general thesis?" I asked. As a member of the judge's generation, I was anxious to hear the reviewer's judgment.

"It's that Judge Garza was able to combine a successful career as a lawyer and a judge and maintain his Mexican-American roots at the same time. The book details his early years as a relatively secure child in a large middle-class family of Mexican immigrants who operated a hardware store in Brownsville, Texas. It shows his early encounters with hardship, racism, and exclusion and how he fought back by trying harder. It traces his college and law school career at the University of Texas, one of only two Mexican-American students in his law school class, and then his rise in Democratic politics and the state bar, all concluding in his appointment as the nation's first Mexican-American federal judge."

"Wasn't he once offered a cabinet position?" I asked.

"U.S. Attorney General during the Carter administration," Rodrigo replied. "He turned it down because he didn't want to uproot his family. Later he received an appointment to the Fifth Circuit. Serving during a time of intense civil rights activity, he handed down many well respected decisions, especially in the areas of labor law where his familiarity with working class people and conditions enabled him to write opinions notable for their progressivism."

"He sounds like a commendable human being," I observed. "In some ways he reminds me of some of the early African-American federal judges of my own generation who struggled to validate themselves in a skeptical world while trying to hand down rulings that advanced the cause of social justice."

"A difficult balancing act," Rodrigo acknowledged. "But I think that with Judge Garza it was harder, somehow. And this brings me back to what we were talking about at the conference."

"Harder because of who he was, or because of social conditions at the time he went on the bench?" I asked.

"Both," Rodrigo replied. "He was appointed during a time of intense ferment, almost all on behalf of blacks. The Chicano movement came much later. His own community, Brownsville, was more than eighty percent Spanish-speaking. Many people were poor, but according to his biographer this resulted more from structural poverty and a lack of jobs than from outright discrimination. Nor did the legal system consider Chicanos a suspect class. Like the Indochinese and other Asian groups, they occupied a sort of limbo—minorities, but not clearly entitled to the special protection of civil rights law."

"Don't the Lat-Crits have a special name for this?" I asked.

"The black-white binary," Rodrigo replied, "an idea that's just now emerging as a means of understanding American civil rights law and the place of nonblack groups in it. The idea is that the structure of antidiscrimination law is dichotomous. It assumes you are either black or white. If you're neither, you have trouble making claims or even having them understood in racial terms at all."

"I think I follow you," I replied. "But could you fill it out a little more? Assuming that our system does incorporate such a dichotomy, how does that render nonblack minority groups one-down, as opposed to, say, one-up, compared to blacks?"

"That's the next step," Rodrigo replied. "At the conference, no one had worked that out fully. Reading about Judge Garza helped me crystallize my thoughts."

"Every time a new movement springs up in the law, it's stimulating," I said. "I remember the ferment when Critical Race Theory came into the world not too many years ago. And, if you can believe it, I was actually around when critical legal studies emerged nearly thirty years ago."

"You have been teaching a long time," Rodrigo replied, giving me a quick look. "And that's why I want to run past you some things I've been thinking about in the wake of the conference."

"Ask away," I said. "How long does the drive to your place take?"

"About forty-five minutes since they built the new airport." Rodrigo eased past a group of slow-moving trucks, accelerated the little sports car smoothly to sixty miles-per-hour, then said: "You remember, Professor, how critical legal studies early on developed the notion of the fundamental contradiction?"

"Of course," I replied. "At the time a breathtaking breakthrough, it explains many of the strains and tensions running through our system of law and politics. It led to powerful critiques of the public-private distinction, judicial indeterminacy, and rights. Were the Latinos at your conference working on something similar?"

"I think we were," Rodrigo replied. "It's that very same black-white binary. If the reigning paradigm identifies only one group as central, everyone else is likely to suffer. Not only that, members of other groups are apt to think of themselves as black or white. It's quite a disabling instrument. We may have to blast the dichotomy—embrace the full multifariousness of life—if we're ever going to get anywhere."

"You put it rather dramatically," I said, smiling at my young friend and protégé to let him know I appreciated his enthusiasm for ideas, even if it was sometimes a little superheated. "I suppose any rigid structure inhibits flexibility during times of change. But I think you started to say this had something to do with Judge Garza."

"I don't want to be too negative," Rodrigo said. "He was a genuine pioneer, for which we should all be grateful. But he never really developed much class consciousness—or, if he did, he kept it pretty secret. He went around the Mexican-American community extolling individualism and telling his countrymen and women that they could rise and accomplish the American dream through hard work, just as he had. He detested discrimination and slurs aimed at Chicanos and Mexicans, but attributed them to individual failures on the part of particular Anglos, not to anything systemic. As a young man he worked for an agency that ran the Texas Rangers, despite their history of brutal mistreatment of his people. He sold war bonds, backed America's role in wars, and encouraged young Mexicans to enlist. He praised all things American, and even ruled against the plaintiffs in *Partida v. Castaneda,* an early case presenting the issue of whether segregation and discrimination aimed against Mexican Americans are redressable."

"He was overruled by the Supreme Court, as I recall," I said.

"Fortunately," Rodrigo agreed. "Garza began—and even ended—with good social instincts and a love of justice. But the black-white racial binary made it difficult for him to think of himself or his group in effective legal terms—as a people with a history of conquest and brutal treatment in need of redress. If you don't have a class analysis—and the binary assures that you don't—all you can do is urge your countrymen to work harder, and those who are oppressing them to back off—as individuals, that is. You'll rule against your people, Jehovah's Witnesses, and other minorities, as he did, and oppose federal welfare programs for the poor and intervention on behalf of prisoners and the institutionalized."

"Didn't I read somewhere that early litigators arguing on behalf of Chicanos and other Latino groups pursued something called the 'other white' strategy?" I asked.

"They did," Rodrigo replied. "It's the logical extension of black-white binary thinking. The only way to get relief is to maintain that your client, a Mexican American or Puerto Rican, say, is white and thus should not be the object of social discrimination."

"Not exactly empowering," I commented wryly. "But I believe you were going to tell me of other ways the binary does its pernicious work."

"In addition to the way just mentioned—namely that it fetters our own minds," Rodrigo said, "preventing us from articulating, or even imagining, how our victimization is a serious, group-based form of oppression."

"You must do so, and in the most complete fashion possible," I said. "If the binary is to serve as Latinos' fundamental contradiction, you have to spell out exactly how this structure of thought renders your people one-down. Otherwise, it's simply an observation, a descriptive statement no more useful than 'many Latinos speak Spanish,' or 'many have ancestors from Latin America or the Caribbean,' or 'a certain judge with good social instincts stopped just short of a civil rights breakthrough.'"

"I agree," Rodrigo replied. "Without such an explanation, the insight kind of runs out of gas." He sneaked a quick peek at his instrument panel, then—"Which reminds me, we'll need a quick stop for fuel before we get home."

"Let me buy," I suggested. "You were kind to come get me in the middle of your evening."

Rodrigo waved my offer aside. "Your listening to my thoughts will be payment enough. We're our best sounding boards, I think."

"That we are," I agreed. "So, what are your ideas on how the black-white paradigm injures Latinos and other nonwhite groups?"

THE BLACK-WHITE PARADIGM AND THE SOCIAL REPRODUCTION OF INEQUALITY: DOCTRINE'S ROLE

"As you know, Professor, the mainstay of American civil rights law is the Equal Protection Clause. Rooted in Reconstruction-era activism and aimed at the wholly laudable purpose of redressing slavery, that clause nevertheless produces and reproduces inequality for Latino people."

"The Equal Protection Clause?" I replied, raising my eyebrows. "That crown jewel in our jurisprudence, centerpiece of justice, and source of civil rights breakthroughs like *Brown v. Board of Education*? It's *this* that you think subordinates and injures Latinos? That's paradoxical, to put it mildly. I think I need to hear more."

"Let me try," Rodrigo replied calmly. "An analogy occurred to me on the way back from my conference. Consider a different constitutional principle, namely, protection of the right of property. How does that function in a society like ours?"

"I suppose you're going to say that it benefits the haves, while disadvantaging or leaving as they are the have-nots, thus increasing the gap between the propertied and those who have less of that commodity."

"Exactly," Rodrigo replied. "And the same is true of other constitutional principles. The Free Speech Clause increases the influence of those who are articulate and can afford microphones, TV air time, and so on. In the same way, the Equal Protection Clause produces a social good, namely equality, for those falling under its coverage—blacks and whites. These it genuinely helps—at least on occasion. But it leaves everyone else unprotected. The gap between blacks and other groups of color grows, all other things being equal. Even Judge Garza advocated on behalf of *maquiladoras* and declined to find Mexican Americans a minority group."

"It sounds strange when you first hear it," I said. "The idea of the Equal Protection Clause producing inequality. But you may have a point. As with those other clauses, the black-white paradigm could marginalize Latinos because of the way the clause and the other Civil War amendments aimed at redressing injustices to blacks."

"I've thought of two other doctrinal sources of inequality," Rodrigo added. "Would you like to hear them?"

"Of course," I said. "I assume they also have to do with the black-white paradigm?"

"They do. The first is the very notion of civil rights. In American law, this means rights bestowed by the civil polity. But Latinos—many of them, at any rate—are not members of that polity. Rather, they want to immigrate here. In this respect they stand on a different footing from blacks. I'm sure you know, Professor, that the plenary power doctrine in immigration law means that someone desiring to immigrate to the U.S. has no power, enforceable in court, to compel equal treatment. U.S. immigration law can be as racist and discriminatory as Congress wishes."

"Immigrants have due process rights, for example to a hearing," I pointed out.

"But only once they're here," Rodrigo replied. "Not to get here in the first place. Since many Latinos, like Asians, come from somewhere else, this limitation affects them drastically. Yet it is inherent in our liberal notion of civil rights and implicit in the black-white binary. Blacks, and even Indians, were here originally or from very early days. Once society decided to count them as citizens, their thoughts and preferences began to figure into the political equation. Even if they were often outvoted and oppressed, their voices at least counted. A Mexican peasant desiring to immigrate in search of a better life, or a Guatemalan village activist fearful that the government wants to kill him, or a Chinese boat person does not count. They can come here only at sufferance, only if Congress decides to let them in."

"For example, through a Bracero program, a student visa, or some other category benefiting the U.S., such as that for investors," I added.

"Judge Garza even cooperated with mass roundups and deportations of undocumented aliens," Rodrigo interjected. "He pioneered mass hearings, rather than individualized adjudication of their cases. He was quite proud of this innovation, believing that it reduced the misery of the detainees, since it shortened the period of time they had to languish in jail and freed space for other, more serious offenders."

"Because the aliens had not been lawfully admitted, they had few rights, except to bare-bones procedural due process," I said. "Judge Garza's legal training did not equip him with a theory for understanding their predicament. It would have taken a judicial genius to pioneer a new approach, especially back then."

"That's true even today," Rodrigo replied, eyeing his gas gauge nervously. "As a society, we seem to have taken a detour on the way to justice. And I'm afraid that you and I will have to take one ourselves if I don't see a gas station soon."

"I have towing insurance," I said half-facetiously. "But I'm sure we won't need it. What's your second doctrinal source of inequality?"

"It's related to the one I just mentioned," Rodrigo said, scrutinizing the approaching off-ramp. "No station there. We'll have to wait until the next one. I'm sure you've heard, Professor, of the self-definition theory of nationhood?"

"In immigration law, you mean?" I asked. Rodrigo nodded. "I have. Going back to an article and a book by Peter Schuck, the argument holds that nations have the inherent right to decide how to define themselves. Otherwise, any group could force a nation to undergo radical transformation merely by moving here. Tapping neorepublican principles, the argument has proved influential in the immigration debate by supplying an ostensibly neutral principle for limiting immigration. And I suppose you think something is wrong with it?"

"I do," Rodrigo replied. "The current contours of the U.S. citizenry are shaped by past immigration policies, which were overtly racist. Recently, those policies have eased somewhat, but only a little. Thus, to ask a body of citizens like ours what sort of person they would like to let in is to invite the answer: as nonthreatening and as much like us as possible. And probably in small numbers, too. If we were a more diverse society, that would not be so bad. But the way things stand, the principle of national self-determination that Schuck and others tout merely reproduces more of the same. Oh, good, there's one and it's still open."

While Rodrigo pumped gas and I cleaned the windshield, we continued as follows: "So, Rodrigo, you think you have found the DNA, so to speak, that reproduces inequality for Chicanos and Hispanics. A triple dynamic, inherent in equal protection doctrine and contractarian politics, that excludes and injures Latinos."

"Yes, but more than mere doctrine holds us back. If it were just that, we could make gains by working outside the legal arena, by mobilizing and educating, for example. Now, let's see, how do I get a receipt?"

"I think you push that button," I said.

"Oh, there it is," Rodrigo said. "They're all a little different."

"Like Latinos and blacks," I quipped.

Rodrigo smiled, and a few seconds later we were easing back onto the freeway with a full tank of gas. "Something happened at the conference that I think you'll find interesting. It illustrates a third way binary thinking injures Latinos. Would you like to hear?"

A FURTHER EXPLANATION: THE OUT-OF-MIND PHENOMENON

I nodded vigorously. "I love conference dynamics. Something zany happens at almost every one. I'd love to hear."

"It's not all that earthshaking," Rodrigo replied. "But I think it captures something. The conference, as I mentioned, featured a star-studded cast. Attendance was fairly good, even though the event was held in the law school, near the edge of campus. The curious thing is that only one law professor from the huge host faculty showed up. The dean, who had been scheduled to introduce the keynote speaker, begged off at the last minute pleading important business, and sent the associate dean instead. And even he didn't stay to hear the address itself."

"Maybe they were just busy," I said a little lamely, trying to excuse my colleagues at that other school, several of whom I knew personally.

"I'm sure that's true," Rodrigo conceded. "But suppose the eminent panel of conferees had been black, consisting of Derrick Bell, Cornel West, John Hope Franklin, Leon Higginbotham, and others of that stature. In fact, the Latino speakers were just as stellar in terms of reputation and standing in their fields."

"Are you saying that attendance would have been better?" I asked.

"I'm not sure it would have been better," Rodrigo replied. "But I suspect the law faculty would have put in at least token appearances. They would have gushed over the speakers, shaken their hands warmly, and told them how glad they were that they were here, how much the students needed them, and so on. They would have shown solidarity and engaged in at least a few minutes of chitchat before, of course, taking off for their offices and their next manuscripts."

"I hope you're not saying their failure to show up was a deliberate affront?" I asked.

"More likely just a matter of priorities. On any given day, dozens of major events take place at a large university. The professors probably saw the conference as just one of many possible demands on their time, like that reception for the married students or that lecture on Proust being held across campus. No conspiracy or conscious boycott operated, but the result was the same: they didn't show up. If we'd been blacks, they would have. It's as simple as that."

"I know that faculty pretty well," I said. "What you recount is surprising. They're all liberals and deep-dyed supporters of civil rights."

"I wouldn't doubt it," Rodrigo replied. "The faculty know, on some level, that Latinos have terrible troubles and need help. But the classic, the *essential* racial group is blacks. If you're a liberal law professor, you donate time to the NAACP Legal Defense Fund. When someone mentions 'civil rights,' you immediately think black."

"And so Latinos are simply out of mind because of the black-white binary," I added.

"We're not part of the mindset or discourse. People don't think of us in connection with civil rights struggles. Another mechanism is geographical. Many Latinos, Chicanos for example, don't live in the cities. They're farmworkers or field hands. But when you think of civil rights, you immediately think of city problems—like gangs, urban blight, segregated run-down schools, and unemployment—that afflict mainly blacks."

"Puerto Ricans are by-and-large an urban group," I pointed out.

"True, and some urban programs do include them. But many Latinos fall almost entirely outside traditional civil rights consciousness, even though their struggles with pesticides, insecticides, field sanitation, and education for their kids are just as serious as those of inner-city dwellers."

"I'm beginning to see the force of the black-white paradigm," I interjected. "It looks like it really does render Latinos one-down."

"And I hope you'll help me figure out more ways that it does. We've touched on three."

"I'm game. What are your thoughts?"

PRACTICAL CONSEQUENCES OF THE BLACK-WHITE PARADIGM

"I think the paradigm not only has doctrinal and conceptual consequences, limiting the way we think of race and racism, concrete real-world ones as well."

"Do you have an example?"

"Let's say you're an employer or state bureaucrat distributing benefits, contracts, or jobs. You can give a job, say, to one of two equally qualified candidates. One's a black, the other a Latino. You probably give it to the black. The black can sue you. He or she has all those civil rights statutes written with him or her in mind. To be sure, courts have held that Latinos may also sue for discrimination. But the employer may not know that. And the Equal Protection Clause does not protect brown litigants as unconditionally and amply as it does blacks. The binary makes the black the prototypical civil rights plaintiff. Recall Judge Garza's ruling in the Texas school discrimination case. When people read of Latinos suing for school or job discrimination, they are always a little surprised."

"Latinos ought to publicize this fact," I said.

"That's the problem. We have fewer leaders who could do so. Affirmative action produced a generation of college-trained black leaders and professionals beginning about thirty years ago. Today, these people are mayors of cities and members of Congress. That body boasts a longstanding Black Caucus, but only a much smaller and more recently formed Hispanic one. And, despite Judge Garza's breakthrough, the entire federal bench includes fewer than thirty Latino judges today. It contains many more black ones, even though the two groups' numbers are almost the same in the general population. And the reason is simple: affirmative action started earlier with blacks. Even today, the average employer thinks of affirmative action in black, not Puerto Rican, Laotian, or Chicano terms. A Laotian or Chicano law teaching candidate shows up, and even liberal law faculty have to remind themselves, 'Oh, yes, they qualify for affirmative action, too.'"

"That's a problem of mindset and conception," I said. "The way society thinks of a group influences the way it behaves toward them. If you're out of mind because everyone is thinking in dichotomous terms, how successful will you be in having your needs noticed and addressed? Listeners may even decide you're at fault for your own predicament, a whiner when you call attention to the way no one attended your conference," I warned my young protégé.

SYMBOL, MYTH, AND THE ROLE OF THE BLACK-WHITE BINARY

"I'll be careful," Rodrigo agreed. "But it's interesting to notice why it's necessary. I think the black-white binary conveys to everyone that there's just one group worth worrying about. People conveniently forget that the early settlers exterminated ninety-five percent of the Indian population, or that many Puerto Rican, Chicano, and Indochinese families are just as poor and desperate as black ones. Recall how much poverty haunted Brownsville where Judge Garza grew up. But only the one group, blacks, has moral standing to demand attention and solicitude. Those others don't. And to make absolutely sure they don't, we deploy appropriate myths and images. Asians are the model minority—smart, quiet, sure to rise in a generation or two, Mexicans are happy-go-lucky cartoon characters or shady actors who sneak across the border, earn some money, and then send it to their families back home. No one today could get away with speaking of blacks in such disparaging terms. But as recently as the 1960s the national Frito-Lay corporation used the logo of a sleeping Mexican bandito, hat pulled over his eyes, dozing under a cactus. Even Judge Garza ran across some of that. And the imagery the political right deploys in the English-only and immigration reform campaigns is nearly as vicious: Latinos come across as criminals, welfare leeches, and drug dealers. If we were part of the civil rights paradigm, no one would dare do this, at least so openly."

"And you think the black-white paradigm is the reason?" I asked.

"Not alone," Rodrigo replied. "But it supplies the conditions that allow it to happen. If one's prevailing cultural image is not that of a noble warrior, like Martin Luther King, but of someone who takes siestas or steals jobs from deserving Americans, why would anyone want to help you?"

"In some ways, those images of Latinos are even more devastating than the ones society has disseminated about blacks, overtly until very recently, and covertly today. They justify society not only in ignoring your misery but in making war against you."

"I'm sure you've heard of the militarized border that is just beginning," Rodrigo interjected.

"I have, and of the imagery deployed by the political right to justify it—the 'waves of immigrants,' the 'horde of welfare recipients,' the 'tide' of brown-skinned welfare mothers just waiting to have babies here so they can gain citizenship, the unassimilability of Latino people and their dubious loyalty."

"Even though Latino servicemen and women have given their lives and won medals for heroism far out of proportion to their numbers and exceeding those of every other racial group," Rodrigo interjected.

"Like Reynaldo Garza and his son, war heroes."

"Right. And consider the issue of language. If an immigrant French couple speak French to each other or English with a French accent, that's considered a sign of high status and culture. A Mexican worker speaks Spanish and he or she is considered stupid or disloyal."

"Here we are," Rodrigo announced, sliding the little car into a driveway. Glancing at a lighted window, he added, "Giannina's still up. You must have a bite with us before retiring."

* * *

A little later I was comfortably ensconced in the hide-a-bed the two young people had graciously opened up for me, reviewing my papers for the Legal Services board meeting I was to attend the next day. As my eyes pored over columns of figures in the plastic-covered binder the chairperson had sent as background reading, my mind kept wandering back to the conversation in the car. I recalled how it had begun with Rodrigo's recounting of Judge Garza's life and career, then continued with his startling announcement that the Equal Protection Clause of the Constitution, with its implicit creation of a black-white binary, functioned as a subordinating instrument and producer of inequality for Latinos. I recalled how Rodrigo had showed that additional forces operate in concert with that paradigm, magnifying its effect—the out-of-mind phenomenon, geography, asset-hoarding, political influence, and cultural imagery—some operating on a practical level, others on a level of myth and narrative.

As I rather sleepily underlined facts and figures for the discussion the next day, I kept coming back to this and other conversations Rodrigo and I had had recently about the role of nonblack groups in America's future. Would a country which I had served for more than forty years as a professor and civil rights advocate adjust peaceably to a century in which whites will begin to be outnumbered by blacks and browns? And would those two minorities be able to work together toward mutual goals—or would the current factionalism and distrust continue into the future, with groups of color competing for crumbs while majoritarian rule continued unabated?

Would the civil rights community prove flexible enough to modify the black-white binary to include other groups? Or would it decide petulantly that broadening vistas to include groups such as Latinos and Asians is too much trouble? For their part, would the young Lat-Crits be content with a new, richer paradigm, or would they aim at an anti-paradigm in which the very concept of race and different races dissolves? Old habits die hard, I thought, recalling the nearly all-white law faculty that had failed to show up for Rodrigo's conference. The more nuanced understanding of race of which Rodrigo spoke would not come easily. I wondered if these issues would replay themselves at tomorrow's board meeting and recalled, with a start, that a neighborhood group had written to our secretary recently questioning the lack of Spanish-speaking attorneys in two cities within our region.

I checked to see that the alarm clock was set early enough that Rodrigo, Giannina, and I could continue the conversation over breakfast tomorrow.

DERRICK BELL'S TOOLKIT
Fit to Dismantle That Famous House?

BLUEBEARD'S CASTLE

In the world of literature and music, *Bluebeard's Castle* is both a French fairy tale and an opera by Béla Bartók. Both tell the story of a nobleman who marries a series of women and spirits them away to his castle, where they remain hidden for the rest of their lives. In Bartók's version, the principal character, Judith, Bluebeard's fourth wife, finds herself attracted to the "strange and awe-inspiring" noble whose heart she hopes to touch with the humanizing power of her love. Despite her family's warnings and the evidence of her senses, she allows herself to become entranced with Bluebeard and takes increasing risks as their relationship develops. When Judith visits Bluebeard's castle, she finds a forbidding, windowless fortress so damp and sunless that, in a signature aria, she sings that the very stones must be weeping.

Walking along a central hallway one day, Judith spies a series of seven locked doors. Hoping to find a ray of light to relieve the castle's gloom, Judith asks Bluebeard to throw them open. He refuses, asking her to accept him on faith. But she persists, certain that the rooms will contain what her hopes tell her must be there—some sign that life with Bluebeard will hold more than the all-pervading dreariness that envelops his castle. When she finally persuades Bluebeard to open the doors and peers inside, she discovers a series of vistas each more horrifying than the last—instruments of torture and hoards of wealth, all stained by blood. Undaunted, Judith insists on admission to the final room. Over Bluebeard's objections she enters, fearing the worst—that she will find the murdered corpses of Bluebeard's three previous wives. Instead, the door opens to reveal that Bluebeard has not murdered them. Far from it, they are quite alive, pale and bedecked in jewels, crowns, and splendid dresses. As they advance, Bluebeard seizes the wide-eyed Judith, who pleads for mercy. But to no avail: Bluebeard drapes her with shining raiment, crown, and jewels, and she slowly, inevitably, takes her place with the others behind the closed doors.

For Bell, Judith's fate is an allegory for blacks' hopes and fears and a metaphor for American racial progress. The seven locked rooms of the castle correspond to major developments in civil rights history such as *Brown v. Board of Education* and 1960s-era civil rights laws. Judith's hope as she opens each door mirrors the black community's celebrations following each milestone; her disappointment, that of African Americans as each advance inevitably is cut back by narrow judicial interpretation, foot dragging, and delay. Bell takes issue with Martin Luther King, Jr., who wrote that "the line of progress [may] never [be] straight," but that a traveler who perseveres will nevertheless "see the city again, closer by." Instead, just as

Bluebeard shuts Judith away when she opens the final door, so America will always shrink from the light so that "[d]isappointed, resigned to our fate, we will watch as the betrayal of our dreams is retired to some somber chamber while the stage grows dark and the curtain falls."

JUDITH'S PREDICAMENT AS METAPHOR FOR AFRICAN-AMERICAN HOPES

Why did Bell choose a French fairy tale to illustrate a point about African-American history and experience? Perhaps to illustrate a universal truth about empowered groups' cynical use of hope to keep the peasantry in line. Perhaps, too, Bell found himself drawn to the story of Bluebeard because he saw himself in Judith, whose transformation from besotted idealist to disillusioned bride mirrors, in some respects, Bell's own life. As the opera opens, Judith entertains a vision of an ideal life with Bluebeard and, despite warnings, takes risks to achieve it. When she finally gains access to the castle, she recognizes it for what it is—just as Bell, despite his early hopes, now recognizes the reality of a persistently racist country. Despite her growing horrific realization, Judith clings to the faith that her marriage will succeed, just as civil rights activists once clung to the hope of a better world.

The force of Bluebeard's story lies in its use of repetition, the seven doors standing in for milestones in black history, but also serving to highlight the maddening similarity of each step, with its repeat cycle of curiosity, hope, revelation, and disappointment. Similarly, the eerie image of the imprisoned brides, coma-like in their consciousness, is driven home through repetition. Three, now four, seemingly identical, pale, imprisoned women forcefully remind us of the fate of a people who fail to grasp their situation or who listen to dreamers who tell them that salvation lies just around the corner.

BLUEBEARD'S CASTLE AND THE ARCHITECTURE OF RACE

In Bell's allegory, Judith could have avoided her predicament by staying home and tending her garden, just as Bell, the sometime cultural nationalist, has encouraged his fellow African Americans to foreswear integration and settle instead for building strong communities. As I will argue later, she need not abjure love entirely but should instead seek it with a more steadfast suitor.

We might begin by taking a closer look at the architecture of that castle with its arrangement of rooms and the relationships they set up among Bluebeard's four wives. Like an Eastern potentate with a harem, Bluebeard may be playing them off against each other, maintaining everything nicely under control. For example, at the very time *Brown v. Board of Education* announced a ringing breakthrough for black schoolchildren, U.S. Attorney General Herbert Brownell was ordering Operation Wetback, a massive roundup of Mexicans, many of them United States citizens, for deportation to Mexico. Recall, as well, how just a few years earlier, a presidential decree had ordered all Japanese Americans living on the West Coast to wartime detention centers, many losing farms and businesses in the process.

By the same token, during Reconstruction southern planters refused to hire the newly freed blacks, instead bringing in Mexicans and Asians to carry out the work the slaves previously performed. In similar fashion, Texas school authorities in the wake of *Brown* certified certain schools desegregated after cynically arranging pupil assignment so that the schools were fifty percent black, fifty percent Mexican American.

Ignoring how society racializes one group at the expense of another, then, is risky business. To understand when one is being manipulated or used to suppress someone else, each minority group must attend to the broader scale. Castle doors may be opening and shutting in a more complex sequence than we will realize if we focus only on the fortunes of one occupant.

When Bell carries out this larger exploration, the desperate urgency that he illustrated through the Bluebeard metaphor will gain even more force. He will be able to show that what minorities saw as social and legal advances actually moved us closer to the forfeiture of our dreams, and how the dominant society arranged it so. Like Judith, we will learn to be skeptical because "neither love nor life can be sustained on unearned trust." This is even more so because the tyrannical Bluebeard, like some of today's conservatives, rationalizes that he did his bedecked, bejeweled, but still imprisoned wives a favor.

Knocking on the Castle Door: The Black-White Binary of Race
Judith's entrancement with Bluebeard may stand as a metaphor for the dichotomous quality that afflicts much racial thought today. As scholars such as Juan Perea have pointed out, traditional civil rights thinking deems a single group paradigmatic, with the experiences and concerns of other groups receiving attention only insofar as they succeed in analogizing themselves to this group. Binary thinking often accompanies "exceptionalism," the belief that one's group is, in fact, so unusual as to justify special treatment, as well as nationalism, the belief that the primary business of a minority group should be to look after its own interests.

Consider now, the many ways that binary thinking—like Judith's initial refusal to consider the fates of Bluebeard's three previous wives—can end up harming even the group whose fortunes one is inclined to place at the center.

Shifting Tides: How Society Arranges Progress for One Group to Coincide with Repression of Another
The history of minority groups in America reveals that while one group is gaining ground, another is often losing it. From 1846 to 1848, the United States waged a bloodthirsty and imperialist war against Mexico in which it seized roughly one-half of Mexico's territory (and later colluded with crafty lawyers and land-hungry Anglos to cheat the Mexicans who chose to remain in the United States of their lands guaranteed under the Treaty of Guadalupe Hidalgo). Yet only a few years later, the

North fought an equally bloody war against the South, ostensibly to free the slaves. During Reconstruction (1865 to 1877), slavery was disbanded, the Equal Protection Clause was ratified, and black suffrage was written into law. Yet, this generosity did not extend to Native Americans: In 1871, Congress passed the Indian Appropriations Act, providing that no Indian nation would be recognized as independent and capable of entering into a treaty with the United States. A few years later, the Dawes Act broke up land held jointly by tribes, resulting in the loss of nearly two-thirds of Indian lands. In 1879, Article XIX of the California constitution made it a crime for any corporation to employ Chinese workers. And in 1882 Congress passed the Chinese Exclusion Laws that were soon upheld in *Chae Chan Ping v. United States*. Goodwill toward one group, then, does not necessarily translate into the same for others.

In 1913, California's Alien Land Law made it illegal for aliens ineligible for naturalization to lease land for more than three years, a measure that devastated the Japanese, many of whom derived their livelihood from agriculture. A few years later, Congress *eased* immigration quotas for Mexicans because they were needed by large farm owners. Go figure.

During the first half of this century, Indian boarding schools sought to erase Indian history and culture, while California segregated black and Chinese schoolchildren to preserve the purity of young Anglo girls. Yet, in 1944, *Lopez v. Seccombe* found segregation of Mexicans from public parks to violate the Equal Protection Clause, and a short time later a federal court declared California's practice of requiring Mexican-American children to attend separate schools unconstitutional. And, in a horrific twist, in the 1940s, the United States softened its stance toward domestic minorities, who were needed in the war industries and as cannon fodder on the front, but turned its back on Jews fleeing the Holocaust.

Shortly after the war, at a time when vistas were beginning to open up for returning black servicemen, Congress reversed its policy of giving United States citizenship to Filipino World War II veterans. Even today, the patchwork of progress for one group coming with retrenchment for another continues. For example, at a time when Indian litigators are winning striking breakthroughs for tribes, California has been passing a series of anti-Latino measures, including English-Only, Proposition 187, and restrictions on bilingual education.

Affirmative Pitting of One Disadvantaged Group against the Other
Not only does binary thinking conceal the checkerboard of racial progress and retrenchment, it can conceal the way dominant society often casts minority groups against one another, to the detriment of both. For example, in early colonial America, white servants had been treated poorly. In 1705, however, when the slave population was growing, Virginia gave white servants more rights than they had enjoyed before, to keep them from joining forces with slaves. In the same era, plantation owners treated house slaves (frequently lighter skinned than their outdoor counterparts) slightly better than those in the fields, recruited some of them to spy on their brothers and sisters outdoors, and rewarded them for turning in dissidents.

In the years immediately following the Civil War, southern plantation owners urged replacing their former slaves, whom they were loath to hire for wages, with Chinese labor. They succeeded: In 1868, Congress approved the Burlingame Treaty with China, under which larger numbers of Chinese could travel to the United States. Immediately following the Civil War, the Army recruited newly freed slaves to serve as Buffalo Soldiers putting down Indian rebellions in the West.

In *People v. Hall,* the California Supreme Court used legal restrictions on blacks and Native Americans to justify banning Chinese from testifying against whites in criminal trials. The court wrote:

> It can hardly be supposed that any Legislature would attempt ... excluding domestic negroes and Indians, who not unfrequently have correct notions of their obligations to society, and turning loose upon the community the more degraded tribes of the same species, who have nothing in common with us, in language, country or laws.

Similarly, Justice Harlan's dissent in *Plessy v. Ferguson* staunchly rebuked segregation for blacks, but supported his point by disparaging the Chinese, who had the right to ride with whites in Louisiana's railroad cars. And, in 1912, when the House of Representatives debated American citizenship for Puerto Ricans, politicians used the supposed failure of other minority groups to justify withholding rights from the newly colonized.

During California's Proposition 187 campaign, proponents curried black votes by portraying Mexican immigrants as competitors for black jobs. Earlier, even the sainted George Sánchez exhorted his fellow Mexican Americans to oppose further immigration from Mexico, on the ground that it would hurt Mexican Americans already here.

Overidentification with Whites
Sometimes the pitting of one minority group against another, inherent in binary approaches to race, takes the form of exaggerated identification with whites at the expense of other groups. For example, early in Mississippi's history, Asians sought to be declared white so that they could attend schools for whites. Early litigators followed a similar "other white" policy on behalf of Mexican Americans, arguing that segregation of Mexican Americans was illegal because the law countenanced only the variety directed against blacks or Asians.

Chinese on the West Coast responded indignantly to *People v. Hall,* the Chinese testimony case, on the grounds that it treated them the same as supposedly inferior Negroes and Indians. Later, Asian immigrants sought to acquire United States citizenship but learned that a naturalization statute that had stood on the books for 150 years, beginning in 1790, denied citizenship to anyone other than whites. In a series of cases, some of which reached the United States Supreme Court, Asians from China, Japan, and India sought to prove that they were white.

Anglocentric norms of beauty divide the Latino and black communities, enabling those who most closely conform to white standards to gain jobs and social acceptance, and sometimes to look down on their darker-skinned brothers and sisters. Box-checking also enables those of white or near-white appearance to benefit from affirmative action without suffering the worst forms of social stigma and exclusion.

Interference with Moral Insight and Generalization

Binary thinking can also impair moral insight and reasoning for whites. Justice John Harlan, author of the famous dissent in *Plessy v. Ferguson,* wrote many shockingly disparaging lines on the Chinese in that case and elsewhere. Similarly, others have pointed out how Earl Warren, who enjoys towering fame as a liberal justice who supported civil rights for blacks and, as governor of California, put an end to school segregation for Asian and Mexican-American schoolchildren, was a prime mover in the effort to remove Japanese Americans to concentration camps in the beginning months of World War II. Until recently, most historians and biographers embraced the official version in which Warren played at most a minor role. It seems quite likely that binary thinking made possible the selective empathy that enabled these two figures to misstep as they did.

Binary thinking can easily allow one to believe that America made only one historical mistake—slavery. If so, the prime order of business is to redress that mistake; the concerns of other groups would come into play only insofar as they resemble, in kind and seriousness, that one great mistake. But simplifications of that form are always debatable, never necessary, and rarely wise. As a leading Native American scholar put it: "To the Indian people it has seemed quite unfair that churches and government agencies concentrated their efforts primarily on the blacks. By defining the problem as one of race and making race refer solely to black, Indians were systematically excluded from consideration." The truth is that all the groups are exceptional; each has been racialized in different ways; none is the paradigm or template for the others.

Blacks were enslaved. Indians were massacred and then removed to the West. Japanese Americans were relocated in the other direction. African Americans are stereotyped as bestial or happy-go-lucky, depending on society's shifting needs; Asians, as crafty, derivative copycats or soulless drones; Mexicans as hot-tempered, romantic, or close to the earth. Blacks are racialized by reason of their color; Latinos, Indians, and Asians on that basis but also by reason of their accent, national origin, and, sometimes, religion as well. All these groups were sought as sources of labor; Indians and Mexicans, as sources of land. Puerto Ricans, Indians, and Mexicans are racialized by reason of conquest. Latinos, Indians, and Asians are pressured to assimilate; blacks to do the opposite. The matrix of race and racialization thus is constantly shifting, sometimes overlapping, for the four main groups.

This differential racialization renders binary thinking deeply problematic. Consider the recent trial of Ronald Ebens for the murder of Vincent Chin, whom he beat to death for being a "Jap" supposedly responsible for the loss of jobs in the automobile industry. After Ebens's first trial in Detroit, which resulted in a twenty-five year jail sentence, was overturned for technical reasons, his attorney moved for a change of venue on the ground that Ebens could not be tried fairly in that city. The motion was successful, and the second trial was held in Cincinnati, where Ebens was acquitted. A United States Commission on Civil Rights report speculated that the acquittal resulted from the limitations of the black-white paradigm of race, which may have misled the Cincinnati jury, sitting in a city where Asian Americans are few, into disbelieving that racism against Asians played a part in the crime.

"You're So Special": When Minorities Succumb to the Siren Song of Uniqueness

Black-white or any other kind of binary thinking can also warp minorities' views of themselves and their relation to whites. As social scientists know, Caucasians occasionally select a particular minority group as a favorite, usually a small, non-threatening one, and make that group overseers of the others or tokens to rebut any inference that the dominant group is racist. Minorities may also identify with whites in hopes of gaining status or benefits under specific statutes, such as the naturalization statute, that limit benefits to whites. The siren song of specialness may also predispose a minority group to believe that it is uniquely victimized and entitled to special consideration from iniquitous whites. Latino exceptionalists, for example, sometimes point out (if only privately) that Latinos have the worst rates of poverty and school dropout; are soon to be the largest group of color in the United States; fought bravely in many foreign wars and earned numerous medals and commendations; and are racialized in perhaps the greatest variety of ways of any group, including language, accent, immigration status, perceived foreignness, conquered status, and certain particularly virulent stereotypes. Needless to say, specialness lies entirely in the eye of the beholder and can be maintained only by presenting a particular interpretation of history as the only true one.

Impairment of the Ability to Generalize and Learn from History: Reinventing the Wheel

Binary thinking and exceptionalism also impair the ability to learn from history; they doom one to reinvent the wheel. For example, when recent scholars put forward the theory of interest convergence to account for the ebb and flow of black fortunes, the theory came as a genuine breakthrough, enabling readers to understand a vital facet of blacks' experience. Yet, the long train of Indian treaty violations, as well as Mexicans' treatment in the wake of the Treaty of Guadalupe Hidalgo, might have led commentators to arrive at that insight earlier and to mold it into a broader, more powerful form. By the same token, the treatment of Asians, with the group first favored, then disfavored when conditions change, might have inspired a similar, more nuanced theory. And in Mexican-American jurisprudence, *Mendez v. Westminster School District,* decided seven years before *Brown v. Board of Education,* marked the first time a major court expressly departed from the rule of *Plessy v. Ferguson* in a challenge to *de jure* segregation. Had it not been for a single alert litigator on the staff of the NAACP Legal Defense Fund who recognized the case's importance and insisted that the organization participate in *Mendez* as amicus, *Mendez* would have been lost to African Americans and the road to *Brown* would have been harder and longer. Finally, when Mexican Americans were demanding their rights, George Sánchez, anticipating one of the arguments that the NAACP used to great effect in *Brown*—namely, that continued discrimination against blacks endangered the United States' moral leadership in the uncommitted world—argued that mistreatment of Latinos in the United States could end up injuring the country's relations with Latin America. Earlier, the Japanese in California had effectively deployed a similar argument when San Francisco enacted a host of demeaning rules.

Writings by Derrick Bell and Gerald Rosenberg pointing out the limitations of legal reform for minorities are foreshadowed in the experience of American Indians when the state of Georgia refused to abide by the Supreme Court's ruling in *Worcester v. Georgia* and President Andrew Jackson did nothing to enforce it. After Bell wrote his signature *Chronicle of the Space Traders,* Michael Olivas observed that Latino and Cherokee populations experienced literal removal several times thereafter.

Impairment of Coalitions

Finally, dichotomous thought impairs groups' abilities to forge useful coalitions. For example, neither the NAACP nor any other predominantly African-American organization filed an amicus brief challenging Japanese internment in *Korematsu v. United States,* or in any of the other cases contesting that practice. Earlier, the League of United Latin American Citizens (LULAC), a politically moderate litigation organization for Latinos, distanced itself from other minority groups and even from darker-skinned Latinos by pursuing the "other white" strategy. And in Northern California, Asians, Mexican Americans, and blacks recently have been at loggerheads over admission to Lowell High School and UC-Berkeley.

Sometimes, minority groups do put aside differences and work together successfully. For example, Chinese- and Spanish-speaking parents successfully challenged monolingual instruction in San Francisco in *Lau v. Nichols.* Jews and blacks marched hand in hand in the sixties. A coalition of California Latinos and Asians collaborated in striking down Proposition 187, which denied social services and public education to undocumented immigrants. And another coalition of minority groups has been working to change the nearly all-white lineup on current television programs.

The school desegregation case *Mendez v. Westminster School District,* which (as I described earlier) was a rare exception to the inability of minority groups to generalize from other groups' experiences, is worth recounting in some detail. By the 1920s, Mexican immigration had made Mexican Americans the largest minority group in California. Although state law did not require school districts to segregate Mexican-American schoolchildren, pressure from Anglo parents led most school boards to do so on the pretext that the Mexican children's language difficulties made this in their best educational interest. On March 2, 1945, a small group of Mexican-American parents filed suit in federal district court to enjoin that practice. The court ruled, nearly a year later, that because California lacked a segregation statute, the doctrine of "separate but equal" did not apply. Moreover, it found that sound educational reasons did not support separation of the Mexican children, that separation stigmatized them, and ruled the practice unconstitutional.

The school districts appealed to the Ninth Circuit Court of Appeals, at which point the case came to the attention of the American Jewish Congress and the NAACP Legal Defense Fund. The NAACP's amicus brief, prepared by Robert Carter, advanced many of the same arguments the attorneys for the Mexican plaintiffs had put forward in the trial court, but added a new one based not on legal doctrine or precedent, but on social science. Relying heavily on data collected by Ambrose Caliver, an African-American researcher employed by the U.S. Department of Education, Carter argued that racial segregation would inevitably lead to inferior schools for minorities because few school districts could afford the cost of a dual system and would inevitably cut corners with the schools for Mexicans and blacks. Citing the work of Gunnar Myrdal and others, Carter also argued that racial segregation demoralized and produced poor citizenship among minority individuals and thus contravened public policy.

The NAACP's brief was cautious and incremental in arguing that segregation invariably led to spending differentials. At the same time, its social science was rudimentary, relying as it did on studies of the adverse effects of segregation in general, rather than on ones showing that segregated education harmed minority schoolchildren. A second brief authored by a group of social scientists and submitted by lawyer and historian Carey McWilliams supplied many of the ingredients missing from the NAACP's brief. The social scientists marshalled studies showing that young children were especially vulnerable to the crippling effects of forced racial separation and quick to absorb the lesson of inferiority. This more narrowly targeted argument was the very one the NAACP would adopt, years later, in *Brown v. Board of Education.*

Although the Ninth Circuit affirmed the trial court opinion, it did so on the narrow ground that California law lacked any provision for the segregation of the Mexican schoolchildren. Two months later, Governor Earl Warren eliminated that loophole by signing a bill repealing all of California's statutes requiring racial segregation. Thus, official segregation in California came to an end.

While the appeal was pending, the NAACP sent their brief to William Hastie, one of the principal figures in the campaign against segregated schooling. Quickly appreciating its significance, Hastie wrote to Thurgood Marshall, encouraging him to develop the argument contained in the social scientists' brief "with as little delay as possible." Marshall agreed, and assigned Annette H. Peyser, a young staff member with a background in social science, to do so. She did, and other social scientists, learning of the NAACP's interest, pursued their own studies of the intrinsic harm of forced racial separation, many of which found their way into the graduate school litigation cases and ultimately into *Brown* itself.

The *Mendez* case demonstrates that narrow nationalism not only deprives one of the opportunity to join with other groups, it can also close one off from the experiences and lessons of others. It can conceal how the American caste system, in a complex dance, disadvantages one group at one time and advantages it at another. It can disguise the way American society often affirmatively pits groups against one another, using them as agents of each other's subordination, or uses mistreatment of one group as a template for discrimination against another. Because almost all racial binaries consist of a nonwhite group paired with whites, they predispose outgroups to focus excessively on whites, patterning themselves after and trying to gain concessions from them, or aiming to assimilate into white society.

WHAT CAN WE DO?

Minority groups in the United States should consider abandoning all binaries, narrow nationalisms, and strategies that focus on cutting the most favorable possible deal with whites, and instead set up a secondary market in which they negotiate selectively with each other. For example, instead of approaching the establishment supplicatingly, in hopes of a more favorable admission formula at an elite school or university system, Asians might approach African Americans with the offer of a bargain. That bargain might be an agreement on the part of the latter group to support Asians with respect to an issue important to them—for example, easing immigration restrictions or supporting bilingual education in public schools—in return for their own promise not to pursue quite so intensely rollbacks in affirmative action or set-asides for black contractors. The idea would be for minority groups to assess their own preferences and make tradeoffs that may bring gains for all concerned. Some controversies may turn out to be polycentric, presenting win-win possibilities so that negotiation can advance goals important to both sides without compromising anything either group deems vital. Like a small community that sets up an informal system of barter, exchanging jobs and services moneylessly, thus reducing sales and income taxes, this approach would reduce the number of times minorities approach whites hat in hand. Some gains may be achievable by means of collective action alone. When it is necessary to approach whites for something, a nonbinary framework allows that approach to be made in full force. It also deprives vested interests of the opportunity to profit from flattery, false compliments, and mock sympathy ("Oh, your terrible history. Your group is so special. Why don't we. . . .").

Ignoring the siren song of binaries opens up new possibilities for coalitions based on level-headed assessment of the chances for mutual gain. It liberates one from dependence on a system that has advanced minority interests at best sporadically and unpredictably. It takes interest convergence to a new dimension.

Bluebeard's Castle could just as easily have served as an allegory about gender imbalance and the social construction of marriage between unequals. Although Bell does not draw this lesson from it, it is certainly as implicit in the French fairy tale as the lesson Bell extracts about black progress. Seen through this other lens, a straightforward solution, one that Judith apparently never contemplated, would have been to engage in collaborative action with Bluebeard's three previous wives against their common oppressor, the gloomy noble bent on subjugating them all—in short, an injection of feminist solidarity. Persisting in an unsuccessful strategy, waging it with more and more energy, can prove a counsel of despair. Sometimes, as with the black-white binary, one needs to turn a thought structure on its side, look at it from a different angle, and gain some needed distance from it, before the path to liberation becomes clear.

PART VII
Politics and Critique

The wall between law and politics has never been impermeable. Classroom discussions frequently focus on how case holdings affect policy decisions. And, of course, lawmakers often enact laws with a policy goal in mind. Delgado's writings on politics and critique extend his analysis of law into the broader reaches of social policy and culture, which legal scholarship frequently does not address adequately.

In "Shadowboxing" he shows how legal rules reflect cultural power invisibly and seemingly naturally.

In "Rodrigo's Seventh Chronicle," Rodrigo startles the Professor by declaring that the Enlightenment was, and continues to be, a source of racial oppression, and that democracy simply maintains it.

The Professor meets Giannina's mother, Teresa, and is smitten in "Rodrigo's Remonstrance," a satirical essay somewhat reminiscent of Jonathan Swift's "Modest Proposal." During a social visit at Teresa's condominium, during which those present discuss a number of books, Rodrigo puts forth the outrageous premise that minorities would benefit from treatment as endangered species as do certain animals under the Endangered Species Act.

"Rodrigo's Roadmap" introduces Rodrigo's friend Lazlo Kowalski, a conservative colleague at Rodrigo's law school. By chance, they encounter the Professor at a conference and talk about whether the free market is capable of driving out racism. Rodrigo posits that law and economics scholars ignore or discount the problem of evil. The Professor doubts that economic analysis can address the knotty problems of social realities such as race relations. Laz proposes a left-right synthesis of race-neutral programs designed to help the poor of every race.

Delgado asks the question, "To whom should the nonwhite poor turn for help?" in "Zero-Based Racial Politics." After evaluating the best-case arguments that could be made to each of the two dominant political parties in the United States on behalf of the poor, he puts forth an answer that may be surprising.

Shadowboxing
An Essay on Power

It is important to know when we are being gulled, manipulated, and duped. It is even more important to know when we are unwittingly doing this to ourselves—when we are using shopworn legal scripts and counterscripts, going around endlessly in circles, getting nowhere. Understanding how we use predictable arguments to rebut other predictable arguments in a predictable sequence—"The plaintiff should have the freedom to do X," "No—the defendant should have the security not to have X done to her"; "The law should be flexible, permitting us to do justice in particular cases," "No—the law must be determinate; only bright-line rules are administrable and safe"—frees us to focus on real-world questions that do matter. We can begin to see how the actions we take as lawyers, law students, and legal scholars advance or retard principles we hold dear. We can see where the scripts come from and, perhaps, how to write new and better ones.

AN EXAMPLE: "SUBJECTIVE" VERSUS "OBJECTIVE" STANDARDS

Everyone knows that in many areas the law prefers "objective" over "subjective" standards for judging conduct. Tort law uses the reasonable person doctrine, contract law applies objective rules to determine when a contract has been formed and what its terms mean, and so forth. Where does this preference come from, and what does it say about ourselves and our legal culture? Does the objective-subjective distinction hold up under analysis? When we rehearse the familiar arguments in favor of one approach or the other, what are we doing, and what is at stake?

Consider the standards used in three areas: cigarette warnings, informed consent to medical treatment, and date rape. Tobacco companies defend their marketing of a product known to cause cancer, heart disease, and a host of other illnesses by invoking the narratives of *freedom* and *consent*. The warnings they place on cigarette packages are visible and easy to read. Purchasers who smoke despite these warnings must be deemed to consent to the risks of that activity; any more effective measure would unacceptably impair freedom of action. To the objections that some consumers are addicted, will ignore the warnings, or will bow to social pressure, the manufacturers reply that the warnings are what an ordinary consumer living in our society would expect when purchasing a somewhat hazardous product, and that no further effort on their part is necessary.

One aspect of the debate on cigarette warnings was before the Supreme Court a few years ago. In *Cipollone v. Liggett Group, Inc.*, a widow whose husband died of smoking-induced lung disease sued a large cigarette manufacturer for damages. The issue was whether federal law, which requires only the current labeling, supersedes state tort law, under which a stricter standard of liability might be applied to cases like the Cipollones'. Not surprisingly, the defendant advocated application of the more formal, and more easily satisfied, federal standard; the plaintiff, the more flexible state-law tort approach.

The law of informed consent to medical treatment operates in a similar fashion. Before performing medical operations or other invasive procedures, doctors must communicate to the patient what a reasonable person would want to know about the material risks and benefits of the procedure, and obtain the patient's consent. It is immaterial whether the patient has an undisclosed or highly personalized fear or preference that, if known, would have called for further information or a different course of action. The law requires only the doctor's initial disclosure of "objective" information.

Some physicians, to be sure, may go further, asking, "Is there anything else you are concerned about?" But it is the rare doctor who asks the patient about her specific feelings and attitudes toward pain, incapacity, dependency, death, risk aversiveness, reproductive faculties, and religion—a few of the matters that could bear significantly on a medical decision. Answers to these questions might suggest to the doctor the necessity of further discussions with the patient, further disclosures, or a different course of treatment.

The case law of informed consent makes clear, however, that the physician's duty to disclose is simpler and more easily satisfied. The leading case in this area, *Cobbs v. Grant*, requires that the doctor disclose to the patient the reasonable risks and complications of the contemplated procedure and, beyond this, what a competent member of the medical community would disclose. Although more exacting standards have been proposed, they are not yet the law.

The debate on date rape exhibits a similar structure: men generally prefer an objective standard, women a more broad-based, subjective one. If a man can truthfully report that a woman accompanied him without protest, did not resist his advances, and began disrobing when he did, the man wants those actions to be deemed consent. For many date-rape activists, however, that is only the beginning of the story. Under a subjective standard, other factors come into play. We also need to know whether the woman felt coerced or intimidated. Perhaps they were at a party where they drank too much liquor. Perhaps the woman felt social pressure to pair off. Perhaps she was afraid to say no, afraid of ostracism or of having to go home alone in the dark if the man grew disgusted and left. Perhaps the atmosphere was such that a woman could not easily say no.

Men generally find this type of response infuriating: in their view, women just want to be able to change their minds, depending on what happens later—how he behaves (does he send flowers?), how she feels in the morning, whether or not she becomes pregnant. Men want the woman's outward behavior at the time of the incident to be conclusive: if a reasonable observer would interpret her actions to signal willingness to have sex, that should end the inquiry. She consented. A more individualized approach would chill legitimate courtship behavior, encourage bogus claims, and be impossible to adjudicate. Additionally, it might patronize, encouraging women to see themselves as weak, easily led, and in need of protection.

WHAT THE SUBJECTIVE-OBJECTIVE DEBATE SHOWS—AND CONCEALS

Underlying these stylized debates about subjective versus objective standards is a well-hidden issue of cultural *power,* one neatly concealed by elaborate arguments that predictably invoke predictable "principle." These arguments invite us to take sides for or against abstract values that lie on either side of a well-worn analytical divide, having remarkably little to do with what is at stake. The arguments mystify and sidetrack, rendering us helpless in the face of powerful repeat players like corporations, human experimenters, action-loving surgeons, and sexually aggressive men.

How does this happen? Notice that in many cases it is the stronger party—the tobacco company, surgeon, or male date—that wants to apply an objective standard to a key event. The doctor wants the law to require disclosure only of the risks and benefits the average patient would find material. The male partygoer wants the law to ignore the woman's subjective thoughts in favor of her outward manifestations and words. The tobacco company wants the warning on the package to be a stopper. Generally, the law complies.

What explains the stronger party's preference for an objective approach, and the other's demand for a more personalized one? It is not that one approach is more principled, more just, or even more likely to produce a certain result than the other. Rather, the answer lies in issues of power and culture. It is now almost a commonplace that we construct the social world. We do this through stories, narratives, myths, and symbols—by using tools that create images, categories, and pictures. Over time, through repetition, the dominant stories seem to become true, natural, "the way things are." Recently, outsider jurisprudence has been developing means, principally "counterstorytelling," to displace or overturn these comfortable majoritarian myths and narratives.

The debate on objective and subjective standards touches on these issues of world-making and the social construction of reality. Powerful actors, such as tobacco companies and male dates, want objective standards applied to them simply because these standards always, and already, reflect them and their culture. These actors have been in power; their subjectivity long ago was deemed "objective" and imposed on the world. Now their ideas about meaning, action, and fairness are built into our culture, into our view of male-female, doctor-patient, and manufacturer-consumer relations.

It is no surprise, then, that judgment under an "objective" (or reasonable person) standard generally will favor the stronger party. This, however, is not always the case: Rules that too predictably and reliably favored the strong would be declared unprincipled. The stronger actor must be able to see his favorite principles as fair and just—ones that a reasonable society would rely upon in contested situations. He must be able to depict the current standards as integral to justice, freedom, fairness, and administrability—to everything short of the American Way itself (and maybe even that, since societies that regulate these relationships more closely are paternalistic, and verge on [shhh!] socialism).

HOW OBJECTIVITY DOES ITS WORK

We have cleverly built power's view of the appropriate standard of conduct into the very term *fair*. Thus, the stronger party is able to have his way and see himself as principled at the same time.

Imagine, for example, a man's likely reaction to the suggestion that subjective considerations—a woman's mood, her sense of pressure or intimidation, how she felt about the man, her unexpressed fear of reprisals if she did not go ahead—ought to play a part in determining whether the man is guilty of rape. Most men find this suggestion offensive; it requires them to do something they are not accustomed to doing. "Why," they say, "I'd have to be a mind reader before I could have sex with anybody." "Who knows, anyway, what internal inhibitions the woman might have been harboring?" And "what if the woman simply changed her mind later and charged me with rape?"

What we never notice is that women can "read" men's minds perfectly well. The male perspective is right out there in the world, plain as day, inscribed in culture, song, and myth—in all the prevailing narratives. These narratives tell us that men want and are entitled to sex, that it is a prime function of women to give it to them, and that unless something unusual happens, the act of sex is ordinary and blameless. We believe these things because that is the way we have constructed women, men, and "normal" sexual intercourse.

Notice what the objective standard renders irrelevant: a downcast look; ambivalence; the question, "Do you really think we should?"; slowness in following the man's lead; a reputation for sexual selectivity; virginity; youth; and innocence. Indeed, only a loud firm "no" counts, and probably only if it is repeated several times, overheard by others, and accompanied by forceful body language such as pushing the man and walking away briskly.

Yet society and law accept only this latter message (or something like it), and not the former, more nuanced ones, to mean refusal. Why? The "objective" approach is not inherently better or more fair. Rather, it is accepted because it embodies the sense of the stronger party, who centuries ago found himself in a position to dictate what permission meant. Allowing ourselves to be drawn into reflexive, predictable arguments about administrability, fairness, stability, and ease of determination points us away from what really counts: the way in which stronger parties have managed to inscribe their views and interests into "external" culture, so that we are now enamored with that way of judging action. First, we read our values and preferences into the culture; then we pretend to consult that culture meekly and humbly in order to judge our own acts. A nice trick if you can get away with it.

WHY NOT A SUBJECTIVE STANDARD? ON BEING "UNPRINCIPLED" ON PRINCIPLE

"But it wouldn't be *fair* to require more. A man would virtually have to carry out a half-hour cross-examination before going to bed with a woman." (Men, of course, have no difficulty quizzing women—or each other, for that matter—at length when deciding whether to enter into a business partnership or deal, looking for ambivalence, doubt, or strength of motivation.) A cigarette manufacturer would have to place a blinking neon sign on every pack of cigarettes. (Fine—cigarette manufacturers do just that when they install billboards aimed at creating demand and convincing new consumers that placing a burning carcinogenic object in their mouths is desirable and a path to social acceptance.) To get their message *into* your minds, stronger parties are perfectly willing to go to great effort and expense. But to find out whether you are *willing* to do what they want, oh no, we must rely on simple, easily ascertained "objective" factors.

The subordinate party, naturally, prefers the subjective standard. No matter how limited one's resources or range of options, no matter how unequal one's bargaining position, at least one's thoughts are free. Small wonder that the recent legal-storytelling movement holds such appeal to people of color, women, gays and lesbians. Stories inject a new narrative into our society. They demand attention; if aptly told, they win acceptance or, at a minimum, respect. This is why women demand to tell their account of forced sex, why cancer victims insist that their smoking was a redressable harm despite the tobacco companies' pathetic warnings, and why patient advocates demand a fundamental restructuring of the doctor-patient relationship.

A FINAL EXAMPLE AND CONCLUSION

I began by observing that law-talk can lull and gull us, tricking us into thinking that categories like objective and subjective and the stylized debates that swirl about them really count when in fact they either collapse or appear trivial when viewed from the perspective of cultural power. If we allow ourselves to believe that these categories do matter, we can easily expend much energy replicating predictable, scripted arguments—and in this way, the law turns once-progressive people into harmless technocrats.

But this happens in a second way as well, when we borrow *their* tools for *our* projects without sensing the danger in that use. For example, a recent article by a critical race scholar proposes a novel approach to the impact-intent dichotomy in antidiscrimination law. Most persons of majority race, including judges, are not prepared to see subtle forms of "institutional" or "latter-day" racism in the absence of vicious intent. That is, "impact" alone is not enough. To bridge the gap between currently unredressable, unintentional discrimination and the redressable, intentional kind, one author proposes that the law recognize a third, *unconscious* form of redressable discrimination. So far, so good. But his article goes on to propose a "cultural meaning test" for this sort of unconscious racism. Under this test, unconscious racism is redressable if, in light of prevailing cultural meanings and understandings, the action is racist. It is no defense that the actor did not *intend* racial harm; if persons in the culture would reasonably interpret his act as racially offensive, the court will as well.

Although the above mentioned article has won an enthusiastic reception from moderate-liberal writers, the cultural-meaning test takes the teeth out of his proposal. Majority society has *defined* racial reality in such a way that relatively few acts are racist. "Racism" is limited to those rare individual (not institutional) acts of a vicious, indefensible, shocking sort. It tends to be associated with persons of another class, who have little political influence and lack the ability to structure society in such a way that your and my forms of racism are condemned. The author would have done better to couple his suggestion with proposals to change the legal culture, as the storytelling movement sets out to do. Instead, he proposes small doctrinal adjustments within that culture which will prove ineffective because they do not consider the systems of power and knowledge within which all interpretive acts take place.

* * *

Sometimes a gestalt switch is necessary. As in a drawing by Escher, a figure will stand out only if we focus on the background and ignore the foreground at which we have been staring. If we constantly skirmish with the legal foreground when it is the background that has causal efficacy, we are unlikely to get anywhere. I propose that in many cases it will behoove us to examine the legal background—the bundle of assumptions, baselines, presuppositions, and received wisdoms—against which the familiar interpretive work of courts and legislatures takes place. Sometimes, all the rest is shadowboxing.

Rodrigo's Seventh Chronicle
Race, Democracy, and the State

The familiar voice in my receiver gave me quite a start: "Professor, it's me, Rodrigo Crenshaw. I'm at the corner grocery store just down the block from your building."

I had been getting a number of calls from former students wanting to know if I would serve as a reference for the bar examiners or an employer. After making a quick gestalt switch, I said: "Sorry it took me a minute to recognize your voice. Come on up if you have time. It's been a while."

In a few minutes, the tall, lanky Rodrigo was standing in my doorway. An African-American LL.M. student at the famous university across town, the brilliant young firebrand had entered my life about a year ago when he sought me out for career advice. The son of a U.S. serviceman and an Italian mother, Rodrigo had been educated in Italy, where his father was serving. He graduated from the base high school, then attended an Italian university and law school on government scholarships, graduating close to the top of his law school class. He and I had met a number of times to discuss critical thought, cultural history, law and economics, and the U.S. racial scene.

"How has your summer been going, Professor?" Rodrigo cast his eyes over my desk. "Looks like you've got your blue books done."

"I had to grade fast this year, because—did I tell you?—I received a grant to spend a month at a study center in northern Italy. I just got back, in fact."

"I didn't know. The last time we talked, I was so wrapped up in my own problems I neglected to find out about your plans. So, what did you think of my old country?"

"I loved it. The countryside and food were great. I'm sure I've put on a couple of pounds. And I used the time at the center to finish that book we talked about before."

"Were the working conditions good?"

"Ideal. It's right by a lake. I thought of writing you, but they said the mail takes weeks. I would have called you soon, if you hadn't showed up first."

"The government's been in turmoil. Did that affect your trip?"

"No—all was calm so far as I could tell. You have relatives there, though, right?"

Rodrigo nodded yes. "In Bologna, mainly."

"Are they okay?"

"Fine. I talked to them last week. They say it's no worse than usual. You probably know that in Italy, as in many parliamentary democracies, the government changes easily and often."

"And not just the national government," I offered. "Regional and even city governments vary. You can travel three miles and be in a completely different regime. In one town, the government can be centrist or socialist. The next town over can be communist, and so on."

"I know. It makes life there interesting. When I came to the States, I went through the reverse adjustment. Here, you have only two basic approaches to politics, each linked with a competing conception of the state. Things seemed to me static, almost boring. Of course, there's nothing European students love better than to sit in a café and discuss politics."

"Do you miss the ferment there?"

"A little. I couldn't help being struck by the contrast. Here, twenty different theories or approaches to law vie for acceptance, ranging from right-wing law and economics to left-wing critical race theories, like those you and your friends are developing. Yet, thinking about the *state* seems frozen at a fairly simple level."

"Compared to elsewhere, you mean?"

"Yes, it's remarkably dichotomous. For example, I've noticed that exactly one-half of my professors think government should be large and powerful, an agent for change."

"We both know what political party they are apt to belong to."

"Of course. And the others believe in the minimalist state. For them the larger the government, the more harm it is likely to do. Then, there are the communitarians and civic republicans, who want greater identification between the citizen and the state. But aside from those, the possibilities seem quite limited. My friend and fellow LL.M. student Ali says he almost never runs into a fellow Marxist."

"A growing number of the students are libertarians," I commented.

"I've noticed that," Rodrigo agreed. "They strike me as a variant of Republicans, even if they don't identify with that party. Their fascination with deregulation, personal privacy, and laissez-faire economics reminds me of the strain of political thinking that prevailed during your period of rapid expansion a century ago."

"But you were saying that all those categories were played out."

"I think so, Professor. For example, consider the age-old problem of race—something both of us care deeply about. Proponents of both the activist and quietist state say they have our interests at heart. Yet people of color seem to do no better in the one regime than in the other. In some respects, we have the worst possible situation here."

I made a mental note to ask Rodrigo something about that later if the opportunity arose, but resisted the temptation for now. Instead I said, as non-committally as possible: "Some of us have written about that."

"I know."

"And I suppose you think the solution to our social ills is bound up with the concept of the state in some fashion, so that a different form of government is a necessary step toward resolving those problems?"

"As always, it's easier to see what's wrong with the current system than to figure out what to put in its place. But if you have the time, Professor, I'd love to run some ideas past you. I'm thinking of using them for the last part of my dissertation; a draft is due by the end of the summer."

"I'd be happy to listen. As always, I'm sure I'll learn as much as you. Would you like some dinner?"

"Giannina and I just ate. But I'd be glad to join you for a snack."

"The two of you remain on good terms, I assume?"

"Yes, we're doing just fine."

"I'm glad to hear it." As I gathered up my keys and sweater, I asked, "And what are your plans?"

"Oh, I've got a teaching job! My friend Ali got one, too. Mine's in the Midwest. I'm not sure what Giannina and I are going to do. We're getting along really well after that rift I told you about. But she's reluctant to leave the city, where she has all her writing contacts."

"Sounds like a difficult decision," I commiserated. "I know couples who have tried commuting. Some find it grueling; for others, it's not so bad. There's a little dessert shop just down the street," I said. "Can I interest you?"

"Great. I can always eat dessert," my young friend said with enthusiasm.

IN WHICH RODRIGO EXPLAINS THE CONNECTION BETWEEN RACISM AND DEMOCRACY

A few minutes later, we were comfortably seated in the pastry shop down the block from the law school. After selecting our desserts from a tray the waiter brought, I said:

"You were saying something about the relationship between government and racism, Rodrigo. Something about our form being the worst of all for minorities. I'm sure you mean in theory because, in practice, other cultures are just as bad, if not worse."

"Both in theory and in practice, Professor. It may sound troubling."

"It certainly does," I burst in. "What about Cambodia? What about ethnic cleansing? What about the religious tyranny of Iran? And what about the honorable moments of our own history, like *Brown v. Board of Education*?"

"Let me explain, Professor," Rodrigo replied mildly. "There is plenty of blame to go around. Other cultures have been vicious, too. But they have tended to victimize outsiders, generally nonmembers or historic enemies. We—I mean Western democracies—are practically alone in our systematic mistreatment of our own minorities. And this is a major problem for any theory of government—understanding and regulating the relation between the majority and the minority, I mean."

"You have a theory, I assume?" Rodrigo brightened, whether at my question or the arrival of the waiter with our desserts, I couldn't tell. "What are you having?"

I looked at his plate. "Flan," he replied.

"Looks good," I said, taking a spoonful of my own lemon sherbet. "Now tell me about your theory of government and race."

"I didn't mean to be too harsh earlier, Professor. Your—I mean our—system has some of the best formal values in the world. We have language declaring that all men and women are equal, about the brotherhood of man, and so on. On the Fourth of July, when all the flags are flying, and on a few other occasions of an official nature Americans can be counted on to be genuinely fair minded, genuinely antiracist."

"A few of them can be counted on at other times, too," I interjected.

"To be sure. Yet in moments of informality, those same Americans feel free to tell an ethnic joke, to complain about blacks, or talk to a woman condescendingly."

"We've all seen that. We know that there are certain places, bars and the like, where we are not safe. And we know that even those white folks who we can ordinarily trust, who would not think of saying anything hurtful, change. At certain times, in a certain atmosphere, at a certain party, in the company of certain others—you have to watch out."

"I think the axis has something to do with fairness and formality," Rodrigo said. "On formal occasions, such as in court, when serving on a jury perhaps, the average American can sometimes get beyond race. You have all those reminders—the flag, the robes, the judge, the solemn words—that cue you that this is an occasion where the formal values, the higher, official ones, are to preponderate. Other, more intimate occasions do not evoke those same values. The same person can be racist one minute, then nonracist the next, depending on the setting."

"Interesting," I replied. "I think I agree with you. But what about a country like South Africa?"

"There the situation is exactly reversed. The public values, until recently, were officially racist. But on occasion South African whites could be counted on to show real compassion in their private lives. If you were a black and in trouble of some sort, a private citizen, not the government, would be your most likely source of help."

"Maybe that's why American blacks like big government and historically have looked to the Democratic Party and the federal government as our salvation."

"I think it may have something to do with that," Rodrigo replied. "But more and more, it's beginning to appear that that is a vain hope. Neither political party does much for us. Our fortunes are little better under the bigger-spending Democrats than under the less-is-more Republicans."

"I agree. And so, I gather you think we need some wholly new approach?"

"I do," Rodrigo replied. "We can't rely on formality forever. Otherwise, our young people will get jobs in exactly two areas—sports and the Army. Superimposed on the entire system is a layer of anti-black sentiment. To get beyond racism, to make any sort of inroads, we must do more than look for the chinks in the system, the few islands of relative safety. We must first understand, then do something about, the system that demeans and submerges our people at every turn."

"A large undertaking, Rodrigo. Would you like to discuss it over coffee?" We had both finished our dessert. Rodrigo looked as though he could handle another one.

"Or, would you like something more to eat? My sherbet was very good."

"No thanks, Professor. Just coffee. Understanding what's wrong is not too hard. I can lay it out for you in a few minutes. Where to go from there is another matter. Waiter!"

Rodrigo had caught the attention of the waiter circulating behind me. Soon we were sipping cappuccino, decaffeinated on my part, the real thing on his. After a moment, he began: "Professor, have you read Catharine MacKinnon's work?"

"Of course. I admire it greatly. Her analyses of the operation of patriarchy are at once illuminating and hard-hitting. She has written several pieces on sexual harassment of women in the workplace, and on pornography. Her book *Feminism Unmodified* is a classic in its time, but she has written much more."

"Then you know how she regards sexuality as the essence of women's subordination."

"I do. It's one of her more controversial theses. She says that the sexualization of woman, the construction of her in that role, is the very instrument of her oppression, and not in any contingent or means-ends sense. It is not possible to be a female sexual being in our society and not be relegated to second-class status. Sexuality is women's subordination, pure and simple. It doesn't just happen that women are both sexualized and oppressed. They are two opposite sides of the same coin."

"And had you thought whether something similar is true for us, Professor—whether some parallel mechanism accounts for our subordination?"

I was silent for a moment. I reflected on such theories as socio-economic competition, the colonized mind, interest-convergence, and various psychological theories that authorities had put forward to explain the persistence of racism.

"I'm not sure I can think of anything precisely similar, if you mean a simple psychological or political mechanism, like sexuality, that accounts for black subordination and the maintenance of a racist regime. I suppose you have one to propose?"

"I think it's democracy," he replied.

"Democracy?" I was thunderstruck. "The crowning achievement of the West, the legacy of Athens and Rome, the jewel in political theory. You think it's this that explains white-over-black power relations and the oppression of our people?"

"Yes," Rodrigo replied with the remarkable insouciance that was his trademark, "at least one variant of it. Western-style democracies, even with their formal, for-public-consumption rhetoric of equality, brotherhood, and all the rest, basically don't mean it. Whether they ever could change to be fair toward minorities, nonconformists, and other outsiders, I seriously doubt. I think minorities always have done better—relatively speaking—and will continue to do better—in other types of regimes. And this is systemic and intrinsic, not accidental."

"Rodrigo, of all the things we have discussed, this idea of yours strikes me as the most counter-intuitive. I can think of innumerable counter-examples. But let me put them on hold for a moment. I want to learn more about your—how shall I put it?—jaded attitude toward the West. What on earth do you see in democracy that renders it the root of our mistreatment of minorities?"

"It's the idea of Enlightenment," Rodrigo answered. "It functions for minorities as sex and sexualization do for women. You recall MacKinnon's thesis. She holds that sexuality, or, rather society's construction of it, is the very medium of women's subordination. I think Enlightenment-style Western democracy is its parallel, the source of black people's subordination. Not just in a causal sense. Rather, racism and Enlightenment are the same thing. They go together; they are opposite sides of the same coin."

I recalled a powerful scene in the movie *Malcolm X*, in which the young Malcolm received an introduction to systematic color-imagery in the words of Webster's dictionary by his prison mentor. I asked Rodrigo, "Do you mean the way in which color-imagery and symbols operate to devalue dark skin and place a premium on white?"

"That and much more," Rodrigo replied. "I think the system of imagery, the metaphors, the myths and stories of Snow White, white man's burden, dark villains and continents, and the rest are but surface manifestations of something deeper, something that lies at the heart of Western-style government and politics."

"And this something distributes power, privileges, social roles, disapproval and approval, niceness and its opposite—and has to do with Enlightenment philosophy?"

"Yes. The word itself is no accident. Locke wrote essays justifying slavery. Hobbes, Mill, and even Rousseau either did the same or wrote of a hierarchy of cultures and the natural subservience of the darker-skinned ones to the lighter. The Framers of the United States Constitution used color imagery. Many were slaveowners. The few who decried slavery publicly nevertheless thought people like you and me were inferior and devised schemes to send our 'unfortunate' dark-skinned forefathers, as they called them, back to Africa; others blithely justified the institution as the lesser of two evils."

"Perhaps that was a historical anachronism which Western society has outlived. No one would advocate those things today except the lunatic fringe. Indeed, less than two centuries after the period you are describing, Quakers and others were turning Enlightenment ideas around to challenge slavery."

"I don't think it was simply a stage, something we have outgrown. The Framers put in place a structure of government that is inherently biased against the minority. They thought they were establishing a perfect machine, one predicated on the separation of powers and similar doctrines that would assure that it remained forever in perfect balance, like the heavens, whose celestial laws of dynamics and motion Galileo, Descartes, and Newton described. Such a perfect machine could scarcely need serious systemic correction—that would be contrary to its nature. Intrinsic to Enlightenment thought are the ideas of order, balance, symmetry, and control. So, the idea of perfection, of perfect arrangement, made it hard for the minority group to get its pleas heard or taken seriously. It remains so today. Have you ever tried to get a white person to take complaints of racism seriously?"

"It's not easy. They either deny them, or say racism lies in the past. If you point out an example they can't deny—the black Nobel Prize winner denied a job in favor of a no-good high-school dropout white—they say, 'well, things are better now than they used to be, don't we have to admit that?'"

Rodrigo smiled, then said: "It's part of the idea of perfectionism, which in turn is an integral part of Enlightenment philosophy."

"And that makes us seem like ingrates for complaining. But you mentioned that you had more."

"I do. Another component of Enlightenment thought is the idea of hierarchy—of one culture or mode of thought being always and forever better than another. Light over dark. Enlightened over savage. We over they. Think of all the light-type words with favorable connotations—'enlightened,' 'brilliant,' 'insightful.' Enlightenment implies a progression, with ourselves—which originally meant Western white male aristocrats in lace shirts—at the top. Our class, you see, knows mathematics, physics, the laws of motion and philosophy, while *they* are benighted, ignorant, superstitious, mired in darkness. Naturally, it should fall our lot to develop theories of government, and to run things. We have sanitation and they don't."

"Quite a combination," I replied, ironically. "A balanced, perfect machine. And our own class in charge, pulling the levers. The one confers authority, legitimacy. The other assures stasis, resists challenge. But perhaps we're dealing with benevolent despots, ones who are wise and compassionate. That wouldn't be too bad. Consider the Western missionaries, for example. Surely they did some good." I was determined to play the devil's advocate as long as possible.

"You're right," Rodrigo conceded, "except for one thing. Enlightenment thought and politics imply exclusion, imply disdain for those falling outside the charmed circle. It is not a warm, embracing philosophy, like some you might have run into in the villages and small towns of my country, Professor. In its images, metaphors, and foundations it has exclusion and cruelty built in."

"I'm not sure what you mean. Are you referring to something more than the near-universal human tendency to prefer, to be most comfortable with, to trust, one's own kind?"

"I am. Enlightenment thought is exclusionary by its very nature. Consider what a beam of light does. It illuminates a narrow circle or band, leaving the rest unlit. It attracts the eye there, discourages it from going to the rest. That is the guiding metaphor of Enlightenment thought, and it has exclusion built in. And I don't mean in any accidental, contingent sense, but inherently and necessarily. Any political system, such as democracy, built on such a foundation will be bad for the minority. It is not just happenstance that Western democracies pioneered the slave trade, plantation system, coolie labor, Native American relocation, and Bracero programs. The United States was one of the last western countries to abandon slavery. It maintains and tightens strict immigration controls at the very time when other countries are loosening them. The West used color imagery to justify empire—recall the white man's burden—as well as the Discovery Doctrine to force Native Americans off their ancestral lands. Domination and exclusion are implicit in the idea of democracy. All can't govern, literally—that would be impossible. And in the West, the basis of that exclusion is color, followed by sex and property, in that order."

"I thought you said sex was the basis of female subjugation."

"I said sexuality, or rather, MacKinnon did. The way society constructs sexualized woman is the very means of her subordination. You can't have sex, as currently understood, and female equality at the same time. But that's her thesis. Mine is that democracy is the counterpart mechanism for us. If you are black or

Mexican, you should flee Enlightenment-based democracies like mad, assuming you have any choice. Enlightenment philosophy is the very means by which you are rendered a nonperson, always one-down. A thousand myths and tales, a thousand scripts, plots, narratives and stories will paint you as hapless, primitive, savage, lascivious, and not-so-smart, suitable only for menial work. It's as rigid a system as the Middle Ages, yet harder to change because it's all informal and implicit. There is nothing to rebel against. Indeed, the formal guarantees are impeccably egalitarian. A black person can be president, even though none ever has, and only three of us have ever been in the Senate."

"Then why are you here?" I asked. "You just said black persons should flee this place, yet you took a teaching job in the Midwest!"

"I have a mission," Rodrigo replied levelly, "as I mentioned before. Besides, I was born here. We have work to do."

"And the thing we have to work on is that which we have all been taught to treasure—democracy, which you see as the means of our oppression?"

"The very instrument," Rodrigo replied cheerfully. "Liberal democracy and racial subordination go hand in hand, like the sun, moon, and stars. Enlightenment is to racism as sexuality is to women's oppression—the very means by which we are kept down."

"And to think I once studied mathematics and Descartes," I shuddered in mock disbelief. "Rodrigo, do you have any idea how paradoxical your equation is? Democracy as the very source not just of majoritarian oppression—many have warned of that—but of racism, of steady, enduring, systemic subjugation on the basis of color!"

"All truth is paradoxical," Rodrigo replied. "It starts out with a question, goes underneath what is accepted."

"There are paradoxes and then there are paradoxes. As I have done more than once, I must encourage you to keep these ideas to yourself, at least until you are finished with your degree and have tenure. I see nothing but trouble ahead if you air them too freely. Our white friends have a healthy self-image. For them, Enlightenment philosophy is the crown jewel of civilization, the pride of Western culture. To portray it as the source of bigotry and oppression—that way lies trouble. If I were you, Rodrigo, I would keep these ideas of yours quiet for a while."

Rodrigo looked at me mildly. "I know you're on my side, Professor. I appreciate your counsel."

"Besides," I added, "there's an economic side to all this. It's very complex, having to do with laissez-faire capitalism, a companion system to what you call Enlightenment political thought. Lately, a whole approach to law, called law-and-economics, has sprung up dedicated to exploring this aspect of law and governance. Its practitioners maintain that everything should be efficient. How does your indictment of Western liberalism deal with this? It's not particularly liberal or romantic, but pretends to be hard-headed science."

"I've actually given it some thought. Will you scold me if I tell you about it?"

"No, please, I'd love to hear."

IN WHICH RODRIGO EXPLAINS THE CONNECTION BETWEEN RACISM AND FREE MARKET ECONOMICS

"The scientific trappings of economics are no guarantee against racism," Rodrigo began. "You recall what anthropologists were saying about us as late as 1925. Note the parallels—both free market economics and Enlightenment political philosophy are erected on mechanistic premises. The one visualizes government as a grand, noble machine, perfectly in balance, as we mentioned. The other regards economic activity in much the same way, as a broad summation of private choices, endlessly and forever perfecting itself as stronger actors and businesses drive out weaker ones. Processes, products, inventions, and services get better over time. People trade things—services and labor—and the whole system improves ineluctably and endlessly. The less regulation, the better, for if people act according to their own self-interest—pursue their own gain—society will be better off. We'll have more jobs, products, services, and wealth."

"And I'm sure you see some flaw in this design?" I asked.

"A kind of flaw. One the seriousness of which depends on your position in society. Some might regard it as minor. For others, it would be more serious."

"And I gather those others are us—people like you and me?"

"Yes. I was discussing this with Ali the other day. Are you familiar with Garrett Hardin's refutation of socialist economics?"

I searched my memory. "Do you mean his work on lifeboat ethics, or the tragedy of the commons?"

"The latter mostly, although the former comes into play as well. In his famous article he points out that socialism—any form of collective organization, really—has a built-in difficulty, namely the free rider problem."

"You mean the individual who agrees to the collectivist arrangement but with an unspoken reservation. This person is happy to have the village or group set aside land—or any other resource—for common use. He uses it, but when it comes his turn to pay or care for it, mowing it for example, he shirks. One of the other ninety-nine members of the cooperative has to step in. After a while, people start to notice that certain members of the collective are drawing a share of the crops but not doing the work. So, the whole thing falls apart. Socialism contains the seeds of its own self-destruction, since everyone learns, sooner or later, that they can do better by investing as little as possible."

"But doesn't this hold true just for lazy people, a small fraction of any group?"

"No. It holds true for the industrious just as well. By inconspicuously withdrawing from the collective enterprise, remaining members in name only, they can devote the extra time to private activity—making shoes, for example. That way, they get both shoes and crops. The others get just crops."

"So socialism is flawed, and tends in time to flip-flop over into capitalism," I said in summary. "But I gather you had something different to point out."

"Oh, yes," Rodrigo replied, taking a quick gulp of his cappuccino and draining his cup. "Without controls, collectivism tends to decay. But the same thing happens with free market capitalism. A mirror image flaw lies on the other side, one with special implications for minorities."

"Do you mean the way in which color preferences exclude us from market transactions, deny us access to trades? People just won't deal with us, at least if a white person is equally available."

"We talked about that before. And I think what we said then holds true: The market does not cure racism, but accentuates it. But on thinking about it a little more, I believe I've found an even more basic mechanism that generates a climate in which vulnerable groups, particularly those of color, cannot flourish."

"I'd love to hear what you have to say. But, first, how about a refill? Or would you like more dessert?"

"Fine. All this talking makes me hungry."

I caught the waiter's eye and gestured Rodrigo to continue.

"Individualistic market economics teaches everyone to seek his or her own profit, to rely on his or her own resources and effort to support himself through life. Yet there must be rules and laws, against stealing or setting fire to your competitor's shop, for example, requiring the payment of taxes, and so on."

"Our friends in the law-and-economics movement would set that level as low as possible."

"But even they believe there must be some laws to assure security, public safety, and some degree of social cooperation. Yet even that minimal level tends to erode under market pressures, with the result that Western societies get rougher and rougher over time."

"More or less the opposite of Hardin's thesis, but for capitalism," I commented.

"And, as I mentioned, with sobering consequences for minorities and other outsider groups. In a free market society, every actor is rewarded for coming as close to the line as possible. A merchant who cuts corners, who takes liberties with labor, fair-weights-and-measures, tax and reporting requirements will have an edge on competitors who are more law abiding, more generous toward their staffs, and so on. When everyone learns this and begins to do the same, by a sort of tacit agreement the line moves back. Eventually the legislature formalizes the new line. Driving speeds on the freeway are a good example. Even people who would like to drive slowly and safely can't."

"And you think the same holds true for matters of race?"

"Yes. Even those whites who would otherwise care about us, who left to their own devices would work for a nonracist society, don't. They lose interest, devote themselves to their own concerns, drop out of the civil rights movement."

"I've seen it happen with my own students. Even the ones who begin law school as idealists, wanting to help the poor and downtrodden, change. By the time they graduate, they are ready to go into corporate practice, or become house counsel for the rest of their lives—anything other than the public interest work that attracted them to law in the first place."

"I've noticed that, too. Competitive pressures drive out altruistic, other-regarding impulses. Pretty soon, the formal rules change, and we don't even notice how this happens. If a free market society does contain an impoverished or minority group, all things being equal, that group's situation will worsen over time because the majority will come to care less and less about it, will be willing to devote fewer and fewer resources to redressing its needs. Eventually, things get so bad, competition so cut-throat, the agony of the inner city so intense, that society intervenes. We pass a few laws, establish a few programs, and we all feel much better."

"It *is* like Hardin's thesis," I mused. "And it certainly accords with historical experience. The last twenty years for us have been some of the worst I've seen. And certain earlier periods of rapid economic development—or times of economic distress and competition—saw the introduction of harsh measures against Asians, Mexicans, and other immigrant groups."

"And I think these resurgences of nativism are not simply aberrations, Professor, but markers in what is generally a steady decline in civility, generosity, and tolerance. All of this, of course, has very real consequences for our people."

"In a way, Rodrigo, your thesis is similar to the counter-majoritarian difficulty that many have pointed out in connection with judicial review, but includes it as a special case. Enlightenment-based, Western-style democracy poses not just the possibility, but the near-certainty of domination and rough treatment of minorities—a treatment that comes in time to seem more and more natural and deserved—and less and less in need of correction. Legal self-seeking comes to be defined as what white people do."

Just then, the waiter arrived with a tray of tempting looking desserts. "Those look good. Have one. This is on me," I said.

As we started on our desserts, I recapitulated what I had heard. "So, Rodrigo, you believe that the source of our troubles lies with Enlightenment philosophy. You've deployed cognitive psychology to show how that outlook generates a willingness to disdain others and works together with color imagery to assure that our people are always despised and disdained. You have said that Enlightenment notions are for blacks what sexuality is for women, the very means by which society constructs and justifies our subordination. In democracy not all can have a voice. Enlightenment democracy assures that we are the ones who don't. And even if we could be heard, the perfectionist strain that Enlightenment breeds makes criticism seem like flyspecking, making the listener prone to ask questions like, 'But aren't you better off than you were in Africa?'

"Further, you have argued that free market capitalism works together with Enlightenment political thought to keep blacks and other people of color down. In a kind of reversal of Garrett Hardin's thesis, you urged that capitalism eventually destroys fellow-feeling and identification with the group. Those who start out caring for us go off to tend their own gardens lest they get too far behind the competition. I agree with you on most of these points. But is there not still hope? Is not democracy an open social arrangement, one in which talented outsiders like yourself may work for change? If not, what's the point of struggle?"

Rodrigo took a mouthful of his raspberry torte and looked up. "It's not particularly open, at least compared with other social systems. And whether there's any point in struggling, I think everyone must decide for himself. The system does resist change, both practically and on a level of theory. Have you noticed how uninterested most Americans are in hearing about their own racial injustices?"

"I have. And I assume you attribute this to the same factors of perfectionism and the sense of one's own culture's infallibility that make change difficult," I ventured.

"Yes, those plus the other things we talked about earlier. Color imagery and the cognitive psychology of visual imagery and light make it difficult for persons in the society to focus for long on the troubles of outsiders. Plus recall law's contribution to freezing things."

"Locke-ing things in, so to speak," I quipped.

"Interesting double entendre," Rodrigo shot back. "Mind if I steal it?"

"Not at all. You've been doing most of the talking today. I've gotten much more out of this discussion than you."

"You're the one who encouraged me to pursue this vein of thought in the first place. I can never thank you enough. You're a good mentor and friend."

I marveled, once again, at how even grizzled old veterans like me learn at least as much from our students as they from us. Even their half-formed ideas often trigger responsive ones in our minds, enabling us to go on in what is often an arid and desolate landscape.

[Rodrigo next explains how racism becomes locked in, explaining the role of Calvinism and intense individualism in American thought. The two friends then part as follows.]

CONCLUSION

As I rode rather sleepily homeward through the dark streets, I reflected on what we had said. Rodrigo's ideas on Enlightenment as the source of racial oppression seemed to me plausible, even powerful. I wondered how his new colleagues would see them, and how they would receive this new *wunderkind* with his audacious ideas. I wondered whether the racial problems of our people were really rooted in some basic flaw of our form of government, so that only a radical reconception of the state could enable us to go beyond cosmetic changes and periodic peaks of progress. Like many, I had grown up thinking that democracy was a good thing, and it pained me to hear Rodrigo's remorseless indictment, on fairness and formality grounds, perfectionism, color imagery, the association with Calvinism and individualistic mindset, law's contribution to stasis, and free market economics.

I thought how kind and courteous, almost tender, Rodrigo had been of my aging frailties in calling an early halt to the evening and hailing a cab for me. Was that not a root example of democracy, namely, considering the other person's feelings? Or was it socialism?

My reverie didn't last long. "We're here, Professor," the cabby said in a voice just this side of sharpness. I paid, trudged up the steps to my building, and prepared to deal with jet-lag and the new week.

~

Rodrigo's Remonstrance
Love and Despair in an Age of Indifference

"Professor, is that you?"

The familiar voice from behind me gave me quite a start. Wheeling around so suddenly that my cart almost collided with that of an oncoming shopper, a young woman who smiled at me indulgently, I sputtered, "Rodrigo! What are you doing here?"

The tall, smiling youth stepped out from behind his cart, shook my hand warmly, and said, "Giannina and I are in town for a few days, staying with her mother, who has a time-share condo here. She uses it every summer to get away from the Florida heat. The two of them are making plans for when the baby comes. We tried calling you, but the school says your voice mail has been down."

"I never much cared for the new technology," I said, then motioned toward his supermarket basket, which was piled high. "Looks like you're stocking up."

"Giannina's mom has to start over every time she comes to town, because the previous tenants have to clean everything out. She gave me quite a shopping list."

"I've got a long one myself," I said, easing my basket along the aisle and motioning him to follow. "What a nice surprise. We must get together before the two of you go back."

"Giannina made me promise to set something up. I was going to drop by your office on the way home. Mrs. Pellegrini said we should invite you over for tea. She's interested in meeting you. Oh, here are the anchovies." Rodrigo took a large tin and added it to his already overflowing basket.

"I'd be honored," I said. "How is Giannina doing these days?"

"Fine, except that she has these strange cravings. Just the other day, she wanted a peanut butter sandwich with anchovies on the side."

I smiled, remembering the time, many years ago, when my late wife had been pregnant with my own two daughters. "And what is her mom like?"

"You'll like her," Rodrigo said. "She's an ardent environmentalist. In fact, she's at a meeting of the local wildlife federation right now."

"Then I know just the present for her," I said as I reached for a long, narrow box of transparent sandwich wrap that I used to pack my lunches for work. Then, after a pause to allow a pair of fast-moving teenagers with baskets speeding down the aisle to clear us, I said, "And what are you working on these days?"

"Oh," replied Rodrigo, frowning and peering closely at two pricing labels for almost identical-looking packages of crackers. "Let's see, this one looks like it's ... twenty-four cents an ounce, while this other one ... okay, I'll take this one ... oh, what am I working on. Well, I've got my vacation reading right out in the car, as a matter of fact—four books on the current racial situation. An advance copy of the National Urban League's annual *State of Black America,* Terry Eastland's diatribe against affirmative action, Bowen and Bok's *The Shape of the River,* and Paul Barrett's *The Good Black.*"

"That's quite an assortment," I said, slowing down to round the corner of the aisle and head down the next. "What made you select those four?"

"Just keeping up on my reading." Rodrigo paused a moment at the meat counter to scrutinize some pink-looking filets of salmon. "Mmmm. Those look good. Giannina and her mother love salmon. But, as I was saying, after reading three of them and nearly finishing the fourth, a hypothesis occurred to me. I was just starting to talk it over with Giannina when an old friend stopped by with a baby present, so we had to put it on hold. Maybe we can discuss it when you come for tea."

"Sounds good to me," I said. "I've read Eastland, which struck me as a particularly remorseless dissection of affirmative action, as cold and uncaring as I've seen. And of course I've read Bowen and Bok, which everybody has been talking about—even the tables and charts. I asked the librarian to get me *The Good Black* the other day. But I haven't seen the latest from the Urban League."

"I can lend it to you when we get outside," Rodrigo said, fishing his credit card out of his wallet and holding it in his teeth as he slid a heavy bottle of water onto the lower rack of his shopping cart. "Giannina's mom drinks only the bottled kind. She said we would too, if we saw *A Civil Action.* Oh good, there's not much of a line."

Rodrigo paused as our cashier rang up the items and handed him the bill. He examined it quickly, then handed the cashier his credit card. "My mother-in-law said to give you these coupons," he said.

Minutes later, we were wheeling our baskets through the supermarket's huge parking lot. "Hey, you parked practically next to me," Rodrigo said. He opened the hatchback of his and Giannina's little car, and I helped him stow his groceries inside.

"Thanks," Rodrigo said, opening up the back passenger-side door and reaching inside. "Here's that book. Now, let me help you with your stuff."

He did, and after exchanging phone numbers and promising to get together soon, we drove off to our respective destinations. Rodrigo was true to his word. When I returned to my apartment, I heard Giannina's familiar voice on the answering machine inviting me to her mom's place the following Thursday for tea and thanking me for making sure that Rodrigo got all the food items she wanted—especially the anchovies.

IN WHICH RODRIGO, GIANNINA, MRS. PELLEGRINI, AND I MEET TO DISCUSS AMERICA'S RACIAL PREDICAMENT

"Good afternoon," I said. "Are you Mrs. Pellegrini?"

The handsome, white-haired woman standing at the doorway took my hand, smiled warmly, and invited me inside. "You must be 'the Professor.' Welcome. Giannina has told me so much about you. It looks like you brought something."

"It's for you," I said, handing over a package I had wrapped myself. "Open it now, if you like."

While ushering me into the attractive, sunlit condominium, Mrs. Pellegrini tilted her head and looked at my rectangular, flat package with interest. "It must be a stuffed animal," she joked.

As she began removing the wrapping paper, I said, "I hope you don't already have one. Rodrigo told me you're an environmentalist."

"Oh, an animal clock!" she exclaimed, clapping her hands together. "A friend of mine has the bird kind that plays songs every hour on the hour. I've always wanted one like this." Looking at it closely, she said, "I've got the perfect place for it." As she picked it up and motioned me to follow her in the direction of the kitchen, I heard the sound of familiar voices and noted to myself the resemblance between mother and daughter.

An attractive woman—maybe after the young ones leave, I'll ask her to lunch. I hope Giannina won't be scandalized, I thought, and cautioned myself not to be too forward. Perhaps a sedate invitation to a lecture at my university, followed by a bite to eat at a campus restaurant. Surely the young people could not object; she is, after all, about the age my late wife would have been had she lived. And I *had* been wanting to learn more about environmentalism, especially the new environmental justice movement. But I warned myself to proceed discreetly, remembering how the young often did not like to think of their elders as having a social life and not wanting to jeopardize the fine relationship I enjoyed with Rodrigo and Giannina.

"Oh, there you are," Giannina said, looking up from some two-person cooking project with which she and Rodrigo were busily engaged. "We hope you like Italian soup. We're making it for later, in case we get hungry after tea and cookies. What do you have there, Mom?"

Mrs. Pellegrini showed the two young people her present, which brought much laughter and exclamations as she plugged it in and turned the hands to the various animal positions.

"There's a way to turn it off at night, if you want," I said. "The instructions are in that plastic bag over there. The warranty, too."

Rodrigo covered the large pot, adjusted the heat to low simmer, and took off his white chef's apron. "Come on out," he said. "Everything's ready."

We followed Giannina as she carried the tea and cookies on a tray to the dining area adjacent to the kitchen and placed them down on the table, which I noticed was nicely set. A far cry from my bachelor simplicity, I thought, then looked up again at Mrs. Pellegrini, who was adjusting a spray of yellow flowers in a glass bowl on the table.

"Have a seat, Professor. Why don't you sit over here next to me? That way, we can keep an eye on the young people and make sure they don't get into trouble."

I laughed and pulled the chair out for her. She smiled, thanked me, then said, "I know Rodrigo and Giannina have been waiting all week to talk to you about some books they've been reading. Go ahead and don't worry about me. I taught government and U.S. history at the community college before I retired. I know next to nothing about law, but am willing to make the effort."

Rodrigo thanked her and immediately got up and brought four familiar-looking books from the hutch nearby and set them next to himself on the table.

"May I offer you a refill, Professor, before my son-in-law gets started?" Mrs. Pellegrini asked. "By the way, you can call me Teresa."

As Rodrigo looked up expectantly, I took the bait. "And so, Rodrigo, you have a hypothesis of some sort. Something that occurred to you on reading those four books?"

"I do," Rodrigo said, smiling. (He's never at a loss for an intriguing theory. Their baby is going to be really something, I thought, catching a glimpse of Giannina's mother out of the corner of my eye as she reached to pass around a plate of some sort of homemade cookies.)

But instead of pursuing Rodrigo's theory right away, I said, "Before you jump into that, maybe we should take turns summarizing those books. Your mother-in-law may not have read them all."

As Mrs. Pellegrini smiled appreciatively, Rodrigo looked up at Giannina and said, "Why don't you start?"

[Eds. After discussing the four books, the friends continue as follows.]

We were all silent for a minute, absorbing the bleak quandary our analysis [Eds. Of the four books] had left us in. Then, I looked over at Rodrigo. "I believe you were going to tell us about a hypothesis of some sort. I hope it has to do with a way African Americans and other people of color can break out of doomed or self-defeating strategies like the ones the four books cover."

When Mrs. Pellegrini also nodded encouragingly, Rodrigo picked up his cup and saucer and said, "Giannina and I think we need to clear away some of the clutter and start over with some new approaches, including one or two we think will knock your socks off. Speaking of clutter, why don't we clear the table. Would everyone like soup and bread?"

We all nodded and carried the dirty dishes into the kitchen in exchange for bowls from Mrs. Pellegrini into which Giannina ladled out servings of steaming soup with colorful vegetables floating on top. As we filed back into the living room, I noticed that Mrs. Pellegrini allowed the young people to go ahead of us. I took advantage of the moment to pose the possibility of lunch next week and was delighted when she quickly agreed. "I'll call you tomorrow," I said, then wondered if Giannina, just ahead of us, had overheard. Did I just imagine that she smiled at me slightly as we sat down again? I quickly looked away. Come now, I thought to myself, I am, after all, nearly seventy years old and a widower. We old-timers are entitled to a little companionship from time to time, are we not?

IN WHICH RODRIGO AND GIANNINA PUT FORWARD SEVERAL NEW THEORIES FOR CIVIL RIGHTS PROTECTION

I pulled myself together as Rodrigo began.

"Well, as you can imagine, I think we need some wholly new approaches. Those four books show that litigation has been producing fewer gains, affirmative action is probably on the way out, and self-help aids only those who have something to invest. Playing it straight—assimilation—exacts a terrible cost and even then guarantees no sure reward."

As Rodrigo paused for effect, Mrs. Pellegrini asked if I would like some coffee. As she leaned close I noticed the faint scent of apricots. I nodded gratefully, "Decaf, if you have it," after which she took orders from the others.

"Talk about something else," she asked, disappearing into the kitchen. While Teresa was away, I asked Giannina a little about her family history and learned that Teresa had grown up in Sardinia, off the coast of Italy, where her father, a captain in the Italian navy, had been assigned to an outpost. After he died, she and her daughter emigrated to Canada, spending several years in Toronto, then relocated to New York where Teresa worked as a translator for the United Nations. I learned that in addition to loving animals and wildlife, Teresa was a devotee of the theater. Aha! I thought, remembering that my campus's theater department was about to start a run of Beckett's *Waiting for Godot* and relishing the possibility of attending it with the beauteous Teresa.

I snapped to attention as our hostess emerged from the kitchen with a tray full of coffee cups and two decanters of coffee. Placing them on the table and looking over at her son-in-law, she said, "Now, where were we?"

"Rodrigo was about to entertain us with his thoughts on the future of civil rights theory," I said. "Since traditional approaches are not working, new ones need to be explored."

"I have a few in mind," Rodrigo said. "Giannina and I were thinking about this recently in connection with a grant application we were filling out." He looked over at his wife expectantly.

[Eds. Giannina and Rodrigo present three new approaches to minority protection—international human rights law, jury nullification, and class-based affirmative action. They then continue as follows.]

Environmental Law

"Rodrigo and I were just starting to discuss this the other day," Giannina began. "We didn't get very far, because something intervened and we had to put our discussion on hold. Then, as our trip approached, we thought we'd wait and get your input."

"I gather you're referring to the environmental justice movement," Teresa asked. (Giannina nodded.) "That's been a big issue in my organization. The board is thinking of polling the membership to see if they want to move into this area in a serious way."

"What are the prospects?" Rodrigo asked.

"Fairly good, I think. The membership is liberal, and the idea of joining a movement that examines the siting of biohazards in minority communities should appeal to many members. No one could quarrel with distributing toxic waste sites, sewage treatment plants, and similar noxious installations equitably instead of concentrating them in poor communities. The board is also considering adding arsenic, lead, and rats—big-city hazards that afflict slums and minority neighborhoods—to our list of environmental concerns."

"You said no one could quarrel with these objectives, Mom. But courts do. I've been learning about the litigation history of the environmental justice movement in my reading group. Most of the cases find that the plaintiffs have no cause of action. If they sue under the Fourteenth Amendment or a civil rights statute, they lose because they can't prove discriminatory intent. In most cases, the company or utility located the nuisance where it did, not because it hates black or brown people, but because the land is cheap or the residents unlikely to object as vociferously as they might if the biohazard were placed in Beverly Hills."

"And one or two cases that were not brought under civil rights laws, but under environmental statutes, fared only slightly better, if I recall," I added. "These laws don't require intent, but the usual solution is to remand the case for a fuller hearing. If the court or agency below skipped steps or moved too fast, the remedy is to slow things down and do it again."

"And in the meantime, Native American children are playing on radioactive waste piled up on the reservation," Teresa added, sadly. "So, what's the solution?"

Species Protection

"We're almost afraid to say it," Rodrigo said. "We think it's a different environmental statute: the federal Endangered Species Act. For people, we mean."

"Do you mean that we should ask Congress or the courts to declare blacks, Chicanos, and Indians endangered species?" I asked, thunderstruck. When Giannina and Rodrigo nodded, a little warily, I continued, "What an audacious idea. It reminds me of something I read by Chris Stone, but in reverse. I also read somewhere that only 900 Ute Indians are left in Colorado, all the rest having been slaughtered early in history or wiped out by white man's diseases, and that almost twenty-five percent of American Indian women of childbearing age have been sterilized, many at U.S. Public Health Service hospitals. And, of course, the black community sometimes describes African-American males as an endangered species, constantly harassed by the police and plagued by high rates of homicide, high blood pressure, incarceration, and early death. As we mentioned, infant mortality and sudden infant death rates are much higher in the African-American community than among suburban whites. So, I suppose that in a sense African Americans, Indians, and Chicanos are endangered. The Urban League study certainly shows that for blacks. But are you suggesting that the Endangered Species Act (ESA) should, literally, be applied to them—that blacks should have standing, as it were?"

"Yes," Rodrigo said with conviction. "Even though the idea sounds novel when you first hear it, no insurmountable barrier prevents its being done, either by judicial construction or express legislative amendment. People are animals, too. We're all part of the great web of life. Protecting humans beings is certainly as worthy a goal as safeguarding snail darters."

"This idea of yours definitely takes a little getting used to," I said. "I hope it wasn't in your grant proposal." [Eds. Rodrigo and Giannina recently applied for a grant to open a liberal think tank.] Rodrigo smiled and shook his head. "But I don't want to reject it out of hand." I foresaw some interesting sessions down the road with Teresa, learning more about killer whales and spotted owls while getting to know each other better, but my curiosity got the better of me. "How about a quick tutorial on the ESA and what it provides?"

"Sure," Giannina said. "Our study group was reading up on it. And, I bet Mom can help us fill in the gaps."

[Eds. Giannina provides a quick review of the ESA.]

"That's quite a statute," I said, feeling that I now knew enough to understand my young colleagues' astonishing proposal. "Thanks for sketching it out for me. But do the three of you really think it might be extended to human beings and communities of color?" Rodrigo and Giannina nodded. "I still have huge doubts. But I can see why you might find it attractive. It draws, potentially at least, on all the approaches you've mentioned today. It would take the best aspects of international human rights law, in that it demands that we treat minorities humanely—like animals." My three companions smiled at the irony. "Teresa just now mentioned that the international human rights approach frames things in such a way as to have an embarrassment potential that could lead to a healthy result. Calling attention to the way the United States treats animals better than some minorities can certainly do that."

"Most dogs have doghouses; people even worry about displaced prairie dogs. Yet the United States, unlike many Western industrialized countries, has a homelessness problem," Giannina interjected. "Most dogs and cats get vaccinations and a nutritionally balanced diet. The FDA monitors animal products to make sure this is so. Yet, many ghetto kids get neither."

"Not just that," Rodrigo added. "In some cities, dogs and cats have their own private cemeteries, with gravestones and carved monuments. Many indigent people have to resign themselves to a much less fancy disposal of their remains. In fact, I was just reading that in certain counties in Colorado where the sugar beet industry attracts large numbers of migrant workers from Mexico, local governments have persuaded the state legislature to pass a bill prohibiting the use of public funds for burial of indigents, whose remains would instead go to a medical school for dissection. The bill struck terror in the hearts of Chicano field workers, many of whom bought burial insurance they could scarcely afford."

"Many cities have boutique dog kennels for pets whose owners are going on vacation. And in Los Angeles, a dog or cat that is neurotic or acts out can be taken to a psychoanalyst for therapy," I added. "Not to mention obedience training."

"The other day," Rodrigo added, "Giannina and I saw a TV program showing a team of veterinarians who were trying to diagnose and cure a sick eagle. The bird, which had no broken bones or other obvious injuries, was listless and apathetic. They finally concluded it was suffering from lead poisoning."

"Just like many black children in inner cities," I said. "Many show dangerous levels of lead in their bloodstreams from old, peeling walls that were painted with lead-based paint. It would be ironic if the eagle received first-class medical attention while the children did not."

"Lead poisoning leads to permanent brain injury and impaired mental functioning," Teresa added. "So, pointing out the way we treat people less solicitously than some animals should at least get people's attention."

After a pause I added, "Last month, I read about a New Zealand group that is seeking human rights for higher apes. They point out that the great apes share many human characteristics, such as self-awareness, the ability to reason, and empathy—the capacity to imagine what others are feeling. I'm starting to come around to your position. In some respects, our society treats animals—pets, anyway—better than it treats the urban poor. And your suggestion is that we point this out and ask for equal treatment?"

"Well, yes," Rodrigo replied. "I don't think that's too much to ask."

"At least it's an arresting analogy," I conceded. "And it does recall affirmative action arguments in urging that people receive at least as much consideration as animals."

We were all silent for a moment. Then Rodrigo said, "Positive law in the United States protects flags, state flowers, agricultural products from defamation, and the institution of heterosexual marriage. It would be ironic if it could not protect poor African Americans, Asians, and immigrant farm laborers just as assiduously."

After another pause, Giannina said, "And do the two of you see how all this ties in with another approach we discussed—judicial and jury nullification?"

When I must have looked blank, she continued, "Imagine the effect of minority scholars advocating for inclusion of minorities under endangered species protection! Whole new areas of debate might open up; people would need to confront that, at least in the environmental arena, the law treats minorities worse than it treats animals. One of the chief benefits of nullification is its ability to force attention on law reform and the role of racist cops and unpopular drug laws. The ESA approach has some of the same potential."

"Even if not directly enacted," I said. "And I suppose you think the ESA approach borrows from class-based affirmative action, as well?"

"That's right," she continued. "As we know all too well, conservatives like Eastland and increasingly the courts insist that any affirmative action program based on race is unconstitutional. But the notion of 'endangered species,' if extended as we urge, would include *any* human community that presently bears or is likely to bear a disproportionate burden of environmental hazards. Worded this way, it should easily survive a charge of reverse discrimination."

"You've got me half sold," I replied. "Although at first I thought it was off the wall, I now see how your proposal is at least rhetorically and strategically appealing. But could it really be put into effect, do you think?"

"A five-part argument suggests so," Rodrigo replied. "The first two parts have to do with emotions and plausibility, the last three with logic and analogical reasoning."

"Stranger things have happened," I said. "Go ahead."

ARGUMENTS HAVING TO DO WITH PLAUSIBILITY AND WHITE RESISTANCE

Otherness and Familiarity; Terror and Reassurance

"Have you ever noticed how a certain type of Euro-American thinks nothing of lavishing affection on an African-American or Latino baby?" Rodrigo began.

"You mean on sidewalks and in supermarkets, that sort of thing?"

"Yes. They coo over the infant, say how cute he or she is. They'll stop the mother, who may be walking the baby in a pram, and ask the baby's name and how old it is. If the toddler is standing, the white person may pat him or her on the head. They demonstrate genuine affection."

"And you don't think it's a facade, to show how liberal the white is?"

"No," Rodrigo replied. "In contrast to African-American male teenagers and adults, who strike terror in Euro-American hearts especially when walking in groups on a darkened street, African-American babies seem safe and cute, like little animals. Their hearts go out to them."

"I see where you are going," I said. "The idea is to frame the problem in a way the dominant group will accept. Affirmative action won't work because whites hate to think of themselves as guilty participants in an iniquitous scheme or undeserving beneficiaries of privilege. It also requires that they think of black and brown people as victims, when to their way of thinking these people are getting away with all the jobs and advantages—while others in their group are committing crimes. International human rights law, while intriguing, won't work because Anglo Americans don't like to think of their country as an international terrorist or violator of human rights—even if it is. But your endangered species approach only asks them to think of minority people as small animals. Quite unthreatening, even appealing. It's a little demeaning, but heaven knows, we need all the help we can get. What's your other argument?"

Interest Convergence
"It's simply interest convergence. As you know, Derrick Bell and, before him, Charles Beard, proposed that the twists and turns of blacks' racial fortunes in the United States respond not so much to altruism or evolving notions of decency as to the self-interest of elite whites. Bell refined this notion in the form of 'racial realism,' which holds that African Americans and other people of color must realize that their fortunes are unlikely to improve significantly, and that the only thing left is struggle."

I looked up at Teresa and was intrigued when she seemed familiar with this idea. As though reading my mind, she said, "I'm familiar with Bell, even used some of his work in one of my classes. And I can see how the ESA approach would converge with the interests of the wildlife federation, at least. We have a lot of trouble getting minorities on board. The environmental movement is often accused of being the province of white elites. If minorities see that the movement is on their side, they are more likely to lend their support. The environmental movement will gather strength at the same time as environmental racism will weaken. There you have it: interest convergence. And so, my friends, what do you think?"

"I think Mom is onto something," Giannina said. "I also agree with the more general argument you two made. White people hate being made to feel guilty or like the bearers of undeserved privilege. One thing they do like is animals. If we could get them to see African-American adults, just as they do small black children, as animals, they might be kinder."

"Their treatment is, indeed, at times inhuman," I mused. "Police stop us, even if we are business executives taking a commuter train to work. Early in our history, whites stole the lands of Mexicans and Indians, rioted against the Chinese, and passed racist immigration laws against groups of color and southern Europeans merely looking for a better life. Treating us as full equals may be an unreasonable goal. Sadly, the best we can hope for may be to be treated like spotted owls or wild mustangs."

"Someone once wrote that American society feels about the African-American community roughly as it does about saving the whales," Teresa added. "Perhaps it is even less committed to making things better for African Americans; the whales, at least, are not threatening anyone. But I think you said you had a final argument for making this happen?"

* * *

To Protect the Intrinsic Value of Human Life
"Oh!" Rodrigo started, having been lost in reflection for a moment. "Our next argument is simple. Animal lovers love the ESA. To them the statute finds its justification in its generous protection of the animals they hold dear. But surely human life is just as worthy of protection as that of animals such as Preble's Meadow jumping

mice. I don't mean to be speciesist about it, but, after all, we're surely as deserving of protection as a snail darter."

"I certainly hope our fellow citizens agree," I said. "Which raises a question, at least in my mind: Why do you think the ESA has not been extended to people?"

"I think elitism plays a role," Giannina replied. "Environmentalists love their playgrounds, while poor, environmentally threatened minorities have too much to worry about to be concerned with Bambi's safety. Their kids are inhaling carcinogens and dodging rats all day long! Wildlife concerns are an unaffordable luxury when you're surrounded by smokestacks and toxic waste dumps."

"Another reason might be that minorities, except for Indians, are not in danger of extinction. Instead, minority population numbers are increasing. What do you say about that?" I asked, determined to press my two young friends as long as possible.

"That's true," Giannina replied, "but the Act does not require that a species be at imminent risk of extinction, only that it be endangered. Am I right, Mom?"

"You're right," Teresa replied. "But an analogy from hunting comes to mind. I'm sure you've heard deer hunters insist that their favorite sport is necessary to thin the herd."

"I've heard that," I said. "They say that if X number of deer were not killed every year, the population would rapidly increase so that a deer would eventually be standing on every square inch of land."

"But we all know that's not true," Teresa replied. "Most wild animals automatically adjust their procreative rate to the amount of food available. If hunters stopped their barbaric sport, the number of wildlife would increase, but just for a short time, until equilibrium was reached."

"And the three of you think that something similar operates in poor, American minority communities?" I asked.

"It seems likely," said Giannina. "Anthropologists tell us that in other societies, poor farmers have more children, because many of the children die young, and so the parents produce more to have enough to help them with the farm and to take care of them in their old age."

"Better prospects and a higher standard of living may be the best contraceptive," Teresa added. "There's nothing like hope to start women thinking about the future in positive terms. What's true in other societies may hold here, as well."

"So that the seemingly high reproductive rate in United States minority communities may be a function of desperation—of the high homicide rates, poor nutrition, and the blighted life choices that society offers them?" I asked.

"It's at least a plausible hypothesis," Rodrigo added. "Everyone knows the middle and upper classes have much smaller families than everyone else. If the high reproductive rate of the minority poor is a function of terrible living conditions, with constant threats like those the deer receive from the hunters, then the term 'endangered' might well, plausibly, be applied to them despite their numbers' remaining constant or even growing."

Just then, Teresa's new clock, which until then had remained silent, let out a thunderous bellow; I imagined the sound of a buffalo or similar animal. "Oh, my," I said, looking up. "It's five o'clock already. Time certainly flies...."

"When you're having fun," said Giannina with an impish smile. "Well, you two had better set up your date if you're going on one. For our part, Rodrigo and I need to get going. Our Lamaze class starts in half an hour, and we don't want to be late. We could drop you off, Professor. It's on our way."

Minutes later, I was taking my leave of Teresa ("By the way, call me Gus"), and walking down the steps wishing we had had more time. As I stooped over to get into the back seat of Rodrigo and Giannina's little car, I said something vaguely complimentary to Giannina about her mother—I think, how rare it is to find a Euro-American of her generation with such a passionate commitment to both racial equality and environmentalism.

As Rodrigo smoothly accelerated into the traffic in the direction of the women's center and my apartment, Giannina gave me a quick, but warm smile, and said, "She's a rare species. We'll all have to take good care to keep her well. Even without a statute."

I resolved that I, at least, would do my part, and looked forward to my meeting with Teresa on Wednesday and a new chapter that I hoped would include talk of children, race, the environment—and each other. I reminded myself, as well, to ask her (perhaps after we built up some rapport) whether she thought Giannina and Rodrigo meant their proposal about minority communities and the Endangered Species Act seriously or were proposing it only for effect. Just then, I heard a sudden intake of breath, Giannina said "Watch it!" and Rodrigo braked sharply to avoid a squirrel skittering across the roadway.

Well, well, I thought. I think I have my answer.

Rodrigo's Roadmap

Is the Marketplace Theory for Eradicating Discrimination a Blind Alley?

SOLILOQUY

It had been a glorious day in this quaint town in the Great Northwoods of Michigan. Outside, sunshine filtered through the massive hardwood trees, giving the underlying grounds a dappled effect. Stately, flat-bottomed clouds punctuated the sky, moving slowly as though keeping time with the hands of the great clock at campus center. The sudden peal of distant chimes reminded me that the final session of a surprisingly stimulating conference on privatizing hydroelectric energy production was drawing to a close. I had decided to attend because—aside from being on sabbatical and in the region visiting friends—I was interested in environmental theory, having done a small amount of writing in this area earlier in my career. My hope that the location would draw some representatives of the famous Chicago school of law and economics had been realized. In fact, the closing panel featured two individuals whom I had most hoped to see—Richard Posner and Rodrigo's colleague, Lazlo Kowalski, a young scholar with a growing reputation. As expected, they came out in favor of free market solutions with minimal regulation of the hydroelectric industry.

My interest whetted by an earlier conversation with Rodrigo, I had been reading up on the law-and-economics movement, which has ascended to a position of great prominence over the last twenty years, and hoped to gain some additional insight from the speakers. Although I found the movement's work elegant and even logically compelling, some of their underlying assumptions concerning human nature troubled me. If the premises from which these scholars derived their views were wrong, did this mean that their advocacy of free market mechanisms at the expense of environmental regulation was fatally flawed?

In particular, I was skeptical of the notion that "rational" actors in a free market would always, or even generally, act in a self-interested manner to maximize satisfaction, and that this would benefit the social good. If the hope that we would do better by doing less—that society would be better with less government—was wrong, then the implications were profound. Perhaps it was my romanticism for the civil rights spirit of the 1960s. Perhaps I was simply set in my liberal ways. Nevertheless, I had great difficulty with the notion that eliminating governmental intervention would lead to greater good for those already at the bottom of the social heap—women, gays, the poor, the homeless, racial and ethnic minorities, and new immigrants. I still felt in my bones that it was necessary to provide for government regulation of human nature, which I perceived as much more complex than the blithe prose of law and economics suggested.

It seemed to me that people act for a variety of reasons, some economic, some emotional, and others that can only be described as incomprehensible. Any attempt to assume human motive seemed inherently problematic; we cannot, after all, look inside another's head or heart. To bypass this problem, the law-and-economics scholars employ the market as the medium for communicating human preferences. Assuming an autonomy free of force or coercion, the market becomes a proxy for inferring volition or motive on the part of individuals engaged in transactions. Further assuming that the parties have sufficient information, the motive for any free market transaction is presumably that both sides will be made better, or at least not worse, off. Moreover, encouraging a system of such exchanges will increase the wealth or utility of society as a whole.

I am not at all averse to economics or economic theory, which I regard as a powerful way of conceptualizing our lives under a capitalist system. What bothered me was its application to apparently non-economic phenomena, such as racial discrimination. Beginning with Gary Becker's ground-breaking work in 1957, law and economics had come to dominate discussion in many areas that I, at least, felt were ill-suited to it. In particular, I was perturbed by how easily so many accepted that economic analysis could explain the mysteries of human nature. If we have not been able to make significant headway in unraveling many of the most intractable—some would say delicious—secrets of life in over two thousand years, why would one suppose that economic theory could succeed? Perhaps I was being merely romantic, but I rebelled against the thought of reducing human complexity to numbers and graphs. Indeed, I thought it dangerous to allow economics to dictate non-economic social realities, such as race relations, as a growing chorus of conservative voices in think tanks and Congress were beginning to urge, many going so far as to insist on the complete repeal of all our civil rights laws.

As the day's final program came to an end, the sun was just dipping below the stone facade of the clock tower outside the window. The hands read 5:35 but I was feeling weary. It is remarkable how tiring it can be to sit and listen to people talk for nine straight hours—or was it my advancing age? I made a mental note to go to bed early and get a fresh start in the morning. However, I first wanted to see if I could speak with Laz, who had just finished answering questions from the audience and was smiling as everyone clapped enthusiastically. As the crowd began to disperse, he was surrounded by a small group of students, professors, and journalists, all wanting to say something personally to him.

Deciding to seek him out later, I headed out from the lecture room into the fading sunshine in the direction of my hotel. The sound of the school band, practicing off in the distance, made me smile briefly, remembering my own undergraduate days. Too bad I did not take more courses in economics, I thought. My interest in law and economics, and its possible mismatch in areas such as racial discrimination, stemmed from a 1985 article by Robin West, in which she argued that Richard Posner, in implicitly following the Kantian moral tradition of autonomy, justified the principle of "wealth maximization" on the basis of consent. Because wealth maximizing transactions promote autonomy, they are morally attractive; and because participants in a transaction, even unwitting losers, have at least implicitly consented to the transfer in the hopes of maximizing their personal satisfaction, they are morally legitimate. Wealth maximization thus becomes, for Posner, a moral imperative with which the state should not interfere, except to correct injustices stemming from fraud, force, or other forms of interpersonal abuse that negate free choice.

West's insight is that law and economics oversimplifies human nature. In particular, it fails to account for masochistic, self-abasing tendencies. According to West, "[W]e as a people are more authoritarian and submissive than the depictions of our nature relied upon by mainstream liberal theorists." If consent is a moral trump, as the law-and-economics scholars assert, then free market transactions are insulated from critique, regardless of their inescapable tendency to produce winners and losers, haves and have-nots, rich and poor. West primarily focuses on the victimization side of the equation. Using the disturbing stories of Franz Kafka, she shows a "disjunction between a system that formally and outwardly insists upon the legitimating function of consent and a human personality that inwardly and persistently seeks the security of authority." Kafka's terrifying stories illuminate the resulting alienation—the gap between outward descriptions and inward experience—that typifies our modern world and is "deeply familiar" to the contemporary individual at the *existential level. West criticizes Posner's vision of the social world as "unfamiliar" because his hypothetical characters possess "welfare-maximizing inner worlds" that correspond artificially with the overly simplified outer world of free market economics.*

Just then, I passed a campus kiosk covered with flyers announcing a rich array of coming events, including a lecture by Dinesh D'Souza on hate-speech codes. Knowing that he would undoubtedly speak out against regulation in this area, I wondered idly what he proposed to replace it. Probably nothing, I mused. This reminded me that I wanted to explore another, implicit side of West's equation: authoritarian, cruel tendencies in human nature. Authority and submission are sides of the same coin. If some individuals in the modern world seek out submission to authority, then some must also seek out an authoritarian role. It is really, as economists would express it, a matter of supply and demand. If modern individuals desire submitting to authority, there must be authoritarian individuals to whom one submits. If our social structure tolerates authoritarianism, then certain individuals will be channeled into authoritarian roles while others will locate themselves on the other side, submitting to this authority. Indeed, a neo-Nietzschean such as Michel Foucault, a favorite of my friend Rodrigo, would probably argue that modern institutions of authority, such as penology or psychoanalysis, actually are designed to produce and replicate authoritarian and submissive sets of individuals.

West focused on the victims in Kafka's stories as a means of criticizing Posner's "simplistic and false psychological theory of human motivation." I wanted to focus on law-and-economics scholars' failure to account for evil as a major factor in human motivation. In allowing such a small role for state regulation of racism and other forms of cruelty, I believed that the law-and-economics scholars were simply mistaken in holding that free markets would, by themselves, rectify such human shortcomings. I had the inescapable conviction that evil, or moral wrong, such as racial prejudice, was both socially constructed and biologically based. People are naturally hostile and territorial towards outsiders; this innate hostility would not simply go away if the government retreated and let people function according to a free market system. By rendering an inadequate account of human evil, the normative implications of free market ideologies were thus dangerously conservative.

I was shaken from my thoughts by voices. A small knot of conference-goers was converging on the hotel. My walk had taken longer than anticipated and, realizing that I had not eaten since morning, stirred a mighty hunger within me. Upon entering the hotel, I went straight to the restaurant, a homely, generic place with a menu posted on an easel that seemed to feature American cuisine. I would have preferred to go out and sample some of the local ethnic fare but my appetite was overpowering. I sat down and ordered a hot turkey sandwich and a dinner salad. After the waiter left, I looked around the room and spotted none other than Lazlo Kowalski, and who should be sitting next to him but Rodrigo! Seated in a booth on the opposite side of the restaurant, they were talking animatedly. I waited until a pause in their conversation, then half stood and waved in their direction. Laz immediately spied me, stood up, smiled, and waved for me to join them. Catching the waiter's eye to let him know I was moving, I picked up my table setting and water glass and joined my young friends.

"Professor!" Rodrigo exclaimed, shaking my hand warmly and gesturing me to sit down. "We were just talking about you. What are you doing here? It's great to see you!"

"I'm on sabbatical and visiting some friends in the region," I answered. "I dropped by hoping to catch a glimpse of Laz and maybe learn something about environmental law. Are you attending the conference?"

"No. Giannina and I are here for something much more mundane—her sister's baby's christening. We got in just this afternoon. I dropped by to offer Laz moral support."

"I didn't see you inside," I said.

"It's a big auditorium," Rodrigo said. "And packed. I thought Laz did a great job, especially afterward in the Q and A."

Laz grinned appreciatively, just as the waiter arrived to ask, "Are you gentlemen ready to order?"

My two young friends did, Laz a cold-cut combo, Rodrigo a steak ("medium rare, please"), after which we continued:

"So, what brought you here, Professor?" Laz asked, smiling to show that he was pleased I had shown up. "You're not switching sides, are you?"

"Not at my age, I'm afraid," I said. "Although I do have an amateur's interest in law and economics. Rodrigo and I had a long conversation once about its relation to racism and civil rights."

"He told me," Laz replied. "Too bad I wasn't there, but we didn't know each other then."

"It would have benefited from your contribution," I acknowledged. "But if you have the time—and you, too, Rodrigo [I nodded across the table at my friend]—I'd love to revisit the issue. A number of books have come out recently...."

Rodrigo held up one hand to suggest a pause, while he rummaged for a moment in his briefcase, which was resting on the floor at the foot of his chair.

"Including one I've just been reading," he said, holding up a slender black volume with familiar-looking silver printing on its cover.

"That's one I had in mind," I said. "The other one's by Stephan and Abigail Thernstrom. Both books advocate cutting back programs designed to assure equal opportunity for blacks and other minorities."

"I've read both of those," Laz said animatedly. "And I'd love to talk about them. Building on the framework laid down by early law-and-economics scholars such as Epstein, Becker, and Posner, Charles Murray argues that the country's antidiscrimination laws ought to be jettisoned. The Thernstroms argue that the country's commitment to affirmative action should go, too. And it may surprise you to know that I agree, with the Thernstroms, at least."

Rodrigo and I must have looked aghast, for Laz quickly continued: "Not because I oppose minorities' advances, for as you know I'm a well-wisher, being the son of immigrants myself. But conservative principles and ordinary common sense show that these programs really do people of color little good, while greatly increasing resistance by my side and by working-class whites. I think they also increase stigma for high-achieving blacks and Chicanos. I didn't think so before, but I do now."

"Well," I said, drawing a deep breath. "We do have a lot to talk about. Do the two of you have some time?"

RODRIGO, LAZ, AND THE PROFESSOR RESOLVE TO DISCUSS ARGUMENTS AGAINST OUR NATIONAL CIVIL RIGHTS ARMAMENTARIUM, BEGINNING WITH A BRIEF TREATMENT OF WOMEN AND JOBS

Laz and Rodrigo both smiled with anticipation, but before we could begin, the waiter arrived with our food. "Dig in, everybody," I said, and for the next few minutes we ate in tacit silence. Then Rodrigo looked up:

"Giannina and I were discussing one aspect of this the other day. She had just read some news stories about the lack of women managers and executives. Her analysis might suggest how minorities of color will fare under a regime, like Laz's, of no civil rights enforcement."

"I didn't say *no* civil rights enforcement," Laz said pointedly. "As you know, I detest racism. I just don't think that governmental programs are the best way to combat it. Actually, I have some ideas that even the two of you might approve of. I can run them past you later, if you like. [Rodrigo and I both nodded.] But, for now, I'd love to hear what Giannina had to say about women in the job market."

"Okay," Rodrigo agreed. "But only if you promise to tell us your ideas, Laz. [When Laz said sure, Rodrigo continued as follows.] Well, back to Giannina. We were talking about some of the same books the professor just mentioned. She said that women's experiences cast doubt on the ability of the free market to redress sexism."

"Oh?" said Laz, looking up a little skeptically. "I just read that women are now well over fifty percent of undergraduates at the nation's colleges. It seems to me only a matter of time before the job market sees them distributed, if not evenly, at least in large numbers, virtually everywhere."

"She wouldn't dispute that," Rodrigo replied. "In fact, she argued that changes in the job market, not kindness, were what prompted affirmative action programs in the first place. You'd concede, wouldn't you, Laz, that white women have been the main beneficiaries of affirmative action?"

Laz grinned ironically. "Absolutely."

"In that case, recall what was going on in the country right around the time affirmative action got rolling in the mid- and late 1960s."

"A civil rights revolution?" Laz queried. "Marchers in the streets? Two Democratic regimes in a row?"

"Those, too," Rodrigo said. "But Giannina was thinking of the job market. Transistors had just been invented. It must have been clear to elite groups that we were in the early stages of a technological revolution that would ultimately lead to an information-based society. And what kind of workers would that society need in large numbers?"

We were both silent for a moment. "Women?" Laz finally ventured.

"Exactly," Rodrigo replied. "Giannina pointed out that the new data-processing industries would need millions of new workers. Clean, neat, and careful, to process data in, and process data out. The new workers would need to be conscientious and hard-working, but not very ambitious, because few of these jobs led anywhere. And who would be the perfect workers to fill these new jobs?"

"I see where you're going," Laz interjected. "But, sobering as your analysis is—and, mind you, I'm not so sure that these jobs go nowhere—doesn't it just prove my point? The market worked. Women returned to the workforce, got jobs, lots of them, and all without having Big Brother looking over everybody's shoulder."

"That happened, but only to a point," Rodrigo agreed. "Two kinds of limitations set in."

"What kinds?"

"The first is the glass ceiling that a federal commission recently documented. That limitation, which sets in at some point in practically every woman's career, stops her from advancing beyond that point. The reason the glass ceiling is there in the first place is that some of the women who entered the marketplace were not content with entry- and mid-level jobs. They began to compete with men, insisting on consideration for middle-management positions, partnerships in accounting and law firms, and the like."

"So the point of affirmative action was to admit women, but in just the right numbers and for just the right low-level jobs. Not too competitive, not too highly paid. Ingenious," I said sadly.

"The idea was to assure a supply of compliant, conscientious workers to operate computers, do legal research, and other forms of paper-pushing. It was not to revolutionize the workplace, much less to employ black men."

"Hmmm," Laz said. "I'll have to think about that. What's the second limiting principle?"

"Childbirth," Rodrigo replied. "Too few babies were being born—white ones, anyway. Recall that raft of books, most written by conservatives, lamenting the 'birth dearth'? They warned that white women were having too few babies, while minority women were having too many. The precious national gene pool was deteriorating. According to some of them, we were losing several IQ points per generation. It was time to get white women out of the workplace and back in the bedrooms."

"It is interesting that the family-values movement sprang up right around the time you are thinking of," I said.

"About 1990, just as women's gains were cresting. Giannina pointed that out, too."

"Intriguing!" Laz commented. "I don't agree totally with what she says. But her theory of the market's unseen limitations, which click in when women's progress reaches a certain point, has the ring of truth. It reminds me of Derrick Bell's interest-convergence theory, which explains the twists and turns of blacks' fortunes in terms of the class interests of elite whites. That theory I definitely agree with. But, speaking of Bell, you mentioned that Giannina thought her theory might apply to people of color. What specifically did she say about race?"

"Unfortunately, we never got to finish that discussion. So, working that out is up to us."

"I'm game, if you are," I said, then paused for the waiter who had just appeared at our table to ask how we found our food. "Fine," we said in unison, and, after topping off our water glasses, he departed. As he left, Rodrigo resumed speaking.

"I have a theory I can run past you, if you like. And, because it's a critique of law and economics, Laz, I'd love your comments. It'll also enable us to discuss those two books we mentioned. In fact, they're what stimulated Giannina's and my discussion."

"Too bad she's not here, so we could benefit from her insights," I lamented. "Didn't you tell me once that she majored in economics?"

"She did," Rodrigo replied.

RODRIGO, LAZ, AND THE PROFESSOR DISCUSS WHETHER THE MARKET WILL CURE RACISM

After pausing for the waiter to remove our plates, I turned to Rodrigo. "I've had some thoughts on this myself, prompted by a marvelous article by Robin West. And Laz, I hope you'll jump in whenever you think we're wrong. We need you to keep us honest. Don't be silent just because you're outnumbered."

Laz smiled and said quietly, "Don't worry," so Rodrigo began:

"My theory has four parts, all converging on the account of evil in the work of liberals, classic as well as modern." (I smiled inwardly as I realized my young protégé and I had been thinking along the same lines.) "Both seem to think that racism and other forms of power-tripping will go away if we simply let the free market function. Four arguments suggest this is very unlikely."

"Before you two get into that," Laz spoke up, "I wonder if it doesn't make sense to lay out, if only briefly, the case that it will. That way, we'll all have a common understanding of what the argument is that we're critiquing."

Rodrigo and I nodded agreement, a little abashed (in my case, at least) that we hadn't thought to do that first. "Laz, why don't you do the honors. Those two books we just mentioned might be a good starting point."

[Eds. After discussing recent books advocating laissez-faire approaches to racial discrimination, the three settled down, Rodrigo took a last swig of his coffee, looked up, and began.]

"As you know, I'm convinced that in a nation such as ours, with a long history of white-over-color subordination, racism will not wither away by itself. But let me start with a thought experiment or two."

"I love your thought experiments," Laz said. "Fire away."

"You and I were talking about this before. It has to do with the unthinkable. Imagine a rural state, say Minnesota. The legislature is concerned about the high toll in deaths and accidents caused by teenage drivers. So, it decides to allow children to obtain driver's licenses at age eleven. Studies show that many children this age would make very good, careful drivers. With the new change, young Johnny can help Dad and Mom on the farm. He can drive the tractor a few miles along County Road 5 from the back twenty to the front fifty, which is a big help. At the age of sixteen, however, Johnny must surrender his license until age twenty-six, at which time he can get it back again."

"So the overall accident rate goes down with all those dangerous teenage drivers off the road. And Dad gets some help on the farm," Laz said.

"Exactly," Rodrigo said. "But would other states emulate Minnesota's example? No. The sight of little twelve-year olds, hunched over the steering wheel, carefully and responsibly driving Mom to church, would fly in the face of society's conception of children. Children are supposed to be dependent, small, 'cute,' in need of protection. The notion that some of them might turn out to be safer drivers than older teenagers and young adults goes against the grain. No other state would follow Minnesota's lead. Even that state itself might repeal the law."

"And you think this has some bearing on the market and race?" Laz interjected.

"Yes," Rodrigo replied. "Minorities labor under similar stereotypes. Even if one firm prospered by hiring a brilliant black or Chicano chief executive officer, others would not rush to follow suit. They would be certain that something would go wrong with the other firm and its CEO—maybe he or she would be fired for graft. Or, if the minority executive proceeded to double profits year after year, they would simply pronounce him or her an exception. The next black that applied would be ruled out for some reason."

Laz furrowed his brow. "I'm not so sure," he replied. "Profits that large should give the racist competitor pause. But if you're right, why should that be?"

"It's because extra-market forces, like stereotyping and internalized, scarcely visible preconceptions so strongly support racism. The thick web of culture, language, and institutional inertia discourages the competitive frenzy that marketplace advocates place their faith in. If the market brings changes, they will come at best slowly and painfully. In the short run, minorities in the marketplace will confront a host of pseudo-economic stereotypes, like that they're 'dull,' 'lazy,' or 'of bad character.'"

"But this isn't because of any market failure, it's because of false information," Laz retorted. "As the market starts to work, businesses will gain exposure to more black and brown workers and learn that their stereotypes are false and the taste for discrimination costly."

"But there you are," Rodrigo replied, leaning forward excitedly. "You and your friends—nothing personal, Laz, you know you're my pal—are making what we might call a category mistake, like asking 'What color is the number seven?' To see racism as a matter of private taste is to mistake its very nature. It's a public harm, one that warps the entire fabric of social and political life. Racism should be condemned socially, by all of society, and one means of doing so is by affirmative action and other forms of intervention in the free market."

"Well, are you saying that blacks and Chicanos somehow fall outside the free market?" Laz asked incredulously.

"Yes, in a way. Slaves were not part of the free market, except as chattels. They could not buy their freedom, and the same is true of their successors today. A rich black or Latino is still subject to police harassment merely by reason of driving a nice car or walking the streets at night. No, Laz, racial equality is a public good which the private marketplace cannot easily, or quickly, bring about. It demands a pre-allocative normative reckoning by society as a whole. Only once the difficult normative questions have been faced up to does the market become a viable means of effectuating those normative decisions, including the very basic one of who is an equal member of society."

"Political decisions have costs," Laz said. "And who is to say that society will make the right ones? We could decree fair treatment and hire an army of police to watch out for any show of racism. But blacks and Latinos would still, in most cases, be stuck in dead-end, private sector jobs."

"We should make the effort, nevertheless," Rodrigo replied. "As my thought experiments show, the market just won't drive out racism. Thinking it will is a category mistake. Waiting around for the market to catch up with our public ideals is morally unacceptable. If we believe in equality, we must condition the market and ourselves to break down long-standing barriers to freedom for all."

Laz shook his head and smiled in spite of himself. "Interesting thought experiments, Rodrigo. I especially like the eleven-year-old drivers. And your distinction between public and private commitments and category mistakes does give me pause. But you'll need more than that to make a believer out of me."

Rodrigo's First Argument: Cultural Texts Show the Ubiquity of the Problem of Evil

"Okay," Rodrigo said. "Consider how four types of evidence converge on the necessity of constraining the problem of evil: cultural texts, social science studies of helping behavior, evolutionary science, and cross-cultural studies."

"Hmmm," said Laz. "I'm curious to see where you're going. I've often thought that you bleeding-heart types lacked an adequate account of human evil, visible in your treatment of crime and criminals, for example. But now it seems you are going to use this against my side. I'm all ears."

"You'll have to decide for yourself which way the argument cuts," Rodrigo said. "The marketplace argument, which owes its origin to early utilitarians like Bentham, Mill, and Smith, is almost entirely forward-looking. If one course of action doesn't work, try another. This may account for the cheerful, social-engineering character of liberal civil rights law that all three of us have noted, as well as the short attention span of liberals who, once having put a plan or law in place, think the problem is solved and want to move on to another one, such as saving the whales."

I wanted to move back to Rodrigo's evidence. "And by cultural texts, I assume you mean ones such as Shakespeare, Melville, and the Bible, which recognize the human impulse to harm enemies, distrust foreigners, and conquer and enslave other societies?" I asked.

"Those and more," Rodrigo answered. "They all show humans struggling with the impulse to war against and suppress others. Human nature, of course, also contains a generous and benevolent impulse, as Adam Smith recognized. But it is, unfortunately, limited mainly to persons we know well."

"I think I can see where you are going," I interjected. "It's amazing—I was reflecting just this afternoon on Robin West's classic exchange with Richard Posner. Are you familiar with her Harvard article?"

When the two young scholars, who had entered teaching recently, nodded a little uncertainly, I elaborated as follows:

"Robin West, professor of law at Georgetown, criticized Richard Posner, and implicitly the entire law-and-economics school, for rendering an imperfect view of human nature. Basing their theories on a view of mankind as interested in satisfying basic needs, Posner and his colleagues put forward a mechanism, namely the market, and a medium, namely economic exchanges, to enable the maximization of that satisfaction. In their view, exchanges and contracts, such as for labor, entered into freely by autonomous individuals ordinarily ought to be left alone, because they should be presumed to advance the interests and well being of the parties who negotiated them. Even if one of the parties turns out to be the loser in a transaction, say an investment, allowing such exchanges benefits all of society and so should win the endorsement even of those who occasionally lose. They, too, benefit from the overall wealth and freedom such a regime of free market rules brings."

Laz asked, "And I suppose West took issue with that basic premise?"

"She did. Drawing on great literature, especially the stories of Franz Kafka, she shows that, in addition to a happiness-maximizing impulse, men and women have a darker side that causes us to surrender our autonomy and to allow ourselves to be dominated and made miserable."

"That sounds like classical masochism," Laz said. "I agree that some people behave that way, although some of my fellow conservatives probably would quarrel over how much. Conservatives, as you know, tend not to be very interested in unconscious motives. Richard Posner, in a reply to Professor West, said as much, if I recall. But I gather you're emphasizing something different in human nature?"

"Yes," I said. "The flip side of what she emphasized, in fact. Sadism—although that word may be a little more psychoanalytic than I would like. What I mean is that cultural texts, as well as the human record, show a recurring tendency to want to dominate and mistreat others. Early man limited his fellow feeling to members of his family or clan. Today, even though our sympathies are more universalistic, we still tolerate economic exploitation by ruthless capitalism in Latin America and Russia. And famines in Africa or poverty in our inner cities draw less attention than troubles on our doorsteps."

"Out of sight, out of mind," Rodrigo interjected. "But with respect to the law-and-economics school and its account of racism, your point is . . . ?"

"The cultural record shows that we are apt to be much less generous with people of other races. The English language alone boasts a rich vocabulary including xenophobia, chauvinism, and racism, as well as an extensive set of words that stereotype and demean others merely on the basis of their skin color. This implies that, left to their own devices, humans will not choose to deal with others whom they regard as different. They will not hire, trade with, or in general bring them into their circles of regard. They may engage in economic exchanges with them, such as renting hotel rooms or seeking them out as clients, but only if others of their own kind are unavailable."

"This makes me think of that Minnesota thought experiment," Laz mused. "I think I have a reply, but go on. I'd like to hear the other arguments against the marketplace theory first."

Rodrigo's Second Argument: Biology and the Study of Other Species Discloses That Many Adopt Strategies Similar to Human Ones

"My second argument proceeds by induction," Rodrigo said. "Consider how other species engage in similar behavior. I hasten to add that I don't mean that biology is destiny, nor that every species kills for pleasure—most don't. Human beings, after all, have free will, or at least our political and legal institutions assume so. But seeing how other species, including ones closely related to us, adopt strategies that defend territory or exclude competitors from food, light, or other necessities of life shows that we can't safely rely on innate human goodness, or the market, to curb such behavior among ourselves."

"I can think of works like Konrad Lorenz's *On Aggression*," I added. "And Jane Goodall's work, which shows that the great apes not only cooperate but fight, and sometimes kill, to advance group interests in breeding, territory, and food. Sometimes they do it for what she can only describe as the fun of it. These and other works show how some species see to their own survival by attacking others, even ones closely related to them."

"You're not saying that these animal studies prove something about human behavior, are you?" Laz asked. "Because humans are different. We have souls. We have speech. We have an ideal, not just a material, nature. If parents indoctrinate children with a sense of right and wrong, certain realms *may* be left safely to the market. People are just fundamentally different from a flock of sheep or a group of untrained dogs that might require constant watching—regulation, if you will."

"I don't want to make too much of the naturalistic argument," Rodrigo conceded. "It just puts us on notice not to assume too much. My next argument addresses specifically human behavior. Ready to move on?"

It was late, and I was starting to flag. Rodrigo must have noticed, for he said "I hope we're not wearing you out, Professor. You've been up longer than we have. Want to postpone the rest until breakfast?"

"No, no," I insisted. "I'm going strong. I want to hear the last two prongs of your argument. But I could use a cup of tea."

Laz immediately looked around, attracted the waiter's attention, and seconds later we were placing orders. More coffee for my two young friends (whose iron constitutions caused me, once again, to marvel—coffee this late would have me tossing and turning all night) and a soothing chamomile tea for me. Then, Rodrigo continued:

Rodrigo's Third Argument: Studies of Helping Behavior in Cross-Race Situations Cast Doubt on the Ability of Free Choice and Deregulation to Drive out Racism

"Good idea, Professor. I'm a little bushed myself," Rodrigo admitted. "But I can go through my last two arguments quickly. I'm sure the two of you are familiar with the social science literature dealing with so-called helping behavior in cross-race situations, and also with the role of influence on cognition?"

"We were talking about the first group of studies before," I said. "But maybe not the second. Why don't you summarize them for us."

The waiter set down our steaming beverages, and I motioned surreptitiously for the check. Rodrigo objected, but I waved him aside: "I'm on sabbatical. Please be my guests." The two exchanged glances, and I knew I would have a battle on my hands later, so I said, "We'll see. But why don't you go on." Rodrigo took the bait. As he did so, I stealthily removed my credit card from my wallet, which I had been holding in my lap.

"A host of social science studies explore what people do in cross-race situations. In a typical one, the scientist has a black female assistant stage an accident in which she spills a bag of groceries. Later, a white one does the same thing, and they record what happens. Sometimes they do something similar with stranded motorists. The studies show that people go to the aid of persons of their own race more readily than to persons of another race or ethnicity. Some researchers explain the results in terms of 'norm theory.' We respond to persons in need according to how normal or abnormal their plight seems to us. Famines in Biafra evoke little response because we think they are normal in that part of the world. But if our middle-class neighbor shows up at our doorstep, not having eaten in two days because of losing his or her job, we immediately rush to his or her aid."

"I remember that line of experiments," I said, "and see how they fortify your argument. If an economic exchange is the kind that can also help the other person, say a hiring decision, then one might well unconsciously look for people like oneself—freckle-faced blondes of European descent, if one is like that, rather than black men with Afros, even if they have Ph.D's. This skews the marketplace in favor of any group who can exercise discretion not to deal. But what's the second line of experiments?"

"I was thinking of studies, such as Stanley Milgram's and Solomon Asch's, of authority and mindset. Are you familiar with these?"

Laz said, "I know about Milgram and his studies of obedience. In a series of articles and a book, he described experiments that show how people behave when commanded by authority figures. In one, he hooked up volunteers, who did not know the purpose of the experiment, to a fake console with a series of switches. The doctor, wearing a white coat, explained that the purpose of the study was learning and reinforcement, and that they were to be the teacher, administering small electric shocks to a learner in another room. The doctor warned the volunteer, however, never to flip the switches beyond a certain point, as this could administer a potentially lethal dose of electricity. As the experiment proceeded, the doctor directed the teachers to administer higher and higher doses of electricity, each of which led to louder and louder shrieks from the other room. The cries were emitted, of course, by trained actors and were completely fake. Although all of the volunteers showed distress over what they were doing, fidgeting and sweating, most followed the directions of the doctor, even to the point of administering what they believed could be a lethal jolt of electricity to a fellow human being. Afterward, many confronted the realization that, like good Nazis, they had done what an authority figure commanded even though they might have killed another human being."

"And the other line of experiments," Rodrigo continued, "while not quite so graphic, is just as well known. Asch and his collaborators held up cards with lines drawn on them and asked a group of volunteers to identify which of two matched in length. All except one were confederates of the experimenter and instructed to vote for the wrong line. The idea was to see if group pressure would cause the subject who was not in the know to go along."

"I read about those studies," I interjected. "In most cases, the subject did so. And, afterward it turned out that many acquiesced not just to avoid trouble or to get the experiment over with, but because group dynamics actually changed what they saw."

"I see how these studies help your side," Laz said. "As with your eleven-year-old driver example, they suggest that people won't trade with perfectly acceptable partners of another race because, as Milgram's and Asch's studies show, they have adopted the racist assumptions of the society they inhabit. Again, I have some reservations, because I think people have more free will than that. But, let's hear your fourth argument."

**Rodrigo's Fourth Argument: Studies of Other Societies,
and of Particular Institutions in Our Own, Show That
Highly Formal Settings Elicit the Least Racism**
"My final point also proceeds by induction. Damn! Those are some fast hands, Professor!" I had just snatched the bill from the waiter, who had arrived bearing it on a small tray.

"You can say what you will about altruism in mixed-race settings," I replied with a smile, "but in this one, I'm paying. My salary's much higher than yours, and

I've learned many a new wrinkle today. You young scholars don't realize how much we old timers learn from upstarts like you. Especially when it comes to recent currents, such as marketplace theory and social science studies, that came along after we got our start. So, consider it even. We can split breakfast if we're all up that early. Want to eat together?"

Laz and Rodrigo glanced at each other. "We were going to go for a quick run, then grab a bite before we catch our flight back. Want to join us?"

"I did bring my running shoes," I said. "But I'm sure you two will want to set a faster pace than I can go comfortably—just as you do in intellectual conversation. Why don't we start out together, then you can go on ahead at some point. I'll finish my run and meet you back here at, say, eight-thirty?"

"Perfect," said Laz. "Let's meet outside the hotel at seven. The desk clerk said they have running maps for guests."

Having settled our morning plans, Laz and I sat back expectantly. After the waiter refilled our cups, Rodrigo looked up.

"My final argument draws on empirical and cross-cultural studies. For example, in connection with hate speech, a specific form of racism, writers have been studying the effect of formal rules. Basing their conclusions both on the nature of prejudice and on the success of Canada and certain European societies in bridling it, these scholars have developed what they call the 'fairness and formality' hypothesis. Are you familiar with it?"

"I've read about it," Laz said. "It holds that formal institutions are apt to diminish, not just the amount of racism expressed in behavior, but the very impulse itself. Formality, such as the robes, flags, and other paraphernalia of a court proceeding, reminds all present that the higher values of the American creed are to predominate. Informal settings, such as those that characterize alternative dispute resolution, present fewer such reminders and so, all other things being equal, are apt to call up more prejudice. Scholars have used this to explain why racism is relatively absent in settings like the military and sports, which contain many formal rules and so afford less scope for discretion. They have also used it to compare the record of relatively laissez-faire societies such as the United States to that of societies such as Canada, Great Britain, Italy, and Germany, which believe in freedom of expression but nevertheless forbid racist and anti-Semitic speech."

"And so you agree that, all things being equal, formality offers better prospects for discouraging prejudice than its opposite?" Rodrigo asked.

"I would," Laz conceded. "Like most conservatives, I have no problem with formality. And I see how it argues for regulation, not laissez-faire and markets, as a means of controlling racism. And, although I don't draw quite the same conclusion you do from your four-part argument, I concede that you've shown a chink, maybe a large one, in the armor of the law-and-economics movement and that of some of my more complacent libertarian colleagues. Racism does present a unique challenge to free market philosophy. Your thought experiments plant the seed of doubt, and your four types of evidence drive it home: We cannot sit back complacently, rake in profits, and rationalize that the system that benefits us and our class is best for those at the bottom of the hierarchy too. Self-respecting conservatives must do better than that!"

"Can you do better, Laz?" I asked. I respected the young man's intelligence and candor. His befriending of Rodrigo, a year younger than he, junior on his faculty, and poles apart politically, spoke volumes for Laz's fair-mindedness and generosity. I hoped he had a proposal, and despite the late hour was delighted when he said:

LAZ PROPOSES A CULTURAL SYNTHESIS: A RACE-NEUTRAL PROGRAM ON WHICH LEFT AND RIGHT MIGHT AGREE

"Actually, I've been giving this some thought. As you know, Professor, my own parents were immigrants. I was raised to detest discrimination of any kind. I believe all men and women are entitled to rise according to their merits, without artificial barriers or preferences. At the same time, I agree with Rodrigo that merit is, to some degree, constructed, and is apt at any point in history to favor those activities that the empowered group does well. I also agree that with respect to race, neutral, process-oriented market strategies are not apt to pick out members of minority groups for advancement and beneficial trade. But the Thernstroms and Murray do make valid points. Formal governmental programs aimed exclusively at blacks and Latinos institutionalize bureaucracy, deprive people of the opportunity to act out of generosity by converting everything into an obligation, foster a hand-out mentality among the beneficiaries, stigmatize able minorities, and stir up hostility among working-class whites, like my family. The trick is to find something that minimizes these costs while allowing suffering populations, until recently mired in slavery and Jim Crow laws, to move ahead."

Rodrigo looked up with an expression that I can only describe as a mixture of wariness and hope. "Go ahead, Laz. I'm anxious to hear your thoughts."

Glancing quickly over at me, Laz began. "The American public is tired of race-conscious remedies. Although one can quarrel over what the polls mean, it's only a matter of time before affirmative action and similar programs targeted specifically at minorities come to an end. The question is what to replace them with."

"Aren't they necessary to counter the effects of past discrimination, level the playing field, and allow enough professionals of color to enter the ranks to serve as role models?" Rodrigo asked.

"I agree that those things are important, and it's inexcusable that the Thernstroms offer no replacement for them. I think, however, the answer is color-neutral programs that help *all* those who are poor and disadvantaged. These would include special consideration in college admissions for anyone who can show that he or she was raised under impoverished circumstances. They would also include special outreach to inner-city schools and programs to create jobs and ameliorate urban blight. Many of the problems of the ghettos and barrios are not racial in nature, but economic. What's needed is universal programs. Not only will these be more palatable to the white middle class, they will help the truly poor and deserving. The son or daughter of the black or Chicano brain surgeon may not get special help, but why should they? At the same time, the child of Ukrainian immigrants who is the first in his or her family to attend college would get special consideration. Remedial programs like those we have in place now don't help desperately poor blacks, who can't get into college or win construction contracts even with a helping hand. My programs would."

Laz had been speaking quietly and urgently. Finally Rodrigo spoke. "Laz, your proposal reminds me of William Julius Wilson's recent book on the decreasing significance of race. And, much as I respect your humanism and commitment to equal rights, I doubt it will fill the bill. Even under universal programs, blacks will end up receiving short shrift unless the programs have a race-conscious component or are monitored extremely carefully. Those in charge, even with the best will in the world, will not distribute jobs and other benefits evenly among whites and minorities. Ellis Cose showed that even black executives and law partners suffer racism every day. It's true that we must deal with poverty, crime, drugs, and lack of services in the cities. But race will always remain a separate and independent subordinating factor. Blacks are not just white people who happen not to have any money right now. Pretending that race doesn't count is an evasion."

"Pretending that black people's problems are all due to race is also an evasion," Laz said evenly. "And programs based on race are social dynamite. They single out beneficiaries by an easily identifiable physical factor—one that bears a lot of historical baggage, I might add. If you could give aid directly to the black poor, which I admit are in great need of it, and could do it quietly and for a short time without being discovered, I might favor it. But you can't do that in a society such as ours. And if you did do it openly, you'd just foster resentment and make matters worse."

"You could try educating white people to accept it," Rodrigo ventured. "Economic conditions are a little better than they have been for a time. The pie is expanding. Giving a job to A does not mean taking one from B."

"But programs that change the infrastructure are much better. They last forever," Laz replied. "And they have a cascading effect. Create more jobs in the inner city or the manufacturing sector, and you put more money into the pockets of the poor. Some will open small businesses, or send their children to community colleges, when before they couldn't afford it."

"I feel the attraction of your approach," Rodrigo conceded. "And I, too, welcome the day when race does not matter. But, for now, it does. Perhaps there's no way out of the trap, and we just have to muddle through, using whatever degree of remedial race-consciousness society will tolerate, while hoping that broad, race-neutral programs aimed at the poor in general will provide some incidental relief. I just hope it happens before the poor of color sink into an irreversible, never-ending downward spiral."

"One last thing you two liberals might want to consider, given your wary views on law and economics, is the difference between allowing free market forces to rule and using market incentives to induce certain kinds of behavior. For example, in environmental law, the first approach would entail allowing the national forests to be sold to whoever values them the most—environmentalists or timber companies. The second incentive approach would correspond to using 'pollution permits' which polluters must buy in order to pollute, but which they can sell if they become cleaner. This might work with affirmative action." Laz sat back with an expectant expression.

"You mean companies with good records of hiring blacks could, say, sell their surplus brownie points, so to speak, to firms who don't like them?" I asked.

"Exactly," Laz said. "This should satisfy even Charles Murray, because his main objection to antidiscrimination laws is that they force people to do what they may not want to do, namely satisfy their taste for discrimination. It also requires a lesser role for government...."

"Which should keep Murray happy," I interjected.

"Indeed," Laz said. "Government would not need to ride herd on every company and every transaction, because the sales of these discrimination permits would go on privately, between companies."

"Perhaps the two broad sorts of programs—race-neutral and race-conscious—will work together," I said, sensing that our discussion was about to come to an end and hoping to set the stage for tomorrow's. "As white folks begin to see that the new programs, such as job training, benefit them and their struggling counterparts, their empathy and receptiveness to dealing with the special problems of racism may soften. The two sorts of plans, then, may work together, each being a necessary precondition of the other."

"An intriguing suggestion, Professor," Laz said, brightening and pushing his chair back from the table. "I'd love to know how your and Rodrigo's observations on human nature fit into it. Why don't we talk about it more tomorrow morning. Rodrigo and I have afternoon classes to teach back home tomorrow, so we might want to get a few hours of sleep."

"I'm game," said Rodrigo. "It's almost ten."

As we stood up and started walking toward the elevator to our rooms, Laz turned to me and said, "If there's one thing I think we can all agree on, it's that the combination of the Thernstroms' anti–affirmative action proposal and the Murray libertarian suggestion to eliminate or water down all the civil rights laws is lethal. It would leave people of color with little protection, requiring them to pull themselves up by their bootstraps, something not even white immigrants managed to accomplish unaided. We all agree that the market alone won't drive out racism or do much to alleviate the special problems of the underclass of color. Laws forbidding racial discrimination will remain necessary into the foreseeable future. Whether we can do more than that is open to debate. The two of you think we can. The Thernstroms disagree. I say we can target poverty of all kinds, black or white. Will this improve conditions for your people quickly enough to turn things around? I wish I knew."

"It's a topic for another day," I said, yawning.

Rodrigo pressed the "UP" button. "And maybe another book," he smiled.

ZERO-BASED RACIAL POLITICS
An Evaluation of Three Best-Case Arguments on Behalf of the Nonwhite Underclass

Every index of black and brown misery today warrants alarm. Blacks' income, net wealth, educational attainment, life expectancy, infant mortality, drug addiction, and incarceration are worse than those of whites. On most of these measures, the black-white gap is increasing, and on some, blacks stand worse off today than they did ten or even twenty years ago. Latinos are even poorer and more segregated in schools than blacks.

To whom should the nonwhite poor turn for help? The black and brown middle class is too small to carry out a rescue operation of the magnitude needed. A coalition, if only temporary, with some segment of white society will be necessary—but which one? The traditional answer has been liberals, especially those of the moderate persuasion associated with the Democratic Party. Yet, if careful reflection shows that a better alliance is possible, a realignment should not be out of the question. The continuing decline of the poor is surely a predicament no less urgent than that of a corporation whose earnings have dropped and whose shareholders are at risk of not receiving their accustomed dividends. Faced with this sort of stringency, corporations have imposed zero-based financing, requiring that longstanding operating practices be justified or cut. Might the nonwhite poor do something similar?

The time has come to ask the zero-basis question: In a society with power divided almost equally between two political groups, one conservative, one liberal, which is the more likely source of aid for the nonwhite poor? I begin by selecting two legal and political positions that share much of the power in the United States: the moderate right and the moderate left. I identify and evaluate what I consider the "best case" arguments that spokesmen for the poor could make to each of these groups. I identify the premises of each argument and assess its cogency and rhetorical force.

This approach, which proceeds by means of a two-by-two matrix, leads to a surprising conclusion: The arguments to the right turn out to be both more analytically sound and more convincing than the ones to the left. The nonwhite poor, several million strong, should therefore reconsider their historic alignment with moderate liberalism and enter into a dialogue with the other side.

Two premises underlie my analysis: disaggregation and competition. The former holds that we should be open to the possibility that a political group whose positions we admire on certain issues (*e.g.,* the environment, military spending) may not be the best in other areas (*e.g.,* support for the poor). The latter holds that nonwhites will do better if they force majority-dominated interest blocs to compete for their votes and support; alliances that are too automatic will eventually yield suboptimal results.

THE ARGUMENT TO THE MODERATE LEFT

The nonwhite poor can offer a number of reasons why liberals should support social welfare services. They can argue that support is the morally right thing to do because it is helpful to the individuals concerned, good for society as a whole, and an integral part of combating discrimination. These are, indeed, arguments that liberals have themselves made often.

The moral argument dates back at least to the Elizabethan Poor Laws, which drew a distinction between the "worthy poor" and paupers. The "worthy poor"—such as the blind, the aged, and the handicapped—were those in need through no fault of their own. They were distinguished from paupers—such as the lazy, the demoralized, and the drunk—who deserved their fate. It was society's obligation to make sure that members of the first group did not decline into the second. This notion that assistance is morally required struck a chord in the hearts of post–Civil War progressives that still resonates in today's proponents of liberal social philosophy.

The moral rightness of helping the worthy poor has surfaced this century in welfare legislation grounded in New Deal principles, court decisions, and political rhetoric. Basic fairness through income redistribution was a driving impetus in the passage of legislation such as the Social Security Act, the Fair Labor Standards Act, and the progressive income tax. Beginning around 1950, state courts began striking down "suitable home" provisions in Aid to Families with Dependent Children (AFDC) distribution schemes. Courts found these provisions, which terminated benefits if the mother was found to be engaging in extramarital sex, to unfairly punish the children (who were still "worthy"). These judicial decisions foreshadowed the Fleming Rulings, which codified the rules developed in the courts. President Lyndon Johnson echoed the sentiment when he declared, ["We should wage war on poverty] because it is right that we should."

A related argument for affording assistance to the poor—that it is possible to do so and hence we should—is related to the first and also has a lineage extending from post–Civil War progressivism to modern-day liberal dogma. In 1869, Henry George lamented that the United States was a land of "private fortunes" side by side with "poverty and degradation." This same sentiment surfaced almost 100 years later in both the Economic Opportunity Act of 1964, which sought to eliminate "the paradox of poverty in the midst of plenty," and statements of the AFL-CIO Executive Council such as, "[n]o nation in the history of the world has a greater capability of lifting all of its people above the level of want." Though not relying directly on a "moral rightness" argument, those who frame the issue this way imply that society should aid the poor because it is irrational not to do so.

A second argument for welfare assistance, that it will help people as individuals, rests on the liberal principles of equality of opportunity and equality of treatment. The poor need assistance to overcome the effects of social isolation and limited aspirations and "to achieve at least minimal dignity." Sometimes these altruistic appeals accompany pragmatism. In 1928, George Bernard Shaw wrote that "though the rich end of town can avoid living with the poor end, it cannot avoid dying with it when the plague comes." President Johnson noted that "helping some will increase the prosperity of all"; President Kennedy said, "[i]f a free society cannot help the many who are poor, it cannot save the few who are rich." The Kerner Commission warned of riots and warring camps of blacks and whites if the United States did not bring poverty and racism under control.

The final liberal argument for assistance to the poor is that it is an integral part of protecting minority groups from discrimination. Many liberals believe that racism and poverty are inextricably linked and must be solved together. In this view, government assistance to the poor is a vehicle to effect social change and a necessary component of the liberal agenda.

Evaluating the Liberal Argument for Social Assistance

It is not difficult to convince liberals that their position must entail welfare assistance to the poor. The difficulty lies in deciding what level of assistance the poor need and mobilizing support for it. Essentially, the arguments appeal to altruism; they speak to our finest instincts and tap sources deeply embedded in the Judeo-Christian tradition. Yet they come without a yardstick. Once we decide to give to a deserving individual or group, how much should we give? It is vitally necessary to develop a measure: In times of financial stringency it is easy to balance away ill-defined rights of unpopular groups like the poor.

The current weakening of the motivating principle that liberalism relies on for support of social welfare presents an equally serious problem. This principle, altruism, is strongest and most reliable when:

1. we fear that the same misfortune (illness, being out of work) may befall us;
2. those who suffer the misfortune confront us daily and are highly visible;
3. those who suffer strike us as being like ourselves;
4. those who suffer appear blameless with respect to their own condition;
5. our failure to give conflicts with another value we hold or our own self-concept (i.e., as a loving and generous people);
6. those in need are appealing or attractive.

All six conditions are likely to continue to weaken. Few to whom any appeal would be directed fear becoming poor or homeless themselves. Moreover, geographic separation of the rich and the poor is increasing; few readers of this chapter have much daily contact with inner-city ghettos or pockets of deep rural poverty. The unfortunates we do see wandering the streets are not like us, nor are most of them particularly appealing. Further, with the scaling down of the Cold War, we no longer find domestic poverty a public-relations liability. Nor do our institutions preach altruism with their previous fervor. We are more concerned with self and material well-being and are ready to blame the poor for their own poverty; we are "conscienced out." Liberals are more interested in issues like the environment and military spending (which may be of low priority to the nonwhite underclass), than with subsistence welfare for the needy. The altruistic appeal thus today provides a weak basis for asserting an obligation to provide social welfare to the nonwhite poor.

THE ARGUMENT TO THE RIGHT

Conservative thought emphasizes self-reliance, the free marketplace, and as little governmental intervention as possible. Accordingly, one might think that the right is an unpromising source of support for the nonwhite poor. Indeed, nonwhite populations and the poor have generally sought coalition with various strands of leftism. Yet this reliance may be misplaced; conservative principles may be a better source of succor for the poor than has hitherto been thought.

Why the Principled Right Should Support Social Programs for the Nonwhite Poor

Conservatives believe in a free marketplace in which actors make exchanges based on self-interest. A worker exchanges labor in return for wages; an investor or entrepreneur, money or ideas in the hope of a return. Those who act imprudently will fail and be replaced by others who offer a better product or better labor, or invest more wisely.

This general approach yields a powerful argument for aid to the poor. A certain amount of "cultural capital" is an essential precondition for entry into most marketplaces. One who, from birth, lacks a minimum level of acculturation and training will be unable to make exchanges and will suffer exclusion from the marketplace. It is as though society set up a game of Monopoly, invited everyone to play, but refused to issue paper money to a few. Once a person receives the means to make exchanges, if he or she squanders it—by making a foolish investment or continually coming to work late and getting fired—we may conclude that the person deserves his or her poverty and refuse to render aid. But we cannot say this of the abject always-poor. We have never issued them the wherewithal to compete; they have never had anything to exchange. This the conservative cannot allow, because his or her theory is based on exchanges. Consequently, conservatives must support a certain minimum level of public services for the poor.

What level? And, are we in danger of dropping below it today? The following thought experiment provides both a yardstick and an answer. Imagine an inner-city youth born to a welfare mother. His home is a crowded, noisy tenement in a public housing project. He has never met his father. The neighborhood schools are in disarray, the teachers demoralized, discipline nonexistent, truancy high. Vicious gangs dominate the streets. To survive, the boy must join one of them, all of which teach a brutal ethic of crime, drugs, opposition to authority, and control of turf. By the age of sixteen, the young man has been convicted of several offenses and dropped out of school.

Imagine that this youth approaches you, the reader, a lawyer in a respected law firm or a professor at a major university. He tells you he needs a job. He offers to deliver your legal messages, clean your office after hours, shelve books in your library. Most readers' reaction would be entirely predictable: No. The youth lacks the cultural capital to work for you or anyone else. He is unlikely to know basic things he needs to function in your world. He is alien, he is "Other." You would fear him; you would prefer to hire someone with a greater foothold in your world. I would do the same.

Principled conservatives cannot allow youths like the one in the example to exist. Yet they do, in large numbers, their education, nutrition, medical care, and nurturing falling below the minimum necessary to enable them to enter into exchanges with people like you and me. They effectively are rendered economic nonpersons, unable to enter legitimate marketplaces, hold jobs, make investments, and purchase property. The conservative is not only logically bound to remedy this problem, he or she should be strongly motivated to do so. Youths like the one in the thought experiment would be entitled to revolt, violently if necessary, against society. Our system has little, if any, claim to their loyalty. They would be justified in taking by force the essential life commodities that society has failed to provide them. Conservatives have a greater stake than others in seeing that this does not happen. Often wealthier than their liberal counterparts, they have the most to lose from the crime and disruption that results from unmet human needs. More attuned to business values, conservatives may react sympathetically to job training that will help meet the threat of foreign competition, while at the same time reducing crime and disruption.

One area where similar arguments gain a hearing is bankruptcy. The institution of bankruptcy, favored by conservatives and liberals alike, aims to accomplish two principal purposes. First, it permits individuals to avoid the discouragement and suppression of productivity that can result from an unpayable amount of debt. The second purpose is humanitarian: Experience teaches that the free market produces persons who find themselves saddled with overwhelming debt through no fault of their own. These victims of our rough-and-ready system deserve a second chance. Next time their fortunes may improve; we are not yet ready to write them off.

Both arguments apply at least as strongly to the youth of my imaginary example. A businessperson whose venture fails gets a "fresh start." The youth, by contrast, needs *a* start; unlike the entrepreneur, he never had one. Unless the youth has an opportunity to enter into exchanges, society will never benefit from whatever labor, inventions, and enterprise he may have produced. Moreover, the youth, deprived of any meaningful opportunity to rise, can scarcely be blamed for his condition. Both the social-utility and humanitarian reasons for bankruptcy apply with equal or greater force to individuals whose chances in life are near zero, who have been "bankrupt since birth."

Evaluating the Argument to the Right
Possible weaknesses in the argument to the right include: (1) that conservatives care mainly about business values, and welfare spending is inimical to the business climate; and (2) that the right hate the poor and are unlikely to wish to have much to do with them.

It is true that subsistence programs for the poor will raise taxes and so may have a short-term negative impact on the economy. But a much greater threat to the economy stems from foreign competition—by the rapidly expanding economies of China, India, and other emerging countries. A principal reason why these countries threaten our markets is that they benefit from highly motivated and educated workforces. American business leaders recognize that to compete, the pool of United States workers able to handle demanding, technical work must grow. As minorities become an even larger proportion of the United States population, educational and job training programs for members of these groups will be increasingly essential to a healthy economy.

It may also be true that some on the political right hold a visceral dislike for the poor: their perceived sexuality, high reproductive rate, music, and disinclination to work. Yet at least some conservatives are eager to help nonwhites who are struggling to rise. Witness the recent instances in which wealthy industrialists and churches have promised to sponsor the education of inner-city children who agree to stay out of trouble. Further, the right and the nonwhite poor are arguably natural allies on certain issues, such as the environment and military spending. Both oppose drugs and favor strong families and religion. These convergences favor a coalition, particularly if the right recognized that it could enable them to win several million votes and administer a final, stinging defeat for the left. Finally, because those on the right are often more deeply religious than those on the left, appeals based on basic human dignity and Judeo-Christian values may move them more than they move others.

[Eds. Delgado next reviews three Supreme Court cases that decline to find a constitutional imperative to alleviate poverty.]

The nonwhite poor's predicament is acute and worsening. Because Supreme Court cases indicate the poor can expect little help from the courts, their best avenue for relief will be the political arena, where their increasing numbers offer at least the cold comfort that majority-race groups will need to take them seriously. Evaluation of "best case" arguments shows that the nonwhite poor's most logical ally is the principled right. The argument to the right has not been fully articulated, yet it is both more cogent and more likely to be heeded than those to the left.

To gain the attention of any majoritarian political group, the poor will need to be strident, demanding, and willing to engage in disruption if need be—in a word, radical. Yet once mobilized, their best friends, in a paradox worthy of our times, may be members of the principled right rather than their now tepid traditional allies, the moderate left.

PART VIII
Affirmative Action

Though in 2003 the U.S. Supreme Court decided to let stand restricted affirmative action plans in higher education, the debate over those policies' efficacy and legitimacy still continues. Some states have passed referenda that forbid affirmative action in publicly funded universities, and the issue, in large part, remains unresolved.

In an essay based on the Hugo Black annual lecture at the University of Alabama law school, "Ten Arguments against Affirmative Action—How Valid?" Delgado reviews what happened to the minority members of his own law school class at the University of California at Berkeley after they graduated. After demonstrating that their success rates equaled those of nonminority members of the class, he presents ten common arguments against affirmative action policies in higher education, and then rebuts them.

In "Rodrigo's Tenth Chronicle," Rodrigo makes his final appearance in this volume during an earlier stage in his life when he has just become friends with Laz, a conservative colleague at the law school where they are both teaching. The Professor, a panelist at a conference for new law professors, encounters Rodrigo and Laz. Together they discuss affirmative action. Rodrigo audaciously deconstructs the concept of merit, showing how it reflects societal norms. Laz counters that merit can serve as a bulwark against racism. The two decide to explore the issue further in a conference they decide to launch on race and class.

1998 Hugo L. Black Lecture
Ten Arguments against Affirmative Action—How Valid?

Not long ago, I stood in front of another university audience like this one, speaking on a similar, although not identical, subject—diversity. A certain irony attended the occasion, the graduation of the 1996 class at Boalt Hall, the law school where I myself graduated many years ago. As it turns out, my class at Boalt was the first to experience a fully diversified student body throughout all three years; the one I addressed was likely to be the last. [Eds. Because of Proposition 209, which eliminated affirmative action in California.]

Let me paint the scene for you. Here was the Greek Theater, a giant outdoor bowl surrounded by eucalyptus trees and overflowing with the most diverse imaginable crowd of proud parents, brothers, sisters, and other relatives of the graduates sitting on stage, waiting for the speeches to end and the magic moment to arrive when they would collect that coveted diploma. Large Chicano families with young children mingled with equally large African American ones from all over the nation. And, of course, Asian and white families were liberally sprinkled among them. Earlier a steel marimba band had played salsa music under the sun, cutting to Pomp and Circumstance when it was time for the procession. I was struck by how perfectly inaptly certain critics and even defenders of diversity and affirmative action frame the debate about them. Diversity is not a heavy-handed obligation, risky social experiment, or vengeful righting of the scales, but a giant *celebration.* Like a party, a graduation, a meal at a good ethnic restaurant, or international travel, diversity should be a source of pleasure, wonderment, delight. Not at all a win-lose proposition, diversity can be a win for *everyone,* white, black, brown, Native American, or anything else, opening the door to new ideas, skills, and experiences.

But, of course, not everyone sees it that way. Others see diversity in the same way some motorists cruising a large, crowded parking lot see the handful of parking spaces reserved for the disabled, certain that if it had not been for those few reserved slots, they would be safely parked by now.

On day one, most law school deans greet the entering class with a welcoming address in the course of which they tell them a little bit about each other. My own class, if I recall, included a professional ballet dancer, several small business owners, and a clown from the Barnum and Bailey Circus. It also contained a number of social workers, community activists, and organizers looking for new skills in the struggle against poverty and inequality.

That was how we entered. My class was about thirty percent minority, like the one I was about to address. Curious where all that diversity *went,* I asked administrators at Boalt to do a bit of research and tell me where my fellow students of color, and women, too—for then law schools were also making special efforts to raise the numbers of women enrolled—all products of affirmative action, wound up. Did they all flunk out, fail the bar exam, or assimilate silently into obscure, gray corners of the corporate kingdom?

Here is a small sample of what I learned. They all passed the bar exam, after which a certain Paul, who sat opposite me in class, became CEO of Broadway Federal Bank, the largest African American–owned financial institution in the United States. I wish I had gotten to know him better! Six classmates of color became state judges, including Lance Ito, who even then seemed bound for distinction. Richard was recently nominated to the Ninth Circuit. Jose, the chief justice of the Supreme Court of the Northern Mariana Islands. Jennifer became a hearing judge for the Merit Systems Protection Board of California. Ted, executive corporate counsel for Wells Fargo—another person I wish I had gotten to know better. Ginger, deputy administrator of the U.S. Small Business Administration. Charles, a partner at Davis Wright Tremaine. Frank, U.S. Congressperson, Texas. Thomas, solicitor for the U.S. Department of Labor and deputy inspector general of the Energy Department. Ned, partner at Paul Hastings, in San Francisco. Richard, partner, Rivkin Radler. Susan, Kate, and Laura, professors of law at Washington University of St. Louis, Duke University, and Georgetown, respectively. Jessica, pioneering female managing partner of a major law firm (Heller Ehrman). Lois, executive director of Children Now. Claudia, U.S. District Court judge. Not to mention three more law firm partners, a New York State Supreme Court judge, a Goldman Fund executive, a director of Lawyers Committee on Civil Rights, another professor of law, a state bar presiding judge, and one state bar president. And, of course, Yours Truly, professional typist. As you know, the Cassandras and detractors of affirmative action warn that we are in danger of sacrificing quality. Well, you certainly could not tell it from that list. I have never felt so much like an under-achiever.

At the law school where I taught recently, in each of the last several years the minority students, many of whom were admitted under diversity programs with lower LSATs than the others, graduated at the same rate, found jobs more quickly, and earned a slightly higher entering salary than their classmates as a group. Not only that, they obtained prestigious positions, such as judicial clerkships or university professorships, at a slightly higher rate. Certainly, all the students were smart, capable, and went on to fine careers, but the diversity part of the party did as well as the rest. Moreover, my travels around the country convince me that what is true at that school is true elsewhere: attend the tenth- or twentieth-year reunion of the black or minority students association, and you find yourself in a roomful of extremely distinguished people. Do not mistake what I am saying: law schools, like other social institutions, should be trying constantly to improve the quality of all of those they admit, train, and turn loose on the world. But higher education is one of the few things that America emphatically does right—our universities are the envy of the world, every year unfailingly attracting the best foreign students—and diversity is one of those programs we do right, as well.

I sometimes think that defending diversity is like having to justify a really good party or celebration. Why would anyone need to? Yet, as I mentioned, some people focus on the three reserved slots in the parking lot rather than the tiny displacement rate and great social utility of setting aside these spaces. The next part of my talk is aimed at them and the principal arguments they tend to assert.

I will *not* be discussing here reasons that argue in *favor* of affirmative action, just ones against it. I favor it, obviously, believing its benefits practically self-evident. If you are conservative, these are my answers to your arguments; if liberal, tools you can use to defend your position.

The first argument is the one from stigma. A paternalistic argument, it holds that we should reject affirmative action, even though most people of color support it, because it would only hurt them. If they knew their own self-interest, they would oppose it. This argument tends to come from liberals who genuinely like minorities but worry about their black friend with an IQ of 149 who may be unfairly labeled an affirmative-action baby. It is also made by some principled conservatives who fear affirmative action will do more harm than good and do not want that harm to befall blacks. And it is also made disingenuously by people who do not much like blacks or Mexicans at all, much less care if they are stigmatized, but think it a good argument against something they dislike.

The stigma argument holds that affirmative action will hurt all blacks, Mexicans, Asians, and so forth, even those who got to the top by their own merits. In the absence of other information, observers will assume that they did so with the aid of the unseen hand. The argument is empirical. It holds that if you do X, something unfortunate will happen. But stigmatization and stereotyping of people of color in the media and movies have either held constant or decreased in the roughly thirty-year period that affirmative action has been in place. Before this time, stereotyping of blacks and other minorities was rampant—groveling maids and Aunt Jemimas, shoot-you-in-the-back Mexicans, "ugh-want-um" Indians, and more. Many states had laws on the books forbidding interracial marriage until 1967, when *Loving v. Virginia* declared them unconstitutional. What more stigmatic message could exist than that—a law that says that if you are black or Asian, you are unfit to marry a white?

Stigma is in plentiful supply still, but it predates and operates independently of affirmative action. Consider that almost all universities admit athletes, musicians for the school orchestra, holders of ROTC scholarships, and legacy candidates (sons or daughters of wealthy alums) with SATs and grades considerably lower than those of the students regularly admitted. *Does the star quarterback feel stigmatized?*

Most schools employ a geographical preference, favoring students from far away, even though they all study from the same textbooks and watch the same television programs. When Stanford admits a student from rural New Hampshire with numbers a little lower than those of the genius from Marin County, California, does the New Hampshire student feel stigmatized or regard himself or herself as a case of affirmative action? Do veterans, who receive special consideration in federal job programs, feel stigmatized because of the way they got their jobs? Does a disabled person feel stigmatized when he or she goes up a ramp to a restaurant or public building that was installed pursuant to federal law? No, it is only people of color who are said to be. An odd selectivity, in my opinion.

The second argument is that affirmative action helps those blacks and other minorities who need it least: the proverbial son or daughter of the black neurosurgeon who got into Stanford or Harvard under an affirmative action program. This, too, is an empirical claim, and unlike the first one has a small grain of truth to it. The students of color who get into Stanford, Berkeley or Alabama are apt not to be the ones whose parents were dope fiends and dropped out of inner-city schools at age eight, but a little higher up the socioeconomic ladder. But the social status of whites at top schools is even higher. A straight-line correlation links standardized test scores and family income; zip codes predict LSAT scores better than those scores predict law school grades. At one law school at which I once taught, the average family income, in today's terms, was over $120,000. *Are we not also helping those whites who need it least?*

The black middle class, a few of whose sons and daughters do get into colleges through affirmative action, is indeed growing; but as writer Andrew Hacker points out, it stands on quite a different footing from that of the white middle class. A black family with a yearly income of $75,000 is apt to consist of a bus driver making $45,000 and a nurse earning $30,000, while the white family is apt to consist of a male engineer making that total and a mother who stays home or works part-time. Just as black poverty is different from the white kind—it tends to last forever—black membership in the middle class is more insecure than that of whites. Blacks fall from the middle class more often and suddenly. Their children are more likely to be downwardly mobile. Even those who reach comfortable professional status, making $250,000 a year or more, according to Ellis Cose, endure racial insults and lockouts on account of their color. I personally have had conservatives virtually cross-examine me, certain that I must be the son of Eva Peron, a Venezuelan oil magnate, or a brown neurosurgeon. When they learn I am instead the son of a Mexican orphan who immigrated to the United States at the age of fifteen without a cent to his name and a woman from the tenement district of Chicago, they act puzzled and disappointed. They *know* there has to be a brown neurosurgeon in there somewhere.

Consider how we also apply this argument unevenly. The unstated assumption is that we should put all our resources where they are most needed, namely into dirt-poor blacks and Mexicans. But we do not apply the same standard to professors who ask for no morning classes or want all their classes in a three-day block. We do not tell them, "Shame on you. You have no business worrying about that when the real problem is cancer, AIDS, children in Appalachia, or secretaries who are going blind from staring at computer display terminals all day long." We simply accommodate them because they are our friends, and we want to please them. But with middle class blacks it seems unnatural to us that they should have advanced so far and shameful that they would want even more.

The fact is that race is probably the best measure of social disadvantage that we have, even better than poverty. If you compare the prospects of a group of middle-income blacks from families earning, say, $55,000 to those of relatively poor whites making $30,000, you will find that the white kids, on the average, have better life prospects than the blacks. In many parts of the country, a black with a college degree earns as much as a white high school drop-out.

A third argument is that affirmative action operates like an unfortunate stairstep, admitting to top schools students of color who otherwise would go to middle-tier ones, and so on down the line. The result, according to writers such as Lino Graglia, Richard Sander, and Abigail Thernstrom, is that minority students always end up over their heads. One who would have done well at Fordham instead gets into Harvard, where he or she is supposedly miserable, scores in the bottom of his or her class, considers suicide, and possibly drops out, when the same individual would have been happier and better adjusted had he or she studied in the more forgiving atmosphere of a second-tier school. Like the two previous arguments, this one is paternalistic, professing concern for minorities and using that as a basis for phasing out a program that helps them. It, too, relies on an empirical premise: namely, that affirmative action harms its beneficiaries. But this premise is difficult to maintain in the face of the generally high morale, camaraderie, and success record of minorities at my university and elsewhere. A recent book by two university presidents shows that at elite colleges, which deploy affirmative action aggressively, blacks, at least, earn degrees at a rate within a few percentage points of whites and go on to careers of great success.

It also assumes that exposure to first-rate education is not good for you but *bad,* that attending a school with a favorable student-faculty ratio and studying under nationally acclaimed professors is good for whites, but not for blacks. This is truly paradoxical, and I am surprised bright people assert it. Rich people of all eras have been sending their sons and daughters not to the worst, but the best schools they could get them into, sometimes bending the rules to do so. There is little reason to believe that what is true for whites is not true for blacks, Mexicans, and other minorities.

The staircase argument also presupposes the argument from *merit,* namely that blacks and others of color on the average have less going for them and that facilitating their entry into law schools, jobs, and other charmed circles violates that sacred principle. This is argument number four. How would you like to be operated on by a surgeon who got into medical school not because of his or her scientific ability but skin color, the argument goes. In many ways this is a central criticism of affirmative action, but it, too, begs the question. Now, I am not one to maintain that every person of color is hardworking, trusty, thrifty, smart, and loyal. There is a range, just as with white people. But the merit argument holds that affirmative action generally, or always, places underqualified workers and students into jobs or slots over more highly qualified ones, presumably white or Asian. Once again, I am not saying that there is no such thing as an incompetent black or Mexican, any more than anyone could sensibly maintain that no whites squander inheritances, make poor use of their opportunities, or are just plain underpowered. But I defy anyone to produce evidence that the average level of services has gone down in the United States over the thirty years or so of affirmative action. The United States economy has taken nose dives from time to time, but these have been more the product of short-sighted behavior in executive suites, here and abroad, than on the part of hardworking immigrants and minorities working in restaurants, cutting grass, burning the midnight oil in the library, and doing a thousand other things, usually efficiently and for low wages.

It ends up, then, that the meritocrat is stuck with SAT scores and the like, where minorities do indeed, on the average, score lower. Does that mean they lack merit? Of course not, unless by merit you simply *mean* scoring high on a three-hour, multiple choice test taken on a Saturday in October. The SAT, until recently, included items about polo mallets, lacrosse, and regattas. How likely is a poor kid from the inner city to spend his or her weekend playing lacrosse or attending regattas? The SAT's originator, Carl Campbell Brigham, was an unabashed white supremacist and the author of *A Study of American Intelligence* (1923), in which he warned that southern European immigrants and minorities were swamping the country with their inferior genes, at the expense of those of superior European stock. He also warned against interbreeding and urged that we close our borders. Two years later, he became director of the College Board's testing program, in which capacity he borrowed racial classifications for his test data from Madison Grant's *The Passing of the Great Race*, a white supremacist tract. The test's purpose was to confirm the superiority of white test takers, pure and simple. You might think today's testing organizations would have repudiated his teaching, but the Educational Testing Service library today bears his name.

The SAT is eminently coachable. The director of one of the prominent test-coaching companies, which charges over $1000 for its services, boasted that his organization is able to boost the score of the average test taker by 185 points. Thirty percent improved by 250 or more. How many struggling minority families will be able to afford those services?

A further problem for merit advocates in educational settings like this one is what I call the paradox of distributed merit. The paradox lies in the moral irrationality of using merit criteria to distribute goods that can give the recipient a boost in an attribute that forms a part of the very same set of merit criteria used for distributive purposes. It would be like a paint store that only sold yellow paint for houses that were already yellow. If law school can boost anyone's LSAT—and we say that the purpose of law classes is to get you to think like a lawyer—it becomes irrational to insist on an absurdly high test score as a condition of entrance.

Consider, also, how contingent ideas of merit are. LSAT scores do predict law school first-year grades. But they also reflect the backgrounds and training and advantages of those who thrive under them, as well as correspond to the law firm jobs and prestigious clerkships some of the students will hold after they graduate. Identifying the LSAT as a predictor of grades, or even of later job performance, tells us only that this narrow test picks people who thrive in particular types of situations. Yet those situations are contingent, not necessary. Change the rules, and any test becomes more, or less, valid. Raise or lower the hoop in a basketball game six inches, and you radically change the definition of who has merit. Change the legal curriculum, or the way law is practiced, so that it becomes more cooperative or empathic, and half the current first-year class might not get in.

The fifth argument is that affirmative action establishes group rights, something the Constitution has never recognized and that is especially dangerous in a democracy. But the Constitutional Convention included only white men, who provided for political representation only for people like themselves. The document they drew up provided for the institution of slavery in no fewer than six clauses, as group-based a set of rights as you are likely to find: One group was entitled to own another. A century later, the Thirteenth and Fourteenth Amendments abolished that, but Jim Crow and separate-but-equal laws maintained a system of group rights for nearly 100 more years. To say that a paltry program of affirmative action that benefits a few blacks and Mexicans a year violates a long-standing principle is an odd way to read history. We give rights to groups all the time, for example, through favorable tax treatment, veterans' preferences, senior citizen discounts, and many other ways. Like the other arguments, this one turns out to be quite selective: groups turn out to be troublesome only if they look different from ourselves.

The sixth argument against affirmative action is that affirmative action injures relations between the races, producing resentment among whites, and maybe Asians, who blame blacks for their every defeat and trouble in life. *Unlike* most of the other arguments, this one may well contain a grain of truth. But the solution is not to abolish affirmative action; rather, it is to explain to whites how very little actual displacement is occurring. Admissions directors around the country will tell you that every year the most indignant protests they receive are from white applicants who would not have gotten in even if affirmative action did not exist. The few who are displaced, right at the margin, right at the very bottom, and so who have to go to the immediately next-best school—Yale, say, instead of Harvard, or Seattle University rather than Washington—are just not that hugely disadvantaged, at least compared to the hungry and determined black kid who struggled up from a broken home and substandard schools but nevertheless has real intellectual ability. A lot of things cause working-class Caucasians to suffer real hardship these days, including profit-driven corporations that send jobs to Third World countries, close factories at the drop of a hat, and spend their time and energy gobbling up each other instead of carrying out research and development, all in hopes of making a quick buck. These short-sighted, profit-driven actions cause a substantial loss of jobs, certainly many times more than that caused by a few blacks or Latinos moving up.

If one were looking for actions that limit the hopes of white individuals interested in getting into undergraduate and professional schools, one would find dozens of policies traceable right to elite sources and government, such as a Congress that is cutting student loans and a medical profession that maintains an artificially low supply of doctors and medical schools. All of us have cause to be upset over the increasing gap between the poor and the rich in this country and diminishing upward mobility. But to blame the one and one half percent impact on professional and graduate school enrollment traceable to affirmative action is to miss much of what is really going on.

The next argument is not empirical but ideological. It holds that affirmative action is reverse discrimination. But huge differences separate "No blacks need apply" from a program that gives blacks a moderate boost vis-à-vis whites. For one, the purpose of affirmative action is remedial. Whites-only drinking fountains and workplaces were not aimed at remedying anything: not historical injustice against whites, nor anything else. The purpose of affirmative action is radically different from that of the old-fashioned, black- and Mexican-hating kind, namely to help a historically marginalized group acquire the tools to enter society on an equal basis. Relatively little displacement occurs, as I mentioned earlier—about one and one half percent, as in the parking lot example—while the earlier regime of "whites only need apply" excluded blacks one hundred percent. In dozens of situations, the purpose and setting in which something is done makes a large difference; otherwise, capital punishment would be the same as murder.

The eighth argument, that affirmative action violates the principle of color blindness, is another armchair argument that simply does not hold water. Our legal system, from the beginning, has been intensely color conscious, as well as conscious of sex or gender. And this was so not just in the early years of slavery and Indian conquest, but continued on a formal level until very recently, and does on an informal one today. Every single large-scale test of social prejudice reveals that Americans are highly color conscious. In a typical example, testers from a university or governmental agency, one white, one black, go to check out apartments, apply for jobs, buy things in stores, or apply for a loan. As alike as possible in income, education, age, personality, etc., the two testers nevertheless report radically different experiences. For society, then, to say, "We cannot take account of race" simply ratifies and allows the unchecked accumulation of private prejudice.

The ninth argument holds that affirmative action balkanizes, encouraging people to regard themselves as members of small groups, jealously guarding their positions vis-à-vis each other, rather than being simply Americans. It promotes antagonism, ethnic strife, and a racial spoils system in which the momentary victor, today's majority, gets to take advantage of all the others or get even for imagined past sins.

But balkanization, properly understood, means small groups or nations feuding, endlessly and senselessly reliving old grievances and settling old scores. It does not mean small groups who have been deprived of their birthright and share of America's bounty making demands on the larger society for redress. That is not balkanization, but something quite different and, in many cases, wholly legitimate.

The last few years have, indeed, seen an increase in tensions among outgroups, such as Koreans versus blacks, blacks versus Jews, blacks versus Hispanics, and so on. But this is not so much because of affirmative action as it is because America has been slow to extend its bounty. Raising the income level of groups of color to a decent minimum would greatly ameliorate inter-group tension. Changing our racist immigration and licensing rules also would help. Many Korean merchants who run grocery stores in the inner city, for example, hold professional degrees, are pharmacists and teachers back in their home countries, but cannot practice their professions here. That is why they open small stores in Brooklyn or south-central Los Angeles, where, unsurprisingly, they sometimes come into conflict with the people who live there.

The final argument is that we do not need affirmative action—all we have to do is to enforce anti-discrimination laws currently on the books. Ending all discrimination would, of course, help a great deal, although it would do little for those who lead blighted lives now from the legacy of slavery, Jim Crow laws, and a century of neglect. Recall the runner on the starting line for a race whose officials scrupulously monitor for cheating, bumping, and other unfair tactics. Their scruples do little good because the race itself is unfair.

But a second reason counsels that we should not rest content with existing laws against discrimination. The civil rights laws, even more than others, are radically flouted and underenforced. A 1987 survey by the University of Chicago showed that seventy percent of employers in that city acknowledged making distinctions based on race and ethnicity. Yet only a small proportion of those making such decisions—on the order of one or two percent—have a complaint filed against them. Litigation is expensive; many valid complaints are not brought because of difficulties of proof or because the victim decides "what's the use?" A federal survey estimated that between two and four million cases of housing discrimination occur in this country per year. Affirmative action must remain as a supplement for imperfect enforcement of the law.

A variant of this argument charges that affirmative action penalizes persons who did not own slaves or run plantations. This innocence argument is a corollary of one we considered earlier, namely that affirmative action benefits those who need it least. Is it true that affirmative action punishes innocent whites for the sins of their fathers? No. When a university sets up a program to allow in a slightly larger number of blacks and Latinos, its purpose is far from punishing whites. If anything it wants to broaden their education by exposing them to a new range of experiences and ideas. When a university decides to let in Naval ROTC scholarship holders, tuba players for the band, quarterbacks who can throw a football seventy yards, veterans, or the sons and daughters of wealthy alums, is it trying to *punish* physics majors, the nonmusical, or pacifists? If it sets up a geographical quota for students from far away, is it punishing the locals because their fathers and mothers committed the sin of having them be born in the state where the school is located? No. It is only with blacks and Latinos that we find unfairness in a modest mechanism that lets a few of them get ahead.

White people, even ones who had no part in the plantation economy, still benefit from the development it brought the South, just as all of us benefit from the railroads the Chinese built, the farm labor of Mexicans, and the ruthless seizure of Indian lands. Our friends and children benefit from the informal set of privileges, favors, and courtesies we extend each other and from which blacks and Mexicans are almost entirely excluded. Such practices include the artfully crafted letter of recommendation that gets an erratic student into a fine college, the summer job one of Dad's or Mom's friends offers at the last minute, the teacher who discusses the extra-credit assignment with a favorite student that enables him or her to raise a B-plus in an Honors course to an A-minus. These are all examples of white privilege, an invisible system of courtesies and favors that has been going on for centuries and that constitutes, in one way of looking at it, history's largest affirmative action program:

benefits, jobs, and other forms of help awarded not on the basis of merit but acquaintance, friendship, or other morally irrelevant, nonmeritocratic criteria.

[Eds. Delgado next considers a number of ways to tailor race-conscious admissions programs to render them safe from attacks on constitutional grounds.]

One possibility would be to roll with the punches and take seriously proposals to abandon race-based affirmative action, now highly unpopular, in favor of a version based on socioeconomic status or underprivilege, but with a twist. First, notice that programs of this sort, which give bonus points for childhood poverty, broken homes, frequent moves, and so on, present three problems for those who take racial justice seriously. First, the number of poor whites greatly exceeds that of poor blacks and browns, so that these programs would do relatively little to help those who are disadvantaged on both scores. Deeming race one disadvantaging factor among many would help, but only so much. Second, one confronts the "top of the bottom" problem. Current race-based affirmative action plans draw criticism because they are said to favor middle-class blacks, Mexicans, and other minorities over the very poor. Colleges who recruit from the pool of all minority applicants naturally look with greatest favor on those who require the least adjustment and are most likely to succeed, namely those who are most like their usual pool of middle-class whites. With a shift to socioeconomic status (SES), colleges will examine the pool of disadvantaged applicants and choose those at the top of that pool, with high grades and test scores, most of whom will be white.

A third problem is that black or brown poverty is qualitatively different from the white kind. It tends to last forever, as I mentioned, while poor whites remain that way for just a generation or two, after which the kids move up. For all these reasons, substituting socioeconomic status for race is apt to do little to promote racial justice.

One change would help a great deal. We might take the idea of social class seriously and devise a program based on SES that not only gives a helping hand to those on the bottom of the scale, but corrects, or discounts, for some of those at the top. Imagine a youth from a socially prominent and well-heeled family who earns 1200 on the SAT and has a grade point average of 3.1 from a famous prep school. This student has enjoyed tutors, summer camps, and European travel while growing up. Indulgent teachers, aware of his famous family name, gave him extra-credit assignments and other help to shore up a sagging grade and make sure that he earned at least a B. As the time for taking the SAT rolled around, the youth took a prep course costing over $1000. All of us in education know students like this—socially advantaged, rich, and often fairly dull. Their college application essays describe how hard they worked to make the cross-country team and how it fortified their character. Sometimes you read about them in the news, years later, when they flunk the bar exam for the third time.

Contrast this applicant with a Chicano youth sporting an SAT of 1160 and a GPA of 3.4 from an inner-city school, who stepped in when Dad went to jail, took care of his or her younger brothers and sisters, delivered a paper route, and wrote an application essay explaining how to apply Cesar Chavez's ideas of religiously based, collectivist social organization to the *urban* working poor. I would pick the Mexican kid, and I bet most of you would, too. I would also be inclined to apply a system of discounting or penalty points to the very large number of bland, paradise-lost kids, like the ones I described, who made little use of their opportunities, have little idea what they want to do in life, and who our experience as educators tells us are likely to disappoint but who clutter up the field for the rest who really deserve and will benefit from a college education. Just as conservatives correctly point out that diversity cannot be a constitutionally valid reason for admission purposes if we apply it selectively, we should tailor programs based on socioeconomic advantage and disadvantage as I have suggested, that is, across the board.

My suggestion may not conquer all unfairness in the way health, education, and other social goods are allocated, but could be a start in the right direction. It might *even* have appealed to a certain Supreme Court justice, long dead, with Alabama roots, a checkered record on racial justice but an undying commitment to workers, the poor, and the common person.

Rodrigo's Tenth Chronicle
Merit and Affirmative Action

INTRODUCTION: IN WHICH RODRIGO AND I MEET BY CHANCE AT THE NEW PROFESSORS CONFERENCE AND I LEARN OF A RECENT EVENT AT HIS SCHOOL

I had just put down my papers from the talk that, as one of three graybeards, I had just given to a roomful of eager new professors when a familiar face materialized in front of me.

"Rodrigo! I didn't see you in the room. Where were you sitting?"

"Over there," my young friend and protégé replied, "behind Henry Abercrombie. He's a giant—I'm not surprised you didn't see me. That was a great talk."

"Thanks," I said. "They called me up at the last minute. I didn't have much time to prepare. Have you been here for the entire conference?"

"I have. My dean is good about paying for this sort of thing. She sent both of us new professors—Barney, over there, and me."

"It's a lot different than when I was starting out," I said. "We were sent straight into the classroom with the casebook and our own notes. It was sink or swim—no teachers' manuals, no conferences like this one, and often no older hands to give us advice. Most of us were the only professors of color at our schools. Do you have any company in that respect?"

"Barney is Asian," Rodrigo said. "We get along great, even though he teaches tax. And there's Elaine, the assistant dean. She's black and teaches professional responsibility."

"Not bad," I replied. "This session looks like it's breaking up." I pointed to the crowd starting to straggle out of the auditorium. The conference staff was already busy changing the name tags on the speakers' table in preparation for the next session. "Do you want to go somewhere for a drink or a bite to eat?"

"I'd love to," Rodrigo replied with alacrity. "I got up early for the constitutional law session and missed breakfast. I was going to go to the session on networking, but I'd much rather talk with you."

As we filed out of the conference room, I asked Rodrigo how he liked his new job.

"It's great," he said. "I love the students. I'm teaching two new preps, but I have this terrific research assistant. It looks like we may actually get some writing done. Maybe you and I can talk about that later. But something curious happened just last week that I'd like your opinion on. Perhaps we could discuss it over dinner."

"I'm famished," I said. "Public speaking always makes me hungry. Have you found a good place to eat around here?"

"There's a decent sandwich shop up on the mezzanine. But yesterday Barney and a few of us went to this little Middle Eastern restaurant a couple of blocks away. The food is good and the prices reasonable. I think they start serving dinner at five."

"Middle Eastern sounds good to me," I said. "So, what happened at your school?"

Rodrigo fell silent for a moment as we rode down in the elevator in the company of a few strangers and one of my acquaintances. When we got out, he continued. "It concerns the way I got appointed. I'm not worried or upset. But I thought it was curious and made a note to ask you about it sometime. By the way, did you know you were not listed on the program?"

"I spoke last year," I explained, "but this year they had a last-minute cancellation. I agreed to help them out, and now I'm glad I did. I'll get to do two of my favorite things—eat Middle Eastern food and talk with you!"

We set out down the crowded city sidewalk. "I can vouch for the food," Rodrigo said, "but I don't know how much you'll get out of the conversation because it'll be mostly about me. The incident did get me thinking, though, about the whole issue of merit. We've talked about this a little before, but my thoughts have gone further, thanks to the incident at my school."

"I'm sure you'll notice this, Rodrigo, if you haven't found it out already. We older hands get just as much from our younger colleagues as they do from us. Our conversations over this last year have stimulated many thoughts in my mind, and not a few book chapters. Sometimes I think *you're* the mentor and I'm the pupil."

Rodrigo waved aside the compliment. "What happened concerns a colleague of mine named Kowalski—an interesting guy from a poor background. He's got a brilliant law school record and terrific publications despite being in only his second year of teaching. Kowalski came to my office the other day. It's no secret that he's conservative—in fact is faculty advisor to the local Federalist Society. But he's a nice guy. When I started teaching, he offered me his teaching notes and tried to be really helpful."

"So, what did you learn from your conservative and presumably Polish friend?"

"That my appointment was part of the school's affirmative action policy. At my school they call it a special opportunity appointment. Nobody had bothered to mention this to me, not even the dean. Kowalski dropped this bombshell in the course of a discussion we were having on affirmative action and then was taken aback and apologetic when he discovered that I hadn't known about it. He had cited my appointment as an example of the way affirmative action works. He pointed out that he himself had not been eligible for a special opportunity appointment even though his own parents emigrated to this country when he was two, were poor, and lived in a rough neighborhood. Meanwhile, I, as an African American, was eligible for preferential treatment."

"Sounds like the two of you must have had a—how shall I say?—tense conversation. I hope it came out that your own credentials are also quite impressive."

"He already knew that. And it *was* tense until I told him that I saw no problem with being hired that way if the school used the special funds from the president's office to hire an additional professor that they otherwise would not have been able to hire."

"In other words, you didn't displace anyone, not even the proverbial 'more highly qualified white,'" I said. "And did that get you off the hook with Kowalski?"

"More or less. We went on to have a good talk about affirmative action and merit. He kept insisting that, present company excepted, affirmative action is unprincipled because it gives the edge to someone on the basis of a morally irrelevant factor, namely race. He also worried that it would end up stigmatizing even professors like me because everyone would assume we had inferior credentials and did not really deserve our professorships. It also could cause tensions between whites and blacks because the former would assume that whenever they lost out on an appointment, job, or other opportunity, it must have been because a black or other minority person won out."

"These are the standard arguments," I observed. "And as you know, they all have answers. Oh, here we are." We were both silent as we entered the small, homey restaurant. The maitre d' ushered us to a booth decorated with Persian bric-a-brac.

We seated ourselves, and Rodrigo continued as follows:

"I know, and I gave them. But then the conversation took a different turn. He cited an argument I had heard mentioned, in D'Souza and elsewhere, that the multiculturalism movement, not racism, is driving the recent wave of racist incidents, graffiti, and name-calling on campuses. According to this view, minority groups who are calling for theme houses, special dormitories, and anti-hate-speech rules are misdiagnosing the situation. They have only themselves to blame—or, more precisely, affirmative action—and the cure is less, not more, of what they demand. This, in turn, led to a discussion of the whole idea of merit, but we had to postpone it to go to a faculty meeting."

I made a face. "Now *there's* an institution whose merit really ought to come under scrutiny. And I gather you've had some further thoughts on the whole question—merit, I mean?"

"I have. Do you have time to listen? Oh, here comes our waiter."

We immersed ourselves in the menu while the waiter stood patiently. We gave our orders—kabob for Rodrigo, vegetarian couscous for me—and then continued as follows:

IN WHICH RODRIGO AND I EXPLORE THE CONNECTION BETWEEN MARKETS AND MERIT

"Professor, have you ever noticed how conservatives seem to love the First Amendment?"

"I have. But lots of old-line constitutionalists, including some who consider themselves liberal, do too. You see this strange alliance with hate-speech codes. Conservatives like Dinesh D'Souza hate them, of course. But they have allies in moderately leftist, progressive organizations like the ACLU. Every time a college thinks of enacting such a code to protect minorities and gays against the tide of vicious insults and name-calling that has been welling up these days, the conservatives say that Western civilization is ending, and the ACLU files suit. It's an odd alliance, somewhat like the way the religious right and radical feminists often find themselves on the same side fighting pornography, but, of course, in reverse."

"Politics makes strange bedfellows," Rodrigo added. "Is that how the expression goes?"

Rodrigo, who had spent the last half of his life growing up in Italy, sometimes misused an expression or idiom. But this time I nodded. "Exactly right. And what moral do you draw from this, Rodrigo?"

After a moment of thought, Rodrigo replied, "I wonder if you saw the recent *New Republic* cover story that asked, 'Is the First Amendment Racist?'" I indicated that I had. "The author's answer, of course, was no and that minorities and others clamoring for hate-speech regulations are deeply misguided."

"And I gather that you think that it is—racist, I mean?"

"Not inherently," Rodrigo responded. "But what I find intriguing is the way in which conservatives and traditionalists, people who basically don't want blacks changing position too rapidly, are enamored of the First Amendment. Consider that throughout history, top satirists and commentators have scrupulously reserved their sharpest slings and arrows for the high and mighty, for kings and other public officials who abused their power, and so on. Never, or rarely, did they use their wit to put down the halt, the lame, and the poor."

(Ah, he knows *that* idiom, I thought. He catches on fast.)

"A root word of humor is humus," I interjected. "Like earth. Humor brings the powerful down to earth. That's a principal function of satire. The Roman emperors employed slaves to follow them during victory parades and celebrations, whispering, 'Thou art but a man.' Nobility of all ages employed jesters to mock their mannerisms and prevent them from becoming too enamored of themselves. But I gather you think all of this has something to do with the First Amendment."

"It does. The First Amendment is a marketplace mechanism, like many others. One of its functions is to assure that life's victors continue winning—in this case, speaking more effectively than others and thereby convincing themselves that their positions are right. The top satirists, Molière, Swift, Twain, and in more modern times, columnists like Russell Baker, have carefully avoided making fun of the poor, minorities, and those of lower station and power than themselves. These individuals are already lowly, like humus, down to earth. But the First Amendment can't capture this simple moral intuition. Indeed, I believe one of its functions is to blind us to this asymmetry, to the way in which vituperative speech aimed at the poor, or gays, or minorities stands on a very different moral footing from criticism of government or the powerful."

"The First Amendment treats all speech alike. You have just as much right to criticize the Italian or U.S. government as a campus bully has to tell you to go back to Africa."

"An example of decontextualized, neutrality-based jurisprudence, as we discussed before," I added. "And deeply mistaken."

"One could argue," Rodrigo added, "that this perverse application of First Amendment principles violates the equality principle. It makes us dumb, deprives us of the ability to see differences that matter. Treating unequals as though they were equal is just as much a violation of equality as treating equals unequally. It also enables life's winners to think they won fair and square. When the campus bully notices that next year there are fewer blacks on campus because they have dropped out or transferred to a less racist institution ..."

"Like Morehouse," I ventured.

"Exactly," Rodrigo continued. "Resegregation is a real problem. Black colleges are increasing enrollment just as the numbers of black students in large, white-dominated colleges are declining. Parents of color are opting to send their sons and daughters to historically black colleges where the climate will be less racist. And one of the reasons is the reign of terror and catcalls that our First Amendment purist friends insist continue unabated."

"A friend of mine is doing that very thing," I mused. "Sending his kid to Morehouse, that is. Yet our ACLU friends insist that hate speech remain unregulated. The First Amendment must be a seamless web. But we were talking about merit. I assume you see a connection."

"Oh yes," Rodrigo resumed, furrowing his brow slightly. "Let me bring myself back on track. I was going to make the point that all formalist devices, like merit, free speech, and the economic free market of trades and exchanges, serve a similar purpose. They decontextualize the transaction and so enable the powerful to exclude from consideration past actions, like slavery and female subjugation, that have effects even today which prevent some from entering the competition on equal terms. In fact, the First Amendment is a special case of merit. The First Amendment is designed to winnow out meritorious from nonmeritorious speech and ideas. Supposedly, through a clash of ideas, the truth, the most robust idea of all, will emerge. Thus, if one culture is dominant, it must deserve to be that way. Our ideas competed against those other, more easygoing, ones and won. It was a fair fight. Merit serves the same function in slightly different spheres."

"It does this by consolidating advantage. Any society's elites will deem what they do well as constitutive of merit, thus assuring that their own positions become even more secure. Merit is a resource attractor. Those who have it make more money and gain more power. They use that money and power to purchase more increments of merit for themselves and their children."

"The rich get richer."

"Not always," I interjected. "They send their children to the best schools, where some flunk out. But others go on to be rich. The gap between the haves and the have-nots gets greater every generation, and one reason is this host of seemingly neutral market-type mechanisms that assure that everyone has exactly the same chance—all the while ignoring that it takes a microphone to speak effectively, a college education to become a neurosurgeon, and so on."

"Merit supplies a defense to an equal protection challenge," Rodrigo added. "If society distributes a good to A and not to B, courts will sustain the distribution if the government can show that A had more merit than B, i.e., was more deserving. But what you are saying is that the pre-existing level of merit may be skewed, and that supposedly neutral mechanisms prevent us from seeing this."

"Not only seeing, but even looking for it," I replied. "There is no reason to. If A is more deserving of the job than B, why should we even inquire into how he or she came to deserve it? He may have had greater opportunities than B, may have had more solicitous parents or teachers. Better known people may have written him letters of recommendation. When he was a teenager, perhaps he got a summer job or internship through a family connection. A friendly teacher may have proposed an extra credit assignment that changed a B plus into an A minus, or helped him get into an honors section of a class that an equally talented black or working class kid might not have gotten into."

"Yet white people do not see it that way," Rodrigo replied. "Anytime a black gets somewhere by means of an affirmative action program, they are certain that *this* is an affront to principle, that it is unfair to innocent whites. Even our liberal defenders consider affirmative action a perilous program, designed to work for a short time only and fraught with many risks, such as stigmatization of able blacks."

"So Rodrigo," I summarized, "you identify two kinds of racism. The old kind is overt and takes the form of laws and social practices that expressly treat blacks and others of color worse than whites. But another takes the form of facially neutral laws and practices that require the decisionmaker to ignore history, context, and things that everybody knows are important. Merit is a prominent example of such a mechanism."

Rodrigo nodded, but quickly added: "I know what you're going to say, Professor. I've made only a start. And you're right. Kowalski pointed that out—my argument is merely formal. I must go on and give affirmative reasons why merit often serves dishonorable ends. He kept saying that merit *could* deflect us from seeing important things, including those that lie in the past. But he said that he didn't think there were many such things today, and that, on balance, a merit-based scheme is apt to be fairer to minorities than one that relies on discretion, like affirmative action. He said my categories were not exclusive, and that he personally knew people without a racist bone in their bodies who nevertheless believed in merit. He also pointed out how his father and mother rose from abject poverty. He kept saying he meant no offense, but affirmative action could only produce lazy, unmotivated beneficiaries—and sullen, resentful whites convinced that minorities are responsible for every setback and defeat they suffer in life. He also inquired whether I felt stigmatized on account of the way I was hired and seemed surprised when I said no."

"Of course, you did graduate near the top of your class at the oldest law school in the world, own an LL.M. degree from a top U.S. institution, and are the winner of two competitions for student writing. Still, Kowalski sounds like a great foil."

Rodrigo waved aside my attempt at praise. "Laz keeps me on my toes, makes me think—just as you do, Professor. Oh, and did I mention that he's not opposed to speech codes? He says racist speech is disgusting and has nothing to do with the First Amendment—like many conservatives, he also supports regulating pornography. All this even though he opposes affirmative action and thinks it lies at the root of many of our troubles. If you've got the time, I could run past you some things I've been thinking about in the wake of our discussion."

I nodded enthusiastically, reminding my brilliant young protégé, once again, how much I got out of our conversations. I sat back expectantly.

RODRIGO'S THREE REASONS WHY MERIT OFTEN SERVES DISHONORABLE ENDS, PROMOTES RACISM, AND DEEPENS MINORITIES' PREDICAMENT

"My thoughts mainly have to do with the connection that Kowalski persuaded me to make between merit and discrimination. Why don't we take them up one by one. Oh, here's our food!" We were silent while the waiter served our sumptuous-looking dinners.

"This looks great," Rodrigo said. "Usually I like trying different restaurants, but this one was so good last time that I'm glad I came back."

When I beamed my own approval, he continued: "As I mentioned, my arguments fall into three groups. One set is analytical and has to do with the way merit operates, on a discursive and conceptual level, to strengthen the hand of the powerful at the expense of the disempowered. A second has to do with the after-the-fact quality of neutral, marketplace-type mechanisms, that is, the way they enable life's winners to justify the status quo. And a final critique is historical, showing connections between today's meritocrats and those of former, more racist times. How's your couscous?"

Rodrigo's First Argument: Merit's Majoritarian Nature Guarantees the Ascendancy of Elite Groups

"Great, for vegetarian fare," I replied. "You probably know my doctor told me to cut down on meat. It's hard, especially when you're traveling. So I'm glad you brought me here. Even in my old meat-eating days I loved Middle Eastern food."

Rodrigo gave me a sympathetic look. "Giannina is mostly vegetarian, too. So, I have some idea of what you're going through. Want to hear the first argument?"

"Whenever you're ready," I said, taking a forkful of steaming hot couscous.

"The first problem I have with the idea of merit has to do with its majoritarian nature. Writers contributing to the critique of normativity in legal thought, among others, have pointed this out. Merit is what the victors impose. No conquering people ever took a close look at the conquered, their culture, ways, and appearance, and pronounced them superior to their own versions. Those in power always make that which they do best the standard of merit. This is true at all times in history, including our own. The SAT, for example, has test items about athletic and recreational activities prominent in white, middle- and upper-class culture. Graduate programs often emphasize linear, rationalistic thought over other kinds, and so on."

"There's the famous chitlins test," I mused, half-seriously, wondering if Rodrigo, who grew up in Italy but was half African American, had heard of such a thing. [Eds. The chitlins test contains items that are commonly known in the black community. Most whites score very low, while most African Americans score close to 100 percent.]

He smiled appreciatively and went on. "Not only does this type of test disadvantage the poor, minorities, and anyone else whose upbringing and experience differ from the norm, it also can punish women, many of whom have strengths and approaches that differ from those of their male counterparts. A man might choose to sit down with a calculator and a legal pad while a woman might start by thinking and talking about a decision with others. The man might believe that the logic stemming from his own reasoning skills can solve the problem without consultation with others. A woman, on the other hand, may tend to believe that a collective decision is the most likely to succeed and to be accepted by others, who may or may not be touched by the decision in the same way that she is. But because men tend to be in charge of most things in this world, including hiring and admissions decisions, they will look for the skills that have worked for them. Not surprisingly, they will find these skills predominantly in other men. When a woman has skills that men deem important, she will, of course, be hired, but only because she has this male-defined set of skills. Frequently the woman's skills will include the ability to read and understand the people she has to work with and to motivate coworkers and subordinates. These abilities are necessary for the smooth operation of the workplace and the campus, but it is often left to chance that they will reside in the same people who possess the level of logical and analytical skills the evaluative committees demand. Therefore, imposition of the male standard not only discriminates against women, it also robs the group or institution of the diversity that makes it effective."

"I think you and I discussed something similar before," I said. "Did we not agree that two candidates, one white and one black—or one male, one female, for that matter—will often compete for the same position? Both are equally capable of doing a stellar job. But the interview, or job test, rewards the candidate who has the greatest store of cultural capital, the one who soaked up knowledge so easily at his father's or mother's knee. The household had the right kind of music and books. The dinner table conversation taught precisely the mannerisms, conversational patterns, and small talk skills that the employer finds comforting, familiar, and reassuring. The more conventional candidate gets the job, even though the other one could have done just as well, maybe better."

"Exactly," Rodrigo replied. "And it never ceases to amaze me how tenaciously elite groups resist a realignment of merit that you would think would benefit them as well. Racism—any form of irrationality, really—is economically inefficient and bad for a society. So is a merit scheme that rejects the contributions of a major sector. Oh, but before I forget, I told Kowalski all this, and do you know what his answer was?"

"No, what?"

"He said that all this may be true, but that *formal* racism ended with the Civil Rights Act in 1964. Now, the only kind lies in attitudes, unconscious predispositions, that sort of thing. Formally the playing field is level, and if the merit criteria are biased, the solution is to change them, not advocate dangerously inegalitarian measures like affirmative action—which, by the way, he insisted on calling 'reverse discrimination.'"

I winced. "And how did you deal with this objection?"

Rodrigo's Second Argument: Merit's After-the-Fact, Apologetic Function

"Historically. I pointed out that the emphasis on merit began in earnest in 1964. He got the connection quickly. Formal racism was phased out, veiled or nonformal racism came in—racism under the guise of excellence, fairness, equal opportunity, all the things that make up the constellation of attitudes and standards we call 'merit.'"

"True," I acknowledged. "And if memory serves me correctly [I was much older than Rodrigo], that is more or less what happened. Before 1964 white males benefited from old-fashioned laws that cut down on the competition by eliminating blacks and women, and from old-boy networks by which they helped each other. The events of 1964 changed just the first part—the other remained intact. In fact, merit today is a principal means by which empowered people who have been to the best colleges, taken the same tests, know each other, and talk the same way, ensure that they and their class remain in charge. It's especially important today when the population is changing. In some parts of the country, whites are already in the minority. Merit mechanisms ensure that their class remains in power a little longer."

"Not only that," Rodrigo added. "Conditions are different. The era of rapid economic growth is over. The pie is beginning to shrink. Merit, a principal measure of distributive justice, assumes even greater prominence."

"I'm not sure I follow you," I said. "With a shrinking pie, isn't it even more important to have clear-cut rules and standards to determine how to distribute that pie? Perhaps your problem with merit is not with the concept itself, but with the way society applies it. Merit is a kind of formalization. Many of us have written of the connection between fairness and formality, the way in which courtroom rules related to the presentation of evidence, allowing both sides a prescribed time to speak, and so on, promote fairness and reduce prejudice. They confine discretion, which could easily be used against the minority, the woman, or other disempowered litigant."

"Good point," Rodrigo conceded. "The trouble is that merit is an example of the wrong kind of formality. It excludes morally relevant data, particularly events that happened in the past. It prevents us from considering another principle of distributive justice, namely reparations or making amends. Blacks, Chicanos, and Native Americans were formally oppressed throughout our history by the many mechanisms with which you and I are familiar. The merit advocate says, 'Let's ignore all that and start being perfectly fair right now. How high did you score on the SAT?'"

"A test that, as we said, examines only a narrow range of skills, mainly of linear-type thought. White folks are perfectly willing to look to the past, if that is where their merit badges lie, but not to ours if those pasts show disadvantage and hurdles surmounted. Of course, if *their* past includes a grandfather who immigrated from Ireland or a poor Baltic nation, they'll remind us of that over and over, overlooking the corporate dynasty the family established in between."

"A dynasty that may have taken real energy and talent to set up," Rodrigo pointed out, "but that nevertheless profited from the advantage white skin conferred."

"So you're saying we can't be concerned just with distributing the pie fairly. We have to ask who set the table, invited the guests, and made the place cards."

"Exactly," Rodrigo exclaimed. "And the place card example is perfect. Conservatives would probably be irritated at the suggestion that merit is comparable to etiquette. But in some ways it is. All cultures have utensils for eating, but they vary and no one set is necessarily better than any other. [Rodrigo indicated a group of diners on the other side of the restaurant who were seated on cushions and using their fingers instead of the more usual chairs and silverware.] All have ways of assigning places to guests. In some, tradition prescribes who sits where; in others, place cards are used. Much the same is true of merit. Each society is organized in a particular way and has rules—which they call merit—to ensure that their organizational system continues undisturbed. But the organization and the assignment of roles is, to a very large extent, arbitrary. Move the basketball hoop up or down six inches and you radically change the distribution of who has merit. Add items related to love, compassion, or intercultural awareness and you have a completely different SAT."

"But Rodrigo, if two candidates have exactly equal merit for a job, and one is white and the other is black ..."

"They're not equal," Rodrigo interjected. "The black probably has come further. They are equal only if you arbitrarily decide that overcoming advantage is not a component of merit. Many whites receive inheritances; most people of color do not. Whites often benefit from artfully crafted letters of recommendation. When a teacher proposes an extra credit assignment that allows them to receive an A-minus in an honors course, a neighbor gives them a summer job, or their father stakes them to their first home mortgage, they consider that normal, not a part of race and class advantage. Yet it is. You might even consider it a form of affirmative action—a system of rewards and resources bestowed without regard to merit."

"There are exceptions," I pointed out. "The black middle class is growing. And the minority old-boy network looks after its own, as well."

"I know there are exceptions," Rodrigo replied. "But all too few. Ones of another kind—what I call 'cultural exceptions'—come up much more often."

"I'm not sure what you mean by the term."

"Take a case close to hand. Law school teaching candidates are supposed to be hired because of their teaching and scholarly potential. But merit, like most legal terms, gets applied against a background of cultural assumptions, presuppositions, understandings, and implied exceptions, most of which operate against our people. Imagine two candidates for a faculty position, one white and one black. Let's suppose both served on law review and dutifully wrote the same well-researched note, heavy on case analysis. Both made the finalist round in moot court, and so are likely to be good teachers as well—to whatever extent one can predict that."

"But the white gets the job, right?"

"Usually, yes. It turns out that the white had a more pleasant demeanor, was deemed better at small talk, went to a well-known private school. The black seemed tighter, a little intense. The white comes recommended by a more well-known professor. The white ends up getting the job."

"But isn't the solution, then, to assure that *true* meritocratic criteria are applied and not those other self-serving, counterfeit ones? Wouldn't it be better to insist that appointment committees steadfastly refuse to look at these other race- and class-based traits—ones that do not bear on teaching fitness, but simply render the candidate more familiar, more comfortable, more like one's own kind?"

"That *would* be a start," Rodrigo conceded. "But the number of presumptions and implied exceptions is virtually infinite, including things like dress, hair, intonation, demeanor, sports played, hobbies, travel experiences, and so on. One's checklist would have to be very long indeed."

After a short pause, I added: "Every now and then a school hires one of us with credentials just short of the Thurgood Marshall type—say, somebody who graduated fifteenth in his or her class and had a gilded three years as the star trial attorney in the district attorney's office. When this happens, everyone—including our friend Kowalski, I'm afraid—will go around muttering about the iniquities of affirmative action and unfairness to innocent whites. Sometimes I point out that many of their most esteemed colleagues, hired under either the meritocratic criteria or the second kind, fall woefully short on any standard of professional excellence. One hasn't written anything in fifteen years. Another is such a notoriously weak classroom teacher that his enrollments are close to zero."

"Hmmm," Rodrigo said. "I think we have a couple like that at my school. And what happens when you point this out?"

"They always say that there's a reason. The first professor wrote the definitive work on nonprofit corporations twenty-five years ago and is obviously germinating another, equally good article. The notorious classroom teacher is simply demanding, or else has other talents, perhaps delivering great annual lectures to the bar, which is good public relations for the school."

"So merit criteria end up being applied against a host of background forces—meanings, excuses, understandings, practices, notions of what any commonsense institution would do—that favor whites. Whites were in a position of power long ago, years before the merit criteria were written into the faculty code. That code naturally is interpreted against the backdrop of these forces. And so, even the most scrupulously fair-minded appointments committee ends up hiring whites and passing over blacks."

We were both silent for a minute while the waiter picked up our empty plates and asked whether we would like to see the dessert menu. We looked at each other, Rodrigo nodded enthusiastically, and I said, "Let's have a look."

A minute later I said to Rodrigo, "You mentioned a series of considerations concerning the way merit criteria are *applied*. The ones you have mentioned so far seem to me to be intrinsic to the concept itself or to the language game of which it is a part. I'd love to hear your thoughts regarding merit's application. But before we move on, do you have more to say about the logical aspect?"

"No, I'm just about ready to move on," Rodrigo said, looking around to see if the waiter was nearby. I marveled at my rail-thin young friend's appetite while wrestling with my conscience over whether to have dessert or not. "Just one more thing."

"What is it?"

"We previously observed that conquering nations, like elite groups today, always impose their own merit criteria on the people they subjugate." I nodded. "Ideas about merit and notions of cultural superiority always find use to justify conquest and colonialism. Recall, for example, the white man's burden of Kipling, the Conquistadores who brought the blessing of Christianity to Native Americans, the wrath of Allah that fueled the invading Moorish armies, and, in our time, banana-boat diplomacy that installed puppet regimes in Latin America to bring the people the miracles of democracy."

"Yes, go on."

"What I wanted to mention is that less idealistic nations, those with less normative zeal, were much more reluctant to impose their own merit criteria, and, as a result, were less oppressive victors. The early Romans, for example, did not demonize their slaves. They did not have to. The Romans were not Christians, and so had no need to paint their slaves as base, unsaved heathens. They did not, in other words, have to deem them normatively bad, lacking in merit. Our society, on the other hand, does need to do so, in order to justify our own bad acts. Thus, we demonize our enemies in war, and our own minority populations as well. We employ backwards reasoning: the subjugated *must* be bad, we treated them so badly. And we are more prone to this rationalization than a more cheerfully secular group of conquerors, such as the Romans. Merit-based ideas help us live comfortably despite the discrepancy between our ideals and the reality of the poverty and blighted lives that we see all around us."

"Whites *hate* merit plans," I mused, "when they are applied against them. School teachers' unions oppose merit plans with a passion. And don't even try to get a law faculty to take seriously the idea of doing away with tenure and evaluating every professor on a year-to-year basis."

Rodrigo smiled in appreciation of my suggestion, then said: "That's all I have under the first head. Ready for the application?"

"That *and* dessert," I said, which made Rodrigo smile even more.

Rodrigo's Third Reason: Merit Rules Disadvantage Minorities and the Disempowered Even When Applied by the Most Fair-Minded of Administrators

"Those look great," Rodrigo said, staring eagerly at the dessert tray. "What's that one?" he asked the waiter.

The waiter explained and withdrew after taking our orders, a variegated flan for Rodrigo ("They have something similar in Italy"), and for me a banana pudding that the waiter promised was low in calories.

After the waiter disappeared from view, I said, "So, Rodrigo, you think merit operates to harm and disadvantage minorities not only in its structure, but also practically, in the real world? I assume you mean something other than the ordinary disparate impact that the Supreme Court finds insufficient in employment settings except when an extremely over-general exam is used to screen out, say, state plumbers or custodians."

"I am familiar with that line of cases. I was thinking of something even more pernicious. Earlier, you and I were talking about the canonical effect of certain words and social practices. There is nothing more canonical than merit. A canonical practice or meaning resists change almost by definition, for it is one of the prime mechanisms we apply to determine when change is desirable."

"That means that our notion of merit is very slow to change," I said. "I agree with that. Look how laggardly our acceptance of multiculturalism has been, and how campus curricular reform has sparked such resistance."

"In part that's because changes in required courses and book lists come with the implied statement that these new authors and subjects are worth learning about. Persons who believe that only the Western greats are properly on that list naturally protest."

"Take a case we discovered at my old school. My friend Ali and I were on a faculty-student committee charged with revising the first-year curriculum. I was the LL.M. delegate, Ali the alternate. We were doing some fact checking in the placement office when we discovered something interesting. The minority students, many of whom had been admitted under affirmative action programs and with lower indices, were graduating at virtually the same rate as the rest of the class. Not only that, they were getting jobs and passing the bar at similar rates and even making more money—not a lot more, but still more. Moreover, a slightly *higher* percentage were going into prestigious jobs like teaching and clerking for federal judges. All the students, of course, were brilliant, and virtually all did quite well in later life. But the minorities were doing as well as the others and, in some cases, better. All this despite entering credentials that were, on average, considerably lower than those of the regularly admitted students."

"And what moral did you draw from this?" I asked.

"I thought immediately that the LSAT must be encoding some form of cultural preference for the whites, who had higher scores than the minorities, but ended up doing little, if any, better. But most of my classmates advanced a different theory."

"What conclusion did they draw?"

"First, they were suspicious of my figures and wanted to know where I had gotten them. When I said the alumni affairs office, they were dumbfounded. Many of them insisted that the results must be the product of affirmative action in wider society—judges and employers offering the helping hand to the less qualified minority, and so on."

"And that's what you mean by the canonical function of merit, right?"

"Yes. The whole point of the canon is to defend itself, to insist that countervailing evidence justify itself in terms of the canonical idea. So, when the ostensibly less meritorious minorities did well, it must be attributable to a further derogation of merit, namely favoritism in wider circles, like the job market. Canonical ideas resist change, insist that new evidence be interpreted in light of them, a near-impossible task for the proponent of social change."

"Merit goes along with what is placed at the center, with the 'I.' If those others are succeeding, it must be because they are getting unfair help. Canonical narratives of all kinds exist largely for that purpose: rationalizing and justifying the way things are," I concluded.

Rodrigo nodded. But resolving to play the devil's advocate as long as possible, I added, "But Rodrigo, what about when you and I grade bluebooks. Aren't we applying merit criteria? Don't we apply merit criteria every day in life? Say I go to the grocery store and buy a dozen Grade A potatoes. Am I guilty of buying into a canonical sin, of reinforcing the status quo? I have to eat, and I want to eat the best quality potatoes. What's so wrong with that?"

"Nothing," Rodrigo replied, taking a last bite of his flan and scrutinizing the bottom of his dish to see if there was any more. "But grading people, especially for something as long-term as a job or seat in law school, differs radically from grading potatoes. When the grocer grades potatoes, the potato is static. It will be bought and eaten within a short time. The grocer properly applies a freeze-frame approach, looking only at the potato as it is now—its color, texture, shape. It is irrelevant how far the potato has come or how far it is likely to go in the future. People, however, are dynamic. Imagine a super-potato from another planet. Would you like to buy and eat one merely because right now it resembled all those other ordinary ones sitting in the grocer's bin?"

I smiled at Rodrigo's example, and he continued as follows: "I ran across a great example in a magazine I found on the plane that I took here," Rodrigo said. "An ad by U.S. English, which opposes bilingual education for Hispanics and others, was entitled, 'Why a Hispanic Heads an Organization Called U.S. English.' The ad explained the group's position by employing the rhetoric of equal opportunity. Even though it wishes to force everyone, including the foreign-born, to stop speaking their native languages and struggle along as best they can in English, the organization described itself as entirely egalitarian." Rodrigo fished out the ad and read: "'On the job and in the schools, we're supporting projects that will ensure that all Americans have the chance to learn the language of equal opportunity.'"

"Equal opportunity?" I asked. "That sounds like Orwellian doublespeak."

"Not really," Rodrigo replied. "If you adopt the organization's view of linguistic merit—namely, speaking English—their position is quite consistent. Once you accept that, everything else follows, including the part about equal opportunity."

"Of course, one might hold that it is better to be bilingual than monolingual," I said vehemently, recalling my own struggles to learn Italian early in life and then again more recently in preparation for a trip to Italy. "One could hold that speaking more than one language is an advantage, a sign of a cultured person."

"In that case, the organization and its agenda would appear vulgar and xenophobic. But if your mission [Rodrigo looked again at the ad] is the preservation of our common bond through a common language," Rodrigo said as he took another look at the ad, "then speaking other languages, by definition, threatens that goal."

"I'll take cosmopolitanism," I said. "But it *is* odd that the organization urges repression of linguistic minorities under the banner of equal opportunity."

"It's all in the definition," Rodrigo replied. "If your goal is forcing everyone to speak English, then your program will seem to you like equal opportunity. It treats native speakers of English and immigrants alike: everyone must speak the official language. And this is true in general. If you exclude from the definition of merit what another group values, likes to do, and does well, they will naturally turn out to be meritless. And your actions in coercing them to learn what *you* deem important will seem well-intentioned, fair, and just—a favor to the benighted."

"So, you believe that merit is not only biased, it's also undemocratic because it inexorably leads to tyranny of the majority. But surely we need *some* criteria. Otherwise you'd be calling for lazy, unqualified people to get desirable jobs—people who don't deserve and haven't earned them."

"Not at all," Rodrigo replied mildly. "Slackers get jobs right now. The economy of this country is sinking, its productivity and quality of life at low ebb. The workforces of many Asian countries are as productive as ours, and their children attend school for more hours and earn higher scores on standardized tests. Our traditional merit criteria are ensuring mediocrity. It's quite alarming."

"And you think that our preoccupation with merit is the cause?"

"It's one," Rodrigo replied. "Unless constantly revised, merit causes complacency, like the British aristocracy, a millstone around Great Britain's neck. The more absorbed in merit a system becomes, the worse it will fare in world competition."

"It produces a slack people," I added.

"So it does. And so we have come full circle once again," Rodrigo replied. "Oh, here comes our waiter."

"Would you gentlemen like some coffee?" he asked. We each looked at the other. "I believe there was one final point about history that we were going to explore," Rodrigo said, noncommittally. "I'm going strong, but you've had a long day."

I hesitated. The coffee looked good. We both nodded to the waiter. Just then Rodrigo looked past my shoulder and with a shock of recognition said, "Kowalski! What are you doing here?"

I turned to see a strikingly pale young man, about Rodrigo's age, with a neat suit, short hair, and an alert, sparkling expression. I half-stood, Rodrigo introduced us, and I invited Kowalski to sit down. It turned out that he had just arrived for a morning panel the next day on tenure. "We were just discussing merit," Rodrigo said. "Would you care to join us?"

"I'd be pleased to," Kowalski said. "Although I'm just here for a snack. Looks like the two of you are nearly finished."

"Please stay," I said. "Rodrigo was going to give me the last chapter of a conversation he says was inspired by you. He was going to review the history of merit and meritocracy in the United States and draw some lessons." I turned to Rodrigo. "I hope I'm not putting you on the spot."

"Oh, no," Rodrigo replied. "Laz and I tell each other everything. Nothing scandalizes him, even my most wild-eyed radical ideas. He loves debate and, as you will see, is capable of holding his own on anything. Right, Laz?"

The pale young man smiled and said, "We'll see. I get as much out of Rodrigo's challenges as he gets out of mine. I'd love to hear what you have to say." He gestured toward the waiter, ordered a spicy dish—I complimented him on his choice—and Rodrigo began:

IN WHICH RODRIGO AND HIS FRIEND DEBATE MERIT'S HISTORY AND WHAT IT MEANS FOR TODAY

"I'm really happy you showed up, Laz," Rodrigo said. "I didn't know you were coming. The Professor and I were talking about some of the same things you and I discussed the other day."

"Still resisting merit, eh?" Kowalski said. "Ironic—the most brilliant member of our faculty, and still deconstructing his own talent and distinction. I think you liberals are just uncomfortable with your own smarts, your own status. Such levelers. Too bad." Kowalski smiled warmly to let us know he meant nothing personal.

"Touché," Rodrigo replied good-naturedly. "But even if you are right about liberals on a personal level, a host of irrationalities and problems afflict merit, even more than the ones you and I were talking about before. The Professor and I developed them further just now. If you like, I can bring you up to date when we get home. Actually, what flight are you on? Are you flying home tomorrow?"

It turned out that the two young scholars were indeed on the same flight. They quickly made plans to phone the airline and change their seat assignments to sit together. "I've got the 800-number somewhere," Rodrigo said. "Maybe I'll do it as soon as we get back to the hotel." He caught the waiter's eye, indicated we would indeed like coffee, and resumed his colloquy.

"I'm sure both of you know how the early anthropologists, up to the period of Franz Boas, were fascinated by the idea of proving racial differences, particularly ones having to do with intelligence and cranial capacity."

"Most of these have been discredited," Kowalski said quietly. "No one of my political persuasion would give them any credit today. That was a disgraceful chapter in our history. I hope you are not going to tar the entire idea of merit with the brush of the early extreme pseudoscientific meritocrats."

"No one subscribes to the crude versions of those early race-IQ theories," Rodrigo said. "But the history of the idea is still relevant. In many respects today's most strident meritocrats are straight-line descendants of the late nineteenth and early twentieth century ones. And in some respects, their agenda and arguments are exactly the same. Consider the SAT, administered by the Educational Testing Service for the College Board. Until recently, the test had items that would be familiar only to upper-class families. It is eminently coachable. The director of one test-coaching company recently declared that his organization could boost the score of the average test-taker by many points. Thirty percent improved by 250 or more. Because of the high price charged, the children of the wealthy are more likely to be able to take the course."

"I must admit I took such a course myself," Kowalski said. "Twice, in fact. Whether it helped my score or not, I don't know. But my parents were not at all rich, as you know. I saved up the money because I wanted to do well. If the test disadvantages poor kids, isn't the solution to eliminate unfair items and make sure that the cram courses offer scholarships for poor kids who can't afford them?"

"That would be a start," Rodrigo said. "But I think the whole enterprise ought to come under scrutiny. The test's principal originator, Carl Brigham Campbell, was an out and out white supremacist who published a book that warned that immigrants were swamping the country at the expense of those with superior European genes and warned against interbreeding and too much immigration. Two years later, he became director of the College Board's testing program, where he based the first test on earlier Army tests that eugenicists liked because they confirmed their prejudices. In both tests, whites, of course, came out on top. It is no different today: Merit is up-to-date bigotry."

"I had not heard about that history. It's appalling," Kowalski said. "But I'm not sure what it has to do with today. No one advocates those distasteful notions any more. And isn't merit the best protector blacks have against intolerance? How else can you dispel negative stereotypes, except by succeeding, being successful, demonstrating your merit?"

"That's just what we are prevented from doing," Rodrigo replied. "Remember those test items about regattas. They actually had an item like that on the version of the LSAT I took. I knew what the word meant because it's similar to one in Italian. However, if I'd been a smart but poor ghetto kid, I might have failed that item. Fairness, including fairness in testing, is always a contested concept, always relative to someone's interests, perspectives, and purposes. It does not stand outside experience in some external realm. It's a matter of what we deem important. And the *we* is generally those who are in a position to assure that their own merits, values, standing, and excellence remain untouched."

"I still think you are putting too much emphasis on early history," Kowalski said. "The test may have been biased back then, and maybe a regatta or two creeps in even now. But ETS employs expert test validators who comb the items for bias. And surely you cannot believe that applicants do not differ in legal aptitude. You're a teacher! Rodrigo, you see those differences every day, every time you teach a class or grade a bluebook. What's wrong with trying to see that legal education is not wasted on those who simply can't get it, on whom it won't take hold? You do no favor by admitting someone who has so little talent for analysis that every law school class is a torment, every exam a humiliation. And if they don't pass the bar, they've wasted three years."

"The Professor and I were talking about bar results, jobs, and so on, before you came in. But I'd like to return to history, if the two of you don't mind. And no, Laz, I don't think that the history of an idea is irrelevant to its current function and understanding. Some of the modern conservative and neoconservative writers sound themes remarkably similar to ones from that more overtly racist era. [Rodrigo pointed out the book his friend had been carrying that now lay on the booth seat next to him.] Jared Taylor is an example, but some of the more moderate conservatives and neoliberals say the same things."

"Patrick Moynihan says that blacks in the urban underclass are evolving into a new and different species, cut off from the rest of civilized society and developing mores and a culture of their own, passed down from mother to son. Speciation, he calls it," I remarked.

"And he's a Democrat!" Rodrigo exclaimed. "Then there's Arthur Schlesinger, who is from the same party. His recent book, *The Disuniting of America,* tells how the recent ethnic upsurge is tearing the country apart. He posits that multiculturalism and identity politics are weakening the Anglocentric culture that formerly bonded us together, making us a single nation. He says this is not only bad for the country, but also for minorities. For the American tradition is 'the unique sauce of individual liberty, political democracy, the rule of law, human rights, and cultural freedom.' Collectivist cultures, by contrast—and by those he means us, I'm afraid—'have stamped with utmost brutality on human rights.' He considers them tribalistic, despotic, superstitious, and fanatical. It is absurd that society is asked to give those cultures equal respect. White guilt, he says, can be pushed too far."

"I've read that book," Kowalski said. "And it is possible that it overstates. Other cultures, including my own, have given America much of what it has to be proud of, ranging from some of its best music to its top scientists, and even," he noted as he gestured toward his plate full of steaming dolma-type delicacies, "its finest food. Yet, I think he has a point when he says that the American synthesis has an inevitable Anglo-Saxon coloration. If so, he is not amiss in portraying racial separatism and separate dorms for blacks as forms of balkanization."

"I'm not so sure why it has to be that way," Rodrigo replied mildly. "*The Passing of the Great Race* echoed some of the same themes, warning of chaos and disorder. Immigration continued, yet the evils the author warned of did not come to pass. Some of the 'English-Only' people sound some of the same alarms. Their theory of language is that English ought to reign supreme, that its sacred texts, including the Bible and Shakespeare, are the only guarantors against barbarism. The problem I have is that there is a match, virtually a one-to-one correspondence, between the new writers and the old ones who wrote tracts about white supremacy. Lawrence Auster's 1990 book warns that we are seeing the end of Western civilization in recent immigration reform acts, which modestly relax the previous restrictions against immigration from the Third World. Richard Brookhiser, senior editor at *National Review*, writes in his book, *The Way of the Wasp*, that Anglo traits such as conscience, antisensitivity, industry, and success deserve primacy over the opposite cultural traits that minorities and foreigners bring, namely self, creativity, gratification, and group-mindedness. If we allow the latter traits to submerge the former, America is sure to lose the way. These ideas resemble nothing so much as those of Henry Pratt Fairchild in *The Melting Pot Mistake*, a 1920s-era tract against immigration. So, you see that today's meritocrats and test advocates have much to live down. Both their current and their old champions base their arguments, implicitly and explicitly, on racial superiority and xenophobia."

"So, Rodrigo," I said. "You are saying that an appeal to a unity based on Anglo-Saxon values is inherently racist."

"Yes, and so is pandering to fears of balkanization. As a recent author put it, ideas are only intelligible within the particular circumstances that gave rise to them and in which they are circulated. Thus, an appeal in today's climate to national unity, assimilation, or against balkanization is deeply racist."

"So is one to merit," I added, "for the same reasons."

"Rodrigo, you two have me half convinced," Kowalski conceded. "But only half. The history you recounted is certainly distasteful—although no more so than other chapters we could name, including express quotas against Jews at top universities, and 'No Irish Need Apply' rules in effect in certain Northeastern cities for at least as long as the repulsive testing and IQ theories you mentioned. And I'll remind you that one still hears Polish jokes even today. But I still think that merit, properly applied, can serve as the best guarantor against racism and bias. Look at sports. As you yourself pointed out, blacks dominate, simply because they're faster and have more drive. Other spheres could yield in similar fashion. Look at you, for example. You and Barney are two of our most recent hires and among our best by any measure.

Global standards of merit, like the SAT, may be unfair, overbroad, and prone to the kinds of abuses you detailed. But I don't see how you can deny *local,* or contextualized merit—speed, in a hundred-yard dash, teaching ability in a law school, spelling ability in an editor. You liberals believe in contextualizing everything. Isn't that the solution to your problems with merit?"

Rodrigo replied: "That may help somewhat. But merit still excludes, and in an especially pernicious way. The Professor and I were discussing some of these things before."

At the mention of my name, I shook my head, recognizing with a start that the relaxed reverie into which I had lapsed was drifting perilously close to dozing.

"The Professor is looking tired," Rodrigo said. "He's had a long day. Maybe we'd better call it quits for now."

"I'm going strong," I protested. "I just need another cup of coffee."

"We'll walk you back," Laz said, taking my elbow as I stood up. "I've finished my food, and my rambunctious buddy and I both have early sessions tomorrow morning."

CONCLUSION: EXIT RODRIGO ON A NOTE OF RACE-AND-CLASS RECONCILIATION

Our meeting soon broke up. We walked in near silence back to the hotel. Rodrigo spoke only once, to remind his friend to ask him about something later. Within ten minutes I was in my hotel bed, sleeping the sleep of the dead. I saw Laz and Rodrigo only briefly the following morning, in the hotel lobby. They were engaged in an animated discussion. But I had a feeling I would hear from the two young scholars, one conservative, one radical—yet seemingly best friends. My hunch turned out to be true. Only two days after I got back, I received a lengthy letter from Rodrigo in my law school mailbox. Written on recycled paper (his trademark), it contained a torrent of words, concluding with the following:

"... And so, Professor, after our long talk on the plane back home, we each realized that the other was both right and wrong. After hearing more of Laz's story, I've concluded that European ethnics can experience headwinds just as great as those our people suffer, the element of skin color excepted. (Did I tell you that Laz, despite his obvious brilliance, went to a community college?) Much cruelty and unfairness proceed under the banner of class, which is often as great a disadvantaging factor as race, and nearly always a cross-cutting one. Moreover, affirmative action merely shifts the cost of racial remedies onto those least able to protest—blue-collar whites like Alan Bakke or Laz's siblings—neatly exempting the high-achieving son or daughter of a blueblood family.

"For his part, Kowalski finally came around to my belief that we must fundamentally re-evaluate merit standards and their use. He also agrees that affirmative action generates its own pool problem through a sort of self-fulfilling prophecy. He added that the West's slipping economic position is especially troubling, as it is likely to close off opportunities not just for blacks, but also for upwardly mobile white ethnics. He said his people have a kind of 'second sight' or double consciousness, like ours. Outsiders to some extent, they also have seen the way entire cultures can sink, as in Eastern Europe, with their superstructure, leadership, and cultures essentially intact.

"For my part, I agreed—somewhat reluctantly to be sure, but Laz's logic is unassailable—that minorities ought never, except in the narrowest circumstances, accept affirmative action. Doing so splits the poor community along color lines and reinscribes the current merit standards just that much deeper. It also reinforces the belief that people of color are unworthy and need affirmative action, when the reality is that society needs *them* and their contributions at least as much as we need society.

"So, Laz and I declared a pact, a sort of truce, which we plan to publicize to our groups and to everyone who will listen. We'll start by holding a conference. The general idea would be that minorities will forswear affirmative action unless it also includes poor whites. White ethnics and people of color would agree to work together to subvert and replace the array of standards, social practices, and old-boy networks that now hold back both. We believe the critique of merit, far from being a sour-grapes venture, leads inexorably to a bold, hopeful coalition in which two numerically large groups—minorities and ethnic whites—work together to lift the yokes of racism and classism that oppress each, and that end up, as we've seen, linked. Until now this linkage between racism and classism had not been demonstrated. Now that it has been, will you and your friends join us in the last, the final, and the most important, subversion of all? Here are a range of dates we are thinking of for the conference. We're getting the money for your speaker's fee. Will you come?"

Annotated Bibliography

BOOKS

Race and Races: Cases and Resources for a Diverse America, 2d ed. St. Paul: West Group, 2007 (with Perea, Harris, Stefancic, and Wildman).

The Politics of Fear and the Republican Ascendancy. Boulder: Paradigm Publishers, 2006 (with M. Gonzalez).

The Derrick Bell Reader. New York: New York University Press, 2005 (with Stefancic).

How Lawyers Lose Their Way: A Profession Fails Its Creative Minds. Durham, NC: Duke University Press, 2005 (with Stefancic).

Understanding Words That Wound. Boulder: Westview Press, 2004 (with Stefancic).

Justice at War: Civil Liberties and Civil Rights During Times of Crisis. New York: New York University Press, 2003.

Jurisprudence—Classical and Contemporary: From Natural Law to Postmodernism, 2d ed. St. Paul: West Group, 2002 (with Hayman and Levit).

Critical Race Theory: An Introduction. New York: New York University Press, 2001 (with Stefancic).

Critical Race Theory: The Cutting Edge, 2d ed. Philadelphia: Temple University Press, 2000 (with Stefancic).

When Equality Ends: Stories of Race and Resistance. Boulder: Westview Press, 1999.

The Latino/a Condition: A Critical Reader. New York: New York University Press, 1998 (with Stefancic).

Critical White Studies: Looking Behind the Mirror. Philadelphia: Temple University Press, 1997 (with Stefancic).

Must We Defend Nazis? Hate Speech, Pornography, and the New First Amendment. New York: New York University Press, 1997 (with Stefancic).

No Mercy: How Conservative Think Tanks and Foundations Changed America's Social Agenda. Philadelphia: Temple University Press, 1996 (with Stefancic).

The Coming Race War? And Other Apocalyptic Tales of America After Affirmative Action and Welfare. New York: New York University Press, 1996.

The Price We Pay: The Case Against Racist Speech, Hate Propaganda, and Pornography. New York: Hill and Wang, 1995 (with Lederer).

The Rodrigo Chronicles: Conversations About America and Race. New York: New York University Press, 1995.

Failed Revolutions: Social Reform and the Limits of Legal Imagination. Boulder: Westview Press, 1994 (with Stefancic).

Words That Wound: Critical Race Theory, Assaultive Speech, and the First Amendment. Boulder: Westview Press, 1993 (with Matsuda, Lawrence, and Crenshaw).

ARTICLES

The Current Landscape of Race: Old Targets, New Opportunities, 104 Mich. L. Rev. 1269 (2006). Argues that recent scholarship on race has neglected two topics that ought to be on the agenda of every civil rights scholar: white privilege and the black-white binary of race. Shows how this oversight mars a number of recent books, and demonstrates how including these features can provide a fuller, more accurate account of race.

Rodrigo's Roundelay: Hernandez v. Texas *and the Interest-Convergence Dilemma,* 41 Harv. C.R.-C.L. L. Rev. 23 (2006). Argues that a critical race theory tool—interest convergence—explains *Hernandez v. Texas,* a leading Latino civil rights decision. Reviews historical evidence to show that this breakthrough Supreme Court decision, a companion to *Brown v. Board of Education,* came about not as a result of evolving social standards, the force of precedent, or an act of conscience on the part of the Supreme Court. Instead, it appeared because elite decision makers were concerned over the specter of Latin American communism and domestic activism.

Shooting the Messenger (book review), 30 Am. Ind. L. Rev. 477 (2006). Reviews a recent book by Ward Churchill on America's role in world affairs. Shows how Churchill's criticism of U.S. foreign policy is not as baseless as some of his critics assert and that, though not flawless, his book provides valuable insight into how our detractors see us. Analyzes Churchill's argument that the stockbrokers, investment bankers, and FBI agents killed in the World Trade Center disaster were, in effect, "little Eichmans" who richly deserved their fate.

Si Se Puede, but Who Gets the Gravy? 11 Mich. J. Race and L. 9 (2005). Introduces "critical rap theory" as a mode of legal analysis. Chronicles the parallel rise of critical race theory and the new conservatism beginning in the 1980s. Makes a series of praxis-based recommendations for advancement of the left, including making critical teaching "hotter," reaching solutions through interest-convergence strategies, and drawing on other disciplines, like postcolonial literature, for new sources of ideas.

Rodrigo and Revisionism: Relearning the Lessons of History, 99 Nw. U. L. Rev. 805 (2005). Discusses how *Brown v. Board of Education* exacerbated the situation for Latinos by reinforcing the black-white binary in U.S. civil rights law. Summarizes and reviews a recent book by Ian Haney López that sets out a theory of the relation among violence, protest, and racial self-identity. States that Latinos missed the mark by patterning activism and reform on black civil rights gains. Suggests that Latinos instead embrace a new self-understanding where conquest, not slavery, serves as the decisive story of origin and the basis for novel litigation strategies.

Locating Latinos in the Field of Civil Rights: Assessing the Neoliberal Case for Radical Exclusion, 83 Tex. L. Rev. 489 (2005). Exposes the unique position Latinos occupy—whereas conservatives think they pose a threat to Anglocentric tradition, liberals increasingly disclaim them for exploiting resources reserved for "traditional" minorities, like blacks or Native Americans. Probes and critically analyzes the latter position. Surveys a history of anti-Latino nativism and advises on the desirability of Latino assimilation with the white majority.

Nigger (book review), 1 STAN. C.R.-C.L. L. REV. 1 (2005). Reviews a book by Randall Kennedy that finds nothing inherently wrong with the word *nigger*. Argues that Kennedy ignores the term's disreputable history as well as the power of hate speech, generally, to denigrate and marginalize its victims. Shows how ignoring these features can easily lead to violence, even of the mass variety, and argues that courts should pay more, not less, attention to the harms of hate speech.

The Racial Double Helix: Watson, Crick, and Brown v. Board of Education, 47 How. L.J. 473 (2004) (principal coauthor). Shows how courts and the law of evidence carve up the stories of marginalized defendants and transform them beyond recognition. Asks how society replicates itself and why segregation persists fifty years after *Brown*. Summarizes the contributions of Derrick Bell in understanding the replication of racial relations: explains how culture replicates itself, considers a set of homeo-mechanisms concerning interest convergence, and explores different racialization, including the part played by landmark legal decisions like *Brown*.

About Your Masthead: A Preliminary Inquiry into the Compatibility of Civil Rights and Civil Liberties, 39 HARV. C.R.-C.L. L. REV. 1 (2004). Examines the relationship between civil liberties and civil rights, showing several instances where they are entirely compatible. Explores the tensions and strains between civil rights and liberties using the classic example of the hate speech controversy. Looks to the source of these tensions and offers some thoughts on how to live with them.

Crossroads and Blind Alleys: A Critical Examination of Recent Writing about Race, 82 TEX. L. REV. 121 (2003). Documents the general shift within critical race theory from racial realism toward discourse-based analysis and racial idealism. Summarizes a new reader, pointing out that its content is almost entirely discourse analysis. Explains the limits of that approach. Proposes that critical race theory return to its realist roots and suggests issues that the next major volume of critical race writing should address.

White Interests and Civil Rights Realism: Rodrigo's Bittersweet Epiphany, 101 MICH. L. REV. 1201 (2003). Exposes the true goal of civil rights law: to advance white majority interests. Shows how civil rights laws preserve some degree of racism. Explains how the "right amount" of racism preserves white privilege and protects white psychic well-being. Examines the present race discourse and outlines a new civil rights strategy—one that accounts for the centrality of white interests in current thought.

Linking Arms: Recent Books on Interracial Coalition as an Avenue of Reform, 88 CORNELL L. REV. 855 (2003). Examines interminority coalition as a means of promoting social reform. Summarizes and contrasts a recent book by Lani Guinier and Gerald Torres with one by Eric Yamamoto. Explores the underlying logic of coalitional method. Points out that when race is an element, coalition making becomes more problematic. Details the history of interminority coalition and opines that maintaining solidarity has been unsuccessful. Concludes that reformers should replace coalition, a means of achieving reform, with social justice, a substantive goal.

Explaining the Rise and Fall of African American Fortunes—Interest Convergence and Civil Rights Gains, 37 HARV. C.R.-C.L. L. REV. 369 (2002). Examines the rise and fall of minority fortunes through a racial realist or materialist lens. Focuses on a recent book by Mary Dudziak that demonstrates how the self-interest of elite groups fueled breakthroughs for blacks in order to advance U.S. strategic objectives in the Cold War with international communism. Surveys the shifting fates of prominent black radicals and political groups.

Where Is My Body? Stanley Fish's Long Goodbye to Law, 99 MICH. L. REV. 1370 (2001). Summarizes and reviews a book by Stanley Fish, an English and law professor. Focuses on Fish's antifoundationalist themes such as hate speech, affirmative action, and religion. Recommends a practical antinormative approach, similar to Fish's, to guard against thuggery operating under the guise of principle. Argues that tuning our moral convictions in to this approach can help us remember to support what we need to support and resist what we need to resist while navigating the "body of law."

Thinking about Race and Races: Reflections and Responses, 89 CAL. L. REV. 1653 (2001) (with Perea, Wildman, and A. Harris). The authors of a recent casebook reflect upon its publication and America's racial state of affairs. Responds to comments provided by the casebook's independent reviewers.

Two Ways to Think about Race: Reflections on the Id, the Ego, and Other Reformist Theories of Equal Protection, 89 GEO. L.J. 2279 (2001). Demonstrates how idealist theories like those of Charles Lawrence, which explain racial dynamics in terms of thoughts, words, and internal urges, are analytically incomplete. Argues that attending to the material side of race and racism confers a number of benefits while at the same time avoiding drawbacks associated with the idealist approach. Proposes ultimately that critical race theory return to its materialist roots, and encourages it to make common cause with the incipient movement for economic democracy.

Official Elitism or Institutional Self-Interest? 10 Reasons Why UC-Davis Should Abandon the LSAT (and Why Other Good Law Schools Should Follow Suit), 34 U.C. DAVIS L. REV. 593 (2001) (principal coauthor). Traces the history of the standardized testing industry with a focus on the Law School Admissions Test (LSAT). Shows how standardized testing limits minority achievement in higher education. Criticizes the supposedly "objective" content of standardized tests and offers strategies to reform the admissions process at institutions of higher learning.

California's Racial History and Constitutional Rationales for Race-Conscious Decision Making in Higher Education, 47 UCLA L. REV. 1521 (2000) (principal coauthor). Documents California's ambivalent treatment of minorities from the state's inception through the present. Focuses on events that have excluded or prevented minorities from educational advancement. Reviews the case law of affirmative action and argues a remedial justification for it.

Goodbye to Hammurabi: Analyzing the Atavistic Appeal of Restorative Justice, 52 STAN. L. REV. 751 (2000). Discusses restorative justice, a recent dynamic movement that addresses the effects of crime on communities. Reviews the origins and ideology of restorative justice and offers both an internal and external critique of the movement. Assesses the deficiencies of the current system with a focus on the interests of minorities, young offenders, and the disabled. Offers suggestions for strengthening community bonds while dealing fairly and consistently with those who have breached them.

Derrick Bell's Toolkit—Fit to Dismantle That Famous House? 75 N.Y.U. L. REV. 283 (2000). Discusses how United States antidiscrimination law embraces a black-white binary paradigm of race where nonblack minorities must compare their situation to African Americans to gain redress. Uses an allegorical text by Derrick Bell to show how thinking within that narrow binary harms all groups: it weakens solidarity, reduces opportunities for coalition, deprives one group of the benefits of the others' experiences, makes one overly dependent on the approval of the white establishment, and sets one up for ultimate disappointment.

Toward a Legal Realist View of the First Amendment (review essay), 113 HARV. L. REV. 778 (2000). Argues that First Amendment law has circumvented the reforms of legal realism by persisting in a mechanical jurisprudence that values formalistic rules at the expense of policy and context. Analyzes a recent text by Steven Shiffrin that recommends higher levels of First Amendment protection when speech is in the form of dissent or infringes on entrenched or dominant interests. Discusses how this "dissent-based" approach to the First Amendment has merit, with a focus on hate speech. Urges a number of practical solutions to the problems inherent in regulating hate speech.

Rodrigo's Remonstrance: Love and Despair in an Age of Indifference—Should Humans Have Standing? 88 GEO. L.J. 263 (2000) (principal coauthor). Discusses four books dealing with America's racial predicament. Explores a range of topics that affect black fortunes, including unemployment, education, and affirmative action. Presents several possibilities for protecting the interests of racial minorities: the invocation of international human rights law, jury nullification, class-based affirmative action, and a novel application of environmental law.

Race-Sensitive Admissions in Higher Education: Commentary on How the Supreme Court Is Likely to Rule, 26 J. BLACKS HIGHER EDUC., Winter 1999/2000, at 100 (principal coauthor). Suggests possible outcomes of a future Supreme Court ruling on affirmative action in student admissions to higher education. Examines other Supreme Court decisions and assesses the impact that different justices and different presidents would have on an affirmative action ruling as related to educational legislature.

Canadian Critical Race Theory: Racism and the Law, by Carol A. Aylward, http://www.cjsonline.ca/ reviews/critrace.html, Canadian Journal of Sociology Online, 1999 (principal coauthor). Reviews a book by Carol Aylward that introduces critical race theory and proposes a novel approach for lawyers representing black clients.

Making Pets: Social Workers, "Problem Groups," and the Role of SPCA—Getting a Little More Precise About Racialized Narratives, 77 TEX. L. REV. 1571 (1999). Responds to Anthony Alfieri, whose recent work examines the rhetorical meaning of race in everyday legal practice. Applauds and summarizes Alfieri's conclusions. Shows how Alfieri's inquiry allows jurisprudence to accommodate changing social mores and prevent embarrassing and obsolete decisions. Suggests that we broaden his inquiry to address civil as well as criminal trials and nonwhite minorities other than African Americans.

Home-grown Racism: Colorado's Historic Embrace—and Denial—of Equal Opportunity in Higher Education, 70 U. COLO. L. REV. 703 (1999) (principal coauthor). Addresses Colorado's treatment of minorities from when it was a territory up through the present day. Focuses on the obstacles and conditions that have historically prevented the educational advancement of minorities. Reviews the case law of affirmative action in higher education and argues a remedial justification for it. Shows how major sectors of Colorado's economy have severely mistreated persons of color.

Rodrigo's Committee Assignment: A Skeptical Look at Judicial Independence, 72 S. CAL. L. REV. 425 (1999). Discusses the unique political pressures that judges face and considers the role of impeachment within the federal judiciary. Uses the Professor's recent run-in with the law as a catalyst to examine a range of phenomena that undermine judicial neutrality. Presents eight discrete factors that potentially contribute to a lack of independence among judges.

The Repeal of Reticence: A History of America's Cultural and Legal Struggles over Free Speech, Obscenity, Sexual Liberation, and Modern Art, by Rochelle Gurstein (book review), 562 ANNALS AMER. ACAD. POL. AND SOC. SCI. 226 (1999). Reviews a recent book by Rochelle Gurstein that denounces the circus-like atmosphere of today's public discourse and charts the demise of a certain "reticent sensibility" valuing politeness, tact, and discretion.

Is American Law Inherently Racist? 15 T.M. COOLEY L. REV. 361 (1998). Chronicles a debate between Delgado and Professor Daniel Farber over whether racism is inherent in American law.

Ten Arguments against Affirmative Action—How Valid? 50 ALA. L. REV. 135 (1998). Critically analyzes ten arguments against affirmative action that touch on a wide variety of subtopics, including standardized testing, the possibility of "reverse discrimination," and the controversial idea of group rights.

Rodrigo's Roadmap: Is the Marketplace Theory for Eradicating Discrimination a Blind Alley? 93 Nw. U. L. REV. 215 (1998). Questions how well the law and economics movement interfaces with noneconomic phenomena such as racial discrimination. Summarizes and discusses two books that offer economic arguments against the existence of national civil rights protections and affirmative action. Posits that the market will not drive out racism on its own. Marshals cultural texts, social science, evolutionary science, and cross-cultural studies in favor of this assertion.

Rodrigo's Bookbag: Brimelow, Bork, Murray, and D'Souza—Recent Conservative Thought and the End of Equality, 50 STAN. L. REV. 1929 (1998). Reviews three recent books by conservative authors and discusses the resurgence of inequality in the United States. Examines the relationship between liberty and equality in welfare capitalism. Shows how the American commitment to equality necessitates increasing dehumanization of the poor. Sets forth four definitional mechanisms that undermine Latino equality.

Rodrigo's Book of Manners: How to Conduct a Conversation on Race—Standing, Imperial Scholarship, and Beyond, 86 GEO. L.J. 1051 (1998). Responds to several critics of critical race theory. Discusses whether the espousal of multiculturalism truly represents an assault on truth, and whether criticism of conventional standards of merit constitutes an implicit attack on Jews and Asians. Addresses the claim that legal storytelling and narrative jurisprudence fall outside the realm of serious scholarship, as some critics believe. Proposes a series of rules for conducting scholarly conversations about heated topics such as race.

Are Hate-Speech Rules Constitutional Heresy? A Reply to Stephen G. Gey, 146 U. PA. L. REV. 865 (1998). Responds to an article by Stephen Gey, who strenuously disagreed with several proposals to regulate racist and misogynistic hate speech. Points out how Gey's argument is devoid of public policy concerns. Addresses Gey's central premise about governmental control of speech and examines some of his subordinate issues about hate-speech regulation—for example, that minorities should not write about hate speech because they are blinded by self-interest. Concludes with a perspective for understanding social resistance, including articles like Gey's.

Critical Race Theory: Past, Present, and Future, 51 CURRENT LEGAL PROBS. 467 (1998) (principal coauthor). Reflects on critical race theory's history. Assesses the present-day situation and maps out challenges for the future.

Editor's Introduction, Symposium on the Relation Between Scholarship and Teaching, 73 CHI.-KENT L. REV. 749 (1998). Queries the relationship between scholarship and teaching. Recommends a large-scale statistical study to illuminate the connection between the pedagogical skill and the scholarly distinction of a professor. Suggests various considerations and evaluative criteria for such a study.

Rodrigo's Fifteenth Chronicle: Racial Mixture, Latino-Critical Scholarship, and the Black-White Binary, 75 TEX. L. REV. 1181 (1997). Uses the biography of a Mexican American federal judge as catalyst to discuss current legal problems facing Latinos. Explains the "black-white binary," the notion that American civil rights laws are dichotomous and exclude those who are neither black nor white. Shows how the civil rights amendments to the Constitution may amplify inequality for those who fall outside the black-white paradigm. Lays out further theoretical and concrete consequences for Latinos caught outside the black-white binary, suggesting future inquiries for Latino critical scholars.

Why Universities Are Morally Obligated to Strive for Diversity: Restoring the Remedial Rationale for Affirmative Action, 68 U. COLO. L. REV. 1165 (1997). Proposes a renewed focus on the remedial rationale for affirmative action, which posits that such a program is necessary to redress past discrimination. Outlines the theoretical advantages of the remedial approach. Exposes in detail how public institutions of higher learning have historically given minorities short shrift.

Rodrigo's Fourteenth Chronicle: American Apocalypse, 32 HARV. C.R.-C.L. L. REV. 275 (1997). Rodrigo's conservative colleague, Laz, advocates for an equal-opportunity theory of welfare reform. Discusses an impending racial war and disfavored treatment of minorities. Theorizes that these occurrences would represent reactionary behavior aimed at defeating the inevitable shift of demographic, and hence democratic, power into minority hands. Cautions against essentialism and explores in depth the peculiar position of Latinos in America's racial future.

Rodrigo's Thirteenth Chronicle: Legal Formalism and Law's Discontents, 95 MICH. L. REV. 1105 (1997). Asks how legal formalism contributes to the unhappiness of legal professionals as well as women's and minorities' disenchantment with law school. Examines the public's disappointment with the legal profession. Shows how formalism and doctrinalism ultimately deflect us from things that matter.

Rodrigo's Twelfth Chronicle: The Problem of the Shanty, 85 GEO. L.J. 667 (1997). Discusses the inadequate housing situation in impoverished shantytowns at the Texas border. Criticizes mainstream liberal solutions to those problems on account of their mildness and inefficacy. Shows how law and economics fails to cure or explain the problem of the shanty. Proposes a solution whereby the government takes a more active role in curing inequities. Suggests a variety of self-help remedies for the impoverished underclass.

Conflict as Pathology: An Essay for Trina Grillo, 81 MINN. L. REV. 1391 (1997). Reviews Trina Grillo's critique of alternative dispute resolution (ADR) and discusses how informal disputing may not benefit impecunious or small-stakes disputants. Speculates about what Professor Grillo may have added to the critique of ADR had her career not ended. Undermines the ADR movement by pointing out that conflict is not necessarily pathology and that informality tends to incite prejudice. Explains the current popularity of the ADR movement through ideological and temporal considerations.

Outsider Scholars: The Early Stories, 71 CHI.-KENT L. REV. 1001 (1996) (coauthor). Casts scrutiny on the situation of outsider legal scholars ten to fifteen years earlier, before the relative mainstreaming of their work. Analyzes the results of a questionnaire polling prominent voices early in the movement. Documents the historical distortion of outsider scholarship by law review editors. Reveals that early outsider scholars had difficulty getting work published and were often discouraged from pursuing critical or feminist themes.

The Colonial Scholar: Do Outsider Authors Replicate the Citation Practices of the Insiders, but in Reverse? 71 CHI.-KENT L. REV. 969 (1996). Examines whether outsider scholars—crits, feminists, and critical race theorists—engage in an insular practice by citing each other's work and ignoring the contribution of mainstream civil rights scholars. Analyzes qualitative and quantitative data that suggest that this is not the case.

Playing Favorites, 74 TEX. L. REV. 1223 (1996). Reveals Delgado's favorite case as *City of Richmond v. J. A. Croson Co.,* the "minority set-asides case," which held that remedying generalized societal discrimination is not a legitimate state interest. Favors this case because it demonstrates the instrumentalist approach: law is a means to an end, useful for some things and not for others. Frames the case as prophecy, foreshadowing the demise of minority gains.

Coughlin's Complaint: How to Disparage Outsider Writing, One Year Later, 82 VA. L. REV. 95 (1996). Replies to Professor Coughlin's article that disparages autobiography in outsider scholarship. Examines the interplay between Coughlin's theory of autobiography and her conclusions with respect to outsider scholarship in general. Focuses on Coughlin's treatment of Delgado's writing, in particular. Offers words of caution and advice for white feminists who study writers of color.

Apologize and Move On? Finding a Remedy for Pornography, Insult, and Hate Speech (book review), 67 U. COLO. L. REV. 93 (1996) (principal coauthor). Summarizes and discusses a book by Richard Abel that asks when an apology should suffice to close public or private disputes involving hate speech. Provides a brief overview of the hate speech controversy. Argues that apology as a solution is too mild and trivializes the harm of racist and sexist speech. Suggests that the apology option suffers from often insurmountable practical and theoretical shortcomings. Concludes with suggestions for proper hate speech remedies.

Rodrigo's Eleventh Chronicle: Empathy and False Empathy, 84 CAL. L. REV. 61 (1996). Exposes the myth that society empathizes with minorities through the concept of "false empathy," where a white person believes s/he identifies with a minority when in fact that person only does so in a slight, superficial way. Shows how empathy reproduces hierarchy and why genuine sympathy is in short supply. Proposes a "due process of storytelling," an ability to speak openly of an injustice without the typical strictures of the legal system.

"The Speech We Hate": First Amendment Totalism, the ACLU, and the Principle of Dialogic Politics, 27 ARIZ. ST. L.J. 1281 (1995) (principal coauthor). Takes issue with the purist First Amendment position—the belief that hate speech deserves protection precisely because it is unpopular and that to protect speech of one sort, it is necessary to protect another. Demonstrates how the argument is paradoxical and lacks foundation. Shows how the argument's contradictions disappear once one understands that hate speech now sits at the center of First Amendment ideology, while political speech has shifted to the periphery.

Stark Karst: Law's Promise, Law's Expression (book review), 93 MICH. L. REV. 1460 (1995). Summarizes and discusses a book by Stark Karst that examines the "social issues agenda" of the new right—political opportunism that rails against reproductive autonomy, paints welfare recipients as leeches, and seeks to minimize the role of women and gays in the military. Looks at the cultural causation behind this trend. Shows how the symbolic forms of the agenda facilitate its eventual entrenchment in reality. Concludes that Karst understates the extent of America's predicament and suggests a more critical approach.

Rodrigo's Tenth Chronicle: Merit and Affirmative Action, 83 Geo. L.J. 1711 (1995). Deconstructs "merit," the source of supposedly objective standards. Shows how merit is what the victors impose and that it functions as a sort of etiquette, excusing self-interested acts of the majority. Gives multiple examples of how merit rules disadvantage minorities. Explores the history of merit and its present-day implications. Ultimately proposes a reevaluation of merit instead of affirmative action programs.

Rodrigo's Final Chronicle: Cultural Power, the Law Reviews, and the Attack on Narrative Jurisprudence, 68 S. Cal. L. Rev. 545 (1995). Discusses, in dialogic form, the critique of narrative scholarship within the legal academy. Cautions budding academics about the risks involved in using the narrative technique to explore ideology and mindset. Discusses the attack on student-edited legal journals, in part because they are receptive to this mode of scholarship. Situates the internal critique of narrative scholarship within the broader frame of society and the omnipresent "cultural weight" that resists change.

Cosmopolitanism Inside Out: International Norms and the Struggle for Civil Rights and Local Justice, 27 Conn. L. Rev. 773 (1995) (principal coauthor). Points out the benefit of the shift toward international human rights law as a source of aid for minority groups. Sketches out one mode of attack on the international shift in the minority rights movement: "cosmopolitanism," the notion that an ideal being severs his or her roots and eschews identity politics. Discusses the virtues and defects of the cosmopolitan ideal as a standard for national and international behavior. Cautions reformers who may be tempted to place too much faith in international human rights as a source of progressive arguments and change.

Critical Race Theory, An Annotated Bibliography 1993: A Year of Transition, 66 U. Colo. L. Rev. 159 (1995) (principal coauthor). Updates Delgado's earlier annotated bibliography. Lists and annotates the major entries within the critical race theory corpus of work. Sets forth a revised set of overarching themes within the CRT movement and identifies them within the selected works.

The Social Construction of Brown v. Board of Education: *Law Reform and the Reconstructive Paradox,* 36 Wm. and Mary L. Rev. 547 (1995) (principal coauthor). Advances a novel perspective on *Brown* that focuses on societal events contemporaneous to that decision. Summarizes the shortcomings and accomplishments of *Brown* using the current debate over campus hate speech rules as an illustrative device. Points out how the current debate exemplifies the backward drift in civil rights gains. Sets forth a "reconstructive paradox" that shows why society erroneously believes the legal system can effect significant change in matters such as race.

Rodrigo's Ninth Chronicle: Race, Legal Instrumentalism, and the Rule of Law, 143 U. Pa. L. Rev. 379 (1994). Reconciles mainstream civil rights law with the more pessimistic racial realist (critical race theory) version. Explains and defends legal instrumentalism. Shows how self-interest, not idealism, is the best course for reformers and demonstrates the shortcomings of interest convergence with the dominant group.

The Neoconservative Case Against Hate-Speech Regulation—Lively, D'Souza, Gates, Carter, and the Toughlove Crowd, 47 Vand. L. Rev. 1807 (1994) (principal coauthor). Examines the intersection of the hate-speech controversy, neoconservatives, and the politics of denial. Reviews the history of the campus hate-speech controversy and analyzes a group of arguments associated with the neoconservative or "toughlove" position. Theorizes that neoconservatives oppose speech regulation because it ultimately threatens a key conservative tenet: the level playing field.

Foreword, Essays on Hate-Speech, 82 CAL. L. REV. 847 (1994). Introduces two essays that address how society resists change in the context of the hate speech controversy. Indicates that together, both forms of resistance are powerful brakes on the transformation of our attitudes about regulating speech. Points out, however, that both essays offer practical solutions to assist reformers in effecting change.

Hateful Speech, Loving Communities: Why Our Notion of "A Just Balance" Changes So Slowly, 82 CAL. L. REV. 851 (1994) (principal coauthor). Identifies one reason why proponents of hate-speech regulation encounter resistance—often, it is the stubborn manner in which we frame the two core values at stake, equal dignity and freedom of speech. Illustrates the shortcomings of judicial balancing as a solution to the tension between these values. Uses narrative theory to demonstrate how society prevents canonical ideas and social structures from rapid change. Explores routes that reformers may pursue when attempting to advance efforts at regulating hate speech.

Pressure Valves and Bloodied Chickens: An Analysis of Paternalistic Objections to Hate Speech Regulation, 82 CAL. L. REV. 871 (1994) (principal coauthor). Identifies a second brake on the movement to regulate hate speech: paternalistic objections, which purport to know what is best for the group seeking protection. Reviews the history of campus antiracism rules in great detail. Offers practical instruction on how to draft regulations that both protect minorities and stay within permissible constitutional boundaries.

Scorn, 35 WM. AND MARY L. REV. 1061 (1994) (principal coauthor). Analyzes the use of scornful humor by the Supreme Court. Details the various types of scathing speech, including satire, parody, mockery, irony, and sarcasm. Explains how the Justices unleash scornful humor—against litigants, lawyers, ideas, and each other. Argues that the Court should reserve its scorn for powerful actors but should avoid it when confronted with society's poor and outcast.

Imposition, 35 WM. AND MARY L. REV. 1025 (1994) (principal coauthor). Demonstrates how courts and commentators employ language of imposition, which entails exasperation and fatigue, when confronted with the demands of minorities, prisoners, and other outsider groups. Explains how such narratives construct reality in opposition to outsider reform. Details and explains common scenarios and the mechanisms that deploy the language of imposition. Shows how such language is reactionary in the sense that it surfaces at pivotal moments in the reform movement.

Rodrigo's Eighth Chronicle: Black Crime, White Fears—On the Social Construction of Threat, 80 VA. L. REV. 503 (1994). Discusses how society has constructed African Americans unfairly, especially with regard to criminal behavior. Rodrigo shows how statistics fail to support the assumption that black crime is more damaging to society than crime perpetrated by other groups. Explains how the construction of "crime" favors whites—for example, white-collar crimes and war crimes, traditionally nonblack crimes, are rarely prosecuted.

Rodrigo's Seventh Chronicle: Race, Democracy, and the State, 41 UCLA L. REV. 721 (1994). Considers how democracy and the state both sit at the root of racism and points out how this is a natural extension of Enlightenment principles. Explores the link between free market economics, individualist competitiveness, and racism. Suggests shifting toward a collectivist model based on love and the act of hugging.

First Amendment Formalism Is Giving Way to First Amendment Legal Realism, 29 HARV. C.R.-C.L. L. REV. 169 (1994). Argues that the old formalist view of speech as an instrument for testing ideas and promoting social progress is transforming into a more nuanced and socially responsible view: First Amendment legal realism. Gives multiple examples of how First Amendment formalism legitimizes the status quo, slows social reform, and fails society when dealing with social ills like racism or sexism. Posits the inevitable demise of formalism and the growing influence of realist ideas.

Comments on Mary Becker, 64 U. COLO. L. REV. 1051 (1993). Broadly surveys the accomplishments of minority scholars in the legal academy. Discusses the recent emergence of narrative jurisprudence and the variable structure of the First Amendment.

Rodrigo's Sixth Chronicle: Intersections, Essences, and the Dilemma of Social Reform, 68 N.Y.U. L. REV. 639 (1993). Uses a recent controversy at Rodrigo's law school as a springboard to discuss the essentialism debate: is there one essential sisterhood, one unitary feminine nature, or are there many that split along racial lines? Points out how the essentialism debate has serious implications for persons who lie at the intersection of two marginalized identities. Advises the social reformer with an intersectional identity not to compromise his or her interests to form a larger coalition. Sketches the contours of a theory of antiessentialism and the relation of small groups to social change. Discusses the role of oppositional groups in effecting social change.

Rodrigo's Fifth Chronicle: Civitas, Civil Wrongs, and the Politics of Denial, 45 STAN. L. REV. 1581 (1993). Discusses the highly normative turn legal education has taken and points out the intense preoccupation with professional responsibility. Counsels the legal profession to confront racial and economic problems directly instead of engaging in denial and normative discussion. Shows how this direct approach would allow outsider discourse and insights to pierce the nonproductive, predictable, and normative dialogue that rarely goes anywhere.

Rodrigo's Fourth Chronicle: Neutrality and Stasis in Antidiscrimination Law, 45 STAN. L. REV. 1133 (1993). Discusses the difficulty of redressing social harms through neutral legal and social rules. Rodrigo, Delgado's alter ego, argues that in a society such as ours, even a decision maker with the most pristine social conscience and no trace of overt racism will still make decisions adverse to minorities. Analyzes the cultural backdrop of our society and legal system, concluding that it has much more efficacy than law on the books. Notes that even race-conscious rules intended to protect and benefit minorities generally end up making matters worse. Offers a number of cultural and structural reasons for the persistence of racism even where society's formal rules condemn it.

Rodrigo's Third Chronicle: Care, Competition, and the Redemptive Tragedy of Race, 81 CAL. L. REV. 387 (1993). Outlines a civil rights strategy based on love. Proposes socialized caregiving as a strategy to redeem the marginalized and forgotten. Points out the value of the free market economy in the productive sector. Suggests that synergy between these two sectors will ensure a successful future for the caregiving sector. Proposes a mythic framework and a novel form of coercion to move us toward an ideal society.

Rodrigo's Second Chronicle: The Economics and Politics of Race, 91 MICH. L. REV. 1183 (1993). Presents a dialogue between Rodrigo Crenshaw (the author's fictional alter ego) and his mentor. Discusses the economic marketplace's potential to eliminate racism: might nonracist businesses outcompete those that discriminate? Rodrigo argues that racism would multiply within a capitalist economy because of stereotypes and Western myths that hold blacks and other minorities in a subordinate position.

Five Months Later (The Trial Court Opinion), 71 TEX. L. REV. 1011 (1993). Offers a fictional trial opinion, written by a federal judge, that upholds minority hiring plans at a number of law schools. Complements a prior article by Michael Paulsen where the same judge ruled against law schools at the summary judgment stage, when sued by a white applicant for a law teaching position. Reveals how case law and social policy lend themselves to a defense of race-conscious hiring practices. Suggests that a "two-pile" hiring system may pander to disappointed white applicants.

On Telling Stories in School: A Reply to Farber and Sherry, 46 VAND. L. REV. 665 (1993). Responds to multiple criticisms of critical race theory, especially those directed at the use of narrative. Counsels that narrative jurisprudence is only one of critical race theory's tools and that criticism of it should not be imputed to the entire field. Acknowledges the diversity of outsider voices and narrative forms. Concludes that mainstream academics should postpone evaluation of outsider scholarship due to lack of mutually acceptable criteria.

The Inward Turn in Outsider Jurisprudence, 34 WM. AND MARY L. REV. 741 (1993). Focuses on two developments within outsider jurisprudence: the call for standards to judge radical feminist or critical race scholarship, and antiessentialism, the practice of these groups in identifying more specific subgroups within themselves. Argues that standards are unnecessary at present and potentially harmful. Advocates for an acceptance of antiessentialism as a normal phenomenon. Argues that both movements represent a response to power shifts and paradigmatic evolution.

A Shifting Balance: Freedom of Expression and Hate-Speech Restriction (book review), 78 IOWA L. REV. 737 (1993) (coauthor). Explores the hate-speech debate in a comparative context that may ultimately shed light on the domestic controversy. Reviews a collection of papers delivered at an international conference addressing regulation of hate speech and freedom of expression. Employs the comparative perspective to dispel common myths favoring the antiregulation position.

Critical Race Theory: An Annotated Bibliography, 79 VA. L. REV. 461 (1993) (principal coauthor). Lists and annotates the major entries within the critical race theory corpus of work. Sets forth the overarching themes within the CRT movement and identifies them within the selected works.

Pornography and Harm to Women: "No Empirical Evidence?" 53 OHIO ST. L.J. 1037 (1992) (principal coauthor). Considers social responses surrounding the pornography controversy as a method of generating a general theory of social regression. Offers a concise history of media depictions of women, including pornography. Explains why those who oppose reform do not see pornography as a serious harm. Concludes by suggesting ways reformers might eschew the strictures of the status quo and ensure a degree of social reform.

Images of the Outsider in American Law and Culture: Can Free Expression Remedy Systemic Social Ills? 77 CORNELL L. REV. 1258 (1992) (principal coauthor). Shows how conventional First Amendment doctrine is most helpful in connection with clearly bounded disputes yet fails to assist us when confronted with the most pressing systemic social ills, like racism or sexism. Traces a history of racist minority stereotypes. Points out how the indefensible nature of these images becomes apparent well after the fact, because historical actors cannot control their consciousness when limited by time and positionality—despite a belief to the contrary, termed the "empathic fallacy." Shows how the U.S. system of free speech not only fails to correct the repression and abuse subjugated groups must face but often deepens their dilemma. Sets forth a program of social reform and a new, variable theory of the First Amendment.

Zero-Based Racial Politics and an Infinity-Based Response: Will Endless Talking Cure America's Racial Ills? 80 GEO. L.J. 1879 (1992). Sets forth three reasons why intergroup dialogue is unlikely to remedy society's current racial problems. Demonstrates how normative discourse poses certain problems for aspiring reformers. Explores what remains once we understand the limited value of conversationalism and counsels progressive scholars to focus their efforts on an antiracist agenda.

A Comment on Aleinikoff, 63 U. COLO. L. REV. 383 (1992). Discusses a recent article by Aleinikoff on the continuing significance of racism as seen through a constitutional lens. Points to the rigidity of the prevailing mindset and other reasons to show why his article will receive less attention than it deserves. Suggests paths for future scholarship and praxis.

Legal Scholarship: Insiders, Outsiders, Editors, 63 U. COLO. L. REV. 717 (1992). Comments on three articles included in a symposium on the state of legal scholarship. Discusses a range of topics, including how editors think, the empirical study of scholarship, and the debate over the lack of standardized criteria in new critical writing.

Shadowboxing: An Essay on Power, 77 CORNELL L. REV 813 (1992). Deconstructs the law's preference for "objective" over "subjective" standards when judging conduct. Shows how the preference for "objective" standards caters to the established regime and favors the majoritarian or stronger parties to a lawsuit.

The Imperial Scholar Revisited: How to Marginalize Outsider Writing, Ten Years Later, 140 U. PA. L. REV. 1349 (1992). Queries the state of affairs now that critical race theorists and radical feminists have entered the legal academy. Revisits the original article, *The Imperial Scholar,* and investigates whether twenty-six "imperial scholars" continue to operate in an insular fashion that marginalizes outsider and minority academics. Documents how mainstream scholars cite outsider scholars generally. Concludes that those who control the terms of discourse will marginalize outsider writing as long as possible.

Rodrigo's Chronicle, 101 YALE L.J. 1357 (1992). Introduces Rodrigo Crenshaw (the author's fictional alter ego). Discusses, in dialogic form, the shortcomings of standardized testing in the legal academy. Shows how the law school hiring market disfavors minority scholars. Situates current Western dominance within a world history of culture and power. Discusses the rise of the right and society's cyclical embrace of minorities.

Derrick Bell's Racial Realism: A Comment on White Optimism and Black Despair, 24 CONN. L. REV. 527 (1992). Assesses the charges of pessimism leveled at Derrick Bell and his brand of racial realism. Offers reasons for the "optimism gap" between Bell and his critics. Discusses how the psychology of race and the current wave of antiminority sentiment may be responsible. Concludes that pessimistic messages still advance racial reform.

Our Better Natures: A Revisionist View of Joseph Sax's Public Trust Theory of Environmental Protection, and Some Dark Thoughts on the Possibility of Law Reform, 44 VAND. L. REV. 1209 (1991). Criticizes a theory of environmental protection—that humans should act as trustees for our natural resources. Outlines Sax's original proposal and how society has adopted it. Shows how the public trust theory is ineffective and has stalled competing approaches to conservation efforts. Sets forth general strategies for legal reform.

Campus Antiracism Rules: Constitutional Narratives in Collision, 85 NW. U. L. REV. 343 (1991). Discusses issues that arise when campuses enact rules to prohibit disparaging remarks based on one's sexual orientation, ethnicity, or religion. Surveys the extent of racism on campuses and resulting university responses. Looks for guidance in social-science research and the experiences of other Western nations. Shows how individual actors tend to characterize the problem in one of two ways, either as a free speech or an equal protection issue—each leading to drastically different results. Bridges the gap between these positions, showing how speech regulation can preserve core First Amendment values while being faithful to the guarantees of the Fourteenth Amendment.

Recasting the American Race Problem, 79 CAL. L. REV. 1389 (1991). Argues that many of the defects of liberalism can be remedied by attending to broader perspectives offered by critical thought. Shows that the principle of formal equality promotes subordination of people of color because racism is the norm in our society. Posits that formal equality will only single out highly visible deviations from a racist status quo.

Enormous Anomaly? Left-Right Parallels in Recent Writing About Race, 91 COLUM. L. REV. 1547 (1991). Reviews several recent books by scholars of the new right and the CRT left. Points out their shared dissatisfaction with liberalism and the moderate-left civil rights program that has dominated the U.S. political and social scene since the early 1960s. Argues that liberalism today is practically bankrupt as a source of civil rights reform.

Outsider Jurisprudence and the Electronic Revolution: Will Technology Help or Hinder the Cause of Law Reform? 52 OHIO ST. L.J. 847 (1991) (coauthor). Exposes the developing intersection of two forces in the law: outsider jurisprudence and the electronic transformation of media. Describes each of these movements, then offers predictions about their convergence. Offers suggestions to ensure that computerization facilitates law reform and unites the two forces into a powerful impetus for legal and social change.

Norms and Narratives: Can Judges Avoid Serious Moral Error? 69 TEX. L. REV. 1929 (1991) (principal coauthor). Presents a history of embarrassingly inhumane judicial decisions that trod on the rights of minorities. Examines the merits of the Law and Literature movement and considers whether reading a well-written, deeply felt counternarrative can save a judge from history's condemnation. Concludes that the redemptive effect of counternarrative may be weak in the case of judges, yet suggests other means by which reform-minded lawyers can make limited progress.

Pep Talks for the Poor: A Reply and Remonstrance on the Evils of Scapegoating, 71 B.U. L. REV. 525 (1991). Replies to the recent writing of Robin West who advises outgroups to relinquish their dependence on the courts and instead to engage the citizenry and the legislature for much-needed reforms. Disagrees with this approach and argues that this proposal ignores history. Catalogues myriad defects in West's proposal. Searches for the source of West's viewpoint, as she is generally a progressive scholar. Discusses what reformers should be doing at present.

Moves, 139 U. PA. L. REV. 1071 (1991). Addresses the emergent critique of normativity and anticipates likely responses to it as a series of "moves." Suggests that critics will characterize the critique as self-contradictory or contradicted by the old order. Anticipates charges of nihilism, essentialism, and other forms of attack.

Norms and Normal Science: Toward a Critique of Normativity in Legal Thought, 139 U. PA. L. REV. 933 (1991). Unmasks the normative reductionism of modern legal thought through discursive and empirical analysis. Explores three related ways that society currently employs normative thought. Anticipates questions regarding paradigm change and the critique of "normal science." Concludes that the critique of normativity fails to threaten the cause of social reformation any more than earlier critiques of law as logic or law as empirical science.

Derrick Bell's Chronicle of the Space Traders: Would the U.S. Sacrifice People of Color If the Price Were Right? 62 U. COLO. L. REV. 321 (1991) (principal coauthor). Examines the plausibility of Bell's famous allegory, where white America sells its black citizens to an advanced race of extraterrestrial aliens. Concludes that the story has the ring of truth—history shows that when nonwhite populations stand in the way of westward expansion, they are summarily relocated or exterminated. Optimistically revises Bell's account to reach a new conclusion wherein the American people reject the trade.

Affirmative Action as Majoritarian Device: Or, Do You Really Want to Be a Role Model? 89 Mich. L. Rev. 1222 (1991). Considers why scholars of color have grown increasingly skeptical about affirmative action's utility and how it frames the issue of minority representation. Criticizes the "role model argument" in favor of affirmative action—the notion that minorities who benefit from affirmative action will set a good example and uplift their people. Proposes that professionals of color eschew the "role model" function and seek out more authentic and vital relationships with their constituent communities.

Brewer's Plea: Critical Thoughts on Common Cause, 44 Vand. L. Rev. 1 (1991). Takes issue with Scott Brewer's foreword to the *Harvard Law Review* colloquy on Randall Kennedy's critique of the CRT movement. Brewer calls for both parties to work toward common goals; Delgado questions whether such common goals exist and, if so, whether the time is right for coalition politics.

Zero-Based Racial Politics: An Evaluation of Three Best-Case Arguments on Behalf of the Nonwhite Underclass, 78 Geo. L.J. 1929 (1990). Asks the zero-basis question: in a society with two dominant political groups, one conservative and one liberal, which is the more likely source of aid for the nonwhite poor? Identifies and considers the "best case" arguments on behalf of the poor for each of these groups—also includes a third political group based in communitarian social welfare theory. Concludes, surprisingly, that the right may offer the impoverished more than leftist groups.

Mindset and Metaphor: A Response to Randall Kennedy's Racial Critiques of Legal Academia, 103 Harv. L. Rev. 1872 (1990). Shows that Randall Kennedy's disagreements with three CRT authors stem from certain presuppositions and metaphors that authors of Kennedy's persuasion subscribe to and deploy.

Panthers and Pinstripes: The Case of Ezra Pound and Archibald MacLeish, 63 S. Cal. L. Rev. 907 (1990) (coauthor). Provides biographical treatment of Pound, an Imagist poet, and MacLeish, a noted lawyer–poet–public servant. Points out that while the men had little in common, MacLeish was instrumental in effecting Pound's release from an asylum in 1958. Offers two theories addressing MacLeish's role and motivation for freeing Pound. Uses the case of these extraordinary men to ask whether contemporary lawyers can preserve a degree of humanism while practicing law.

Judicial Influences and the Inside-Outside Dichotomy: A Comment on Professor Nagel, 61 U. Colo. L. Rev. 711 (1990). Explores the boundaries of pressure and protest aimed at influencing judges. Suggests that the indeterminate, open texture of the law fuels societal demand for judges to isolate themselves from external pressures. Contrasts this view of judging with the view held by legal formalists. Points out that silences are facially indeterminate.

Approach-Avoidance in Law School Hiring: Is the Law a WASP? 34 St. Louis L.J. 631 (1990). Considers diversity hiring on law school faculties as an example of unconscious racism and subordination through mindset and preference. Points out certain stumbling blocks that have kept minorities and women off of law faculties. Makes several proposals to reform the hiring system.

When a Story Is Just a Story: Does Voice Really Matter? 76 Va. L. Rev. 95 (1990). Analyzes an article criticizing the assertion that some scholars write in a distinct "voice" by virtue of their marginal status. Summarizes how conventional liberal discourse views the issue of voice. Contrasts that view with outsider perspectives and illuminates the paradigmatic gap between critical race theory and more mainstream systems of belief.

On Taking Back Our Civil Rights Promises: When Equality Doesn't Compute, 1989 Wis. L. Rev. 579. Observes how advances in technology and sophisticated methods of statistical proof increasingly assist civil rights attorneys in proving inequality. Shows how the law resists such change by redefining legal doctrine in order to make civil rights violations unredressable. Concludes that at a certain point, society will no longer be able to disregard the law's departure from traditional notions of justice.

Why Do We Tell the Same Stories? Law Reform, Critical Librarianship, and the Triple Helix Dilemma, 42 STAN. L. REV. 207 (1989) (principal coauthor). Explores how professional research and indexing systems create and maintain the strictures of Western tradition. Describes the principal systems and shows how they have developed. Illustrates the shackling effect of existing systems, using civil rights law as an example. Indicates that we can sometimes circumvent this effect by using the current coordinate systems against themselves.

Storytelling for Oppositionists and Others: A Plea for Narrative, 87 MICH. L. REV. 2411 (1989). Explains how storytelling changes mindset, shatters complacency, and challenges the status quo. Gives multiple examples of how stories construct reality. Reveals the positive psychic effects of storytelling for outsider groups. Argues that members of the majority should listen to stories of all kinds to enrich their own reality.

Minority Law Professors' Lives: The Bell-Delgado Survey, 24 HARV. C.R.-C.L. L. REV. 349 (1989). Considers the fortunes of minority law professors in the past few decades, from promising beginnings to stalled gains. Discusses the results of a survey of minority law professors, which gauged their experiences through questionnaires and in-depth interviews. Reveals how minority law professors reported their experiences within eleven discrete categories, including academic freedom, institutional climate, research support, relations with students, and relations with colleagues. Concludes with the sobering news that pain and stress afflict many minority law professors who encounter subtle racism, exclusion from social networks, and a host of other professional impediments.

Critical Legal Studies and the Realities of Race—Does the Fundamental Contradiction Have a Corollary? 23 HARV. C.R.-C.L. L. REV. 407 (1988). Discusses the differing perceptions of racism among majoritarian identities and minorities. Explains how the majority rarely has conscious encounters with racism, whereas minority reality is steeped in it. Considers how this feature arises and traces out its consequences through sociolegal theorizing. Shows how the race-charged quality of the world in which minority people live affects the way they strike various balances between formal protections (e.g., rights) and informal community.

ADR and the Dispossessed: Recent Books About the Deformalization Movement, 13 LAW AND SOC. INQUIRY 145 (1988). Broadly surveys the writing on Alternative Dispute Resolution (ADR). Summarizes three recent books that approach ADR from a critical perspective. Compares ADR with formal adjudication processes in terms of function and underlying politics. Shows how deformalized justice can blur litigants' rights and how prejudice and bias can infiltrate ADR.

The Politics of Workplace Reforms: Recent Works on Parental Leave and a Father-Daughter Dialogue, 40 RUTGERS L. REV. 1031 (1988) (principal coauthor). Examines parental work leave from multiple perspectives and summarizes the literature to date. Discusses, in dialogic form, the social, normative, and political implications for women considering parental leave. Points out how certain workplace reforms allow a glimpse of a world free of gender inequality.

Derrick Bell and the Ideology of Racial Reform: Will We Ever Be Saved? 97 YALE L.J. 923 (1988). Reviews and summarizes a book by Derrick Bell that shows how U.S. civil rights law is not aimed at improving conditions for blacks, except on the rare occasions when doing so coincides with whites' self-interest. Demonstrates the value of Bell's use of narrative, as it probes the strains and weaknesses of the accounts by which we organize experience. Contrasts the rigidity and coerciveness of traditional legal methods with counterstories that bridge the gap between majoritarian ideals and the life of outsiders; such stories may spur intergroup dialogue and contribute to a more equitable construction of reality.

The Ethereal Scholar: Does Critical Legal Studies Have What Minorities Want? 22 Harv. C.R.-C.L. L. Rev. 301 (1987). Suggests that the schism between Critical Legal Studies (CLS) and minorities derives from a fundamental difference between the aims of CLS and the needs of minorities. Investigates aspects of the CLS program and explains why some are troublesome for minorities. Reveals how a common theme of the CLS critique—the advocacy of informality—ignores the need for structure in containing and eliminating racism. Describes what a radical political program must include to serve the interests of minorities and outlines the social arrangements that could help minorities flourish.

Protecting Autonomy and Personhood in Human Subjects Research, 11 S. Ill. U. L.J. 1147 (1987) (coauthor). Recounts recent criticisms of the Health and Human Services guidelines in that they inadequately protect personhood and autonomy in human subjects research. Examines proposals to enhance human subjects protection. Argues to reform halfhearted or pressured disclosures. Details the problems inherent in "deception" research and suggests closer monitoring and "informed deceit" provisions. Advocates for increased training and education in the ethics of human research.

Informed Consent in Human Experimentation: Bridging the Gap Between Ethical Thought and Current Practice, 34 UCLA L. Rev. 67 (1986) (principal coauthor). Proceeds from the widespread belief that informed consent requires an elevated standard in the context of "research" or other experimental procedures. Reviews the current approach to safeguarding the interests of human subjects participating in biomedical and psychological research. Summarizes the usual rationales for protecting consent in human research and proposes three additional reasons. Points out the inadequacies of current protections in light of these rationales. Proposes amending the federal regulations to guarantee necessary protection. Concludes by setting forth a possible judicial remedy available to victims when researchers breach the regulations.

How to Write a Law Review Article, 20 U.S.F. L. Rev. 445 (1986). Offers guidance on how to write a law review article. Discusses the virtues of the law review article as opposed to other forms of expression. Details the different varieties of law review articles. Counsels on research strategies and the dilemma of picking a topic. Talks about the importance of footnotes in composing an article. Offers a short primer on the publication process.

Fairness and Formality: Minimizing the Risk of Prejudice in Alternative Dispute Resolution, 1985 Wis. L. Rev. 1359 (1985) (principal coauthor). Presents an overview of Alternative Dispute Resolution and conducts a contrasting survey of its counterpart, in-court justice. Concludes, based on social science literature, that ADR is likely to increase the risk of prejudicial behavior. Summarizes left-wing political criticisms of ADR. Queries the significance of a possible increased risk of prejudice resulting from ADR. Suggests ways of lessening prejudice without sacrificing the benefits of ADR.

The Author Replies, 3 Law and Ineq. 261 (1985) (reply to Robert O'Neil). Revisits the thesis of Delgado's *Imperial Scholar* article and briefly addresses a recent reaction to it.

"Rotten Social Background": Should the Criminal Law Recognize a Defense of Severe Environmental Deprivation? 3 Law and Ineq. 9 (1985). Considers whether socioeconomic deprivation, also known as rotten social background (RSB), could be used as a criminal defense.

Summarizes some of the social scientific and medical literature on the contribution of environmental deprivation to criminal behavior. Canvasses existing criminal defenses and analyzes their capacity to accommodate RSB factors. Identifies the forms an RSB defense might assume and the costs and benefits of each option.

Fact, Norm, and Standard of Review—The Case of Homosexuality, 10 U. DAYTON L. REV. 575 (1985). Points out how gay rights cases arouse strong pro or con attitudes, thereby masking relevant legal issues that are only apparent in hindsight. Identifies the factual and normative questions that courts must address when deciding the rights of homosexuals. Reveals the interdependent nature of these questions. Sets forth a checklist of these issues aimed at ensuring substantive completeness in adjudication.

The Language of the Arms Race: Should the People Limit Government Speech? 64 B.U. L. REV. 961 (1984). Examines the negative implication of the First Amendment: what results when the people wish to silence a state actor or one part of the government wishes to silence another? Discusses the case for limiting government speech in the context of nuclear armaments and strategy. Theorizes that the executive branch dissembles ideas in this area and that its one-sided views may not be corrected in the marketplace of ideas due to widely shared human response mechanisms and official secrecy. Considers how the situation interfaces with democratic response theory and proposes various remedies.

When Religious Exercise Is Not Free: Deprogramming and the Constitutional Status of Coercively Induced Belief, 37 VAND. L. REV. 1071 (1984). Revisits an earlier article by Delgado, *Religious Totalism*, and replies to its critics. Reviews what happens in many instances of cult joining. Offers a conceptual account that justifies deprogramming of cult members who are unable to comprehend or surmount the coercive and deceptive influences that led to their commitment. Addresses constitutional problems that are triggered in the event that deprogramming should affect religious belief. Discusses deprogramming and whether it is capable of remedying the situation of vulnerable cult inductees without violating constitutional norms.

Inequality "From the Top": Applying an Ancient Prohibition to an Emerging Problem of Distributive Justice, 32 UCLA L. REV. 100 (1984). Focuses on the government's allocation of resources among sectors of the population and how such activity may erode equality. Examines Supreme Court doctrine dealing with giving. Proposes a new test for official giving, based on two little-used constitutional provisions, the antinobility clauses, and traces their history and development. Addresses the strengths and weaknesses of an antinobility approach. Illustrates analysis under the approach through examples.

The Imperial Scholar: Reflections on a Review of Civil Rights Literature, 132 U. PA. L. REV. 561 (1984). Points out how minority scholars are severely underrepresented in the field of civil rights theory. Suggests that white scholars systematically occupy and exclude minorities from this field. Shows how white scholars engage in an insular practice by citing each other's work and ignoring the contribution of minority scholars. Discusses the benefits of an inclusive civil rights discourse and offers strategies to achieve such a goal.

Can Science Be Inopportune? Constitutional Validity of Governmental Restrictions on Race-IQ Research, 31 UCLA L. REV. 128 (1983). Examines the permissibility of state action prohibiting the pursuit of new scientific knowledge on the ground that it is inopportune. Employs possible race-based differentials in intellectual endowment (the "IQ controversy") as an example to explore potential conflict between the state and the scientific community. Identifies the individual and social interests at stake in the IQ

Professor Delgado Replies, 18 Harv. C.R.-C.L. L. Rev. 593 (1983) (reply to Marjorie Heins). Responds to a critique of Delgado's seminal article, *Words That Wound,* which proposes a tort action for racial insults or name-calling. Illuminates the divide between First Amendment absolutists and those who advocate for legal recourse against the harms of racism. Unmasks the politico-moral standing of the article's critic.

Beyond Sindell: *Relaxation of Cause-in-Fact Rules for Indeterminate Plaintiffs,* 70 Cal. L. Rev. 881 (1982). Discusses a pro-plaintiff doctrine that shifts the burden of proof onto all defendants when an indeterminate defendant is at fault. Explores the feasibility of a reversal of this situation, namely, whether an "indeterminate plaintiff," as part of a larger class, could proceed in court. Evaluates policy grounds for developing the new doctrine and points out particular scenarios where extension of the preexisting doctrine would prove useful. Anticipates objections to the proposal and responds to them.

The Moralist as Expert Witness, 62 B.U. L. Rev. 869 (1982). Examines the role of moral, ethical or religious authorities when testifying as expert witnesses. Describes the potential functions of such expert witnesses and reviews evidentiary rules relating to them. Sets forth criteria to ensure that moral experts actually aid courts in their adjudicative function, without usurping their authority. Concludes by sanctioning the testimony of moral experts in certain situations.

Words That Wound: A Tort Action for Racial Insults, Epithets, and Name-Calling, 17 Harv. C.R.-C.L. L. Rev. 133 (1982). Advocates for an independent tort action to counter racial slurs. Documents the severe and extensive harm that racism continues to impose on American society. Examines how current legal doctrine fails to protect minorities from racial insults. Blueprints a cause of action against race-based insults. Anticipates possible objections to the proposal and responds to them.

"Concurrence" in Quotes: A Critical Assessment of Chief Justice Burger's Objections to a Right to Treatment for the Involuntarily Confined Mentally Ill, 15 U.C. Davis L. Rev. 527 (1982) (principal coauthor). Identifies and evaluates Chief Justice Burger's objections to a right to treatment for the involuntarily confined mentally ill. Points out how some of those objections only address a constitutional right while others aim at any type of right to treatment. Evaluates several of these objections based on doctrinal or institutional considerations and considers possible abuse of the right to treatment. Discusses four recent theories supporting a right to treatment and situates them within Chief Justice Burger's critique. Concludes that a right to treatment survives despite Burger's objections.

Cults and Conversion: The Case for Informed Consent, 16 Ga. L. Rev. 533 (1982). Argues for the requirement of informed consent in the case of religious conversion. Demonstrates how such a requirement is plausible in a First Amendment context and necessary to avoid injury to recruits. Sets forth a composite model of the cult-joining process, identifying points where consent issues arise. Considers possible remedies to enforce an informed consent requirement and anticipates possible objections to those remedies.

Death: Multiple Definitions or a Single Standard? 54 S. Cal. L. Rev. 1323 (1981) (coauthor). Deconstructs "death" and explores the implications of adopting a contextual or functional approach to defining it. Examines several areas where the decision to regard an individual as dead has significant legal and social consequences: double-indemnity life insurance, autopsy, burial, and organ transplantation. Endorses an approach that tailors the definition of death to the area in question.

Law School Admissions Study, Mexican-American Legal Defense and Education Fund (book review), 32 HASTINGS L.J. 1777 (1981) (coauthor). Reviews an admissions study examining the situation of Mexican Americans in connection with legal institutions of higher learning.

Active Rationality in Judicial Review, 64 MINN. L. REV. 467 (1980). Discusses the general requirement that laws be rational and make sense. Examines the duty courts may owe to criminal defendants facing prosecution under irrational statutes—often involving drug crime. Considers the elements of the prima facie case that could challenge irrational statutes. Analyzes possible arguments against courts being able to actively intervene on behalf of defendants.

To Tell the Truth: Physicians' Obligation to Disclose Medical Mistakes, 28 UCLA L. REV. 52 (1980) (coauthor). Discusses the need for a duty to disclose, showing that the medical community does not effectively self-regulate. Emphasizes the importance of such a duty in light of the inherent inequality between patient and doctor. Establishes the plausibility of the duty to disclose. Outlines the prima facie case for, and defenses to, an action for breach of the proposed duty to disclose. Anticipates objections to the duty of disclosure and responds to them.

Religious Totalism as Slavery, 9 N.Y.U. REV. L. AND SOC. CHANGE 51 (1980). Argues that viewing religious totalism as a form of slavery, triggering the Thirteenth Amendment, illuminates the legal problems it poses as well as possible solutions. Attempts a comparative exercise that matches slavery case law with cases involving religious cults. Discusses four values fundamental to the Thirteenth Amendment and how cult behavior offends those values. Explores possible remedies if one concludes that religious totalism constitutes slavery.

A Response to Professor Dressler, 63 MINN. L. REV. 361 (1979). Responds to criticism of Delgado's earlier article setting forth a defense theory for "brainwashed" individuals. Refines and strengthens the original thesis. Refutes the claim that the original thesis is both underinclusive and overinclusive through an example. Shows how even ideologically coerced defendants merit such a defense despite retaining some degree of "free choice."

Ascription of Criminal States of Mind: Toward a Defense Theory for the Coercively Persuaded ("Brainwashed") Defendant, 63 MINN. L. REV. 1 (1978). Sets forth and details the concept of superimposed *mens rea* (criminal intent that is not the actor's own), which often afflicts victims of thought reform. Establishes the plausibility of such a concept through an example. Reviews existing legal doctrines to understand how analogous concepts of transferred mental states can relieve the actor of liability in other contexts. Concludes that the presence of an implanted *mens rea* may form the basis for a tenable new defense theory. Offers criteria for determining when such a transfer has occurred and considers possible objections to the new defense.

God, Galileo, and Government: Toward Constitutional Protection for Scientific Inquiry, 53 WASH. L. REV. 349 (1978) (principal coauthor). Examines the applicability of existing constitutional doctrine to state action that prohibits, burdens, or declines to fund scientific research merely because the state considers the area "inappropriate." Tenders and examines the thesis that governmental decisions to regulate scientific inquiry implicate highly protected constitutional values by virtue of the possible scientific knowledge at stake.

Religious Totalism: Gentle and Ungentle Persuasion Under the First Amendment, 51 S. CAL. L. REV. 1 (1977). Explores the legal and social issues posed by the recruiting and indoctrinating activities of religious cults, especially those raised by the prospect of state intervention. Reviews the psychiatric and medical literature relating to religiously motivated thought reform. Considers how the First Amendment may not protect cults engaging in physical and psychological harm. Anticipates the defense that such harm may be consensual and explores the legal significance of such a claim. Details and analyzes the process of induction with a focus on voluntariness since the legal system is typically reluctant to limit the self-regarding actions of adults. Sets forth a comprehensive range of legal solutions addressing the problem of religious totalism.

Organically Induced Behavioral Change in Correctional Institutions: Release Decisions and the "New Man" Phenomenon, 50 S. CAL. L. REV. 215 (1977). Briefly surveys the current biological model of aggressive behavior and discusses the principal treatment modalities. Suggests that currently available techniques may correct the violent propensities of certain inmates so that they no longer pose a risk to society. Reviews developments in prison law suggesting that courts will entitle organically treated offenders to release under certain circumstances. Explores the parameters of this "right to release" and sketches a procedural machinery by which courts could hear organic rehabilitation claims.

Euthanasia Reconsidered—The Choice of Death as an Aspect of the Right of Privacy, 17 ARIZ. L. REV. 474 (1975). Evaluates and agrees with the thesis that decisions relating to death deserve constitutional protection by virtue of the right of privacy. Analyzes the parameters of such a right. Considers possible state interests against a right to die, including some that are substantial and may circumscribe the interest of one who elects death.

The Legal Education of Chicano Students: A Study in Mutual Accommodation and Cultural Conflict, 5 N.M. L. REV. 177 (1975) (coauthor). Assesses the situation of special admissions programs targeting Chicanos. Reviews the development of these special admissions programs. Explores the law school experience for Chicanos, focusing on their backgrounds and how they adapt to law school. Concludes with several institutional mechanisms that promote inclusion of Chicanos, including curricular change and special education programs.

Minority Students and the Legal Curriculum: An Experiment at Berkeley, 63 CAL. L. REV. 751 (1975). Describes the difficulties and rewards of offering a law school course specifically focused on legal issues facing Mexican Americans. Details a curriculum and shows how such a course requires limited institutional resources. Reveals the overwhelming value of such a course in linking the traditional law school curriculum with the problems of the barrio.

Mexican-Americans as a Legally Cognizable Class Under Rule 23 and the Equal Protection Clause, 50 NOTRE DAME L. REV. 393 (1975) (principal coauthor). Reviews the status of Chicanos as a class under current decisional law. Reveals, for the first time, a fundamental incongruity: while those who discriminate against Chicanos can tell who they are, courts and judges cannot, leaving many wrongs without a remedy. Addresses the difficulty courts encounter in perceiving Chicanos as a class and discusses a number of characteristics that may help delineate such a class. Concludes that certain attributes when subject to narrowing techniques under Rule 23 are sufficiently distinct to enable courts to certify Chicano subclasses for litigation purposes.

Parental Preferences and Selective Abortion: A Commentary on Roe v. Wade, Doe v. Bolton, *and the Shape of Things to Come,* 1974 WASH. U. L.Q. 203 (principal coauthor). Discusses whether a woman's right to privacy extends to selective abortion based on characteristics of the fetus. Presents a series of hypothetical yet realistic selective abortion scenarios. Explores the ethical underpinnings and social ramifications of the "right" to selective abortion. Questions the balance between the state's interest and a woman's right to privacy in this context.

College Searches and Seizures: Students, Privacy, and the Fourth Amendment, 26 HASTINGS L.J. 57 (1974). Points out how an emphasis on institutional order and discipline diminishes the Fourth Amendment rights of college students. Analyzes case law and the legal doctrines that apply when university officials enter the room of a college student with neither a search warrant nor consent. Sets forth a set of model guidelines for university administrators to help them avoid illegal searches and seizures that violate student rights.

Note, *Jury Selection: Vicinage Requirement,* People v. Jones, 62 CAL. L. REV. 536 (1974). Examines the policy considerations involved in selecting a jury from outside a criminal defendant's vicinage, as required by the Sixth Amendment. Presents multiple meanings of the word *vicinage* and the resulting implications for defendants. Advocates for a flexible construction that accounts for policy and is tailored to the facts of a specific case.

Comment, *Underprivileged Communications: Extension of the Psychotherapist-Patient Privilege to Patients of Psychiatric Social Workers,* 61 CAL. L. REV. 1050 (1973). Analyzes the consequences of the legislature's failure to extend the psychotherapist-patient privilege to patients of psychiatric social workers. Details problems that the denial of this privilege poses for the parties involved. Analyzes similarities between the existing privilege and the proposed one. Sets forth a variety of theories courts could use to extend the privilege.

Index

AALS. *See* Association of American Law Schools
ACLU. *See* American Civil Liberties Union
ADR. *See* alternative dispute resolution
affirmative action, 159; arguments against, 365–75; arguments for, 171–72; balkanization and, 372; casts doubts on competence of minorities, 57; displacement and, 371, 377; diversity rationale for, 99; merit and, 375–95; nonblack groups and, 293; quotas and, 110; race neutral, 353–54; remedial rational for, 99, 372; social class remedy and, 394–95; special opportunity appointments and, 377; top of the bottom problem of, 374
African Americans. *See* blacks
agony tales, 55, 56, 63
Alfieri, Anthony, 88
Al-Hammar X, and law school hiring story, 13–15
Alien Land Law, 97, 299
alienation, 270
All Rise (Reynaldo Garza), 286
alternative dispute resolution (ADR), 99–100
altruism, motivations for, 358
American Civil Liberties Union (ACLU), as opponent of hate speech codes, 378
Anarchy and Elegance (Chris Goodrich), 187
animals: aggression in, 349; treated better than humans, 333–34
antidiscrimination law, 98; closing the gap in, 260–61; neutrality in, 101, 107
anti-essentialism: Angela Harris and, 264, 265; antinominalist argument and, 264; Kimberle Crenshaw and, 268–69; relation of small groups to social change and, 273–76. *See also* essentialism
Arlington Heights v. Metropolitan Housing Development Corp., and retreat from *Brown*, 250
Asch, Solomon, and group pressure experiment, 350
assimilation: risks of, with dominant group, 152, 270–82
Association of American Law Schools (AALS): annual conference of, 52; testing industry and, 198, 206
assumptions: role of, in legal decisionmaking, 105–16
attestors: role of, in determining legitimacy of minority achievement, 147–48
authoritarian personality, and racism, 228, 340–41

backlash, against minorities, 30–31
Bartók, Béla, 296
Beauharnais v. Illinois, 230
Bell, Derrick, 93–96, 174; critique of, 138–39, 296–305; public-interest lawyers and, 76; racial realism and, 140; role at Harvard, 55
Beyond Love, problem of being, 44–51, 146
bilingualism: benefits of, 389; Proposition 187 (California) and, 299
billable hours, 180
binary, black-white. *See* black-white binary of race
binary thinking, 298
Black Panthers, 143

Black Power movement, and end of civil rights era, 161
blacks: anticommunism and, 152–53; changing images of, 64–65; living conditions of, 47–48, 61; middle class, and affirmative action, 368–69; as the Other, 19, 45, 49, 51, 146
black-white binary of race, 287–95; coalitions and, 303–05; as impediment to racial progress, 297–305; practical consequences of, 293–94; remedies for, 305; symbolic effect of, 294–95
blood pressure, and hate speech, 213
Bluebeard's Castle, 296–97
Boalt Hall (law school) graduation, 365
bridge people, 50
Brigham, Carl Campbell, 198, 370, 391
Brown v. Board of Education: Equal Protection Clause and, 289; failure to generalize and, 245–52; as favorite of liberal legal theory, 192; impact of, 45, 60–61, 95, 271; as impediment to Latino progress, 289–90; interest convergence and, 150–52; interpretations of effectiveness of, 243; retreat from, 250–51; social construction of, 243–53
Buffalo Soldiers, and Native Americans, 162, 300
Burlingame Treaty, 300

campus speech codes, 84, 220, 225–34, 239, 244–45, 378. *See also* First Amendment; free speech; hate speech
canonical thinking, 267, 276–77, 279
capital, cultural. *See* cultural capital
capital punishment, 130
capitalism, 37–38; détente with socialism and, 35–43; law and economics and, 339; synergy with caregiving sector and, 39, 41. *See also* free market economics
caregiving activities: incompatibility of, with profit motive, 37; socializing the cost of, 36–43
Carrington, Paul, 176
Carter, Robert, 304
category mistake, 346–47
Chae Chan Ping v. United States, 97
Chaplinsky v. New Hampshire, 230
Chavez, César: pragmatic attitude toward the law and, 143

checkerboard of racial progress, 296–305
Chicanos. *See* Mexican Americans
children: impact of racism on, 215–16; social construction of, 346
Chin, Vincent, 301–02
Chinese Exclusion Act, 97, 299
chitlins test, 382
cigarette warnings, and objective versus subjective standard, 309–10
Cipollone v. Liggett Group, Inc., 309
City of Memphis v. Greene, and retreat from *Brown*, 249
City of Richmond v. J.A. Croson Co., and retreat from *Brown*, 250–51
civil rights: doctrinal entrenchment and, 258; white scholarship about, 167–75
Civil Rights Act (1964), 383
Civil Rights Cases, and harsh treatment of blacks, 250
civil rights movement: end of, 161; foundations and, 156, 162
Civil War, aftermath of, 299
Clark, Kenneth: on self-worth, 212
class: advantage and hate speech, 235–36; affirmative action based on, 394–95
Clean Water Act, and public trust doctrine, 254
clean your room, meaning of, 105, 246
Clinton, President William: national dialogue on race and, x
CLS. *See* critical legal studies
coalition(s): algebra of interracial, 155–56; as civil rights strategy, 270–73; hierarchy and, 158; historical differences and, 159–60; leadership and, 157; party politics and, 158–59; role of multiple consciousness in, 274; social reform and, 154–63
Cobbs v. Grant, 310
coercion: new form of, needed in civil rights enforcement, 46–49
Cold War, and civil rights, 150–51
College Board, 198, 391
color imagery, 320
colorblindness, 95, 98, 103–09; affirmative action and, 372
communism, and American blacks, 152–53
competition, socioeconomic: theory of racism and, 80
computers: role of, in law reform, 258–61
confrontation theory, for controlling racism,

228–29
Congress of Racial Equality, 156
consciousness, double. *See* double consciousness
consciousness, false. *See* false consciousness
consent: role of, in market transactions, 340
conservatives: arguments for, to support social welfare, 359–61
contradiction-closing cases, 116
corporations, and the law, 145
counterstories, 4, 18, 55–56; anonymous leaflet, 15–17; about law school hiring, 13–15; mental health and, 18; use of by Mexican Americans, 18; use of by slaves, 18. *See also* stories and storytelling
courts: as agents of pain and death, 93–94; allowable narratives and, 93–94; difficulty of addressing racism through, 115; struggle for racial justice and, 142; trial rules and, 88
credibility: effect of racist imagery on, 224–25; hate speech and, 237
Crenshaw, duke of, 71
Crenshaw, Geneva. *See* Geneva Crenshaw
Crenshaw, Kimberle, and anti-essentialism, 268–69
Crenshaw, Rodrigo. *See* Rodrigo Crenshaw
Crick, Francis: and DNA, 95
crime: black, compared to white, 117–37; black underclass and, 120; corporate, 125–26, 133–36; social construction of black, 120–24, 127, 136; statistics, 125–26, 129–31; street, 127; upward mobility and, 123; by white ethnic groups, 123; white-collar, 125–26, 128, 131–33, 134, 145
criminal justice system, differential treatment within, 74, 128–29
critical legal studies (CLS), 176, 192; methodology, 192
critical race theory (CRT). *See* counterstories; differential racialization; interest convergence; legal instrumentalism; neutral principles; racism; social construction; stories and storytelling
cross-burning case. *See* R.A.V. v. City of St. Paul
CRT. *See* critical race theory
cultural background, and impact on rules, 105

cultural capital, 383; lack of, by nonwhite poor, 359
cultural nationalism, 141; disadvantages of, 304
cultural weight, of social practices, 60–61

date rape, and objective versus subjective standards, 310–11
Dawes Act, 97, 299
decline of the West. *See* West, decline of
Delgado, Richard: life and career of, xi–xii
democracy: as obstacle for racial reform, 319–27; as source of racism, 317–20, 322
Democratic Party, 318; and zero-based racial politics, 356–61
demoralization, and racist imagery, 224
Dewey, John, 280, 281
differential racialization, 97–98, 301–02
discrimination, 50, 338; intersectional, 268–69; law, 98; proof of, with computers, 258–61; remedies and, 107; by universities, 99
Dissent, Injustice, and the Meanings of America (Steve Shiffrin), 234–40
distributive justice argument, as basis for affirmative action, 171–72
Disuniting of America, The (Arthur Schlesinger), 392
diversity, ways to think about, 365. *See also* affirmative action
diversity rationale. *See* affirmative action
DNA: cultural, 93–100; scientific concept of, 95
doctrinalism: debate about value of, 184–95; legal education and, 193–94; mechanical quality of, 184; women and minorities and, 194. *See also* legal formalism
dominant discourses, 188
double consciousness, 26, 76; role of, in coalitions, 274
Dred Scott v. Sandford, and harsh treatment of blacks, 251
D'Souza, Dinesh, 31; and argument against multiculturalism, 377
Du Bois, W.E.B.: double consciousness and, 26, 274; expulsion from NAACP and, 152
due process, structural. *See* structural due process
due process of storytelling, 82–85

dumping, toxic: as a crime, 129
duties: positive and negative, under law, 114

economics. *See* law and economics.
Educational Testing Service (ETS), 198, 391
Edwards, Judge Harry, 176, 177, 195
electric car competition, and intelligence, 202
eleven-year-old drivers, Minnesota's licensing of, 346
empathic fallacy, 57, 76, 158, 219, 221
empathy, 50, 69–89; in courtrooms, 85–88; failure of, in imperial scholarship, 170–71; law and, 82; in short supply, 79–80, 81; theory of, 75. *See also* false empathy
Endangered Species Act: for minorities, 332–37; public trust doctrine and, 254
English-only laws, 251, 286, 299; black support of, 157
Enlightenment: as exclusionary, 321; as justification for empire, 321; light and color imagery of, 321; as obstacle for racial reform, 324–27; as source of racism, 319–27
environmental justice, 332
environmental protection, public trust doctrine of, 58, 253–58
Equal Protection Clause, as barrier to Latino progress, 289–91
equality: formal, 109–11; of opportunity versus results, 109–14; statistics about, 258–61
Erie v. Tompkins, 190–91
essentialism, 262–82; interracial coalitions and, 157; in legal storytelling, 54; Martha Fineman and, 265–66; as power move, 268; relational, 267; strategic, 270. *See also* anti-essentialism
Ethnic Notions (Marlon Riggs), 218
ETS. *See* Educational Testing Service
everything must change at once, 59–61, 244. *See also* reconstructive paradox
evil: problem of, in human nature, 341, 347–49
exceptionalism, 298, 301, 302

fairness and formality, 318, 352–53
fallacy, empathic. *See* empathic fallacy
fallout, atomic: as a crime, 129
false consciousness, 26, 75, 76, 270

false empathy, 69–89; and religiosity, 80; and reproduction of hierarchy, 78; theory of, 76. *See also* empathy
family: African and Latino, care, 31; white, as source of crime, 132–34
Farber, Daniel, 54, 66
Fineman, Martha, and essentialism, 265–66
First Amendment: absolutism, 237; exceptions to, 224; freedom of speech and, 218, 221, 223; hate speech and, 226–27, 229–31; inability to redress hate speech and, 56–57, 83; legal realism, 234–40; as marketplace mechanism, 379. *See also* campus speech codes; free speech; hate speech
Ford Foundation, and cooptation of black radicalism, 162
foreign competition, and U.S. nonwhite poor, 361
formalism. *See* legal formalism
Fourteenth Amendment, and hate speech, 226, 227, 231–32
free market economics: critique of, 322–26; flaws of, 323–24; inability of, to eradicate racism, 345–47; as source of racism, 324. *See also* capitalism
free rider problem, 47, 49, 323
free speech: apologetic function of, 224; campus speech codes and, 220; civil rights and, 238; disadvantages of, as cure for racism, 222–23; exceptions to, 223, 230, 234; marketplace of ideas and, 221, 223, 224; stigma-pictures of subordinated groups and, 232–33; systemic social ills and, 218; uses of, 230. *See also* campus speech codes; First Amendment; hate speech
Freeman, Alan, 84, 87
fundamental contradiction, 288, 289

Gandhi, Mahatma, 142
Garza, Reynaldo, 286–88, 290
gene pool, deterioration of, 251, 344, 391
Geneva Crenshaw, 21
Giannina: family history of, 331; law school and, 182, 183; as a playwright, 103, 188
Gonzalez, Corky, 156
Good Samaritan. *See* helping behavior
GPA (grade-point average), and law school admissions, 202

Graduate Record Exam (GRE), 198
Gramsci, Antonio: and false consciousness, 75, 76
Greenawalt, Kent: and free speech controversy, 231
group(s): harsh treatment of, of color, 251; rights and affirmative action, 371; small, and social change, 262–82

Hacker, Andrew (*Two Nations*), 45–46, 49–50
Harris, Angela: and anti-essentialism, 264–65
hate speech, 56, 83, 84–85, 211–40; blood pressure and, 213; campus, and First Amendment, 56–57; class advantage and, 235–36; credibility and, 237; elements of cause of action for, 216–17; fate of Professor's articles about, 56–57, 64; First Amendment and, 226–27, 229–31; Fourteenth Amendment and, 226, 227, 231–32; harms of, 214–17, 230–31, 234–35; homeostat of, 236; legal formalism and, 113; marketplace of ideas and, 224, 236, 237; "more speech" argument against, 215, 219–20; pre-political normative reckoning and, 240; psychological consequences of, 212, 213; silencing and, 245; stereotypes and, 215. *See also* campus speech codes; First Amendment; free speech
hate speech codes. *See* campus speech codes
helix: racial double, 93–100; triple, of racial reality, 96
helping behavior: experiments on, 79, 80, 146; persistence of racism and, 350
Hispanics. *See* Latinos
Hobbes, Thomas: and social compact theory, 47
Hollow Hope (Gerald Rosenberg), 108, 115, 116
homeostat: of civil rights law, 45, 116; of hate speech, 236; of social change, 68
human nature, and economic model, 339–41
humor, 4. *See also* satire
hunger: role of, in social change, 280–81
hybrid vigor, as an argument for tolerating minorities, 32

images: of black criminals, 123, 136; of blacks on TV, 46; changing, of blacks, 65, 147–48; creators of racial, 218; functional use of negative, 64–65; use of racial, to subordinate minority groups, 294. *See also* stereotypes
immigration, 159; and plenary power doctrine, 290
imperial scholarship, 167–75; citation practice of, 167–69; defects in, 169–72; emphasis on procedure in, 170–71; explanations for, 173–75; legal instrumentalism and, 153; remedies for, 174–75. *See also* stereotypes
Indian Appropriations Act, 97, 299
informed consent, objective versus subjective standard, 310
ingroups, benefits of stories to, 19–20
Inquispro (computer), 73–74
institutional analysis, Harvard school of, 190
instrumentalism, legal. *See* legal instrumentalism
intelligence, multiple, 199, 382–83
interest convergence, 139, 302; *Brown v. Board of Education* and, 45; class interest of elite whites and, 345; disadvantage of, as a strategy, 149–53; environmental-law remedy and, 336; legal instrumentalism and, 141, 149–53; as a mechanism of social replication, 97–98; role of, in law reform, 273–75; women and, 34–45. *See also* self-interest
interracial coalition. *See* coalition(s)
intersectionality, 268–69

Japanese-American internment, 298, 301; NAACP and, 162, 303
John Henry, story of fictional job applicant, 6–17
judges: backgrounds of, 190–91; narcissism of some, in dismissing legal scholarship, 195
judicial system. *See* courts
justice first, then peace (slogan), 282

Kafka, Franz, 340–41
King, Jr., Martin Luther: and no obligation to obey unjust laws, 142–43
Kuhn, Thomas, 188

laissez faire economics. *See* free market economics

424 *Index*

LatCrits, 285–86
Latinos, 285–95; invisibility of, because of black-white binary, 292–93. *See also* Mexican Americans
law: corporations' lack of reverence for, 145; disaggregating function of, 88; inability of, to effect social change, 59, 243–52; proceduralism and, 143; utilitarian view of, 143–44
law and economics: rationality and, 339; as a type of formalism, 98
law reform, difficulty of, 243–61
law reviews, attack on student-edited, 58–59, 67
Law School Admissions Council (LSAC), 198
Law School Admissions Test (LSAT), 197–207; correlation between, and first-year grades, 200; deficiencies of, 21–22; increasing reliance on, 196; reducing reliance on, 205–07; scores of minority students and, 201, 366
Law School Data Assembly Service (LSDAS), 198–99
law school hiring, 385–86; dynamics of, 22–25; process of, 6–17, 106, 111
law students, career aspirations of, 40, 60
lawyers: attitudes of public toward, 178–79, 188; client narratives and, 86–87; courtroom rules and, 86–88; decline of civility among, 186; discontent of, 179–97; as hired guns, 182, 184; law practice and, 196; lawyering as an art and, 185, 188; most-admired, 179; personal lives of, 180–81; public interest, and civil rights cases, 86; social reform and, 87
Lazlo Kowalski, friend of Rodrigo, 184–85, 339, 341–55
legal capitalism, 182
legal decisionmaking, assumptions of, 105–16
legal education: case method and, 193–94; clinical classes, 185; competitive aspect of, 186; formalism and, 196. *See also* Socratic method
legal formalism, 98; anarchy and elegance and, 187–89; colorblindness and, 98; equality and, 109–11; *Erie v. Tompkins* and, 190–91; moral sense and, 193; precedent and, 187; reductionism and, 194;

schizophrenia and, 194–95; as source of law's discontents, 175–97. *See also* doctrinalism
legal instrumentalism, 137–53; as a civil rights strategy, 141–53; defined, 141; legitimacy of, 144–45; pragmatism and, 141, 143
legal realism, and First Amendment, 234–40
legal rules: effect of objective and subjective, on more empowered party or class, 309–14
legal scholarship: acceptance of critical, 26, 58; citation practice in, 167–68; criteria for judging, 54–55; defects of, 25, 30
legal storytelling. *See* stories and storytelling
level playing field, 68, 103–04, 235, 237
liberals: arguments for, to support social welfare, 357–59
linear thinking, 27, 28
litigants, and empathy, 82–85
litigation: ineffectiveness of, for social change, 82–85, 252
Locke, John, 226, 320
Lopez v. Seccombe, 299
Lopez Tijerina v. Henry, 173
love, 40–41, 50–51; exclusion of poor blacks from social network of, 43. *See also* empathy
Lowell High School (San Francisco), and Chinese community, 162, 303
LSAT. *See* Law School Admissions Test

MacKinnon, Catharine, 84, 87; concept of neutrality and, 103; sexuality and subordination and, 318–19, 321
Madison Plan, University of Wisconsin, xii
male bonding, 268
Malinche, La, 77, 78
marching in the right or wrong direction, 270–71, 273
market incentives: use of, to control racism in workplaces, 355
marketplace of ideas, 57; apologetic function of, 224; in free speech, 221, 223; hate speech and, 236, 237
marketplace theory, for eradicating racism, 338–55
markets, and connection to merit, 378–81
Marshall, Justice Thurgood, 87
master-slave perceptions, 274

Index 425

McClesky v. Kemp, 252
McCrate Report, 176, 177
medical procedures, botched: as crimes, 128–29
Mendez v. Westminster School District, 302–04; contribution to *Brown* litigation strategy, 303–04
mental and psychosomatic illness, and racist remarks, 212
merit: affirmative action and, 57, 369, 375–95; apologetic function of, 383–87; canonical function of, 387, 388; conquering nations and, 386; criteria of, 57, 106; disadvantaging functions of, to minorities, 387; as formalization, 384; majoritarian nature of, 382–83; paradox of distributed, 370; preoccupation with, and cultural decline, 392–93; principle of, 31; race and class advantage and, 384–85; teachers unions and, 387
metaphors: amnesia and stroke as destroyers of memory, 94; bankrupt since birth, 360; baseball, 103; basketball hoop and merit, 384; Bluebeard's Castle, 296–97; cresting wave, 27, 28, 32, 34; deer herd, size of, 337; jogging suits, 51–52; lawn chemicals, 106–07; minstrel show, 175; riveters, 195; Ulysses and trust doctrine, 58; vending machine, 117–18; weeds, 147
Mexican Americans: early history, 97; as a legally cognizable class, 173–74; and *Mendez v. Westminster*, 302–04; and other white strategy, 162, 288, 300, 303; racialization of, 301. *See also* Latinos
Milgram, Stanley: and obedience experiment, 350–51
military, and racism, 352
mindset, 3–4, 17
minority groups, and overidentification with whites, 300–01, 302
minority poor, and high reproductive rate, 337
minority students, success rate of, 275–76, 365–66
Mountains Without Handrails (Joseph Sax), 257
Muslims, solidarity with, 162
myth: of law's efficacy, 143–44; of law's objectivity, 192; of level playing field, 139; of a new civil rights, 46–49; of racial progress, 138–40

NAACP Legal Defense Fund: Japanese-American internment and, 162, 303; role in *Mendez* and *Brown*, 302–04; W.E.B. Du Bois and, 152
narrative(s): as antidotes for racism, 221–22; client, 87, 93; constitutional, about free speech, 225–34; dominant, of racism, 220–21; killed by courts, 93–94; role of, in interpreting legal decisions, 247–48; role of, in meanings, 246; role of, in social practices, 247. *See also* stories and storytelling
narrativity, critique of, 52–69
National Environmental Policy Act (NEPA), and public trust doctrine, 253–54
nationalism. *See* cultural nationalism
nationhood, self-definition theory of, 291
neutral principles: antidiscrimination law and, 103–09; argument against affirmative action, 171–72; equality and, 96, 109–14; freeze-frame approach and, 113; hiring and, 8, 106; immigration policy and, 291
nonlawyers, and civil rights movement, 86
norm theory, 79, 81, 350
normativity: as impediment for law reform, 272–73; role of, in limiting legal reform, 257; the rule of law and, 143; self-centeredness of, 272
nullification, by judge or jury, 334
nurturing activities. *See* caregiving activities

obedience to authority, 351
objective versus subjective distinction. *See* legal rules
ontogeny recapitulates phylogeny, 62–68
Operation Wetback, 297
opportunity, equality of, 109–11
optimism-pessimism gap, 140, 151
outgroups: benefits of stories to, 18–19; manipulation of, 97–98

panethnic groups, 158
paradox. *See* reconstructive paradox
past achievements, as predictors of law school success, 206
patriarchy, 264, 267, 319

People v. Hall, 300
perfection: idea of, and the Enlightenment, 320
perseveration, 31, 142, 267
perspective, 267; perpetrator, 84, 172; role of, in perceptions of racism, 222
pessimism, racial. *See* racial realism
pitting one group against another, 97–98, 296–305
platitudes, contradictory pairs of, 194
playing field, level. *See* level playing field
pleading rules, 82, 84, 86
plenary power doctrine, and immigration, 290
Plessy v. Ferguson, 249, 250; Justice Harlan's opinion disparaging Chinese and, 300, 301
political correctness, 148–49, 251
poor: black, 61; laws, 357; law's treatment of, women, 252; programs to aid, nonwhite underclass, 357
positivism, legal, 187–88
Posner, Richard, 348; wealth maximization and, 340–41
poverty. *See* poor
power: cultural, 21–22, 52–69; objective rules and, 309–14
precedent: First Amendment and, 187; narratives and, 88
principles, neutral. *See* neutral principles
procurement fraud. *See* crime, white-collar
promises, taking back civil rights, 258–61
Proposition 187 (California): effect of, on bilingualism, 299
Proposition 209 (California): effect of, on affirmative action, 365
public trust, theory of environmental protection, 58, 253–58
Puerto Ricans, debate over citizenship, 300
Pure Politics (Girardeau Spann), 61, 104, 141

quotas, 110

race: dominant narrative and, 220–21; as a measure of social disadvantage, 368–69; traitor, 89
race-and-class reconciliation, 394–95
race-conscious admissions. *See* affirmative action

racial double helix. *See* helix
racial insults. *See* hate speech
racial memorabilia, in museums, 218
racial politics, zero-based approach to, 356–61
racial progress, checkerboard of, 296–305
racial realism, 138–41
racial remedies: costs of, placed on people of color, 107, 171–72
racial slurs. *See* hate speech
racial voice, legal instrumentalism as argument for, 153
racism: authoritarian personality and, 228; as a category mistake, 346–47; children and, 214, 215–16; class hierarchy and, 213–14, 235–36; confrontation theory for controlling, 228–29; democracy and, 319–27; Enlightenment and, 319–27; formal, 383; formal rules and, 229; formality and, 352; free market economics and, 323–26; as a group harm, 232; harms to perpetrator and, 213, 235; homeostat of, 45, 116; hydraulic theory of, 229; inability of free market to eradicate, 345–53; the military and, 352; parenting by minority persons and, 212; persistence of, 112–13; psychological, physical, and pecuniary harms of, 211–14; quantity of, in world, 222; socioeconomic competition and, 80; socioeconomic theories of, 228; sports and, 352; time warp aspect of, 313–14; unconscious, 313–14
rape. *See* date rape
R.A.V. v. City of St. Paul, 83, 234
realism, legal. *See* legal realism
realism, racial. *See* racial realism
reconstructive paradox, 89, 243–53; definition of, 248–49; "everything must change at once," 59–61, 244
redemption, societal, 51
remedial rationale. *See* affirmative action
reparations argument: for African Americans, 157–58, 160; as basis for affirmative action, 171, 172
Republican Party, and zero-based racial politics, 356–61
results, equality of, 109–11
reverse discrimination, and affirmative action, 371–72, 383

rights: of association, 96; of groups versus individuals, 233
rights-talk, and normativity, 272
Robeson, Paul: as sacrificial lamb, 152
Rodrigo Crenshaw: disappearance of, 33, 68–69; early life of, 315; introduction of, 20–21; job interviews and, 137–38; kidnapping by Irish nationalist group, 71–72; libel show and, 102–03; LL.M. program and, 21, 33, 35; lover's quarrel and, 263; LSAT and, 21–22, 33; military service in Italy and, 32, 33; origins of, ix; printout and, 34; printout, on crime statistics and, 125–31; secret of social healing and, 50; student writing competition and, 35–36, 42–43, 103; theories of social reform and, 44–51, 273–82; Women's Law Caucus and, 262–82
Roe v. Wade, effect of, 272
Romans, and treatment of slaves, 386–87
rule of law, 47, 174; legal instrumentalism and, 137–54
rules of evidence, and suppression of nonstandard narratives, 93–94

sabotage, warning of risk of, 32, 49
San Antonio Independent School District v. Rodriguez, and retreat from Brown, 250
Sanchez, George: and mistreatment of Latinos, 303
SAT. *See* Scholastic Achievement Test
satire, 378–79
Sax, Joseph: and public trust doctrine, 58, 253–58
Schlesinger, Arthur, 392
scholarship, imperial. *See* imperial scholarship
scholarship, legal. *See* legal scholarship
Scholastic Achievement Test (SAT), 198–206; coachable nature of, 370, 391
Schuck, Peter: and theory of nationhood, 291
segregation: *Brown* decision and, 59–61; Latino, in schools, 298, 302–04
self-hatred and self-doubt, and racist remarks, 212
self-help, 141
self-interest: of corporations and nations, 145; of imperial scholars, 172; as strategy for minorities, 146–49; white, and black

justice, 271. *See also* interest convergence
sentencing: disparities in, 130; guidelines and role of discretion, 74
Serving Two Masters (Derrick Bell), 54, 76, 86, 170
Settlement House movement, 75–76, 78
shadowboxing, and legal rules, 309–14
Sherry, Suzanna, 54, 66
Shiffrin, Steve, 234–40
slavery: deaths from, as a crime, 130; white women and, 160–61
slurs. *See* hate speech
social change: coalitions and, 154–63; relation of small groups to, 273–77; role of malcontent groups in, 279–82
social construction: of blacks, 146, 147; of blacks as criminals, 120, 123–24, 127; of *Brown*, 243–53; of children, 346; of racial stigma, 232–33; of social reality, 5, 19, 311; of teenagers, 122, 124; of threat, 117–37
social reform movements, 282; instrumentalism and, 142–44; resistance to, 65–66. *See also* law reform
social welfare, 356–61
socialism: flaws of, 323; reconciliation with capitalism, 35–43
socioeconomic differences: demonstrating, with computers, 258–61
socioeconomic status, and victimization by racism, 212
Socratic method, as source of students' discontent, 182, 185, 186, 194
solidarity: essentialism and, 157; group differences and, 159–60, 270–71, 277; in interracial coalitions, 156, 162–63; need for, 277
South Africa, racism in, 318
Space Traders, Chronicle of the (Derrick Bell), 56
species, endangered. *See* endangered species
sports, and racism, 352
stairstep argument, against affirmative action, 369
standardized tests and testing: affirmative action and, 199; analogies in, 200; arguments against, 199–205; chitlins test, 382; correlation of economic status and scores with, 201, 202; cultural knowledge and, 202–03; deficiencies of, 197–205;

errors in, 199; history of, 198–99; hype in, industry, 204; inability to predict future achievements, 204; legacy admits and, 200–01; negative correlations with race and, 202–03; reform of, 205–07; stereotype threat and, 237; study of, by Lani Guinier, 201; test prep courses and, 201, 370; U.S. Dept. of Education guidelines for, 203; zip codes as predictors of scores and, 201
standing: doctrine of, 88; lack of, in imperial scholarship, 169–70, 175
statistical analysis, of inequalities, 259
status quo: affirmative action and, 373; invisibility of, 275; manipulation of, 25
Steele, Claude: and stereotype threat, 235
stereotype threat, 235, 237
stereotypes: of Asian Americans, 219, 301; of blacks, 136, 218, 219, 301; functional theory of, 64–65, 219; of Indians, 219; of Mexicans, 219, 301; racial, as barrier to free market, 346. *See also* images
stigma, and affirmative action, 367–68, 377
stigma-pictures. *See* stereotypes
stories and storytelling, 3–20, 62, 311, 313; benefits of, to ingroups, 19; benefits of, to outgroups, 18–19; in court, 84, 85–86, 93–94; critique of, 53–62; due process of, 85; majoritarian, 5, 56; resistance to, 63–64, 66; risks of, 53–54; stock story, 5, 6–8; U.S. story of origins and, 260–61; use of, in legal scholarship, 54, 62. *See also* counterstorytelling
structural determinism, 96–98
structural due process, 191–92
student conduct codes. *See* campus speech codes
subjective versus objective distinction. *See* legal rules
submissive personality, 340–41, 351
success rate, of minority graduates, 275–76, 365–66

teenagers: as drivers, 346; social construction of, 122, 124
Teresa Pellegrini, and the Professor meet, 329–38
terrorism. *See* sabotage
testing industry. *See* standardized tests and testing

text: interpretations of, against background of meanings, 246
thinking: canonical, 267, 276–77, 279; different styles of, 200; linear, 27, 28
time warp, aspect of racism, 220
tobacco companies. *See* cigarette warnings
tort action, for hate speech and epithets, 211–17
trashing, 192
Treaty of Guadalupe Hidalgo, 97, 298
Tribe, Laurence: and structural due process, 191–92
triumphalism, 271
trusts. *See* public trust
Two Nations (Andrew Hacker), 42, 44, 45, 46, 48, 49
tyranny of the ordinary, 192

unconscious racism, and cultural meaning test, 313–14
underclass, programs to aid nonwhite, 356–61
United States v. Carolene Products Co., 170, 240
United States, and war with Mexico (1846–1848), 97, 298
U.S. English, 389
utility argument, as basis for affirmative action, 171

Van Alstyne, William: and critique of legal storytelling, 66
Van den Berghe, Pierre: on racial prejudice, 216
victim(s): blaming, 108; empathy and, 87
video arcade, 53
Visigoths: self-destruction of, by incessant warfare, 32

Warren, Earl: end of segregation in California and, 304; Japanese Americans and, 301
wars: undeclared, as a crime, 129–30
Washington v. Davis: intent requirement and, 83; retreat from *Brown* and, 250
Watson, James: and DNA, 95
Wechsler, Herbert: and critique of *Brown*, 95–96
welfare. *See* social welfare
West, decline of, 27–32

West, Robin: critique of law and economics, 340, 345, 348–49
Wheatley, Phillis, 148
white-collar crime. *See* crime, white-collar
white privilege, 336, 373–74
whiteness: appeal of, as impediment to interracial coalition, 156
whites: economic advantages of, 202; innocent, and affirmative action, 373; working-class, and blacks, 97
witnesses: treatment of, at trial, 85
Wittgenstein, Ludwig, 264, 267
women: as beneficiaries of affirmative action, 343; childbirth and, 344; essentialism-anti-essentialism debate and, 262–82; glass ceilings and, 344; job market and, 343–44; law's treatment of poor, 252; subordination and, 318–19, 321; white, in plantation society, 160–61; willingness to have sex, 310–11
words that wound. *See* hate speech
World Trade Center, and nationalism, 281
Wright, Judge Skelly: and legal scholarship about Warren Court, 169

zero-based approach, to racial politics, 356–61

About the Author and Editors

Richard Delgado is University Distinguished Professor and Derrick Bell Fellow at the University of Pittsburgh School of Law. He is author, with Jean Stefancic, of *No Mercy: How Conservative Think Tanks and Foundations Changed America's Social Agenda* (Temple University Press 1996).

Adrien Katherine Wing is Bessie Dutton Murray Professor of Law and Associate Dean for Faculty Development at the University of Iowa College of Law.

Jean Stefancic is Research Professor of Law and Derrick Bell Scholar at the University of Pittsburgh School of Law.